Societies of Peace: Past, Present, and Future offers a comprehensive study of matri- archal societies. It is an outstanding representation of the intellectual exchanges at the First and Second World Congresses on Matriarchal Studies. Texas State University-San Marcos was honoured to host the 2005 Congress; our faculty and students experienced inspirational and thought-provoking discourse from scholars, mainly women, from around the world. There is a wealth of insightful work in the book from the clarity in Heide Goettner-Abendroth's article on definitions, and Genevieve Vaughan's discussion of matriarchal societies as alternatives to market- based societies, and through the historical articles documenting past and present societies and their contributions and issues. From the discussion of Barbara Alice Mann of the Bear Clan of the Ohio Seneca, Iroquois, to Lamu Gatusa of Mosuo, Yunnan of Southwest China, the work is a rich and provocative reading experience. I look forward to the book's availability in our university library.

—Sandra Mayo, Director, Center for Multicultural and Gender Studies, Texas State University-San Marcos/U.S.A.

Ground breaking feminist scholarship on matriarchal societies. Urgently needed insights for recreating equality, economic justice, and peace.

—Linda Christiansen-Ruffman, Professor of Sociology and Women's Studies, Saint Mary's University, Halifax/Canada

Throughout the ages patriarchal capitalism has co-opted human energy and knowledge, in order to control and dominate other human beings—and the natural world. But in today's twenty-first century reality, the worldview of ma- triarchy understands all forms of life as being interconnected with each other. Women should rise and reclaim matriarchy for the needs of our present reality, and for future prosperity.

—Wahu Kaara, Executive Director of Kenya Debt Relief Network (KENDREN), Kenya

This is a powerful life-affirming political book. The feminist theory, vision and practice reported in this volume draws its strength from humanity's common matriarchal history—uncovered, honoured and analyzed here by women from Africa, Asia, the Pacific, Europe and the Americas. Deep personal and academic knowledge of, and reflection on, surviving matriarchal elements in some of the contributors' own Indigenous cultures and archaeological accounts of lost cultures by others, shape the book's ambitious and fully realized theoretical and political project. Common principles found in vastly different matriarchal societies across time and space are potent guides in our continuing struggle to recover the humanity and harmony lost to patriarchy not so long ago in the scale of these things. The global dialogues and solidarities among women reflected in this book, as much as its inspiring content, give us hope that this new world is possible.

—Angela Miles, author of *Integrative Feminisms* and Professor of Sociology, OISE/University of Toronto, Canada

Modern Matriarchal Studies is to be commended for supplying clear historical, anthropological, philosophical, and sociological evidence demonstrating that a balanced society has never ceased to exist. This society of peace between genders, among generations, and between humans and nature—as well as of motherly gift giving—still exists, although as a maltreated packhorse under the saddle of exploitative, patriarchal, trans-national corporate enterprise. Matriarchal Studies provide vital inspiration for humanity's quest of life-nurturing ways to build a new culture, and helps avoid returning to the fundamental error human civilization has fallen prey for the past 4000-6000 years.

—Johannes Heimrath, Executive Director of The Club of Budapest, WorldShift Network, Germany/Hungaria

Throughout my life long radical feminist and peace activism I have strived to create a new world, I however felt that we lacked a vision of this "new world." This book offers me the answer: the gift-giving matriarchies show me the vision and Matriarchal Studies offer me the theory.

—Erella Shadmi, Peace activist, Israel

I am delighted to enthusiastically endorse this groundbreaking compilation of papers edited by Heide Goettner-Abendroth. These papers are the result of two very important conferences on the new field of Matriarchal Studies the second of which I was very fortunate to attend. The diversity and breadth of these papers, many by members of present day matriarchal societies throughout the world, is astonishing and inspiring. Heide Goettner-Abendroth as the director of these conferences and Genevieve Vaughan as the sponsor of the second conference should be congratulated for their stellar achievement.

—Cristina Biaggi, editor of *The Rule of Mars: Readings on the Origins, History and Impact of Patriarchy*, New York/USA

SOCIETIES OF PEACE
Matriarchies Past, Present and Future

SELECTED PAPERS
FIRST WORLD CONGRESS ON MATRIARCHAL STUDIES, 2003
SECOND WORLD CONGRESS ON MATRIARCHAL STUDIES, 2005

EDITED BY HEIDE GOETTNER-ABENDROTH

INANNA PUBLICATIONS AND EDUCATION INC.
TORONTO, CANADA

Published in Canada by Inanna Publications and Education Inc.
210 Founders College, York University
4700 Keele Street, Toronto, Ontario M3J 1P3
Telephone: (416) 736-5356 Fax (416) 736-5765
Email: inanna@yorku.ca Web site: www.yorku.ca/inanna

Printed and Bound in Canada.

Cover Design: Val Fullard
Interior Design: Luciana Ricciutelli

Library and Archives Canada Cataloguing in Publication

World Congress on Matriarchal Studies (1st : 2003 : Luxembourg, Luxembourg)
    Societies of peace : matriarchies past, present and future : selected papers, first World Congress on Matriarchal Studies, 2003, second World Congress on Matriarchal Studies, 2005 / edited by Heide Goettner-Abendroth.

Includes bibliographical references.
ISBN 978-0-9782233-5-9

1. Matriarchy--Congresses. 2. Women--Social conditions--Congresses. I. Göttner-Abendroth, Heide, 1941- II. World Congress on Matriarchal Studies (2nd : 2005 : Austin, Tex.) III. Title.

GN479.5.S63 2008   306.83   C2008-906371-6

This book is dedicated to Genevieve Vaughan
who gave a most generous gift so that the new paradigm of modern
Matriarchal Studies might come to light around the world.

Contents

Part V. Past – Theory of History

Part VI. Past Matriarchal Societies

Europe

North Africa, Israel, Japan

Acknowledgements

The Two World Congresses

The generosity of several individuals and groups made it possible for this new paradigm of peaceful societies to come to light. Particular appreciation for their support of both World Congresses is due to: Marie-Josée Jacobs, Minister of Family and Women's Affairs (Luxembourg); Genevieve Vaughan, the Foundation for a Compassionate Society (Austin, USA); Hans Boeckler Stiftung (Duessel-dorf, Germany); UNNA-Stiftung (Duesseldorf, Germany); Fonds National de la Recherche (Luxembourg); Mediengruppe Kulturell Kreative (Berlin, Germany); Gerda-Weiler-Stiftung (Ulm, Germany); Maecenia Stiftung (Frankfurt, Germany); Association of the International Academy HAGIA (Germany).

The great success of both World Congresses depended on the expertise of the lecturers. We are deeply grateful to those who brought their knowledge, wisdom and creativity to bear on all aspects of this work.

Profound thanks to the presenters from various Indigenous traditions, who, at the 2005 conference, offered their traditional prayers and ritual celebrations at the beginning of each day. Their inspiring contributions grounded all our work, with one representative from each continent where matriarchal peoples reside: Dona Enriquetas Contrereas (Zapoteca, Central America), Barbara Alice Mann (Seneca, North America), Gad Osafo (Akan, West Africa), and Patricia Mukhim (Khasi, Asia).

This Book

The publication of this book was made possible through the generosity and com-mitment of: Genevieve Vaughan, The Foundation for a Compassionate Society (Austin, USA); UNNA-Stiftung, Duesseldorf (Germany); and the Association of the International Academy HAGIA (Germany).

Many thanks also to Luciana Ricciutelli, Editor-in-Chief at Inanna Publications and Education Inc. for her kind help with this manuscript. We are delighted that, with Inanna's support, this book could come to fruition.

HEIDE GOETTNER-ABENDROTH

Introduction

Matriarchy and Modern Matriarchal Studies

B ringing the world back into balance means creating equilibrium and peace at every level: between the sexes, the generations, and different social groups. This is the chief objective of all efforts to achieve a sustainable society. Over the past decades a new socio-cultural science offering definitive insights for this process has been developed: research on matriarchal societies, known as Modern Matriarchal Studies. Presenting concrete social alternatives to the unsolved problems of western societies, Modern Matriarchal Studies holds great political potential, offering practical solutions developed out of the long experience of these very different cultures.

Before Modern Matriarchal Studies was inaugurated 30 years ago, matriarchies had been sporadically investigated by western social sciences, but this exploration was constrained and distorted by European gender paradigms, worldviews, and religious beliefs. In most cases, matriarchal societies have gone unrecognized by western social sciences, or have been classed as merely matrilineal. An accurate distinction would acknowledge that while matriarchal societies always pass goods and honour down through the maternal line, they are equally characterized by having their means of livelihood—the economy—rest in women's hands. This gives women a very strong position in these cultures, and that is why they are called "matriarchies." Widespread misconceptions notwithstanding, women's strong position in these societies does not mean that matriarchies are women's autocracies. Rather, in matriarchies women's power is counterbalanced by men's power, so that neither gender dominates the other. The governing principle of these societies is balance, rather than domination.

In general, matriarchal societies are based on gender equality. Their social rules have developed out of thousands of years of experience, and demonstrate a perfectly balanced relationship between women's and men's spheres of action—an ongoing relationship maintained through codes of conduct. All political decisions are reached through consensus among community members, and thoroughly worked out principles and social guidelines ensure that unanimity will eventually be achieved on each issue. The resulting social structure is non-violent, and enables a peaceful life for all. Matriarchally-formed societies—contrary to domination-oriented

1

patriarchal societies—are needs-oriented and inclusive. Their social structures, still in use today, are not only optimal for both sexes, but they also engender respect for the unique qualities of different generations: there exists neither a battle of the sexes nor a generation gap. Every aspect of society—economic and political, social and cultural—is governed by principles of consensus-building and achieving harmony among all members. With their socially balanced economic systems, matriarchal societies are sustainable with regard to nature and its resources; they are societies that respect all life on earth. The principle of balance between the sexes, between generations, and between humans and nature constitutes their fundamental ethical value.

Demonstrably, matriarchal societies are true societies of peace. They are non-violent, and their relationships lack the interpersonal, social, and economic barbarism so prevalent in patriarchal societies, particularly in western civilizations. Though mistakenly judged as primitive, or as insignificant ethnic groups, these are cultures in the fullest sense of the word. Today the largest of these matriarchal societies comprise up to several million people, with very distinct divisions of labour. Their history as peoples and societies is long and fascinating, and full of extraordinary contributions to human development and culture.

Modern Matriarchal Studies researchers have brought to light characteristic patterns of these cultures through anthropological and historical investigation. In their study of existing matriarchal societies, researchers have uncovered elaborate regulations to implement principles of balance and peace. This has led them to conclude that perfectly balanced "gender democracies" of matriarchal cultures are not based on abstract principles, but on practical experience and long tradition.

Matriarchy research has also rediscovered the history of Neolithic and Bronze Age matriarchal cultures, whose roots go back far beyond the advent of patriarchal forms of society. These studies uncover our cultural roots, adding a new dimension to the cultural history of humanity, which has otherwise been approached from a male-centric perspective.

Modern Matriarchal Studies thus brings to light a significant human spiritual and social heritage that has been achieved specifically by women. This contributes to a better understanding of the overall social and cultural history of our earliest beginnings, including women's pivotal role as creators of culture, and as the maintainers of society's structures. This deeper knowledge of history is still being suppressed and silenced today, preventing understanding and negatively impacting on women's present situation. But it is impossible to understand the current situation, especially regarding women, without a deeper understanding of the history. Due to such progress in knowledge and insight, Modern Matriarchal Studies is fundamentally changing our view of history, and eventually will lead to a complete change in our worldview. Modern Matriarchal Studies is thus creating a new cultural history and social paradigm.

The Two World Congresses on Matriarchal Studies

At two World Congresses on Matriarchal Studies, these largely misunderstood matriarchal societies were presented to a wider public. In 2003, the First World Congress on Matriarchal Studies, "Societies in Balance," took place in Luxembourg. Chiefly sponsored by that country's Minister of Family and Women's Affairs, Marie-Josée Jacobs, it was organized and guided by Heide Goettner-Abendroth, founding director of International Academy HAGIA for Modern Matriarchal Studies, in Germany. It was a ground-breaking event that brought together for the first time international scholars who had previously been working on this issue in relative isolation from each other. A milestone with great historical implications for Matriarchal Studies in general, it grew out of Academy HAGIA's international contacts and enabled a wide-ranging, alternative scientific community to come into its own.

In 2004, Genevieve Vaughan invited Heide Goettner-Abendroth to bring the new field of Modern Matriarchal Studies to the United States. (Genevieve Vaughan, who participated in the first World Congress, is the founding director of the Center for the Study of the Gift Economy in Austin, Texas.) After a year of friendly collaboration between Goettner-Abendroth in Germany and Vaughan in the USA, the Second World Congress on Matriarchal Studies, "Societies of Peace," was held in 2005 in San Marcos, Texas. It took place thanks to Vaughan's generous sponsorship, and was chaired by Goettner-Abendroth.

The Second World Congress went beyond what had been achieved by the Congress in 2003. Co-sponsors included Sandra Mayo, Center for Multicultural and Gender Studies of Texas State University, San Marcos; Indigenous Women's Network; Institute of Archaeomythology; Reformed Congregation of the Goddess International; Women's International League for Peace and Freedom (WILPF), and the Women's Spirituality Program of the California Institute of Integral Studies, all based in the United States. It included Indigenous researchers, mostly women and some men, from many of the world's still existing matriarchal societies. They came from North, Central and South America; from North, West and South Africa; from Asia, including China, Sumatra, and India. This made the Second World Congress a significant intercultural event, and set an unparalleled precedent with respect to the meeting of Indigenous matriarchal speakers from all over the world. Dressed in their symbol-filled, traditional costumes, they spoke not only about the matriarchal patterns their societies have preserved, but also about the societal and political problems that colonization has brought to their communities. In this way, they corrected distorted perspectives often held by non-Indigenous peoples, and shared with the audience the non-violent social order of their communities. These are places where all living creatures—humans, animals, and nature—are respected, and where reciprocal equality—regardless of sex and age—is practised.

As in 2003 in Luxembourg, the last part of the 2005 Congress was dedicated to presentations by renown scholars from the USA and Europe on historical theories and research on past matriarchal societies and matriarchal symbolism. This opened new possibilities of communication between researchers from those two continents, as did lectures on the origins of domination and patriarchy. Overall, the creative impact of women's contribution to human development was celebrated throughout the Congress.

Seen as a whole, presentations at both Matriarchal Studies Congresses demonstrate a new research area that has effectively become a social science in its own right, and which now emerges as a new paradigm of human history and society. Furthermore, in their own ways, the presenters at both Congresses are all working with new, complex methodologies that both integrate and transgress many traditional scientific disciplines, such as ethnology, anthropology, archaeology, history, theology, folklore and oral traditions, the arts, and linguistics.

The Congresses were received with great enthusiasm, both in Europe and the United States. The audience participated actively in the discussion periods, and extra hours of dialogue had to be added to the schedule to accommodate the enthusiasm. While the first Congress filled the European Parliament's famous Hémicycle Hall in Luxembourg with participants from many European countries and the USA, the second one, at the University Performing Arts Center in San Marcos, Texas, hosted participants from all over the world: Canada, Mexico, Haïti, Costa Rica, Brazil, Bolivia, Nepal, India, Pakistan, the Philippines, Israel, Turkey, Uzbekistan, Germany, Switzerland, and Italy, among others. Participants were women of all ages, and included academics, researchers, and political activists.

At the end of the second Congress, a common political declaration was formulated. Speakers and participants shared ideas on how to generate concrete alternatives and practical solutions to the patriarchal system of exploitation, and on steps to promote the re-establishment of peaceful societies. After the declaration was finished, several groups formed to take action on specific issues that had arisen out of the Congress: resistance to building "big box" stores; concern about the murders of women factory workers in Mexico; changing the political climate in the USA; and rebuilding the women's movement from the perspective of Modern Matriarchal Studies.

This declaration, included at the end of this book, emphasizes the political significance of both Congresses, and of Modern Matriarchal Studies. The short and long term consequences of these extraordinary events are still unfolding and cannot be predicted at this point.

In addition to the scholarly and political aspects of the Congress, expressions of matriarchally-influenced art and spirituality included photography, decorative arts, sculpture, and textiles. Artists working in other broadcast and film media were also represented, and documentary films made about both Congresses. Further, the entire proceedings of the second Congress were also broadcast on-line by FIRE (Costa Rica): <www.fire.or.cr> and taped for radio by WINGS (Canada).

Introducing this Book

This book presents a selection of represenative presentations that demonstrate the breadth and depth of today's Modern Matriarchal Studies. Like the congresses themselves, the book is divided into sections dedicated to the continents the presenters came from. This reflects the widespread occurrence of matriarchal cultures around the world today, whose existence is often vehemently denied by the countries they occur in. Many of these societies are in danger of being undermined by patriarchal powers, and face losing their fascinating traditional cultures. In some cases they are threatened with total extinction, if not genocide. In light of this, Modern Matriarchal Studies is all the more urgently called on to bring these cultures to light, allowing their profound significance to be valued, and thus to be of support to them insofar as possible. Particularly important in this regard are the personal accounts presented by speakers from existing matriarchies. Out of all this material arises a perspective on a form of society and culture that is utterly unlike what we have been accustomed to.

Woven through all these contributions are the decades-long investigative efforts of researchers, the highlights of which are included here. By presenting a range of these contributions, this book offers readers an opportunity to become familiar with this new socio-cultural science, enabling them to bring it into various other contexts in which they work and live.

In order to convey the differences between the approach taken by Modern Matriarchal Studies to matriarchy research and that adopted by traditional patriarchal theorists, Part I is dedicated to the Theory and Politics of Matriarchal Societies. In the first article, *Heide Goettner-Abendroth* (Germany) outlines a new definition of matriarchy in which she characterizes the deep structure of this form of society, emphasizing its economic, social, political, and spiritual contexts, and the way it permeates all aspects of society. This definition is based on her cross-cultural research on still-existing matriarchies worldwide. By demonstrating that matriarchies are economically-balanced societies, egalitarian in the relationship between the sexes and between generations, and consensus-based in their politics, she provides a scientific foundation for further research. Furthermore, she shows that matriarchal peoples have developed a very effective system of principles and social codes enabling humans to live in peace with each other and in harmony with nature; this could be of utmost political relevance to our vision of the future.

In her article, *Claudia von Werlhof* (Austria) concentrates on the fact that non-matriarchal societies did not appear in the world fully formed as "patriarchies," but developed over time and are still developing today. She shows that key mechanisms in the development of patriarchal society have been regarded as embodying a superior form of society, one that naturally overcame and replaced matriarchies with something purportedly better, more highly developed, and more evolved spiritually. For her, patriarchy's ultimate utopia is a world from which motherhood and mothers have disappeared; it is characterized by a "war system" in which war has replaced other values to become the main principle of social organization, economics, politics, technology, science, and the relationship with nature, gender. and the future. With the globalization that characterizes this terminal phase of patriarchy, the effects of this war system are being felt today more strongly than ever before.

Genevieve Vaughan's (USA) article discusses matriarchal society as an alternative to market-based society, not only because of matriarchal cultural values, marriage arrangements, and structures of cohesion, but also because of their economic principles. She emphasizes that a mode of distribution based on mothering principles and satisfying needs directly is more functional for everyone than a market economy based on self-interest. She makes explicit that the manhood agenda in patriarchy imposes goals consonant with the market and opposed to gift giving/mothering, while female identity in patriarchy is directed towards caring for occupants of artificially-constructed male gender roles. Interactions between socially-constructed genders are grafted onto market interactions, with exchange on the one hand and invisible gift-giving on the other. She stresses the importance of understanding and healing these pathological patterns in order to create matriarchal societies of peace.

Part II features articles about some existing matriarchal societies of America and Oceania, beginning with North and Central America: *Barbara Alice Mann* (Bear Clan of the Ohio Seneca, Iroquois, USA) presents the Iroquoian model of woman-power—an ancient, highly-developed system among American Indians. Mann shows that all eastern Nations recognized the political, economic, spiritual, and social roles of Clan Mothers as the power brokers of their people; in the twelfth century, Iroquois adopted these roles directly into their Constitution. In fact, by law, the men's councils still may not consider a matter that has not been discussed by the women and forwarded to them by the women's consensus. She tells us that when U.S. feminists learned of this system, they held up the Iroquoian *Gantowisas,* or Official Women, as their model of the possible.

Veronika Bennholdt-Thomsen (Germany) presents the Juchitecan society of ethnic Isthmus Zapotecs (Isthmus of Tehuantepec, Southern Mexico). In a country where "Indigenous" is nearly synonymous with "poor," Juchitecans are well nourished and relatively well-to-do. Their wealth comes from a well-functioning regional economy based on women traders' work. She describes the principles that maintain Juchitecan economy and society as matriarchal, and considers whether this example could be used elsewhere for transforming globalized economies into non-patriarchal, regional ones.

Dona Enriqueta Contreras (Zapoteca, Oaxaca / Mexico) talks about her people, the Sierra Juarez Zapotecs of Oaxaca, as a cultural matriarchy. In presenting this pre-Columbian society as devoted to reverence for nature and equality between the sexes, she notes the respect for both female and male shamans. She explains that their deities represent aspects of nature, and despite the imposition of European Christian male-centered, patriarchal ideals, her people's connection with nature has survived the holocaust of that first fateful meeting five centuries ago. They continue to revere nature, renewing their bond as a commitment to the sanctity of Mother Earth.

The following articles present matriarchal societies of South America: *Antje Olowaili* (Germany) presents her research on the Kuna Culture of Panama's Caribbean coast, a very close, politically semi-independent community that celebrates each girl individually. She shows that although Kuna men hunt, fish, and provide all the food, women distribute it and rule the house. Since marriage is matrilocal, the eldest mother in the clan has most of the power. And women and men live in strictly delineated spheres, each with their own roles.

In her article, *Carolyn Heath* (Great Britain) tells of the Shipibo, an Indigenous Upper Amazon people. She explores the power relations between Shipibo men and women, discovering factors that contribute to Shipibo women's unique self-confidence. It has been asserted that "Shipibo women enjoy more rights, freedom, individual fulfilment and spontaneity than women of other cultures can dream of" (Gebhart-Sayer 1984). To test the veracity of this affirmation, Heath explores Shipibo women's power in four spheres: family, economics, politics, and spirituality, concluding that strong elements of matriarchal organization are present in Shipibo society.

Many matriarchal elements still exist in Indigenous societies in Oceania, as discussed in the following contributions: *Mililani Trask* (Hawaii) tells us that long before western scientists and academics debated theories of evolution, Hawaiians knew and recited the evolution of the universe, the earth, and all of its life forms. She says that in both ancient and modern times, Hawaiians have understood that the evolution of life arises from the female, and that the balance of life is maintained by women. This understanding pervaded traditional Hawaiian society and laid the foundation for all aspects of the social order of the Hawaiian matrilineal culture.

Taimalieutu Kiwi Tamasese (Samoa and New Zealand) states that culture is not static, but resembles the flow of a river. She points out the impact of European colonization on Indigenous Samoan culture, especially in regard to gender arrangements. She tells us that in pre-contact times, the primary family relationship in matrilineal Samoa was actually between brother and sister. The brother would look to the sister as his sacred covenant, and would serve her throughout her life—including generating her children. When missionaries arrived, they changed the sacred covenantal relationship into one between people and God, modeling this relationship on European gender arrangements between women and men. Tamasese informs us that today, Indigenous Samoans are in the process of restoring the social, political, and religious sacredness of womanhood in general, as well as that of women in families, communities, and societies.

Part III is dedicated to existing matriarchal societies of Africa, and begins with articles on West and South Africa: *Wilhelmina J. Donkoh* (Akan, Ghana/West Africa) discusses female leadership among her people, the Asante, who constitute one of the principal groups of matrilineal Akan-speaking people in the modern state of Ghana. She points out that an identifying Akan characteristic is descent through the female line and that traditionally important social and economic institutions as property ownership and inheritance are based on blood affiliation to the mother's lineage. Women among the Akan are thus expected to play a unique role in ensuring the perpetuation of the lineage, and female leaders among the Asante play a central role within the Asante socio-political system. Her examination reveals that when female leaders have transcended gender boundaries and become diplomats or political heads, their actions have tended to foster greater social cohesion.

Gad A. Osafo (Akan, Ghana and Germany) gives an overview of the Akan healing heritage, traceable as far back as 4000 years ago. Traditional medicine practiced by the Akan and other ethnic groups of Ghana are, for 50 percent of the population, the only readily available remedy for health imbalances ("dis-ease"). He finds that Indigenous ancestral medicine is not only closely associated with cultural practices, but is also intimately associated with Akan religious beliefs. Medicine/healing exhibits two procedural components, which he characterizes as the spiritual/psychic aspect, and the process of applying material medicine. He reports that the custodian of this heritage in the matrilineal group is the *Obaapanying/Aberewa* (elderly woman), who also is—directly or indirectly—the spiritual head of the family.

In her contribution, *Cécile Keller* (Switzerland) shows that in matriarchal societies such as the Akan and the Iroquois, medicine has always been in the hands of women. She notes that healing methods include treatment of the body and guidance of the soul and consciousness, with the matriarchal mythology and cosmology of that culture being activated to reconnect the afflicted person to their own worldview and social community. Keller emphasizes that in addition to providing a sense of security for the individual being treated, this method can also be used to treat collective problems.

Bernedette Muthien (Khoisan, South Africa) says violence and inequity are inextricably tied to patriarchy and the dominator system. Though prevalent now, she says cultural systems of patriarchy and domination are not inevitable, citing the Khoisan of Southern Africa and other pre-patriarchal societies as examples of harmonious, gender-continuous, non-violent lifestyles. She hints at historical records and modern texts that reflect numerous examples of the Khoisan's originally peaceful, non-violent, and egalitarian ways of life, drawing on many lessons embedded in Khoisan culture that can be adapted to reduce current violence and improve present society.

The following contributions present matriarchal societies of North Africa: In her article, *Hélène Claudot-Hawad* (France) asks what it means today, in Tuareg society, to be a woman or a man, and reflects on the images, roles, and standards, reciprocal rights and duties, social and symbolic functions, evoked by these categories. In her article she conveys the nature, significance, and contemporary manifestations of male and female gender categories by putting them back in the contexts from which they arose: an original nomadic society that gives a pre-eminent role to the "feminine." She indicates that the Tuareg culture promotes a woman-centered system; the existence of these principles contradicts the theory that male dominance over women is universal in nomadic societies.

Fatimata Oualet Halatine (Imajaghen or Tuareg, Central Sahara) speaks of her personal journey, typical of today's Tuareg women, towards modernity. She tells us that her family's roots were in the bush, where her mother owned a large herd, and that when her parents moved into a town, she lost the socio-economic advantages of her traditional environment. She also discovered that people spoke of African women as being exploited, and were unaware that many African women have a privileged position and are free. She reports, however, that Tuareg women are currently discovering the workplace, and they work hard. This change has led to a crisis: much ancient knowledge has now been lost, and the future is uncertain.

Makilam's (Kabyle/Berber, Algeria and Germany) article presents the Berbers, said to be the oldest culture of Northern Africa; today they live in Morocco, Algeria, and Tunisia. She demonstrates the way her people, the Berbers of Kabylia, have retained many of their pre-Islamic customs, maintaining traditional Kabyle women's arts such as pottery and weaving, which are accompanied by rites and practices that build on magical relationships and unity between humans and nature. According to Grasshoff, the cosmology of Kabyle women is closely connected to their art, and is expressed in the decoration of ceramics and weaving that constitute a secret language among women, with motifs directly related to femininity and fertility. This secret script is passed on exclusively from mother to daughter.

In Part IV, some existing matriarchal societies in contemporary Asia are presented. The first two articles in this section focus on India. *Patricia Mukhim* (Khasi, Meghalaya/Northeast India) shows that her Khasi society is fairly egalitarian, without caste or class systems prevalent in other Indian societies. She discusses the situation of the Khasi matrilineal system today. She tells us that descent or lineage is still based on the female line, and ancestral property passes through the youngest daughter or the "Khatduh," whose role is that of a custodian. Along with ancestral property, the youngest daughter also inherits substantial responsibilities. Mukhim demonstrates the underpinnings of Khasi matriliny and its survival in the midst of surrounding patrilineal and patriarchal societies. She also analyzes disruptions that threaten to replace matriliny with an apparently more gender-balanced system, and demonstrates the tough resistance such initiatives face in her society.

In her article, *Savithri Shanker de Tourreil* (Nayar, Kerala/Southwest India and Canada) looks at some of the changes among her own people, the matrilineal Nayar. From her interviews with three generations of Nayar women—mother, daughter, and granddaughter groups—she provides first-hand information on the changes, among other things, in desirability of girl babies. While they used to be wanted, welcomed, and prayed for by the oldest female and male generation in the kin group, this has changed drastically in recent times. She also demonstrates distinctive configurations and changes among Nayars in the dynamics of power, control, and privilege among both male and female members of the extended family.

The following articles are dedicated to the matriarchal people on Sumatra: *Peggy Reeves Sanday* (USA) presents a conceptual framework for rethinking matriarchy, based on her long-term ethnography of the Minangkabau of West Sumatra,

Indonesia. The Minangkabau are unique in that they identify themselves as a matriarchy. She characterizes the Minangkabau culture as exhibiting an ethic of gender balance and dedication to negotiation and peaceful conflict resolution. In addition to their women-centeredness, the Minangkabau are proudly Islamic, which adds to the mystery Sanday sees in this unusual society. In this article, she discusses the lessons we can learn from the Minangkabau in our quest for world peace.

In her contribution, *Usria Dhavida* (Minangkabau, Sumatra/Indonesia) addresses the role of Minangkabau women in her society. She examines the meaning of queenly sovereignty in West Sumatra through a description of the symbol of "Bundo Kanduang," the legendary Queen Mother of the Minangkabau people, whose story is told in their national myth. She sees this symbol of divine queenship as a model of social life for the Minangkabau, as demonstrated in women's ceremonial activities in village life.

Finally, the last group of articles in this section focus on matriarchal societies in China: *Yan Ruxian* (Beijing, China) presents the matrilineal kinship system and terminology of the Mosuo people in Yunnan, China, which, as she shows, are centred around the mother. The matrilineal families of the Mosuo are mostly headed by women, and consist of members with pure matrilineal blood ties. Property is passed down through female inheritance as well. The sexual life of adults takes the form of a "visiting marriage," and the relationship between men and women is a sexual partnership. This matrilineal cultural system has a long history in local communities, exerting a strong impact on social life. However, Yan notes that today, while many people continue to follow their matrilineal traditions in their day-to-day lives, local communist government leaders are male.

Lamu Gatusa (Shi Gaofeng) (Mosuo, Yunnan/Southwest China) elaborates on some of the issues covered in Yan's article. He tells us that although the Mosuo culture is woman-centered, the role of males in the culture is not underestimated. This creates an equal relationship between men and women that is seen in family patterns, as well as in property and marriage patterns. This equal relationship is evident in Mosuo people's "visiting marriage," in which the partners remain largely independent personally, emotionally, and economically. They have neither sexual nor economic privileges, and as a result, their relationship is a purely natural one of equal association.

Hengde Danshilacuo (He Mei) (Mosuo, Yunnan/Southwest China) complements what has been said about her Mosuo culture in the previous two articles. Since Mosuo follow a matriarchal system, and most people live their whole lives in the maternal family home, never marrying their lovers, Mosuo family structure is very different from others in China. Hengde describes how the current Mosuo family structure came into being. She compares Mosuo family structure with that of China as a whole, and outlines the advantages and limitations of the former, briefly discussing ways to preserve it.

In her article, *Shanshan Du* (China and USA) proposes several socio-cultural frameworks that foster balance, harmony, and equality between the sexes and among individuals in some non-industrial societies. The first model, "maternal centrality," is typically manifested in matriarchal societies, whereas within the framework of gender "insignificance," the symbolic elaboration of "men," "women," and their relationships is scarce and socially insignificant. In the third model, "gender unity," men and women are identified with each other as members of higher social categories, and are expected to perform joint social roles. Through an ethnographic study of the Lahu people of Southwest China, she finally demonstrates how gender equality has become a by-product of the worldview of gender unity.

After presenting several of the existing matriarchal societies across the globe—without which we cannot understand what "matriarchy" is—the book addresses the scope of research on matriarchal societies of the past. This research is also a relatively new development, which clearly shows that in early in human history, societies with matriarchal structures were widely distributed around the world. This means that a long matriarchal cultural epoch must have existed—and in some places it still exists—chronologically preceding patriarchies. This new perspective signals a revolutionary transformation in our historical worldview: the scientific and political consequences are unimaginable.

To introduce these ideas, Part V is dedicated to the Theory of History of Matriarchal Society: In the first contribution, *Riane Eisler* (USA) looks at cultural evolution from the perspective of two underlying possibilities for structuring social systems: the "domination model" and the "partnership model." She traces the cultural evolution of western societies from prehistory to the present in terms of the underlying tension between these two basic alternatives for cultural organization. In her cultural transformation theory, she suggests that shifts from one model to the other are possible in times of extreme social and technological disequilibrium, asserting that there is strong evidence of such a shift during our prehistory. She finds that in the current massive technological and social dislocation, another fundamental shift is possible—to a world oriented more towards partnership than domination.

A critically important aspect of the struggle for our future are theories of human cultural origins. Here the research of Lithuanian/American archaeologist Marija Gimbutas (1921-1994) plays a crucial role, as introduced by *Joan Marler* (USA), who notes that Gimbutas was a pioneer in the study of the symbolic imagery of the earliest farming peoples of Europe. Gimbutas examined thousands of anthropomorphic and zoomorphic sculptures, elegant vessels and cult equipment from the "Old European" cultures of Southeast Europe (6500-3500 BC). This wealth of examples indicates the centrality of women's activities and their roles as creators of culture—leading to a completely new picture of the Neolithic epoch. Marler explains that the concept of matriarchy as a nuanced model of "society in balance" provides an insightful lens through which to view the pre-Indo-European cultures of Old Europe.

In her article, *Annette Kuhn* (Germany) looks at transitions of matriarchal power in the symbolic and social sphere in history. She finds that when women tell stories, they usually make use of an older, more universal pattern of thought, one that is based on women's experiences within matriarchal societies of the past and present. According to Kuhn, this older pattern of female thinking becomes a force in history and contributes to a more human and universal view of society, politics, and power.

In Part VI, articles address matriarchal elements that point to the existence of matriarchal societies in the past. The examples are drawn from many corners of the world: Europe, North Africa, Israel, and Japan. The following articles in this section present matriarchal research on Europe: *Michael Dames* (Great Britain) shows that the abundant archaeological evidence for pre-Christian goddess worship in Britain and Ireland is supported by folklore, folk customs, place names, and medieval writings. Each strand of evidence can be scientifically analyzed, but to uncover the original quality of goddess mythology, he thinks a poetic synthesis of all these strands should be attempted. Instead of the modern cult of objectivity, a pre-Socratic empathy is required. He believes that the archaic offers a new methodology with which to mend a torn world.

Kurt Derungs (Switzerland) broadens this view with his "landscape mythology." He tells us that besides developing a peaceful social structure, matriarchies have also produced an outstanding ecology and mythology of landscape. He finds that in the naming of landscapes (mountains, rivers, lakes, hills, and so on), in burial site symbolism, in architecture, in rituals and mythology, Indigenous cultures have documented ancient knowledge in which principles of matriarchal philosophy of nature can be read. He gives several examples from still existing matriarchal societies.

In her contribution, *Kaarina Kailo* (Finland) confirms the idea that folklore studies can corroborate the historical possibility of ancient matriarchal societies. She discusses the case of a possible gynocentric Finno-Ugric matriarchy based on cross-cultural Northern evidence from archaeology to ethnography and folklore studies. She revisits Finnish studies on the Finnish Helka Festival in light of the new definition of matriarchy, and shows how this and other archaic rituals can help us reconsider the matriarchal worldview of Northern European peoples. Furthermore, she argues that one cannot explore matriarchal times without a bold and radical shift of methodological paradigms and theoretical attitudes.

Lucia Chiavola Birnbaum (Italy and USA) argues that the oldest deity worshipped by homo sapiens is that of a "dark mother" in Central and Southern Africa. Prehistoric signs of this figure were carried by African migrants after 50,000 BCE to the caves and cliffs of all continents. She tells us that c. 25,000 BCE, these signs were transmuted into venerated female images found all around the Mediterranean area, and in the Middle East, the Far East, and in the Americas. In the Christian epoch, she says these became "black Madonnas," but that the legacy of the African "dark mother" is evident in all representations of dark-skinned women divinities on every continent. This contribution to matriarchal studies concentrates on the island of Sardinia.

The following contributions present traces of past matriarchal societies in North Africa, Israel and Japan: *Vicki Noble* (USA) discusses how the Amazons got their name, indicating that ancient civilizations were composed of goddess-worshipping clans governed by women, where marriage as we know it probably didn't exist. As with contemporary Mosuo in China, women would have been free to take lovers, while their children would be raised by the clan as a whole. Noble states that when patriarchal tribes entered territories occupied by matriarchal peoples, the lack of obvious roles for husbands and fathers was in glaring contrast to their own practices. Scythians, for example, lived next door to matriarchal Sarmatians, among whom were women warriors and priests. She hypothesizes that these Scythians would have called the Sarmatians "Amazons," meaning, "no-husband-ones."

Marguerite Rigoglioso (USA) continues this topic with her research on Libyan Amazons (Tunisia). She explains that ancient historian Diodorus Siculus described various female warrior tribes of North Africa known as "Amazons," while Herodotus provided ethnographic detail on what were possibly matriarchal tribes of antiquity. In her article, Rigoglioso presents preliminary archaeological, ethnographic, semiotic, and linguistic evidence gathered from her recent research expedition to Tunisia that she states may attest to the historical existence of the "Libyan" or North African Amazons. She considers whether certain matriarchal aspects of Imazighen/Amazigh (Berber) cultures, local religious practices and legends, and ancient Berber symbols could be remnants of Amazon culture.

In her article, *Christa Mulack* (Germany) provides a new perspective on the Hebrew Bible, one of the most patriarchal texts of western tradition. Yet, the thorough study of this text, in combination with Matriarchal Studies, sheds light on other aspects of biblical literature, such as ancient passages with clearly matriarchal content. The discovery of these textual treasures allows her to identify a pre-Israelite goddess underlying many texts coming from the culture of ancient Palestine. As a consequence, she finds it necessary to abandon the conviction that Israel began with a patriarchal culture and society possessing a primordial monotheism.

Susan Gail Carter (USA) talks about what she calls the "matristic" roots of Japan. According to her, a strong case can be made that matriarchy preceded patriarchy in Japan. Using a set of seven cultural indicators, she sets forth the hypothesis that Japan's prehistory (and proto-history) was matriarchal and provided fertile ground for the myth of Amaterasu-o-mi-kami and her emergence in female form. Carter finds that this goddess's spiritual reign and survival today as the preeminent deity in the Shinto pantheon can, in part, be attributed to the remaining traces of this earlier matriarchal culture.

In Part VII, the question of the origins of patriarchy is discussed. Understanding the origins of patriarchy is one of the most urgent tasks of Modern Matriarchal Studies, because up until now, no adequate explanation has been given for the rise of patrarichy in almost all corners of the world. In order to be able to analyze present patriarchal societies, including western societies, it is necessary to understand on a deep level what caused the shift from the matriarchal form of society to the patriarchal one on different continents. There can be no understanding of the current global crisis without an understand ing of the history of the patriarchal system at the root of this crisis.

James DeMeo (USA) maintains that the origins of patriarchy lie in the ancient desertification of Central Asia and Northern Africa, a huge region he calls "Saharasia." He explains that the anthropological data, and a correlated global archaeological/historical survey, suggest a source region for what he calls armoured "patristic" or dominator cultures within Saharasia mainly after 4000 BCE. He demonstrates that around that time, Saharasia began to change from a semi-forested savanna into desert, with subsequent famine-driven outward migrations. According to him, this is the genesis of the great Indo-Aryan and Semitic cultural migrations which are characterized by patriarchal societal organization.

Heide Goettner-Abendroth (Germany) argues that it is impossible to hypothesize about the historical origins of patriarchy without first having researched the structure of matriarchial societies prior to the rise of patriarchy. This is necessary in order to expose false assumptions about the constituent causes that brought patriarchal structures into existence that may be rooted in patriarchal worldviews. To clarify how this happens, Goettner-Abendroth challenges some of the popular—but incorrect—hypotheses about the rise of patriarchy, and then proposes an answer to the question of *why* the matriarchal form of society gave way to the patriarchal form. This change took place at different times in different ways all over the world, and is still going on today. She briefly outlines the most important steps in this transformational process.

Finally, Part VIII is dedicated to Matriarchal Politics. It presents the Declaration developed on the final day of the Second World Congress. The presenters, as well as many participants, expressed their ideas on how to generate concrete alternatives and practical solutions to the patriarchal system of exploitation, and explored steps that could be taken to promote the re-establishment of peaceful societies. The Declaration emphasizes the political significance of both congresses, and of Modern Matriarchal Studies in general, and demonstrates that international matriarchal politics stands in opposition to white supremacist patriarchal capitalist homogenization and the globalization of misery. It stands for egalitarianism, diversity and the economics of the heart. Several matriarchal societies still exist around the world, proposing an alternative, life-affirming model to patriarchal raptor capitalism. In this way, many awakened women and men are about to create working matriarchal models as component parts of a new humane society.

Part I
Theory and Politics of Matriarchal Societies

HEIDE GOETTNER-ABENDROTH

The Deep Structure of Matriarchal Society

Findings and Political Relevance of Modern Matriarchal Societies

Despite all the hostility directed against modern Matriarchal Studies, it is not possible to disregard its findings. It presents us with a well-balanced, egalitarian and basically peaceful society that can exist without life-destroying inventions like wars of conquest and the rule of dominance. This is why I am convinced that matriarchy is needed in the struggle for a humane world.

—Heide Goettner-Abendroth

The term "matriarchy" needs to be redefined. For women, *reclaiming* this term means reclaiming the knowledge about cultures that have been mainly created by women. We are not obliged to follow the current, male-biased understanding of the term "matriarchy" as meaning "rule of women" or "domination by the mothers." Matriarchy is commonly interpreted this way because it seems an obvious parallel to "patriarchy." In fact, the Greek word *arché* has a double meaning. It means "beginning" as well as "domination." "Matriarchy" can thus be translated more accurately as "the mothers from the beginning."

"Patriarchy," on the other hand, translates correctly as "domination by the fathers." Patriarchy could also be translated as "the fathers from the beginning," but this led to "domination by the fathers," because not having any natural right to "beginning" means that men had to enforce their right to be "first" through domination. By the same token, since mothers clearly *are* the beginning, because of their capacity to bring forth life, they have no need to enforce their place in the social order by domination.

When I began doing research on matriarchal societies, a task to which I have devoted my entire life, I began with my own culture and investigated the social and mythological patterns of pre-patriarchal times in the early history of Europe, the Mediterranean region, and the Middle East (Goettner-Abendroth 1995). I did my research as a European philosopher, occupied with philosophy and the history of cultures. From the very beginning this was a task that required a deep critique of patriarchy.

I could not, however, continue confining my study to these regions, because in these areas the early matriarchal cultures were destroyed and what remains are only fragments and remnants, distorted by many layers of later interpretations, and thus not sufficient to provide a complete picture of matriarchal societies. I subsequently decided to familiarize myself with anthropological research that had been done on this topic. In the anthropological sources I found the same prejudices about matriarchal cultures as I had in historical research, and this led me to broaden my criticism of patriarchal ideology. During the last fifteen years, using critical analysis and cross-cultural studies, I have uncovered a more complete picture of matriarchal societies, and developed the full definition that I now use in my research on matriarchies (Goettner-Abendroth 1988-1995, 1991 and 1999, 2000).

I never intended, however, that my results should speak for Indigenous peoples, nor would I pretend that my analysis of the deep structure of this type of society could elucidate one of these societies completely and in detail, or could be applied to all Indigenous societies. This task can only be fulfilled by years of field work in many corners of the world, and can best be done by Indigenous researchers into their own societies.

My explication of "matriarchy" is much more than a simple definition. First, it sets out the deep structure of the social form called "matriarchy." This structural definition is an effective intellectual tool that can be used to uncover matriarchal structures in cultures both past and present.

Second, this structural definition forms the basis of a comprehensive theory on matriarchal societies. But this is not a theory set in stone; it can be used and continuously developed by each researcher who is interested.

Third, this theory is based on a hybrid methodology that includes historical and anthropological research as well as all the other relevant disciplines. It cannot be developed from one discipline only, thus, in this sense it is truly multidisciplinary. All fields of socio-cultural sciences must be used together to re-cover the vast yet suppressed knowledge of matriarchies and the newly-emerging modern Matriarchal Studies.

Even if matriarchal studies started more than 140 years ago with the pioneering theories of Johann Jakob Bachofen (1861) and Lewis Henry Morgan (1851), their research didn't have a true scientific foundation because of the lack of a clear definition of this type of society, and because patriarchally-biased presuppositions distorted their findings. This situation has continued. Up until recently, research in the field of matriarchy—often reported on under false categories—has lacked scientific definition of matriarchy and an elaborated methodology, in spite of the existence of several competent studies and extensive data collection. This absence of scientific rigour opens up the door to the emotional and ideological entanglements that have been a burden for this socio-cultural science from the very beginning. Patriarchy itself has not been critically considered in the treatment of this subject, while stereotypical views of women—and a neurotic fear of women's alleged power—has often confused the issues.

In 1978, I started to publish a theoretical framework for research on matriarchies that in the meantime has been further developed (Goettner-Abendroth 1978). It provides a new basis for this field of knowledge, thus making way for

Modern Matriarchal Studies. This new research differs in several ways from previous matriarchal studies:

1. It articulates a structural definition of "matriarchy," including specific definitions of terms which present the deep structure of these societies.[2]
2. From this starting point a comprehensive theory is developed (Goettner-Abendroth 2004).
3. It uses an explicit multidisciplinary methodology, in which different socio-cultural sciences are combined logically.
4. It presents a systematic method for criticism of the patriarchally-biased ideology that characterizes the existing social and cultural sciences concerning the subject "matriarchy."

In this way, a new socio-cultural science has been created, one that represents a new paradigm. I call it the "matriarchy paradigm." The central tenet of this paradigm is that women have not only created society and culture over long periods of human history, but that all subsequent cultural developments originated there and are based on these societies.

A new paradigm emerges when the old one has lost its credibility and starts to decay. This new approach, the matriarchy paradigm, can be used to clarify many open questions that the patriarchal paradigm could not satisfactorily resolve. It has political relevance as well: it must not stay confined to academia because, as a new worldview, it affects society and the individuals within it. It is not dependent on one particular individual; rather, it "erupts" simultaneously in many different ways and at many different places because the time is ripe for it. It comes into being out of a spiritual and political need, one that no one planned and no one ordered.

Several scholars, working independently of each other, are now expressing the matriarchy paradigm for the first time, while maintaining their own specific emphases and perspectives (see, for example, Bennholdt-Thomsen 1994; Claudot-Hawad 1984, 1993; Grasshoff 1996; Mann 2000; Gimbutas 1989, 1991; Eisler 1987). Some of these scholars hold differing perspectives, and some of their results might not be consonant with each other. Not all of them call this form of society by the same name; it is variously referred to as "matrifocal," "matristic," "matricentric," or a "glycanic" society. However, this does not weaken the new paradigm. On the contrary, as with every young science, each of these researchers advance the process of developing new knowledge. The scholars involved in this exciting process have one subject in common: a radical new perception of society and culture, one that completely replaces the patriarchal worldview.

The Deep Structure of Matriarchal Society

The research findings of Modern Matriarchal Studies contradict the ideology of universal male dominance and universal patriarchy. Modern Matriarchal Studies is concerned with investigating and presenting non-patriarchal societies: those that have existed in the past and those that are, to some degree, still with us now. Because all over the world today, Indigenous peoples in Asia, Africa, the Americas, and the Pacific area foster cultures that show matriarchal patterns in their age-old traditions. These patterns are not just a reversal of patriarchy, with women somehow ruling over men—as the usual misinterpretations would have it—rather they are, without exception, gender-egalitarian societies. Additionally, most of them are egalitarian societies on the whole. That means, hierarchies, classes, and the domination of one gender by the other are unknown to them. They are societies that are free of domination, but are stabilized by certain guidelines and codes social interaction.

With matriarchies, equality does not mean a mere levelling of differences. The natural differences between the genders and the generations are respected and honoured, but the differences do not necessarily lead to hierarchies, as is common in patriarchy. The different genders and generations each have their own value and dignity, and through a system of complementary activities, are dependent on each other.

We can see this at all levels of society: the economic level, the social level, the political level, and also the cultural level (which includes worldview and faith). More precisely, matriarchies are societies with complementary equality, where great care is taken to provide a balance. This applies to the balance between genders, among generations, and between humans and nature; it creates an attitude of peacemaking. In turn, this is what makes matriarchies so attractive to those looking for a new philosophy and a new vision to support the creation of a just and peaceful society.

Some of these still existing matriarchal societies are the Mosuo, Yao, Miao and Tan peoples in China; the Chiang people of Tibet; the Minangkabau of Sumatra; the Ainu of Japan; the Trobrianders of Melanesia in the Pacific; the Khasi and Garo in Northeast India, and the Nayar in Southeast India; the Bantu of Central Africa; the Akan and Ashanti peoples in West Africa; the Berbers and Tuareg of North Africa; the Arawak peoples of South America; the Cuna and Juchitecan societies of Central America; and, the Hopi and Pueblo peoples as well as the Iroquois peoples of North America, just to name the main ones. Even though their concrete patterns of societal organization differ, they all show the same characteristics that allow them to be called "matriarchal societies." It is similar with patriarchal societies, which show many differences from their beginnings as warrior societies via patriarchal theocracies and empires to present-day capitalist patriarchies, but their intrinsic features are the same and can be found throughout their history. Matriarchal societies also had a long history—even longer than the history of patriarchal societies—so it is no surprise that the still existing concrete societies of this type differ among each other. But this does not concern their principles, which make their common deep structure visible.

Today, all matriarchal peoples are in danger of losing their traditional cultures—or have already lost them. I have portrayed matriarchal societies in their socio-cultural and historical context, according to the anthropological and historical evidence available in my main work, *Matriarchy* (published in Germany in 1991/1999 and 2000). Additionally, I have published a monograph about the Mosuo people in *Matriarchy in Southern China* (published in Germany in 1998). From these studies, and through a careful, inductive process, I have reached the conclusions from which I derive my arguments.[3] Based on cross-cultural examination of case after case, I have outlined the structures and regulative mechanisms that function across all levels of matriarchal societies. In this way, the deep structure of matriarchal society emerged. I refer to four different levels of society: (1) the economic level; (2) the level of social patterns; (3) the level of political decision-making; and, (4) the level of culture, worldview, and spirituality.

1. The Economic Level

At the economic level, matriarchies are most often agricultural societies, but not exclusively so. According to a system that is identical with the lines of kinship and the patterns of marriage, goods circulate as gifts. This system prevents goods from being accumulated by one special person or one special group and is hence, a system of mutual aid. Thus, the principles of economic equality are consciously maintained, and the society remains non-accumulating and egalitarian.

The people enjoy perfect mutuality for every advantage or disadvantage in terms of acquiring goods is mediated by social guidelines. For example, at the village festivals, wealthy clans invite all the people in the village to be their guests. These wealthy clan members organize the banquet, the rituals, the music, and dances of one of the annual festivals, and they give away their wealth as an unconditional gift to all their neighbours. They do not gain anything by it but honour. At the next festival another lucky clan will outdo itself by inviting everybody in the village or neighbourhood, and will entertain all and distribute gifts. The matriarchal economy can thus be called a "gift economy" in the truest sense (see Vaughan 1997).[4]

Therefore, on the economic level matriarchies create a balanced economy, which is the fundamental basis for peace. Due to these features, I call matriarchies, at this level, *societies of economic reciprocity, balanced by gift-giving*.

2. The Social Level

At the social level, matriarchal societies are founded on motherhood and are based on the clan. Motherhood is perceived as the most important function in each society, for mothering creates the new generations that are the future of society. It is necessary, however, to clarify two points here:

1) In matriarchies, it is not necessary to be a biological mother in order to be acknowledged as a woman, because matriarchies practice the common motherhood of a group of sisters. Each individual sister does not necessarily have children, but together they are all "mothers" of any children that any of the women have. Matriarchal motherhood is founded on the freedom of women to decide on their

own about whether or not to have biological children. Furthermore, each female elder is referred to as "mother," which is an honourary title.

2) In matriarchies, mothering, which originates as a biological fact, is accorded such great importance that it is transformed into a cultural model. This model is much more appropriate to the human condition than the way patriarchies conceptualize and use motherhood. Of course, patriarchies depend on motherhood just as much as any culture does, but patriarchies contrive to make the importance of motherhood invisible. This ends up making women, and especially mothers, into slaves or chattel.

In matriarchal societies, people live together in large kinship groups formed according to the principle of *matriliny*; that is, kinship is acknowledged exclusively via the female line. The clan's name, and all social positions and political titles, are passed on through the mother's line. Such a matri-clan consists at least of three generations of women and the directly related men who are the brothers of each generation of women. Generally, the matri-clan lives in one big clan-house. The women live there permanently, because daughters and granddaughters never leave the clan-house of their mother when they marry. This is called *matrilocality*.

What is most important is the fact that women have the power of disposition over the goods and the houses of the clan, especially over the sources of nourishment. All the goods are given to the clan mother, the matriarch, and she distributes them equally among the members of the clan. This characteristic feature of women's power over the disposition of goods, besides matrilinearity and matrilocality, grants women such a strong position that these societies are accurately called "matriarchal" (and are thus not merely matrilineal).

The different clans are connected to each other by marriage patterns, especially the system of reciprocal marriage between two clan groups. Marriage between two clans is not marriage between individuals, but rather a communal marriage. It is an ancient custom of bonding between two clans, and an effective system of mutual aid.

The married people do not leave the houses of their mothers, but stay in their own matri-clans. In places where the most ancient patterns are still in use, men practice "visiting marriage," going to their lover's or spouse's clan house to meet them. But there they are only guests overnight, and they must leave in the morning. They have no rights and duties with regard to the children of their spouses, but instead they have rights and duties in the houses of their own mothers, and act as "social fathers" for the children of their own sisters.

Due to additional patterns of marriage between all clans, everyone in a matriarchal village or neighbourhood of a town is related to everyone else by birth or by marriage. These nets of relationship are intentionally produced to form a "big family" of the people, where everybody is "mother" or "sister" or "brother" to all, which results in creating bonds of love and care among equals. Therefore, I call matriarchies *non-hierarchical, horizontal societies of matrilineal kinship*.

3. The Political Level

The decisive factor for a society of peace is the process of making political decisions. In matriarchal societies, political practice follows the principle of consensus, which means *unanimity* for each decision. Matriarchal societies are well-organized to actualize this principle, and practise it along the lines of matriarchal kinship. In the clan-house, women and men meet in a council where domestic matters are discussed. Everybody has only one vote, even the matriarch, and no member of the household is excluded. After thorough discussion, each decision is taken by consensus. This is the basis for real equality.

The same is true for the entire village. When matters concerning the whole village are to be discussed, delegates from every clan house meet in the village council. These delegates can be the matriarchs of the clans, or the brothers and sons they have chosen to represent the clan. No decision concerning the whole village may be taken without the consensus of all clan houses. This means that these delegates do not make decisions themselves; they simply communicate the decisions that have been made in their clan houses. They maintain the communication system of the village and move back and forth between the village council and the clan houses until the entire village reaches consensus.

The same applies at the regional level. Delegates from all villages meet to discuss the decisions of their communities in the regional council. Again, the delegates function only as bearers of communication. The delegates of the villages move back and forth between the village council and the regional council, and the delegates of the clan houses likewise move between the village council and the clan houses, until all individuals of the region have reached consensus. The source of all the politics are the clan houses where the people live, and in this way, a true "grassroots democracy" is put into practice. The foundation for this political system is an economy of reciprocity, based on gift-giving, and the "big family" of a society of matrilineal kinship.

Therefore, from the political point of view, I call matriarchies *egalitarian societies of consensus*. These political patterns do not allow for the accumulation of political power. In exactly this sense, they are free of domination. They have no class of rulers and no class of suppressed people; that is, they have no "enforcement bodies" like warriors or police, nor do they have controlling and punishing institutions necessary to establish domination.

Matriarchies are all egalitarian at least in terms of gender—they have no gender hierarchy and are true *gender-egalitarian societies*. For many matriarchal societies, the social order is completely egalitarian at both local and regional levels. In the course of their long history under varying conditions, some matriarchal societies developed certain hierarchical patterns at the local or regional levels, based on the most traditional society-founding clans. Sometimes, queendoms/kingdoms developed from these, maintaining gender-egalitarian patterns throughout the society—including the highest offices—and refraining from imposing tributes on their peoples. Clearly, their structures are completely different from those of patriarchal kingdoms formed by conquest and, consequently, of patriarchal empires based on exploitation.

4. The Level of Culture, Worldview, and Spirituality

Such a societal system would not function as a whole if there were not a deep, supporting and all-permeating spiritual attitude. This is the case with all matriarchies. At the spiritual and cultural level, matriarchal societies do not have religions based on a God who is invisible, untouchable, and incomprehensible—but omnipotent. On the contrary, in matriarchy, divinity is immanent, for the whole world is regarded as divine—as feminine divine. This is evident in the widely held concept of the universe as the Great Creatress who created everything, and of the earth as the Great Mother who brings forth every living being. Everything is endowed with divinity, each woman and man, each plant and animal, the smallest pebble and the biggest star.

In such a culture, everything is spiritual. In their festivals, following the cycle of the seasons and the cycle of life, everything is celebrated: nature in its manifold expressions; the different clans with their different tasks; the different genders and generations with their specific abilities following the principle, "Diversity is wealth." There is no separation between sacred and secular, so everyday tasks—such as sowing and harvesting, cooking and weaving, building a house and making a journey—also have ritual significance. Furthermore, there is no absolute difference between the living and the dead, for the "dead" are living male and female ancestors who will return as new-born children into their clans. The veneration of the ancestors, especially the ancestresses, is a marked characteristic.

In an all-permeating sense, these societies are sacred ones. If nature is regarded as holy, including the whole earth and the cosmos, then humans worship nature and live in peace with Her in order to best ensure their own welfare.

Therefore, on the spiritual level, I define matriarchies as *sacred societies and cultures of the Feminine Divine*.

In recent times most traditional matriarchal societies—which reflect the deep structure outlined here—break down or have broken down due to patriarchal societies. The causes of this cultural destruction are colonization by different patriarchal empires; Christian, Islamic, and Buddhist missionizing; the mass tourism of modern times; intrusion of the market economy and new technology that fosters the male ego and destroys the clan system; and, industrialization to profit ruling states and global corporations. Some of them are passionately fighting for their survival, rights, and cultural identity.

Political Relevance of Modern Matriarchal Studies

This outline shows that modern Matriarchal Studies deals with knowledge about non-patriarchal egalitarian economical, social, political, and cultural patterns, which are basically peaceful. This knowledge is urgently needed in this late phase of globally destructive patriarchy.

Today, it is becoming increasingly clear that matriarchal patterns have great significance for both present and future societies. For matriarchies are not abstract *utopias*, constructed according to philosophical concepts that could never be implemented. On the contrary, they have existed throughout long historical periods until today. They embody an enormous amount of intellectual creativity and practical experience, and belong indispensably to humankind's cultural store of knowledge. Their precepts show how life can be organized in such a way that it is based on the unconditional fulfillment of needs, is non-violent, and is simply *humane*.

This is why it is important to recognize the political significance of matriarchal patterns as a way of solving current problems. Matriarchal societies can show us the path to new egalitarian societies that combine spirituality with politics to create another kind of economy and, hence, another kind of society. Their economics, politics, social organization, and spirituality are interconnected, and the purpose of all of it is to provide a good life for everybody; this common good is assured through their organizational structures and conventions. Of course, we can not go back and simply transfer historical patterns to the present. For example, the blood-relatedness of the clans, or their sole dependence on agriculture, is not necessarily appropriate today. History and its accompanying social changes cannot be turned backwards. However, for our own path toward new egalitarian societies, we can gain much stimulation and great insight from these matriarchal patterns, which have been tried and tested over millennia.

Economically, we have arrived at a position where it is no longer possible to increase the amount of large-scale industrial growth, and further inflate the western standard of living without running the risk of totally annihilating the biosphere of the earth. A way out of this—one that has been discussed by several scholars—is subsistence economy, based on local and regional units (see, for example, von Werlhof, Bennholdt-Thomsen and Faraclas 2001). These communities work frugally and self-sufficiently, and the resulting quality of life is more important to them than producing a great quantity of goods. It is important to support the still existing subsistence economies the world over, and create new ones everywhere. Women are the mainstays of these economic structures and the societies that are based on them. They need to be supported and helped to expand by our own subsistence creations, so that such economies cannot be absorbed into the global market. This regionalization, in which women guide the economy, is a matriarchal principle.

On the *social level,* it is important to stop the increasing "atomization" of society. It drives people deeper and deeper into desperation and loneliness, causing disease and providing fertile ground for violence and war. What is necessary is the support and creation of affinity groups and intentional communities of different kinds: they can be neighbourhood associations or regional networks, they may be traditional existing communities, or alternative new ones. These groups are not just interest groups—interest groups are quickly created, but just as easily disbanded. The affinity groups, rather, are formed on the basis of a spiritual-philosophical rapport between the members. This is the basis for creating a symbolic clan as a group of *siblings by choice*. Here, there is far more commitment than there is in a mere interest group.

As a matriarchal principle, such affinity groups, which can form affinity clans of siblings by choice, are initiated, directed, and kept going by women. Right now women can instigate such groups, and many women have already done so. The decisive factors are the needs of women—and especially of children, who are the future of humanity. The focus here is not men's desire for power and dominion, which has led to patriarchal, extended families and political men's clubs and associations that exclude and oppress women. The symbolic matri-clans, based on siblings by choice, integrate men fully, but do so according to a set of values based on mutual care and love instead of power. Men have a better life in this kind of society than they do under patriarchy. It would be a political aim to actualize or support the creation of such communities in every possible way.

On the *level of political decision-making*, the matriarchal consensus principle is of utmost importance for a truly egalitarian society. This can be practised in the here and now, anywhere and everywhere. The consensus principle is the foundation for building new matriarchal communities. At the same time, it prevents splinter groups, cliques, or individuals from dominating the society. It brings about a balance between the genders and also between the generations as the youth and the elderly have the same standing as everybody else. Furthermore, consensus is a genuine democratic principle, for it provides what formal democracy promises, but never delivers.

Following this principle, small units of these new matri-clans are the true decision-makers, but this can only be practised up to the regional level. According to the subsistence perspective, flourishing and self-sufficient regions are the political aim—not the big nation states, state unions, and superpowers, which are merely serving to increase the power of the wealthy elite and reduce individuals to "human resources."

On the *spiritual-cultural level*, we are bound to bid farewell to all hierarchical religions with a transcendent view of the divine and a claim to the total truth. This has led to the vilification of creation, the environment, and humankind itself—particularly of its women. Instead, the aim is a re-enchantment and sanctification of the world as a whole. According to matriarchal vision, everything in the world is divine. This leads to everything being honoured and celebrated in a free and creative way: nature in her manifold appearances and various beings, as well as the multiplicity of human individuals and communities. It means celebrating the different genders and generations and honouring their special skills and abilities as their different "dignities." Many women today have already begun to do this. In this way, matriarchal spirituality, practised among women, is once again about to infuse all aspects of everday life, although there is no dogma and no teaching, and no one is forced to believe; instead there is the continuous, manifold celebration of life and the visible world.

In this sense, the path to new egalitarian societies can only be holistic, without being vague. It has to be concrete, without getting lost in disconnected details. New egalitarian societies could follow what I call the "Matriarchal Model," which sets out a clear vision and practical guidelines to a better future for all of us. Thus, matriarchies can be our guiding light towards a just and peaceful world-society.

Translation by Karen Smith

Heide Goettner-Abendroth has published various books on matriarchal society and culture and is the founding mother of Modern Matriarchal Studies. In 1980, she was visiting professor at the University of Montreal (Canada) and, in 1992, at the University of Innsbruck (Austria). In 1986, she founded the International Academy HAGIA: Academy for Modern Matriarchal Studies and Matriarchal Spirituality in Germany. Recent publications include The Dancing Goddess: Principles of a Matriarchal Aesthetic *(1991);* The Goddess and Her Heros: Matriarchal Religion in Mythology, Fairy-Tales, and Literature *(1995). Her main work on Matriarchy (published in three volumes 1988, 1991, 2000 in Germany) is now translated into English. She organized and guided two World Congresses on Matriarchal Studies (2003 and 2005) which are presented in this book. She is one of the 1,000 "Peace Women" all over the world who have been nominated by the Swiss Peace Initiative for the Nobel Peace Prize in 2005.*

[1]Motto on my personal website <www.goettner-abendroth.de>.
[2]Independently of my research, Peggy Reeves Sanday (2002) also re-defined "matriarchy" in her research on the Minangkabau.
[3]For an extensive bibliography of this scholarship see Goettner-Abendroth: *Das Matriarchat,* three volumes (this work is now translated into English). See also Goettner-Abendroth 1998, 1999.
[4]The "gift economy" is based on maternal values in the sense that such an economy cares for everybody and nurtures all its members. It does not allow the goods of the many to be hoarded in the hands of few (see Vaughan 1997).

References

Bachofen, J. J. 1967. *Myth, Religion, and Mother Right: Selected Writings of J. J. Bachofen.* 1861. Princeton: Princeton University Press.
Bennholdt-Thomsen, Veronika. 1994. *Juchitàn—Stadt der Frauen. Vom Leben im Matriarchat.* Reinbek bei Hamburg: Verlag Rowohlt.
Claudot-Hawad, Hélène. 1984. "Femme Idéale et Femme Sociale chez les Touaregs de l'Ahaggar." *Production pastorale et société,* Nr. 14, Paris.
Claudot-Hawad, Hélène. 1993. *Les Touaregs: Portrait en fragments.* Aix-en-Provence: Edisud.
Eisler, Riane. 1987. *The Chalice and the Blade: Our History, Our Future.* San

Francisco: Harper and Row.

Gimbutas, Marija. 1989. *The Language of the Goddess: Unearthing the Hidden-Symbols of Western Civilization*. San Francisco: Harper and Row.

Gimbutas, Marija. 1991. *The Civilization of the Goddess: The World of Old Europe*. Ed. Joan Marler. San Francisco: HarperSanFrancisco.

Goettner-Abendroth, Heide. 1978. "Zur Methodologie der Frauenforschung am Beispiel einer Theorie des Matriarchats" ("Towards a Methodology for Women's Studies Exemplified by a Theory of Matriarchy"). *Dokumentation der Tagung "Frauenforschung in den Sozialwissenschaften."* Munich: Deutsches Jugendinstitut.

Goettner-Abendroth, Heide. 1988-1995. *Das Matriarchat I. Geschichte seiner Erforschung (Matriarchy I. History of Research)*. Stuttgart: Verlag Kohlhammer.

Goettner-Abendroth, Heide. 1991 and 1999. *Das Matriarchat II.1. Stammesgesellschaften in Ostasien, Indonesien, Ozeanien (Matriarchy II.1. Matriarchal Societies in East Asia, Indonesia, and Pacific Area)*. Stuttgart: Verlag Kohlhammer.

Goettner-Abendroth, Heide. 1995. *The Goddess and her Heros: Matriarchal Mythology*. Stow: Anthony Publishing Company. (First published in German: *Die Göttin und ihr Heros* München: Verlag Frauenoffensive, 1980.)

Goettner-Abendroth, Heide. 1998. *Matriarchat in Südchina: Eine Forschungsreise zu den Mosuo (Matriarchy in South China: Research Among the Mosuo People)*. Stuttgart: Verlag Kohlhammer.

Goettner-Abendroth, Heide. 1999. "The Structure of Matriarchal Society. Exemplified by the Society of the Mosuo in China." Ed. Joan Marler. *ReVision* 3 (21): 31-35.

Goettner-Abendroth, Heide. 2000. *Das Matriarchat II.2. Stammesgesellschaften in Amerika, Indien, Afrika (Matriarchy II.2. Matriarchal Societies in America, India, Africa)*. Stuttgart: Verlag Kohlhammer.

Goettner-Abendroth, Heide. 2004. "Matriarchal Society: Definition and Theory." *Il Dono/The Gift: A Feminist Analysis*. Ed. Genevieve Vaughan. *Athanor* 15 (8). Rome: Meltemi. 69-80.

Grasshoff, Malika. 1996. *La Magie des femmes kabyles et l'unité de la société traditionnelle*. Paris: L'Harmattan.

Mann, Barbara. 2000. *Iroquoian Women: The Gantowisas*. New York: Peter Lang.

Morgan, Lewis Henry. 1965 [1851]. *League of the Ho-dé-no-sau-nee, or Iroquois*. Rochester: Sage and Brother.

Sanday, Peggy Reeves. 2002. *Women at the Center: Life in a Modern Matriarchy*. Ithaca: Cornell University Press.

Vaughan, Genevieve. 1997. *For-Giving. A Feminist Criticism of Exchange*. Austin: Plain View Press.

von Werlhof, Claudia, Veronika Bennholdt-Thomsen and Nicholas Faraclas, eds. 2001. *There Is an Alternative: Subsistence and Worldwide Resistance to Corporate Globalization*. London: Zed Books.

CLAUDIA VON WERLHOF

The Utopia of a Motherless World

Patriarchy as War-System

I am sorry, but we still live in patriarchy! It is, therefore, my task to make clear what that really means. Because, patriarchy is not only a threat to matriarchal societies still alive on earth and of matriarchy as a sort of "second culture" within patriarchy, but it is also a threat to humankind as a whole, including the patriarchs themselves.

—Claudia von Werlhof (2001, 2003, 2005)

Hypothesis: Patriarchy is a "Dark" Utopia

A "deep" analysis of patriarchy shows:

1) Patriarchy tries to build a "new paradise" on earth.
2) The way to this paradise is war.
3) The new paradise is supposed to be a motherless world.

Patriarchy, therefore, is a "dark" utopia. As a utopia against the world and against women it has to be forced upon the world and women, if it is going to be realized.

Patriarchy is a "Civilization" Dependent on Matriarchy

Patriarchies never existed based on their own capacities and never had their own independent civilizations, but developed only after the conquest of matriarchal societies. Seen from this perspective, patriarchy is a social process still evolving. What is called civilization today is a dependent (patriarchal) civilization that has been built upon matriarchy, or what is left of it, up to the present day and every-where on the globe. In reality, patriarchy is a mixed society, which still depends on matriarchy for its life.

The utopia of patriarchy consists in becoming totally independent from matri-archy. The question is, nevertheless, can patriarchy develop into an independent civilization, and if so, what will happen when the last vestiges of matriarchy have been destroyed?

29

Patriarchy is "Militarization" Instead of "Civilization": A Developing "War-System"

What is the real meaning of war?

Matriarchal societies are societies of peace. But patriarchy came into the world by conquest, by war. War is not just violence, but organized mass violence, based on calculated planning.

After the conquest the war continues. It becomes institutionalized. The war takes the form of the State. The new order is more militarized than civilized, because it has to be protected from being dissolved by the people, and by life. Thus, war is not the exception, as is normally assumed, but the rule in patriarchy.

We can say that the new society becomes a system because, in contrast to matriarchal society, it is based on systematic contradictions within society and between society and nature. The belief in violence becomes the general religion of patriarchy. Violence is looked upon as the main truth in life (Girard 1972).

A complete, "pure," closed war-system that is embracing all spheres of society and nature is the utopia of patriarchy.

What is the real meaning of the patriarch, the "father"?

Let us explore what "patriarch" or "father" means. The analysis of the etymology shows: Fathers are allegedly legitimate rulers over conquered paradises that have been transformed into kingdoms/empires of the sky and on earth; fathers are supposed to be the real creators of life and wealth, being somehow mothers, too; fathers seem to have the knowledge about the secrets and miracles of creation from the beginning of time, so that there is neither an independent mother, nor a Goddess anymore; and the mother has been defined away or reduced to an attribute of the almighty cosmic-and-earthly ruling Father-God, who has stolen her power and wisdom (Budge 1969, 1978; Frankenberg 1985; Walker 1988; *The American Heritage Dictionary* 2001). Thus, the Father-God is a fiction in contrast to the Mother-Goddess as a reality.

The earthly fathers and patriarchs, therefore, get into a difficult situation. They have to prove in reality that they are able to create, that this creation is the highest and best, and that they can even replace the supposedly lower forms of existing creation. This is their utopia. The question now becomes: What is it that fathers create? And how are they doing it?

What are patriarchal meanings of death and life? How are death and life related to patriarchal creation?

The first patriarchal creation is "creation" out of destruction. The looting that takes place during war provides wealth and life to warriors and their society (Mies 1986). Hence, the cult of the artificially produced second, supposedly good, death, the death under control, the non-natural death, that occurs through war, murder, torture, rape, and other forms and techniques of violence.

The second main creation of patriarchy is a so-called creation out of nothing.

It is based on the invention of a fictitious life and world beyond the existing one, a metaphysical, supposedly existing second, higher and better, life and world (Plato 1994).

We can be certain that the world had never before been perceived as divided in that way. We can further assume that foreign invaders invented a world beyond the existing one because they had to explain where they came from in order to legitimize their rule. In sum, patriarchal acting and thinking follow the same principles:

1. Negate what existed before conquest by destroying it, usurping it, perverting it, transforming it, trying to do without it, and, as long as it still exists, looking down on it as bad, low, wrong, and sinful.

2. Make propaganda for utopia, a supposedly better world than the one that is still remembered as having existed before the conquest.

3. Invent a division between supposedly good and supposedly evil worlds, justifying the principle of "divide and conquer."

4. Feel legitimized to start to realize the utopia of a "better" world by a "creation" that consists of the plunder of the existing supposedly evil world, and by the "creations" of the supposed "good," metaphysical world, the world of the "higher" and "holy" creation.

The metaphysical world is the model of a utopia that will have to be materialized on earth (Sloterdijk and Macho 1991). However, in reality, the patriarchs as the "fathers" still depend on women and nature. This is why they are desperately trying to accelerate progress.

How the alchemist tried and still tries to become the first concrete utopian father

Why is the new "creation" destructive even after war, in so-called "peaceful" times? The analysis of patriarchal creation beyond immediate war can be undertaken by using a new concept of alchemy and of the alchemist who is helping to expand the war-system to non-military, if not all spheres, of life. "War is the father of all things!" as Heraclitus put it. If we look at the methods and principles of about 5000 years of alchemical processes and manipulations, we see that they have become typically patriarchal: "Divide and rule!" "Solve et Coagula!" (Werlhof 1997, 2000, 2001, 2004).

The first step in the alchemical process of "creation" is called "mortification," from the Latin word mors, or death. Mortification means bringing death to living matter. This occurs in order to take control over matter and is mostly done by using fire (see Eliade 1980). This is most probably due to the war-tradition. The process finishes with a sort of black matter, which is considered to be the primordial matter, materia prima or massa confusa, out of which—so the alchemist supposes—life came into being. At that point, the alchemist thinks to start at point zero of creation like God himself, but on earth.

In the case of working with metals as matter, the alchemist continues his work based on the "black matter" as his *materia prima* which he has produced in the first step. In a second step, the alchemist tries to produce silver, which he calls "white matter," by adding mercury as "semen" into the *materia prima*, mostly lead, the lowest in the supposed hierarchy of metals. In a third step, the alchemist tries to produce alchemical "gold,"which he calls "yellow matter," by adding sulpher as "semen" into the silver. Gold is considered the highest of all matter. The substances, which the alchemist is putting together, are supposedly male and female. The lower matter is thought of as female, the higher matter and the "semen" is perceived to be male.

Using pyrotechnics (a melting process in the alchemist's oven that looks like an artificial uterus) the "chemical marriage," a perversion of the concept of the "holy marriage" in matriarchy, takes place. It is said (see Eliade 1980) that if the melting process during one of its stages is not successful, a woman has to be sacrificed, usually the female assistant of the alchemist, who must then jump into the oven. That seems to have worked.

In a fourth step, "red matter," a form of red gold or a red powder, can eventually result from adding "coral semen" into the gold (cf. Schütt 2000). This substance is next to what is called the "philosopher's stone," matter that contains all the creative life forces that will finally allow the alchemist to become a godlike creator.

The alchemical process can also occur using as a base plants or animals, organic or inorganic substances. It depends on the type of "creation" the alchemist is interested in. If human life is concerned, the alchemical process occurs with a base of human blood and sperm with which the alchemist tries to produce a *homunculus,* or little man, in a test-tube. For this creation, no mother is needed aside from female blood as "substance," and no biological father is needed aside from sperm as "substance." The "marriage" occurs in a test-tube, which again looks like an artificial uterus. At the top is the alchemist as the father who is inventing, leading, and controlling the procedure.

The alchemist's intent is to create a utopian life, a life *u-topos*, which means that it is life or matter without a genuine place on earth, without origin, without a navel, without the participation of real persons—except the alchemist himself—without a concrete locality, without love, and *without a mother*, especially without mother earth. This idea is central to all his creations, not only when human life itself is concerned. Gold, for instance, is seen as a mature child of mother earth. When extracting the different metals out of mother earth's womb, the alchemist considers them to be immature children of mother earth, which he is receiving by forcing her to abort them. By transforming the immature metals/children into mature ones, namely gold, he thinks he is helping mother earth to be faster, more efficient, and even more perfect in her birth-giving processes, so that finally the alchemist himself becomes the real creator.

The alchemist wants to become an independent creator who is able to force life into existence. Hence, the "philosopher's stone," the paradoxical combination of an artificially created higher matter with something perceived as the essence of life, with which the alchemist is able to create life not only independently from mothers, but also independently from women and nature as such. Only then is *creation out of the nothing* possible.

But the problem of the general alchemical procedure is that there is dead matter —after its "mortification"—brought together with other more or less dead matter that has been abstracted and isolated from its original surroundings. The creation of real, new life in this way is, in fact, impossible. The alchemist in antiquity seems to have had a mechanical view of nature and life, but in reality life is not created mechanically. In modern times, the mechanical view has become the foundation of progress and, as such, modern alchemy is confronted with its constant failure. It thus sought to overcome this problem by combining dead matter with living matter. This is the principle behind the invention of the development of the *cyborg* today, which is conceived of as a mixture of a living being and machine (see Haraway 1983).

Generally, ways to combine dead matter with living matter was the result of industrialization which brought about a new technology, the machine, and a definition of living human labour linked to, and combined with, the machine(ry). During the work day, the labourer himself—the first cyborg actually—was transformed into a combination of something living with something dead, the machine(ry). From this stems the definition of a human being's labour power as something that can be disposed of as a commodity and be sold to the owner of the machine(ry). The labourer is thus a combination of separate parts, namely his labour power, which belonged to the machine, and himself, as a living being. In this way, the labourer, even without the machine, was seen as a combination of a living matter and something that did not belong to him, an abstract labour potential that could be sold to the machine owner.[1] The labourer from then on—like a cyborg—was neither really alive nor really dead, but rather a living machine, a commodity, living a life that is half dead because it has to be given away/sold as part of the labour process.

This modern, capitalist perspective on the labourer and his experience of the labour process show how much alchemical thinking and organizing has been implemented since the beginning of modern economy and the introduction of machine technology, which since then has gone unnoticed. This is because modernity is seen as a full success and therefore it never wants to be seen in relation to a pre-modern alchemy that failed.

Today the *hybrid,* a combination of living matter with other living matter, as can be observed in all forms of life-industries—as in bio-chemical, reproductive, and genetic engineering (see Rifkin 1998)—can be seen as another way to avoid a further failure of alchemy. In any case, modern alchemy cannot renounce life as such. But it is always influencing more deeply life cycles and life processes, changing them from within. Jeremy Rifkin (1983) calls this "algeny," a mixture of alchemy and genetics.

Though the pre-industrial alchemist was thinking according to machine-principles of destruction through division and re-combination, the machine as such had not yet been invented. But the modern sciences—though they would deny it because alchemy failed to produce gold and life—took over the methodological principles of alchemy as well as its aims. This endeavour is now called modern production and technological progress. I, therefore, consider alchemy to belong not only to patriarchy as a whole, but to have been adapted to modernity, too. In reality, the machine saved patriarchal alchemy from disappearing from the world. The machine is the most important invention of alchemy during modernity. And saying this implies its present and future failure as well, as its method of *creation by destruction* is maintained, if not generalized, by machine technology. Counteracting its mortal effects by integrating living matter into the alchemical process will not help in the long run. On the contrary, this integration will only widen the range of beings that are going to experience a loss of life or its damage to death.

It is clear that nearly nobody wants to hear this today. In the meantime, methods of alchemy have spread to all spheres of society, so that we can speak of the development of what I call an *alchemical system*, a system of seemingly "peaceful" destruction, a paradox typical of patriarchy.

The alchemist, like the modern scientist, too, has a patriarchal view of the world. He does not want to create the same as women and nature do. He sees himself as helping nature to become the supposedly better, higher life, and to get there faster than it would by natural evolution. He believes that nature and matter *want* to be improved and agree with being sacrificed for patriarchal development. He does not see himself as being needlessly destructive, because for him violence is needed for creation, and his creation is a higher creation. He never looks from "below," from the point of view of matter itself, because he sees himself as being part of the "holy rule" of the fathers and as being "above" matter and natural life. He always looks down from his metaphysical, "spiritual," "higher," and more "noble" point of view. The *sacrifice* he is demanding from matter, women, and nature is self-evident to him. Progress needs sacrifices—from others.

Patriarchal alchemy helped change the view of nature and women completely before modernity. The alchemist is not looking with enchantment into the world; he does not respect the forms that nature brings into existence; he does not wonder about the beauty and grace of Her beings. On the contrary, his mind is gloomy. He works with tricks, fraud, and violence against nature; he is competing with her as his ovens and test-tubes show, and he has no emotional problem with being Her murderer. For him, sex and death belong to each other in more than one way. He is already on the way to modern rationality (Kutschmann 1986).

The alchemist is somebody who tries to find a new male identity within patriarchy, a form of patriarchal maleness or "masculation" (Vaughan 1997) that is not exactly like the warrior, the ruler, or the priest, but a combination of the three, and—in modern terms—of a patriarchal scientist and engineer: the *concrete utopian "father."* Until modern times, the alchemists were exceptions. Few men were dedicating their lives to alchemy. This is changing with modernity. Not contemplation, but action is wanted. The time for the alchemist is now or never.

The War-System is Expanding by Becoming an "Alchemical System."

The alchemists wanted to achieve too much too early. The project of realizing patriarchy needed a broader foundation. There was no direct path to utopia. Today we can identify what have become the results of modern alchemy.

What is a commodity?

Alchemy had to go through capitalism, the so-called "Great Transformation" (Polanyi 1978) that transformed women into the first "black matter" of modernity, its first basic raw material (Federici 2004). In this way, women became the (subjected) "nature" of modern society and its first living machine and/or commodity, equipped with a form of labour power *without* value, price, or wage—in contrast to men. "Black matter" and women in modern society are considered a natural resource that can freely be appropriated. After the witch hunts, women became "housewives" and "housewifized" (Mies, Bennholdt-Thomsen and von Werlhof 1988), a sort of natural commodity or commodified nature that had previously gone through the process of alchemical "mortification."

In general, capitalism can be defined as a society in which all things, including people and nature, are sought to be transformed into commodities in order to profit from them (Wallerstein 1974), respectively into "capital," which takes the form of machinery, "command over labour," or the money that bears interest (Marx 1974: 168, 381, 391, 400, 424, 447). Capitalist technology, the machine(ry), is the method for how this transformation is occurring. I call it modern alchemy.

Capitalist economy, then, is the way to transform the commodity into money and profit by building up a new market, the capitalist world-market for commodities. In this way, modern economy is alchemy as well. It does not produce gold as the highest form of wealth, but money as the highest form of wealth. Gold is replaced by money (in fact the gold-standard of money is no longer used), and gold is as well generally replaced by capital (see Binswanger 1985).

So what does the transformation of nature and life into commodities, machinery, hierarchies, and money really mean? And is it not true that we consider this process to be the foundation of western society as, allegedly, the highest civilization ever, one that is creating a new paradise on earth?

As we have seen already, alchemy, including its modern version, is not creating or producing life or gold as such, but something else. In the phase of mortification it produces raw materials by killing nature and women in the meaning of a female "culture." When dead things are forced together in the factory they come out as "commodities," as *double-dead* things. They are dead because of their mortification into "raw materials" and because of using up labour power during their production process. The past life of nature and the past life of the labourer are composing the commodity. Commodities, therefore, are not just dead, but dead forever. This is a completely new situation on earth, because natural death is normally followed by new life. On the contrary, the systematic artificial death we are confronted with in modernity is not followed by life because this possibility is systematically excluded by "alchemical" destruction of the natural life-death cycle. With this type of death, life does not go on any more.

Furthermore the new form of death is paradoxical. It is not just passive, but actively threatening and even destroying its environment, too, as if we existed in a world of zombies. This death is dangerous. It is like a post-death-"life" that is as aggressive, mortal, and warlike as its own production and destruction have been. Even after death this war continues. Patriarchal "creation," therefore, does not lead to an artificial new paradise but to an artificial hell on earth.

The more de-naturalization has taken place in the production process of the commodity, the more probable that it ends as special waste. This waste is a threat to life and to the earth as such, like nuclear, electronic, chemical, and plastic waste. Always more waste, even organic waste, cannot be recycled within the natural environment any more, because it has turned into poison.

This poison is a result of the fact that the commodity arose from a process of systematic and large-scale life-destruction. The way of the commodity is paved with violent death from the beginning to the end. Like a vampire that is neither dead, nor alive, the commodity has absorbed life, turning it into capital. Karl Marx defined capital as "past, dead labour," "labour that once was," but without drawing out the necessary consequences (1974: 247, 209, 271, 446).

Another example of a mortal life-death combination is the genetically modified organism (GMO), be it plants or animals. These organisms are dangerous and even lethal to other plants and animals. They root them out. They are aggressive. On the other hand, their life is weak. Most of them are purposely infertile, like "terminator" seeds. With some GMOs, mostly animals, we do not know what the consequences of their existence will/might be. In the end, new "life forms" will have killed older life forms, whilst dying out themselves (Verhaag 2004). Only death forever will be left over.

Genetic engineering, which means "birth-giving war arts," started to create its own "life forms" by forcing different genes of different species together, producing the GMO. The GMO is a living commodity, a machine made out of nature-parts, consisting of a combination of at least two different living genes. It has no genealogy, no natural history, no mother, no morphological field, and no species to which it belongs. It knows no stability, no meaning in itself and no place in the cycle of death and life. It is not embedded within nature and not related to bio-diversity. It is utopian. It is irreversible. And it is like a contagious, lethal, epidemic disease. From this point of view, it becomes apparent that instead of getting life and death under control, patriarchal creation is causing a new kind of life and death that are completely *out* of control.

Only in its appearance does the commodity seem to be related to nature and life in a positive way, and this is why people become confused with the perversion of "fetishism" (Marx 1974: 85-98), which means that they believe in this appearance of the commodity, as if it is even more alive than nature, better than nature, and is therefore able to fulfill real needs for a happy life. In the meantime, people even believe that commodities stand for life and that nature is dead, turning everything upside down. This helps modern alchemists' propaganda claims for the production of a better and higher matter and for the necessity of the "creative destruction" of the world.

After having created the reality of a bad world, the new alchemists ask us to help create a good one. This new creation now seems to be the only answer to the catastrophes of the former. Patriarchy is tautology: The problems that have to be challenged first had to be created. Without these problems, there would be no need for patriarchy. In this way, it is not utopia that materializes, but dystopia—the opposite of utopia. It is utopia as a self-made catastrophe

What is money today?

Capitalist money contains all the former steps of the alchemy process, all former life, violence and death. Fetishists paradoxically perceive it as more alive than anything else. They are assured by the fact that modern money as a system is organized as if it is "fertile." Via the interest it generates, it can be seen as growing as though it were "getting children and grandchildren" (Binswanger 1985), so that people forget about real fertility as an ability of nature alone, and do not find it scandalous when nature is systematically rendered infertile and destroyed. Money has thus become a sort of "philosopher's stone," a concentration of life energy with which you can create more life wherever and whenever you want.

But, money is neither alive, nor fertile, nor does it create life. It is a violent fiction, like everything in patriarchy. It is the emptiness, the No-thing that is left over after the Great Transformation took place that started to liquidate matter, nature, and people, leaving them behind for the "liquidity" of the money system. There is no creation out of nothing. There has only been a "creation" *of* nothing.

What is the response of nature?

The time in which these facts remain hidden is disappearing rapidly. This is seen in ecology. The question is: How is nature responding? Her reactions are a mirror for us. Today, She is showing everybody that She does not agree with being taken as "base" matter for a supposedly higher creation. Nature does not want to be transformed into an alchemical paradise. Now She, too, is beyond human control instead of being dominated by modern man. Now She shows that She is not at all dead matter, but a living being that reacts actively and powerfully against the violence with which She is treated. This can be seen very clearly in climate changes and global warming—*global warning*.

When the Catholic missionary Bonifacius, some 1300 years ago, cut the holy oak tree of the pagans in Saxony, this act mocked the pagan's belief system; they believed that the sky would fall down now that the oak tree was no longer holding it up any more. The sky did not fall down. In reality, however, when seen from a spiritual point of view, it did. We have only just recognized this, as the consequences of this kind of behaviour against nature can no longer be denied.

Nevertheless, there is no way back from abstraction into interconnectedness. You cannot transform money, the commodity, the machine, capital, or a GMO back into living nature again. What has been killed this way cannot be brought to life again. Alchemy is a one-way undertaking only.

Others call it the law of entropy. Once the energy that you have produced out of matter is in the world, you cannot get it back any more. And as alchemy is basically a form of pyrotechnics, it has helped to transform large parts of global matter into energy—another one of our modern "philosopher's stones." Hence its result, global warming.

And, look at "nuclear alchemy" (Easlea 1986), which tries to divide and rule over atoms, the tiniest spirit-matter of life, that holds together life as such, so that the most terrible violence is needed in order to divide it. Believe it or not, nuclear alchemists think the same way all alchemists do: that even the use of nuclear violence is creating new life on earth (Caldicott 2002). Of course, they neither consider the dead of today, nor those of the future who are sacrificed before they have been born (Anders 1994). Progress always seems to need more sacrifice, even in face of the fact that nuclear poisoning can never again be reversed. For nuclear alchemists, the curse can never be greater than the blessings they think they are bringing to the world.

Most people do not look at the transformation processes of nature that accompany commodity production, because they believe in the creative aspect of modern economy and technology. Those who do look at the destruction that occurs consider this economy a "creative" destruction (Schumpeter 1962). This is an (unconscious) alchemical way of understanding capitalist patriarchy, which means that for the sake of a possible creation, the destruction that occurs at the same time is not taken seriously.

The destruction that is necessary for the maintenance and expansion of capitalist transformation has become global and always more rapid, penetrating all spheres of life at the macro and micro levels. Global treaties like the General Agreement on Trade in Services, the GATS of the World Trade Organization, are organizing the final transformation into commodities of everything that has escaped this process so far (Mies and Werlhof 2003). They call it privatization. It is the only way to maintain capitalist growth—the growth of profits *made out of life*. Those who advocate this policy are all alchemists. They literally want to liquidate everything forever. Furthermore, they even organize the liquidation of the future in order to appropriate its potentials now.

Most people do not understand the alchemical character of capitalist (including "socialist") economy and technology. Like the Left, most people consider the transformation of life and nature in general into commodities to be productive instead of destructive. They do not care about ecology. They do not care about women, children, and about themselves. Generally, there is an "optimistic" perspective towards the future. Otherwise, they would have discovered how the transformation into commodities, machinery, money, capital, and the overall "command over labour" not only affects in-organic, but also organic, matter, including their own lives. They do not see that the perpetrators are and will be affected as well.

What is the response of people?

It started with the transformation of women into "witches" and then into housewives. Regarding this change, what are the problems of human ecology that we are facing today?

While people were told to become intelligent, healthy, wealthy, democratic, free, sensitive, civilized, equal, strong, and beautiful, the opposite is true. Something within us, something of our lives, our work, our behaviour, our thoughts, our feelings, our future, has become commodified. We have, at least partly, become capital. We have become living machines. We are obeying nearly every order we are given. We seek a mimesis with money as if it were the "transcendental subject" of mankind (Sohn-Rethel 1970). We are still alive, but only partly. We are told that it is only our labour-power and not ourselves that is used as a commodity. So we think we are free people with a free life.

In reality, there is no separation between us and our labour power. It is our life-energy, eros, brain, fantasy, creativity, imagination, dreams, sex, soul, and spirit that is subsumed in our transformation into a commodity. The separation between us and our labour-power is a fiction. If we are treated like commodities, we are forced to transform our life energy accordingly. We are called upon to kill parts of ourselves, divide and conquer ourselves, purify ourselves, take special abilities out of ourselves, force them together again, and then try to re-configure ourselves, *believing* that all this will lead to the best life we can possibly have. Emotionally we have to identify with this "self-alchemization," and enter into a mimetic relationship with ourselves as commodities, not as living beings. How much of me is capital already? How long can I make money out of my life, energy, body, brain, organs, labour, myself? How long can I function like a machine? How long can I do whatever I am ordered to do? Until I become a killer-solider, or an Eichmann (Genth 2002)?

Karl Marx (1974: 765) called the violence that we are committing against ourselves "economic violence" in contrast to the direct, "political" violence that comes from outside. The slave, he said, had to be forced to go to work (1974: 447, 624, 765). We force ourselves to go to work. This is one of the differences between today and former periods in history. We have learned to internalize the system, the commodity, the machine, the command, the capital. We have been conditioned to identify with those processes that rob and loot our lives and those of others worldwide. We gain our identity from becoming "like them," the capitalists, the modern alchemists, and the system itself. We apparently had no choice: we perverted our mimesis, fantasy, intelligence, energy, and feelings to become more and more like the system, the machine(ery) itself. We submitted to the system and let it define who we are. Finally, we ourselves are responsible for the system. Without us it would be dead. But we gave life to it and transformed it into a "living machine." Without our consent it would immediately break down (Holloway 2006). We, in reality, produced the paradox of a "living system," because we fed it constantly. By feeding the "creation out of destruction" of the alchemical system, we behave like perverted patriarchal "mothers" within an alchemical system of "fathers."

We are called to justify this partial suicide of ourselves and the partial murder of others as progress and development. In reality it is a deadly alienation and separation from inter-connectedness with life that we are forcing upon ourselves and our children. As a result, we get further away from the power of life, and become more and more helpless. In turn, our children become more and more frustrated and angry.

Once our labour-power is not only used as a commodity, but has become a commodity, the commodification-process does not stop. We may experience being treated like a *materia prima*, like raw material, like a "dividual" instead of the in-dividual. Or, we are chosen as a "substance," as an expert, for example. We are forced together with other "experts," forming a unit that has to function for projects defined by others. Such a project is a marriage, too: the female and the male "element" are bound together for the sake of the state as the alchemical father. The sacrifice is up to the woman and/as the mother (for a historical comparison, see Treusch-Dieter 2001).

Nobody is left out. We are all facing the fact that parts of our lives have been damaged, stolen, destroyed, and transformed into their opposite. Therefore, we feel weak, half-dead, and burnt-out. We do not love life any more; joy and laughter have disappeared. We have stopped playing and cannot feel anything anymore. When we do allow ourselves to feel, we feel something negative, because we are frightened, frustrated, greedy, depressed, and aggressive. And we don't know why.

We do not understand what the procedure of alchemical "creation" comprises. Neither the sciences, nor the Left, not to speak of "Gender-Studies" à la Judith Butler (1991), is helping us in this respect. On the contrary, we are being led even deeper into the alchemical darkness of the realization of patriarchal utopia, called modernity. We therefore have to change the way we think and feel about it.

Finally, we have to stop to make the wrong choices in order to justify what we have done to ourselves and others in order to make us believe that we have reached a "better" and "higher" life. We are drawing false consequences out of our dilemma. We run into addiction, because the life perspective has been taken away from us. We go deeper and deeper into delusion, becoming more and more like machines, abstract like capital, fictitious and empty like money, or believers in the supposed holiness of command. Our faith in the alchemical wonder of a metaphysical world on earth makes us blind to reality. We believe in a "life after nature" or in the "post-natural human" (see Bruiger 2006).

Patriarchy is the Dys-topia of a Motherless World, But We Can Do Something About It

Together with the war-system and its contraction into the alchemical system of capitalist patriarchy, western civilization and western peoples became murderers first and now we are on route to suicide. We do not need more than a few hundred years. The accumulation of capital turns out to be the accumulation of eternal death. There is no infinite production—if it is destruction—on a finite globe. There are no "renewable resources." There is nothing that is able to replace what has been destroyed: soil, food, water, forests, cultures, peoples, subsistence, the gift, love, and even parts of the interconnectedness of life. I call it *West End*.

The dark secret of patriarchy, the violence that is trying to literally annihilate life and death on earth, is coming to light in ourselves. For a long period of time, peoples, and especially women, have tried to remain "good people," even when they had to go through war, misery, and despair. Today, it seems that this form of resistance is disappearing rapidly, especially in the North of the World System, women included. The rationality that we have developed turns into its opposite, that is, irrationality and fundamentalism.

The spirit in which "production" takes place and the character of the alchemical methods used for this production of commodities are falling back on us like a boomerang.

We are prisoners, in jail, behaving like inmates. This is because that is what we have become. We have to, therefore, break out.

We are confronted with the urgent need for an alternative, if we want to survive this war.

We know that a commodity, that money, capital, a machine, cannot be transformed back into living nature. Our only hope is that we are *not totally* commodified, machinized, monetarized, alchemized, housewifized, patriarchalized, and enslaved.

We can remember what of our life's potential that has not been totally absorbed by self-alchemization and strengthen ourselves again.

We can remember what is left of matriarchy as a "second culture" within and outside of us.

We can join with people and communities that are struggling for the same.

We can defend what is alive within us and others and strengthen it against the destruction within us, them and around us.

We can learn to struggle in favour of life on the globe, and struggle to get patriarchy out of our bodies, minds, behaviour, emotions, and fantasies.

We can learn to use our mimetic capacities in order to get closer to mother earth again.

We can experiment with gift-giving.

We can start to lose faith in violence and trust in life on earth.

We can defend ourselves against those who are looking at life from the perspective of the death they produce.

We have to start to recognize what life, earth, nature, natural death, and the Goddess, really mean, because never in history has there been a society that knew less about them.

We, therefore, have to start to revert what has been perverted: Life into death and death into life, eternal death into a so-called paradise. We have to put back on its feet what has been turned upside down. We have to get rid of the confusion of our minds.

We have to become strong and we have to strengthen ourselves mutually, because patriarchs do not joke at all. When the patriarchs begin to understand that their whole system is failing, when the truth about the last five or seven thousand years of patriarchy is recognized, the patriarchs will not simply give up. Their philosopher's stone is the bomb. Therefore, we have to "*take the toys out of the hands of the boys.*"

Because, without nearly any matriarchal vestiges and without nearly any life on the globe, when nearly everything is on the tilt toward death forever, when the earth has nearly everywhere turned into hell, we then will not be able to invent a new matriarchal or post-patriarchal civilization.

So, let us do something now. Let us find out how to get rid of utopia and dystopia, the patriarchal hell, and how to get to the roots of "topia."

The *u-topos* as the non-local, the non-vernacular, the opposite of concrete life, of the concrete mother and living matter, the abstract, the fiction, the nowhere, the No-thing, he motherless world will then disappear; maybe slowly, but it will.

Claudia von Werlhof is the mother of a son, and professor of Women's Studies at the Institute for Political Sciences, University of Innsbruck, Austria, since 1988. She co-founded Women's Studies and Research in Germany, when Assistant Professor in the Department of Sociology at the University of Bielefeld. She has conducted years of field research in Latin America. Her work demonstrates trans-disciplinary attempts to define a feminist theory of society and nature that knows about matriarchy and knows how to analyze patriarchy, the new paradigm of the "Critical Theory of Patriarchy." She is an activist against globalization as the globalization of capitalist patriarchy and modern alchemy, and has published numerous books and articles in different languages. At the moment she is preparing an international conference about "Ways to a Different Civilization?" in 2010 in Austria.

[1]On the problems with the definition of the labour power under capitalism, see Marx 1(974: 192-330, 391-460).

References

Anders, Günther. 1994. *Die Antiquiertheit des Menschen.* München: Verlag Beck.

Binswanger, Christoph. 1985. *Geld und Magie.* Stuttgart: Verlag Weitbrecht.

Bruiger, Dan. *Second Nature: The Man-Made World of Idealism, Technology and Power.* Victoria, BC: Leftfieldpress

Budge, E. A. Wallis. 1969. *The Gods of the Egyptians.* Vol. 2. New York: Dover.

Budge, E. A. Wallis. 1978. *An Egyptian Hieroglyphic Dictionary.* Vol. 2. New York: Dover.

Butler, Judith. 1991. *Das Unbehagen der Geschlechter.* Frankfurt: Suhrkamp.

Caldicott, Helen. 2002. *The New Nuclear Danger: George W. Bush's Military-In-*

dustrial Complex. New York: New Press.

Easlea, Brian. 1986. *Die Väter der Vernichtung. Männlichkeit, Naturwissenschaftler und der nukleare Rüstungswettlauf.* Reinbek: Verlag Rowohlt.

Eliade, Mircea. 1980. *Schmiede und Alchemisten.* Stuttgart: Verlag Klett-Cotta.

Federici, Silvia. 2004. *Caliban and the Witch: Women, the Body and Primitive Accumulation.* New York: Autonomedia

Frankenberg, Gisela von. 1985. *Kulturvergleichendes Lexikon.* Bonn: Verlag Gisela Meussling.

Genth, Renate. 2002. *Über Maschinisierung und Mimesis. Erfindungsgeist und mimetische Begabung im Widerstreit und ihre Bedeutung für das Mensch-Maschine-Verhältnis.* Frankfurt and New York: Verlag Peter Lang.

Girard, René. 1972. *La violence et le sacré.* Paris: Éditions Bernard Grasset.

Haraway, Donna. 1983. "A Manifesto for Cyborgs: Science, Technology and Socialist Feminism in the 1980s."*Socialist Revolution* 80: 65-107.

Holloway, John. 2006. *Die Welt verändern ohne die Macht zu übernehmen.* Münster: Westfälisches Dampfboot.

Marx, Karl. 1974. *Marx-Engels-Werke.* Vol. 23. *Das Kapital 1.* Berlin: Verlag Dietz.

Mies, Maria. 1986. *Patriarchy and Accumulation on a World Scale: Women in the International Division of Labour.* London: Zed Books.

Mies, Maria. 2005. *Krieg ohne Grenzen. Die neue Kolonisierung der Welt.* Köln: PapyRossa.

Mies, Maria, and Claudia von Werlhof, eds. 2003. *Lizenz zum Plündern. Das Multilaterale Abkommen über Investitionen – MAI. Globalisierung der Konzernherrschaft, und was wir dagegen tun können.* Hamburg: Verlag EVA.

Mies, Maria, Veronika Bennholdt-Thomsen, and Claudia von Werlhof. 1988. *Women: The Last Colony.* London: Zed Books.

Plato. 1994. *Sämtliche Werke.* Vol. 2. Reinbek: Verlag Rowohlt.

Polanyi, Karl. 1978. *The Great Transformation: Politische und ökonomische Ursprünge von Gesellschaften und Wirtschaftssystemen.* Frankfurt: Verlag Suhrkamp.

Rifkin, Jeremy. 1983. *Algeny.* New York: The Viking Press.

Rifkin, Jeremy. 1998. *The Biotech Century.* New York: Tarcher/Putnam

Schütt, Hans Werner: *Auf der Suche nach dem Stein der Weisen. Die Geschichte der Alchemie.* München: Beck

Schumpeter, Josef. 1962. *Capitalism, Socialism, and Democracy.* New York: Harper Torchbooks.

Sloterdijk, Peter, and Thomas Macho, eds. 1991. *Weltrevolution der Seele: Ein Lese- und Arbeitsbuch der Gnosis.* Vol 2. Gütersloh: Verlag Artemis and Winkler.

Sohn-Rethel, Alfred. 1970. *Geistige und körperliche Arbeit: Zur Theorie der gesellschaftlichen Synthesis,* Frankfurt: Verlag Suhrkamp.

The American Heritage Dictionary 2001. New York: Dell-Random.

Treusch-Dieter, Gerburg. 2001. *Die Heilige Hochzeit. Studien zur Totenbraut.* Herbolzheim: Verlag Centaurus.

Vaughan, Genevieve. 1997. *For-Giving: A Feminist Criticism of Exchange.* Austin:

Plain View Press.

Verhaag, Bertram. 2004. *Leben außer Kontrolle.* München: Verlag Denkmalfilm.

Walker, Barbara. 1988. *The Woman's Dictionary of Symbols and Sacred Objects.* New York: Harper & Row.

Wallerstein, Immanuel. 1974. "The Rise and Future Demise of the World Capitalist System: Concepts for Comparative Analysis." *Comparative Studies in Society and History* 16 (4): 387-415.

Werlhof, Claudia von. 1997. "Ökonomie, die praktische Seite der Religion. Wirtschaft als Gottesbeweis und die Methode der Alchemie." *Ökonomie (M)macht Angst.* Eds. Ulla Ernst et al. Frankfurt and New York: Verlag Peter Lang. 95-121.

Werlhof, Claudia von. 2000. "Patriarchat als Alchemistisches System. Die (Z)ErSetzung des Lebendigen." *Optimierung und Zerstörung. Intertheoretische Analysen zum Menschlich-Lebendigen.* Ed. Maria Wolf. Innsbruck: Verlag Studia. 13-31.

Werlhof, Claudia von. 2001. "Losing Faith in Progress. Capitalist Patriarchy as an 'Alchemical System.'" *There is an Alternative: Subsistence and Worldwide Resistance to Corporate Globalization.* Eds. Veronika Bennholdt-Thomsen, Nicholas Faraclas, and Claudia von Werlhof. London: Zed Books. 15-40.

Werlhof, Claudia von. 2004. "Using, Producing, and Replacing Life? Alchemy as Theory and Practice in Capitalism." *The Modern World-System in the Longue Durée.* Ed. Immanuel Wallerstein. Boulder, CO: Paradigm Press. 65-78.

Werlhof, Claudia von. 2006. "Patriarchy as Negation of Matriarchy: The Perspective of a Delusion." *Gesellschaft in Balance. Dokumentation des 1. Weltkongresses für Matriarchatsforschung.* Ed. Heide Goettner-Abendroth. Stuttgart: Edition HAGIA und Verlag Kohlhammer.

Werlhof, Claudia von. 2007. "Capitalist Patriarchy and the Struggle for a 'Deep' Alternative." *Women and the Gift Economy: A Radically Different Worldview is Possible.* Ed. Genevieve Vaughan. Toronto: Inanna Publications. 139-153.

GENEVIEVE VAUGHAN

Matriarchy and the Gift Economy

Matriarchy demonstrates gender equality on the basis of the female model. In the last decades feminists have insisted on equality with men according to a male model (or standard) and within a culture, which consists mainly of institutions based on (dominant) male models, imaginaries, and representations. In fact, a society based on patriarchal capitalism creates the illusion that this is a reality to which there is no alternative and from which there is no way out. The best that can be done by women seems to be an improvement of their own status within existing institutions. This illusion is toxic and must be dispelled if we are ever going to be able to create a peaceful world.

Much energy is employed in achieving equal pay for women in male institutions, equal rights before male law and equal opportunity in patriarchal schools, religions, businesses, and corporations. While these attempts have empowered some women and liberated them from ignorance and domestic slavery, the patriarchal institutions of our society have a life of their own so that they are indifferent to the participation of individuals and continue as self-perpetuating social forms without being fundamentally changed by the equal participation of women. Moreover, the improvements in gender relations at the individual level in countries like the U.S. have taken place with a parallel displacement of male dominant behaviour onto class and national levels so that hyper-masculinity is considered normal when it is practiced by capitalists, corporations, and countries. In fact, their hyper-masculine behaviour is not even recognized as having anything to do with gender. It is just considered standard policy.

What we need to do in this situation is to radically shift from the norm of the male gender construction to the norm of the mother. A recent theory in cognitive psychology proposes that we have prototypes of categories. For example, for middle-class USA, a robin would be the prototype or exemplar, the best example of the category "bird" (Rosch 1999 [1978]; Lakoff 1987). I believe we do this also with our category of "human," and the male has been the prototype of the category "human" for patriarchy. In order to radically change patriarchal institutions and perhaps reestablish matriarchies we would need to make the mother the prototype of the category "human." That would mean that the nurturing characteristics of the mother would be considered human, not just a female characteristic. Since the male exemplar or norm has permeated society everywhere, we need to be able to recognize it and find or imagine the alternative in all the many places it exists.

Energy needs to be employed in radically changing the institutions and the premises on which they are constructed so that both male and female human beings can find a context where they can practice their maternal humanity.

At present, the contexts of patriarchal capitalism discredit caring and make other-orientation almost impossible, or they find a way of using it to make money or at least to establish control—witness the New Orleans disaster (Jurgens 2008). They over-value the logic of exchange and success in the market while making gift-giving appear to be just an individual quirk, a self-indulgence, or a kind of ego tripping attempt at saintliness.

Even equality itself as a criterion is based on male models and the market where what is equal to what and how much, are the main issues (identity logic). The drive to become the one at the top (the prototype) and exercise power-over is a value for patriarchy but not for matriarchy. This allows for egalitarianism in matriarchy that is based on the appreciation of diversity. In fact, the process of the socialization of children requires that the other, the different, who is a small baby, be respected for her or his diversity and brought "up" to the same level as the mother. The domination of children, like the domination of adults, is part of the patriarchal (masculated) mode. This does not mean that women cannot dominate but that when they are doing it they are enacting a logic of behaviour that is patriarchal, not matriarchal.

Patriarchies have overtaken matriarchies because some of the patriarchal values are self-confirming, like violence and power over. This has created hybrid societies that do not recognize themselves as such.

We can also look at these two kinds of societies as based on two ways of behaving economically, two economic logics. One is gift-giving, the direct satisfaction of needs. The other is exchange, giving in order to receive an equivalent. These two ways of meeting needs constitute two modes of distribution. Gift-giving, which is evident in mothering, has a logic of its own, which is unrecognized by patriarchy. It is transitive and creates positive relationships, subjectivities, and communities. Gift-giving takes place not only in mothering but it permeates society, and exchange, which seems to stand alone, could not take place without it. We can look at gift-giving as the basis of an alternative economic way, which, at present, has been overtaken by an economy based on the logic of exchange and the market.

Exchange, giving in order to receive an equivalent, is different from gift-giving. Where gift-giving creates solidarity and trust, exchange creates adversarial stances of each against all, as each person tries to get more than the others from the transactions. Gift- giving creates bonds while exchange breaks them. Exchange requires measurement and quantification while gift-giving is mainly qualitative. Exchange is ego-oriented while gift-giving is other-oriented. Exchange is intransitive while gift-giving is transitive. In fact, exchange, which is only a double gift, a gift turned back on itself, actually cancels the gift by the equal return.

This cancellation of the gift makes the market an appropriate environment for patriarchy. In fact, the motivations of patriarchy—competition, hierarchy, domination, accumulation for power over—have been incarnated in the market to such an extent that we can call our system patriarchal capitalism or capitalist patriarchy.

Gift-givers give to the exchange economy as their other, and the exchange economy, motivated by patriarchy, takes from the gift economy.

Patriarchies are based on male identities constructed in opposition to mothering, and they are locked into a parasitic relation with gift economies internally. They also seek to recreate these relations externally, forcing other patriarchal groups to give to them. Thus, hyper-masculine behaviour is justified by the market and the market resonates with the male gender identity.

However patriarchies began originally, they are recreated in every male child that is born because of our practice of educating boys into a gender category opposite to that of their mothers, even at a time when mothers are intensely practicing gift-giving towards their children. Then, mothers, as well as their girl children, adapt to care especially for the boys who are learning to be non-giving human beings. But actually gift-giving is the basis of our humanity—men's as well—so this gender distinction sets up some basic, important, and pervasive paradoxes that influence our lives at all levels, and which are at the root of patriarchy and capitalism.

Matriarchies have communicative economies. That is, economies based on giving and receiving material goods that reinforce the material and spiritual subjectivity of the receiver and the positive other-oriented agency of the giver. These effects allow the development of relations among givers and receivers as well as among all of the members of communities in which gifts freely circulate. This kind of society requires a certain egalitarianism because the development of hierarchy forces more gifts to be given to those at the top (capturing them and holding them there, or wasting them).

Patriarchies can function with important gift aspects, but they usually constrain the gifts to flow from the many to the few, through taxes, tributes, and even slavery backed up by police and military hierarchies. Power over can be defined as this control of the flow of gifts. Because gift economies would be more life-affirming and positive for everyone, since no one would have to submit to force to get their own and others' needs met, the market and patriarchy, which value competition, compete with gift economies and win. In fact, patriarchal capitalism is deeply threatened by the gift economy.

Colonialism can be seen in this light as the take over of other economies, many of which were gift economies, in order to establish and control a flow of gifts from them towards the colonizing countries. The invasion of the Americas can be seen as the take over of Indigenous American territories and the seizure of their gifts, made more ferocious by the fact that many of them had gift economies. Indigenous cultures had to be assimilated and eliminated in order to avoid proposing the gift economy model instead of the Patriarchal Capitalist model.

Markets impose distribution without gift-giving, because the goods and services are given in order to receive an equal exchange. The exchange cancels the gift and changes other-orientation to ego-orientation. Markets are intransitive, non-communicative economies and the relations they create are adversarial, ego-oriented, and atomistic. What the members of the community have in common is their non-community, their intransitive material non-communication of private property. They give something in order not to give it, to keep its value, so as to be able give it again in the form of money, and satisfy their own needs. Instead of giving value to the other they give value to the self, using the need of the other as means rather than as an end in itself. While markets may appear better than forced labour and slavery they are not the neutral and neuter, ungendered, just and autonomous constructions they are purported to be.

Actually, they float on a sea of gifts. Housework, which would add 40 percent more to the Gross National Product in the U.S. (more in some other countries) if it were monetized, is a gift women are giving to the market economy. If profit is seen as coming from surplus value, the value of the worker's labour beyond what is covered in the salary, it can also be considered as made up of free gifts from the worker to the capitalist (even if from the workers' point of view the gifts are forced.) Anytime one person pays more for something than it is worth, s/he is giving a free gift to the seller. So profit is actually made up of gifts. Remittances from immigrants in the North to people in their home countries are gifts now amounting to billions of dollars. But actually all the free acts of kindness and community that we practice on a daily basis can be considered gifts and part of an economy of kindness that softens the market and makes it liveable. Gifts at all levels have been misdefined or ignored by Patriarchy, but we can make them visible as part of a thread which connects them in a positive way.

Capitalist markets are markets infused with the competitive values of patriarchy, which drive the exchangers to accumulate more gifts in order to leverage power over others. The ego-orientation of exchange fits with the ego-orientation of patriarchal men as each person competes with others and strives towards domination. While the market may appear to be better than patriarchy as such, it is a process that hides the giving of gifts by the many to the few and displaces what was previously read as a biological or hereditary advantage of males in patriarchy onto more primitive and seemingly ungendered factors such as risk, luck, and virtue.

I say these factors are more primitive just for the reason that they are part of what we might call a folk theory that justifies categorization as male. Males are born male by luck, or perhaps deserve to be male by (some kind of prenatal superiority) or the superiority of their spirits. We can even say that by being born they risked becoming females but by their good fortune they were placed in the superior category. Later they have to "deserve" their manly privilege by hard work and by the same kind of individuation and atomization the market process provides. Masculinity is not a biologically based gender identity, but an identity formed by an ideological process that can be embraced by women as well as men, and by people from all cultures. I believe it is this ideological (gender) process that is incarnated in the market, and allows everyone to strive to be put in privileged categories by having instead of lacking.

Taking this false male gender construction as the standard broadens the false judgment that males are not like their gift-giving mothers, so that it extends to everyone. Thus we say that humans are basically not-giving, but that some humans are forced by others to give, and that they are thus victims, while those who have the power (to make others give to them) are admired as successful predators.

The victims are supposedly unlucky, incompetent, afraid to risk, and lacking in manly abilities (like being aggressive and staying the course). Those who are biologically female ("have-nots") are more likely to be victims. They are born to be failed predators. They are the prey in what I call "raptor capitalism." Similarly, race and class categories privilege those in power and condemn everyone else to the giving victim role. By incarnating this gender construction in the market, the values of the European male gender construction have been given an independent existence outside of the normal flow of time and history. Moreover, this incarnation has permitted everyone to embrace these values or forced them to embrace them because there is the penalty of poverty and death by hunger and disease for failure or non-compliance. Thus, women and people of non-privileged cultures can presumably compete to be in the superior European (male "have") category. However, they seldom, if ever, succeed.

This "raptor capitalist" vision of society and gender is not only false but it does not allow a starting place for change.

Economics textbooks begin with the idea that the market is the way scarce goods are distributed. They do not mention that the market itself is often the cause of the scarcity of the goods. The commodification of goods and services transforms them from abundant gifts to scarce commodities, and allows the accumulation of wealth by the few at the expense of the many. This is particularly evident now in globalization with the seizure of water and seeds and even life forms by corporations, so that things that were once a means of giving, abundantly available for the taking, have been absorbed into the market, and can only be had at a price.

The explanation of the market and capitalism, starting with the gift economy and the female standard, which includes rather than rejects mothering, lets us look at predatory behaviour as an aberration and at gift-givers as positive agents who are temporarily trapped and exploited by a system based on an illusory gender construction.

This problematic European male gender construction does not have to do primarily with sex but with the foundations of economics. That is, how people get their material needs met. How are needs met in society? Patriarchy says that one gender, the male, will not meet needs as mothers do. In the socialization of children this implies that in order to take up a male social and sexual role as an *adult,* the child has to give up the maternal *economic* identity from his earliest days, and, the corresponding cultural or super-structural identity. For children, this economic identity has to do with very detailed gift-giving and receiving on a daily basis. It is the stuff of life itself and the primary relation creating interaction. Making an adult sex role contingent on the child's adopting a certain economic behaviour, places him in a situation of exchange already, because sex becomes the reward or payoff for not-giving behaviour. That is, he gives up gift-giving and will eventually be allowed to be a male sex agent if he can act according to the manhood agenda and become a subject of the market, as a breadwinner. Thus, boys are already in an if/then, *do ut des* mode as they grow up.

Since gift-giving and receiving are the way we construct human relationships, boys are placed in a problematic situation when they are turned away from the gift economy as children. A substitute for giving is made available to them, which is hitting. In fact, hitting, like giving, reaches out and touches the other person, and establishes a relationship—though one of harm rather than of nurture. Furthermore, it establishes a relationship of hierarchy rather than mutuality. Gratuitous hitting calls for pay back, and so fights begin, on the basis of exchange, revenge and "honour." Backyard brawls prepare boys not only for participation in the market but for wars fought on the market principles of escalating exchanges of blows, attacks, and reprisals, in the struggle to establish national male dominance. The loser nation is forced to give up and give to the winner, and, in the process take on a female position.

Markets and exchange have early capillary roots in manipulation, bribery, and education through punishment and reward. These are interactions, which validate exchange, and impose it on children, socializing them away from gift-giving. There are many other cultural influences that validate the market.

Even religions that otherwise might propose the gift model are Patriarchal and unquestioningly promote exchange. For example, look at the Judeo-Christian idea of payment for original sin. There are many areas in which gifts are given within an in-group, creating community within an otherwise Patriarchal institution. For example, in the military there is much solidarity and reciprocal help that is given among soldiers on and off the battlefield. Community is created which actually strengthens the kind of military exchanges (attacks and reprisals) it is possible to undertake.

The hybrid societies of matriarchy-patriarchy are awkward constructions in which the givers give to the not-givers, and the not-givers use force to keep the givers in their female or nurturing position. Many paradoxes and double binds occur in these hybrid societies, which are schizophrenogenic, causing disassociation and denial as well as vulnerability to lies and manipulation. In fact, lies function according to the logic of exchange, as they are told to satisfy the need of the giver, not the communicative need of the receiver.

Matriarchies do not divide males from females economically in childhood as Patriarchies do. Adult males are still expected to behave economically like their mothers. They can do this while maintaining a sexual behaviour that is like their father's or mother's brother's or other male model's. They do not have to reject mothering economics in order to become sexually adequate males.

Heterosexuality, therefore, does not in itself depend on males rejecting mothering economics or values, which derive from and are functional to gift-giving.

It is not surprising that many people are attempting to challenge gender categories, but they seem to do it more regarding sex than economics. Changing gender roles appears to regard only homosexuality and transgender while the economic aspects of gender are ignored or only understood in terms of equal opportunity within the patriarchal capitalist institutions. This renders the gender challenge of the Gay, Lesbian, Bisexual, and Transexual (GLBT) movement much weaker and less political than it could otherwise be. I believe that a movement that embraces adult gift-based economic behaviour can challenge patriarchal capitalism. Breaking the connection between masculine sexuality and the rejection of gift-giving would eliminate much of the motivation towards capitalist accumulation. It is (male) gender as an economic identity that is the problem. Sexuality outside of patriarchy is only another way of giving and receiving.

In matriarchies the continuity between mothering and adult economic behaviour is not broken. The connection also remains intact between mothering and symbolic behavior like language, and between mothering and epistemology.

The maternal character of the environment is recognized by Matriarchies and gift economies. Mothered children who recognize the fact that they have been mothered, and have participated in and not rejected a gift economy, can use this gift interaction when interpreting other phenomena. An epistemology, which interprets perception as the reception of gifts from our surroundings, allows a respect for and appreciation of nature and gratitude for nature's gifts—in which we can include our own capacity to receive—whether nature is personalized or not. Technology is the extension of the instrumentalization of humans in exchange to the instrumentalization of nature. Rather than dominating or instrumentalizing nature as masculated men do, gift economies and Matriarchies cooperate with nature. The market has a neutral or a neuter objective face, which is projected into a concept of nature as an object. In so doing, human nature, including the body, which is produced by the mother and nurtured by mothering economics, is treated as an object. The gift aspects of humanity and of nature are thus denied and the processes of competition, hierarchy (the great chain of being), and sexual dominance are attributed to objectified nature itself.

In order to choose a differently gendered economy, and thereby change the approach to nature as well, it seems that people have to create social experiments or be dropouts from the system, which penalizes them because, due to the scarcity artificially created by the market, they do not usually have access to the means of giving. Instead we need to collectively challenge the gendered character of the market: dismantle patriarchal capitalism, and replace it with generalized mothering economic behaviour. At the same time we need to challenge the way we construct masculinity in opposition to mothering.

I do not think it is likely that we can reinstate matriarchies quickly, but I think we do have to do something quickly. What we can do is to analyze and challenge the male gender construction so as to make it clear that it is artificial and unnecessary, and that the combination of patriarchy and capitalism is what is bringing our planet to immanent disaster. I believe we need to reveal that the values expressed in the ideology of patriarchal capitalism are false, pernicious, and harmful to everyone, to the very men who try to put them into effect as well as to society as a whole. They are a translation of gift-giving into a neuter or aggressive "male" mode.

I suggest putting the pieces of the puzzle in different, unfamiliar places. First, change the standard from male to female and hold in abeyance the idea of standard itself and of equality itself—both based on the logic of identity which I see as a distressed constituent part of the male gender construction.

Consequently, we should change what the movement is focused on—not on the assimilation of women but on a radical change in the institutions towards a maternal model. Challenge and change the gender construction of men by separating sexuality from economics. Value gift-giving and liberate it from its relation of host to the not-giving parasitic system. As institutions change towards maternal values and maternal economics, hyper-masculine behaviour will no longer be adaptive or admirable. These are just a few pieces of the puzzle. The first step in rearranging them is defining gift-giving as economic.

*Genevieve Vaughan is an independent researcher. In 1963, she moved to Italy from her native Texas. Her two early essays "Communication and Exchange" (*Semiotica 1980) *and "Saussure and Vigotsky via Marx" (*Ars semiotica 1981) *deal with language and economics. In 1978, she became a feminist, participating since then in the Italian, U.S., and international feminist movements. In 1983, she returned to Austin, Texas, where she created the Foundation for a Compassionate Society (1987-2005), an all-woman activist foundation, which initiated many innovative projects based on the politicization of "women's values." In 1997, she published her book,* For-Giving: A Feminist Criticism of Exchange, *and in 2004, she edited* Athanor, The Gift: A Feminist Analysis. *In 2007,* Women and the Gift Economy: A Radically Different Worldview is Possible, *was published by Inanna Publications. This book is a collection of essays from the 2004 conference on the gift economy, which she organized in Las Vegas. She also co organized the 2005 conference on Matriarchal Studies in San Marcos Texas under the direction of Heide Goettner-Abendroth, from which a number of essays in this volume derive. She is active in the feminist, anti-globalization, and peace movements. She coordinates the International Feminists for a Gift Economy network, a group of activists and academics devoted to promoting the gift paradigm. A film on her life,* Giving for Giving, *was produced in 2007 and aired on Free Speeech TV. The film and many of her books and essays are available free on her website www.gift-economy.com.*

References

Caille, Alain, and Jacques Godbout. 1998. *The World of the Gift.* Montreal: McGill-Queen's University Press.

Bennholdt-Thomson,Veronika, N. Faraclas, and Claudia von Werlhof, eds. 2001. *There is an Alternative: Subsistence and Worldwide Resistence to Corporate Globalization.* London: Zed Books.

Goettner-Abendroth, Heide. 1991. *Das Matriarchat II, 1. Stammesgesellschaften in Ostasien, Indonesien, Ozeanien.* Stuttgart: Kohlhammer-Verlag.

Goettner-Abendroth, Heide. 2000. *Das Matriarchat II, 2. Stammesgesellschaften in Amerika, Indien, Afrika.* Stuttgart: Kohlhammer-Verlag.

Goux, Jean-Joseph. 1990. *Symbolic Economies: After Marx and Freud.* Ithaca: Cornell University Press.

Hyde, Lewis. 1979. *The Gift: Imagination and the Erotic Life of Property.* New York: Random House.

Jurgens, Rick. 2008. "Avoiding Home Repair Fraud:Lessons from Hurricane Katrina." Boston: National Consumer Law Center.

Lakoff, George. 1987. *Women, Fire and Dangerous Things: What Categories Reveal about the Mind.* Chicago: University of Chicago Press.

Marx, Karl. 1930. *Capital in Two Volumes: Volume One.* 1867. London: J. M. Dent and Sons, Ltd.

Mauss, Marcel. 1990. *The Gift: The Form and Reason for Exchange in Archaic Societies.* 1923-24. London: Routledge.

Mies, Maria. 1998. *Patriarchy and Accumulation on a World Scale.* 1986. London: Zed Books.

Rosch, Eleanor. 1999. In S. Laurens and E.Margoulis eds. *Concepts: Core Readings.* 1978. Boston. MIT Press.

Sanday, Peggy. 2002. *Women at the Center: Life in a Modern Matriarch.* Ithaca: Cornell University Press.

Taylor, John R. 2003. *Linguistic Categorization.* Oxford: Oxford University Press.

Vaughan, Genevieve 1980. "Communication and Exchange." *Semiotica* 29 (1-2): 113-143.

Vaughan, Genevieve. 1981. "Saussure and Vygotsky via Marx." *Ars semiotica, International Journal of American Semiotic* 4: 57-83.

Vaughan, Genevieve. 1997. *For-Giving: A Feminist Criticism of Exchange.* Austin: Plain View and Anomaly Press.

Vaughan, Genevieve. 2004. "The Exemplar and the Gift." *Semiotica, Journal of the International Association for Semiotic Studies* 148 (4): 95-118.

Vaughan, Genevieve. 2006. *Homo Donans.* Available online: <www.gift-economy. com>.

Vaughan, Genevieve, ed. 2004. *The Gift. Il Dono, A Feminist Analysis. Athanor: Semiotica, Filosofia, Arte, Letteratura* 15 (8). Roma: Meltemi Editore.

Violi, Patrizia. 2001. *Meaning and Experience.* Bloomington: The University of Indiana Press.

Vygotsky, Lev Semenovich. 1962. *Thought and Language.* Cambridge: The MIT Press.

Part II
Existing Matriarchal Societies –
America and Oceania

BARBARA ALICE MANN

"They Are the Soul of the Councils"

The Iroquoian Model of Woman-Power

I am continually astounded by the apparently fixed idea of even left-of-centre academics that women are, by definition, a powerless group. Feminist theorists generally propose social sabotage as a woman's tactic—for society could not possibly be constructed by women; linguists figure that deviation from standard language is due to low status people who are assumed to be women; and, should anyone in the crowd mention high status women, why, the conversation must be about the ancient, and emphatically lost world of the Mesopotamian Goddess.

All this leaves me shaking my head and wondering sadly how American feminists, especially, can have forgotten the model and the inspiration of their own movement, the *Gantowisas*, that is, the Iroquoian woman acting in her capacity as a public official. The *Gantowisas*, or woman of the sisterhood of the lineage, boldly led her nation in politics, economics, social life, and spirituality. She was more than a little instrumental in creating the constitutional government that established their civil, political, economic, social, and spiritual rights.

The notion of such formalized woman-power may startle Europeans and their descendants, but it is an old and mature idea among Native Americans, especially those east of the Mississippi River. All eastern Nations recognized the political, economic, spiritual, and social roles of Clan Mothers. Women were and, among traditionalists, remain the power brokers of their people, but, in the twelfth century, the Iroquois codified these roles directly into the Haudenosaunee Constitution, traditionally known to the *Ongwe Howeh* (Iroquois) as the Great and Binding Law of Peace.

Thus, while there is much I could speak about, it seems to me that the most fruitful offering I can make is to tell you the history of how the *Ongwe Howeh* (Iroquois) created our generous, egalitarian, woman-centred, and—not coincidentally—peaceful government. Among Native peoples, it is axiomatic that no one can understand the fruit of a tree without first knowing its roots. It is only in watching a thing grow that we can understand its medicine, to replicate and make it work for us.

The Constitution of the Haudenosaunee, or People of the Longhouse, was ratified by popular vote by the Seneca, Cayuga, Onondaga, Oneida, and Mohawk in the year 1142—sixty-three years before the Magna Carta was signed. The Great

Law represented a hard-fought victory for the forces of peace and justice, settling a civil war that had been raging for over a century. Women generally, and their head Clan Mother, particularly, were instrumental in all phases of the struggle. Variously known in tradition as the *Jigonsaseh*, the Great Woman, the Mother of Nations, and the Peace Queen, the *Jigonsaseh* was key at every stage, from the war of liberation to the constitutional peace that followed.

To understand the civil war leading up to the Iroquoian Constitution, readers need to know that the power structure immediately preceding Iroquoian democracy was the Priesthood of the Mound Builders. The Mound Builders were an ancient North American culture that dated back in Ohio (the first eastern home of the Iroquois) to 2450 Before the Common Era (BCE), contemporaneous with the inception of ancient Egypt. I do not have time to go into the long, long history of the Mound culture bringing us into the eleventh century, when the Iroquoian civil war began, so I will just give a few glimpses of its structure.

The ruling Priesthood was a male elite enjoying a stranglehold on power, maintained largely through terror and brutality. In particular, the Priests specialized in spiritual terrorism, for instance, claiming the power over life and death, and casting lethal disease on dissenters. They eventually became very corrupt, using their absolute power to wage massive wars through a military caste that was under their command. They laid claim to and hoarded all commodities produced by the lower classes. They also kidnapped and gang-raped any young woman who caught their fancy, only discarding her once she was too battered and broken to be attractive to them any longer. The Mound-Builder economy included female farming but depended heavily on male hunting.

Around the ninth century, the people in Ohio became restless under this heavy-handed system. A number of flights from Mound Builder communities began. In particular, Iroquoian women got fed up with male domination and simply walked away from it. For instance, the people who became the Mohawks left Ohio under the leadership of a Clan Mother named *Gaihonariosk*. First, she led them into Québec, above the St. Lawrence River, but found the growing season too short there. After a number of years in Québec, she stood up and walked south into eastern New York, where the growing season was just right for bounteous harvests. The majority of people followed her, although some remained in the north, becoming the Laurentians, whom Jacques Cartier encountered in 1534.

Gaihonariosk was not the only Clan Mother to walk away from the Priests. Another woman led the people who were to become the Attiwendaronk, or the so-called "Neutrals," to Ontario. This woman was the direct ancestor of the *Jigonsaseh* of the Constitutional era. Her people, in particular, crafted a new form of government, based on agriculture, in which women and men shared power, and the will of the people was sacred. It is no accident that around 800, the first modern corn cropping began in Ontario as the staple food of the people. Archaeologists can literally pinpoint the movement of *Zea Mays*, which we call the Grandmother Corn, our oldest strain, moving from Ontario into New York, starting around

900. It was also no accident that corn cropping, a replacement for hunting, spread south, from Ontario into New York, western Pennsylvania, and Ohio.

In woodlands culture, people send out "Emissaries of Peace" when they have great new ideas to announce. For instance, when the Seneca invented bow-and-arrow technology around 500, the men sent emissaries to their allies to share the discovery. Similarly, in the tenth century, the Attiwendaronks began sending female emissaries south with the news of the Three Sisters—Corn, Beans, and Squash—with instructions on how best to grow them, starting a sea change in economic organization in the east. Before that time, the Priests had known of, and even grown, corn ceremonially, but it was not allowed to the people as food.

In North American Native culture, it is a law that any messenger from one group to another must:

1. Be sent by a recognized authority in the first group;
2. Bring a helpful message to the second group; and,
3. Be welcomed by a recognized authority in that second group.

The fact that the female leaders of Corn Way camps south of Ontario were welcoming these messengers and accepting their corn-cropping messages was a huge challenge to the Priesthood.

The upshot was a very nasty, ideological war that raged throughout the eleventh century over whether corn-cropping democracy or Mound-Builder Priesthood would prevail. The active leader of the Corn Way was the important Clan Mother, the *Jigonsaseh*, who had personally brought not only corn-cropping, but also a message about how to organize a participatory culture.

There are many traditions about the *Jigonsaseh* of this period. One tradition shows her dressed as a warrior. Her body paint was green, the colour of growing corn, and covered her entirely. Her headdress was made of yellow corn tassels. She was reputed to be an expert canoeist.

The Priests sent a powerful speaker to confront her, saying, "Who are you, strange woman? Who sent you? Who welcomed your strange message?" The Priests then gathered up as many of her children (i.e., followers) as they could find, tied them in a cornfield, and set the field on fire. They could not find the *Jigonsaseh* or many of her followers, who escaped by canoe. Throughout the long war, the Priesthood put a heavy price on her head, but she skillfully escaped every assassination attempt.

The chief Priest of the Mound culture was *Adodaroh*, a powerful and insane shaman. Descriptions of him are very colourful. His body was crooked. His feet were like duck's feet and his penis was so long, he wrapped it three times around his waist. (A bloated penis symbolized killing power, and three is the traditional number of warnings given before drastic action is taken.) Priests came from the Snake Clan, and *Adodaroh* wore live snakes wound into his long hair, writhing with his every step. He also wore the hollowed-out heads of snakes on his finger-tips, wiggling at everyone he spoke to. His medicine was strong; he could call up tornados and make waves run high. (These were references to the Great Horned Serpent, which is the male symbol of Earth.)

What was clearly happening was a bid for female power, with the war fought over land usage (female farming or male hunting) and governmental format (priesthood or democracy). In addition to the *Jigonsaseh*, leader of the Corn Way, there was the Peacemaker, a man also from Ontario, sent down to bring a message of peace to that troubled land.

The elder, hence more powerful, of these two figures was the *Jigonsaseh*. When the Peacemaker came down, he was scarcely out of his teens, with no real credentials beyond his message. His first act was to seek out the *Jigonsaseh* and ask for her to ally her Corn Way with his peace proposal. He needed her; she did not need him.

Instead of rushing into his arms crying, "My hero!," she negotiated hard-nosed terms into his proposed constitution, granting women sweeping powers. Only then, did she agree to support his peace cause. The powers that the *Jigonsaseh* put into the Constitution include:

•*Ne G shasdensä*, the sacred will of the people, is one of the three foundational principles (the other two are *Ne Gai'i hwiio,* high ethics, and *Ne Skeñ'non*, public health and welfare);
•Women as *sole* counsellors at the local, or "grassroots," level of government;
•Women as the *sole* keepers of peace and war;
•Women as the *sole* keepers of Mother Earth;
•Women as the *sole* keepers of lineages and "names."

Taken together, these powers put Clan Mothers in the driver's seat of the new League. A Clan Mother is a woman who has passed menopause and has been elected to office by her peers, because they recognize her as wise, quick, intelligent, and forceful. There is no simpering allowed.

The grand finale of this story is how the power of the Priesthood was dashed. How differently this story would have gone had it been European. Towns would have been taken, and armies slain. The winning Queen's men would have killed the losing King, with the murder celebrated in song as holy vengeance. Then, men would have taken over the new government, and later histories might briefly mention how pretty and sweet-tempered the Queen was. None of this describes the outcome of the Iroquoian civil war.

First, the civil war wound down as more and more people simply refused to fight. Many defected to the Corn Way, including *Ayonwantha*, the one-time top Lieutenant of *Adodaroh*. Towards the end, the Priests were isolated, with few loyalists remaining. The war collapsed entirely when *Adodaroh* ceased to struggle against the peace by agreeing to come into the Corn Camp. The strategy to bring him around came from the *Jigonsaseh*. It is important to understand what she did here, because it bespeaks a mindset that is essential to tracing the roots of peace.

Among Native North Americans, it is important to grasp consensus. Anyone who stands against the people, as a whole, has cast himself into outer darkness. Therefore, the *Jigonsaseh* determined to show *Adodaroh* just how far outside of consensus he stood by asking all the people of all Five Nations to gather on the shores of the lake surrounding his island. From his lodging, no matter in what direction he looked, he saw thousands of people, going about life in the Corn Way, as he stood alone for the Priest Way.

Once that point was made, the *Jigonsaseh* sent the Peacemaker and *Ayonwantha* to his island, not to kill him, but to make him an offer he could not refuse: if he came over to the Corn Camp, he would be named the First Chairman of the Men's Grand Council. It was her medicine song the Peacemaker and *Ayonwantha* sang, to overcome the storm he called up, as they paddled to his island. Once they arrived, in view of the situation, *Adodaroh* accepted the offer immediately, holding the council together. All subsequent chairmen of the Men's councils have been called the *Adodaroh*, because, in woodlands culture, when an historic official does a notable job in office, the office, itself, is thereafter named after that person.

The war was won, the Great Law was recited to all the people, including the significant women's roles enshrined in that law. Collaboration, not domination, was key.

This collaboration was based on an ancient and bedrock perception of woodlands culture that the Iroquois shorthand as "The Direction of the Sky." It is the notion that TWO MAKE ONE. In eastern woodlands culture, ONE does not, *can* not, exist as a free-standing entity. In order to have ONE, there must first be TWO.

This is not a "duality." Western terms like "duality" are heavily loaded with Manichean expectations that kill rather than illuminate Native thought. The base number of western (monotheistic) cultures is One: There is one God. This has ramifications throughout the culture: People have one life, one soul, one true love. In such a system, two of anything means a competition is at hand, often violent.

Only one of the two can be the true expression; the other is necessarily fraudulent, debased—the "evil" twin—and must be destroyed, or at least, contained; hence, for instance, the famous western "battle of the sexes."

Nothing of the sort is implied in "The Direction of the Sky," because the base number of woodlands cultures is TWO. Everything that exists, exists by halves, at once independent yet interdependent. The two halves are commonly presented as Breath (Sky) and Blood (Earth) (or west of the Mississippi, as Air and Water, respectively). This has ramifications throughout the culture. Twinned pairs, cooperating to maintain creation, are spotted everywhere: male and female; farm and forest; day and night; youth and old age. Everyone has, for instance, two indwelling spirits, a Sky spirit from her father, and an Earth spirit from her mother, so that a person with only one spirit is necessarily deformed, demented, probably dangerous.

This Twinship Principle is presented graphically as "The Direction of the Sky," or East to West, that is, the line that Brother Sun runs every day in the Sky. The only reason that a singular direction exists is because East and West first existed. There is no "Direction of the Sky" without its two pinions, East and West. Furthermore, East and West are absolutely equal. They have different attributes, but in essence, they are equal. If East were destroyed, West could not be found. If there were no West, East would not exist. The singular "Direction of the Sky" only comes into existence after East and West cooperate.

Government is seen in the same way. As I mentioned, one of the primary echoes of the Twinship Principle is Male and Female. Male is associated with Sky and East, and Female is associated with Earth and West. (There is also a North-South axis with similar properties.) Obviously, such important coordinates must be expressed in any successful power structure. Governmentally, then, Twinship expresses as the Local (or female) and the Federal (or male) levels, with all matters revolving in a circle from one to the other.

I have to stop to clarify a point, because in western, especially U.S., culture, the local and the federal levels are arranged hierarchically, with the local level receiving lip service, but no real power. This is absolutely *not* the way the Iroquois League arranged local and federal relationships. Remember "The Direction of the Sky"—*both* are required.

In the League, the local level is the level of the grassroots of Mother Earth, where the sacred will of the people is first gleaned, as it bubbles up to the surface of consciousness. It is, therefore, the female level, sometimes called the "Mother" side of the League. The federal level is the male or Sky side, farther away from the grassroots, where messages must be relayed rather than taken, first hand. The Mother or Earth side of the League is run by the Clan Mothers. The Firekeeper (or executive) of their level is the *Jigonsaseh*.

No, she is not nine hundred years old, at least, not personally. The first Head Clan Mother of the League was the *Jigonsaseh* of its founding. All subsequent Head Clan Mothers are honoured to be called by her name—*Jigonsaseh*—in the same way that all Chairmen are called *Adodaroh*. Mothers of all the Clans met in council at Gaustauyea, a place in western New York. The local level is, then, the Clan Level of Government.

The Father side of the League is run by the Men's Grand Council, under the Keeping (executive administration) of the Onondagas. The Men's Council meets by nation, rather than by Clan, in Onondaga, in central New York. The Chairman is the *Adodaroh*, named after the first chairman of the League.

The Women's Clan Council is the most powerful of the two bodies, not the least because the Clan Mothers consider all matters first. By law, *the men cannot consider an issue that the women have not first discussed and forwarded to them.* In other words, women set the agenda of the League. Since the men must raise issues through their Clan Mothers, if there is an issue the Mothers want dead, they simply table it, and it goes no farther.

In this way, for instance, the Clan Mothers refused for fifty years to consider accepting the *Gaiwiyo* of Sganyadaiyoh (the heavily Christianized and woman-crushing *Code of Handsome Lake*) from moving forward. It was only in 1848, after every Clan Mother of Handsome Lake's generation was dead, that the *Code* was sent to the men. It was not coincidental that, in 1848, the U.S. government imposed a "civilized" constitution on the Iroquois, which forbade women's participation in anything but childbirth. U.S.-chosen "chiefs" then approved *The Code*, which U.S. officials smiled upon. By the way, Seneca women did not get back the right to vote until 1964.

Traditionally, before all this "civilizing," if the women did not like what the men had done with an issue, they reintroduced it in their own council, reformulating it to their liking, and sending it forward again, or not, as they saw fit. This power granted women judicial review of men's actions, which could be essentially struck down. The men could not strike down women's actions.

The right to call or end wars was also exclusively a women's prerogative. First, let me mention that traditional Native wars were nothing like European wars. There was no attempt to kill everyone in sight or burn down people's houses and fields. This was seen as barbaric and demented, an echo of the corrupt Priest-hood. What we had, traditionally, amounted to martial arts competitions; we had our own forms of martial arts in which competitors entered the field and sized up the competition, squaring off against someone about their own size and skill level. There was no honour in besting a weakling or a youth with little practice in the art. At least among the Iroquois, women compete, too. If anyone died, or was seriously hurt, it was considered a calamity. Refreshment breaks were called between matches. The first European chroniclers were amazed by these goings-on, describing Native "wars" as leaping and dancing.

After Europeans arrived with their proxy wars and gunpowder, things got more hectic, but still, young men and women went for one engagement only. If they decided along the way that the war was not a good idea, they went home without fighting. They also chose their own leaders. The object of Native "war" was to take captives, not for "slavery," as is still luridly maintained in some western texts, but for adoption as full citizens.

Back to the right to call war—the Clan Mother's right is connected to another firm law in the woodlands, which says women and children have the absolute right to peace, safety, and security. Towards this end, the women, not the men, store all weapons of war. Women's right to peace and security may only be waived by women and children through the Clan Mothers.

Not too many grandmothers are willing to sacrifice their grandchildren for nothing. Thus, the cause has to be very important for the women to give the men black wampum, that is, to tell the Men's Council that it may do as it pleases. Even then, the grandfathers on the Men's Council may reject war as an option, calling for peace councils instead. The notion that war *must* be waged, just because it is possible, is absent from Native thought. War is absolutely the last recourse, never taken lightly.

In 1783, the Clan Mothers in Ohio gave the men black wampum because the settlers were seeking to steal their hard-won homeland after the Revolution. Rather than running to war, just because they had permission, the men sought out one peace council after another, from 1784 to 1791, at which time, the U.S. government sent the U.S. Army under General Arthur St. Clair to seize Ohio by force. Only then, in a huge Men's Council at Auglaize, Ohio, did the Grandfathers vote to take up arms. (They won, by the way.)

Even in the present, traditional women are still covertly calling or stopping wars. Perhaps readers remember the troubles at Oka, in Québec, in 1990. Settlers wanted to put a golf course over a sacred site, but the Mohawk people opposed further seizure of their land, let alone sacred land for such a purpose. Matters came to blows, with young men and women keeping armed guard at the site. When the settler police took them into custody, the media played up the inherent "savagery" of the Iroquois by reporting that a woman was keeping their armory in her bathtub. In fact, the Clan Mother was acting in full accordance with her obligation to keep, and, when it was called for, distribute arms in a war she had called.

I do not have time to go into the full range of women's economic rights to Mother Earth. Although it is one of the *Jigonsaseh*'s provisions in the Constitution, it is an entire talk, all by itself. Suffice it here to say that women owned not only all the earth, but also all the fruits garnered from Mother Earth. This means that women, alone, controlled and distributed the goods and services necessary to life. No one went without, while anyone had anything. Sharing, not hoarding, was the law.

Naming may not sound like much, but it, too, is a vital power. Names have medicine connected to them. The women, alone, name new babies, people who have been adopted into clans, and individuals put in public office. This last is commonly called "nomination" in western literature, but that is misleading. It sounds as though someone can overrule the Mothers. No one can. The Clan Mothers get together, decide on the right person to fill an open position, and that is that.

There are some caveats. First, a woman cannot name her own son or daughter to power, for obvious reasons. Second, women only have naming rights within their own Clans. Western commentators gravely misunderstand both propositions. Instead of seeing that both rules are *restrictions* of power, they ignore the first and focus on the second to conclude that the system was oligarchic. They claim that the system was bound to fail, since power would consolidate in fewer and fewer hands. Poppycock.

First, western commentators are confused by diction, because the titles of Clan office are spoken of as being "inherited." Offices are "inherited" by Clan, but only in the same way that U.S. Congressional Districts are "inherited" by the state they are in. Political organization is the point, not family power. Having a Congressional district in one's state is not the same thing as inheriting wealth and title from a great-aunt. Clans do jealously guard their right to offices, just as any state wants to keep a certain number of Congressmen, but this is political, not familial. Clans were (and are) the equivalent of political parties.

Second, clans were far larger than western commentators imagine. Typically, with their stripped-down, nuclear family norms, westerners think that "clan" means first cousins, aunts, and uncles, the "extended family" of the west. That is not what a clan is. Thousands of people belong to any one clan. Each clan has members in distant cities. By and large, each Clan Mother will personally know only a handful of the candidates. This is why Clan Mothers get together to talk over the whole pool of candidates and their qualifications. After a lot of deliberation and negotiation, the person seen as having the most merit for the position is agreed upon. It is a job application process.

De-naming is part of naming. Just as women appoint men and women to office, they can impeach wrong-doers. Again, dissatisfaction bubbles up from the grassroots. Complaints go to the Clan Mothers. The standard here is first to investigate and make sure the complaints are valid. No one is called on the carpet unless credible evidence shows that he or she has acted amiss. If that is established, the offender receives three warnings before impeachment is contemplated, let alone taken.

Clan Mothers use this power carefully. There is no good in giving permission to tit-for-tat spite-fests. If someone lodges a petty complaint, it is the lodger, not the office-holder, who will be rebuked. To be impeached, an officer must affront the will of the people, honour, and public welfare. In the past, by the way, the primary crime for which a Clan Mother or Chief was deposed was converting to Christianity.

These facts of Iroquoian government are hardly state secrets. Anyone who has looked into the record has come away with this portrait of the *Gantowisas*. Many people today know that the Iroquoian Constitution was one model for the U.S. Constitution. Such points as power deriving from the will of the governed, freedom of speech and conscience, the interaction at federal and state levels, and impeachment of officials are pulled up, and rightly, for comparison. I often wonder, however, what the U.S. would look like had the Iroquoian model been truly followed, so that:

•only women, acting in close consultation with their constituents put people in office;
•women alone decided the agenda of the nation;
•all-female committees investigated allegations of official wrongdoing;
•women officials, only, impeached errant officials;
•women held and distributed all goods and services necessary to life; and
•women, alone, called—and called off—wars.

I believe that much of the posturing that constitutes modern politics would wither into nothingness. When whole cultures exist that allow young, and even adolescent, men to shush women, including elder women, I am not at all surprised that those same cultures rush to aggression as their first option. Cultures run by Grandmothers do not easily opt for war. Instead, they speak to one another, as the Iroquoian women did to the Lenape women in the seventeenth century, when Europeans urged us to war against one another for their own, selfish ends.

The Lenape and Iroquois Grandmothers sat down and consulted together, saying, "Look at the strong and beautiful children we've both raised. Did we go through childbirth and devote decades to the nurture and care of these magnificent youths just to watch them die in senseless quarrels, fights not even of our own making? No, surely we are stronger together than apart. As friends, we will be renown among all nations. For what we do here, the Lenapes will be acclaimed as wise judges, and the Iroquois as tender friends, and the precious Youth of both will live to rejoice in their own grandchildren, in peace and security." In the end, the Lenape Grandmothers voted to come into the League. We did not make war, but peace with one another.

Now, replicating this today is not as simple as just replacing male with female representatives. The so-called "West" reinforces models of patriarchy, dominance, and oppression as "natural" at every turn, while viciously colonizing, demonizing, and, when possible, demolishing those cultures based on equality, cooperation, and sharing, so that just replacing men with women results in tokens and toadies continuing the old forms. (Think: Condoleeza Rice.) Aggression and allegiance to domination will still exist. It takes time for egalitarian values to sink in culture-wide.

This does not mean that I despair of an egalitarian, interdependent, and gentle future, or that I think active steps towards it should be discouraged. I say, run to such a future as fast as possible, but, in the process, resist the mandate to dominate, oppress, or monopolize. Realize that quotidian actions must accompany intellectual re-education. The historical model is there, in the history of the *Jigonsaseh*. Yes, she did fight for her life when physically attacked, but the *Jigonsaseh* did not conquer her way to the Constitution. She negotiated with rivals, incorporated former enemies, offered food to war parties confronting her, provided shared prosperity to her followers, and stood up courageously, for the whole of her centenarian life, to all the forces of patriarchy raged against her.

She thereby *convinced* people that her Corn Way was the best available approach to civics. People simply walked away from the Priests and into her community. It took a century, but the lived example of an open, social group that—no matter what was happening to it—practiced sharing, equality, and participation eventually left the Priesthood without a single follower. With no one left to listen to, or be terrified by Priestly threats of violence, and no one left to carry out their ordered attacks against their enemies, the Priesthood collapsed. Patriarchy, oppression, and dominance fell by its own weight.

Barbara Alice Mann lives, teaches, researches, and writes in Ohio, the homeland of her Seneca ancestors for the last 1,500 years. She is the author of The Tainted Gift: The Disease Method of Frontier Advance *(2009);* The Land of the Three Miamis: A Traditional Narrative of the Iroquois in Ohio *(2006);* George Washington's War on Native America, 1779–1782 *(2005);* Iroquoian Women: The Gantowisas *(2000/2004); and* Native Americans, Archaeologists, and the

Mounds *(2003); editor and author of* Native American Speakers of the Eastern Woodlands *(2001); and co-editor and main contributor of* Encyclopedia of the Haudenosaunee (Iroquois Confederacy) *(2000). She has also authored numerous journal articles and book chapters, including "Euro-forming the Data" and "A Sign in the Sky" (1997). She is currently a Lecturer in the English Department at the University of Toledo.*

References

Allen, Paula Gunn. 1985. "Kochinnenako in Academe: Three Approaches to Interpreting a Keres Indian Tale." *North Dakota Quarterly* (Spring): 84-106.

Allen, Paula Gunn. 1986. *The Sacred Hoop: Recovering the Feminine in American Indian Traditions.* Boston: Beacon Press.

Anderson, Karen. 1991. *Chain Her by One Foot: The Subjugation of Native Women in Seventeenth-Century New France.* New York: Routledge.

Battaille, Gretchen M., ed. 2000. *Native American Representations: First Encounters, Distorted Images, and Literary Appropriations.* Lincoln: University of Nebraska Press.

Bonvillain, Nancy. 1989. "Gender Relations in Native North America." *American Indian Culture and Research Journal* 13.2: 1-28.

Bonvillain, Nancy. 1997. *Native American Medicine.* Philadelphia: Chelsea House Publishers.

Brown, Judith K. 1970. "Economic Organization and the Position of Women among the Iroquois." *Ethnohistory* 17 (3/4) (Summer/Fall): 151-67.

Calloway, Colin. 1987. *Crown and Calumet: British-Indian Relations, 1783–1815.* Norman: University of Oklahoma Press.

Charlevoix, Pierre de. 1966. *Journal of a Voyage to North America,* 2 Vols. 1761. Ann Arbor: University Microfilms, Inc.

Cronon, William. 1983. *Changes in the Land: Indians, Colonists, and the Ecology of New England.* New York: Hill and Wang.

Handbook of North American Indians. 1978. Washington, DC: Smithsonian Institution.

Heckewelder, John. 1971. *History, Manners, and Customs of the Indian Nations Who Once Inhabited Pennsylvania and the Neighboring States.* The First American Frontier Series. 1820, 1876. New York: Arno Press and The New York Times.

Hitakonan'laxk (Tree Beard). 1994. *The Grandfathers Speak: Native American Folk Tales of the Lenape People.* New York: Interlink Books.

Jensen, Joan M. 1990. "Native American Women and Agriculture: A Seneca Case Study." *Unequal Sisters: A Multicultural Reader in U.S. Women's History.* Eds. Ellen Carol DeBois and Vicki L. Ruiz. New York: Routledge.51-65.

Johansen, Bruce E. 1982. *Forgotten Founders: Benjamin Franklin, the Iroquois and the Rationale for the American Revolution.* Opifswich: Gambit Incorporated, Publishers.

Keoke, Emory D., and Kay M. Poterfield. 2003. *American Indian Contributions to the World: 15,000 Years of Inventions and Innovations.* New York: Facts on File, Inc.

Lafitau, Joseph François. 1974. *Customs of the American Indians Compared with the Customs of Primitive Times.* 2 Vols. Eds. and Trans. William N. Fenton and Elizabeth L. Moore. 1724. Toronto: The Champlain Society.

Lahontan, Louis Armand, Baron de. 1905. *New Voyages to North America.* Ed. R. G. Thwaites. 2 Vols. 1703. Chicago: A. C. McClure & Co.

Lescarbot, Marc. 1968. *The History of New France.* 3 Vols. A Facsimile of the 1907 Champlain Society Edition 1609. New York: Greenwood Press.

Lindestrom, Peter. 1925. *Geographia Americae with an Account of the Delaware Indians.* Trans. Amandus Johnson. Philadelphia: The Swedish Colonial Society.

Lowes, Warren. 1986. *Indian Giver: A Legacy of North American Native Peoples.* Penticton B.C, Theytus Books.

Lyons, Oren, and John Mohawk, eds. 1998. *Exiled in the Land of the Free: Democracy, Indian Nations, and the U.S. Constitution.* Santa Fe: Clear Light.

Mann, Barbara Alice, ed. 1998. "Euro-Forming the Data."*Debating Democracy.* Santa Fe: Clear Light Press. 160-90.

Mann, Barbara Alice. 2000. *Iroquoian Women: The Gantowisas.* New York: Peter Lang Publishing.

Mann, Barbara Alice. 2006. *Land of the Three Miamis: A Traditional Narrative of the Iroquois in Ohio.* Toledo: University of Toledo, Urban Affairs Center Press.

Mann, Barbara Alice. 2003. *Native Americans, Archaeologists, and the Mounds.* New York: Peter Lang Publishing.

Mann, Barbara A., and Jerry L. Fields. 1997. "A Sign in the Sky: Dating the League of the Haudenosaunee." *American Indian Culture and Research Journal* 21.2: 105-63.

Mann, Charles C. 2005. *1491: New Revelations of the Americas before Columbus.* New York: Random House, Inc.

McElwain, Thomas. 1978. *Mythological Tales and the Allegany Seneca: A Study of the Socio-Religious Context of Traditional Oral Phenomena in an Iroquois Community.* Stockholm Studies in Comparative Religion, no. 17.

Mooney, James. 1900. "Myths of the Cherokee." *Nineteenth Annual Report of the Bureau of American Ethnology, 1897–1898.* Washington D.C.: Government Printing Office.

Morgan, Lewis Henry. 1901. *League of the Haudenosaunee, or Iroquois,* 2 Vols. 1851. New York: Burt Franklin.

Parker, Arthur C. 1989. *Seneca Myths and Folk Tales.* 1927. Lincoln: University of Nebraska Press.

Richter, Daniel. 1992. *The Ordeal of the Longhouse: The Peoples of the Iroquois League in the Era of European Colonization.* Chapel Hill: University of North Carolina Press.

Rothenberg, Diane. 1978. "Erosion of Power: An Economic Basis for the Selective Conservatism of Seneca Women in the Nineteenth Century." *Western Canadian Journal of Anthropology* 6.3: 106-122.

Sagard, Gabriel. 1939. *The Long Journey to the Country of the Hurons*. Ed. George M. Wrong. Trans. H. H. Langton. 1632. Toronto: The Champlain Society.

Seaver, James E. 1990. *A Narrative of the Life of Mrs. Mary Jemison*. 1823. Syracuse: Syracuse University Press.

Silverberg, Robert. 1968. *Mound Builders of Ancient America: The Archaeology of a Myth*. Greenwich: New York Graphic Society, Ltd.

Thwaites, Reuben Gold, ed. 1959. *The Jesuit Relations: Travels and Explorations of the Jesuit Missionaries in New France, 1610–1791*, 73 Vols. 1896–1901. New York: Pageant Book .

Wall, Steve. 1993. *Wisdom's Daughters: Conversations with Women Elders of Native America*. New York: Harper Perennial.

Wallace Anthony F. C. 1947. "Women, Land, and Society: Three Aspects of Aboriginal Delaware Life." *Pennsylvania Archaeologist* 17 (1-4): 1-36.

VERONIKA BENNHOLDT-THOMSEN

Matriarchal Principles for Economies and Societies of Today

What We Can Learn from Juchitán

Nowadays, we live in the most pronounced, dark ages of patriarchy. The number of wars is increasing. The economy itself is seen as a battlefield, an economy of competition. The basic principle of patriarchal power has been perfected extensively: Women and nature are being denied fertility and productivity in the symbolic as well as in the real order. In the classical patriarchies man installs himself as the birther and life giver.[1] In Christianity the death of Jesus, the son of God brings eternal life to humankind. In this last actual phase of capitalist patriarchy it is not even man himself who is seen as life-giving anymore. The final perversion is that dead financial capital alone is seen as the source of all growth. This viewpoint and attitude is being promoted and translated into reality in this present state of globalizing capitalism.

Many social measures that have formerly been used to support local and Indigenous productivity are being suspended by World Trade Organization (WTO) regulations—this is called deregulation—so that unfettered profiteering may rule and capitalism may continue to grow unbounded. The result, the perishing of hundreds of thousands of people is well known to the International Monetary Fund (IMF) and the World Bank, on which the WTO is based, nevertheless, deregulation is abiding by enforced opening of harbours and the abandonment of custom barriers. Merciless! We are living in a time in which our civilization is undergoing a rapid change and in which old values are being overthrown. The human, or rather the humane, is being driven completely out of the economy. This has never happened before, even in the most cruel patriarchal societies.

But I am certain this inhumane project will fail. It contradicts human nature. It is still women who bear children, they have daughters and the sons have mothers. This guarantees that compassion and caregiving will not die out completely. As Genevieve Vaughan states, this is not so much based on the biology of the mother, but on the biology of the children. "If someone does not take care of their needs, they will suffer and die" (2002: 35). And still there are places in this world where motherly caregiving predominates as a social principle; in other words, there are local societies in existence that preserve matriarchal principles. To investigate these societies and disseminate knowledge about them is of eminent importance, to confront the wolf-like, neo-liberal, globally publicized new "civilizing" process with different economic practices and values.

Juchitán is an Indigenous town in the southern part of Mexico with approximately 100,000 inhabitants. It is located in the centre of a region 75 kilometres wide and 100 kilometres long (= or 62.1 miles) on the Isthmus of Tehuantepec, in the Pacific coastal plain. Here the Isthmus-Zapotecs live, surrounded by, as well as living with other ethnic groups. The Isthmus-Zapotecs do not deny women, and nature, their fertility and productivity; on the contrary, these qualities are explicitly attributed to them. The economy lies visibly in female hands; the trade is women's territory exclusively. Men are farmers, fishermen, craftsmen, and labourers, who hand over their products to the women, who in turn process and market their products, and manage the money. There are no female farmers or fisherwomen. When women work on a handicraft, it is an explicit female craft, mostly in food processing (considered a handicraft in this society). There are no wage workers. Likewise they are not the housewife of a farmer or a fisherman, a craftsman or a wage worker. Housewives do not exist in Juchitán. Every woman has her own trade and her own independent social and economic position.

The town belongs to the women. This is, on the one hand, based on the fact that the houses are the property of the women. Father-houses do not exist; only the house of the mother exists. Matrilocality is also reflected in the different towns' districts, which are, more or less, settling areas of matriarchal clans. This is because the mother hands down her house to the youngest daughter and helps other daughters build their houses on her terrain. When a woman gets married, the man moves into her house. He moves back to his mother's house should the relationship dissolve, which is a frequent occurrence.

On the other hand, the town also belongs to the women as they are the leading actresses on the social stage. The ceremonies and rituals of the big festivals, the social events par excellence, are women's domain, and accord women and their families' social prestige. It is via this extension that the man gets to participate in the festivals. This represents one aspect of female genealogy and matrilinearity. It is part of the social career of every woman, mostly during later years, to have been the "matron"—in Spanish *mayordoma*—of at least one Vela, one of the big festivals. The rituals and commitments related to the *mayordoma*, last the whole year. Several hundred to 3000 people congregate every day during the actual four days of celebration. The biggest responsibility and the highest costs are carried by the *mayordoma*. The more generous she is, the more she is esteemed. This is the prestige-economy principle. It is not those who own, keep, or horde plenty who receive honour, but the one who gives, so that it can be consumed together. There are thirty-five Velas each year: most take place during May, shortly before the rainy season, and most carry the traits of seasonal and fertility festivals, even though many are dedicated to Catholic saints.

By and large, Juchitán's Catholicism is syncretistic and shows clear traits of nature worship. The centralism and hierarchy of the Catholic Church is also thwarted in Juchitán. The house altar is the most important ritual place in the house. Ceremonies for different life stages are celebrated there, as well as spiritual healing rites performed by the matriarch. The veneration of the ancestress also plays an important role. Every Sunday, the grave site of the ancestors is visited and decorated with fresh flowers. The most important celebration at the cemetery is Palm Sunday, the turn from the dry season of winter to the rainy season of summer and the start of the new growing season. This unusual connection between the celebration of the death of their ancestors and the cycle of Christian death and resurrection festivals is unique throughout Mexico. A matriarchal tradition is clearly being asserted here.

Formal political offices, such as mayor or council officer, are usually held by men. Women do not regard political representation as their role; this is true of other matriarchal societies. Even so, there are female council members occasionally, and in other places on the Isthmus one can find female mayors as well.

In spite of clear matriarchal elements, patriarchy is just as clearly present in Juchitán, because Juchitán is not outside the patriarchal world. This is why the answers to the following questions are even more revealing: How are the people of this society able to maintain their different, matriarchally oriented culture, economy, and social structure? Where do the deciding differences to capitalist patriarchy lie? And what are the mechanisms that are able to reproduce them?

1. Economic, cultural, and social life are not separate in Juchitán.

This fact is already recognisable in small details. Prices of goods on the market are not calculated in an abstract fixed manner, which would be the same for everyone. They are flexible, depending on the level of the "reciprocating account" between the market-woman and the customer. The principle of reciprocity rules in Juchitàn, in all aspects of life. Of course this only works because the participants know each other and are not dependent on some faraway supermarket finance. In our globalized times, contrary to Juchitán, the exchange of goods is becoming more and more anonymous, and money is becoming an increasingly abstract variable. Money is ceasing to be a means of exchange, which should enable easier communication between the participants, but is actually estranging them from one another. Values important in Juchitàn, however, are human respect, thoughtfulness, and consideration for the circumstances of the other person. They also mould the economy, and money is part of this value system. What governs here is a "moral economy," which enables each and everyone to find the means by which they can can sustain themselves and their families, and thus ensure their survival.

2. Life in Juchitán is geared to subsistence in contrast to other societies geared to the world-market and superfluous consumption.

Subsistence is what everybody needs for everyday survival, including material and immaterial needs, food and drink, a roof , spiritual nourishment, and conviviality. The basis for subsistence production is self-sufficiency—not the self-seeking self-sufficiency of an autarchy, hostile to community, as the isolated subject of present-day patriarchal society would straight away imagine—but a moral self-sufficient economy which includes the needs of others in the community. Subsistence orientation creates and ensures the local regional economy.

3. Motherliness is a cultural and economic principle.

Motherliness remains the structural principle of social reproduction. The motherly economic caring of women has not been subjected to a man in form of housewife service, nor has it been usurped by men calling themselves "the bread-winners." There are no private housewives in Juchitán, instead, all of Juchitàn is one big household, based on the division of labour. The division of labour between women in the area of provisioning is highly developed and complex. An expert in a particular chicken dish, for example, does not need to know how to wash, starch, and iron the lace of the festival garments or how to steer a car—these are other woman's tasks.

In western patriarchal societies many women reject subsistence provisioning as a female task because they are not able to imagine performing this task without being subordinated to a man and a family. Thus, the women's movement of the western world has rejected subsistence orientation, and this has paradoxically intensified the patriarchal global capitalist economy. Instead of freeing provisioning production from its status of non-work and non-economical, freeing it of the social invisibility and creating a concept of motherly-economics, most western women see their "salvation" in wage work that is abstract and alienating.

4. The women of Juchitán do not aim for wage work.

Every woman is a trader, of one kind or another, in the provisioning economy with its high division of labour. Women exchange their products and services against money, hence as a commodity, and it is therefore why their work itself is not turned into a commodity. Wage work means, as we should remember, that the workforce itself becomes a commodity. For a Juchiteca, it is a question of honour and self-consciousness to carry out her particular skills independently and masterfully. It is her greatest aim in life to be her own boss.

In this way there is a more or less "wage-work-free zone" in existence. This prevented the *maquilas*, the world market factories that use cheap female labour everywhere else, from becoming successful, in spite of the fact that the development plan of the Mexican government has tried hard to establish *maquilas* in the area. As a result, the Zapotecs of the Isthmus enjoy a relatively high level of prosperity. Misery and begging as well as malnutrition are almost unknown. In the rest of Mexico it is especially the indigenous areas that are suffering most. Under the coordination of Ursula Oswald, we conducted a nutritional research project in Juchitàn, which was especially revealing. A focus was put on five–year-old children, because the damage from malnutrition in this age group lasts for life. The results were surprising; these children were on average better nourished than the same age group of children in the USA. The reason for this lies in their own mothers' masterful skills in the food trade, and in trade generally, as it has resulted in holding together the regional and local economy. Farmers, fishermen, and craftsmen prefer to put their yields into the hands of women instead of selling them to anonymous brokers. On the one hand, this integrates the men substantially into the local, female-run prestige economy, and on the other hand, this protects the creation of value within the region, instead of out to the anonymous world market. In short, a female affected culture protects the caregiving economy, and the care-giving economy in turn protects the matriarchal culture.

In conclusion, what can we learn from Juchitán? We should learn that we women have to get involved in the economy in an explicit, concerted, and systematic way. Matriarchally-oriented women, be they conscious feminists or not, be they scientists or not, know how a humane economy works, and can and must assert this fiercely against a patriarchy ever increasing in cruelty. It is not true that economists, managers, and bankers are the experts in economic questions—it is women! This self-confidence, this unquestioned conviction, is what we can learn from the Juchitecan women. The first step we can take, immediately and everywhere, is the creation and strengthening of local food systems and the giving of overall support to the local and regional provisioning economy

Translation by Jutta Ried and Catherine Caulwell

Veronika Bennholdt-Thomsen is a German social anthropologist specializing in Rural Sociology,, Economic Anthropology, and Women's Studies. She has lived and worked as a researcher for many years in Mexico. Her main emphasis is on peasant economy and feminist research in Latin America and Europe. She is the director of the Institute of Theory and Praxis of Subsistence in Bielefeld, Germany. She is presently a Visiting Professor at the University for Culture of the Soil, Vienna, Austria.

[1] See Maurice Godelier's book, *The Making of Great Men: Male Domination and Power among the New Guinea Baruya* (1986) with regard to this practice among the New Guinea Baruya.

References

Bennholdt-Thomsen, Veronika, ed. 1994 and 1997. *Juchitán Stadt der Frauen. Vom Leben im Matriarchat.* Reinbek: Rowohlt.

Bennholdt-Thomsen, Veronika. 1994. "Musches, das dritte Geschlecht." *Juchitán Stadt der Frauen. Vom Leben im Matriarchat.* Ed. Veronika Bennholdt-Thomsen. Reinbek: Rowohlt. 192-213.

Bennholdt-Thomsen, Veronika, Mechtild Müser, and Cornelia Suhan. 2000. *Frauen Wirtschaft, Juchitán – Mexikos Stadt der Frauen.* München: Frederking & Thaler.

Bennholdt-Thomsen, Veronika, Nicholas Faraclas, and Claudia von Werlhof, eds. 2001. *There is an Alternative. Subsistence and Worldwide Resistence to Corporate Globalization.* London: Zed Books.

Giebeler, Cornelia. 1994. "Politik ist Männersache – Die COCEI und die Frauen." *Juchitán Stadt der Frauen. Vom Leben im Matriarchat.* Ed. Veronika Bennholdt-Thomsen. Reinbek: Rowohlt. 89-108.

Godelier, Maurice. 1986. *The Making of Great Men: Male Domination and Power among the New Guinea Baruya.* Cambridge University Press.

Holzer, Brigitte. 1994. "Ökonomie der Feste, Feste als Ökonomie." *Juchitán Stadt der Frauen. Vom Leben im Matriarchat.* Ed. Veronika Bennholdt-Thomsen. Reinbek: Rowohlt. 48-64.

Holzer, Brigitte. 1996. *Subsistenzorientierung Als "widerständige Anpassung" an die Moderne in Juchitán, Oaxaca, México.* Frankfurt au Main: Peter Lang.

Mies, Maria. 1995. "Zwischen Rambo und Märchenprinz." *Reader zum 1. Männerkongress von Bündnis 90 / Die Grünen NRW* am 28.5.1994 in Wuppertal, 7-12.

Müller, Christa. 1994. "Frauenliebe in einer frauenzentrierten Gesellschaft." *Juchitán Stadt der Frauen. Vom Leben im Matriarchat.* Ed. Veronika Bennholdt-Thomsen. Reinbek: Rowohlt. 214-228.

DOÑA ENRIQUETA CONTRERAS

Matriarchal Values Among the Sierra Juárez Zapotecs of Oaxaca

D oña Enriqueta Contreras is a descendant of a long line of Zapotecan shamans that date back to 500 B.C. in Oaxaca, Mexico, which is one of the most sought out archeological sites in MesoAmerica. Her grandmother, a mid-wife, healer, seer, and shapeshifter, lived to be ninety-five years old. Traditionally, in the Zapotecan culture, shamans included both men and women. The rulers of the day honoured and resoected shamanic decisions and actions because shamans held the interests of the community to be their first priority. The Zapotecan Sierra Juárez com-munities, to this day, refer to themselves as "Los Pueblos Mancomunados," or "United Communities." The Zapotecs (self-named as the "People of the Clouds") of the Sierra Juárez are a dialect-specific group that have continuously lived and continue to reside in the nine-thousand feet above sea level foot pine forests just north of Oaxaca City, Mexico. These isolated communities, though not exempt from the effects of the Spanish invasion, managed to preserve their spiritual, traditional medicine, and communal heritage: all strongly survive today. —Mary Margaret Návar

I believe each and every one of us has within our hearts a hidden feeling and that this feeling is moving us to find a channel of energy, light, and hope. A hope that someday will touch us deeply in our hearts so that we may see life from another perspective.

I am Zapotecan from the Northern Sierra of the state of Oaxaca. I speak my own native language. There is a law, considered sacred, that has been handed down to us from our ancestors. Zapotecan culture in the Sierra Juárez is based on four life principles: first, everything has life; second, reverence for Mother Nature; third, reverence for our ancestors; and fourth, the relationship between human beings and Mother Nature. These four principles have been the foundation of our laws in our communities for thousands and thousands of years. Despite the invasion of the Spaniards, and their intention to destroy our culture and kill off our *curanderos* (healers), we have survived and are still here today. This has unified our communities. There is equality between our communities and between men and women. Beginning from the nucleus of the family, our grandparents, our ancestors, taught us a value called "respect." The mutual respect that is found at the heart of the family has made our communities "united" communities. As the

Sierra Juárez is located to the north, at quite a distance from Oaxaca, we sometimes refer to ourselves as living in the "corner of the forgotten." But our hearts live and continue to shine because we have preserved and continue to conserve our culture. And we have preserved all our traditions, despite our poverty.

Our communities have survived because of a phenomenon known as *el trueque* or "exchange." *El téquio* or "community service" is the responsibility we share for serving our communities, a responsibility that applies to both men and women. We all work together, hand in hand, on any project that is taken on for the benefit of our community. There are no differences here; men, as well as women, have the same rights, because we, as human beings, all deserve respect. When respect lives and shines in a community, everything follows the right path. All these values have been preserved. For example, in our state of Oaxaca, the festival of *La Guelaguetza* is celebrated yearly on the eighteenth of July, which in our native language of Zapotecan means "you give to me, and I give to you." This is a sacred ritual that persists and exists in each and every heart of the mountain people. Our people respect Mother Nature and care for her, because she is one and the same with Mother Earth. There is no separation between humans and Mother Nature. All children from an early age are inculcated with the value of respect. Expensive toys are never bought for children, because it destroys their intuition and creativity. All the children in the Sierra are barefooted, shivering from cold, but they are protected by Mother Nature.

All of our women work for the collective or communal good. Women must carry out their duties as assigned to them by our village elders. There is no distinction, despite the fact that we never had the opportunity to go to school—we never learned to form the letter "O" by its roundness—but we remain aware of our responsibilities as mothers and as citizens of our community. When we travel to big cities, we see sad panoramas that hurt and affect us in the deepest part of our being. What effect is politics having? What effect is bureaucracy having? What effect is money having? It is sickening the souls of the powerful. Daily we see the rich are getting richer and the poor are getting poorer. But payback will begin. The wealthy have lots of money, but they won't be able to eat it. The poor farm workers who cultivate the earth are connected with this sacred divinity: the spirits of the Earth. They may not have money but they will have something to eat.

In our villages, our community members are united in sorrow, in joy, and in death. And united we all work for the common good, especially for our children. We don't want to leave them the inheritance that these Northern countries are leaving to their children: we want to leave them an inheritance of peace, of light, and of hope.

Let us open that false door where we have stored all our resentments, and where we have forgotten our great responsibility as the women that we are. As human beings, we have an enormous responsibility to make a change on Planet Earth. Let us bring ourselves to consciousness, because today we see a lot of people that are in fear: many people are running from one place to another. Why are we so afraid? For it is what we have sowed that we are now harvesting. Our own behaviour is terrifying us. We have contaminated Mother Earth with chemicals and trash. We are destroying her. No one wants to build a new world, but everyone is afraid of what is going to happen to it. Let us raise our awareness, and with all these sudden changes that are happening, let us give thanks to the Great Creator of the Universe and the Mother Earth because everything has life: the clouds, water, air, fire, nature, we who walk on two feet, and the winged-ones. Everything has life and deserves great respect. And if we start to collaborate on nourishing our Mother Earth again, we will still have time to make changes. So, in fact, we will not eventually destroy ourselves.

We are all one: mentally, physically, and spiritually. Let us connect ourselves to the Mother Earth and open our hearts and remember that within us, there is a great and powerful divinity. Because nobody is going to fix this world; it is the women of the world who are going to have to do it. Women must take back their authority.

Translation by Mary Margaret Návar

Doña Enriqueta Contreras grew up in the arms of the Zapotecan forest in Oaxaca, Mexico. True to her ancestors, she learned the ways of the wilderness at the young age of seven as a goat-herder in the Sierra Juárez learning the power of nature, herbs, and water. Curious and gifted with a fearless commitment to help her people, Doña Enriqueta became a midwife at age seventeen serving the broad Oaxacan community of Zapotecan villages on foot and horseback. In fifty years of service as a midwife, she has never lost a child or a mother in childbirth. Her extraordinary gifts as a healer and a "seer" are widely known in Mexico, the United States, Europe, and Canada. She speaks often at conferences and offers workshops on a variety of topics ranging from midwifery to preparation of natural medicines, to spiritual connections with Nature and Mother Earth.

References (added by Mary Margaret Návar)

Berlin, Heinrich. 1988: *Idolatría y superstición entre los indios de Oaxaca*. México D.F.: Ediciones Toledo.

Butterworth, Douglas. 1962. "Relaciones of Oaxaca from the Sixteenth to the Eighteenth Century." Ed. John Paddock. *Boletín de Estudios Oaxaqueños*. Boletín 23. México D.F.: México City College.

Carmichael, James H. 1959: "Balsolobre on Idolatry in Oaxaca." Ed. John Paddock. *Boletín de Estudios Oaxaqueños*. Boletín 13. México D.F.: México City College.

Caso, Alfonso. 1962. "The Mixtec and Zapotec Cultures: The Zapotecs." Trans. John Paddock. *Boletín de Estudios Oaxaqueños*. Boletín 21. México D.F.: México City College.

Cline, Howard F. 1964. "The Relaciones Geográficas of the Spanish Indies, 1577-

1586." *Hispanic American Historical Review* 44: 341-376.

Esparza, Manuel, ed. 1994. *Relaciones Geográficas de Oaxaca, 1777-1778.* México D. F.: Centro de Investigaciones y Estudios Superiores en Antropología Social.

Lawrence, D. H. 1927. *Mornings in Mexico.* London: William Heinemann Ltd.

Marcus, Joyce. 1998. *Women's Ritual in Formative Oaxaca.* Memoirs of the Museum of Anthropology. Ann Arbor: University of Michigan.

Marcus, Joyce, and Ken V. Flannery. 2000. "Ancient Zapotec Ritual and Religion." Eds. M. Smith and M. Masson. *Ancient Civilizations of Mesoamerica.* Malden: Blackwell Publishing.

Noriega, Raul, Carmen Cook de Leonard and Julio R. Moctezuma, eds. 1982. *Esplendor de México Antiguo.* Mexico D.F.: Centro de Invesitgaciones Antropológicas de México.

Parsons, Elsie Clews. 1936. *Mitla Town of Souls.* Chicago: University of Chicago Press.

Starr, Jean. 1987. "Zapotec Religious Practices in the Valley of Oaxaca. An Analysis of the Relaciones Geográficas of Phillip II." *Canadian Journal of Native Studies* 7 (2): 367-384.

ANTJE OLOWAILI

"Goldmother Bore Human Children into the World"

The Culture of the Kuna

The Kuna live on about 60 of the 300 islands of the Caribbean San Blas archipelago on the Atlantic coast side of Panama, as well as in a few bush villages on the mainland nearby. According to differing sources, the population varies between 30,000 inhabitants in 1993 and 50,000 in 2005. The people belong to the language family of the Chibcha, one of the formerly flourishing high cultures in Northwest Columbia. For a long time the Kuna lived in the rainforest of Darién. During the siege of the Spanish conquerors they fled to the Panama coast and to the Coral islands. There they live—densely crowded but in harmony with each other. Each village community is close-knit. The Kuna owe their autonomy as an Indian people to their distinct communal sensibility. In the *Dule* revolution of 1925, they freed themselves of the occupational power of Panama and now, officially accredited, they call their territory *Kuna Yala*: the Kuna mountains.

Their way of life is very much in tune with nature and is, at the same time, spiritual. Many of their daily activities are of a ritual character and almost each object in use is pregnant with symbolic content. In this article, I show how the Kuna faith, cultural expressions, and social structures are strongly connected, and how, as a result, the Kuna, people who venerate Mother Earth, also respect and protect women.

Regrettably, increasing contact with the outside world and adaptation to this world, has transformed and/or masked the traditional way of life on some islands. This can be attributed to the influence of the Catholic Church, commercial allurements of the capitalist economy, and politics of life in Panama City, as well as the impact of increasing tourism in the area, and last, but not least, drug traffic passing by from Colombia to Panama. It manifests itself in schools, bamboo churches, healthcare units, bamboo hotels, radio and television, trade (for money, instead of goods exchange), ready-made clothes, and consumption of processed food. Nevertheless, I would like to focus on the basic patterns, that have existed for millennia, of community life and the unique creed of the Kuna that still permeates the Kuna lifestyle.

As an art student, during 1992-1994, I travelled through Latin America. On this journey, I unexpectedly met the Kuna and was fascinated by them. I stayed and shared their life for a year, first as a patient of the medicine man, then as a village member, and finally as a child adopted by a shaman and his wife.

On a multitude of islands and especially in the bush villages, completely cut off from the outside world, I came to know a community in which women played a very special role and where each girl celebrated; a culture in which history and ritual knowledge is kept in song; a life in which the laughter of children chases away hurricanes. A worldview opened up to me where women prophets descend upon golden disks to earth and tell of a Great Mother who has given birth to all earthly beings—mountains and rivers, forests, animals and humans—and tell of a Great Father who helped her in this creation.

The Creation

Nana is the Kuna word for mother. *Nana Dummad,* the Great Mother, gave birth to human children according to the creation story of the Kuna, the *Anmar Danikid Igala,* or translated: "Path on which we have come."

Baba is the Kuna word for father. *Baba Dummad,* the Great Father, is the word for God. But different from the Christian belief, this word includes the mother. In the spiritual songs handed down since primeval times, *Baba* and *Nana* are always mentioned together. To speak about a father—that is how the old chiefs explain it in their evening assemblies of the village community—presupposes the existence of a mother. Therefore, the belief in God as Creator includes the existence of a Goddess who gives birth to life in this world. "All of nature is created in this way: flowers, trees, animals, and humans. This is what the old Nele have sung to us and we continue to sing it for you: Father is inconceivable without Mother."

In the Kuna cosmology *Baba* and *Nana* are a unity, a creative pair. They created the earth, a joy for all beings, and for the plants and animals that live on her. At the very end they created *Olodule*—gold humans, which is what the Kuna call themselves—as guardians and protectors of the earth. They put the *Olodule* onto the fertile Mother Earth so that they could sow and harvest her and bring her into blossom.

From my shamanic foster father, Olokinwinapi, I learned what essentially is so simple but difficult to understand with patriarchal thought patterns: "Mother Earth does not belong to us. We belong to her because she has brought us forth, therefore, we have to share her fruits with all her children—humans and animals. Sharing is important because: *Anmar belagwable gwenatgan*—we are all brothers and sisters."

This conviction (which each Kuna child is taught early on) creates a life in harmony with all living and soulful beings—beings that include beyond the various peoples, animals, plants, stones, rivers, wind, the sky, the earth, the sea, and manifold spirits. They know that nothing exists separately, therefore, each individual has a place and is part of the great whole in their community. We are all brothers and sisters, and this does not exclude any animal or small leaf on a tree.

The Life

Life in a Kuna village is simple, at one with the surrounding nature and in the deepest soul relationship with all plants, animals, and spirits. The Kuna eat what they can cultivate in the bush, find by way of hunting or by fishing in the sea—and they fish, hunt, or harvest only that which they also can eat. No super abundance, no accumulation of possessions, no social classes or strata, a thoroughly egalitarian society in which each human with his/her idiosyncracies, capabilities and skills, is respected.

Kuna woman cooking bananas for a ritual meal which will be shared with the village community at the initiation festival of her daughter. Photo: Antje Olowaili, 2005.

The Kuna live closely together in extended families within bamboo huts, the walls of which have many gaps and do not allow for a shutting off against the village community. Embedded in the network of relationships, nobody remains on the outside or lonely: the mad are listened to, the sick are cared for; albinos are treasured as highly gifted; homosexuals or gender role changes are accepted; and old people are highly respected. Loneliness is practically non-existent in Kuna Yala, just as there is no private sphere—and thanks to this closeness, this absence of shut-off rooms and opaque walls, there is no domestic violence against women or children or men.

The central figure of each family is the mother. *Nana*, the most heard word in a Kuna village, names with great respect and love the one who gives life, who nourishes and educates others. Though it is the men who are going out to look for food, who hunt and fish, the women hand out the food and rule the hut.

But women not only prepare and distribute food (and thereby maintain the family), they are also the guardians of the fire. Fire is never allowed to go out in a society embedded in nature. This relationship with fire is essential for the Kuna women because, aside from its destructive power, fire is at the same time the source of life and, in this way, has a direct connection with birthing. "Women at the hearth" is only a perverted patriarchal translation of the ingrained certainty that women and fire belong closely together.

Because marriage is matrilocal, the respected oldest mother of the extended family has the most influence. Husbands—or, let us say, *Sui,* the Kuna word meaning "collectors of food," describes a man who is coupled (because the marriage as a registered institution does not exist in Kuna culture). Husbands who do not behave in accordance with the will of their wives and especially with the will of the mother's mother of the family (those who, for example, are lazy or short-tempered or treacherous or even violent) are expelled without further ado and must return to their mother's hut.

A woman, however, can never be without shelter. All her life she lives in the hut of her mother, and after the death of her mother she herself becomes the matriarch. Once she dies, the hut is transfered to her daughters.

Possessions—as, for example, temporary cultivated land in the bush, golden jewellery, and other goods of the family—are traditionally inherited through the mother's lineage. Although a banana tree plantation or a coconut palm island is for the most part owned by the man who cultivates it, when he becomes old he transfers it to his daughter's "collector of food" or, in many cases, directly to the daughters. In this way, after his death, sources of subsistence remain with the family of his wife. They are not handed over to his son because this son is going to leave his family one day to marry into another family.

Although a woman is always provided for and made secure in her family, she is not free to go where she wants to. Generally—men and women are treated the same—the council of chiefs decides who leaves the home village, be it for a short visit to the neighbouring island or to go to Panama City to work. A woman receives this permission with much more difficulty than a man and, traditionally, only under the condition that she has male protection at her side—usually her husband or father and, in exceptional cases, her mother. This tradition may sometimes have been interpreted as patriarchal control over women, depending on the viewpoint of the observer. But this tradition also points to the inestimable value each woman has for the continued existence of the village community and for her peoples' tribe, whose survival is threatened.

Children are the focal point of the extended family. They enjoy great freedom, are allowed to run about everywhere, to touch everything, to shriek or cry to their heart's content, and to develop according to their own capabilities. No consideration is required of them. They, however, get almost unlimited consideration. Being so strongly affirmed in their self-value, Kuna children, already in

Kuna women ritual drinking at a little girl's festival of offering the hair.
Photo: Antje Olowaili, 2005.

their first years of life, take on responsibility for themselves and for their brothers and sisters. They mature early and often at only four years of age do adult tasks out of their own motivation. For example, they join in collecting food, fishing, fetching water, grating coconuts, or doing the laundry. In a natural way, children contribute out of their own volition, for the welfare of the family, without ever being forced to do so.

The mothers have in this respect a vital role, too, because from them, the children learn more than walking, speaking the mother tongue, and treating others with love. A slogan of the protest march of Indigenous peoples at the five hundredth anniversary of the conquest of America, which ended in Kuna Yala, says: *No necesitamos escuelas. La madre es nuestra maestra en la America Indígena.* "We do not need schools. The mother is our teacher in Indigenous America."

This demonstrates that traditional women's professions as we know them—cook, housewife, educator, teacher, nurse—do not necessarily have to be a means or instrument of oppressing women. On the contrary, as long as these roles are valued as important achievements in the society in which they live, the women who perform these roles are highly esteemed in their community.

The Culture

The culture was brought to the Kuna by *Nele* women prophets. A long time ago, three brothers lived in the rainforest, so sing the chiefs. They hunted for food.

Kuna women proudly selling their collection of mola handicrafts on the island Ukubseni.[1] Photo: Antje Olowaili, 2005.

One day, three beautiful women descended on a golden disk from the sky and brought them the culture. One of them, Nadili, remained with them and became the mother of today's Kuna people. Like Nadili, all Kuna women remain bearers of their culture, and on their bodies, visible to all (and different from the Kuna men) they wear their traditional patterned garment: the *mola*.

Mola

The wonderful hand-sewn *mola* (a blouse of imagery) is internationally known. The *mola* tells stories, in mysterious images and meandering patterns, about the complex cosmos of the life and beliefs of the Kuna. Rites and customs, mythology and history, everyday life in the huts, hunting and fishing, animals and plants, spirits and demons, medicine and dance, all have their place in the *mola*. Every motif has also a symbolic significance. It not only tells a story, but it has a purpose: for example, to provide good fortune for fishing, or protection from diseases.

It is fascinating that in *mola* art the Kuna women seem to perceive the world in which they live by way of patterns rather than objects. Animals, plants, spirits, or humans are never represented in a compact or naturalistic way, but always abstracted as a symbol or screened onto the material in manifold spiral forms, colourful patterns of stripes, dots, and meanderings—just as if the figures and the background are constantly interwoven. This reflects their view of a world in which everything is interconnected.

With their *mola* and *sabure* (hip cloth), *muswe* (head scarf), *olasu* (nose ring) and *wini* (pearl strings for the arms and legs), the Kuna women are a joy to behold for anyone who meets them. But they are, at the same time, heirs to an ancient art of telling stories in images beyond words.

In addition to this cultural aspect, the selling of *mola* images to collectors and tourists represents an important part of the family income to which the women contribute. Thus, with regard to the economy, in many cases, women earn more money than men.

Singing Memory

Different to the women's art of storytelling with images, men in positions of dignity, like chiefs, healers, and visionaries, tell stories with words which are sung. In the past this was called "singing the images." At that time there still existed the old pictographs of the medicine people, whose canon of forms is closely related to the symbols and patterns of the *mola*. And although that written language no longer exists on the islands, the words of the songs are still figurative, symbolic, and older than the everyday language. Therefore, they are incomprehensible to the uninitiated Kuna. They require a "language opener" (*argar*) who translates the ritual songs for the village inhabitants into present-day Kuna language.

Wise men are—as singing keepers of history and religion—the historical memory of their tribe and in this way keep it spiritually alive. Their rich ancient mythology includes the four times the world ended (of which the big flood in Christian mythology is the most recent). Four times human beings have been washed away from the earth surface, the Kuna remember, because their human greed was abusing and destroying mother nature. Today, the Kuna say, there's not much time left before humanity will experience the fifth. It is thus apparent that the Kuna storytelling tradition is many times older than ours. This knowledge is sung for women and men two times per week in singing units of several hours. Sometimes the chiefs of several islands combine their singing, a form of storytelling that can last from three days to one week.

The chiefs (*saila*) and song healers (*kandule*) as well as the shamanic escorts of the dead (*masardule*) sometimes recite ritual songs by heart, which may take several days. The entire Kuna history, their creation story, as well as their shamanic remedies and healing chants, are handed down exclusively in this oral tradition. This achievement of the memory is completely inconceivable to those of us who are used to recording in written form everything that we feel must be remembered. Presumably the old pictographs help with visual memory. A comparison of the pictographic writing system, which still exists in a rudimentary way in the bush villages, with the *mola* signs, suggests that songs and *mola* images speak the same symbolic language and are based on the same secrets of life. Further, the names of traditional *mola* patterns are consistent with words from the ritual songs. From this I conclude that image patterns and sound patterns (of words in chants) are tied together and thus mutually enhance the other's effectiveness.

This interweaving of image and song, of female and male conservation of history, parallel and equal in their respective levels of expression, is a wonderful example of a balance in gender role distribution in my view.

Everyday Songs

Nevertheless, despite the tradition of history-chanting, it can in no way be deduced that for the Kuna the song is typically male. While only the song healers, medicine men, and chiefs sing among the Kuna men, the life of most Kuna women consists, to a large extent, of everyday singing: they sing their children to sleep, they cry their laments for the ill and the dead, and when celebrating they laugh happiness songs about the joy of drinking together. These mostly improvised everyday songs form a constant backdrop of sound to life in a Kuna village.

The Lullaby

The lullaby of a Kuna woman, which is sung frequently during the day with the pumpkin rattle, is called *Koe Bibiye*—an individual song the text and melody of which each woman finds for herself, composed from her very personal wishes and hopes. When Kuna women sing for the children the *Koe Bibiye* to send them to sleep, they give direction to them from the first day of their life, for the rest of their lives, concerning their later roles in the society. They sing of their love for their children and of the care which they wish to receive in turn, as well as the work they will do as adults. You cannot avoid noticing that they sing different songs for the girls and for the boys.

For example, a lullaby for a girl: "My golden child, when you are grown up you will be a beautiful Indian woman. You will have a *Dule* man. Who will it be who comes into our hut to help the father? You are going to bear many children. When your husband and your father return from the mountains, you will be the first one who awaits them at the edge of the island. You will help them to pull the canoe up the beams on the embankment. You will carry what they bring to the hut. This hut is your home forever. Here you are loved and secure. You will never lose it."

A lullaby for a boy: "My little son, you are only with us temporarily. Now this is your home, we will feed you so that you can grow up. We give you our love so that you will never forget us. But when you have grown up, you will leave us. The hut of your wife will be your home. You will work for another family. Today we work for you but you are only a guest in our family. So think of us when you are far away, and come to visit us sometimes. Once you earn a lot of money, then buy us a gas oven."

All these lullabies, lamentations and drinking songs are typically female in Kuna Yala. Aside from the everyday songs, there are also a considerable number of female ritual songs. Performed by healing women, these songs tell, in a fixed word canon, about the initiation and dedication of girls—a taboo for men. Healing women sing about medicine. Women prophets (*nele*) communicate in trance songs with spirits and demons in their subterranean worlds.

Coming of Age Rituals

The various coming of age rituals for girls consist of feasts which last for several days, and in which the whole village participates. In this context belong the *ikko inna*, the celebration of the needle, for the ceremonious piercing of the nose and ears of female babies for their later golden jewellery; *disla inna*, the celebration of the scissors, a ritual shearing of the head of small girls as a sacrificial act for their life after death; and *diwe inna*, the dedication of the coming of age when the first bleeding happens (also called "puberty celebration"), with which the young maturing woman is received into the circle of adult women as the fruitful image of mother earth. Often the latter happens when the girls are eleven or twelve years old. There are no comparable celebrations for boys.

Young girl performing a ritual bath in the puberty chamber, isolated from her family and community, while being initiated by a ritual woman. Photo: Antje Olowaili, 2005.

All these celebrations are lead by old and wise ritual women. Traditionally, menstruation, the fertility cycles, pregnancy, and giving birth are taboo for men. Because of this, everything connected with these rites of passage, all the knowledge, including that of women's medicine and spiritual child bed care (of both mother and child during the first weeks after childbirth), is exclusively handed down from woman to woman: the practical aspects, from mother to daughter, the medicinal knowledge from the healer to her apprentice, and the spiritual aspects of fertility and creation—and with it the significance of the women for the life of the tribe—from the ritual woman to the girl to be dedicated.

There is no comparable secret knowledge for men as life producers. Nor is there a mythical ceremony for their duties as collectors of food, which starts from the day of their living together with a woman, and which is traditionally enacted through the ritual of being captured, sometimes at the age of thirteen or fourteen. The task of looking for food is not a secret. It belongs to a moral set of rules in the bamboo congress (or prayer hut) and is a permanent component of the evening teachings.

Politics

The realm Kuna men explicitly dedicate themselves to is politics. However, it is not taboo for women and there are always individual, active women who participate. The men congregate in the prayer hut each evening, also called congress, and talk about the fate of their island, about improving the infrastructure, matters of conflict, or the practical organization of impending celebrations. Some of them become temporary chiefs, keepers of order or openers of the old ritual language. Others represent their family.

All married men are obliged to participate in these daily assemblies. It is their responsibility to take relevant topics into their families, to discuss them, and then return to the congress to represent the positions of their family members. In this way they make sure that the interests of women are not ignored. If it is necessary, it may also happen that a woman appears in front of the congress and talks to the chief or to the assembled men. She will do this politely, not as a reverent petitioner but rather as a self-assured woman and often with much emotional emphasis.

In this way, both women and men influence the decisions to be made and the daily life in the village. Mothers rule the hut and family life, fathers seek consensus decisions in congress. Power is shared by women and men, though strictly delineated according to their gender roles. Although such delineation, when abolishing the matrilocal marriage or right to live in the hut of the mother and introducing patrilocality, tends to cause a fatal power pattern, in the matrilocal Kuna society, it does not lead to the exertion of power by one gender over the other.

Vision

In the creation story of the Kuna, the *Anmar Danikid Igala*, there is an impressive admonition that the aggressive, belligerent principle should form an outer wall of protection around the community and that in its centre the life-giving principle has its place and is protected. What happens when the principles are interchanged and the aggressive nature is taken into the centre (see patrilocality, male heads of family, etc.) is also described: they change into monsters inimical to life because their aggressive qualities are then channelled wrongly and directed against the members of their own community. Mother Earth and humans will experience unspeakable suffering as a consequence, as the story goes, from the formerly beloved mother who embodied beauty only the bones remain, and the originally gentle movements of the earth change into natural catastrophes—that this already happens in large parts of our world is beyond doubt.

A worldview that centres around the mother is, therefore, not a philosophy of women but a philosophy of life. With the Kuna, this is propagated by men. It is a mystery of life that views a fertile nature and motherhood as the basis of our lives and wishes to live in harmony with both. Neither gender is seen as better or stronger. Women and men form a social, economic, cultural, and spiritual equilibrium.

"Did you know that nature is female?" my shamanic foster father, Olokinwinapi, asked me. "Therefore, she has to be protected just as women have to be protected. Nature and women are the same. Without them, we would not survive one day. Therefore, you can see that a people who honours nature also honours its women and protects them." *Thank you Olokinwinapi!*

Nine Fundamental Matriarchal Tenets of the Kuna Society

1. Living together is matrilocal. When a couple gets together the man moves into the hut of his wife to live with her family, to work with her father and to collect food for her family members.

2. An individual's name is transmitted according to the matrilinear sequence—the family name comes from the mother. The Kuna lived this way before Christian missionaries introduced their patriarchal custom of the father's name into Kuna Yala. Since then the Kuna use both family names, the name of the mother and that of the father.

3. Inheritance is matrilinear. Possession and the goods of the family are inherited through the mother's lineage. For example, if a man owns a coconut palm, this palm remains after his death with the family of his wife. It is not handed over into the possession of his son because this son is going to leave his family one day to marry into another family.

4. The basic economy is in the hands of women—although it is men who collect daily the food from bush and sea. They hand it over, upon arrival at the island, to the women. From this moment onwards, banana, coconut, and fish belong to the women who prepare and distribute them. Because they distribute the food they are seen as the maintainers of the family. In addition to this, the selling of the *mola*, sewn by women, is an important component of the family economy.

5. Women are seen as the source of life. Traditionally, men are not allowed to know or to enquire about menstruation, pregnancy, and childbirth. Formerly this was taboo—and is still so in many villages up to today.

6. Thanks to her capability to sustain her people, the woman is at the centre of the family and family life goes according to her direction.

7. The mother is the teacher in Indigenous America. There is no need for external schools to learn the mother tongue, to live the traditional life and to maintain and care for the traditional Kuna culture in its community.

8. The women are the bearers of their culture—evidence of this are the traditional

garments, the celebratory dedication rituals for girls, the celebration of female puberty, wise women who lead these rituals, and women prophets who descend from the sky on golden disks to bring the culture to the Kuna.

9. The Kuna society is a fundamental egalitarian community. No gender is seen as better or stronger. Both women and men form a social, economic, cultural, and spiritual equilibrium.

Translation from German by Karin Meissenburg and Cathie Dunsford

Antje Olowaili was born in Berlin in 1968. While studying free arts she initiated women's art projects and wrote articles about women's rights in the former GDR. During the years 1992-94 she travelled through Latin America on her own and stayed one year with the Kuna people. There she was adopted by a shaman and his wife and went through months of treatment with indigenous medicine. She learned the Kuna language, their chants, and famous mola sewing art. Her book, Sister of the Sun: One Year in Kuna Yala *was published in Germany in 2004. Today, Antje Olowaili is living and working as an artist and author in Leipzig, Germany.*

[1]Kuna men never take scissors into their hands and sew a *mola* (it is an unspoken taboo), unless they are *omegi* (transgendered men who live as women). In this photograph, the first person from the left is *omegi*.

References

Olowaili, Antje. 2004. *Schwester der Sonne: Ein Jahr in Kuna Yala (Sister of the Sun: One Year in Kuna Yala).* Königstein/Taunus, Germany: Ulrike Helmer Verlag. ISBN 3-89741-138-5.

Olowaili, Antje. 2001. "Solidarität mit Frauen: Luxus oder Kunst? (Solidariry with Women: Luxury or Art?)" *Ihrsinn* 24.

Hübscher, Anneliese. 1998. "The Magic Flare: Paintings of Antje Olowaili." *Letter Arts Review* 14 (4): 2, 18-23.

Hübscher, Anneliese. 1999. "Schriftbilder von Antje Olowaili (Scriptual Paintings of Antje Olowaili)." *Jahresschrift der 8. Internationalen Ausstellung für Künstlerbücher und Handpressendrucke (IAKH).* Frankfurt/Main: Leipzig

CAROLYN HEATH

Women and Power

The Shipibo of the Upper Amazon

The Shipibo have given me power to narrate. The overall aim of this paper is to fulfil an obligation to Shipibo women, to make their voice heard in the west, to give voice to invisibility. Years ago I was travelling in Río Pisqui, the most isolated part of Shipibo territory, when a blind woman called me to her side. "We shall never see your country," she said, "but you shall carry our voices there, that we may be heard." This compelling invitation was later echoed by another woman who sang me a song, which formalized the proposal at a public festival. I see this paper as a continuation of that process.

****

The Shipibo are a lowland Indigenous group living in the Upper Amazon. Some 200,000 tribal people from 63 distinct ethnic groups still inhabit the rainforests of eastern Peru, their survival due partly to the relative inaccessibility of their lands until recent times and partly to the more flexible attitudes of Peruvian authorities compared with neighbouring countries. An estimated 40,000 Shipibo live in 110 villages along the banks of the Ucayali River, a major tributary of the Amazon stretching northwards from Atalaya as far as Orellana. The modern Peruvian city of Pucallpa marks the centre of traditional Shipibo territory. The Shipibo call this place *Mai Joshín* meaning "red earth." The Shipibo were colonized by Spanish missionaries in the sixteenth century. This process did not proceed without a struggle, the Catholic Church acquiring some 30 martyrs in the Ucayali area. The Shipibo way of life is currently threatened by an encroaching capitalist society that is rapidly consuming their habitat—the Amazon rainforest—making the public documentation of their worldview and social organization all the more compelling.

Personal visits to more than 50 ethnic groups in the Upper Amazon confirm my observation that Shipibo women possess an extraordinary degree of self-confidence compared with women from other Amazonian groups. Shipibo women are assertive, independent, vigorous, self-confident, and perceptive. They are extraverted in their social behaviour but intuitive in their use of creative designs to decorate ceramics and textiles.

During the first year of of a Masters degree in Women's Studies, I learned with

92

increasing disbelief that female subordination is universal (Ortner 1974: 69). From personal experience of living closely with the Shipibo for twelve years I can affirm that Shipibo women are in no way subordinated to men; the women's artistic and spiritual power is a major source of their strength and self-confidence. I do not suggest that Shipibo women wield total power but that they share power equally with men. Anthropologists from other corners of the world—Southeast Asia springs to mind—have observed that societies exist in which men and women share power equally, often by assuming complementary roles.

Henrietta Moore reminds us that anthropologists have had to tackle the problem of difference, especially in the way in which gender is experienced. She argues that western concepts are potentially distorting and suggests one should look at what women do in a particular society, their access to resources and the amount of economic and political autonomy they possess (1988: 79). Shelly Errington (1990) observes that ideas about what power is and how prestige should be attained vary cross-culturally. She speaks of the need to discard eurocentric ideas about power and status. Jane Atkinson, speaking of the Wana of Southeast Asia, refers to "gender asymmetry"—"the notion that men and women are seen to be the same sort of beings, differentiated through their activities rather than their fundamental nature" (1990: 79). As the source of humanity both sexes share power equally for the creation of new life (1990: 77). This concept approximates to Shipibo thought.

During the 1970s, feminists argued about the possible existence of matriarchal societies. Matriarchy was conceptualized as the mirror image of patriarchy with women rather than men occupying positions of power. Sherry Ortner claimed that "the search for a genuinely egalitarian, let alone matriarchal, culture had proved fruitless" (1974: 70). Marilyn Strathern spoke scathingly of the need for "debunking the myth of matriarchy" (1996: 38). The actual existence of matriarchal societies was open to doubt until the Naxi Cai Hua of Southwest China were identified in 1977, among others.

The suspicion that Amazonian societies differ from those in other areas prompted an investigation of the literature. Carole Counihan points out that in Amazonian societies women "have a psychological confidence in their identity and power as women" (1999: 72). Matrilineality may well provide a clue as to why they are so confident. In their intensive study of Amazonian societies Joanna Overing and Alan Passes come to the conclusion that "much of technical language of anthropology … is irrelevant to Amazonian societies" (2000: 2). They find that Amazonian Indians are people who stress harmony in everyday life, that many concepts are ungendered and that family and public domains are not separate, but one. They particularly comment on the egalitarian nature of Amazonian society.

A major research question arising from my preoccupation with women's power is: "What are the contributing factors to the unique self-confidence of Shipibo women?" It has been asserted that "[Shipibo] … women enjoy more rights, freedom, individual fulfilment and spontaneity than women of other cultures may ever dream of" (Gebhart-Sayer 1984: 18). To test the veracity of this affirmation

I propose to explore the spheres of power of Shipibo women on four levels: family power, economic power, political power, and spiritual power.

Family Power of Shipibo Women

An investigation of family power calls for a brief analysis of Shipibo kinship patterns. Linda Stone (2000: 121) uses kinship for the cross-cultural study of gender. She suggests that the status or power of women tends to be higher in societies with matrilineal descent patterns (descent through the female line), especially if the society practises matrilocal residence (post-marital residence with the woman's family).

Turning to the work of researchers who have studied the Shipibo, Peter Koepke remarks: "The young girl ... is the treasure of the family, spoiled but carefully disciplined at the same time. She will become matron and director of a future compound and will be respected and looked up to" (Gebhart-Sayer and Koepke 1984: 6). Similarly Peter Roe notes the privileged position of Shipibo women, indicating that the settlement pattern is a matrilocal compound consisting of the household of the matriarch and her daughters. The compound is the focus of loyalties and co-operation (1980: 49). Angelika Gebhart-Sayer (1984) finds that "each compound is inhabited by an extended family or clan in which—ideally— all women are blood relatives and the men are unrelated. Young men move in with the families of their wives....[This] entails a strong social position for the women in both compound and village affairs" (1982: 6). Françoise Morin (1995: 340) also finds evidence for matrilocal residence, observing that the new husband lives together with his in-laws until the first child is born. The couple then move to a separate house in the same family compound. It can, therefore, be confidently asserted that Shipibo society is matrilocal with three generations of women living in the same compound.

Can we assume that Shipibo descent patterns are matrilineal? Linda Stone observes that ethnic groups with matrilocal residence tend to adopt matrilineal descent patterns (200: 65). Annette Weiner points out that "matrilineality gives women a domain of control that men can neither emulate nor infiltrate with any degree of lasting power" (Weiner 1976: 234). Kay Martin and Barbara Voorhies (cited in Sanday 1981: 177) find that "matrilineal structures are accommodating and integrative" and are more likely to be associated with sexual equality.

Morin has undertaken a partial study of Shipibo kinship patterns. She observes that no in-depth study exists and that Shipibo kinship patterns are "exceedingly complex" (1995: 340). Roe affirms that in the past before social dislocation "descent was matrilineal, and to a degree still is" (1982: 55). In a study of thirteen Shipibo villages undertaken in 1978, Roe found that descent was matrilineal. Two years later he describes Shipibo residence patterns as a matrilineal extended family with its nuclear segments occupying separate but contiguous houses in the family compound (1980: 49). Commenting on the power of Shipibo women Roe explained that the very prominent role females play in Shipibo society is based on their prosperity derived from the tourist trade and on the matrilineal-matrilocal basis of their social organization (Roe 1982: 72). Donald Lathrap recorded the cultural dominance of a "corporate core of related women at the centre of Shipibo society" (1983: 192).

However, further consultation with Morin elicits the information that Shipibo kinship patterns are so complex they do not fit comfortably into any preordained pattern. She suggests similarities to a bilateral cognatic kinship pattern (Personal communication 2005). Stone (2000) observes that whereas most societies follow a mode of patrilineal descent, virtually all societies *also* exhibit bilateral kinship whereby the child is considered equally related to both parents, and kin connections are traced over the generations but without the formation of kin groups. In support of this theory, Overing and Passes point out that one of the characteristics of Amazonian societies is that there are no lineages (2000: 1). Errington (1990) also attributes the equality of women in Southeast Asia to bilateral kinship patterns. Morin (1995) finds some evidence for bilateral kinship among the Shipibo. The point to emphasize is that even if the Shipibo are bilateral or have changed from a matrilineal to a bilateral form of kinship, this still encourages more equal gender relationships than in the patrilineal model.

Other family traits in Shipibo society which favour women's power are that as head of household the woman makes all family decisions and commands great respect (Gebhart-Sayer 1986); female children are more highly valued than males because they attract more sons-in-law to the family (Roe 1982); the mother chooses a husband for her daughter, usually from birth (Morin 1995), and if the marriage should fail children remain with their mother in the family compound. Rafael Girard notes the privileged position of the Shipibo woman and observes that she is the one who gives orders in the house "in virtue of the principle that the person who does the work has the right to command" (1958: 245).

The undisputed authority of the mother-in-law, which guarantees the security of her daughter in the family house, is still a permanent feature of Shipibo life (Morin 1995). Shipibo men actively practice mother-in-law avoidance. Both eye contact and direct speech are considered improper. A Shipibo man virtually becomes the slave of his mother-in-law during the first years of marriage. She will test her son-in-law's strength, endurance, patience, and technical skills by commanding him to clear an agricultural plot, build a canoe, or fetch her a coconut from the top of the tree. He hastens to obey. One might say that in Shipibo society men rather than women are the "muted group." Matrimony is easily contracted and easily dissolved. If the husband turns out to be lazy or unfaithful, his mother-in-law, in consultation with her daughter, will send him back to his family.

Another crucial source of power for women is in the distribution of food (Couníhan 1999). I have observed that Shipibo women retain absolute power over the cooking pot. Shipibo women eat together around the fireplace. Men tend to eat in a separate group, but it is the women who allocate the portions of fish, meat, plantains, and manioc to the men, retaining the choice pieces for themselves. Donald Lathrap recalls that James Loriot, a local missionary, told him that for the

Shipibo "the cooking pot is the centre of the universe. The women and children surround this focus and the men are distributed at the periphery, receiving food only at the sufferance of the women" (1985: 100).

Shipibo women are highly respected by Shipibo men. Their natural beauty and colourful clothing is a source of physical attraction and sexual power. Shipibo women enjoy equal rights with men to indulge in promiscuous behaviour. Even when caught *in flagrante* women are not punished.

Economic Power of Shipibo Women

Moore (1988) suggests that a source of women's power is the amount of economic autonomy women possess and their access to resources. Turning now to the economic power of Shipibo women, Lathrap (1985) unreservedly praises the artistic skill of Shipibo: "The existence of a corporate group of women ... has been the essential matrix for the most spectacular achievements of Amazonian art." Using pre-Columbian techniques, Shipibo women produce hand-loomed cotton textiles and exquisite polychrome pottery, which is well-represented in museum collections throughout Europe and the Americas. Craft production is a means of relaxation for Shipibo men and women. To weave, embroider, or make pottery is a woman's favourite pastime. By the age of ten, a girl will have learned essential skills of beadwork, spinning, and embroidery from her mother and elder sisters. If she shows an aptitude for pottery she will begin a long apprenticeship with her maternal grandmother.

Shipibo women enjoy ready access to natural resources essential for craft production. The Ucayali area provides clay, natural oxides, and lacquer for decorating pottery at specific sites well-known to generations of Shipibo women. Tree cotton is grown in the villages. Peter Gow observes that Shipibo design is specialist female knowledge and is "the means of female control over the transformations of material forms" (1990: 94). In his later work on Piro design (a neighbouring ethnic group) Gow finds that the "imaginative control of design increases with age and is a special property of older women" (1999: 242). He points out that designs are products of women's knowledge: "Knowing how to paint with design" (1999: 237).

There is an increasing demand for Shipibo craft products both nationally and internationally. Roe points out that the prominent role females play in Shipibo society is partly due "to their prosperity derived from the tourist trade" (1982: 72) observing that the market for ceramics and textiles has proved a welcome source of income. Shipibo women rely on the sale of craft products for cash income, travelling widely throughout Peru in the course of their commercial activities and leaving their husbands behind in the villages, sometimes for months. Children will remain in the care of their maternal grandmother. Shipibo women travel together in small groups and are as likely to be found selling beadwork on the beaches of Lima as in the Andean city of Cusco. To sum up, Shipibo women have the freedom to travel where they please; also, profits from craft sales belong to

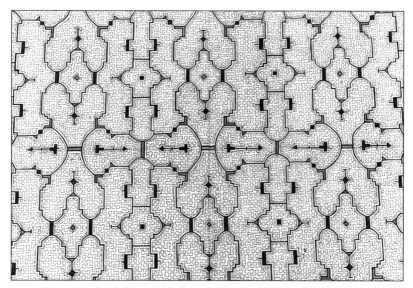

Shipibo cloth painted by Sara Flores Valera, Yarinacocha, 1988.

women entirely. A woman will use the income for personal and family expenses such as school uniforms and books for her children. Some Shipibo women have been able to send their children to university in Lima with the income generated from the sale of textiles and ceramics.

Political Power of Shipibo Women

Overing and Passes confirm the basic characteristics of Amazonian societies: no authority structures, no political structure, no land-holding groups. They emphasize Indigenous antipathy to rules and regulations, hierarchical structures and constraints, pointing out that "the domestic domain and the public domain are not separate, as in western thought, they are one" (2000: 1).

Contemporary Shipibo will tell you that since the arrival of the Spanish the Shipibo have had no overall leader, neither at group level nor at village level, only temporary leaders who might appear at times of war. Roe finds there is "clearly no intervillage, much less overall, tribal political organization" (1982: 39). Morin (1995) confirms the lack of political authority figures in Shipibo society, pointing out that the only male figure with power is the shaman. Since his duty is to resolve conflicts and heal the sick he is likely to be a weak political figure.

In 1974 the Peruvian government introduced a new administrative structure for Indigenous communities. Each village had to elect three "authorities." These unremunerated posts were usually filled by young Shipibo men fluent in Spanish (Morin 1995: 366), but were clearly an external imposition. This is an example of how colonialism has affected traditional power structures of the Shipibo, but the power of women in the family compounds remained unchanged.

Contemporary Shipibo women never fail to attend village meetings where they express their opinions volubly, particularly if displeased when a chorus of protest will be raised. With better education and a growing awareness of opportunities open to them, Shipibo women have begun to enter local politics. By 2002, at least three Shipibo women had been elected as regional representatives in the Ucayali, an impressive achievement.

As a shining example of women's ability to represent the community, I should mention the women's football teams. More than 30 years ago, noticing the excitement generated among Shipibo men by football, Shipibo women organized their own all-female football teams that play regular fixtures against other villages. Football matches are a social event that the whole village turns out to watch. Shipibo women, barefoot and wearing colourful embroidered skirts, have played football at the National Stadium in Lima.

Spiritual Power of Shipibo Women

Any description of Shipibo women's spiritual power requires an analysis of their unique designs and an exploration of their complex but repetitive geometry. Shipibo women are the repositories of a tradition of intricate geometrical design with a highly evolved symbolism. The designs express cosmological beliefs and the Shipibo vision of the universe. The twisting, serpent-like designs are hand-painted on to cotton cloth and on the curving walls of pottery vessels. According to Günter Tessmann (1928), in former times every object in the material universe of the Shipibo was covered with designs, either painted, carved, woven, or embroidered.

In the Shipibo world we find a radically different situation to that in the west. In Shipibo culture women are the creative artists. Art in the Shipibo world, whether applied to textiles or ceramics, was produced primarily for local consumption, with the Shipibo playing the role of both consumer and art critic. No two objects are identical; each piece carries a unique design.

In this paper, the term *spiritual world* is used in opposition to *material world* to distinguish the visible, physical world from the invisible world of the spirit. I use the term *inner world* to refer to the invisible world attainable by Shipibo women and *skyworld* to refer to the invisible world attainable by Shipibo men. I take both worlds to be dimensions of mind and as representing the unconscious.

The aesthetic quality of the work of leading female artists is admired throughout the Ucayali by Shipibo men and women alike. Great artists are thought to be possessed of *shinán,* a brilliant capacity for creativity and innovation (Gebhart-Sayer 1984). The possibilities to manipulate and combine design elements are inexhaustible. "The most respected artists are those who ... possess an ability to come close to the culturally defined limits of innovative liberty or even to expand them; who interpret the style in its highest complexity" (Gebhart-Sayer 1984: 4).

Peggy Sanday refers to societies where women's power has "an inner orientation" (1981: 8). Shipibo women explain that their ability to interpret design comes from their close relationship with the *inner world.* Outstanding Shipibo artists practise fasting and sexual abstinence to enhance their creative ability and their access to that inner world. In the rare event that a woman lacks *shinán,* the ability to reproduce cosmic design, she may request help from the shaman, who will oblige by passing her a sketch on a piece of cloth (Gebhart-Sayer 1986).

Shipibo men are dependent on women for design. A man may carve a war club from tropical hardwood, but it is his wife or sister who will sketch on its surface the designs that will transform an everyday object into a cultural icon. The man will then carve the designs more deeply into the wood (Roe 1979; Morin 1995).

In Shipibo society the shaman is usually, but not always, a man. When he ingests *ayahuasca,* a psychogenic plant *(Banisteriopsis caapi),* to communicate with the *skyworld,* he will perceive the same cosmic designs that Shipibo women reproduce as paintings from the *inner world.* Even on the spiritual plane there is evidence of symmetry; men and women fulfil complementary roles. Shipibo men have access to the *skyworld,* women have access to the *inner world.* Although they will see the same patterns, the shaman will transform the designs he perceives into an acoustic code and use them for healing the sick (Gebhart-Sayer 1986), whereas Shipibo women will reproduce the designs on objects in the material world. Both the *skyworld* and the *inner world* appear to carry equal and complementary status in Shipibo thought.

It is the sheer complexity of Shipibo design that first catches the eye and makes a lasting impression on the observer. Before investigating the *inner world* it is essential to understand an intrinsic aspect of Amazonian societies. Overing and Passes observe that since Amazonian peoples stress convivial harmony in everyday life, the negative features of community living such as anger, jealousy, hate, and greed must be subordinated to the aesthetics of community behaviour which "is not only proper but beautiful and pleasing" (2000: xii). Overing comments on the need of Amazonian peoples "to transform the violent, angry, ugly capricious forces of the universe into constructive, beautiful knowledge and capacities" (2000: 6). The aesthetics of appropriate behaviour for living together in convivial harmony is reflected in the additional requirement that all objects of material culture should be aesthetically pleasing.

Gerardo Reichel-Dolmatoff's (1997) work on the Tukano of the Northwest, particularly in regards to their belief that human society should reproduce cosmic order, has been helpful in understanding cosmological beliefs represented in Shipibo design. This clearly suggests that one of the responsibilities of Shipibo women is, through the repetition of aesthetic design, to create order out of chaos. A similar concept arises in Andean thought where it is believed that the structure of the universe is based on the binary opposition order/chaos. Its cyclical alternation constitutes the rhythm of the universe (Sallnow 1987). The need to maintain order in this world thus becomes of vital importance.

The Shipibo say that the entire visible world is saturated with the invisible patterns of the spirit world. "The whole world is covered with designs," affirm the Shipibo. The designs pass from the visible world to the invisible world and back again, interpenetrating all planes. They appear as black lines on a woman's cream-coloured cotton skirt, emerge in white on the terracotta walls of a pottery vessel, or are carved deeply into the blade of an oar. They reappear in the spiderweb of indigo lines decorating a woman's face or gradually come into focus as liquid is drained from a bowl. Patterns are dynamic, shifting, never static.

Shipibo designs are evenly spaced and interlock loosely giving the impression they could be compressed into a much smaller area or drawn out to cover the whole earth. The viewer senses that only a small portion of the design field has been illustrated and the designs could continue endlessly, were they not limited by the border of the cloth or the contours of the pottery vessel on which they appear. To see a Shipibo painting is to gaze through a window on eternity. Beyond the frame the designs continue in the imagination on an endless trajectory.

Asked to explain her designs a Shipibo woman only smiles and murmurs that her ancestors knew far more than she does. The meaning of sacred designs is not readily divulged to the casual observer. Shipibo women eventually confided some of their ideas to me: "Look! Those twisting lines are serpents," says an old woman, "the boa taught us how to paint." Another woman indicates the night sky filled with stars. "Do you see that up there are many pathways?" she observes. "Here on earth there are also many pathways. Above is the same as below. Our skirts are embroidered with white thread on a black background to represent the stars in the night sky. Our designs show the pathways of light we see in the *skyworld*" (Heath 1988).

Central to Shipibo design is Ronín, the cosmic serpent "who combines all conceivable designs in his skin" (Gebhart-Sayer 1984: 153). In mythological time it was Ronín who showed the design of his magnificent skin to ancestral woman, which has, ever since, inspired her painting. So it would appear that the bold lines of the main pattern represent a coiling snake in stylised form. This is Ronín, the cosmic serpent, who creates the universe and symbolises the deity. At another perceptual level Ronín is, in fact, present in the very structure of the ceramic vessel. The hand-coiled clay imitates the coiled posture of the sleeping cosmic serpent. For the Shipibo, the serpent represents the Amazon River as it winds through the rainforest. The river is a reflection of the Via Lactis, the great sky river sweeping across the heavens. Both of these reflect and are reflected by the cosmic serpent, the energy-bearing current winding through the unconscious, or inner world of the Shipibo.

The principal lines of the design are firmly drawn and set out the basic rhythm of the piece. The greater the length of the main line the more it will be admired. It should twist and turn on itself like a serpent forming endless symmetrical patterns. Now closer, now further apart, now breaking into steps or spirals but never-ending, only merging into new patterns. A long main line forming endless variations on a theme will meet Shipibo aesthetic expectations and enhance the prestige of the artist. Less obtrusive secondary lines run parallel to the main lines providing an echo to the dominant theme but in a minor key. Delicate filler work is then inserted in the spaces between the main lines to cover the background with interlocking figures octagonal in shape. The spaces between the designs form a secondary pattern, so what is initially seen as a positive design on a negative field may also be interpreted in reverse.

So how do Shipibo women explain their designs? Shipibo women see their designs as representing "the world around, the world above and the world within." This corresponds remarkably well with the Andean concept of the three worlds: *kaypacch* (this world), *hanaqpaccha* (the world above, the afterworld), and *ukhupaccha* (the underworld or world within) (Sallnow 1949: 29).

The designs are seen by Shipibo women to represent three levels of perception simultaneously. In the "world of appearances" they are attributed to the sinuous path of the river as it winds across the Amazon floodplain. In the *skyworld* they indicate the pathways between the stars, mark the position of the constellations and echo the flow of the great sky river, the *Via Lactis*. In the *inner world* the designs represent the Cosmic Serpent, the inexhaustible energy source of the unconscious.

Women's Power in Shipibo Origin Myth

Finally, what we can learn about gender symbolism and women's power from Shipibo origin myths? Sanday shows how cosmological beliefs might influence power relations. She argues convincingly that gender symbolism in origin myths is a projection of a people's perception of power in male and female roles. Creation myths tell us something about where people locate the major source of power in the universe: "The duality expressed by male and female principles … establishes in the human world the equilibrium between opposites that underlies the conception of order in the universe" (1981: 90). It is also possible that men and women are co-creators, sharing power equally.

"The Shipibo maintain an extensive and flourishing oral tradition that is chiefly the creation of men" (Roe 1982: 59). The men's oral tradition is balanced by the women's sacred song cycles. Being dynamic in structure, myths can be reinterpreted by the storytellers to account for a new set of circumstances or to reflect new demands imposed on Indigenous peoples by a changing world. The Shipibo creation myth was narrated to me by Octavio Ochavano of Paoyhán in 1975. It might be entitled "Adam and Eve in the Ucayali" (Heath 1988).

The Shipibo creation myth speaks of a great flood in mythical times. The Shipibo man avoids drowning by climbing a *genipa* tree. When the waters subside he climbs down the tree to find a deserted world. Eventually two beautiful women paddling a canoe approach. On impulse he seizes the first woman. "Let me go!" she cries, "I am not for you!" But the man takes her by force. "Fool!" said the woman. "My companion who is the daughter of the *Inca* (God) was to be your wife. I am only her servant. You have made a terrible mistake!" As a result of this union dozens of diminutive human beings issue from between her toes to repopulate the earth.

So the co-creators of the contemporary Shipibo are deemed to be the culture's hero and the Inca's servant. Whereas in the biblical story of Adam and Eve, woman is portrayed as the temptress who offered the forbidden fruit to man, in Shipibo myth woman is not blamed for the primordial error. In Shipibo myth it was the male ancestor who made the catastrophic mistake. Contemporary Shipibo attribute their current problems to this mythological mishap.

If men create and continually re-tell the stories recognizing women's power, this surely indicates that Shipibo men truly share in and agree with the belief that women are their equals. It can be seen from the evidence presented that Shipibo women have every reason to express self-confidence. Shipibo women enjoy family power, economic power, political power, spiritual power, and even mythological power, thus contributing to gender equality in Shipibo society in which power is shared.

Conclusions

In what ways might the knowledge of Shipibo women contribute to a deeper understanding of what it means to be a woman in western societies? The most obvious response was pointed out by Clarissa Pinkola Estés in her popular work *Women Who Run with the Wolves*. She writes: "A woman's creative ability is her most valuable asset ... for it feeds her inwardly at every level: psychic, spiritual, mental, emotive and economic" (1992: 270).

I would suggest that Shipibo women do derive incalculable spiritual power through the constant interpretation and reinterpretation of cosmic beliefs arising from the unconscious and expressed through design. It is this semi-permanent contact with the unconscious that gives Shipibo women a unique source of self-confidence and consequently has a positive effect on gender relations and women's power on the physical plane.

One of the messages from Shipibo women to the west might be: "We never lose contact with the *inner world*. Do not undervalue the unconscious for it is the source of consciousness." In the west, consciousness and the intellect have been valued at the expense of the unconscious and intuition. The two aspects should be harmoniously balanced to ensure psychic stability. As Carl Jung (1972) pointed out: "Rationalism is no guarantee of higher consciousness, but merely of a one-sided one."

Feminist psychoanalyst Gisela Labouvie-Vief (1994) also addresses the great binary of intellect/intuition. She maintains that masculine knowledge (rationality or logos) and feminine knowledge (imagination or mythos) are two complementary dimensions of the mind. She believes that the arbitrary division of the human mind into supposedly masculine and feminine attributes has limited our ability to describe the mind and its development. She suggests we seek to overcome the dualistic way of thinking about mind and see how rationality and imagination may complement each other in every human being. Indigenous groups with non-hierarchical gender patterns such as the Shipibo might well provide a working model of a harmonious society for the western world, one in which the power-balance between men and women is equal: "Not equal and alike, but equal and opposite."

Ursula King (1995) discusses how women's spiritual quest is experienced and explored in the west. She considers the concept of complementarity: "We all have both masculine consciousness which is specialized, analytical and focused and feminine consciousness which is general, intuitive and holistic." King goes on to explain that, "At present a woman (in the west) is valued only if she can operate like a man, with masculine consciousness, in a man's world. Social structures are patriarchal, authority being imposed from above downwards." She argues that emotions, feelings, and psychic sensitivity should be valued as equal to logical thinking as a source of understanding.

I hope I have been able to present an argument which will be meaningful to others by revealing how the traditional designs of Shipibo women might enrich western concepts of what it means to be a woman. If I have succeeded I shall have fulfilled one of my obligations to Shipibo women—to make their voice heard in the west.

The analysis and re-analysis of matriarchy is a new area of academic study in which feminists seek alternatives for western women and a transformation of western society. Certainly, Shipibo women's social and spiritual authority indicates a strong matriarchal organization. It is hoped my research and data will make a useful contribution to the on-going debate.

Carolyn Heath has worked for twenty years as a development consultant in Peru and also for shorter periods in Sri Lanka and Tanzania. In Peru she worked with the Shipibo, an indigenous group of the Upper Amazon, founding the Shipibo cultural centre Maroti Shobo, with the aim of reviving traditional artistic skills and generating income particularly for women. This experience aroused a keen interest in the intricate geometric designs painted by Shipibo women which symbolically represent a Shipibo vision of the cosmos. Returning to UK in 2002, she decided that an academic framework would enhance her fieldwork experience and embarked on the MA Women's Studies at Ruskin College, Oxford. In 2008/09, she organized exhibitions about Amazonian people for PROMPERU in London and Madrid.

References

Atkinson, Jane. 1990. "How Gender Makes a Difference in Wana Society." *Power and Difference: Gender in Island Southeast Asia.* Eds. Jane Atkinson and Shelly Errington. Stanford, CA: Stanford University Press. 59-94.

Counihan, Carole. 1999. *The Anthropology of Foods and Body : Gender, Meaning and Power.* London: Routledge.

Errington, Shelly. 1990. "Recasting Sex, Gender and Power: A Theoretical and Regional Overview." *Power and Difference: Gender in Island Southeast Asia.* Eds. J. Atkinson and S. Errington. Stanford, CA: Stanford University Press. 1-58.

Gebhart-Sayer, Angelika. 1986. "Aesthetic Therapy: An Aspect of Shipibo-Conibo Shamanism." *América Indígena* 46 (1): 190-218.

Gebhart-Sayer, Angelika and Peter Koepke. 1984. *The Cosmos Encoiled: Indian Art of the Peruvian Amazon.* Exhibition Catalogue. New York: Center for Inter-American Relations.

Girard, Rafael. 1958. *Indios Selváticos de la Amazonía.* Peruana, Mexico: Libro Mex Editores.

Gow, Peter 1999: "Piro Designs: Painting as a Meaningful Action in an Amazonian Lived World." *The Journal of the Royal Anthropological Institute* 5 (2): 229-246.

Gow, Peter. 1990. "Could Sangama Read? The Origin of Writing Among the Piro of Eastern Peru." *History and Anthropology* 5: 87-103.

Heath, Carolyn. 2005. "Looking Inwards: What Can We Learn From an Analysis of the Traditional Designs of Shipibo Women?" Unpublished MA thesis. Ruskin College, Oxford, UK.

Heath, Carolyn. 2002. *Una Ventana hacia el Infinito: Arte Shipibo-Conibo.* Lima: ICPNA.

Heath, Carolyn. 1989. "Ani Shëati en el Pueblo Shipibo de San Pablo de Sinuya." *Four Lowland South Amerindian Studies, Technical Reports 1-4.* CIIPR, Puerto Rico.

Heath, Carolyn. 1980. "El Tiempo nos Venció." *Boletín de Lima* 5. Lima, Peru.

Jung, Carl Gustav. 1972. *The Archetypes and the Collective Unconscious. Collected Works. Vol. 9, Part I.* London: Routledge.

King, Ursula. 1995. *Religion and Gender.* Oxford, Blackwell.

Labouvie-Vief, Gisela. 1994. *Psyche and Eros: Mind and Gender in the Life Course.* Cambridge: Cambridge University Press.

Lathrap, Donald. 1970. *The Upper Amazon.* London: Thames and Hudson.

Moore, Henrietta. 1995. "The Cultural Constitution of Gender." *The Polity Reader in Gender Studies.* Cambridge: Polity Press. 14-21.

Moore, Henrietta. 1993. "The Differences Within and the Differences Between." *Gendered Anthropology.* Ed. Teresa del Valle. London: Routledge. 193-204.

Moore, Henrietta. 1988. *Feminism and Anthropology.* Cambridge: Polity Press.

Morin, Françoise. 1995. "Los Shipibo-Conibo." *Guía Etnográfica de la Alta Amazonía.* Vol. III. Eds. Fernando Santos and Frederica Barclay. Washington, Smithsonian Tropical Research Institute. 275-345.

Morin, Françoise. 1973. *Les Shipibo de l'Ucayali: rencontre d'une civilisation Amazonienne et de la civilisation occidentale. Aspects psycho-sociologiques des changements.* Tesis doctoral, Paris, Université de la Sorbonne

Ortner, Sherry 1974: "Is Male to Female as Nature is to Culture?" *Women, Culture and Society.* Eds. M. Rosaldo and L. Lamphere. Stanford, CA: Stanford University Press. 67-87.

Overing, Joanna and Passes, Alan. 2000. *The Anthropology of Love and Anger: The Aesthetics of Conviviality in Native Amazonia.* London: Routledge.

Pinkola Estes, Clarissa. 1992. *Women Who Run with the Wolves: Contacting the*

Power of the Wild Woman. London: Rider.

Reichel-Dolmatoff, Gerardo. 1997. *Rainforest Shamans: Essays on the Tukano Indians of the Northwest Amazon.* Dartington, UK: Themis Books

Roe, Peter .1982. *The Cosmic Zygote: Cosmology in the Amazon Basin.* New Brunswick, NJ: Rutgers University Press.

Roe, Peter. 1980. "Art and Residence Among the Shipibo Indians of Peru: A Study in Micro Acculturation" *American Anthropologist* 82: 42-71.

Roe, Peter. 1979. "Marginal Men: Male Artists Among the Shipibo Indians of Peru." *Anthropológica* 21 (2): 189-221

Sallnow, Michael. 1987. *Pilgrims of the Andes: Regional Cults in Cusco.* Smithsonian Series in Ethnographic Enquiry, Washington DC: Smithsonian Institution Press.

Sanday, Peggy Reeves. 1981. *Female Power and Male Dominance: On the Origins of Sexual Inequality.* Cambridge: Cambridge University Press.

Strathern, Marilyn. 1996. "Gender: Division or Comparison?" *Practising Feminism.* Eds. N. Charles and F. Hughes-Freeland. London: Routledge. 38-60.

Stone, Linda. 2000. *Kinship and Gender: An Introduction.* 3rd ed. Boulder, CO: Westview Press.

Tessmann, Günter. 1928. *Menschen ohne Gott: ein besuch bei den Indianern des Ucayali.* Stuttgart: Strecker und Schröder.

Weiner, Annette. 1976. *Women of Value, Men of Reknown: New Perspectives in Trobriand Exchange.* Austin: University of Texas Press

MILILANI B. TRASK

"Aia Na Ha'ina i Loko o Kakou"

The Answers Lie Within Us

Long before western scientists and academics debated the theories of evolution, Hawaiians knew and recited the evolution of the universe, the earth and all of its life forms. This cosmological worldview is contained in the *Kumulipo*, or creation chant, which also sets forth the cosmogonic genealogy of our peoples and *Akua*, or sacred gods.

The opening verse of the *Kumulipo* describes a period when the earth was in flames, and the heavens churned and unfolded. In the beginning there was night, only night, endless night, the unfathomable dark blue darkness called *Po*. The mysterious female night, without impregnation gave birth to a son, *Kumulipo*, and a daughter *Po ele*. It is from their incestuous mating that the life forms of the sea and earth evolved, beginning with the goddess *Hina*.

In ancient times, as in modern, Hawaiians understood that the evolution of life arises from the female and that the balance of life, male and female principles at their inception, arises from the female. This understanding pervaded traditional Hawaiian society and set the foundation for all aspects of the social order of the Hawaiian matrilineal culture.

The *Kumulipo* recounts and describes the rise of 40,000 life forms over sixteen *wa*, or time periods. Of these life forms, 20,000 were female. Referred to as *Akua*, or divine spirits, it is the female *Akua* that inspires and empowers Hawaiian women and defines their sexuality and feminine nature. *Po*, the primordial night, is the source of life, divinity, and ancestral wisdom for Hawaiian women.

The pantheons of Hawaiian sacred goddesses are reflections of and embody the personality of Hawaiian culture. Thus, Hawaiian women seeking to understand the wisdom of their historical past can inform themselves by understanding the oral histories of their female deities and the ruling chiefesses who emulated and personified what Polynesians call *mana wahine*, the power of the feminine. In Hawaii and Polynesia *mana wahine* was a powerful force that could not be ignored. It dictated the rank of every person through the bloodlines of their mother and their father's mother.

Righteousness (*pono*) is maintained in the Hawaiian traditional perspective by the correct balance of female and male. This gender-based understanding was reflected in every aspect of behaviour and in every human undertaking including farming, fishing, and all other human and non-human activities.

The goddess *Hina* (in Maori, *Hine*) was the *Akua* of women's inland fishing. She protected and empowered women who gathered medicinal herbs and beat *kapa* (cloth). It is *Hina* who births new life, controls the tides and the sequences of the moon. Most importantly, *Hina* demonstrates the role which women as mothers play in awakening and nurturing the potential of men. Our oral histories verify that the god *Maui* slowed the sun's passage for his mother, *Hina,* so that she might have more time to beat her *kapa*. And that it was for *Hina* that *Maui* raised the heavens and created the islands.

Hawaiian goddesses define the arenas of women's power. These include the making of peace (*La'i La'i*), the skill and beauty of dance (*Laka*), and the teachings of childbirth, war, and politics (*Haumea*).

Renowned in Hawaii were the *mo'o*, female lizard dragons, who resided in and protected waterfalls, streams, rivers, and ponds. Their capacity to wage war was matched only by their ability to seduce men with their beauty. Considered dangerous by even the strongest warriors, *mo'o wahine* often devoured or killed their lovers to ensure that they would not pursue other women.

In oppositions to the *mo'o* are the sisters of fire, *Pele* and *Hi'iaka*. The *Pele* legends and *Hula* lore instruct Hawaiian women in the ways of war and love, teach us respect for our elders, and other cultural practices. The sisters embody the positive and negative attributes of womanhood. Their adventures and lives teach us the protocols of feminine practices we need to follow in our daily lives.

In traditional times, Hawaiian women went to war to defend their lands and livelihoods and to protect their children and loved ones. In modern times, Hawaiian women continue to do both, fighting for cultural survival and for a better future for their people.

Mililani B. Trask was born and raised in Hawaii. She is an expert in international law and has served an inaugural term as the United Nations Permanent Forum on Indigenous Issues, Pacific Regional Representative. She is a founding mother of the Indigenous Woman's Network (USA) and the Indigenous Initiative for Peace, a global human rights advocacy collective under the leadership of Nobel Laureate Rigoberta Menchu-Tum. Trask was elected the first Kia Aina (Prime Minister) of Ka Lahui Hawaii (The Sovereign Hawaiian Nation), an Indigenous Hawaiian initiative for self-governance, and has also served as a Trustee of the State of Hawaii Office of Hawaiian Affairs.

TAIMALIEUTU KIWI TAMASESE

Restoring Liberative Elements of Samaon Cultural Gender Arrangements

The work I excitedly share with you is not primarily my own work. It belongs to a whole group of us, both women and men in Samoa. Children have also contributed to it immensely. And the kindness of the many lands with which we fought about these issue and have come to some consensus about. I will conclude with some recommendations.

I begin this presentation with a poem written by a dear friend of mine. He was itaken away from his family at the age of thirteen and sent to New Zealand to complete his education. About a year later he lost his mother: she died in Samoa. He grew up to be one of the main poets in New Zealand and this poem is about his Samoan mother:

My Mother Dances

Through the shadows cast by the moon tonight
the memory of my mother dances
like the flame-red carp I watched
in the black waters of the lake
of the Golden Pavilion in Kyoto.
Such burning grace.
Though I'm ill with my future
and want to confess it to her,
I won't. Not tonight.
For my mother dances
in the Golden Pavilion
of my heart.
How she can dance.
Even the moon is spellbound
with her grace.

About Clothing and Housing

How do we "weave" together the many forms of knowledge to recreate and restore balance in the way that we gender-arrange our world? I am amazed by how similar some of the designs that women adorn their clothing with are between the Pacific and the Amazon region. We are starting to think about the ways in which each of our own cultures has its own gender cultural arrangement, and how some of these arrangements are expressed in women's handicrafts and art.

In Samoa, we say that culture is not static. We use the metaphor of a "flowing river" to describe the transitions that cultures go through. Cultures are interrupted by colonization, education, or religion. Cultures may also be interrupted by internal forces within themselves, or by external forces. These interruptions within our culture's differing aspects create changes. So, the culture of Samoa in September 2005 may have similar elements to the culture of Samoa from 1905. But there are big changes as well.

If we look at housing or garments in Samaon culture, for example, we will see some changes. There are Samoan men and women who still wear our traditional ceremonial dress from pre-missionary times. When the missionaries came, and brought with them their nuns, this impacted local dress. A lot of these changes can also be attributed to the cash economy. The marriage between the cash economy and theology was quite powerful and resulted in a number of changes in the Pacific cultures. Today women are usually covered from our shoulders down, in traditional wear. As Indigenous peoples, we also now dress ourselves in cotton, introduced by the missionaries. Pre-missionary cloth was made with the fibres from the paper-mulberry tree that people used beat into cloth and then extend, layer upon layer, finally putting designs on it.

If we look housing, we will see that our traditional architecture was basically circular and more oval. The roofing was thatched. The first time this traditional architecture was committed to paper was only two or three years ago, when we needed to rebuild a home in the traditional Samoan style. Along the way, we made the choice to adapt our housing to western styles. We make choices about what elements of our culture we take into the future and which elements we drop off. In the end, these kind of choices come with costs. Our choice, for example, to change from mulberry fibres to cotton came with huge costs.

But the cost is not all of it. Might I introduce an idea regarding why cultures make certain choices? For example, people in Texas suffer from the cyclones or hurricanes. In Samoa, we, too, are now very vulnerable to cyclones in the Pacific and with that has come the need to change the materials with which we build our homes. From thatched roofs to timber, we have become very vulnerable, because with big cyclones the timber tends to fly around, which is dangerous for people. Two and a half years ago, a friend of mine, a colleague and relative, decided to go back to one of our villages—we belong to many villages. We went back to the village where my great-great-grandmother came from. At the time there were no traditional Samaon houses or Indigenous-inspired buildings left. So, we decided that whatever house in this village was going to be restored, it should be inspired by Samoan design. Little did we know what we would have to go through to get it done. In the end, we succeeded in restoring a traditional house.

About Gender Arrangements

As for gender arrangement in Samoa, we have our own concepts of manhood and womanhood, the relationship between maleness and femaleness, between masculinity and femininity. We have our own concept of roles, symbols, rituals, and stories—among them multiple stories about our gender arrangements. In a village meeting, when the men want to make a point, they tend to dig up the most negative stories about the women. And when women want to make a point, we also put on the table about how terrible men's decisions are around a certain project. So there are multiple stories within our own culture about our gender arrangements. How do we identify the most liberating stories or narratives of gender arrangements so that we can retell them and continue to retell them in future generations?

How were these gender arrangements structured into families, communities, religious practices, and decision-making bodies and processes? In pre-colonization time, when a child was born female, she was known as a *Tama Sa* or the Sacred Child, and when a child was born male, he was known as the *Tama Tane* or Male Child. The primary familial relationship in Samoa is not between parents and children, as in some cultures, or between grandparents and grandchildren, as in other cultures; it is actually between the brother and the sister. The relationship between the brother and the sister is called the "covenant." The woman is at the core of the household and owns the title to build a family. But it means more: this woman has the power of blessing and cursing, and her female child will inherit the title. Her brother would look to her as his covenant and would serve the sister throughout her life and in the generation of her children. So, in Samoan familial relationships, although I might be married, I have to work in ways that honour this sister-brother relationship. My brother and my male family members will always look after me to ensure that I am represented to my husband and his family as best as they could have me represented. And this goes on throughout my life and throughout the life of my children.

Between 1830 and 1845 missionaries came to Samoa primarily from Great Britain, but there were also Catholics who came form France. They carried with them European-defined patriarchal values and thoughts and arrangements. They brought with them their own cultural guidance and beliefs, their own structures and their own gender arrangements from the west. If you look at gender arrangements in Samoa in pre-colonial times, then you would say that there is "the brother," there is "the sister," and the arrangement between them is a "covenant." When the missionaries came in they brought with them the gender arrangements of their own cultures, which basically divides "men" and "women." These missionaries came into Samoa and proclaimed that the "covenant" between brother and sister was pagan andthey said that only the relationship between people and God is a "covenant!"

Now there is this relationship between people and God. Who is God? God is invisible, however, he is represented on earth by priests and ministers who are all male. Look at the change: the power of blessing and cursing, that used to women's power, became the domain of God. The missionaries insisted it was considered pagan for any woman to bless and to curse. Blesses and curses could only come from the Almighty, who knows all!

Samoan womanhood was displaced. If you look at that cultural changes that were forced on our peoples over time, they usually didn't last long. The cultural changes that are forced on people either through theology or psychology were usually looked upon with doubt. However, if you look at the displacement of Samoan womanhood, the stories about womanhood that were used and actually imposed on us from foreigners, had a different impact.

The Protestant missionaries used the narrative of Eve. According to the Protestants, Eve is the model for all women, but she was also a seductress. She is the one who ate from the apple, and who tempted Adam with the apple. And Adam is quite passive. He just takes a bite of the apple. In telling the story to Aboriginal women, I say, "Look, the snake told Eve that there was this apple and that she could tempt Adam with it." The Aboriginal men say, "Well, friend, if this Adam were Aboriginal, Australian Aboriginal, he would have eaten the snake, not the apple!"

If the missionaries were Catholic, the story they used to displace Samoan womanhood was the story of Mary. Mary is the mother, the mother of all, but also the virgin mother. And I am a deep Catholic believer who's trying to liberate Mary and myself from all of this. Mary is the virgin mother, who is humble but also gracious and generous. She is the woman who offered her son so that he could save the whole world. She is the kind of woman who is represented as kneeling before the cross. But I can't imagine a Samoan mother kneeling before a cross and saying, "Take my son for the whole world!" I can just imagine what a Samoan woman would say and do: "Bring my son down! Give him back to his mother!"

About Working and Trading

Then there were the traders. When we link international histories, at this point in time, in the United States there was a lot of protest against slavery, and the cotton plantations were about to disappear. The Germans had the idea that if the Americans are not going to have slaves working on the cotton plantations anymore, then Samoa would be the place for new cotton fields. There was a need for cotton plantations. But the Samoans didn't see the sense of working from 8:00 am to 4:30 pm in the hot sun. People who live and work in the tropics have their own time arrangements around work. At 5:00 am they would leave for work, be it on the ocean or on the plantation. At 11:00 am they would come home for the lunch hour, and then they would have a long siesta until 2:00 or 3:00 in the afternoon. Following their siesta, when it was cooler, they would go back to their places of work. This was, in the view of the traders, very inefficient. So what did they do? They brought in what they called "indentured labourers." These were

Chinese people from different parts of China. They brought them to Samoa. They would lose their names before the ships arrived in Samoa. They were given a number, then be known by that number and not by their names. The indentured labourers would work the usual 8:00 am to 4:30 pm in the tropical sun. In this way, cotton production was maintained and the plantations were growing. The missionaries contributed their share and actually converted people to wear cotton. We all knew the cotton to be warm, so we accepted wearing cotton and welcomed this change.

About Decision-Making

In our traditional lifestyle, of course, there was no central law. There were many districts and villages, local arrangements and habits, and whatever. But the missionaries wanted to centralize the administration. Like the traditional covenant between man (brother) and woman (sister), there was a similar structure in the village. There was the men's council and the women's council. No decisions could be made by the men's council until it consulted the women's council. Then the decision would go back and a consensus would have to be reached. The women's council would also consult with the men's council if they wanted to see a change in policy within the village.

When the centralized form of government was set up in Samoa, there was no space for this kind of consensus. The women's council was demolished and a parliament was set up that they said would ensure that everybody would have a vote. But how would women be represented in such an arrangement? There was no place for the women's council in this centralized system. You can imagine what happened. Even now, in Samoan parliament, there is now only three or four women parliamentarians. No space for women's council at parliament level; no space for women's council at the economic level. It was a big loss.

At present, of course, there patriarchal ideology dominates in the cash economy machinery. What are the results if there is no space for women in the decision-making process? This is why we have domestic violence, sexual violations, the socio-political marginalization of women, and the loss of dignity for women. The dominating and rational man now has to live with the loss of connection to land, language, traditions, gods, spirits, to women and children.

Restoring Liberative Elements

We want to restore a social, political, and religious place of sacredness of womanhood in general and of women in families, communities, and societies. What we are doing at this moment in time is trying to reclaim the gender arrangements of our past so that our traditional culture will once again be the foundation on which our families are based, and from which they can grow. And we need to restore a place of dignity and honour for men in our families. We have also watched men of our own culture be displaced, but we need them to partner us in development.

We need to bring them back to help us with the recovery of our culture and of the liberative elements—for ourselves, our children, and for the men as well.

What are the implications for this new kind of development in social policies, agencies, and structures?

- Always to be attentive to issues of power differences between men and women;
- Develop an awareness of manhood and womanhood in relationships of domination and oppression;
- Recognize of the different responsibilities of both genders and recover sacred and equitable relationships;
- Making the cultural liberative gender arrangements well-known in order to build new relationships and structures.

We are deliberately doing this in organizational structures. We have an "accountability" mechanism that we are promoting in government, in educational institutions, in community development agencies, social services, and social policy agencies. We are demanding that in matters of gender and of education these organizations need to be directly accountable to women. And in matters of culture, the work of these agencies and institutions need to be made accountable for their policies and services to Indigenous peoples and the peoples of marginalized cultures.

Taimalieutu Kiwi Tamasese is Samoan and works today at The Family Centre in Wellington on Aotearoa or New Zealand, where she is the co-ordinator of the Pacific Section. She specializes in family research as this applies to the Pacific nations and to Pacific people, for example, in relation to mental health, poverty, housing, unemployment, cultural and gender deprivation. In relation to social policy, Kiwi is engaged in the development of new social policy perspectives emanating from various Pacific cultural nationalities. She is also concerned with the impact of government policy decisions on the Pacific Sector of New Zealand society. Further areas of her work include: documenting and analyzing the effects of cultural dislocation upon the Pacific community in New Zealand; a focus upon Pacific youth; and patterns of migration to New Zealand from the Pacific. Kiwi is regularly contracted to speak and advise in areas of applied social policy at national and international levels.

Part III
Existing Matriarchal Societies – Africa

WILHELMINA J. DONKOH

Female Leadership Among the Asante

T he Asante constitute one of the principal groups of the matrilineal Akan-speaking people of the modern state of Ghana. An identifying character-istic of the Akan is descent through the female line. Traditionally, such important socio-economic institutions and customary practices such as mar-riage, ownership of property, and inheritance are based on blood affiliation to the matriliny. Females among the Akan are, thus, expected to play a unique role in ensuring the perpetuation of the lineage and in identifying who qualifies to be a member. At the same time, like other traditional societies, social, economic, and political responsibilities tend to be gender-specific.

This paper develops a theoretical framework that supports its main thesis: that female leaders among the Asante play a central role within the Asante so-cio-political system. The paper examines specific cases in the history of the As-ante where female leaders transcended the "conventional" gender boundaries and operated as diplomats, political heads, refugee leaders, and military heads in relation to the Asante understanding of order and social cohesion. The paper reviews some of the significant literature on the subject being studied and ana-lyzes the principal theories that are relevant for the study of matrilineal societies as tools for examining stereotypical views that women only play mundane roles and function as mere reproductive units. This paper focuses on one matrilineal society to examine and evaluate the performance of women leaders as individu-als, lineage members, and community heads. To do this successfully, it is im-portant to briefly review the origins of the Asante for a clearer understanding of their socio-political systems.

A Review of Relevant Literature and Theoretical Framework

The scientific study of matriarchal societies, otherwise referred to as non-pa-triarchal or women-centred, goes far back in time (see, Morgan 1851; Lloyd 1901; Radcliffe-Brown and Ford 1950; Fortes 1972). Significantly, these studies have not been confined only to societies that have been described as underdevel-oped (Bachofen 1861). In the mid-nineteenth century, such writers as Johann Bachofen were already discussing the legitimacy of the rights of mothers, and how these rights had, over the years, been masked by religion and myths. However, the discussion had become contentious and politicized because, while some writers dismissed the argument as irrelevant, others saw it as the take-off point for the development of a new paradigm in human history. The consolidation of the feminist movement and the consequent growth of feminist scholarship in the mid-twentieth century refueled academic studies on women-centred societies and matriarchy.

The term "matriarchy," as used in the Akan and Asante socio-political context, emphasizes the unique position that women occupy in the society rather than suggesting that women created those cultures. Indeed, like all Akan-speaking people, the Asante social system is based on an intricate network of relationships. The complex social networks that characterize Asante culture usually commences in the female line or through a common ancestress. Therefore, "matriarchy" in the Asante context could accurately be translated as societies whose genesis could be traced to "mothers." Although there is no evidence to suggest that Asante culture was created solely by women, it could be argued that women constituted the integral centre of their society.

Through a multidisciplinary approach in historical research, it is possible to explain how the matrilineal or matrifocal Asante society was traditionally structured through an understanding of how they conceptualized their universe, and organized their social patterns and political events. The core of their socio-political systems is still extant today. Significantly, therefore, the Asante are a living example of the matrifocal form of society.

Asante historiography does acknowledge the overarching significance of the female in social construction. Therefore, women are not presented in Asante history as "the lower class" or "the marginalized" group. At the same time, however, mainstream studies still looked down upon matrilineal/matrifocal societies as sub-developed cultures. This is particularly the case when western constructs and understanding are employed as an interpretation tool. Sometimes, in trying to ascertain what is fair or equitable, logic seems to fall apart when a western interpretation model is employed. For example, answering the question, "Who has the right to succeed to the interstate estate of a deceased person and why?" becomes contentious depending on the lenses through which it is answered. On the one hand, it is accepted that the matrilineage has the right to the body of the deceased and at least a small portion of the deceased's estate. On the other hand, the spouse and children are expected to determine when, how, and where the body would be buried and who bears what cost.

However, the acknowledgement of the rights of the matrilineage shows that the ancient matrilineal traditions of the Asante that have their roots deep in the past still exist. Indeed, they are still available in the form of oral traditions, customs, myths, rites of passage, and folklore. They are called upon on very important occasions such as selection and installation of traditional rulers, during customary judicial processes, and in the performance of such rites of passage as naming ceremonies for new-born babies. To establish a link between the present and the past, it is essential to briefly review the genesis of the Asante.

Asante Ethno-genesis

The Asante, as noted above, constitute part of the Akan-speaking people who inhabit the forest region of the Republic of Ghana. In addition to the Asante Region they are also found in parts of Brong Ahafo, Volta, Eastern, Central, and the Western Regions of Ghana.[1] Writers like Ivor Wilks (1996) have asserted that at the height of their power, Asante political hegemony transcended the modern state of Ghana and extended to parts of the modern republics of the La Cote d'Ivoire in the west, Togo and Benin in the east, and Burkina Faso in the north.

Originally, Asante society was non-literate. Therefore, the Asante tended to preserve knowledge about their past in the form of folktales, oral traditions, appellations, drum language, pottery, and the creation of sacred sites or groves. One could garner valuable information about the Asante past, particularly their origins, worldview, philosophy, and collective memory, from their cultural artefacts. There are many accounts of the origins of the Asante based on oral traditions. While some of the oral accounts assert that the ancestors of the Asante came from the sky, others state that they came from holes in the ground. These oral traditional accounts seem to support the historical evidence that the present-day Asante descended from stone-age cave dwellers who lived in subterranean caves or in caves on mountain tops within the forest belt of Ghana.[2] The oral tradition is supported by archaeological evidence in the form of stone implements, pottery, and caves, which are usually located in sites set aside as sacred groves as well as other artifacts.

One version of the origin accounts asserts that the ancestors of the Asante emerged from a hole in the ground in Asantemanso, near Asumegya, both located to the southwest of Kumase, the traditional capital of the Asanteman (Asante State). One Monday in the far distant past, a worm emerged from the earth followed by seven men, several women, a leopard, and a dog. The worm turned into a woman whose name was Aberewa Musu. All the members of the group, except one man, were nervous about their situation. This man was called Adu Ogyeinea who became their leader. The oral traditions further recount that these men and women from the ground belong to the seven principal Asante *mmusua* or clans (*mmusua* is plural of *abusua*). These are the Aduana, Asene, Asona, Agona, Bretuo, Ekuona, and Oyoko. More will be said about the *abusua* system later. The various abusua groups started to build huts but on the first Wednesday a tree fell upon and killed Adu Ogyeinea. Thus, Wednesday was branded a bad day (*da bone*) for the group. The event and the day on which it occurred were then instituted into an oath. The account further adds that the dog went out and returned to the group with fire in its mouth. He gave the fire to Aberewa Musu who belonged to the Aduana clan. Aberewa Musu used the fire to cook food for the dog. After being fed with cooked food for a while, the dog gained weight so the people also started to cook their food before eating.

119

Another tradition recounts that one day, a hunter went into the forest near a place known today as Asiakwa in the Eastern Region of Ghana. There, he saw the strange sight of a woman who descended from the skies supported by golden ropes and accompanied by a retinue of retainers. This woman beckoned the hunter to come closer. She inquired about his *abusua* and he responded that he belonged to the Oyoko *abusua*. She revealed that she also belonged to the same clan and that her name was Ankyaw Nyame. She exhorted the hunter to go back to the town to invite the townsfolk to gather together the following day to witness a wondrous event. The following day, she failed to appear at the site as promised. A few days later, however, she appeared in Asantemanso about a hundred miles to the northwest of Asiakwa. Ankyaw Nyame later produced children who became the leaders of a settlement that they founded in Kokofu, a few miles away from Asantemanso. It was from this area that some of the people moved out to found such other Asante settlements as Kwaaman, which later became known as Kumase, Nsuta, and Dwaben. The general area where the original settlements of Asumegya, Asantemanso, and Kokofu were founded is today referred to as Amansie, which literally means "the origins of states." Other accounts also refer to much earlier settlements in the auriferous area of Adanse, which literally means "under buildings," where according to Asante traditions, man first built and lived in houses. Both Adanse and Amansie were and are located within the Pra-Offin basin. It could be inferred that the Asante occupied lands rich in minerals like gold, as well as fertile for agricultural purposes.

The historical significance of these oral traditions could be traced to attempts made by a stone-age people to reorganize their society after adopting more sedentary forms of agriculture and production. The accounts also include references to the genesis of socio-political institutions; for instance, attempts to explain the origins of male leadership, the institution of oaths and references, and new forms of food production and preparation. Significantly, all the accounts associate Asante genesis with female ancestors and the abusua system.

Asante Social System

The term *abusua* translates into two English terms: "the clan," which refers to people who are descended from one anthropomorphic ancestress in the distant past, and "the lineage," which refers to people descended from the line of a common ancestress. Every Asante belongs to an *abusua* that could trace its origins to one female ancestor. The Asante, like all other Akan-speaking people, also believe that every human being has three elements: blood (*mogya*), spirit (*sunsum* and *ntoro*), as well as destiny (*nkrabea*). The *mogya* is inherited from the mother, the *sunsum* is provided by the father, while the Supreme Being, Onyankopon, determines the *nkrabea* at birth. Thus, what all members of one *abusua* have in common is the blood coursing through their veins, given to them only by their mothers. They further believe that while one could be certain about who one's mother is, the same certainty cannot be expressed about one's father. There is no such thing as illegitimate children among the Akan/Asante since every child is absorbed into the mother's *abusua*. Legitimacy is conferred upon a child by naming that child, an act typically performed by the father. Where there is no acknowledged father, the mother's lineage reserves the right to name the child. However, there is a caveat regarding girls who become pregnant without first going through the puberty rites that are mandatory rites for all girls. Breaking this important rule is a taboo referred to as *kyiribra*. The couple involved are driven outside the community to live in the forest and have the child there. If they survive, they are eventually re-admitted into the community after purification rites have been performed. Such a child would be admitted into the *abusua*, but will carry a stigma.

As noted above, Asante society is based on the *abusua* or clan system, which, in this context, could be defined as a kinship group of people descended from a common ancestress or through a common female line that is lost in the male line. Traditionally, corporate and jural identities were (and still are) usually transmitted through this same line. Thus, social positions and political titles are usually passed on through the mother's line. Members of an *abusua* include a mother, her daughters, her sons, her grandchildren through her daughters, her uterine siblings—both males and females—and her mother's siblings. While her mother's sisters' children are members of her *abusua*, children of her brothers and her sons are not. Thus, although marriage between members of the *abusua* group is strictly forbidden because it is considered to be incestuous, mothers' brothers' (i.e., uncles) children are encouraged to marry fathers' sisters' children (cross-cousins). Generally, members of the *abusua* group have an *abusua-fie* (lineage home), which is sometimes referred to as the ancestral home. Traditionally, matrilocality is the preferred living arrangement among the Asante with married women never leaving the *abusua-fie* permanently. Sometimes, the group may have more than one house and the oldest of them is referred to as the *fie-panin*. Sometimes, a woman may live in her husband's family house; the reverse is also possible.

Significant Cultural Characteristics of the Asante

Asante culture is based on a complex belief system that acknowledges three levels of existence: the future life of the unborn which is in the spiritual realm, the present physical existence, and life after death in a spiritual realm. They also believe in a pantheon of spirit beings, sometimes referred to as divinities, deities, fetishes, or lesser gods in western literature. They believe that natural phenomena such as rocks, mountains, rivers, and lakes are the dwelling places of these deities who may be either male or female. In addition to these deities, there is a Supreme Being who created everything. This is a male being known to the Akan/Asante as Onyame (the Satisfier) or Onyankopon Kwame (the Omnipotent or Great One, born on a Saturday), who has many accolades as well as attributes. In addition, they look on the earth as the dwelling place of an important female spiritual being that they refer to as Asaase Yaa (Mother Earth, born on a Thursday). Mother Earth is so sacred that Thursdays, her birthday, is kept holy by the Asante. No farm work is done on that day. Forces in the spiritual realm impact directly and indirectly on the lives and affairs of people in the physical realm. The idea of there being male and female spiritual beings in the Asante/Akan system is derived from the sense of achieving balance through harmony.

Reproduction is a very important concern in Akan/Asante society. Thus, a woman who has many children is much honoured, while those who have none are censured and derided. Indeed, the husband of a woman who gives birth to ten or more children is honoured by the wife's lineage with a *Badu Dwan* (the tenth child's sheep). The concept of rebirth is also very strong among the Asante. Dead persons may be directly reborn as small children to the same *abusua* or matrilineage. Women in Asante and Akan societies are greatly respected, because they have the crucial function of reproduction that ensures the continuity of the lineage and, ultimately, the community. In other words, they ensure the renewal and prolongation of the life of the lineage, which constitutes the basic concept of the matrilineal view of life.

The Akan/Asante socio-cultural system acknowledges the dualistic morality of "good" and "evil," but not in the western sense. These concepts manifest in such acts and thoughts that either seek the welfare of the community or undermine the well-being of this same group. Although Akan/Asante society is dualistically structured, moral value is not gendered, i.e., the female and the male are equally good. Thus, Akan/Asante do not regard one sex as inferior or weaker than the other.

Akan/Asante society is very religious and acknowledges spiritual involvement and influence in all that they do. For example, they invite the ancestors to participate in their meals by offering the first morsel of food and drink to the ancestors. Thus, every meal is regarded as a communion. The same principle of the involvement of the ancestors in everyday life guides the naming system among the Akan/Asante. Further, this principle is also used as a basis for explaining the behaviour of people in society. The Akan/Asante believe in the importance of harmony, balance, and being in tune with nature.

Ownership of Property and Inheritance

Although Asante women may not have the absolute power of disposition over the property of the *abusua*, they and their offspring are the key beneficiaries and, therefore, have a keen interest in the group's property. Asante women also have the power to control the sources of nourishment for the husband and other members of her family. The husband is required to provide meat such as game and fish for the woman to cook. However, it is the woman's responsibility to provide vegetables and other forms of food.

It is commonly believed that among the Akan/Asante, nephews inherit the property of their uncles. This view is only partially true and is much more complex. In actual fact, nephews are only one group of potential inheritors. Brothers have a superior claim over that of nephews. Thus, the Asante have the saying: *Niwaa mama nsaae a wofaase nni adee* (Until all of mother's children or the lateral group is exhausted, nephews cannot inherit). In other words, nephews' right to inherit is superseded by that of uncles. Women have the primary responsibility of ensuring the perpetuation of the lineage or *abusua*. This characteristic feature grants Asante women a very strong position within the *abusua* and the society.

An Asante man has rights and responsibilities within his mother's *abusua*. For example, the home of an Asante man is the *abusua-fie* of his mother. At the same time, he is entitled to farm or build on land belonging to the *abusua*. Although biological fatherhood is known among the Asante, and fathers acknowledge their children by giving them names, these children actually belong to their mother's *abusua*. Rather, a father is believed to give his children spiritual protection by automatically passing on to them certain spiritual qualities (*ntoro*) that enjoin them to share his taboos and food prohibitions. The man, however, is closely related to his sister's children, i.e., his nieces and nephews, who are members of his *abusua*. He may play an active role in the care and upbringing of his nieces and nephews, and the personal goods that he passes on are principally for his surviving siblings, nieces, and nephews. The understanding here is that he would have used *abusua* property such as land or gold as the basis for acquiring his own personal property. Asante men function as "social fathers" to their nieces and nephews.

An attempt to provide historical explanation for the phenomenon of transmission of property through the female line is provided in Akan/Asante oral traditions. According to one account, a man fell into debt and decided to pawn one of his own children to raise the money to pay off the debt. His wife refused but his sister offered him one of her sons for the purpose. Consequently, he acknowledged the significance of his sister's act of benevolence. Subsequently, he decreed that when he died, his estate should pass on to his sister and her children as reward for his sister's loyalty.

In traditional Akan/Asante society, although individual accumulation of property is acknowledged, the norm was corporate ownership. This system prevented goods from being accumulated by one special person or one special group. Property was used on behalf of and for the benefit of the entire *abusua* group (Appiah 1990).

Political Decision-making

The process of making political decisions is organized along the lines of matrilineal kinship. In the *abusua-fie*, women and men meet in a council where domestic matters are discussed. All adult members of the lineage are included. After thorough discussion, each decision is taken by consensus. The same is true for the entire village: delegates from every *abusua*, known as the *abusua panin* (lineage elder) or *abusua tire* (lineage heads), meet in the community council, when matters concerning the whole community have to be discussed. These delegates sometimes could be the oldest women of the lineage (the matriarchs), or the brothers and sons they have chosen to represent the lineage. Ordinarily, no decision concerning the entire community may be taken without considerable consensus among the various lineages. This means the delegates, who are discussing the matter, are not the ones who make the decision. It is not in this council that the policy of the community is made, because the delegates function only as bearers of communication from their respective lineages. If the council notices that the various *mmusua* (plural for *abusua*) do not yet agree, the delegates return to the *abusua-fie* to discuss matters further. In this way, consensus is reached within the entire community.

However, the Akan/Asante system is rather complex because despite considerable consensus, there are, at the same time, underlying principles that facilitate the accumulation of political power by those at the helm. There exists a hierarchical system acknowledging the principle that there are more powerful lineages by right of first settlement, purchase of land, or behest of gifts or conquest. These lineages are the ones who provide political leadership at the top. Law and order within Asante is ensured through the establishment of an administrative system. In this category are law enforcement officers including the *abrafo* (executioners), *esen* (court criers), and *sanaafo* (the finance group). Essentially then, there are rulers and subjects, but each group has rights and responsibilities to one another. Thus, while one could describe Asante as a society of consensus at the level of the village, it may not be accurate to characterize it solely as an egalitarian society.

The discussion above has outlined the principal features of the Akan/Asante traditional socio-political system. It has also indicated that the society is hierarchical with identifiable political leaders. The ensuing sections will focus more closely on female leadership among the Asante.

Types of Female Leaders Among the Asante

The Akan, including the Asante, have male and female traditional leaders. The symbol of traditional political office among the Akan is the stool, buttressed by the oath and the sword. Thus, an Akan leader is said to occupy a stool when the person holds political office. He assumes office after swearing an oath using a sword. The stool is the repository of the spirit of political authority. The stool is a pledge to both the living and the dead to protect the community, while the sword represents the protective power of the community. Male office holders or leaders are referred to either as Ohene (plural: Ahemfo) or Odikuro (Adikurofo) depending on their rank. There are also two broad categories of female traditional leaders among the Asante. These are the positions of the Ohemaa and the Obaapanin. This categorization is based on rank or degree of importance. Literally, the titles Ohemaa and Obaapanin among the Akan mean "female Ohene" and "elderly woman" respectively. In Asante, the Asantehemaa is the highest-ranking female leader. Like her male counterpart, the Asantehene, she occupies a unique position of being the first among equals. She has the privilege of being the first to nominate a candidate to occupy the office of the Asantehene.

Collectively, female traditional leaders in Ghana are known as "Queen mothers." This designation, as used in Ghana, is rather misleading as it is, in fact, the title of the royal female who occupies the highest leadership position in the traditional polity, which could be a state, district, or town.[3] Though the office is a traditional Indigenous one, the term "Queen mother" is a concept coined by colonial authorities for the purposes of easy classification. To avoid any confusion, the Indigenous term "Ohemaa/Ahemaa" will be used in this paper as a generic term for traditional female leaders among the Asante.

Traditionally, the Ohemaa is usually related by blood to her male counterpart, who is known as the "Chief," another colonial legacy. The Chief, together with the Ohemaa, played complementary roles to generate balance in accordance with traditional conception and belief. Traditionally, not all ethnic groups in Ghana have this position. For example, most of the ethnic groups in the three northern regions of Ghana do not have female traditional rulers.

To fully appreciate the socio-economic role of the Ohemaa among the Asante, first it is essential to review her traditional position, responsibilities, and privileges, which constituted the basis of her influence upon which her authority today is based. In addition, it is important to consider the criteria for the selection of an Ohemaa that establishes her eminence and, thus, forges the basis of her influence. Second, since the Akan/Asante people have the most advanced form of the position of the Ohemaa in Ghana, this paper shall highlight the case in the discussion below.

Among the Akan/Asante, the Ohemaa is perceived and described traditionally as the "mother" not only of her male counterpart, but also of the entire royal lineage to which she belongs and by extension, the entire polity (see Assimeng 1981).This position is constitutional. However, in actual fact, she could be the biological mother, maternal aunt, cousin, sister, niece, or granddaughter of the chief. The Ohemaa is the feminine link between the living members of the community and those in the spirit world, in accordance with Akan belief and philosophy. Thus, she is recognized as the custodian of the genealogy of the royal lineage and, therefore, knows who qualifies to ascend the stool and who does not.

Despite the importance accorded the Ohemaa, her office appears to be preceded by that of her male counterpart. On the one hand, she is regarded as a most influential and eminent figure in the Ohene's court. Eminent writers like K. A. Busia (1968) and R. S. Rattray (1923), who have commented on the Ohemaa among the Asante, have emphasized her role in the installment of Chiefs. Among other things, her advice is sought during important discussions concerning the entire community as well as those concerning her royal lineage. Indeed, no public discussion commenced until she had arrived at that gathering (see Assimeng 1981; Obeng 1977). Despite the considerable respect accorded her in the Chief's court, her voice is not heard. She is consulted behind the scenes and her opinions and advice are voiced by the men. In addition, she has her own court and elders, where certain cases such as domestic disputes are decided.

Traditionally, the Ohemaa is regarded as the paragon of perfection and epitome of womanhood in the community, since she is selected from among the best members within the royal lineage. She has the responsibility of maintaining high moral standards among the youth in the community. Thus, as the traditional mother of the community, she played an important role in the nubility rites of pubescent girls who have the future responsibility of ensuring the continuity of the community (see Sarpong 1988). She also plays a key role in the marriage and construction of kinship networks within the royal lineage.

Also, instances abound in Asante history where females have assumed such leadership positions as political heads (Adoma Akosua), diplomats (Akyaa Oyiakwan), refugee leaders (Dwaben Ama Seiwaa), and military leaders (Yaa Asantewaa), whose careers cannot be fully discussed within the limited scope of this paper. In all the instances referred to here, the women concerned acted in such ways that transcended perceived gender boundaries.

Criteria for Selection

Traditionally, the Ohemaa had to belong to a particular lineage that supplied members to occupy that office. This was the royal lineage. Membership into this lineage was only through the mother's line. A prospective Ohemaa had to be nominated by the Chief and her candidacy had to be accepted and confirmed by the Chief's elders. She was expected to have such moral qualities as humility, honesty, intelligence, bravery, eloquence, and generosity in addition to strong physical qualities (she cannot be maimed or barren).

The Role of the Ohemaa Today

The discussion above has clearly established that the Ohemaa was traditionally at the centre of her community, and that this was the basis of the considerable influence she exercised. Admittedly, to a limited extent, her influence has declined as a result of changes in modern society such as extensive migrations, acceleration of modern technology, and the spread of foreign culture. Thus, for example, most mothers do not inform the Ohemaa when their daughters reach puberty nor do they perform the necessary rites for them. Sometimes too, the Ahemaa (plural of Ohemaa) are perceived as causing political unrest in their communities, the result of which is economic underdevelopment in their respective areas. In other words, some of their activities are perceived to inhibit improvement in the material well-being of their communities. The explanation given for this state of affairs is that she is considering personal financial gains, as opposed to those principles traditionally prescribed, when determining her choice for Ohene. This often leads to disputed successions and subsequently, long litigations. Sometimes too, the Ohemaa allegedly engage in unlawful sale of land, which often also leads to litigation and unrest.

Despite the perceived negative qualities of some women in this high position, the influence of the Ohemaa, rather than diminishing over time, has survived into the modern era. Indeed, the significance of the office of the Ohemaa in modern times could be deduced from the fact that some areas—which traditionally did not have it—have now adopted it. In other areas too, the office of traditional female officeholders has been strengthened, while new positions like the Nkosuohemaa or the Development Queen have been invented. The office of the Nkosuohene/Nkosuohemaa was first instituted in 1985 by the Asantehene Otumfuo Opoku Ware II on the occasion of the golden jubilee of the restoration of the Asanteman after the British imposition in 1896. The position of the Nkosuohemaa is conferred on any individual who contributes to the development of the community in terms of providing such amenities as building school blocks, public toilets, and providing pipe-borne water and clinics. Such an individual could even be a foreigner such as an African-American or European. Besides, today in several areas within the country where there are Ahemaa, they are seen as partners in development, who source funding both from within their own communities and from outside to undertake projects for the improvement of the material welfare of their subjects. In some cases, the Ahemaa have broken with tradition and taken certain bold initiatives for the betterment of their people.

Concluding Remarks

This paper has presented the view that the basis of socio-political organization among the Akan/Asante is focused on the female line or *abusua*. The Akan/Asante social system is dualistic and reserves a special position for males within the *abusua* in order to achieve harmony and balance. Female leaders among the matrilineal Asante of the forest zone of modern Ghana have indeed played and continue to play a central role within the socio-political system. This position is supported by specific cases in the history of the Asante, which reveal that the Asante socio-political system had female leadership positions such as political heads, diplomats, refugee leaders, and military leaders that transcended perceived gender boundaries. Often, when women functioned in these positions, their actions tended to foster greater social cohesion, although sometimes their motives were so orchestrated that they seemed to serve a much smaller constituency. Further, through a review of the literature and theoretical analysis, this paper has stated that Asante women leaders have brought distinction and honour upon themselves as well as their lineage and the wider Asante community. It is further argued that Asante women and their offspring are key beneficiaries in the gains of the lineage. Thus, when Asante women are in leadership positions, they tend to organize affairs in ways that protect the corporate interest. For example, if the principles underpinning Asante/Akan inheritance system are carefully studied, understood, and applied, many of the litigations about interstate succession that inundate the courts would be avoided.

Wilhelmina J. Donkoh has been teaching history at the Kwame Nkrumah University of Science and Technology, Kumasi, Ghana, since 1979, and has been Head of History there. Her research on colonialism and cultural change among the Asante earned her a Masters and a Ph.D. from the University of Birmingham, UK. She has published and travelled extensively, researching and speaking on a wide range of topics concerning Ghana's history and culture, focusing on tradition and modernity. Her involvement in outreach programs has been extensive. She is currently the Chair of the History, Archives and Library Sub-Committee of the Kumasi Diocese of the Methodist Church of Ghana.

[1]The modern Republic of Ghana is divided into ten administrative regions. The Akan-speaking people could be found in six of them.
[2]In the course of field studies, I have visited some of these sites in the Brong Ahafo and Asante Akyem areas. These sites have been preserved as sacred groves that can only be visited with permission from the appropriate authorities.
[3]Information for this paper is derived mainly from on-going research on Traditional Rulers sponsored by the International Development Research Council (IDRC), Canada, through the Traditional Authority Applied Network (TAARN).

References

Appiah, J. 1990. *Joe Appiah: The Autobiography of an African Patriot.* New York: Praeger Publishers.
Assimeng, M. 1981. *Social Structure of Ghana.* Accra: Ghana Publishing Corporation.
Bachofen, Johann J. 1861. *Das Mutterrecht (Myth, Religion and Mother Right).* Stuttgart: Krais und Hoffmann.
Busia, K. A. 1968. *The Position of the Chief in the Modern Political System of Ashanti.* London: Frank Cass and Co. Ltd.
Fortes, M. 1972. "Kinship and the Social Order: The Legacy of Lewis Henry Morgan." *Current Anthropology* 12 (2): 285-296.
Morgan, Henri, Lewis. 1851. *League of the Ho-de-no-sau-nee or Iroquois.* New York: Burt Franklin.
Obeng, E. E. 1977. *Ancient Ashanti Chieftaincy.* Tema: Ghana Publishing Corporation.
Radcliffe-Brown, A. R. and D. Ford, eds. 1950. *African Systems of Kinship and Marriage.* London: Oxford University Press.
Rattray, R. S. 1923. *Ashanti.* Oxford: Oxford University Press.
Sarpong, P. K. 1988. *Girls' Nubility Rites in Ashanti.* Tema: Ghana Publishing Corporation.
Wilks, I. 1996. *Many Histories, One Nation: Ghana, Past and Present.* Accra: Ghana University Press.

Akan Healing Heritage

Our world is not just what we can see.
—Gad Agyako Osafo

T he entire life of the Akan is religious. This is expressed in sayings such as *Se Onyame pe a ...* (if God wills ...), *Onyame adaworoma ...* (by God's grace), which are repeated several times a day. Symbols are also used to depict Akan religiousness.

Gye Nyame, Biribi wo soro, Nyame Dua

For the Akan, prayer is a dimension of life that transcends and re-interprets every social relationship and social experience. Therefore, prayer plays a central role in the private and social life of the Akan. The significance of prayer to the Akan is a reflection of their submission to, confidence in, and dependance on Onyankopong (God), the deities, and the ancestors. The Akan pray at the beginning of every social gathering. The prayer is in the form of libation pouring:

Libation (Twi Version):

Obaatanpa, Twieduampong, Borebore Onyankopong, wo nsa ni.
Eno Asase Yaa, yewo nkwa mu a yedan wo, yewo owuo mu a yedan wo,
wo nsa ni oo.
Asuo Bosompo, wo nsa ni.
Asuo ... wo nsa ni oo.
Nananom Adikanfoo momegye nsa

Asumsumpa, Abofopa a mowo apuee, atoe benkum ne nifa mo nso mo nsa ni.
Abusua ahoroo nyinaa momogye nsa.
Mo nim nea enti a yefre mo nanso yeeka bio—
mo na mo se "ka na ka bio yenkyi."
Yeda mo ase se saa nhyiamu yi asi pi.
Yeda mo ase se akwantufoo nyinaa mo de won aba asodwee mu
Yesre mo oo, janja na mo ama nhyiamu yi nkoso asodwee mu na
biribi papa mfiri mu mmra.
Won nso a wode won adwene, won ahooden ne won sika de
hyehyee nhyiamu yi, yesre mo, mo nhyira won na mommo nea won de
ahye nhyiamu yi ho ope, pe pe mma won.
Yesre mo jaja se yewie nhiamu yi nso a, jenja ma mode aki yenko
nea yeeko asodwee mu.
Me nso mo ananawa, mesre mo see me kasa a merebekasa yi moma enye kasa pa.
Otwieduampong Onynankopong, Nanom, Asumsumpa ne Abofopa
nsa oo, nsa, nsa.

English translation:

Good mother, the big tree on whom all can lean,
Creator Onyankopong —here is your drink.
Immortal mother Earth, we depend on you whilst living,
we depend on you when we die—here is your drink.
Bountiful deity of the Sea—here is your drink.
River … here is your drink.
Our Grand-Ancestors, come and get a drink.
Benevolent Spirits and Messengers from the east, north, west and south –
here is a drink for you, too.
All our various clans, come and get a drink!
You know why we are calling you,
but you taught us that repetition is not a taboo.
We thank you for making this meeting [the congress] a reality.
We thank you for bringing all these travellers safely here.
We pray to you, we wish that you let this meeting run smoothly
and give birth to beneficial results.
For those who used their brains, or strength, or money
to arrange this congress, we wish and pray that you bless them
and reward them abundantly.
We pray for good health, and we wish that after this congress
you take us back to our various homes safely.
And I, your great-grand-child, I pray that you let my presentation
be a good one.
Omnipotent Onyankopong, Great Ancestors, benevolent Spirits
and goodMessengers—drink, drink, drink!

Who are the Akan?

The Akan are found in Ghana and in the eastern part of the Ivory Coast. In Ghana the Akan consists of seventeen clans, who share a similar linguistic and cultural background. Each clan traces his/her lineage to a single common ancestress. An Akan is therefore a member of the mother's matrilineage which consists of all descendants of both gender, who trace their genealogy through women to one common ancestress.

The Akan have a saying: *Wo na ba ne wo nua* (Your mother's child is your sister/ brother). Every female above a certain age is called *maame,* or mother. Therefore, all female members of the group are either my mothers or sisters.

Inheritance of property—and certain knowledge, especially spiritual— as well as rights and obligations are matrilineal. This is expressed in the saying: *Màgya ba benya deɛ me na ba nya* (I would rather that my mother's child gets it [something good] than my father's child).

The Akan is very proud to belong to a big family. Children are, therefore, cherished with preference for female children. Also, children are deemed to be reincarnated ancestors. For these reasons, childless women are not viewed well in the clan society. The Akan express this in their saying: *Abusua ye dom—wo na ba ne wo nua* (Family is an army—your mother's child is your sister/brother). The Akan child is introduced to spirituality from the day she/he is born by the giving of a soul-name.

Each Akan clan has a totem or two—animals or plants—to which the members of the group have a special relationship.

Akan Concept of Nature

The Akan believe that one's welfare and the welfare of the family and clan is intrinsically woven into harmonious existence with the natural world. Respect and even reverence for the environment is therefore obligatory. As a result, the desire to conquer the natural world or dominate it is not eminent among the Akan.

To safeguard the existence of the Akan, rules of conduct were developed and enforced. Some of these are the Akan "holy orders" or taboos. These holy orders are intended to protect social order, and also, to serve as prevention against individual and collective disequilibrium. Some examples of Akan holy orders include certain days when land tillage or visiting the forest are forbidden. This is to let EnoAsaase Yaa, or Mother Earth, and the spirits of the forest have rest. The holy orders forbid fishing on Tuesdays to give the seas, rivers, and lakes and also the fishermen time to replenish themselves. Fishermen are obliged to throw some of their catch back into the river, lake, or sea as a "sacrifice" to the deity of the river, lake, or sea. A living fish, and never a dead one, is used. It is a taboo to carry a whole bunch of palm fruits from the forest to the house. One is expected to throw some of the seeds in all cardinal directions before returning home. These "orders" are purely environmental protection measures.

It was obligatory for a menstruating Akan woman to separate herself from the rest of the household and live at *mfikyire*, or outside the house. This is because the Akan believed that a menstruating woman acquires the capability to neutralize all spiritual powers except that of the omnipotent Onyankopong (God). A probable consequence of this taboo is that rape is considered a serious crime punishable by ostracization or death. Akan soldiers are on record for abstaining from acts of raping women in conquered areas during the several wars they fought.

It is a taboo for an Akan male to witness, unless absolutely necessary, the mystical process of child delivery. Other taboos cover personal hygiene, eating behaviour, attitudes toward children and elderly persons, murder, adultery, etc. Disregard for such "holy orders" are seen as a threat to the individual, the group in particular, and to human society in general. Violations are dealt with severely. Nevertheless, the Akan strongly believe that the spiritual forces are just and fair. Human actions are what safeguard harmony or cause disequilibrium.

Health and Healing Among the Akan

The Akan concept of health, illness, and healing is directly based on their views about life. Every individual is regarded as composite of spirit (*sunsum*), blood (*mogya*), soul (*okra*), and body (*nipadua*). *Sunsum* is said to be acquired through the *ntoro* (what is this?) of the father. This is regarded as the intangible element which accounts for the character (*sban*), disposition, and intelligence of a person (*asare poku*). It can be trained and is, therefore, mouldable. The *mogya* from the mother, according to the Akan, makes a person a human being. Human blood is, therefore, held in very high esteem. Abrewa Asaase Yaa—Grandmother Earth—as a deity is said to abhor the spilling of human blood. This is why the Akan males are scared of the female who is able to shed her own blood periodically over several years.

Okra, which is Onyame's part in every individual, is said to be the life-giving element in that person. The slightest dissociation of the *okra* from the other components leads to disequilibrium. A long period of separation leading to a complete departure signifies death. Of prime concern to the individual Akan is then the position of her/his soul and spirit in relationship to the world of spirits—the vital forces of life.

The fourth component, the *nipadua* (the body), houses the other parts and is the visible and touchable form. The Akan view their physical body differently from their spiritual body. This is expressed in the Akan saying: *Wo beyeye me dee, fa boro me* (I prefer being assaulted physically to being insulted with words).

Illness as Disequilibrium

As already indicated the position of the *okra* (soul) and *sunsum* (the spirit) in the universe of spirits is of vital importance to the Akan. An individual having a spirit does not automatically make one a member of the world of spirits. She/he is able to join the world of spirits and be on her/his own only after his death. Therefore, while alive she/he is expected to aspire to closest and possibly best relationship with her/his soul. This means, she/he should live an exemplary life to gain recognition as an ancestress/ancestor.

In addition, the Akan believe that an individual does not have the absolute power to determine the course of her/his own life. *Obi dan obi*—everybody is dependent on her/his spiritual environment and must, therefore, be in a position to respond to the spiritual influences and powers around her/him. She/he is a major actor in safeguarding harmony in nature or causing disequilibrium; i.e., disease in her/his own system, or in the physical and spiritual environment.

To the Akan, disequilibrium as illness is ascribed to physical and spiritual (supernatural) causes. The physical causes are said to be elements entering the human system through the natural openings of the body: the digestive system, the ears (especially what we hear), the nose (including bad air), the eyes (especially the things we see), and through the skin. The Akan healers say: *W'adi nakyidee or w'aye nakyidee* (She/he has eaten or done something she/he cannot tolerate).

Among others, supernatural causes might be: punishment by a deity for violation against taboos; withdrawal of help of an ancestress/ancestor or other spiritual helper who is dissatisfied with the behaviour the individual; the act of a bad witch or sorcerer or the spirit of a victim of violent death seeking recognition or revenge; one's own unwholesome thoughts, desires, and acts.

Prevention and Handling of Disequilibrium

To prevent and contain the causes of illness and threats to the individual, family, and clan, the Akan have painfully guarded their healing heritage to the present day. This heritage can be traced as far back as 4000 years ago. In present-day Ghana and parts of Ivory Coast, the Akan healing heritage, along with the art of healing of other ethnic groups, provides health care services for over fifty percent of the population.

The Akan traditional art of healing has three basic features: 1. Religion; 2. Festivals; and, 3. Practitioners.

Religion

The Akan regard the practice of medicine as the gift of Onyankopong (God). This gift is believed to be dispensed through the deities, the ancestresses and ancestors, and other spirits. All the various practitioners acknowledge Onyankopong as the vital force working through them. This is expressed in the following saying: *Se Onyame ma yaree ka wo a, okyere wo eho Aduro* (If God allows illness to befall you, he also shows you the medicine for the cure). Illness is believed to portend a message. The ability to see, hear, smell, and feel which medicine will be helpful and knowing how it must be used is, therefore, of paramount importance.

Festivals

The Akan celebrate about eight major festivals and a number of minor ones. Some festivals are repeated several times a year. Others are celebrated annually. During festivals, communal cleansing, purification, thanksgiving to Onyankopong, veneration of the ancestresses and ancestors, and solicition of help and protection are important features.

This heritage of celebrating festivals is, therefore, a religious-spiritual act of group therapy strengthening the feeling of "we" in the clan. It is a feeling of having people behind you (*me wo nipa wo makyi*)—a strong backbone—which when needed will carry you like the mother does her child. It gives each individual the essence of life through belonging to a group.

Categories of Akan Healing Practitioners

Varieties of healing practitioners are found in traditional Akan society. These can be divided into two main categories: those who practice without invoking supernatural forces; and those who directly apply supernatural aid whether or not they use material remedies.

The first group includes midwives, herbalists, orthopaedic (bone setters and chiro-practitioners), and surgeons. Under the second group are the priestess/ priest-physicians, general practitioners, magicians, and sorcerers.

According to Akan mythology, Odomankoma Onyankopong (the graceful God) and the ancestresses and ancestors first revealed secrets in the use of words and plants as medicine to women. This was to enhance their ability in increasing the size of the clan. This probably explains why the female practitioners are, in general, more efficient than their male counterparts.

Traditional Midwives

The traditional Akan midwife is usually an Obaapanyin (elderly woman) who has completed her childbearing life. In addition to the practice of child delivery Obaapanyin are well-versed in the use of plants and other medicines for pre- and post-natal care and in cutting of the umbilical cord. Unavoidably, they also serve as health, marital, and family counsellors. The relatively large population of the Akan is proof of the good work of these able women.

Herbalists

Professional herbalists are well-versed in the knowledge of plants and other condiments of mineral and animal origin. Their knowledge is acquired from either a family member or through a long period of apprenticeship. These are practitioners who have acquired the art of effectively using their sensory organs to diagnose.

The efficacy of many of the plants used since ancient times by these practitioners have been proved in modern scientific laboratories. Some of these plants are being used worldwide (for example, Okua [Okoubaka aubrevillei]; Kakapenpen [Rawolfia comitoria]; Mmoframofra-nufu [Euphorbia hirta]; Cinca rosea;

Nunum [Ocimum gratissimum]; Omaatwaa [Strophantus hispida]; etc.). Many forms of medical applications in the form of concoctions, teas, poultices, enema, tampons, powders (as snuff or for inoculation through scarification), creams, ointments, and fumigants have been developed by these professionals. The Akan herbalists have made an immense contribution to the development of Ghana's herbal pharmacopoeia. In recent years pressure is being exerted on them to share their knowledge.

Surgeons

Minor and complicated surgery is exercised by various Akan healing practitioners. These include inoculating scarification, light and deep incisions in cases of snake bites and other foreign projectiles in the body.

Ailments affecting bones, muscles, and connective tissues are efficiently treated by the Akan traditional orthopaedic doctors. Their skill in bone-setting of compound fractures, spinal chiropractic, and hydrotherapy are known within and outside the country. The services of these practitioners are being employed by some western doctors.

Religious-Spiritual and Other Practitioners

The modus operandi of the second group of the Akan healing practitioners present an enigma to most western minds. These practitioners work at a level of consciousness different from normal consciousness. The practitioners of this group include: priestess/priest-physicians, general practitioners, magicians, and sorcerers.

The traditional Kan priestess and priest act as mediator between the human and the deity. As a result of their long (three to ten years) and intensive training, the priestesses/priests serve as repository of the myths, customs, rituals, and even history of the clans, as well as their relationship to the deities. In a traditional setting they command a high position in the community. They enstool and disenstool kings and chiefs; act as spiritual leaders; and, advise the king, chief, and elders through divination. In addition to their spiritual functions, the priestesses and priests serve as physicians and psychotherapists. Some of the priestesses/priests have devotees at their shrines.

By virtue of the way the priestesses/priests operate, western minds and Christians have much scepticism about them. It is, however, an open sect and, when nothing else works, people of all levels of education and social standing, including Christian priests in Ghana, consult the traditional priestesses/priests for help. The popular adage "The one who is able to cure is right" holds also for these priestess/priest-physicians.

The General Practitioner

European missionaries coined the confusing name "medicine man" for these practitioners. General practitioners have incorporated the practices of other practitioners in her/his healing activities. Unlike the priestesses/priests they have no deities and, therefore, no shrines and devotees. Some of them claim to have supernatural powers with which they can detect, ward off, and fight evil powers. General practitioners are found in almost every village and town. They are very accessible to everybody at all times and come into focus in many critical situations in the life of individuals and of the community.

Prospects of Traditional Medicine Among the Akan

The latent potential of traditional healing methods have been recognized by many Ghanian scientists and orthodox medical practitioners. Scientific research on traditional medicine and its documentation, exposure of traditional practitioners to the possibilities of improving their methods, and the interaction and cooperation between scientists, orthodox medical practitioners, and traditional practitioners are being intensified officially in Ghana and Africa as a whole.

This is a very welcome development as an improved traditional healing system has many advantages: it is holistic in regards to body, mind, and soul. It is culturally based and therefore offers credibility. It is also easily accessible and much cheaper because medicinal drugs are made from local materials. Without losing its basic essence, the Akan healing heritage will continue to adapt in order to maintain its effective and efficient contribution to the health care of its people.

Knowing what is good for them, the Akan have painfully guarded this heritage until this day despite the onslaught of foreigners who have tried to diminish and eliminate our traditional healing methods, even if convinced of their good intentions. The Akan healing heritage is a treasure our ancestors left for the generations after them. The main actress in safeguarding this treasure of the Akan is the Obaapanyin/Abrewa (the elderly woman). This is why no Akan king, or chief, or elder will dare make a decision without consulting the Abrewa, the living treasure of knowledge and wisdom in Akan society.

Enonom, yeda Onyame ase se ye ye mo mma —
Mothers, we thank Onyame that we are your children.

Gad Agyako Osafo was born in 1945 in Ghana. He is an agriculturalist, engineer (for alternative energies), and a healing practitioner. Since 1998, he runs his own practice for Alternative Healing Methods in Unna, Germany. He has had contact with Songomas in Swaziland, was taught by a priestess-physician as well as by various herbalists in Ghana and Germany.

CÉCILE KELLER

The Practice of Medicine in Matriarchal Societies

I t seems as though I was led by the goddess when I encountered the shamanic
Healing Circle, Quetzalcoatl Lodge (in Switzerland), which I attended for
more than three years. The knowledge held by the Deer Tribe Métis Medicine Society was taught in Europe at the Quetzalcoatl Lodge. This knowledge
stems from the various Indigenous traditions in North, Central, and South
America, and is being preserved and taught by Indian elders called the Twisted
Hairs. Their knowledge is taught in the form of the Medicine Wheels. This is an
old tradition: wheels and circles have always been used to teach about the ways
of the universe. There is nothing linear in the Indigenous worldview, because
linearity is seen as an illusion. There is no beginning and no end (see Flaming
Crystal Mirror 1999: 13-19).

At the time (sixteen years ago), I was studying western medicine in Switzerland and found myself in the throes of a major crisis. The healing rituals and
medicinal knowledge that I was fortunate to experience in this healing circle
brought me back to health, and helped me to discover my own vision.

Later, when I met up with the International Academy HAGIA and Heide
Goettner-Abendroth, I found that what I had experienced in the healing circle
was a medical tradition that, to varying degrees, dates back to matriarchal societies. As a result of the wonderful experience I had at the Healing Circle and from
what I learned at the International Academy HAGIA, I started doing research
on medicine in matriarchal societies. The practice of medicine in matriarchal
societies has not been researched much, and we are only just starting to recognize its importance. I intend to use my knowledge and experience to highlight
the significance and scope of medical systems in matriarchal cultures. This has
great relevance, and could be groundbreaking in many areas for western medi-
cin, which, in many respects, has reached a dead end.

It has not been easy to find written sources, because matriarchal cultures are
mainly oral cultures. The ritual and medical knowledge has been handed down
orally, and often secretly. Only in the last century has this secrecy been lifted by
Indigenous peoples themselves; this has made it possible for outsiders to research
this knowledge.

I applied fairly narrow criteria of acceptability to the sources: they had to be from cultures that were both matrilineal and matrilocal. The single exception is the Mitsogho in Gabun, West Africa. They are matrilineal, but virilocal (inheritance is through the female line, but women live in their husband's house). They were selected because the overall structure of their society shows many characteristic matriarchal patterns. Presumably, matrilocality existed prior to the slow development of virilocality.

Based on the available research on three societies with matriarchal patterns, I have proposed a first definition of medicine in matriarchal societies. One can rightfully assume that this definition also applies to other matriarchal societies. A major research project would be needed to make this clear. There is still much that can, and should, be done in this area.

Mircéa Eliade (1974) and Claude Lévi-Strauss (1967) were the first scientists to honour the healing arts as well as Indigenous cultures' cosmologies and ways of life. These scientists' empirical research demonstrated that these cultures are highly developed, and this attribution freed them from the label of "primitive," a characterization that stems from colonial and Christian attitudes of western civilizations. As far as Indigenous cultures' healing ceremonies go, they were decried as psychopathological. Lévi-Strauss and Eliade contributed valuable, trailblazing work that has fostered a totally different perception of these cultures' healing arts and society.

My main focus is on the Iroquois[1] of North America, specifically the Seneca, one of the six tribes of the Iroquois Confederation, and one that is well-researched and documented. I shall also refer to the Mitsogho people of Gabun, West Africa, as well as the Hopi in Arizona. I shall also include Korean shamanism, which stems from matriarchal tradition in East Asia.

I shall explain the Iroquois concept of medicine; look at the issue of who practices medicine, and how different practitioners of medicine are defined; outline how sickness and health are understood in those societies; investigate how diagnoses are made in these systems; look at the application of matriarchal medicine; explore treatment methods;explore the Iroquois system of medicine societies.

The Concept of Medicine with the Iroquois

Iroquois philosophy has an impersonal, omnipresent power at its centre; this pervades every object and living being. On this spiritual basis, rites, ceremonies, and healing rituals are created (Thiel qtd. in Hirschberg 1988: 106; Baier-Kleinow 1992: 42). In the Iroquois language this power is called *orenda* (Hewitt 1910; Baier-Kleinow 1992: 42) and it is seen as the underlying cause for everything in this world (Van der Leeuw 1964; Baier-Kleinow 1992: 42). The power of *orenda* is in animals, plants, human beings, foremothers, forefathers, elements, and objects. It manifests in natural phenomena. This happens through song, as in the song of the thunder, the wind, and the storm (Hewitt 1902; Baier-Kleinow 1992: 43).

With the help of special practices, such as rituals and ceremonies, which can be studied and acquired, *orenda* can be activated and augmented. Female shamans, for example, have a very large *orenda*. For this process of activation however, a catalyst is necessary: the spoken or sung word, a spell or a song. This is why songs or sung words have such an important meaning in matriarchal cultures (Hewitt 1910; Baier-Kleinow 1992: 43-44).

Based on this understanding of *orenda*, a definition of medicine with the Iroquois can be deduced. "*Orenda* is identical with the concept of medicine. Any object possessing *orenda* is called a medicine" (Converse 1908: 22; Hewitt 1910; Baier-Kleinow 1992: 44).

Who Adminsters Medical Care in Matriarchal Societies

The following persons practice medical care within matriarchal societies, and may be male or female: shamans, medical practitioners, healers, diviners, fortune-tellers, clairvoyants, diagnosticians, as well as medicine societies.

I have consciously chosen the female form in language. I am including the male form in language in this definition while stressing the importance of women, who, in the older traditions, practised medicine, protected knowledge, and passed it on. Scientific literature mentions women only marginally if at all. Almost all medical practitioners, shamans, and healers are male. But from the very earliest ethnographic accounts of the Iroquois, we know that ritual songs and ceremonies, as well as medical knowledge, belonged to certain matri-clans. The women owned this knowledge and passed it on.

The shamanism of Korea also lies almost exclusively in the hands of women. This is evident from the statistics: 95 percent of the shamans of the ecstatic tradition are women (Goettner-Abendroth 1991).

With the Iroquois, a medicine woman is a woman who possesses great *orenda* with healing powers. Or, she possesses special knowledge of medicine plants. She knows many magic practices, such as how to use rattles and invocations, and how to call spirits. Eliade limits the concept of the shaman to mastering the ecstasy technique only. (In his description he only uses the male form of shaman.) With regard to North American tribes, this definition is far too narrow. This is why the term is defined differently in American literature, compared to European literature. The American definition of a shaman is someone who heals through supernatural powers, or is able to cause diseases (Hultkrantz 1973; Baier-Kleinow 1992: 17). This definition includes all medicine women and every variety of fortune-telling, which is not the case with the European definition. I am, therefore, using the American definition.

Eliade believes the ability to go into ecstasy distinguishes the priestess from the shaman. However, in many North American tribes the function of priestess and shaman are combined into one person. This is also true for Korea in pre-patriarchal times. The most prominent women in the tribe—or in the kingdom—were priestesses and shamans; they inherited their profession. The spiritual concerns of the culture were in their hands, and they were also healers and medicine women. In addition, they were visionaries and fortune-tellers (Goettner-Abendroth 1991: 110).

The Concept of Health and Sickness in Matriarchal Societies

The Iroquois derive their concept of health from their worldview. They believe the universe to be made up of polar powers. For a strong *orenda* unity to be created, these two powers have to connect, for this represents a balance of power. Therefore, health is seen as a condition of balance inside and outside of the individual (Isaacs 1978: 824-829; Baier-Kleinow 1992: 72). Each disturbance of this balance is seen as a possible cause for disease. When an organism is out of balance, it is viewed as weak, and therefore prone to attack by spirits who grow angry. They can enter all living beings, including human beings, animals, plants, and animal spirits. Sickness is not simply an imbalance of power, but also involves the presence of an angry spirit. This is why sickness is doubly feared (Bourgeois 1968: 126; Baier-Kleinow 1992: 73).

The Hopi system is made up of transcendent beings, human beings, animals, plants, sun, moon, earth, and stars. Maintaining harmony between the powers of the system is only achievable through a correct lifestyle (Gugel 1997: 169). Part of this is the maintenance of traditions, the correct execution of ceremonies, and ethical ideals. Human misconduct, called *qahopi*, leads to sickness, drought, and crop failure.

The Mitsogho in Gabun view health as a form of balance and harmony in social interaction. This is mirrored in the individual. If a member of the community is sick, the imbalance has to be removed, which affects the community the same way it affects the individual; the sickness simply points out the imbalance (Prins 1987: 58).

The Diagnosis

Traditional diagnosis aims to uncover the reason for an assumed imbalance. So diagnosis is a statement about the cause. The focus of the diagnosis is the search and discovery of the cause, not the symptoms (Isaacs 1978: 828; Baier-Kleinow 1992: 77). This differs from the scientific approach to medicine, where symptoms and the course of the disease are deciding factors in diagnostics, while cause is largely neglected.

Some matriarchal cultures, such as the Mitsogho and the Iroquois, have specially trained diagnosticians. With the Mitsogho, medicine societies are responsible for certain spheres. In the area of health there are two medicine societies for women and one medicine society for men (Prins 1987: 54).One of the women's medicine societies is called Boô; this group also includes fortune-tellers, who are used to divine sickness. During a night ceremony, the woman responsible for the divination takes Iboga. Iboga is a shrub containing a hallucinogenic. The people know the effect of this drug, and are able to regulate it very well. They are also familiar with application and dosage for particular purposes. For them, it is the "bitter wood." But they also call this medicine plant a "wonderful wood" that enables them to see the hidden issues of life. Behind closed doors, the women dance and drum the whole night long, until the cause of the disease is uncovered. The following day, the diagnosis and exact description of treatment is publicly announced in the village square. Then treatment begins (Prins 1987: 60).

The Iroquois call a traditional diagnostician a fortune-teller. She diagnoses the disease based on the person's dreams, by having the dream recounted to her. On the basis of the dream symbols, she prescribes a healing ceremony (Wallace 1959; Linding 1970: 219; Baier-Kleinow 1992: 17, 77).

Application Area of Matriarchal Medicine

Application areas arise from the way these cultures understand sickness and health. They include the individual, the clan, the village, the tribe, nature, even the universe itself. Disease is not something that concerns only the individual. This explains why, most of the time, the whole clan, village, or tribe is part of the healing ceremony.

An example of using medicine to heal nature is given by a Seneca women's medicine society. The Towisas Medicine Society, the Society of Women Planters, carries out healing ceremonies for everyone's well being. This means the ceremony applies to Mother Earth, who, according to Iroquois understanding, needs repeated healing because each cultivation and planting hurts her (Forbes 1981: 11; Baier-Kleinow 1992: 93). These healing rituals re-establish balance between humans and the earth.

Methods of Treatment

Treatment methods are holistic and address the whole person: body, soul, and consciousness, as well as the cosmological worldview. The rituals bring about a re-connection with the cosmological worldview, and with that a connection to the deities, the ancestral spirits, and nature spirits. This in itself is, in the broadest sense, a process of healing. A scenario is set up to call upon, energetically, all spiritual forces of the ancestors, and the deities. Through prayer, ritual songs, and tobacco sacrifice, the goodwill of these spirits is implored, for only they can grant healing. They are the ones who continually grant knowledge of healing to human beings, and this knowledge is reflected in their myths. Often, they appear in the body of the person who calls them, and they speak and act through them.

It is not the practitioner who decides what treatment the patient needs; it is the spirit beings, the ancestors, and the deities who decide this. The practitioner acts in accordance with the spirit and ancestral world and the deities who impart their knowledge to her.

For example, Iroquois treatments are ritualizedusing herbal cures, water treatments such as washing, body cleansing, massage, and communication with spirits. The ritualized treatment takes care of both physical and psychological disorders (Isaacs 1978: 827; Wallace 1959: 75; Baier-Kleinow 1992: 17, 77-78).

Iroquois Peoples' Medicine Societies

By way of illustration, I would like to address the subject of the system of medicine societies with the Seneca, as they have been well-researched (Gugel 1997: 27). Medicine societies have only been institutionalized under the pressure colonial powers exerted on them to acculturate. When I say institutionalized, I rrefer to the process of keeping the cultural and medical knowledge attributed to a matriarchal system, secret from non-Indigenous people. The institutionalization of these associations started on the reservations. Only in recent history has the secrecy been partly lifted (Goettner-Abendroth 2000: 122).

Medicine societies are federations that aim to maintain the health and well-being of individuals, society, nature, the cosmos, the spirit world, the deities, and the ancestors. This is why, even today, the ceremonies have such great importance. Medicine societies are characterized by healing rituals and teaching. They ensure the handing down of medical knowledge and renewal rituals that follow the agricultural cycle. They hold to characteristic creation myths that explain the meaning of the rituals, as well as holy objects, helping spirits, and protective animal spirits (Goettner-Abendroth 2000: 123; Parker 1970; Baier-Kleinow 1992: 16). Another feature is the unchanged rendering of ceremonies and song lyrics, which often contain words not understood even by the members. This is evidence of the great age of these rituals (Gugel 1997: 49).These are secret and not to be passed on to the uninitiated.

Among the medicine societies for women, three belong to the domain of agriculture and two to hunting. The focal point of the women's medicine societies is the healing ceremonies. Nowadays, the agricultural rites are celebrated publicly. I want to cite two examples that provide indirect information on the content of the healing ceremonies, which are not public.

The Towisas Medicine Society is an agricultural society concentrated on the powers of fertility: birth and growth of plant life, animals, and human beings. There are public ceremonies that begin in spring and extend throughout the summer; that is, from the sowing through the harvesting (Goettner-Abendroth 2000: 123).

The Ogiwe Medicine Society, also called The Talkers with the Dead (Converse 1908: 84; Baier-Kleinow 1992: 94) is involved with ceremonies around death, and cultivates a relationship with the dead. The celebration of the dead happens twice yearly, in March and in late Autumn. In this way these two medicine societies build up a complementary ceremonial body depicting the seasonal cycle and the cycle of all living beings (Goettner-Abendroth 2000: 124).

Outsiders are not privy to the healing ceremonies of the Towisas Medicine

Society; women celebrate in private. It can be assumed that since they are celebrating fertility rituals, the healing rituals relate to women's fertility.

Healing ceremonies of the Ogiwe Medicine Society happen outside the ceremonial calendar. They are better known than those of the Towisas Medicine Society. If there are diseases such as loss of appetite, insomnia, nerve disorders, or confusion of spirit, these will be treated by the Ogiwe Medicine Society women, as these diseases are believed to be caused by spirits who are angry because ceremonies for them have not held frequently enough (Fenton and Kurath 1951; Baier-Kleinow 1992. The clairvoyant is of great importance during this ceremony as she identifies the spirit in the patient. The ability to communicate with the spirits is a clairvoyant one, and is highly regarded within the medicine society (Parker 1970: 178; Baier-Kleinow 1992: 106).

To conclude, I would like to make a general comment in reference to the North American medicine societies for women. Most of these have been documented for the Iroquois, the Hopi, the Mandan, and the Hidatsa. The aforementioned Indigenous peoples are all matrilineal and matrilocal. It can be concluded that the medical and cultural knowledge that is being protected and applied by women's medicine societies is very old. Contrary to commonly held views, women's societies are probably older than the men's, since matriarchal societies are older than patriarchal societies.

Translation by Jutta Ried and Karen Smith

Born in 1948 in Cham, Switzerland, Cécile Keller became a doctor in 1994. She has worked as a medical doctor in several hospitals, and from 1999 has worked as a gynaecologist in Switzerland. She also trained from 1993-1995 at the Centre for Shamanistic Wisdom and Knowledge, Quetzalcoatl, in Ronco, Tessin. In 1997, she started training with the International Academy HAGIA for matriarchal spirituality and is now co-director of the Academy.

[1]The term "Iroquois" stems from the time of European colonialism in North America. The correct name is "Haudenosaunee."

References

Baier-Kleinow, Saskia. 1992. "Frauenbünde und die Bedeutung und Rollen der Frauen im Zeremonialwesen der Irokesen." Magisterarbeit (Unpublished Master's thesis), University of Freiburg, Germany.

Bourgeois, Marie J. 1969. *Present-day Health and Illness Beliefs and Practices Among the Seneca Indians*. Dissertation Abstracts, 29, 4488B-4489B. UM 69-9116: 126.

Converse, Harriet Maxwell. 1908. "Myths and Legends of the New York State Iroquois." New York State Museum Bulletin 125: 5-195.

Eliade, Mircéa. 1974. *Schamanismus und archaische Ekstasetechnik.* Frankfurt am Main: Suhrkamp.

Fenton, William N. and Gertrude P. Kurath. 1951. "The Feast of the Dead, or Ghost Dance at Six Nations Reserve, Canada." Ed. William N. Fenton. Symposium on Local Diversity in Iroquois Culture. Washington: Govt. Print. Off. 163.

Flaming Crystal Mirror, Mary. 1999. *Süße Medizin. Die Lehren der Twisted Hairs.* Vol. 1. Tübingen: Vier Welten Verlag.

Forbes, Jack D. 1981. *Die Wétiko-Seuche. Eine indianische Philosophie von Aggression und Gewalt.* Wuppertal: Hammer Verlag.

Goettner-Abendroth, Heide. 1991. "Schamaninnen in Korea." *Das Matriarchat II.1.* Stuttgart: Verlag Kohlhammer. 104-117.

Goettner-Abendroth, Heide. 2000. "Nordamerika: Am Kreuzpunkt südlicher und nördlicher Kulturen." *Das Matriarchat II.2.* Stuttgart: Verlag Kohlhammer. 104-127.

Gugel, Liane. 1997. *Frauenbünde der Indianer Nordamerikas.* Wyk auf Foehr: Verlag für Amerikanistik.

Hewitt, J. N. B. 1910. "Orenda." *Bulletin of the Bureau of American Ethnology* 30 (2): 147-148.

Hewitt, J. N. B. 1902. "Orenda and a Definition of Religion." *American Anthropologist* 4: 33-46.

Isaacs, Hope L. 1978. "American Indian Medicine and Contemporary Health Problems. 1. Toward Improved Health Care for Native Americans. Comparative Perspective on American Indian Medicine Concepts." *New York State Journal of Medicine* 78: 824-829.

Keller, Cécile. 2006. "Medizin in matriarchalen Gesellschaften." *Gesellschaft in Balance. Dokumentation des 1. Weltkongresses für Matriarchatsforschung.* Ed. Heide Goettner-Abendroth. Stuttgart: Edition HAGIA und Verlag Kohlhammer. 266–275.

Lévi-Strauss, Claude. 1967. *Strukturale Anthropologie I.* Frankfurt am Main: Suhrkamp.

Parker, Arthur C. 1970. "Secret Medicine Societies of the Seneca." *American Anthropologist* 11: 161-185.

Prins, M. 1987. "Tabernanthe iboga, die vielseitige Droge Äquatorial-Westafrikas: Divination, Initiation und Besessenheit bei den Mitsogho in Gabu." *Ethnopsychotherapie.* Eds. Christian Scharfetter and Adolf Dittrich. Stuttgart: Ferdinand Enke Verlag. 53–68.

Thiel, Josef F. 1988. "Dynamismus." *Wörterbuch für Völkerkunde.* Ed. W. Hischberg. Berlin: Dietrich Reimer. 106.

Van der Leeuw, Gerardus. 1964. "Macht und theoretisierte Macht." *Religionsethnologie.* Ed. C. A. Schmitz. Frankfurt: Akademische Verlagsanstalt. 51-64.

Wallace, Anthony F. C. 1959. "The Institutionalization of Cathartic and Control Strategies in Iroquois Religious Pscyhotherapy." *Culture and Mental Health, Cross Cultural Studies.* Ed. M. Opler. New York: Macmillan. 63-96.

BERNEDETTE MUTHIEN

Beyond Patriarchy and Violence

The Khoesan and Partnership

M y beautiful mother was a descendant of the Khoe, and my father came from India. I use the term "Khoesan," rather than "Khoekhoe," because of the split in colonial understandings of the Khoe and the San as two separate groups of people. And so not to exclude those who consider themselves San, I use "Khoesan" to embrace both groups in terms of wholeness, completeness, interconnectedness, and interdependence .

Cape Town is nestled on the slopes of ancient Table Mountain, a sacred mountain range that has also become a favourite of tourists. Cape Town is a peninsula so it has the two oceans, the Atlantic and Indian, on either side of it. This is one of the sites that the ancient, Indigenous people, the KhoeSan, used for tracking time and constellations. It is an incredibly powerful site, where dowel sticks, if you use them, move rapidly back and forth. One can also experience this powerful energy with one's hands. These sites were no doubt used for ceremonial purposes. During solstice, the sun strikes the rock in a particular way, which determines many interesting things. While I will not explore sacred geometry, I did want to show where I come from and how privileged I am to be in this place.

I came to Matriarchal Studies in a non-linear way. It began with my return to South Africa from studies in the United States, after our first elections in 1994, to then being immersed in Peace Studies, Conflict Resolution, and Nation Building, immediately after apartheid. And later still I found myself managing a gender violence programme at the African Gender Institute at the University of Cape Town, and trying to understand gender-based violence—why it happens; how it happens. And more significant for me, how we could transcend gender violence. Apart from hearing about Heide Goettner-Abendroth's work, I came to Matriarchal Studies to try to make sense of the intuitions that I was increasingly involved with.

Ubuntu: *I am because I belong*[1]

We are all aware of how very different we are. No two humans are exactly the same, not even "identical" twins. Sometimes, consciously or unconsciously, we are more or less aware of the differences between each of us. Sometimes differences are used by us and/or others for particular purposes, for a particular group of people's interests, in different contexts at different times—like under apartheid, the Nazi Holocaust, Islamic Jihads, and Christian Crusades.

The histories of, and struggles within and over science provide many interesting examples of sameness and difference, and the oneness of all. The tenth-century Arab scholar, Alhazen,[2] informed the work of the French Franciscan monk, René Descartes (1596-1650: "I think therefore I am"), as well as the English scientist, Isaac Newton (1642-1727), both of whom researched the origins, properties, and behaviour of light. Alhazen formulated his theories of vision and light, which debunked the somewhat arrogant and superstitious (assuming humankind is at the centre of everything, including emitting light rays from our eyes!) "ray theory" of the Greek scientist, Euclid, by proving that light enters our eyes in straight lines from everywhere in our environment. He also thoroughly documented reflection and refraction, two phenomena that create rainbows. Subsequently, Descartes suggested that light was white or colour-less, and that rainbows are created when white light is broken down into separate colours. Newton, through experimental observation, proved that white light is created by combining the separate colours of the rainbow, and thus coined the term "spectrum," heralding the dawn of the Age of Enlightenment, whose positive and negative ideologies we still experience at present.

Thus, Descartes argued that from white comes colours, from sameness comes difference and separation (i.e., white light constitutes the rainbow). Newton proved that difference and colours generate white (or colour-lessness) and sameness, so the rainbow constitutes white light, and in doing so, the spectrum creates oneness and unity. Hence, in terms of light, oneness does not encompass diversity (we are all one but different), but diversity encompasses oneness (we are all diverse but one). So if our foundation is diversity, a fluid spectrum of merging primary colours, our natural inclination is to become united, seen as white (colour-less) light. We are both intrinsically parts of spectra, observably different, and simultaneously becoming colour-less. Diversity creates Oneness.

In this observable sense, "I am because I belong," in fluid and multiple ways, to both a part of a spectrum, as well as the colour-less collective. Desmond Tutu asserts that for him, *ubuntu* speaks of the very essence of being human: to be generous, to be hospitable, to be friendly, caring, and compassionate. *You share what you have.* It is to say: "My humanity is caught up, is inextricably bound up, in yours." We belong in a bundle of life.

We say: "A person is a person through other persons." It is not "I think therefore I am." Rather, in Tutu's words, it says: "I am human because I belong. I participate. I share" (1999: 31).

It is in this acknowledgement of diversities and likenesses, and simultaneous acknowledgement of all being part of the greater whole that provides the essential foundations of this discussion, in terms of my understanding of my peoples' spirituality.

I wish to reclaim, celebrate, and live ancient Indigenous knowledge and ways of being still prevalent in societies today, including the Lahu of China (Shanshan Du), the Minangkabau of Indonesia (Peggy Reeves Sanday), the Iroquois of North America (Barbara Mann), the Saami of Finland (Rauna Kuokkanen), and the KhoeSan of Southern Africa (Yvette Abrahams).

Descartian thinking centres on an "I think therefore I am" paradigm, which can be contrasted with the ancient African notion of *ubuntu*: "I exist because I belong," my humanity is inextricably tied up with your humanity (Tutu), and with a community. This *ubuntu* is a concept that extends beyond the individual, and is located within a community, within an acknowledgement of a greater whole. With Descartian "European" thinking, the self's identity is constructed in relation to an Other, e.g., I am a woman because I am not a man; I am black because I am not white; I am African because I am not European, etc. The meaning of the words "Khoe" and "San" is respectively "human." So for Indigenous people the world over, identity is in relation to our humanness, and to humanity and the cosmos as a whole.

Some of the characteristics of Indigenous societies are:

• They are non-violent, i.e., conflict resolution skills are advanced, justice is restorative and not punitive, and the whole community is involved with "perpetrator" and "victim" alike.
• They show respect for all in relation to all: sky, earth, animals, plants, and humans.
• They are gender egalitarian: genders are varied and fluid, and all are respected equally.
• They are beyond heteronormative: all sexualities are respected as fluid, with "queer" and intersexed people respected as "gatekeepers" to the divine.

To the last point: We Africans have to reclaim our ancient fluidities from despots who project their appalling governance through homophobia, which has us killed and raped daily. Fluidities that account for the ancient practice of woman-to-woman marriage in Africa, which the Christian colonials could not entirely eradicate and, hence, still exists today. Fluidities that had colonial administrators in countries like Namibia during the eighteenth century record the KhoeSan as "normatively bisexual," a typical error, since the KhoeSan are not normatively anything but free, with respect and compassion for all. In an age of unprecedented violence, including curative rape of lesbian and bisexual women, there can be no innocents, only wilful ignorants.

A current buzzword is "conscious consumerism," which is as oxymoronic as "military security." The act of consumption is unilateral, one-way, and centred on the individual satisfying an individual need. No amount of products from Fair Trade will fill one's heart with love, or life with fulfilment. The science of cosmology shows us that stars, by their very nature, are dying, and in this act of dying, they emit light and energy for the cosmos. The sun too, by its very nature, gives light and energy to the cosmos. Neither take from the cosmos; they exist to give. And hence, the cosmos models the nature of Indigenous societies, structured as multilateral gift economies, where we fulfil community needs when we can and when we see them, without thought of reciprocity, and where consumption, whether ostensibly conscious or not, is obsolete. So we need to challenge our minds beyond the emptiness of slogans and the latest fashions, and definitely beyond the advertising we ingest even in our sleep.

We are all, each, accountable. And we need understandings of humanity that are visionary, intensely political, and deeply rooted within communities. We need action as much as we need theorizing. And we demand change. Now.

Gender-Based Violence

To understand gender-based violence, and why it happens, one has to understand violence, and why violence happens. As a starting point, the following working definition of "violence" is offered: the harmful action or actions of one person or group against another person or group. Looking at this definition one can see a binary opposition: Us versus Them.

The construction of binary oppositions may stem from a particular identity formation—the ways in which people are taught to view themselves and the world. The conventional modern formation of identity is premised on an understanding of "I am because I am not." So one can find statements such as, I am female because I am not male; I am black because I am not white; I am African because I am not European or North American. This construction of Self fundamentally needs an Other against which to measure itself and its value. In an intrinsically competitive environment, if the Self is to succeed and be valued, it needs to transcend or overpower the Other, and if the Self is to be valued and triumph, the Other of necessity needs to be devalued. This process can be termed "Othering."

Such identity construction, premised on polarity[3] or "Othering," fosters conflict over access to and control of resources. In this way power also becomes a resource, as in "power to" and "power over." This belief system, based on "I am because I have and you don't," can be juxtaposed with one in which there is a more equitable distribution of resources, i.e., a more "diffuse" form of power. Power as a relation between people becomes a contest over resources because it is premised on a flawed belief system centred on Othering and the devaluation of the Other.

Othering and Oppressions

Our understanding of the origins of Othering and oppressions centres on the explication of two fundamental belief systems. Riane Eisler (1987) posits two models, the "partnership model" and the "dominator model." When Eisler refers to the "dominator model," she means the ranking of one half of humanity over the other. She describes the "partnership model," on the other hand, as one in which social relations are primarily based on the principle of linking rather than ranking. In this model—beginning with the most fundamental difference in our species, between male and female—diversity is not equated with either inferiority or superiority (1987: xvii).

Eisler continues to argue that the dominator model is based on domination and force and the power to take life (death), rather than the power to give life (birth) as in the partnership model, where actualization and maximization of individuals' potentials are primordial. Western and modern thinking and beliefs are premised on the dominator model. Societies based on this paradigm are intrinsically unequal, hierarchical, and oppressive. A recent example is modern European imperialism, which constructed the present state system in Africa.

Significantly, the discourse of colonization similarly operates on a system of binary oppositions, such as female-male, black-white, infidel-believer or uncivilized-civilized. This particular way of constructing personal and group identity fosters conflict rather than cooperation, and by its very nature leads to violence. Think, for example, of the Hutu and Tutsi in the Great Lakes. Whether the identities of "Hutu" and "Tutsi" in Rwanda are based on caste or class, ethnicity, or on resources, and whether their identities preceded colonization, is contested by Rwandans themselves, most of whom argue that their ethnic identities are colonial constructs.

However, bearing in mind that the colonization of Africa engendered much violence, we must also not forget that some African forebears traded in other Africans, as the histories of slavery evince. Some Africans, who operated on the construct of "I am because I am not," also oppressed and waged wars against their kinsfolk whom they felt threatened by and whose property they wished to confiscate. These are practices which were exploited and exacerbated by colonization, and which continue to this day.

Partnership and Matriarchy

The dominator model can be juxtaposed with the partnership model, an ancient and Indigenous way of thinking that preceded colonization, and can still be found in societies such as that of the KhoeSan of Southern Africa, and many others all over the world.

The partnership model is premised on harmony and balance, on mutual respect for, and interdependence of each other and the environment, on cooperation rather than conflict. It is personified in the yin/yang symbol, which epitomizes a harmonious integration of all elements into one being, all dancing fluidly together to create a dynamic organism. It perhaps embodies a different tenet like, "I am because I care," "I am because I belong." This sense of caring community in ancient societies[4] is something Carol Lee Flinders has also touched on in her book, *Reclaiming a Life of Value*. In the partnership model, peace and respect are fundamental organizing principles, where power is cooperatively shared.

In this model, "matriarchy" is not necessarily the opposite of patriarchy. Ancient matriarchal societies were not hierarchical, oppressive, and violent (towards men). Instead, they have been shown to be cooperative and peaceful, societies in which men and women were equal and equitably shared resources, even as females were key leaders, spiritually and otherwise, of their societies.[5] African history records the matriarchal rule of, for example, Amanitare and other ancient Nubian queens, as well as the rule of queens of the Akan in North Ghana. Katarina Tomasevski refers to the civilian rule of Neber in Egypt during the Old Kingdom (c. 3100-2345 BCE). She argues that Indigenous Egyptian society was strongly matriarchal:

> Some historians argue that women may, in fact, have "discovered" agriculture in prehistoric times. There are even instances of matrilineal and matriarchal societies in Malaysia, Java, the Philippines, and India. (1993: 1, 2)

Origins of Gender Oppression

In the context of gender, the dominator model presupposes a rigid distinction between the two genders. There are countless examples of modern colonizers imposing and maintaining this separation at the expense of the partnership model; or, in the sense given, matriarchal model of thought.

In Burma, for example, British colonizers noted how "barbaric" the native Burmese were because their genders were not rigidly separated and hierarchized; so, too, with the KhoeSan of Southern Africa. In both cases the colonizers, aided by the requirements of capitalism, worked immensely hard at inculcating gender distinctions in these societies and communities, with horrific results. Heike Becker has shown in her studies of gender-based violence and the San that both colonization and capitalism, as well as apartheid in Southern Africa, caused and exacerbated gender-based violence in the KhoeSan communities in Southern Africa, through the introduction and fostering of rigid and controlled gender distinctions.

Especially in Africa, the impact of colonialism, grounded in monotheistic and patriarchal religious systems,[6] extended beyond the imposition of rigid gender polarities to also subvert traditional constructions of family and partnerships. The Judeo-Christian and colonial model of heterosexual, male-dominated families can be contrasted with Indigenous African family practices, such as woman-to-woman marriage.

While studies about marriages between women have always been limited, Anthonia Uzuegbunam (2001) documents this phenomenon amongst the Igbo in Nigeria, and traces documents relating cases from the 1930s. She asserts that marriages between women are common in East, Southern, and West Africa, as well as the Sudan (2001: 3). She argues that these marriages are initiated by women who are not able to bear children, who join in a (traditional) union with a younger woman who bears the family children after insemination by a carefully selected man. According to Uzuegbunam,

> woman-to-woman marriage in Igboland is portrayed as a flexible op-tion available to women to pursue any number of interests, political, social, economic and personal. The guiding principles therefore are flexibility, heterogeneity and ambiguity. (2001: 11)

She asserts that these relationships are more egalitarian than conventional het-erosexual ones, and that the childbearing partner enters entirely freely into the union, and continues to explain:

> Woman-to-woman marriage in Igboland is not like lesbianism where love and sexual relations are exchanged by same male sex [sic]. Rather, woman-to-woman marriage has stories of love, children, companion-ship, commitment, sexual freedom, vulnerability and empowerment. The woman initiator invites a male with the arrangement for procre-ation and for pleasure. (11)

This centuries-old practice of woman-to-woman marriage, with its intrinsic mutuality and egalitarianism, has been steadily eroded by the colonization of Indigenous African societies.

Man's fear of penetration and/or violation by the "impure" (bisexual) Other, does seem to cast some light on the reasons for his rejection of her. A useful anal-ogy can be drawn between black and white, or colonized and colonizer. The need to increase and maintain the distance between these opposites stems from the fear of the (strangeness/difference of the) Other. However, one could ask what the origins of this fear is. The answer could be found in dominant ideology itself. Ideology is advanced by a group of individuals who would wish to perpetuate their own positions of power and privileged access to resources. Therefore, they would need to subjugate the colonized. Other, and the ideology of fear and hi-erarchical oppositions lends itself well to this form of exploitation; so, too, with the oppression of woman.

Models of Violence

Johan Galtung[7] constructed a model of violence consisting of three key forms of violence, which can be depicted as the three corners of a triangle, with no one corner static. In other words, the triangle can be rotated in any direction, with any one corner at its peak, at any moment in history. The three corners of the triangle are: direct or personal violence; structural or institutional violence; and, cultural violence.

"Direct or personal violence" refers to a direct assault on a person or group, whether physical, verbal or psychological, for example, a man hits a woman.

"Structural violence" refers to violence that is embedded in the very structures or institutions of our societies. Most obvious examples of this include poverty, starvation, and exploitation. Further examples include gender discrimination, racism, xenophobia, and homophobia. Excessively high maternal and infant mortality rates are forms of structural violence, because they are easily avoidable, and affect only specific sectors of the population, i.e., the most marginalized.

"Cultural violence" refers to violence that is perpetuated through our cultures (methods of thinking and being) that is used to justify direct or structural violence. For example, some men argue that a husband is fully entitled to rape his wife, or force her to have sex against her will.

A further example of cultural violence would be "victim blaming" in the case of rape: A man rapes a woman, which would be direct or personal violence. She lays a charge and finds herself in court confronted by legal mechanisms that are not necessarily designed to protect her, such as overworked and disinterested (often male) police, prosecutors, and judges, which is a form of structural violence. Then she is cross-examined by an often male defence attorney who asks her questions like, what she was wearing at the time of the rape, why she was at that place at that time, and making her feel as if she asked and deserved to be raped; hence, the term "victim blaming."

As we can see from this analysis of violence, and gender discrimination and gender-based violence can be found in each form of violence: direct or personal, structural, and cultural.

The antithesis of violence, of course, is peace, and the three forms of violence outlined above would also have corresponding forms of peace. If one eliminates physical assault (including physical forms of gender-based violence) one will experience direct or personal peace. If one eliminates structural violence (including sexism, racism, and homophobia) and transform institutions appropriately, one will experience structural peace. And if one eradicates cultural violence (including methods of thinking and being) one will experience cultural peace.

Thus, it appears that none of these forms of violence, and their respective antitheses, are entirely isolated from the other. For example, one cannot eliminate gender-based violence without transforming institutions, as well as methods of thinking and being. And if one changes cultures of violence into cultures of balance and harmony, one will necessarily eliminate gender-based violence since there will no longer be polar opposites, or the distrust and devaluation of Others.

Conflict, which is not the same as violence, is not necessarily and intrinsically bad, and may contribute to creativity if resolved peacefully. All relations, and all societies, will invariably experience conflict at least some of the time, in part due to differences. It is in acknowledging conflict and differences, and dealing with it constructively and peacefully that creativity and growth can be fostered.

This understanding of violence and peace now allows a more in-depth examination of the concept of "gender-based violence." According to the Committee on the Elimination of Discrimination Against Women (CEDAW) (General Recommendation No 12), gender-based violence is defined as:

Violence that is directed against a woman because she is a woman, or that affects women disproportionately. It includes acts that inflict physical, mental or sexual harm or suffering, and threats of such acts, coercion or arbitrary deprivation of liberty.

The Declaration on the Elimination of Violence Against Women notes three key spheres in which gender-based violence may occur or which may perpetrate and/or condone such violence: the family, the community and the state. [8] December Green adds one further site of gender-based violence, i.e., the economy. The concept of gender-based violence should accordingly be broadened to also include the notion of economic abuse, which has been defined in the South African Domestic Violence Act (1998) to include "the unreasonable deprivation of economic or financial resources or the unreasonable disposal of household effects in which the victim/survivor has an interest."[9]

Gender-based violence, therefore, occurs through the act of being gendered. Through the kinds of identity construction where the Self cannot exist without the Other, and where the Self cannot be valued without devaluing the Other, women are valued as less than men. The CEDAW definition above focuses on women as the subjects of gender-based violence; however, it should be recognized that such violence also affects men, not only as potential victims, but also when they act as perpetrators.

It is ironic that the dominator model, and the ways in which it articulates itself in the construction of contemporary societies, brutalizes everyone, even the oppressor. If one is taught violence, control, and domination as a way of life, one becomes brutalized by it, on all sides of the equation. In this way, even oppressors are victimized by the system and their own violent behaviours (whether physical, institutional, and/or cultural), since they cannot perceive of a more harmonious and compassionate existence. This is most readily evident in cases of family violence, especially in intensely patriarchal contexts where the role of father and provider turns on itself when the patriarch murders the entire family he is meant to protect;[10] so too, when fathers rape daughters as an expression of their right of ownership over female offspring. It is also commonly known that a large proportion of perpetrators of incest are themselves survivors of such violence. The same can be said about war, where no party involved in the conflict is left unscathed by the violence, murder, and carnage.[11]

Violence, murder, and rape exact a toll on the psyche of both perpetrator and survivor/victim, and everyone is (re-)brutalized in the process, even spectators, as those working to combat gender-based violence will attest.

Gender-based violence, as is commonly known, is not about sex or about conflict. It is about control and about power, in keeping with the dominator model. Gender-based violence is fundamentally premised on the ideology of male control over women's productive and reproductive powers, of male control over women's skills and resources, and especially of control over our power to produce future generations of producers. It is also about male control over women's sexuality, which is the key aspect of reproductive powers.

Women's productive powers include agricultural labour, wage labour in domestic service and other industries, as well as the informal sector, e.g., selling goods for small profits. Women's reproductive powers centre on our abilities to give birth and raise children; children who constitute the next generation of producers. Control over present productive capacity, as well as that of future generations, is of critical importance to patriarchy.

As consumers, women buy and use commodities in the home. Hence, women are also caught up in the endlessly repetitive task of using (if not producing) and reproducing by baking, cooking, etc. the commodity. Women also support the production process, apart from their "invaluable" roles as consumers through their domestic work, thus freeing men for labour in the production process and the public sphere. So too, women reproduce the labour force by bearing the next generation of workers and consumers, or surplus accumulators.

A critical psychological dimension of the control of women's sexuality is male insecurity about the origins of their children. Women become impregnated, and without complex and expensive medical tests, a man will never know certainly whether he is the actual father of his female partner's children. This is prominent in male anxiety over and control of female sexuality. But far more fundamental in this dominator model is the need to limit women's mobility and choice to ensure their consistent producing and reproducing of future generations of producers, reproducers, and surplus accumulators.

In addition, with the kind of identity formation discussed earlier of Self-Other, with women devalued as lesser beings than men, women's sexuality is also devalued and of less consequence than that of men.

According to some writers, there are four clear indicators of gender-based violence. In societies where these circumstances prevail, gender-based violence is more likely to occur in more severe forms. The indicators are: economic inequality; existing patterns of using physical violence to resolve conflicts; male authority and control over decision-making; and, restrictions on women's ability to leave the family setting.

All four indicators fit in with the dominator model. In this sense, since violence generically, and gender-based violence specifically, functions on the three axes of Galtung's triangle of violence/peace, it is imperative that attention be paid to factors that exacerbate and contribute to violence, from issues of development and poverty, to HIV/AIDS.

The construction of identities based on polar opposites, and creation of Self versus Other, engenders oppression, inequality, and violence. To get away from this, to get to the root of the violence in all societies, one needs to begin thinking of more harmonious ways of thinking, living, and being and move away from domination towards partnership.

While patriarchy, or the dominator model, has been around for thousands of years, evidence of societies modelled on the partnership or matriarchal model clearly shows that patriarchal rule is not inevitable, and that other more cooperative possibilities do exist. Historical reflections of beyond-patriarchal societies and beyond-patriarchal periods in societies help support a belief in, and conception of, forms of existence and societies that transcend patriarchal rule.

We should remind ourselves that change is possible. Think, for example, of Chinese foot binding, which is now extinct, thanks to socialism. The practice of facial scarring of women in the Sudan and some parts of South Africa, traditionally used as a form of adornment like modern-day cosmetics, is now almost extinct. Other practices from some ethnic groups in South Africa, like the severing of a finger or part of a finger, have been abolished. Female Genital Mutilation (FGM) is also being eradicated across Africa and throughout the world. Hence, no cultural practice is static or unchangeable.

I, therefore, believe that the key to success is to move away from the adversarial nature of the prevailing dominator system, with its inherent violence and oppression, and to move towards partnership by embracing the timeless values of *satyagraha* (non-violent resistance). In the words of Aung San Suu Kyi:

> If a people or a nation can reach their objectives by disciplined and peaceful means, it would be a most honourable and admirable achievement…. Those who have the greater strength should show restraint and tolerance towards those who have less strength…. Democracy is an ideology that allows everyone to stand up according to his beliefs. They should not be threatened or endangered…. Do not because of your greater strength be vengeful towards those who are of weaker strength. (1991: 201, 204)

Mainstreaming Matriarchies

The idea of "matriarchies" in the sense given above is becoming mainstream nowadays. In Europe especially, the most extraordinary thing happens when I speak at conferences, irrespective of its theme—conflict or security, or gender and gender-based violence—and I use the matriarchal model. I originally derived it from Marija Gimbutas (1991) and the popular Riane Eisler (1987), but more lately from Heide Goettner-Abendroth. Participants literally recoil at the mention of "matriarchies." Contrast this bizarre European reaction to a Cape Town weekly newspaper, which published an article on Goddesses, and continues to publish articles that reclaim feminine strength in divinity. This is how mainstream the idea of "matriarchies" is where I come from. I think part of the reason is how embedded various cultures, various societies, and various continents are in terms of how they benefit and buy into a system. I conclude with two of my poems:

conception

corner to corner
full-eyed poppies
wave smiling bollywood heads
on delicate necks
sending whiffs of inovulation
to pulsing orifi
on endless arcs

under cloudy glare
my irises blossom
madonnas' hearts
as my digits float
thru scarred ozone & oiled mantle
wildmaned with the wisdom
of wireless energy
that is you i all
& on...

immaculate

sacred

rows of trees like erect
stick soldiers devoid
of all green
life
throws a line
takes infinite points
so the gaze be/comes an
    orbiting sphere
encompassing intersecting
en/circles circles
till i spin & skid
pebble on pond
within a cosmic ocean
of unimaginable mysteries
crossing eyes fusing souls
with you
immortal divine beloved

Bernedette Muthien is based in Cape Town, South Africa, and is a member of the pan-African gender network, Amanitare, and served on the Executive Council of the International Peace Research Association (IPRA) 2000-2006, for which she was Editor of Publications. She is co-convenor of the Global Political Economy Commission, as well as an active member of the Conflict Resolution & Peacebuilding Commission. She also serves on a number of international advisory boards, including for two international journals, Human Security Studies *and* Queries *(Africa Editor). A former anti-apartheid activist who spent time in prisons during adolescence, Bernedette's life's work is centred on concrete consciousness transformation in the intersecting areas of genders and sexualities, justice and peace. She believes in accessible research and writing, and has published both academic and creative writing (especially poetry) locally and abroad. She is founding director of a registered NGO, called Engender: www.engender.org.za.*

[1]"I am because of you, you are because of me"; individuals and community exist by virtue of their interdependence.

[2]Alhazen is how he is known in the West. Born in Persia during 965, his name is Abu Ali al-Hasan ibn al-Haytham. According to Dick Teresi, Alhazen "was one of Islam's most influential thinkers" (2003: 223).

[3]According to the *Oxford English Reference Dictionary* "polarity" implies two poles with contrary qualities, two opposite tendencies/opinions, while "dualism"

implies being two-fold, duality; theory regarding two independent underlying principles, e.g., mind and matter, form and content, theological forces of good and evil equally balanced in the universe, Christ as both divine and human. So what we have is polarity and what we are striving (back) towards is duality. [Words seem to be missing between "being two-fold, duality; theory regarding two independent underlying principles." First, no logical connection is made between "two-fold" and "duality," nor is it clear what the function of the semicolon is, how it links what comes after with what comes before. Clarify]

[4]It is useful to note that Gimbutas and others, who have studied ancient Europe and the Middle East, assume timeframes going back to 6,000 BC at their earliest. However, more recent excavations in Africa (arguably the birthplace of humankind), including the very recent discoveries at the Sterkfontein Caves in South Africa, show evidence of an intelligent, creative, and cooperative Indigenous society dating back to more than 70,000 BC.

[5]As to the relations between women and men in Old Europe, the archaeological evidence suggests that there was no apparent social superiority of males over females, and, generally, the distribution of goods in the cemeteries of Old Europe points to an egalitarian and clearly non-patriarchal society (Baring and Cashford1991: 56; and Gimbutas1991).

[6]Tomasevski emphasizes that the subjugation of women did not begin "until the advent of the religions, and became more intense as the centuries rolled on" (include citation!)

[7]Galtung's work originated during the 1960s through the 1980s in development/underdevelopment studies, before he made his mark in Peace Studies during the 1990s. His conceptualization of violence drew on the work of other peace researchers, including Robert Johanssen.

[8]Article 2(a) – (c) of the Declaration on the Elimination of Violence Against Women, United Nations General Assembly Resolution 48/104, 20 Dec. 1993.

[9]Sec 1(ix)(b) of the Domestic Violence Act 116 of 1998.

[10]South Africa is an example of a particularly patriarchal society where family murder by a patriarch is routine, especially amongst sectors of society that are highly militarized and/or hierarchized, e.g., the police force.

[11]The excessively high levels of generic societal violence in South Africa, as well as the pandemic of gender-based violence in the country, is said to be one legacy of apartheid, where white boy-soldiers were systematically brutalized in a similar way to the liberation movements' (largely black) youthful combatants. The Vietnam War is said to have had similar effects in both the U.S. and Vietnam.

References

Baring, Anne, and Jules Cashford. 1991. *The Myth of the Goddess: Evolution of an Image*. London: Arkana.

Bennett, Jane. 2000. "Gender-Based Violence in South Africa." *The African Gender Institute Newsletter* 6, University of Cape Town.

Eisler, Riane. 1987. *The Chalice and The Blade: Our History, Our Future.* San Francisco: HarperOne.

Flinders, Carol Lee. 2002. *The Values of Belonging: Rediscovering Balance, Mutuality, Intuition, and Wholeness in a Competitive World.* New York: Harper Collins.

Flinders, Carol Lee. 2002. *Rebalancing the World: Why Women Belong and Men Compete and How to Restore the Ancient Equilibrium.* New York: Harper Collins.

Galtung, Johan. 1996. *Peace by Peaceful Means: Peace and Conflict, Development and Civilization.* London: Sage

Gimbutas, Marija. 1991. *The Civilization of the Goddess: The World of Old Europe.* Ed. Joan Marler. San Francisco: HarperSanFrancisco.

Goettner-Abendroth, Heide. 2004. "Matriarchal Society: Definition and Theory." Ed. Genevieve Vaughan. *The Gift.* Rome: Athanor Books.

Keepin, Will. 2005. "The Fractal Nature of Consciousness." Paper presented at the International Symposium on Science and Mysticism, Indian Institute for Science and Religion, Pune, India, 2-6 January .

Teresi, Dick. 2003. Lost Discoveries: *The Ancient Roots of Modern Science – from the Babylonians to the Maya.* New York: Simon & Schuster.

Tomasevski, Katarina. 1993. *Women and Human Rights.* London: Zed Books.

Tutu, Desmond Mpilo. 1999. *No Future Without Forgiveness.* New York, London: Image Doubleday.

Uzuegbunam, Anthonia. 2001. "Conflict Management Implications of Woman-Woman Marriage among the Igbos of Nigeria." WAAD Third International Conference, Antananarivo, Madagascar, 8-17 October .

HÉLÈNE CLAUDOT-HAWAD

"We Are the Shelter and the Protection"

The Representation of Gender Among the Tuaregs

The condition of these people is a curious thing and their manner of living strange. For the men are not jealous; none of them identifies his descent with that of his father, but rather with that of his maternal uncle; only the sister's sons inherit.... I have seen this only among pagans.... But these people are Muslims.... As for their women, they have absolutely no modesty; in front of their menfolk, they remain totally unveiled....

—Ibn Battuta 1356 (qtd. in Cuoq 1975: 497)

Ever since medieval times, Arab-speaking travellers have regarded the veiled nomads of the Sahara, ancestors of today's Tuaregs and Moors, as strange and exotic figures. These observers were both surprised and shocked by such a society with its seemingly contradictory features—the liberal attitudes of the women and the matrilineal nature of filiation and succession—which co-existed with Islam. Their bewilderment was complete when they were faced with the relationship between men and women. In this they found but further proof of a corrupt and barbaric morality caused, they surmised, by an uncompleted or deformed religious conversion. One day in the year 1352, for example, Ibn Battuta of Tangiers visited a Massufa family from Walata. He was scandalized by the scene before him. While the husband sat peacefully on the rug, his wife was ensconced on the couple's bed, deep in conversation with another man. Profoundly shocked, their guest hastily withdrew, even though his host explained that: "Among our people the relations between men and women are proper and honourable. They arouse no suspicion at all. [Our women] are not like those in your country" (qtd. in Cuoq 1975: 296).

In the nineteenth century, however, these same distinctive features were reinterpreted by European observers as marks of knightly refinement. As such, they served to support another fantastic theory: these people must necessarily be of non-African origin and their social behaviour influenced by Christianity. The French explorer Henri Duveyrier (1865), speaking of the Kel Ahaggar Tuaregs, stated that traces of Christianity are obvious in Tuareg cutoms: monogamy, the respect for women, the horror of stealing and lying, the keeping of one's word.

In their very opposition, these readings tell us more about the foreign observers' own values and social rules than they do about the actual meaning of the practices they describe. What, in fact, does it mean in Tuareg society to be a woman or a man? What images, roles, and standards, what reciprocal rights and duties, what social and symbolic functions, are evoked by these categories? I will try to convey the nature of these categories, their significance, and their modern manifestations by putting them into the context from which they grew and by using data gleaned from the Ahaggar (Algeria), the Aïr (Niger) and the Arabanda (Mali).

Tuareg speech often links the notion of society to that of a "body" (*taghasa*) whose organs are distinct but interdependent. At the end of the nineteenth century, when French colonial troops arrived in the Sahara, the Tuaregs described themselves as a political body composed of four large entities with complex interconnections—in the Northeast the Kel Ajjer, in the Northwest the Kel Ahaggar, in the Southeast the Kel Ayr, and, in the Southwest the Kel Tademmekat—to which could be added a fifth grouping still in a formative stage, the Tagaraygarayt, or " the middle," in a political rather than geographical sense.

This nomadic society is known for its warrior skills and for the originality of its economy, based notably on a remarkable aptitude for mobility in an arid environment with fragile natural resources. Before colonization, it controlled vast territories in the Sahara and the Sahel. During the 1960s, the area where the Tuaregs lived was divided between five new States, due to the de-colonization process: Libya, Algeria, Niger, Mali, and the Upper Volta (the modern Burkina Faso). Several uprisings, from colonial days to the present (the most recent dating from the 1990s in Niger and Mali), have marked the stages of what many Tuaregs feel to be the mutilation of their body, which has been progressively amputated, chopped into pieces, and forced into immobility.

This notion of a "body," with the organic links it implies between the several parts that make up the whole, is reflected in the Tuaregs' theory of social positions and the roles associated with gender.

Tuareg cosmogonic interpretations provide a powerful configuration of the distinction between the sexes and the way in which this distinction is conceptualized and internalized in the collective imagination. Several versions of the origins of the world exist, elaborated by the "initiated" (*imeyawen*), meaning those enlightened people who, in the ascending stages of knowledge, have reached what is considered to be the highest level. These stories are, therefore, not rigid and unchanging, still less are they dogmas, but rather they are theories constructed by those who have attained the realm of this abstract and philosophic knowledge. Thus, some variations of interpretation are to be found; these relate more to form than to content, expressing in varied metaphorical terms an original storyline based on a certain number of similar principles.[1] Let us take here one of these versions, current among the Ikazkazen, before analyzing its main themes.

The Invention of Difference

In the beginning, according to this theory, there was a single being, a single body, encompassing time and space, female and male, the same yet different. The body of this indistinct whole descended through the void and landed on a vague expanse, an undefined space, where it began to move, advancing first towards the East, then towards the North, then the South, next towards the top and finally towards the bottom. At each move, at each point of contact with this unknown space, the body left behind a part of itself. In the first two stages, it set down its heaviest and fullest base material, containing its primordial essence, solid, compact, inert, autonomous, and concentrated. This part of the body was the female part—which broke down in the East into the female-female and in the North into the male-female—whilst the next two stages were associated with the male part, the West being the female-male and the South the male-male. The movement then shifted upwards (the male), and finished by heading downwards (the female), marking the end of the journey. Thus, the motion came full circle, back to the first stage where the vague body sprang forth from the heights of the cosmos. This is why the female, marking the bottom point in this remarkable journey, is, in absolute terms, the top; that is, the point of departure for the initial cycle, and, of all future cycles.

Despite the spreading of the parts, it is still one single body that has set down its lower end and sent forth its extremities. The first part to be set down represents the hard core, the solid base, the inner depths from which a being springs and whence it can withdraw. The other part, lighter and more peripheral, is ever moving, pursuing its forward path.

In this way, during what one might call the "founding cosmic landing," female and male become separate, and time and space are created. The female pole is defined by its precedence, its density, its stability, and completeness in contrast to the male pole that comes after and seems less substantial, allowing itself to be taken further by the initial thrust. But both parts belong to the same whole and are totally interdependent, unable to exist one without the other.

This cosmogonic view sheds light on several essential principles which are fundamental to the Tuaregs' thought symbolism: the first is that the female *came before* the male; the second is that *difference is essential* for progress, that is, for existence in time and space; the third is that *the parts which make up the whole are complementary.*

Upon these three premises are based the Tuareg's different theories of perceiving and classifying the universe, society, individuals, and objects into a complex philosophical system which can be termed holistic, dialectic, and dynamic. Depending on the relative importance given to each of the three initial propositions, several ways of thinking have arisen and are juxtaposed, fuelling the collective debates which take place, sometimes in ritualistic form in oratory jousts between differing protagonists.

Several concrete examples will serve to demonstrate how this matrix of images,

HÉLÈNE CLAUDOT-HAWAD

out of which is constructed an intelligible and deeply internalized model of the world, materializes in various aspects of Tuareg social life.

The Precedence of the Female

Whether descent is matrilineal (as is the case with the majority of Tuareg groupings) or patrilineal, the terms of kinship are remarkably matri-centred[2] and take descent from the mother above that from the father.[3] Thus, a "maternal uncle" is termed literally the "son of the mother's mother" (amalgamated phonetically into *añat ma*); a brother and sister call each other their "mother's children" (*añaten*); the "nephew" and "niece" of a man can be described respectively as the son or daughter of the mother's daughter (*ag elet ma* and *ulet elet ma*). Let us note that a man may also designate his "nephew" as *tégéhé* (*tégézé, tégéshé*) depending on the dialect form), a significant classification in that this term is also used for a part of the body, the "pelvis," linking the back to the belly, and for a vast political area leaguing several confederations of tribes.[4] In contrast, when a woman speaks of the next generation she calls all her descendants, direct or indirect, by the same term, her "children" (*arawen* or *bararen*).

We have seen above how the female element intervenes right from the first mythic stage of the beginnings of the world. In the same way, by making reference to an original female category, a fundamental entity: *ma*, the "mother," children learn to define their close social environment. They learn which relatives with whom they are most comfortable, to whom is directed their affection and with whom they identify. Further, they learn whose direct heirs they are, in family name, in goods, and in powers.

Relationships on the maternal side dictate the line by which rights and inalienable property are transmitted, which in turn allows the community to literally "feed" itself. Indeed, this inheritance from the mother's side is expressed in a food metaphor, that is, "living milk" (*akh iddaren*). Several terms exist to describe this maternal descent, all stressing its encompassing, enveloping, protective, and stabilizing function. The metaphors used may be anatomical, geographical, or architectural: for instance *tasa*, the "belly" (as opposed to *aruri*, the "back," meaning also paternal relatives); *abatul*, the "hollow" or any hole in the ground able, for instance, to catch seeds blown by the wind; *ébawél*, the "bosom"; *témet*, the "womb"; *ehan*, the "tent" or "home" which provides shelter, all notions contrasting with *ténéré*, the desert, or *essuf*, which means the untamed and threatening outer regions, that is, the unknown world.

The idea of the precedence of the female can also be found in descriptions of the founding of Tuareg groups. Families, tribes, confederations, even the whole society trace back their lineage more or less fictionally to ancestors who are nearly all women. In these tales about their origins, the husbands of the founding ancestors were generally unknown, following a pattern that is widespread in the whole Berber area. When the marriage partners did appear, it was always in a sub-human form, be it as *kel essuf*, or genies, weird beings belonging to the invis-

162

ible world, the "void" (*essuf*), the "desert" (*ténéré*), or as savages, brutish, peaceful nonentities in an apparently empty region. These men, belonging to the "void," are remarkable for their lack of existence, humanity, and culture, in contrast to the women, who are the creators of the socialized, humanized, and civilized world. This representation has logical implications for symbolism, ritual, and social practice to which I will turnbelow.

A Plural World

The cosmogonic example we have analyzed above shows that if the construction of the world is commenced by the female, life itself is based on plurality. Existence only begins where there is diversity. Indeed, the world as we know it, defined in time and space, is born when the unity of its original substance—itself eternal—splits into at least two distinct parts.

This is why, from the Tuareg viewpoint, each element, each identifiable being in known space necessarily has an *alter ego* in the realm of the unknown. It is only possible to apprehend reality in all its diverse forms in relation to this twin concept, wherein the universe appears to be organized along two complementary but antagonistic axes.

In this context, the distinction between female and male is only one of many ways in which the fundamental duality of world order is expressed.[5] It is the equivalent, but on a different level, to the central antithesis between the "internal" and the "external" or between the "home" and the "desert." Here woman belongs to the known, ordered, comprehensible, civilized, and protecting world, as opposed to man, who, unpredictable, wild, and dangerous, is associated with the unexplored and uncultivated space.

The essential difference between the female and the male is inculcated into Tuareg children from a very early age. It is expressed in every aspect of social life, highlighted in moral tales, in rules of conduct, and in rituals.

Let us take baptism, for example, which is performed seven days after birth. The scale of the ceremony and the number of those attending vary according to the sex of the baby. In the Aïr, for the baptism of a baby girl, only the mother's close female relatives are present, whereas for a boy the men of the family also attend and the event is celebrated with an animal sacrifice (*taghtest*). But this difference in treatment has a meaning quite other than that assumed perhaps at first glance by an observer, who could see in it the proof of the social inferiority of the female to the male. In fact, the boy is felt to be somebody belonging to the "outside," thus potentially dangerous; this is why the boy will never be called directly by his name (in the same way that one avoids naming a wild and threatening animal), but by a term of kinship that minimizes his new, "foreign," presence among the group of relatives. In contrast, the baby girl's name is used directly, since she is not perceived as an "external" element to be gradually and cautiously integrated into the home. Thus, a lack of need for rituals in her case.

From this we can see the image that Tuareg society has of itself as a community revolving around an "internal" core which is female and matrilineal, ever on its guard against threats from the "exterior" represented by the men brought in to circulate between the lines of descent.

In the same way, the move into adulthood, which takes place a few years after puberty, is accompanied for the girl by a progressive change in dress, but gives rise to no collective celebration beyond the immediate family. The young man, by contrast, has to pass a certain number of tests, each of which consists in a confrontation with the "adverse world," whether natural, metaphysical, social, or political. Thus, the young man has to confront the desert and cope with its dangers—thirst, hunger, loss of direction, loneliness—by using his knowledge and psychological strengths, as well as his cultural and spiritual resources. He has to prove his ability to manage relations with the outside world without being destabilized or alienated. Then, in the course of a ceremony attended by both his female and male relatives, he solemnly receives the veil, the sword, and all the attributes of a man of honour (a good horse or camel, trousers clasped at the waist by a leather thong, etc.). The veil, which is the symbol of his honour and of his humanity, conceals and contains his savage nature. Further, it guarantees control over his male identity, permitting him to live in the female world without endangering society.

For her part, the young woman learns to play her role as "protector" of her lineage by suiting her actions to her function: she must not only defend the reputation of her home, but increase it, knowing for example how to receive guests generously, how to be dazzling in company using her wit, intelligence, culture, and beauty; in a word, knowing how to shine. Her ability to attract is measured in the numbers of visitors, admirers, and suitors who press around her. The fortunate man who gains her favour by distinguishing himself in oratory and poetic jousts or by his warrior exploits, will be invited to join her in her tent. The more rivals there are, the more the woman's powers of attraction become established, helping to increase her reputation and both her own, and her family's, prestige.

One can understand in this context that the "freedom of women" described by foreign travellers fits into a conceptual and moral framework that, though perfectly strict and coherent, differs in every detail from that constructed by monotheistic religions, whether Islamic or Christian.

In order to undertake their preeminent role, the young women receive a complex education. From early childhood, as the seventy-year-old Ghayshena welet Akedima of the Ikazkazen said in 1989,

> we learn that the world is but leaves swirling behind us. We are the shelter and the protection that attracts them.... Woman walks majestically towards the world and condenses it into her own manners, that the world may swirl behind her and that she shall not swirl behind the world.

Thus, although of the same universal human kind, female and male identities are distinct. The female, or "internal," puts down roots for permanence, stability, and sameness. The male, or "external," is part of the unknown, is about change, mobility, and difference.

It is assumed as a fundamental principle that the universe, the body, and society have the same nature, allowing the establishment between these domains of an infinite number of correspondences that define the originality of each part. Woman equates to the inner realm, to the night and the darkness, the dense, the full, the deep, the damp, to the belly, the steady, the cold. In contrast, Man is associated with the outside world, with daylight and clarity, with the void, the dry, the back, with motion, and with heat.

Duality as a Stimulus

These contrasts have an essential function from the Tuareg point of view. They are the source of dynamism. It is this very tension between dissimilar and competing elements that sets them in motion and propels them on a forward trajectory. The contrasting identities clash and thwart each other in a constant state of rivalry that forces them to surpass themselves and advance. Certain codes of behaviour serve to express this rivalry (rendered in Tuareg by the notion of "racing") which appears in every domain, formal or not, in which the pairs meet (family occasions, poetry evenings, political meetings, celebrations, etc.).

A concrete example on the male side may serve to illustrate this. A man of honour, in front of his peers, adopts a pose characterized by a complete stillness of the body, an absolute mastery of all emotion, a total veiling of the face, which includes the eyes, concealed behind a piece of fabric shaped like a visor. Through this extreme restraint, the absolute control of himself, the man displays the high level of his moral principles and his social standing. But, in adopting this imperturbable behaviour, is he not moving very close to the female temperament, mimicking its qualities of stability, density, and independence from external factors? Whereas an individual who behaves in a manner generally considered to be masculine, with flexibility, mobility, reactivity, and aggression, loses respect and is deemed less honourable.

This fact sheds light on two theses: one is that competition transforms the being, permitting it to exceed and transcend its natural state. The other refers back to the theory that proposes that the closest element to the cosmic whole, that is to say perfection (in this case social), is the female: which is why, in his search for excellence, man tries to "feminize" his attitude.

The rivalry between woman and man is revealed in a particularly spectacular way in the wedding ceremony. Even before the knot is tied, indeed, there is a confrontation between the pair; first, between the families preparing for the union, and second, between the future couple. One of the high points of the wedding is, thus, the moment when the fiancée leaves her parents' home to go the nuptial tent. The female procession surrounding her confronts the bridegroom's male escort in a duel of poetry and song where each group champions the merits of its protégé. Both present the marriage as a bad deal. The arguments put forward by the opposing sides against the union reach fever pitch, through a language that is emphatic, sarcastic, sometimes crude and scatological. As the discussion gets more heated, the women try to seize the headdresses of the bridegroom and his representatives, while the men strive to pull off one of the bride's or her companions' bracelets. When one of the two groups succeeds, the battle is over and calm is restored.

In this case, the clash between opposites leads to a development of the crisis, which simmers as soon as one camp takes possession of something belonging to the opponent, thus provoking an exchange (albeit an imposed one).

But the rivalry can also become dangerous and destabilizing if it leads to the annihilation or the weakening of one side in favour of the other, which would result in the suppression of the stimulating duality, a reduction to a monistic structure, and a sinking into immobility. In order to avoid such extremes, it is necessary to ensure constantly that the balance between the two parties is maintained, a concern addressed by ritual and symbolic activities as well as by social institutions.

The Search for Balance

In practice, a return to harmonious relations necessitates mutual concessions, exchanges symbolized in the attempt by the woman to seize the man's headdress and in his taking of her bracelet. Each of them, in appropriating a symbolic part of the other, has evolved and helped his or her partner to evolve also. Touching the top of the bridegroom's head, this is to say, his mind, the volatile element of his body, is a way in which the woman can capture for herself the power to be mobile. The seizure of the female bracelet (*asender*), the very symbol of the culture, is a way in which the man gains the stability required to strengthen him.

The same logical pattern that can be seen in the ritual relationship between men and women is apparent in how they run society, the family, politics, the natural environment, and the spirit realm, based on the need for difference and competition, and counterbalanced by the need for harmony. The exchange between the partners allows for this restoration of a balance; one that is constantly threatened.

If one of the poles of this duality disappears by accident, the only way to resolve the crisis is to recreate the missing part from within the remaining unit. In the field of gender, there are numerous examples to show that when men do not assume their role, it is women who take their place, be it on the battlefield or in the political arena. This allows us to understand the flexibility of the system and the impossibility of fixing in stone the opposing categories. The roles of the opposites, far from being fixed, are determined interactively. Their natures are relative and reversible. The most important would seem to be the preservation of the stimulating competition between partners and, thus, the maintenance of the balance between the different parts of the whole.

Ultimately, the situation most dreaded by this thought-system is a unicity of structure, encompassing only identical and equal elements, a configuration that would end in immobility and extinction.

There are several procedures by which harmony can be restored. On the whole it is a matter of compensating for, or avoiding altogether, an excess of sameness by associating it with the different.

Let us take a very concrete example of this from the realm of everyday clothing. The most prized form of Tuareg dress in the Aïr, for both men and women, consists of wearing one smock or *tikatkaten* (open at the sides) on top of another. The first is white, and the second, which is indigo, is put on over it, with the inside corners elegantly tucked up over the outside ones at arm level. Now, in the spectrum of colours, the female, who is also the internal, is equated with deep, dense, opaque colours like black or indigo. The male, who is the external, corresponds to transparent and pale colours like white and yellow. It is in order to provide a counterbalance to natural order (woman internal and man external) that the *tikatkaten* are put on in the opposite order. To reproduce an identical image of the man/woman pair might create an excess that could be detrimental to general harmony.

Reaching Beyond the Boundaries

Social life is a journey marked out in stages that must be passed through by re-nouncing a part of oneself, of one's originality, of one's difference, symbolically sacrificed in order to avoid separation from the other. This idea is associated with the crucial notion of "sacrifice" (*ekud*) in this society.[6] \

But how can the absolutely fundamental distinction between female and male, upon which is founded the very fabric of social order, be surmounted and at what price? In what is termed traditional Tuareg society, the ultimate offence for a man is to appear in public without his veil or his trousers. Exhibiting anything that calls to mind his membership of a savage, animal, external world, like a beard, moustache, or genitals, is unseemly and threatens the social order.

In contrast, for a woman to expose her face or breasts is permissible. Moreover, her nakedness, though improper to expose completely, is not seen to be bestial or aggressive like a man's; the worst eventuality is that the woman will be made vulnerable by being deprived of the protection of her clothes.

To leave one's head uncovered, one's hair unplaited, or to wear men's trousers are ways in which women, particularly middle-aged women, can clearly refute the social order. In the same way, in terms of behaviour, meaningful transgres-sions would be, for instance, to shout in public, to be aggressive, to be restless and disorganized, to walk briskly or fast, to refuse the hospitality due to guests (which is seen as a very serious deviation).

These transgressions of the Tuaregs' standard rules of behaviour can be inter-preted in several ways. The state of a man without his veil reflects several possible scenarios. The first of these is linked to a figure from past society, the slave, who had no place in the competition of free men. Belonging to the household, the slave was part of the female domain; he was among the "dishes," that is, with access to the fundamental intimacy of the family. This is why, once he had acquired Tuareg humanities (meaning language and culture) and was given his freedom, he was presented with the veil in a ceremony identical to that organized for the adolescent boy, but with one difference: because of his "female" nature, it was not necessary for him to spend seven days in solitude as it was for the freeborn youth.[7]

A second scenario is that in which a madman or a simpleton might involuntarily break the rules of good conduct.

A third possibility is the expression of an assumed rebellion against, and challenging of, existing standards. For example, Kawsen of the Aïr Ikazkazen, leader of the war waged against the French colonial army from 1915 to 1918, imposed a new model of a man of honour, one who would be capable of renouncing the heroic image of the warrior remaining upon the battlefield until victory or death. Instead, the warrior should consent to continue the struggle by other, very diverse means previously judged "inglorious," by using cunning to counter a much better armed enemy. As affirmation of this direct challenge to ancient custom, he appeared before them without his veil.

A final hypothesis would be that of a sublimation or transcending of the polarities in the world below. The man who is not wearing his veil or even his trousers, who chooses to wear instead an unstitched piece of material around his waist, is here a person from the "in-between," the place between two worlds, who, like the initiated or the holy man (*aggag, afaqir, aneslim*), is the link with the invisible realm. As such, he places himself above the rules of society, and thus, above the distinction between the sexes. He no longer needs his male attributes (veil, weapons, trousers).[8]

We come back to the idea that the process by which man may attain perfection is through the neutralization of his dangerous masculinity, which is linked to the unknown, by a symbolic "feminization" that allows him to understand the two natures or two expressions of the difference between the sexes, and, more widely, between the internal and the external. He goes beyond this distinction. Proceeding stage by stage, he finally reaches the far-distant state of the wise man, placed above all social rules and acting as intermediary between vaster spheres.[9]

In contrast, the opposite situation, where, for example, a woman puts on masculine trousers, is not seen in the same light. This eccentric dress behaviour is the same as taking up arms on the battlefield or as becoming chief. Her meaning is quite unequivocally that men are incapable of assuming their role and that she must take their place.[10] But this behaviour does not imply the surmounting of contingencies, that is, her elevation to the female state, where culture counterbalances rough nature, and thus has no need to be tampered with, moulded, or modified for society to be perpetuated.

Expanding Balances

Finally, it is clear that the Tuareg example contradicts the theory that male domi-nance over women is universal. This case also demonstrates just how inadequate are those concepts generally used to analyze and evaluate the "quality" or nature of the relationship between men and women, that is, notions of equality and inequality, if we are to understand those systems that are holistic rather than individualistic, following anthropologist Louis Dumont's analysis (1983).

Among the Tuaregs, the connections set up between the genders are relation-ships that are mutually effective, different but complementary, and of relative equivalence. The principle of balance between these identities, dissimilar yet of similar strength, is not in itself sufficient to characterize the social order, which is built also upon a dynamic conception of social positions. For these latter are merely the successive steps of a universal ascending journey, defining a hierarchi-cal axis on which the precedence of the female over the male (or the older over the younger, the noble over his protégé) is taken for granted. Put differently, in the representation of universal order, it is the "time" factor that leads to the for-mulation of a hierarchical principle. But in this system, neither position nor role is fixed or absolute. All is relative, within a dynamic framework that continually modifies the vertical order of the hierarchy as it does the horizontal order of equivalencies.

It is essential to preserve the bi- or pluri- polarity which underpins the part-nership. Some writers use the term "diarchy" (Fox 1988). In the Tuareg case, the term "polyarchy" would seem more appropriate; it has the advantage of not specifying the number of partners involved in the system, which might equally be described as "dialogical."

An interesting link may be established between this conceptualization of social order and two factors which again underline the originality of Tuareg society: homosexual practices are not recorded in the nomadic milieu[11] and conjugal violence is extremely rare. One might see in this an avoidance of those situations considered threatening to social order by their propensity to unbalance it either through an excess of sameness, or by the destruction of the link between equiva-lent parts of the whole. These facts also show that it would be wrong to suppose that the distinction between the sexes leads necessarily to sexism.

In conclusion, the Tuareg mechanism for understanding the world advocates as an ideal the nomadic model, the "moving on" which, in learning how to in-teract with other spheres, forces progress and growth, an advance at once social, psychological, and spiritual. In order to blossom, one must thus become, in the words of the poet, a "trawler of horizons" (Hawad 1998) —one who discovers new angles of vision, who goes beyond the bounds, who can reconcile the nar-row identities which divide the world, and who continues to open up the realms of the unknown.

Translation by Elizabeth Corp

Hélène Claudot-Hawad is an anthropologist working in the Research Institute of the Muslim and Arabic World (IREMAM) in Aix-en-Provence, which is part of the National Centre for Scientific Research (CNRS) in France. She specializes in the Tuareg world, a society that has been split between five States (Mali, Algeria, Niger, Burkina Faso, and Libya) since the 1960s. Her books focus on the original socio-political organization of the Tuareg, their cultural and ritual manifestations, and the different ways in which, in the modern context, the Tuareg have been trying to extend, change, or accommodate their nomadism. She has translated the work of the Tuareg writer Hawad and other contemporary Tuareg poets.

[1]So that what appears at the beginning of our world as a body of magma born from the vast matter of the universe can also be described in an aquatic setting as a drop of water detached from the ocean-universe.

[2]For a detailed analysis of Tuareg kinship terms, see Claudot-Hawad (1982); Brock (1983); Bernus et al. (1986). The terms quoted in the following example are in *tamahaq* (the other dialect forms being the *tamajaq* and *tamashaq*).

[3]The semantic relationship established by certain speakers between *abba*, "papa" and *aba*, "there is not"—whatever its linguistic validity—is sociologically significant.

[4]For the names given to the body politic and its units, see Claudot-Hawad 1990.

[5]Or what some writers working on other cultural areas call the "dyad"; see Fox (1988); Du (2002).

[6] For the links between élite, honour, and sacrifice, see H. Claudot-Hawad (2001), especially Chapter 6.

[7]On this subject, see Claudot-Hawad (2000).

[8]On this subject, see Claudot-Hawad (1996).

[9]It is possible to see here, as certain writers have done in dealing with other societies, a model of symbolic androgyny demonstrating an ideal of autonomy inherent in every group (see, for example, Glowczewski 2001: 139).

[10]See, for example, the recent case, in the 1990s, of the *tishamuren*, women who took part in the *teshumara*, a movement of protest and subsequent armed uprising among the Tuaregs in Niger and Mali (see, for example, Hawad 1990; Claudot-Hawad and Hawad 1983).

[11]As opposed to zoophylia, a recorded, albeit highly shameful practice.

References

Bernus S., P. Bonte, L. Brock, and H. Claudot, eds. 1986. *Le fils et le neveu: Jeux et enjeu de la parenté touarègue.* Cambridge/Paris: Cambridge University Press.

Brock, L. 1983. *The Tamejjirt: Kinship and Social History in a Tuareg Community.* Unpublished Dissertation, Columbia University, U.S.A.

Claudot-Hawad, Hélène. 1982. *La sémantique au service de l'anthropologie. Re-*

cherchem-méthodologique et application à l'étude de la parenté chez les Touaregs de l'Ahaggar. Paris: CNRS.

Claudot-Hawad, Hélène. 1984. "Femme idéale et femmes sociales chez les Touaregs de l'Ahaggar." *Production pastorale et société* 14: 93-105.

Claudot-Hawad, Hélène. 1989. "Femmes touarègues et pouvoir politique." *Peuples méditerranéens* 48/49.

Claudot-Hawad, Hélène. 1990. "Honneur et politique. Les choix stratégiques des Touaregs durant la colonisation." *Revue du Monde musulman et de la Méditerranée* 57: 11-47.

Claudot-Hawad, Hélène. 1993a. *Les Touaregs: Portrait en fragments*. Aix-en-Provence: Edisud.

Claudot-Hawad, Hélène. 1993b. "La coutume absente ou les métamorphoses contemporainesmdu politique chez les Touaregs." *Le politique dans l'histoire touarègue*. Aix-en-Provence, *Cahiers de l'IREMAM*. 67-86.

Claudot-Hawad, Hélène. 1994. "Cosmogonie touarègue."*Encyclopédie berbère*. Aix-en-Provence: Edisud. 2137-2138

Claudot-Hawad, Hélène. 1996. "Personnages de l'entre-deux: l'initié, l'*aggag*, l'*énad*, le soufi…." *Touaregs et autres Sahariens entre plusieurs mondes. Définitions et redéfinitions de soi et des autres*. Ed. H. Claudot-Hawad. Aix-en-Provence: IREMAM/Edisud.

Claudot-Hawad, Hélène. 2000. "Captif sauvage, esclave enfant, affranchi cousin… La mobilité statutaire chez les Touareg." *Groupes serviles au Sahara*, Ed. M. Villasante-de Beauvais. Paris: CNRS.

Claudot-Hawad, Hélène. 2001. *"Eperonner le monde."Nomadisme, cosmos et politique chez les Touaregs,* Aix-en-Provence: Edisud.

Claudot-Hawad, Hélène, (dir.). 2002. *Voyager d'un point de vue nomade*. Paris: Editions Paris-Méditerranée.

Claudot-Hawad, Hélène. 1987. "Le lait nourricier de la société ou la prolongation de soi chez les Touaregs." *Hériter en pays musulman*. Ed. M. Gast. Paris: CNRS.

Claudot-Hawad, Hélène, ed. 1996a. *Touaregs, Voix solitaires sous l'horizon confisqué*. Paris: Ethnies.

Claudot-Hawad, Hélène. 1996b. *Tourne-tête, le pays déchiqueté. Chants et poèmes touaregs derésistance (1985-1995)*. LaBouilladisse, Amara.

Claudot-Hawad, H. and Hawad. 1983. "Ebawel/essuf, les notions d'"intérieur' et d'"extérieur'chez les Touaregs." *L'Uomo* n°2, Rome.

Cuoq, J. M. 1975. *Recueil des sources arabes concernant l'Afrique Occidentale du VIIIe au XVIe siècle (Bilâd al-Sûdân)*. Paris: CNRS.

Du, Shanshan. 2002. *Chopsticks Only Work in Pairs: Gender Unity and Gender Equality Among the Lahu of Southwest China*. New York: Columbia University Press.

Dumont, H. 1983. *Essais sur l'individualisme. Une perspective anthropologique sur l'idéologie moderne*. Paris: Seuil.

Duveyrier, H. 1864. *Les Touaregs du Nord*. Paris: Challamel Aîné.

Figueiredo, C. 2001. "La conceptualisation du chaud et du froid. Systèmes d'éducation et relations hommes/femmes chez les Touaregs." (Imedédaghen et Kel Adagh, Mali). *Thèse de IIIe cycle*. Paris: EHESS.

Figueiredo, C. 2002. "Le voyage en 'chaud' et 'froid': conceptions thermiques des Touareg." *Voyager d'un point de vue nomade*. Ed. H. Claudot-Hawad. Paris: Editions Paris-Méditerranée. 137-144.

Foucauld C. de and A. Calassanti-Motylinski. 1984. *Textes touaregs en prose*. (Édition critique et traduction par S. Chaker, H. Claudot, M. Gast.) Aix-en-Provence: Edisud.

Fox, J. 1988. *To Speak in Pairs*. Cambridge: Cambridge University Press.

Glowczewski, B. 2001. "Loi des hommes, loi des femmes: identité sexuelle et identité aborigène en Australie." *Sexe relatif ou sexe absolu?* Eds. C. Alès & C. Barraud. Paris: MSH. 135-155.

Hawad. 1990. "La *teshumara*, antidote de l'Etat." *Touaregs. Exil et résistance*. Ed. H. Claudot-Hawad. Paris: Edisud.

Hawad. 1998. *Les Haleurs d'Horizon*. Paris: Edition Maeght.

Welet, Elghelas K. 1996. "Ma maison est ma nation qui est la maison du monde entier." *Voix solitaires sous l'horizon confisqué*. Eds. H. Claudot-Hawad and Hawad. Paris: Ethnies. 191-196.

Welet, Halatine F. 1996. "L'abandon des privilèges. Parcours d'une femme touarègue dans lanModernité." *Repenser l'école*. Paris: Ethnies. 29-38.

FATIMATA OUALET HALATINE

A Tuareg Woman's Journey Towards Modernity

By the time I was born my parents had moved into the town of Goundam, but the family's roots were in the bush. Like my grandfather, my mother owned a large herd: she and my sister had five hundred head of cattle between them. My father was an intellectual, a teacher of Arabic. He gave lessons and he travelled all over the area to teach his pupils. What really surprised me was the total change in my life from the cosseted little Tuareg girl that I was, required to do no work at all, into the woman I am today, a busy working woman with no time off at all, not even on weekends.

I was my father's eldest daughter and was cherished because I was the first. I was like a friend and confidante to my mother. I was privileged to receive both a girl's and a boy's education. It's very special being the eldest child. You become responsible at an early age because you have to look after your younger siblings.

At that time we had a lot of servants. Any hard work was always done by the men. My father and mother came from a background where this was normal, and when Independence came our servants didn't leave us. They were attached to us and even now we still have a close relationship with them, almost as if they were family.

A Love of Learning

I started my education in a French school and later I went for a time to the *medersa* (Koranic school). My father was a progressive thinker, but my mother's family was against going to school. They found it bizarre. Later, in our third school year, when our mother saw that my sisters and I were really committed, she began to support us, agreeing to sell off her herd bit by bit to pay for our education, so that nothing would stop us from working hard, or turn us against our schooling: she didn't want men to distract us, for us to go to the bad or be put off. It was wonderful to see how she changed, how she pursued her ideals.

While I was attending school, I also went to the *medersa*. My father thought that knowledge was something more than just religion. For him, knowledge can be found in all cultures and should be looked for everywhere, while at the same time you should practice your religion, though not in a fanatical way.

We Kel Intesar women received religious education, but less so than the men. There were actually some women in our group who were teachers: they travelled and went to Mecca, or even to places like Azawagh and Chad to bring back Debakar pupils who would stay two, three or four years with them before returning home with their learning.

When I was little, I liked school because I enjoyed mathematics and logic. I was always near the top of the class. I had no other ambition at the time. I simply had a love of learning. I had no ambition to marry either, or to do anything else. It was only later that I thought about having a profession, and in fact I chose lengthy study courses because I didn't think I would ever need to have a job or a means of earning money. Basically gaining culture and knowledge was the only thing that was important to me at the time. Possibly I didn't think about earning my living because I was well provided for. It was when I started work that I began to have other ambitions, and to want to find a job that was more suited to me.

I went to a teacher training college. After that I went to France to study health, nutrition and home economics.

My Independent Journey

I became interested in the condition of women. It seemed to me that French women were far more exploited than Tuareg women, and that was how I became a feminist. I also discovered that people spoke about the exploitation of African women, but that nobody knew about my own society, where the women have a privileged position. In France, I was too disgusted even to attend classes, because no-one listened to me or paid any attention to my particular experience and they made me feel as though what we were studying had nothing to do with me at all. I left without being offered any kind of theory or analysis of the reality I knew and lived.

I returned to my own country and travelled to every part of it, gathering information. I learned how much the condition of women can vary.

When I started work, it made no difference to my mother because she continued to provide for me. I worked in the town where my parents lived. My mother didn't want me to be alone, so I lived at home and she continued to take care of me. I started teaching in secondary schools in various villages. It was a different milieu which I didn't find particularly stimulating.

I was disappointed by the teaching because there's a set syllabus and a schoolteacher can't show any initiative. Teaching should be child-centred, whereas with the syllabus imposed from above, it was dull and boring. So then I decided pursue further studies and I went on to study economics and management at Aix-en-Provence.

Tuareg Woman Have More Freedom

Around that time I got married, but I was too independent to accept my parents choices for me. My parents didn't want me to marry just anyone, and they drove away several possible men, six in all. My parents didn't think any of them were good enough for me. They went on looking. In any case, I hadn't really made up my mind, and once I did so, I married against their wishes. My parents didn't think the choice I made was right for me, but I got married anyway. My father then accepted my decision, but it took my mother a few years to come to terms with the marriage. Later, when I had children, she came round to it and the problems were solved.

My husband was very easy-going and very kind. I made all the decisions, even though he came from a milieu where the women are less free than we are. He was a Peul. Tuareg women are freer than any other women. We are economically independent, we have the right to make decisions, and we are free. I was much too independent for him, too.

The Effects of Schooling

My schooling has transformed my relationships, because I no longer have the time take care of other people. When I'm needed I'm often not there because I'm doing something else which is more important to me. My work has taken me away from my traditional milieu. In my work, I like to do everything I can to achieve the objectives. This demands hard work and patience, which other people don't always like. They want the work done at top speed, whereas I'm very painstaking.

Maybe it was lucky for me that I went to school. It might help me avoid what has happened to my sisters who didn't go to school: their way of life depends on the climate, and they are illiterate, which is a problem because we're living in a cosmopolitan milieu where you need to learn every language if you want to get by. They only speak Tamasheq (the Tuareg language), which makes things difficult for them. They are a bit left out of things, and they can't understand others or make themselves understood.

There are a few young Tuareg girls who go to school but not many, because there's no real supervision and since in my society children are considered very important, our little girls are sheltered. In a modern school, they're not properly supervised; there's nothing to replace the family and so parents are afraid for them. If there was a school where they were looked after a bit better everyone would send their children there. But there are issues with diet, social issues, and lots of other issues which have yet to be resolved. With boys it's easier, because they have to learn to cope, to face up to difficulties. It's thought normal for boys to have a hard time, whereas girls must be protected.

A New Type of Education for Women

Today things have really changed. Tuareg women no longer have the privileged position they once had. They're discovering the workplace, they work with their hands, they fetch water—something they've never done before—they prepare meals, and they're beginning to band together with other women who have also had to learn how to work. Everything's changing.

The Tuareg women tolerate this, because in wartime everyone has to buckle down. This is normal in any crisis. But, what they don't know is what's going to happen after the crisis: will their new situation continue, or will they return to their traditional lifestyle? For now, the crisis is not yet over.

The people who live close to towns have the opportunity to do something other than traditional agricultural activities. They can convert part of their flocks and herds into cash and open bank accounts. But for the rest there's no alternative but to continue the agricultural way of life, as they always have. For the moment, they haven't reached the stage of building up capital. People keep just enough goats for their own survival so the question doesn't arise. In the past, the women built up their fortunes in jewellery and herds, but today they can no longer afford to to do that.

The condition of the women's lives is worse than it was. Today girls are brought up differently. They're taught to work beside their mothers and they do lots of things. You could even say that today women are over-worked compared to a few years ago.

Reviving Traditional Knowledge

Because of the crisis, a lot of ancient knowledge was lost before it could be preserved. For example, the women who knew about plant- and mineral-based medicine have died. During the crisis, health became less important than food, so that the three years of drought have meant that people are less interested in issues that do not affect them personally. In the past it was essentially the women who took care of the sick. Today there are very few women skilled in traditional medicine.

The women had a role in many other areas, too; a knowledge of genealogies and affiliations, of the rights of succession. They were like tape-recorders memorizing everything that happened in society and then, at the right moment, they would intervene in a matter because they knew all the details. They also taught many things, writing, manners, how to behave in different situations, poetry, astrology, geomancy, educational games.

Another thing women specialized in was the making of jewellery and ornaments from pearls and leather. In fact that was how they lived. I think that with support they can continue to make some very beautiful things.

What does the future hold?

Tuareg women are not lagging behind other women, they're following them. Other women have trodden the same path and now the Tuaregs find themselves in a similar position. Maybe Tuareg women will begin to get together, talk about and reconsider their situation, and perhaps build a new world in which they will have a proper status.

Fatimata's words were recorded by H. Claudot-Hawad in February 1990 in Gao (Mali). Fatimata is now living in exile in Mauritania.

Translation by Elizabeth Corp

Fatimata Oualet Halatine, a Touareg woman now residing in Mauretania, was born and grew up in the Timbuktu region of northern Mali (West Africa). After a career as a high school teacher, she continued her studies to obtain a Master's degree in social and economic development. Fatimata now serves as consultant in various development and humanitarian relief projects organized by national and international organizations. Especially important among these activities is her work in several countries with African and European women's organizations.

The Central Position of Women Among the Berber People of Northern Africa

The Four Seasons Life Cycle of a Kabyle Woman

The Kabyles are an ethnic sub-group of the Berber people, today still living in Algeria, Tunisia, and Morocco. They are the oldest known people of Northern Africa. The three most important groups of the Berbers in Algeria are the Chaouias, who live a semi-nomadic lifestyle; the Tuareg, famous the world over as the People of the Desert; and the Kabyles, who are sedentary. I was born in Kabylia and was able to observe how people preserved some of their traditions. This happened in spite of the conversion to Christianity during the Roman Empire and to Islam after the arrival of the Arabs. Some remaining traditions include the veneration of saints, belief in the magic and power of the earth, the sun, the moon, springs, and the rain.

As a young girl I had already learned about the secret code of women, displayed on hand-painted ornamentation on pottery and on the walls of Kabylian houses. It took a long initiation by elderly women potters in the 1980s to enable me to decipher symbols that can only be truly appreciated by women, because these symbols relate directly to femininity and maternity.

The last phase of French colonialism in Algeria, lasting from 1830-1962, marked the end of the traditional life of Kabylian society. After many years of research I have come to the following conclusion: the introduction of written language together with the French educational system was one of the fundamental factors leading to the demise of the traditional lifestyle, a social order which was focused on the woman as mother of the clan. In Kabylia the woman is seen as the "central pillar" of the house. The actual physical pillar in the house receives religious veneration, because the protective house spirit inhabits this structure, and the woman of the house is compared to this spirit—everything rests on her (Genevois 1962: 18).

Scientific research into Kabylian history and culture within French ethnology and historiography was unfortunately based on the assessment factors of a western civilization. For a better understanding it is, therefore, expedient to describe some of the fundamental traits of traditional Kabylian culture. Without this knowledge one cannot understand the central focus of the position of the Kabylian woman.

Main Features of Traditional Kabylian Society

The Spoken Word as Carrier of Cultural Meaning

The Kabyles speak a Berber dialect, a language without script. Since eternity, knowledge has been passed down orally from parent to child via everyday practical applications. The values, conventions, and customs of the rural clan were passed on in the form of legends and myths only in spoken form (*Taqbaylit*). It is very interesting to note that the word *Taqbaylit* means "woman" as well as "Kabylian language." It is the mothers who teach their children to speak this language from birth. Thanks to mothers, the language of communication in the villages is still Kabylian, despite the fact that at first French and, since 1962, Arabic, has been the language taught at school. Since the Kabyles never formed a nation state, right up to the middle of the twentieth century, their cultural continuation found expression only via their oral tradition. There were no written laws, no government administration, no civil registry office, no civil service, and no land registry. The teachings, knowledge, and words of the elders were regarded as holy and as "living books," and, as such, commanded high regard.

Ancestral and Family Veneration

In traditional Kabylian society the distribution of the population in the country was a mosaic of small village-communities. These villages are politically, legally, economically, socially free and independent. Each village resembles a small republic, governed by the elders. This particularity is based on the special social relationship all inhabitants share with each other. When one analyzes the genealogy of the villagers what becomes apparent is that almost everybody is related in some way or other, forming a kinship-group. How people are related to each other is regulated by endogamy, which allows for marriages between people of the same village community (Khellil 1979: 2). In this way, social relationships are based on blood ties and affiliation to the commonly shared land. Furthermore, the social life in the villages is based on a model of a harmonious community through mutual aid and support (*Tiwizi* or *Touiza*). This model requires a collective responsibility of all members of the family, spreading through the whole village. In every aspect Kabyles experienced their social identity as part of the group. Their responsibility is focused on the family, resulting in a sense of connectedness, in which nobody feels isolated, and everybody feels protected by their family. This sense of responsibility is apparent among the living but also exists in reference to the ancestors. One talks of ancestral veneration, or a "religion" of the ancestors.

> There is no clear division between the living and the dead members of a family; the living as much as the dead are all members of the clan, and only the clan is important. Even less distinction is made between the living members of a family. (Mammeri 1938: 404-405)

This ancestral veneration is not based on religious dogma, but is cultivated in everyday life. It is based on tradition, the bloodline through the mother, and finds expression in all social activities. Even Islam could not find entry into Kabylian society without incorporating ancestral veneration. In its specific version of the Marabout Cult, it is seen as equal to the veneration of the saints. Since the women of traditional Kabylian society have been kept from the Arabic and French written language and schooling, Islam has had little influence on them. The religious dimension in their lives is the experience of everyday life in a ritualized contact with nature. Their lives were filled with an aura of magic, for everything they did formed a unity through ritual.

Farming of the Land and Ritualized Practice

Traditional Kabylia is a typical example of a "closed society" based on a subsistence economy. Within the village boundaries, the community lives off the fruits of their land. Worries about productivity, cost-effectiveness, or competition were unknown to them; there was also no ambition to import "foreign products." Bartering was the mode of "business" employed by the different clans to exchange products within the village. The village was at one and the same time the place of production, consumption, and reproduction, making it self-sufficient. In this agrarian society private property simply did not exist. Dwellings and land belonged to the whole family, since the land was inherited as holy entitlement from the ancestors to be passed on to all descendants. In the faith of the Kabyles, protective guardians endowed with invisible life inhabit the earth. Agriculture is, therefore, carried out in accordance with the seasonal cycles so as not to disturb the harvest and its natural development.

Traditionally, Kabyles lived in close contact with nature. As an oral culture they did not have clocks or calendars. The relationship of the people to their natural environment was based on a holistic approach to life. The people looked at themselves as an inherent part of the macro cosmos; they were not separated from nature, as in modern perception. Their rhythm of life corresponded to natural cycles and all rituals were an expression of their deep reverence of the order inherent in the natural world. The performance of rituals ordered the course of each action from its preparation to its final accomplishment. According to an ancient traditional birth ritual, which was passed from mothers to daughters, when mould a piece of pottery, weave a cloth, or turn a fruit of the earth into a staple food, they echo the birth process. There is no division of labour, but chronological steps, one after the other, connected by rituals, which are in turn connected to the cycle of the moon and the sun.

In this way, the sequence of actions followed when producing a piece of pottery is equated to the cycle of vegetation. The clay for the pottery is regarded as animate. Objects formed from it have to be stood up and one waits for it to "grow," like the wheat in spring, and afterwards it has to dry out – just like grain left to dry in the fields. Only after the harvest is the pottery permitted to bake and after, to be decorated. Should the women violate this order they would, according to their understanding, destroy the fertility of the earth.

During my research I had to realize how a western scientific viewpoint and the perspective of many "enlightened" people caused difficulties in understanding the ritualized lifestyle of Kabylian women. Therefore, I developed a new scientific approach: the four-phase approach. It describes a work cycle for the production of a piece of pottery, a staple food or a garment, consistent with the four seasons of the year. One result, which completely surprised me, was that all ritualized activities, be it the moulding of a piece of pottery, the preparation of food, or the production of a garment, closely follow the rules of the espousal between a woman and a man. All subsistence life activities were modelled on the act of human copulation. When working with clay, for example, the potteress forms an object according to her own biology and the laws of reproduction. The development of a piece of pottery is carried out along the lines of the magical ritual of copulation. The potteress uses for this purpose a round ball, symbolizing the feminine in the moon, on top of which a coil of clay is placed representing the man. In the act of weaving, the warp threads, crossed over by the weft thread, serves to unite the two, and thus, represent the mating of two souls. She creates a completely new piece of cloth, a living creation, equalling the birth of a human being (Makilam 1996).

The Ritualized Traditional Life of a Kabylian Woman

I was able to analyze the traditional activities of women with the help of the four-phase model based on the seasons of the year. To depict the change in the body of a woman during the course of her life I employ the same four-phase method, analogous to her material existence. These phases depict a cyclical development corresponding to the four seasons in nature. This simultaneously reveals a cyclical development, for in traditional Kabylian thinking the beginning of human life equals its ending. At the end of the cycle it thus becomes clear how the rituals accompanying the birth process are repeated in the rituals of surrounding death.

Childhood and Youth

Birthing Rites: Birth is Woman's Domain

As in many other cultures, traditional Kabylian society prohibits men being present during childbirth. The Kabylian father withdraws to the village during childbirth, as the secrets surrounding the process are reserved for women alone. All birthing rites are carried out only by women, and hence, never shared with men. Thus, the beginning of a new life through the birthing process is shared only by women.

> The secret of child delivery, i.e., the discovery by the woman that she is creatress of life, is a religious experience, which can not be translated

into the vocabulary of male experience. (Eliade 1972: 165)

An older woman of my kinship group was shocked when she heard that fathers-to-be in western society are frequently present during childbirth. In a derisive yet sad tone, she said to me:

> *You, who think yourselves to be so liberated in Europe, did it have to come to this, that you have to prove to men that life emanates from you and that you are the mothers of their sons? Giving birth to woman after our own fashion is self-evident. But we are also the mothers of the sons and men.*

According to traditional views children do not belong to their parents, but to the clan or kinship-group. When a census is carried out, it is the houses that are counted, not people. To attribute a child to one man and one woman is an individualized social concept. The birth of a child affects the whole village and cannot be separated from other births. For example, the occurrence of several births together in a village within one month is regarded a bad omen. It is said the moon connected them. When a child's growth is stunted and it cries continuously and is generally in poor condition, this too is attributed to the concurrence of births. The mother then resorts to different rituals. For example, in order to revoke the "moon-binding," she has to go out on the second or third day after nightfall to "a meeting with the new moon," and there she will ask the luminary to undo the ill situation. This ritual reveals the close connection between birthing rites and lunar powers. Later I will report how the birth rites are connected with the moon in the magical 40 days after delivery.

In traditional Kabylian society the purpose of life is focused on the family and its continuation. Without marriage no new social groups come into being. Kabyles know the individual does not count if not backed up by a social group. Beginning with puberty young men and women are prepared for their future role as mothers and fathers. There is almost no adolescence, because arranged marriages take place quite early. Therefore, wedding rituals do not refer to the separation of the spouse from their respective families, but to the end of childhood. They celebrate the changeover to their new responsibility, which is understood as the continuation of life's legacy passed on by the ancestors.

In Search of the Bride

According to the anthropologist Claude Lévi-Strauss, the reason why women do not occupy the same place or the same status in human society is because it is the men who exchange the women and not the other way round (1958: 188). The way marriages are arranged and kinship groups organized among the Kabyles show a different picture. It is a society in which the mothers choose their daughters-in-law. Women look for, choose, and find the wife. Whether a man has close relatives or is alone, he would even send out a stranger he trusted, for it is always women one turns to when looking for a wife (At-Ali 1979: 90f).

In traditional Kabylia, women do not go looking for a husband, and men do not go looking for a wife. A wife is chosen for a man by the man's mother. The search for this woman is a long ritual stage, starting with the birth of the son. Supported by their sisters and daughters, the mothers choose the future daughter-in-law. The mothers alone have this task and hurry to get it done, which is why a wedding often takes place during puberty. When a girl menstruates for the first time she instantaneously turns into a young woman, a wife, and a potential mother. The selection of the future bride depends solely on the character and strength of the chosen woman's mother. When the bride is found, the mother of the son informs the father"?

The last-minute-intervention of male relatives is a Kabylian representation of the decision-making process. In effect the selection is the women's domain (mother, sister, aunts, grandmother). Men only intervene to bless the decision, which despite outer appearance is not their domain at all. (Khellil 1979: 63f)

Weddings and Wedding Rituals

Kabylian weddings are never a private affair for the future spouses. There is no consent needed from them. They do not even meet during the wedding preparations. The wedding was originally only the concern of the whole kinship-group and a commitment by one's word of honour. "The character of a wedding is purely a family matter, no church or temple, nor is the official representation of any religion needed" (Laoust-Chantréaux 1990: 188-189). The French, however, introduced a registry at the beginning of the twentieth century.

The wedding rituals are connected with the cycle of nature. Therefore, no weddings are held in May. What was true for the work of the potter, applies to the wedding: the fertility of the freshly seeded soil is not to be disturbed. For this reason weddings are held mostly in October. When the woman is fertilized by the man through sexual union she is likened to the earth, the Earth-Mother of human life (*Terre-Mère*).

The Pregnant Woman: The "Form-Giver"

The Pregnant Woman as Earth-Mother of Humankind

All Native peoples equate woman-mother with the earth. The analogy between the fertile soil and the fertile woman show up clearly in the Kabyle rules surrounding pregnant women. Theses rules are identical for women and the soil. Agriculture is accompanied by rituals similar to those that apply to pregnant women. When a women walks through her flourishing vegetable garden the first time during harvesting season, she opens her belt ritualistically in reverence and silence as she would do before giving birth. She does what a pregnant woman ready to give birth would do, so as to not hinder the growth of the plants. The positive regard given to the belly of a pregnant woman stresses the importance of female creativity during the process of pregnancy. An expression of thankfulness or reverence is still to this day: "*May the belly be blessed which carried you.*"

A woman is compared to a garden with its swelling fruit, like the pumpkin. The moon also "swells" until it is full and round. During her pregnancy a Kabylian woman is not allowed to work the soil, as she would be "shaping" the soil with her work. In so doing she would also analogously form the infant. During pregnancy she will also avoid whitewashing, plastering, or decorating the walls of her house, or making pottery, for this could also have an adverse affect on her or her child's health. Baneful spirits could disrupt or even destroy the life in the womb. The Kabyles believe that childlessness is not to be ascribed to the woman, as this would contradict her fertile and creative abilities. The inability to conceive is always attributed to some magical, supernatural obstacle. This perception is still found nowadays in Algeria. Pregnancy is treated magically and Kabylian women employ difficult rituals, at faraway grottos, holy springs, and the gravesites of ancestors.

The Rituals of Delivery

In Kabylia birth is not a ritual of delivery as in separation, but one of uniting the mother with the child. The Kabylian woman delivers in a squatting position in order to put the infant down on the ground. This ritualized birth position directly onto the ground (*Humi positio*) can be found the world over. Until 1950, this tradition took place in the home exclusively. The birthing process is women's domain and is experienced in the community of older mothers. The midwife-healer, or another experienced woman, the mother-in-law or the mother, holds the birthing, naked woman from behind with her two open hands forming a kind of seat. There is a great spectrum of rites and practices surrounding pregnancy, childbirth, and the period of nursing, but these are not communicated to the outside world.

> This mystery handed down from the ancestors is creating true community among all female members of society, which is the foundation of the life of the society. (Getty 1992: 43)

Motherhood is experienced as a collective occasion. But it means much more. Motherhood for the Kabylian woman spreads magically over the whole natural environment and influences the fertility of the fields and the domestic animals. Based on this understanding, it is possible to explain the birthing and motherhood rites, such as the prohibition for a pregnant woman to work the fields and the special way of dealing with the fire of the hearth. During the whole duration of pregnancy the fire must not be removed from the house. This rule is also observed at the birth of a calf, at weddings, and during the autumn fieldwork.

Mother and Child

The 40 Days After Delivery and Birth

Until the time of delivery the Kabylian woman takes care of all her usual chores; after the delivery she is obliged to adhere to a strict resting time. The fixed time for this is 39 nights, for mother and child. This time is considered the most dangerous time for a mother. Often the woman will spend this time in her mother's house, for her mother will instruct her in all she needs to know. This is why the birth of a daughter is highly valued. The mother cares for the daughter turned mother herself and accompanies her through all the birthing rites. I have searched long for the meaning of theses magical 40 days, which are observed after delivery and likewise after the death of a person. The older women gave the explanation to me: It is connected with the cycle of the moon.

> The lunar phases—appearance, waxing and waning and disappearance of the moon—followed by the reappearance of the same after three pitch-dark night—have played a powerful role in the formation of cyclical worldviews. (Eliade 1969: 104)

During the three days following the birth neither the child nor its mother are allowed to leave the bed or the house. It is prohibited to visit her as the saying goes: "She's got one foot in the grave." Like the dead, both have to disappear from sight for three dark nights, before they can reappear again. Mother and child then hold an additional resting period in the house for seven more nights. During this time they can only have visitors from the immediate family. Only after these ten days of isolation within the family community is the woman allowed to cross over the threshold of the house. But she will only do this after she has observed a number of magical rituals that will protect her from harm. The mother will furthermore wait another 28 nights, a moon-month, before she leaves the compound of the family. Only then, covering the child carefully, is she able to show the child off to the rest of the village. The time of 38 nights or 39 days is finally finished after the woman has ritually visited a well or a sacred place. Only on the fortieth day will the mother resume a normal life again.

Motherhood

Traces of matrilineal relationships show up in rituals after a child's birth, which are celebrated exclusively by the mother and the female members of the clan. Men are excluded from such rituals and women's magical practices such as the beautifying lustration in the moonlight. In the traditional Kabylian society the most common alliance is that of the marriage between cousins. It is not viewed as incestuous when one marries within one's own family group. However, marriage is prohibited in the case of two children who have emerged from the same womb, or been suckled at the same breasts. The bonding created by breast-feeding is perceived to be as strong as the blood bond. The symbolic gesture of offering a breast constitutes an adoption rite, which carries with it a prohibition to marry. The children of the same mother but by different fathers are also seen as full-fledged brothers and sisters.

Maternal lineage can be read from the names children are given: Brothers—

children of one mother—are called *atmaten;* likewise sisters are called *tissetmatin;* one's own brothers are called "sons of my mother" or *aytma,* and the sisters are "daughters of my mother," or *issetma* (Plantade 1988: 46).

If a Kabylian woman is attacked, it is firstly the sons of her mother, her brothers, who stand up to defend her, not her husband or father. The natural mother-child relationship is of such importance that losing one's mother is the worst tragedy to happen. "I did not harm the one whose father I took away, but I left bereft without anything, the one whose mother I took away."

The Older Woman: The Crone

Birth of the Grandchildren

In the eyes of the Kabyles, the woman is the foundation of the house and the family, but her role as woman and mother is only completely fulfilled when she becomes a grandmother. One of the most important tasks a mother can have is the search for the wife for her son, for it ensures the continuation of the family line through her descendants. From early childhood onwards, traditional upbringing of the Kabylian boy is geared toward keeping him close by his mother's house. It is not desirable for the young married man to cut ties to his mother. Traditionally, the daughters also stay in close proximity to their mother, in order to marry a cousin from a neighbouring house. Only at the beginning of the twentieth century did marriages between different villages become more common. By marrying outside the original family kinship-group, women followed the men to settle far away from their mothers and, hence, close to their mothers-in-law, who coordinated all economic affairs of the local family group. The search for a "bride" has become much more difficult these days. As long as the task is still under female guidance, I can attest to the fact that they still concentrate on the same family group and that the descendants of the mother are favoured.

When the first child gets married, the mother calls herself "grandmother" according to her new role, *tamghart* or the Crone. In Kabylian language this word expresses her very honourable position. At the same time her role as mother to her grown-up children lasts to her death. In old Kabylia, the mother cares for the children of her son turned father and at the same time assists her daughter-in-law in her mother role. This is carried out to such a degree that gifts at the birth of a child are handed to the grandmother, not to the mother or father of the child. The relationship between a mother and a daughter is of utmost importance. The mother hands down all her knowledge to the daughter, the heiress of all the mother's wisdom. She is endowed with a "special love."

At the end of her life the grandmother is viewed as a *magi.* In her womb she created human beings, who have been recipients of her nourishment and care. She turns into a weaver who is able to weave together the threads of life of the ancestors with those of her descendants. She was present at every fertility rite and directed all ritualistic-magical work. Based on her experience she often became a midwife and every evening recounted the myth and fairytales she had heard from her mother and passed them on to her grandchildren.

Return to the Earth

In Kabylian mythology, i.e., the narrative of "the first parents of the world," human beings were born from the earth. In this way the Kabyles believe the dead return to the belly of the earth where they came from. The funeral customs are, therefore, similar to the rites associated with the birth of a child. The return to the earth follows the same rituals and progressive stages as the birth of an infant. Any remains of the dead person have to be removed before the third day after death. Within those days the straying soul of the deceased is hovering over the threshold of the door of the house and will return after 40 days. The visit to the cemetery has to be conducted on the third and the fortieth day after the death. The observance of these magical 40 days we find prior to delivery, after delivery and after the funeral. Life takes on an eternal cyclical character, which is continually carried forward in the womb of the mothers. The funeral rituals make clear that death is not perceived as the end of life, but as the cyclical renewal, serving the renewal of all of life, of nature, the earth, and the heavens.

> In the perception of everybody, death is but a changeover in existence, a kind of transit time, and belief in a life after death is all encompassing. One does not say a person is "gone," but that she or he is "heading for another world" (*teruh di-laxert*), for the life down here and the future life is, we are assured, two sisters amazingly alike, whom we will get to know one after the other. (Laoust-Chantréaux 1990: 241)

Conclusion

This four-part analysis represents the methodology and main results of my research on the magical dimension of the position of the Kabylian women. From the cradle to the grave the woman as mother is the protector of life itself; she is the potter, the provider, the weaver of human bonds. Until I developed my specific approach of the "four-phase-method," it was common to view women's lives in two phases, young and old. This two-fold model was later replaced by a three-fold model: girl, woman, and elderly woman. But the great regard given to the mother cannot be fully grasped with either the two-phase, or the three-phase model, as it does not take into account the phase of the pregnancy. When we consider the beginning of a human life as its birth, we do not give credence to the most important phase of the life *in vitro,* the unseen development of a human being inside the womb of the mother. When the beginning of human life is the actual birth of the child, then the unseen development of the human being in the womb of its mother is not perceived as a crucial phase in the mother role. In this way, the time of motherhood is curtailed. Starting with the birth of the child would be equal to starting with fatherhood, thus producing a false equation. The phase of pregnancy is very important for re-establishing the basis for the forgotten roots of humankind. Refusing to honour this vital part of a woman's life denies her as true source and preserving power of life itself. Every Kabyle is raised in deep reverence for their mother and in the awareness that all humankind owes its life to a woman. In this way, the following sentence has to be understood.

The woman carries the life of the man—husband, brother or father— the defender of her honour, in her womb. (Ait-Ali 1979: 98)

The ritualized life of the women, especially of the grandmothers, emphasizes the reverence of mothers. All rituals in the traditional life cycle of a Kabylian woman, which accompany her existence from cradle to grave, show matriarchal structures of previous times. They have been preserved in the life of women. These rituals can be called magical, because they mirror the cosmic creation in human procreation. In this way, women see themselves not only as creatresses of human life, but also as a symbol of the creative power itself. Therefore, they see this creative power in everything they themselves have created, be they objects made from clay, as in pottery, or things made from wool as in woven products. The production process is regarded as magical creation, which corresponds to the act of sexual union between man and woman and the fertility resulting from it. This is shown clearly in the symbolic language of the women via geometric ornamentation on pottery, pieces of weaving, and the walls of houses.

The adoration of the mother was also expressed in the high regard given to the family, as well as in ancestor veneration and in the rituals performed for the natural environment. This spirit of unity—which encompasses the whole of life—regulates, affects, and explains the magic of the women and their traditional customs in traditional Kabylian life.

Translation by Jutta Ried

Makilam is an historian, author, and Indigenous ethnologist of Kabyle lineage. She grew up in a Kabylian village in Algeria until she was seventeen. Her research is permeated by her personal experience and offers previously unpublished material about the rites and myths of a society at the brink of extinction, where women and mothers play central roles. Two of her books, which describe the magical world of the Kabyle women, were published in France in 1996 and 1999. Both were translated into German and English.

References

At-Ali, Belaïd. 1963. *Les cahiers de Belaïd ou la Kabylie d'antan.* Fort-National.
At-Ali, Belaïd. 1979. "Démarches matrimoniales." *Tisuraf* 4-5. Paris.
Eliade, Mircéa. 1972. *Le sacré et le profane.* Paris: Gallimard.
Eliade, Mircéa. 1969. *Le mythe de l'éternel retour.* Paris: Gallimard.

Getty, A. 1992. *La déesse, mère de la nature vivante*. Paris: Editions du seuil.

Genevois, H. 1962. *La famille*. *FDB* 76. Fort-National.

Khellil, Mohand. 1979. "Pratique(s) du mariage aux At-Fliq." *Tisuraf* 4-5. Paris

Khellil, Mohand. 1979. *L'exil kabyle*. Paris: L'Harmattan.

Khellil, Mohand. 1984. *La Kabylie ou l' ancêtre sacrifié*. Paris: L'Harmattan.

Laoust-Chantréaux, Germaine. 1990. *Kabylie côté femmes*. Aix-en-Provence: Edisud.

Lévi-Strauss, Claude. 1958. *Anthropologie structurale*. 1993. Paris: Plon.

Makilam. 2005a. *The Magical Life of Berber Women in Kabylia*. Online: <www.makilam.com>.

Makilam. 2005b. *Symbols and Magic in the Arts of Kabyle Women*. Online: <www.makilam.com>.

Mammeri, Mouloud. 1938. "La société berbère." *Aguedal* 5.

Plantade, Nedjima. 1988. *La guerre des femmes*. Paris: La Boîte à Documents.

Part IV
Existing Matriarchal Societies – Asia

PATRICIA MUKHIM

Khasi Matrilineal Society

Challenges in the Twenty-First Century

The origin of the Khasis who inhabit the hill ranges of North East India and have now a defined space within which they live, which is the State of Meghalaya, is shrouded in mystery because of a lack of historical records. But Khasis believe they are the descendants of the seven celestial families who decided to live on earth long before humankind existed. Legends have it that there were actually sixteen families living in heaven or *ka bneng*. These families came down to the earth for farming, and they descended and ascended the heavenly navel or *sohpet bneng*, which was a ladder joining heaven to earth. One day, seven families came down, and a sinful person in the group cut down the heavenly ladder with his axe. As a result, the seven families had to remain on earth. They are known as the *Hynniew Trep Hynniew Skum*, meaning, the seven hearths and homes.

Like most tribes in North East India, Khasis had an oral tradition until Thomas Jones, a Welsh Christian missionary, taught them the Roman script sometime in 1842. The written script laid the foundation for the development of Khasi literature. Regarding the origin of the Khasis, some anthropologists and historians take the view that Khasis came from South East Asia. Linguists like J. R. Logan suggest that the Khasi have a close relationship with the Mons or Talaings of Pegu and Tenasserim and the Khmers of Cambodia. Logan identifies a tribe called the Paluangs who inhabit the Shan state of Myanmar, as the closest kinsmen of the Khasis. P. R. T. Gurdon (1907) also claims that the Khasis have great affinity with the people of the Far East, especially the Mon Khmer branch of the Austric family.

Khasi society is matrilineal. Descent is derived from the female line. Khasi matriliny makes a clear distinction between *Kur*, relatives from the mother's line, and *Kha*, relatives from the father's clan. The *Kur* or clan is a kinship group. Most clans trace their roots to their great-great grandmothers, *Ki Iawbei Tynrai*, meaning "grandmothers of the root." Descendants of one ancestress of the clan, *Ka Iawbei Tynrai*, are called *shi kur* or "belonging to one clan." The sub-clans are all descendants of one great-grandmother and are known as *shi-kpoh*. The next category is the family or *Iing* (House). In a Khasi home, it is usual for the grandmother, her daughters, and the daughter's children to be living under one roof.

The living grandmother or the matriarch of the family is called *Ka Iawbei Khynraw,* meaning "young grandmother," to distinguish her from the ancestress.

Understanding Khasi Kinship

The Khasi *Kur* or clan grew out of the *Iing* or family. Marriage between members of the same clan is considered taboo, or, *Ka sang ka ma.* Noted American sociologist, G. P. Murdock, points out that, irrespective of all genealogical considerations, patrilineal descent affiliates an individual with a group of kinsmen related to him through males only, while matrilineal descent assigns an individual to a group consisting exclusively of relatives through the females only. Khasi society consistently stresses matrilineal solidarity, which has been reinforced by the religious association of *Ka iing,* the natal or original home. *Ka iing* is the centre of all family rituals. It is the rallying point for the members of the *Kur* and *Kha* (relatives from the mother's clan line and those from the father's clan). Hence *Ka iing* is a social community that brings cohesion and allows children of different relatives to socialize with each other. In this way, they get to know their own kinsmen from the same clan and, thus, do not get romantically involved.

Elders of *Ka iing* have a responsibility to provide moral and ethical training for their younger members. These codes of conduct have been handed down through oral tradition and are known as *Ka Jingsneng Tymmen* or "the aphorisms of the elderly." Khasi religion focuses around the *Iing* as the religious unit. Members of the family gather together for ceremonial occasions such as naming ceremonies, marriages, deaths, and rituals related the internment of bones. The eldest maternal uncle in the family usually officiates as the priest who offers sacrifices to the household deity as an act of appeasement for wrongs committed against her by any members of the family.

Role of *Ka Khatduh*

The youngest daughter or *Ka Khatduh* makes all the necessary preparations for the ritual. The *Khatduh* at the centre of religious observance because it is she who literally is the progenitor of Khasi religion. However, the *Khatduh* is not a priestess.

Ka Iing is also an economic unit in the distribution and sharing of land and property among family members. The *Iing,* having adequate property, usually allocates land to the married daughters so they can set up their own family units. Sons are also given a share of the property for their use. In Khasi society, the *Khatduh* is the custodian of ancestral property, but the actual management and execution of the property is by the maternal uncle/uncles. *Ka Iing* is also a political unit because senior male members are appointed by the *Dorbar Iing* (family council) to represent the *Iing* in the *Dorbar Kur* (clan council). From the *Dorbar Kur* again, male representatives are sent to the *Dorbar Shnong* (the local governance system).

Many writers and the Khasis themselves, when speaking about the *Khatduh's* inheritance rights, tend to speak from a position of surrealism. They presuppose that the *Khatduh* always comes from a wealthy family and, therefore, inherits all the property of her parents. The truth is if the *Iing* does not have any property, then the *Khatduh* carries a huge burden of having to care for her elderly parents and other unmarried sisters and brothers and may, therefore, need help from her more affluent siblings. Many who do not understand the nuances of Khasi matriliny, consider the position of the *Khatduh* to be a very privileged one. However, the *Khatduh's* position is that of the eldest male members in a patriarchal Hindu family. She has to forego much of her freedom and social mobility, because her uppermost concern is the welfare of her parents who are under her care. Very often, even if the *Khatduh* gets a good job outside of her place of residence, she would not be able to take it up because she would not be able to leave her parents.

The *Khatduh* enjoys a certain amount of financial independence because the major share of property remains with her. This gives her the elbow room to manage not just her immediate family, but also the extended family, namely her brothers and sisters' children, aunts, uncles, and sundry relatives. Financial liquidity becomes imperative especially in a female-headed household when the mother has to literally run the family with her own resources.

As stated earlier, though ancestral property passes through the *Khatduh*, she is not really the owner. She is the stewardess or custodian and the maternal uncle is the chief executor. Attempts to sell off ancestral property have often led to court cases, because the property is not exactly unencumbered. Every family member has a stake in it, even though that is not based on the best and most equitable formula. This is the weakest link in the matrilineal chain. It is an area that perhaps requires deeper study because of its propensity to create conflict between individuals of *Ka Iing*, thereby eroding matriliny as a customary practice of matriliny. There are several instances in which a *Khatduh* marrying outside her community leads to her ostracization. Her brothers demand that she cease to be the inheritor/custodian of ancestral property. They often go to court to state their grievances against the *Khatduh*. Fortunately, for matriliny and for women, the State of Meghalaya takes cognizance of customary law and applies it in cases relating to property disputes. Many such disputes are pending with the District Councils while some are settled by the local traditional institution or the *Dorbar Shnong*. However, since the *Dorbar Shnong* is not in a position to settle cases that are adversarial in nature but only those with scope for conciliation, parties most often move to the formal institutions of justice to redress their grievances.

The Khasis did not have any law of inheritance, perhaps because land had not yet been commodified. When the custom first evolved, land had no financial value attached. It was a common property right. Before the advent of Christianity, the Khasis practiced their Indigenous religion. Funerals and other rituals associated with a death in the family were expensive and cumbersome affairs. Perhaps that is the reason why the youngest daughter was vested with the right to partly manage whatever is left behind by her parents; of course, after due consultation with her uncles and brothers, who would, usually, not create any obstacles to her taking on the role of an inheritor. Khasi society is fairly egalitarian. There is no caste or class system as prevails in other Indian societies.

Marriage Among the Khasi

Marriage as an institution came in only after Christianity. Otherwise, Khasi society recognized co-habitation as having the same sanctity as a formal church marriage. Hence, there is no social ostracism when a child is born out of wedlock. Further, Khasi society also accepted polygamy as the husband was in a position to meet the emotional, financial, and material needs of his wives and his offspring.

In one sense, Christianity gave marriage a sanctity that Khasi society and its Indigenous faith could not. Co-habitation makes it easy for the man to abandon his wife, and vice versa. In modern times, this tendency has left marriages brittle, resulting in a trail of psychological trauma for the abandoned partner, as well as the children who invariably live with their mother. If the mother has no means to support herself, things become even more problematic. Often children have to drop out of school because their mother is unable to support their education. They have to take up some kind of work to supplement the family income. Khasis have tended to depend on the strength of the *Iing* or *Kur* (clan).

In the past, the *Kur* looked after its destitute members by providing a cushion against such adversities. But with modernization and the attendant economic challenges, clan ties are weakening. *Ka Iing* is today no longer the source or symbol of family solidarity. Individual households tend to fend for themselves. If the clan helps at all, it is only by way of a one-off donation for meeting emergencies such as sickness or death in a family. As a result, the abandoned woman may be left to fend for herself, because the Christian Church does not come to the rescue of its afflicted members. And the *Iing or Kur* is no longer cohesive. If the woman wants maintenance, she has to fight for it in a court of law.

After marriage, a Khasi man leaves his parental home and lives with his wife's family at least for a couple of months. After that, if the woman he marries is not the *Khatduh,* then the couple is free to start their own family. But a man who marries a *Khatduh* has to live in her *Iing* or matrilocal residence. This creates a problem because a man has no authority over his own conjugal family. His children are brought up under the care of a host of uncles and aunts, a grandmother and grandfather, all of whom maintain some hold over his children. One other unsettling factor for the man is that when he marries he is said to have left for somebody else's home (*leit iing briew*). This creates a sense of insecurity and psychological alienation for the male as it symbolizes that henceforth he will no longer be as close to his matri-kin as he used to be. In a way, a son in a matrilineal society feels the same sense of alienation from his family as a daughter in a patriarchal society feels.

The misconception that sons do not and cannot inherit property is without basis. In Khasi matriliny, if the *Khatduh* has no daughters, her sons may not inherit ancestral property. But they can be gifted with the self-acquired property of their parents. The ancestral property will, however, pass over to the next elder sister's youngest daughter. It is important to perpetuate the religious duties or *Ka Niam Ka Rukom* in the ancestral home. As stated earlier, Khasi matriliny is not is not without its share of stresses. For example, the proclivity of a married man to buy land in his wife's name. Perhaps this is, first, to ensure some kind of tenurial security during his lifetime; or, second, that on his death, his clan (*kur*) and matri-kin do not appropriate the property and leave his wife and children in penury, a phenomenon common among the Jaintias.

Gender Equity and Khasi Society

Although matriliny faces a variety of stressors, compared to other customary practices, women in Meghalaya have a number of advantages:

1. They perpetuate the clan, because, lineage is from the mother's bloodline (*ka kmie kum ka nongpynkha bad kaba pynneh pynsah ia ka jait ka khong*);
2. There is no prevailing dowry system (*ym don ka jingai ne jingshim na ki arliang ha ka shongkha shongman*);
3. Unmarried women are not under any pressure to tie the nuptial knot (*ym don jingpynbor ia ki kynthei ba kin shongkurim*);
4. Marriage is purely by choice and not arranged (*ka shongkha shong-man ka long beit da ka jingiamon lang ki arngut, ym da ka jingpynbor jongno jongno*);
5. Co-habitation (*ka shongkha shongman da ka jingmynjur ki arngut shi tnga*), or what modern couples call "living together" is not taboo.

But, is Khasi society a gender equitable society? What is the status of men vis-à-vis women? There is no doubt that parents unwittingly place greater value on a daughter because she is the perpetuator of the lineage. However, sons are not exactly discriminated against or unwanted. In terms of educational opportunities, by and large, sons and daughters get equal opportunities. But, like all other societies, Khasis also confuse the biological aspect of being men and women with the cultural construct of male and female. Sexual division of labour is very marked. As a rule, men/boys do not cook, or wash dishes or clothes. Among agrarian families, the woman does more than her share of work, beginning at 4:00 or 5:00 in the morning and ending only after everyone has had their evening meal. Women are expected to care for the sick and elderly. They fetch water and gather fuel wood for the home. They are also responsible for the kitchen garden during off-farm seasons and participate in farming during the planting, weeding, and harvesting season. Khasi women have the additional burden of marketing their agricultural products and livestock, apart from the weekly shopping to meet the family domestic requirements, because it is also seen as a woman's domain. Even among the most educated families, where men are expected to be more gender conscious, the woman spends much of her time in the kitchen and the husband will make an excuse saying: "Well, she enjoys her cooking and the kitchen is her empire." No one asks the poor wife, whether she really enjoys the drudgery of cooking, washing, or cleaning over and over again.

At a seminar organized by the Indigenous Women's Resource Center (IWRC), the guest of honour, a Member of the Legislative Assembly, was amused to observe that it is not the Khasi woman who says she is privileged. Actually Khasi men have all along been echoing this rhetoric so much so that women have begun to believe it themselves. Gender equality is not just about property and who inherits it. It is about who does what, and who has access and control over what resources. A piece of property owned by the *Khatduh* is very often administered by her husband or sons. If a Khasi woman is living her life based the gendered division of labour, and is unable to break free of that social liability, how can a society be called gender equitable? If we look at agrarian communities, and these form a major part of the Khasi population, only the male members have contact with government departments. Only male members have access to agricultural training, seeds, fertilizers, etc. Decisions about what crops to grow are taken by men. Again, men have more access to the markets because of their social mobility, whereas women are restricted by their family responsibilities, such as looking after small children and the elderly and other domestic chores.

Studies have been conducted in the West Khasi Hills of Meghalaya by the IWRC on a number of indicators such as decision-making about the purchase of jewelry, sale of livestock, choice of crops and other agricultural products, to determine the level of gender equity. It was found that women might have a say in smaller livestock such as chicken, but that it is men who decide whether to rear cows or pigs and when to sell them and at what price. Decision-making for women was restricted to what are perceived as less important matters. Gender awareness is a new concept, even to the urban population. In fact, women themselves negate their own strengths when they say: "Let men take care of activities outside the home, let them attend the *dorbar*, why should we women interfere?" This sort of remark from educated, well-placed women such as college teachers and professors reveal that Khasi women are a long way away from understanding gender equality.

Matriliny and Poverty

Matriliny does not and has not been able to address the problem of rising poverty among a large section of the rural population, half of whom include women. Land has traditionally been a community resource. People of a particular clan who reside in a particular village for some length of time are considered part and parcel of that village and are allocated land for farming and housing. This land is called the *Ri-Raij*. For the Khasis, the concept of land ownership by individuals is a fairly recent concept, which gained notoriety when land was commodified and a monetary value was placed on it. This happened after the British introduced their concept of governance and began to acquire land for infrastructure. When the Khasis learned about the value of land, there was no stopping them from converting by subterfuge the *Ri-Raij* land into *Ri-Kynti* or individually owned land. However, it is also true that some free-hold lands not owned by anyone have been claimed by particular clans through the process of *skut,* which means claiming as much land as a person could lay his eyes on—literally taking the hills and rivers as natural boundaries.

But this does not seem to have been the good fortune of many other clans. Agriculture is a risky activity and families often mortgage their land to rich moneylenders (tribals) in order to purchase seeds. When the crops fail these families lose their land and become landless. Sometimes they move to another village with the hope of being allocated some *Ri-Raij* land. When they make improvements upon *Ri-Raij* land, they can stake a claim to it and convert it to *Ri-Kynti.* Once land becomes *Ri-Kynti,* the owner is free to do whatever he wishes with it including mortgaging it should exigencies arise.

In rural Meghalaya, women have no idea of family planning or of reproductive rights. Women continue to have children against their wishes and become even more destitute. Empowerment of women is a concept that only more privileged women in cities are familiar with thanks to efforts of some non-governmental organizations and, to some extent, the government itself.

Women and Political Rights

Women in Meghalaya have traditionally been excluded from the *Dorbar Shnong,* which is the traditional local governance system practiced before the advent of the British into the Khasi Hills. The *Dorbar Shnong,* therefore, is a male-centric organism that clings to its traditional base as a sacred right. But in urban Meghalaya women are slowly beginning to assert their rights for inclusion in the *Dorbar Shnong.* Although there is still strong resistance by the male lobby to having women in executive councils of this *Dorbar,* there is also a subtle recognition that women do have something of substance to contribute. However, the nomenclature of the head of this *Dorbar*—the *Rangbah Shnong,* which literally translated means "Village Headman"—automatically debars women from taking up this responsible position. Khasi women need to fight for a more gender-equitable language of inclusion.

Surprisingly, women have for a long time held positions of power and authority in the formal constitutional democratic system of governance. Although they are today a very negligible number—currently only three of the sixty members in the state legislature are women—there are no barriers to their being elected. Women participate actively during the elections. They canvass for votes and make good election agents and polling agents. To date, though, women have tended to campaign for men instead of for themselves. But things are changing and changing fast. Khasi women are currently trying to create political space for themselves.

How Egalitarian and Democratic is Khasi Society?

Outwardly, Khasi society appears egalitarian. But that is not so. In fact, it manifests clear features of an oligarchical system. Although in the early stages of civilization the *Syiem* (chieftain) was chosen from among the lowly members of society to govern, administer, and adjudicate disputes among his villagers, his position has now become that of a "ruler." The institution of *Syiemship* has now assumed the form of a power centre and made the *Syiem* a powerful authority, so much so that he began to acquire land in his own name and the name of his family members. In other words, the *Syiemship* is acquiring the features of royalty as practiced in other states and countries. On the other hand, poverty among the masses is increasing. Rural poverty arising mainly out of landlessness has forced the poor to sell off even their agricultural lands. Today, farmers cultivate on lease-held land with very short tenures. This creates a feeling of deep insecurity. Meghalaya is gradually inching towards a situation where the affluent are acquiring more and more land, while the poor are getting poorer. Since clan ties are weakening, there is no buffer system to prevent people from selling off their land to meet domestic exigencies. The new class of landowners are not necessarily women. This is where matriliny is eroding in Khasi society.

Right of lineage is not without its curses. Because of it, when a couple divorce, the children invariably live with their mother. Since co-habitation is not a social taboo, a man can abandon his wife without paying for his wife or his children's maintenance. The recent Lineage Bill passed by the Khasi Hills District Council and which received the Governor's assent on February 23, 2005, in principle only defines who a Khasi is. The Act says that a child born of a Khasi mother will always be considered Khasi of the *Kur, Jait,* or clan of the Khasi mother, if the person fulfils the following requirements:

1. She/he can speak Khasi, unless prevented from knowing the language by circumstances beyond her/his control;
2. She/he observes and is governed by the Khasi matrilineal system of lineage, the Khasi laws of inheritance and succession, and the Khasi laws of co-sanguinity and kinship;
3. She/he had not, at any time, in writing or otherwise voluntarily renounced the Khasi status;
4. She/he had not adopted the personal law of the non-Khasi father or husband, as the case may be, or a personal law of a society incompatible with Khasi personal laws and customs;
5. She/he had not lost or been deprived of Khasi status by judgment or

order under the provision of this Act;

6. Whose father is or was Khasi and the mother a non-Khasi, and the Khasi father and every such person fulfils the requirements specified in the above clauses, shall be a Khasi, belonging to such Khasi *Kur, Jait,* or clan in accordance with the Khasi customs, applicable to such Khasi father or belonging to such new *Jait* or clan as may be adopted under any prevailing Khasi customs, applicable to the Khasi father or by *Tang Jait;*

7. Every case of *Tang Jait* shall be reported to the registration authority under this Act by the person performing or conducting it, duly confirmed by the Headman of the village or locality concerned present in the ceremony, and the report will contain the relevant information and particulars as may be prescribed.

Tang Jait is a ceremony where a new *Jait* or clan is conferred on a non-Khasi wife of a Khasi male and to all the offspring born to her. For instance, a Khasi male from the *Nongrum Kur* marries a non-Khasi woman. After the rituals of *Tang Jait,* the wife and children are given the new *Jait* of *Khar-Nongrum.* The word *Khar,* which precedes the word *Nongrum,* indicates that the woman is a *dkhar* or a non-Khasi. In recent times, the number of Khasi men marrying outside the Khasi community is on the rise, possibly because of the male urge to perpetuate his clan, which is not possible in case he marries a Khasi. Ironically, lineage is the very issue that unsettles a man in Khasi society. He feels insecure because of the outside world's perception of him as the breeding bull. His second source of insecurity springs from being dispossessed of family inheritance. These are two crucial factors challenging Khasi matriliny at this juncture.

The practice of *Tang Jait* is not new among Khasis. According to oral tradition, in the past, Khasi men have brought non-Khasi women as captives from the plains of Assam and have later married them. Clan names preceded by the word *Khar* (*Kharkongor, Kharphanbuh, Kharkrang,* etc.) are all indications that the above clans are not intrinsically Khasi, but have been integrated into the society through the ritual of *Tang Jait.* However, this custom is rarely practiced anymore. Khasi males marrying non-Khasi women began giving their clan name to their wives and offspring, and continue to do so today. At no point in history was the *Tang Jait* made compulsory. This is the main reason why the District Council has come up with a law that will ensure compliance. Until this time, Khasi identity was very loosely defined. The *Lineage Ac*t gives a legal sanctity to that identity.

Challenges to Khasi Matriliny

Scholars Chae Nakane and Kathleen Gough have pointed out the structural weaknesses in matriliny. Nakane (1967) sees the matrilineal system as a complex one which cannot face the onslaught of radical economic changes. Gough (1961) observes that matrilineal groups seem to be badly hit when their members enter the market-driven economy. Although matrilineal societies may not disintegrate altogether and may, in fact, carry on for decades, they are likely to break down to their minimal segments. Gough feels that patrilineal descent groups are in a better position to weather the storms of a liberal market economy.

By the same logic, L. O. Poewe (1981) believes that the "contradiction between the increasingly social nature of the forces of production and the still private character of appropriation creates the material conditions for the disappearance of the system" (120). Khasi society is today at a crossroads. It is shifting from an agrarian subsistence economy to a market economy. But, besides economic factors, scholars have also noted the basic structural contradictions in Khasi matriliny that threaten its very survival. These factors are listed below.

1. Clearly what is emerging in Khasi matriliny is the tension between the individual (nuclear family) and the matrilineal descent groups such as *Ka Iing, Kpoh*, etc.

2. Khasi society places a man in a very unfavourable position because he is constantly being tested as to whether he is more loyal to his wife and children or to his own family and clan members (matri-kin). However, this conflict between conjugal and natal ties also applies to the *Khatduh* as well.

3. Marriage demands that the man give more time to his conjugal home than to his siblings and parents. Even this creates conflicts. Again, this is true of the woman as well, particularly the *Khatduh* who often has to be the buffer between her parents and her husband, or her siblings and her husband. Living under the same roof inevitably causes a clash of interests and egos.

4. Conflict between ownership and authority, where land is owned by female members but the authority to administer it lies with the male members (maternal uncle).

5. The system of matrilocal residence, where a man moves into his wife's home after marriage yet never has complete authority over his conjugal family, creates rifts that are unspoken but manifest themselves in easy divorces.

6. Khasis and all tribals believe in common property resources and the tribal concept of sharing those resources among all members irrespective of their physical output. This conflicts directly with the concept of individual entrepreneurship. In a globalized economy the harder an individual works the greater is his income. No individual today would be willing to share his earnings with family members who have not invested in his business.

7. Khasi society gives great respect to the maternal uncle. He is present at all important family functions at his matri-kin residence. His nieces and nephews pay heed to his words and are expected to consult him before making any important decisions. In fact, marriages and engagements do hot happen unless the maternal uncle gives his blessing. Naturally, the role of the father is somewhat diminished. However, the same person would play a similar role in his matri-kin as well. So, to that extent, the system seeks its own equity. But what has been observed in Khasi society is that the maternal uncle is often so attached to his

nieces and nephews that he even gives them a share of his property and wealth and makes them his nominees in important official documents. This creates a direct conflict between his own children and his nieces and nephews.

8. More and more Khasi men in urban Meghalaya are marrying non-Khasi women. This could be due to greater social interaction with non-Khasis and non-tribals. However, it could also be because of the dominant male ego, which wants to appropriate the lineage of his children to his own clan without following the ritual of *Tang Jait*. Another reason is the market economy that hitherto made men a non-bankable asset since they do not actually own property for collateral. If a Khasi male marries another Khasi, custom compels him to keep all property including land and other assets in his wife's or children's name. If he marries a non-Khasi he is under no such obligation. All his assets are in his own name much like what happens in patriarchal societies. These aberrations gradually create a schism in kinship laws and erode matriliny in ways that are not immediately discernible, but which will have deeper implications in the future.

Conclusions

What poses a grave threat to Khasi matriliny is that it is hemmed in from all sides by strong patriarchal societies. Ideas of patriarchy and patriliny have already made inroads into the Khasi psyche with the emergence of organizations like *Ka Syngkhong Rympei Thymmai* (Foundation for a New Hearth), which has been in existence for over a decade. Although there is no immediate threat to Khasi matriliny from this Foundation, their ideas are attractive to the Khasi male who perceives that the system has been unfair to him. Gradual changes from matriliny to patriliny are also taking place at the individual family level.

Education, rapid modernization, and the fact that more and more Khasis, both male and female, have moved to urban areas in search of employment, as well as intermarriage with people of patriarchal societies, has weakened matrilineal ties. But this will take time to manifest. Meanwhile, for the protagonists of Khasi matriliny, it has become important to deliberate on these emerging issues, evaluate the strengths, weaknesses, opportunities of, and threats to, the system they seek to defend. Matriliny will need to reinvent itself to cope with new challenges. Its practitioners should have the courage to bring in reforms wherever needed, because at the end of the day, matriliny is advantageous for women.

Patricia Mukhim was born in 1953 in Shillong, Meghalaya, in North East India and is a renowned columnist and social activist. She is currently the Director of the Indigenous Women's Resource Center whose mandate is to train and build the capacities of indigenous women of the North East Province of India, a region largely inhabited by hill tribes with a strong cultural affiliation to the people of South East Asia. Coming from the Khasi matrilineal society, Patricia has interpreted her society for the rest of India and the world through her writings and independent research. For her free and frank views and her commitment towards a liberal democratic ethos, espoused through the columns of leading newspapers in her state and country, Patricia was conferred the Padmashree, a national award in recognition of her social services, by the President of India in March 2000. Earlier in 1996 she won the Chameli Devi Jain award for outstanding woman media-person. In 2003, she joined the North Eastern Institute of Development Studies (NEIDS) at the North Eastern Hill University (India) as Research Advisor.

References

Choudhury, J. N. 1978. *The Khasi Canvas.* Shillong: Jaya Choudhury.

Gough, Kathleen. 1961. "Modern Disintegration of Matrilineal Disintegration of Matrilineal Descent Groups." Eds. D. M. Schneider and K. Gough. *Matrilineal Kinship.* Berkeley: University of California Press.

Gurdon, P. R. T. 1975. *The Khasis.* 1907. New Delhi: Cosmos Publication.

Logan, J. R. *Journal of the Indian Archipelago and Eastern Asia, 1847-57.* 2: 644-652. Singapore: Mission Press.

Murdoch, G. P. 1937. "Correlations of Matrilineal and Patrilineal Institutions." *Studies of the Science of Society.* New Haven: Yale.

Nakane, Chae. 1967. *Garo and Khasi: A Comparative Study in Matrilineal Systems.* Paris: Mouton and Co.

Nongbri, T. 1996. "Problems of Matriliny: A Short Review of the Khasi Kinship Structure." *Kinship and Family in North-East India, Vol. II.* Ed. J. S. Bhandari. New Delhi: Cosmo Publications. 331-345.

Pakyntein, V. 1996. "The Khasi Clan: Changing Religion and its Effects." in, JS., (ed.) *Kinship and Family in North East India.* Ed. J. S. Bhandari. New Delhi: Cosmos Publication.

Poewe, L. O. 1981. *Matrilineal Ideology, Male Female Dynamics in Laupala, Zambia.* London: Academic Press.

War, J. 1992. "Status of Women in Traditional Khasi Culture." *Women in Meghalaya.* Ed. S. Sen. New Delhi: Daya Publishing House. 20-23.

SAVITHRI SHANKER DE TOURREIL

Nayars of Kerala and Matriliny Revisited

I am a Nayar woman from Kerala. Kerala, a narrow coastal strip on the south-west coast of the Indian peninsula, is home to Nayars. Foreign visitors, western historians, and anthropologists have been fascinated by Nayars for a very long time because of their erstwhile matrilineal system of kinship. However, as K. Saradamoni, a contemporary Nayar woman scholar, wryly cautions, Nayars, already by the beginning of the twentieth century, had travelled a long way from textbook descriptions of matriliny (1999: 28). My study over the last twenty years endorses Saradamoni's view. The contemporary ethos of Nayars is still changing, adapting to the new realities of India. This discussion will be in three parts and will focus on a few of the radical changes that have occurred over the last century. First, I present two "scenarios" of Nayars, approximately one hundred years apart, which elucidate the role of women. Second, the evolution of a certain marriage pattern among Nayars helps highlight the contrast between earlier and present times. Third, I look at how styles of Nayar nomenclature have changed. Contemporary styles reflect the new ethos. Fourth, I conclude with the description of a Nayar ritual of yesteryears.

Bounded on the west by the Arabian Sea, Kerala has long been in contact with places as remote as China and ancient Greece and Rome. However, over the last five hundred years, with the Portuguese appearing at the ancient port of Calicut in Kerala in 1498, Nayars, like the rest of the various communities on the sub-continent, have been in closer and continuous contact with waves of European colonizing groups, the last and most important of these being the British, who established themselves as the imperial power ruling India for almost two hundred years until 1947. This imperial rule has had the most radical and transformative impact over the last two centuries when British administration became centralized and spread to practically all corners of the sub-continent. These years have seen fundamental and pervasive changes to the earlier cultural ethos, lifestyle, and self-understanding of Indian people

Along with other Indian communities, matrilineal groups like Nayars have been significantly affected and altered. When compared to Nayars, say, a hundred years earlier, contemporary patterns present striking contrasts. Though old-style matriliny has now been superseded, changes in the Nayar ethos have been neither uniform nor monolithic. Therefore, my discussion of the contemporary scene is open-ended and tentative. My comments are bound to be coloured by a perception that is woman-centred and will reflect my own upbringing as a Nayar in a universe seven decades earlier. How Nayar men would have perceived the same universe is a question that I have not been able to answer accurately from my own perspective. Therefore, this study does not tell the whole story. Nonetheless, given the almost complete absence of Nayar female voices in past research and scholarship, my insights are, I believe, legitimate and significant and complement earlier discourses.

I propose to examine Nayars over the last one hundred years. I have collected material for the period from several sources. These include family history handed down orally through several generations of ancestresses; published ethnographies, histories, memoirs, and travelogues; literary works, dating back over a century; folklore, ballads, legends and myths; and, most recently, data collected by me in the field over the last twenty years. My field work carried out with Nayar women and women of other closely linked communities in Kerala and in the neighbouring States of Tamilnadu and Karnataka has provided understanding and insights which not only illumine the universe of matrilineal Nayars of yesterday, but also enable me to trace "family resemblances" between Nayars and their neighbours in South India.

I shall present two real scenarios. The first dates back to 1903 approximately; the second is from 1980. Both are from my own matrilineal family. I see in these a living metaphor for the history of matriliny, Nayar style. They articulate what it meant to be male or female in the domains of membership, rights, responsibilities, and the continuity of the (matri)lineage.

The Role of Women

Scenario One

About a hundred years ago, my maternal great uncle, that is, my mother's mother's brother (MMB), performed religious austerities and went on pilgrimage. He undertook a pilgrimage to a hilltop shrine in Kerala, considered the most arduous of pilgrimages at the time.

My great uncle was at the time the eldest adult male of the extended matrilineal family. Therefore he was the *karanavan*, the head of the family unit. However, as *karanavan*, he did not own all the assets. He only managed family properties and assets which belonged to everybody. He was the manager and had executive powers to represent the family in the community and before any legally constituted authority. The *karanavan*, the head of the family, had to be an adult male. If at any point in time, there were no adult males, then the eldest adult female would assume the role of head. She had a symmetrical title, *karanavatti,* that is, a female head of family. The *karanavatti* wielded identical powers. Governance under such female heads, though entirely legitimate, happened only rarely in practice. One of the duties of the *karanavan* was to punctiliously carry out traditionally required ritual for all females of his lineage at puberty. Such ritual recognition of female power was required in order to ensure the fortunes, prosperity, and continuity of the lineage. While all Hindu groups in South India, patrilineal and matrilineal, ritually recognized and celebrated female puberty, there was an added dimension and significance to such ritual among Nayars.

Members of a matrilineal family unit (*taravatu*) were related to one another through a common ancestress, namely, mother, grandmother, great grandmother and so on. The lineage could continue only through a female line. From this it becomes clear that, if at any point in time there are no longer any younger females of reproductive age, or if none of the remaining adult females have produced female progeny, the lineage will come to an end. Therefore, matrilineal Nayars need females at every generation to keep the lineage alive and to continue. When faced with the prospect of extinction, a lineage is obliged to adopt young females from another branch of the extended lineage, related through female links, needless to say. The optimum scenario is when such adoption does not become obligatory.

Now, to go back to my great uncle and his pilgrimage: What had necessitated the pilgrimage?

By 1903, two of his younger sisters (my grandmother and her elder sister: MM and MMZ) had given birth to a son each, seven years ago. These two sons would be eligible heirs in their own persons but being male they could not continue the line to the next generation. Seven years later, there was still no daughter born to either of the females of reproductive age, my MM and MMZ. This is a crisis in a Nayar context, as already explained, because without females the lineage cannot go on. The seven-year wait was frustrating and caused anxiety among all members of the family. My great uncle, being the eldest male and *karanavan*, felt his moral and religious responsibility keenly. He wanted to invoke divine grace upon his lineage and started going on pilgrimage and performing religious austerities, hoping that a daughter would soon be born to one or other of his sisters. And it did come about after a seven-year gap. My maternal grandmother gave birth to a girl, the first in her generation. That was my eldest maternal aunt, my MZ, born in 1903, who lived to be 95. Months later, my MMZ also gave birth to a female child.

When my MZ was born there was celebration and rejoicing. The rejoicing that followed a female birth among Nayars (unheard of in patrilineal systems) reveals the matrilineal ethos. It was obvious that my aunt was welcomed primarily as a potential ancestress. However, the actual words of my uncle, while yearning for a niece to appear, capture another key feature of the Nayar matrilineal ethos as well. My mother reports that he specifically stated, and I translate, *please give me a girl for whom I may celebrate the puberty ritual*. The celebration of female puberty rituals was the most elaborate, extravagant and prestigious ritual among Nayars. Men had no parallel ritual, not even in a simple form. For my uncle, to have a niece who would enable him to establish his enviable status in the community was of supreme importance. It should be noted that every female birth was welcomed and celebrated without waiting to see if this infant proved to be fertile on reaching adult status. Female birth was auspicious per se, with no waiting period to check her future fertility. A logical concomitant of matriliny was that a woman always belonged to her natal lineage and was not assimilated to the husband's lineage upon marriage. She remained a permanent fixture and could never be forced to leave. There were, logically, no marriage prestations from her lineage to her husband's family upon marriage. A woman was never seen as a burden in the context of marriage. For Nayars, "the female was at the centre of matriliny and ... she had a civil and legal status independent of men" (Saradamoni 1999: 26).

Scenario Two

The second scenario dates back to 1980. In my mother's generation, an aunt wrote me a letter in which she was weeping and wailing. What was she unhappy about? Her daughter had just given birth to her third child. *Again* a daughter, my aunt moaned. Three daughters! My aunt was not pleased.

This response may be expected in a patrilineal context among the various communities on the sub-continent. However, that Nayars have so rapidly adjusted their perception of female offspring—falling in line with the majority patrilineal perception among the more conservative and orthodox Indians that female children are less desirable than male and are even seen as a burden—disturbs and shocks me.

When the two scenarios are placed side by side, one sees clearly that something in the Nayar ethos has changed today. A hundred years back, female progeny was welcomed, indeed prayed for actively and strenuously.

Nayars are no longer legally matrilineal, thanks to the recent panIndian family laws enacted in the course of the twentieth century. Moreover, the present evolution and lifestyle of urbanized Nayars may further erode any vestigial, de facto matrilineal pockets still struggling to stay alive. I have first-hand information that some Nayars today deliberately take legal steps to be assimilated into the lineage of their fathers/husbands. It appears that today Nayars, even Nayar women, may not in every instance celebrate the arrival of daughters or granddaughters (nieces no longer being in the picture) as they did one hundred years back. Nor is it true that today all Nayars would prefer daughters to sons.

How may one understand the change? One might point to the rise of a cash economy, colonial ideology, homogenization of patriarchy, panIndian legislation favouring patriliny and "disqualifying" matriliny; the individual learning to assert his/her interests as against those of the larger family unit, changing perceptions of one's role and duties within one's family; presentations from the bride's family almost universally demanded at marriage among Nayars, placing a heavy financial burden on the bride's parents; the nuclear family well on the way to take centre stage, and habits of greater consumption and greed; all pan-Indian phenomena. I would conclude that the present Nayar ethos is not even vestigially "matrilineal."

Evolution of a Marriage Pattern

Now I look at one aspect of Nayar marriage patterns in earlier times and even surviving up to the present time, though not very common. It appears to me that this pattern has both an instrumental and an expressive function in the Nayar matrilineal ethos. According to data collected as late as 1887, over 50 percent of Hindu groups in Kerala were matrilineal and some Muslim and Christian groups as well. This pattern of marriage was common to several groups of Hindu people besides Nayars. There is even corroborating data from places as distant from Kerala as Bengal in the nineteenth century, thus endorsing the spread of an older pattern on the sub-continent.

Let me explain the pattern: We are talking of two marriages arranged at the same time in a matrilineage which involve another matrilineage simultaneously in two marriages. Two sister-brother pairs are involved. I shall name one such pair "A" and "B" and the other brother-sister pair shall be "X" and "Y". The young woman, A, is married to the man, X, from another lineage. Simultaneously, B, the brother of A, marries Y, the sister of X. Nayars educated in English, from my grandparents' generation on, used to label it an "exchange" marriage or "mutual" marriage. The sister of the husband is married to the brother of the wife in the other pairing, in each case.

A = X ; B=Y. A and B are sister and brother. X and Y are also sister and brother. The conjugal unit, AX, is related to the other conjugal unit, BY in symmetrical fashion. Wife A's brother B is married to Y, the sister of X, who is A's husband.

Each member of the two couples is related to the partner in a double bond. A's husband is also the brother of A's brother Y's wife. Each woman finds that her husband's sister is married to her brother. Each man is aware that his sister is married to his wife's brother.

Each marriage is thus reinforced by the other marriage. The husband in one unit knows that his sister's well being is in the hands of his own wife's brother. And vice versa. If any member of the conjugal unit is not treated with consideration and respect by the partner, there will be, or could be, negative "fall out" in the other unit. Therefore, it becomes incumbent on each of the four to be mindful of the greater good and solidarity of their families. They have to accept problems and challenges in the marriage without causing a rift or disharmony in the larger entity of two *taravatus* linked together. The demand for compromise and understanding made on each member of the conjugal pair is indeed congruent with the priorities of the larger entity, one's *taravatu*. The individual, husband or wife, has to try to keep peace and avoid conflict for selfish ends. And, more generally, both lineages feel more "related" to each other because of the two linked marriages. A kind of solidarity is achieved between the two lineages.

Instead of only two individuals being united in a conjugal bond, there are now four, two from each lineage.

It is unfortunate that I never did try to find out from traditional matrilineal Nayars what the purpose behind such marriages was, while my mother and grandmother were around. Nor was I able to discover if there was an indigenous term in Malayalam, the language of Kerala, to designate this type of marriage. From my grandfather's generation on, English terms have been used, like "exchange marriage" or "mutual marriage." What is to be noted, in marked contrast to today's practice among a large number of Nayars, is that in matriliny there was no question of dowry to be given along with a bride to the groom's family. Dowry used to exist only among patrilineal groups. Therefore this exchange marriage was not about avoiding dowry presentations in the time of my great uncle or my uncle. However, it is taking this form often nowadays.

By the time my cousins were getting married, say, fifty years back, dowry was beginning to creep in among Nayars, along with the attrition of matriliny. So the exchange marriage provided a neat solution to the problem and pitfalls of dowry, one might argue. But this development is only a recent twist and not congruent with the older matrilineal ethos in which dowry was unheard of. A more traditional, non-urbanized Nayar man, also highly educated, in his sixties, declared unhesitatingly that such marriages were intended to promote "greater solidarity within the extended family." He firmly believed in this explanation and delighted in it. It made him feel good about the old ethos. Indeed Heide Goettner-Abendroth (1999) sees this type of marriage as a characteristic of matriliny/matriarchy. Old style Nayars fit in quite well in this context. The "explanation" offered by the more traditional Nayar man is congruent with the old Nayar ethos. The newer explanation may adumbrate recent changes in the Nayar ethos.

In the older ethos, sisters, female cousins and nieces on the mother's side, were seen as the real heiresses by brothers, male cousins and uncles. Old-style Nayars had internalized the ethos which created in the men a strong sense of duty to take care of these female kin. By and large, Nayar men accepted such a state of affairs as right, ethical and the way things are. And women reciprocated these feelings. It was considered ethical/normative for Nayar women to feel a stronger bond with their brothers and greater loyalty to them than to their sexual partners and vice versa. A Nayar woman was not financially dependent on her sexual partner. She would, most of the time, continue to live in her matrilineal home and her children would be raised by her maternal uncle or brother, in the old days. The usual practice was for the husband to visit in the evening and return home next morning.

The marital bond was not necessarily strong or lasting, though it could have been, if the parties so desired. My great grandmother used to exult in her fidelity and love for her husband. She had a strong and loving bond with her husband until his death. She never remarried. However, by and large, Nayar marriages were, in matriliny, easily dissolved without prejudice or stigma to either party and subsequent unions were the rule rather than the exception. Women and men had greater freedom than in patriliny to terminate sexual partnerships and women who exercised such freedom were not stigmatized or seen as less honourable. The relative unimportance of the conjugal bond, the absence of dowry, the absence of any perception that sexually mature females could be a burden to the lineage, the high value of the female in the order of things, were all essential components of Nayar matriliny. All these components have been affected and altered in the new ethos among Nayars.

Changing Styles in Nayar Nomenclature

A revealing index to the transformation of matriliny in the differing styles of Nayar nomenclature can be found today. It should be noted that in earlier times, in Kerala and in Tamilnadu, its closest neighbour, the style of nomenclature was different from that in Northern India. South Indians used to have, in practice, only their first names with their lineage being indicated along with it, but preceding the first name. Unlike in the West, surnames do not appear to have been affixed in Southern India before the advent of colonial rule. When English education took root, the family/lineage name was represented by an initial or initials as the case warranted. The initial or initials which preceded a person's first name stood for the family, the lineage. Everyone knew which was which. Only the first name was used, as common practice for most occasions. However, during British rule, this system had the effect of treating a person's first name as his/her family name as it followed the intitials.

Let me illustrate from the British style of nomenclature: W. H. Smith is a name which has the family name last and the personal and middle names preceding the family name. But in South India, a typical old-style Tamil name, D. N. Rajagopalan, has to be understood in just the reverse order. The last mentioned name, Rajagopalan, was the first (given) name. The letters D and N stood for the family name and the father's first name respectively. This name followed a patrilineal style. In effect, this style was the opposite of the British style.

In matriliny, among Nayars, a male took the family name of his *taravatu* and the first name of his *karanavan*, often his direct maternal uncle. From my grandfather's time onwards it became the style to put down the initial letter of the name of the *taravatu* (according to the spelling in English) and/or that of the maternal uncle, both preceding his given (first) name. That is, a Nayar man's first name came last, following the *taravatu* name and the maternal uncle's first name, abbreviated into English initials. The same order was followed as in the previous example of D. N. Rajagopalan. My maternal grandfather's full name was formed in this style. He was K. R. Paramesvaran Pillai. K was the first letter of his *taravatu* name when written in English and R was the first letter of his maternal uncle's first name, Raman. Paramesvaran was my grandfather's given name. Pillai denoted an additional group marker among Nayars. Such group markers existed because Nayars were, more accurately, not a single caste but a "caste cluster" and showed many smaller sub-divisions among themselves. Other such marker names included Nayar, Menon, Kurup, Nayanar, Kaimal, Paniker, Karta, Nampyar and many more. These markers were used only in formal or legal contexts. In every day life, people got along with only their given names. More accurate identity could be explained when needed. The *taravatu* name and the uncle's name were expanded in legal documents. Everyone understood the system clearly. Sometimes only the *taravatu* name was affixed before the given name. As is obvious, the style of nomenclature was neither uniform nor monolithic.

To anyone living in Kerala who heard or read the name, K. R. Paramesvaran Pillai, it would be obvious that the owner of the name hailed from a *taravatu* whose name started with K and a *karanavan* whose name started with R and Paramesvaran was his given name. The final unit, Pillai, indicated that his group had this marker. Another name like M. Raman Menon showed that the owner of the name came from a *taravatu* with a name starting with M (the full name being easily accessible if necessary). His *karanavan's* name was not added in this case. His given name was Raman and his group marker was Menon. The name of his *taravatu* was Menonparampil. Therefore, M. Raman Menon was his name for ordinary purposes.

A Nayar woman would most commonly have the name of her mother or the name of her *taravatu*, or both, preceding her given name, the latter coming first. Her given name would be placed last. My chemistry professor's name was K. Parvati Amma. We never wondered what the K stood for. Everyone knew it stood for the *taravatu* name and could easily be discovered. K was Koyip-pillil, her *taravatu*. Parvati was her given name. She did not carry the initial letter of her mother's name. Amma was a honorific suffix used for adult Nayar females. This professor's husband's name was P. K. Madhava Panikker. My professor never styled herself Mrs. Panikker. What intrigued me, even though my ethnographic "gene" was totally dormant at fifteen, was that a couple of class-mates of mine (dubbed "Anglo-Indian") always referred to our professor, Parvati Amma, as Mrs. Panikker. I found it chic and "cool" at the time. However, now I understand that to these Roman Catholic girls of mixed European and Indian parentage, a patrilineal mode of nomenclature must have appealed and felt more "proper" or "civilized".

Through the nineteenth and twentieth centuries, different permutations and combinations were being tried out. One modified style was that sons would receive the first letter (according to the English spelling) of their father's first name and the daughters that of their mothers. These initials preceding the given name stood for one's "roots". So sisters and brothers would have different initials before their first names as if they belonged to different lineages. Another, more modern pattern, was to affix the first letter of the father's first name to sons and daughters alike, completely leaving out matrilineal connections and identity. This was the form chosen by my father and the husbands of my mother's sisters (lawyers, bankers, government officials) and female cousins. It was impossible to figure out our matrilineal identity from our names. In addition to our given names we each had only an initial which stood for our fathers' first name. My siblings and I received the intial S. My mother's eldest sister's children received the initial A, which was the first letter of their father's name. The second elder sister's children also happened to have S as their father's name also started with S! Three sets of maternal cousins, all from the same matrilineage, children of direct sisters, ended up with no mention of their *taravatu* in their names. No information was given about our lineage, no matronymic, no information about our fathers' lineage either.

The pattern at present is again varied and shows different styles. There is no hint, in the large majority of cases, of the mother or her lineage in a child's name. Sometimes even the lineage of the father is not indicated nor his given name. The child takes only the word denoting the marker of the group to which his father belongs. This becomes his/her "family" name. Let us consider a son of M. Raman Menon. The M stands for the father's lineage in the older style. The son, with a given name of Vivek, may be officially registered as Vivek Menon. This name reveals neither the name of his lineage (his father's or his mother's) nor his father's or mother's first name. Menon is a marker common to such a large number of Nayars that one may not be able to identify the roots of this boy at all from only the name. Such nomenclature is leading to anonymity on a large scale as to one's antecedents and caste affiliations. The majority of Nayar children are named today completely identifying them with their fathers only. However, the marker may be just the given name of the father. Or it may be a marker like Menon without further information. Various styles are now current, including, in rare instances, the old matrilineal one. Some innovative parents choose to give both their initials to their children. So the child carries, in abbreviated form, the first names of both father and mother. Both *taravatus* are left out.

Simultaneously, a large majority of Nayar women, upon marriage, style themselves Mrs.—,putting their husband's group marker like Menon or Paniker or Kaimal or whatever, after their first name, symbolically assimilating themselves into their husbands' clan or lineage. If the husband has only his first name and no caste marker word, the wife will title herself Mrs.—, adding the first name of her husband to her own. In effect, her whole name will consist of two given names, hers and her husband's. Such a name would be as illuminating as the name, "Elizabeth Philip" to designate Queen Elizabeth II! Such nomenclature gives no information whatsoever on the matrilineage or patrilineage of the wife or the husband. Nowadays, Nayars seem to be eager to shed any trace of matriliny from their names and more women prefer to be known as Mrs.—, followed by their husband's last name or even first name. The result is a degree of anonymity.

Contemporary styles appear to be in line with panIndian trends. With the ideal of abolishing or de-emphasizing caste, many Hindus, influenced by social reformers in the last two centuries, had been dropping their caste/group marker last names in several regions of the sub-continent. The trends show the strengthening of the conjugal bond among Nayars and the recognition of the nuclear family with Nayar husbands stepping smartly into the seat of authority left vacant by the karanavan of earlier times. One may conclude that Nayar women, at least a considerable percentage, welcome this new role for the husband and are engaged in the process of developing a new perception of one's identitiy and loyalties to the kin group.

A Nayar Ritual of Yesteryears

I shall round out my discussion by describing a ritual of yesteryears, recently chanced upon. My remarks are subjective, hermeneutical, and based on my knowledge of the old Nayar ethos and the significance of symbols in the Hindu ritual universe. My informant is a fifty-five-year-old Nayar woman from North Kerala. I have never come across this ritual anywhere else, in ethnographic accounts or from any other Nayar informant. The ritual is named *Tulaganapati* and involves a younger brother and older sister. I have not been able to obtain any kind of exegesis of this ritual. I shall present it following my informant's account of it and then attempt my own interpretation.

This is a calendrical ritual and is carried out in the month of Tulam which coincides roughly with the number of days under the zodiacal sign of Libra in western astrology. The ritual to be looked at is a post-harvest one and newly harvested rice is used. As Suzanne Hanchett (1987) points out in her study of symbolic structure in Hindu family festivals, rice is a "key" symbol. It is panIndian. Rice takes on different symbolic meanings according to the context, being used for rituals from birth to death. However, the most commonly understood connotation of rice to a Hindu mind is that of prosperity and food.

Rice is the staple all over southern India. Food is identified with the supreme Goddess in the form of Annapurna. One of the Goddess's myriad names, Annapurna embodies her attribute as the deity who fulfils all needs, starting with the basic need for food. "Anna" is a quintessential term for "food." The adjective, "purna," signifies plenitude, perfection in the highest or even mystical sense. "Annapurna" is thus "the nourishing, protecting goddess who fulfils all wants." The word may also be glossed as "she who makes food perfect." The use of rice in this ritual thus links it directly to this Goddess who also bestows fortune, wealth and fertility. In Hindu terms, Annapurna is the purveyor of auspiciousness. Auspiciousness is a predominantly "this-worldly" concept. In the Hindu universe, women are seen as goddesses of the hearth and home, reflections of Annapurna.

Now to look at the ritual of *Tulaganapati*. First, a banana leaf, cut from the narrower end, and filled with auspicious food items like fruit, *sarkara* (lumps of cane sugar), *malar* (popped rice), *aval* (beaten rice), and other indigenous grains and cereals is offered to Ganapati, the deity of auspicious beginnings. This deity is represented by a traditional bronze lamp that is kept lit in front of the leaf. The sister and brother come before Ganapati, fresh from their bath, dressed in clothes rendered ritually pure. In addition to standard attire, the brother will have a thin cotton bath towel with one short end looped around his neck and knotted at the nape. The rest of the material hangs down free on his torso. He picks up the free end and forms a pouch with the cloth. Standing in front of his sister in this posture signifies that he is a supplicant, even a mendicant. The sister now gathers, in her curved palms held together, three scoops of the newly harvested rice and pours it into the pouch.

My informant could not explain the ritual. Here is my interpretation. We have seen how a Nayar male is dependent on his sisters for his heirs and heiresses, in matriliny. Just as, in patriliny, men are dependent on their wives for progeny and propagation of their line, Nayar men, while respecting the taboos of incest, have a primary interest in the fertility of their sisters. While in patriliny the significant female is a wife, in matriliny it is the sister.

As the sister fills her brother's pouch with rice, she is sharing her fertility and magic, goddess-like attributes. The brother may be seen as a prototype for the *karanavan*. Only a sister can bestow this blessing. The sister scooping out rice, symbol of fertility and life, with her own bare hands and pouring it out to her needy and supplicating brother, not once but thrice—three being a magic and auspicious number—creates an eloquent tableau. We witness the symbolic transference of sacred female fertility for the benefit of the larger family unit. The sister thus becomes sacred especially to her male kin. Nayar matrilineal ethos is succinctly, perfectly captured through this ritual.

Savithri Shanker de Tourreil was born in Kerala, South West India, in a matrilineal Nayar homestead with a depth of four generations, with her maternal great grandmother, grandmother, her sisters, great uncle, mother's sisters, brothers, cousins, etc. All education up to a Master's in English Language and Literature, completed in Kerala. She joined as Lecturer in English at the Maharaja's College for Women, in Trivandrum, and taught there for five years. At age 27, she came to Canada, on a Commonwealth Scholarship, to do doctoral studies. She has taught at several Canadian universities and also in Brazil, and is presently member of the Faculty of Religion at Concordia University in Montreal. Ph.D. dissertation and area of specialization: Hindu women's rituals, with special focus of Nayar female centred rituals.

References

Aiyappan, A. 1982. *The Personality of Kerala.* Trivandrum: The Department of Publications, University of Kerala.

Balakrishnan, P. V. 1981. *Matrilineal System in Malabar.* Calicut: Mathrubhumi Press.

Dumont, Louis. 1961. "Les mariages Nayar comme faits indien." *L'Homme* 1: 11-36.

Fuller, C. 1976. *The Nayars Today.* Cambridge: Cambridge University Press.

Goettner-Abendroth, Heide. 1999. "The Structure of Matriarchal Society. Exemplified by the Society of the Mosuo in China." Ed. Joan Marler. *ReVision* 3 (21): 31-35.

Gough, Kathleen. 1959. "The Nayars and the Definition of Marriage." *Journal of the Royal Anthropological Institute of Great Britain and Ireland* 89: 23-34.

Hanchett, Suzanne. 1987. *Coloured Rice: Symbolic Structure in Hindu Family Festivals.* Delhi: Hindustan Publ. Corp.

Moore, Melinda A. 1985. "A New Look at the Nayar Taravad." *Man* 20 (3): 523-541.

Nakane, Chie. 1962. "The Nayar Family in a Disintegrating Matrilineal System." *International Journal of Comparative Sociology* 3: 17-28.

Saradamoni, K. 1999. *Matriliny Transformed: Family, Law and Ideology in Twentieth Century Travancore.* New Delhi: Sage Publications.

Tourreil, Savithri Shanker de. 1995. *Nayars in a South Indian Matrix: A Study Based on Female-Centred Ritual.* Unpublished dissertation, Montréal, Concordia University.

PEGGY REEVES SANDAY

Matriarchal Values and World Peace

The Case of the Minangkabau

One of the largest ethnic groups in Indonesia, numbering some four million in their homeland province of West Sumatra, the Minangkabau are famous in Indonesia for their matrilineal social system, matriarchal values, and dedication to Islam. They are also known for their business acumen and literary flair. Banks, bookstores, and institutions of higher education in the cities, and satellite dishes and schools in the villages make this modern society all the more interesting for its matriarchal values in a world torn by conflict, strife, and male dominance.

From 1981 to 1999 I visited West Sumatra nearly every year to study what the Minangkabau refer to as *adat matriarchaat*, the term they use for their matriarchal customs. In this paper I examine the relationship between these customs and the Minangkabau commitment to peaceful social relations. My goal is to demonstrate that matriarchal values grow out of a social philosophy in which the emphasis is on cooperation. Viewed from the Minangkabau perspective, matriarchy is not about "female rule," but about social principles and values rooted in maternal meanings in which both sexes work together to promote human well-being. Just as they nourish the vulnerable rice seeds in the rice nurseries before planting them in the fields, then keep the young shoots carefully watered and weeded so that they will grow strong, the Minangkabau nourish the weak and vulnerable so that society will be strong (see Sanday 2002).

The following analysis is based on participant-observation of life in a rural village confederacy located in the highland heartland of Minangkabau culture, and interviews with intellectuals and religious officials in the coastal capital city. These sources provide a unique vision of a society in which matriarchal values are expressed both at the level of natural philosophy and as a social reality.

Nature is Our Teacher

The social philosophy of Minangkabau villagers in this area differs dramatically from western ideals stressing competition and "survival of the fittest." Growth in nature is the model on which the Minangkabau construct their social contract. From this model they derive the principle that nurture is the primordial foundation for the social order. This principle is expressed in a well-known proverb:

Take the small knife used for carving
Make a staff from the lintabuang tree
The cover of pinang flowers becomes a winnow
A drop of water becomes the sea
A fist becomes a mountain
Growth in nature is our teacher.

This proverb introduces the animistic foundation for both the Minangkabau *matriarchaat* and matrilineal law. When I asked people for an exegesis of the proverb they usually answered by saying that people derive the rules of culture by observing the benign aspects of nature. Ibu Idar, a female leader and my hostess in the village where I lived, explained that the imitation of nature means that people learn not just from what supports life but also from what destroys it: "Our *adat* teaches us to take the good from *alam* (nature) and throw away the bad," she said.

According to the above proverb, what grows in nature provides the where-withal for rudimentary implements for food and shelter (first three lines.) Social well-being is found in natural growth and fertility (second three lines) according to the dictum that the unfurling, blooming, and expansion of growth in nature provides a lesson for social relations. As plants grow from seedlings, trees from transplanted branches, the sea from a trickle of water, and mountains from a clump of earth, so do people. Like the seedlings of nature, people and emotions must be patiently fed so that they will flower and grow to their fullness and strength. Thus, nurture is the natural law that humans should follow in devising social rules.[1]

Many *adat* leaders and intellectuals in the urban and rural areas of West Sumatra write about the role of nature in *adat* social philosophy. According to Pak Idrus Hakimy (1985), a religious and social leader whose books of proverbs are widely read in the villages and the cities, nature is the source for *adat* rules and beliefs:

We study everything around us: human life, animals, plants, mountains, hills, and rivers. Nature surrounds us in all the events of our lives. We learn from the good in nature and throw away the bad. The rules of *adat* are based in nature. Like nature, *adat* surrounds us.

Taufik Abdullah, a well-known Minangakbau social scientist, cites a proverb that goes one step further to suggest that *adat* is sacred because it is a primordial aspect of nature:

When nothing was existent, the universe did not exist
Neither earth nor sky existed
Adat had already existed. (1972: 231)

218

The principle of matrilineal descent is a corollary of the logic making *adat* imminent in nature. In another interview, Pak Hakimy (1985) had this to say:

Matrilineal *adat* is in accordance with the flora and fauna of nature in which it can be seen that it is the mother who bears the next generation and it is the mother who suckles the young and raises the child. As we all know, Minangkabau *adat* comes from nature according to the proverb *Alam takambang jadi guru* (growth in nature is our teacher.) In nature all that is born into the world is born from the mother, not from the father. Fathers are only known by a confession from the mother. *Adat* knows that the mother is the closest to her children and is therefore more dominant than the father in establishing the character of the generations. Thus, we must protect women and their offspring because they are also weaker than men. Just as the weak becomes the strong in nature, we must make the weaker the stronger in human life. If the mother abandons or doesn't recognize her own child, *adat* exists to recognize the child's descent line and to ensure the child's worldly welfare.

Similar sentiments were expressed by an *adat* leader in the village I lived in for many years. In 1985, Dt. Nago Besar, who was then at the apex of the male *adat* ladder, explained to me that the matrilineal system was originally devised so that children would always have a family, food, and ancestral land. Speaking rhetorically he asked, "If a child is born without a father, or we don't know who the father is, where can the child find *pusaka* (land, titles, and ancestral house) and food? Like growth in nature, we always know from whom the child descends: the mother."

Such sentiments should not be taken as support for the claim made by nineteenth-century evolutionists in Europe and the U.S. that matriliny derives from ignorance about the father's role in conception. The nineteenth century was a time when there was considerable speculation about a period in cultural evolution when women ruled. Whether this period was labelled the time of *mother-right* or matriarchy, there was wide agreement that female rule was prior to patriarchy and was based on ignorance about paternity.[2]

I doubt that ignorance of the father's role in conception explains matriarchal values in any society past or present. One can't help but wonder why western social scientists seem unable to understand the meaning of women-centeredness in anything other than male terms. The Minangkabau are aware of the father's biological role, but chose to ignore it in favour of the social well-being of the mother-child bond. They think that males can fend for themselves, but mothers and their children need social support. As Pak Hakimy (1985) told me:

Here we elevate the weak instead of the strong. Women must be given rights because they are weak. Young men must be sent away from the

219

village to prove their manhood so that there will be no competition between them and their sisters.

This is not to say that there is no role for the father, only that it is not tied to the transmission of ancestral property rights. True to their tendency to emphasize growth rather than competition and aggression, ideas about the role of the father is designed on the model of nurture in nature. Once again a proverb communicates the message:

Fern leaf tendril, balimbing nuts
Shake the shell of a coconut
Plant pepper with the roots
Seat your child and guide your nephew
Think about your village people
Prevent your village from destruction
And keep up the tradition.

The lines of this proverb describe expectations for the roles of father and uncle. Like the inward folding of the fern tendril wrapped around itself, a father should wrap himself around his family, custom, and the affairs of the village. Like the outward curve of the stem of the tendril, the uncle acts as a leader and guides his nephews and nieces. As a father, a man is expected to "seat" his children (that is, love them) and, as an uncle, he must lead his nephews (that is, educate them).

"The uncle comes when he is called by his sister to discipline her children," Pak Hakimy (1985) informed me. "A mother will say to a naughty child: 'Look your uncle is coming. Please be good!' Fathers and uncles are expected to work together to help provide financial support to the families of their sisters and wives," he concluded.

The Importance of Negotiation in Resolving Differences

The Minangkabau place great value on accommodation and consensus in handling conflict. A prime example of how accommodation works is illustrated by the story the Minangkabau tell about how matrilineal *adat* came to be wedded to patrilineal Islam in the course of their history.

The story often begins with a proverb: *Adat came down; Islam came up.* This means that *adat* originated in the interior mountainous heartland of Minangkabau culture long ago, some say before the time of Christ, and went down to the coast. Islam came much later, brought by traders to the coastal regions, sometime between the fourteenth and sixteenth centuries, and went up into the mountains. The two achieved an accommodation and lived in peaceful coexistence until a few well-known Islamic officials who were educated in Mecca sought to purge Minangkabau culture of *adat* customs such as matrilineal descent by force. Those supporting the accommodation of *adat* and Islam stood their ground by forming an alliance in order to defend their sacred *adat* traditions against the purist tendencies of the local Islamist assault.

The struggle brought on the Padri War in the early nineteenth century (1821-1837). The moderate wing won the struggle with the help of the Dutch. The accommodation of *adat* and Islam involved the purging of some *adat* practices (like gambling) and the strengthening of others. Matrilineal descent, the lynchpin of *adat Minangkabau*, was placed in the most sacred of *adat* categories on par with Islam. This is the only *adat* category that is considered so sacred that, like Islam, it cannot be changed. Because both are handed down from the godhead neither contradicts nor competes with the other.

The accommodation of *adat* and Islam in this case is a prime example of the distinction often drawn between cultural and political Islam in the Islamic world. Political Islam (also called Islamism) refers to the wholesale destruction of local culture in the interest of rule by the laws of the Holy Book. Political Islam did not take hold in West Sumatra due to the outcome of the Padri War and the accommodation of *adat* (local custom) and Islam. The accommodation meant that cultural Islam prevailed instead. Cultural Islam is found in those parts of the Islamic world where communities subscribing to the "five pillars" of Islamic practice live in syncretism with traditions that can be traced to centuries-old pre-Islamic traditions.

The importance of cultural Islam in West Sumatra became more apparent to me in the aftermath of the 9/11 disaster in New York. During a visit in August of 2002, the subject of Bin Laden came up a number of times. Although for some he was the Islamic David who confronted the American Goliath, he was not a leader to be followed. The people I talked to said that the Islam they were taught prohibits violence and the use of force. They emphasized the Minangkabau practice of achieving social goals through negotiation and discussion, not force. One man said that his Islamic education stressed the importance of thinking about others. Do unto others as you would have others do unto you, he said in so many words.

The subject of Bin Laden and 9/11 sparked many comments about the perils of globalization. It was clear that people in West Sumatra felt that 9/11 was a cry against globalization in the form it was taking in the world. However, they didn't agree with the Islamist solution. Minangkabau intellectuals worry about two kinds of globalization: western capitalism and anti-western Islamism. Urban professionals and intellectuals reject both forms of globalization as "a clash between two politicized universalisms." They expressed a longing for a more humane model of globalization for their country and the world based on cultural and spiritual values in the context of "democracy building and creating good governance" (*The Jakarta Post* 2002*).* Minangkabau intellectuals proudly say that the social ideology and practices of *adat* represent the first true democracy in the world, going back millennium. Among other things, today, democracy means protecting local culture from the onslaught of western materialism and the imposition of militant Islamism.

Respect for Senior Women

The Minangkabau system of values interweaving accommodation, consensus decision-making, and nurture is upheld by the dominant symbol of *adat matriarchaat* in village life, known as Bundo Kanduang. Bundo Kanduang, which means "my own mother," is both a royal title reserved for the mythical Queen Mother of the Minangkabau, and a title applied to senior women in their ceremonial roles. As a symbolic title, it has mythic, historical, sacred, and deeply personal meanings. The emphasis on "my own mother" reflects the deep emotional attachment the Minangkabau feel for the mother who raised them. The role and meaning of Bundo Kanduang is expressed in the following proverb:

> *Bundo Kanduang is the butterfly of the traditional house*
> *She is the one who owns the key of the clothes chest and the jewelry box*
> *She is the centre where the threads of the fish net meet*
> *She is the finery of the village*
> *She is sovereign through her dignity*
> *The one who is greatly honoured*
> *The one to whom we take all our problems*
> *The one who receives our last wishes when we die.*

The butterfly metaphor in this proverb has aesthetic and social meanings. In Minangkabau weaving and house carving, the butterfly symbolizes the senior woman in full *adat* regalia—finely dressed, laden with gifts, the conveyor of good fortune and good will. In this guise she is *Bundo Kanduang,* our own mother who is the dominant symbol of the common good. The butterfly is also associated with the central pillar of the traditional house, which is the oldest pillar because it is the first erected. Thus, centre, origin, and maternal symbol are joined, an association frequently found in Minangkabau symbology.

Owning the key to the clothes chest and the jewelry box, as mentioned in the second line of the proverb, also carries aesthetic and social meanings. This is a subject that many women discussed with me because it has material implications for the lives of their daughters. In addition to the implication of finery, the clothes and jewelry are part of the sacred *pusaka* (ancestral) objects so important in ceremonial displays and, thus, safeguarded for passing from mother to daughter. The jewelry represents a woman's economic acumen in her ability to translate rice and garden surpluses into gold jewelry as an investment for a daughter's future. The jewelry is money in the bank for cashing in when funds are needed to stage a ceremony, especially a wedding ceremony. The savings may also be called upon for buying livestock as a form of investment.

The clothes in the chest are the *adat* costumes of fine gold or silver weaving handed down from mother to daughter in the wealthier families to don for special *adat* ceremonies. The chest is also the place where the ancestral *kris* (dagger) is stored for use by the males who inherit the ancestral title on ceremonial occasions. Thus, the chest represents the material repository of *adat* as it is passed from one generation to the next.

The idea that the senior woman of the household is "the centre where the threads of the fish net meet," evokes the image of this woman as hostess to the many guests that flow into her house for the life cycle ceremonies she and the women of her lineage organize. Because the ceremonies are so public, sometimes with most of the village attending, it is easy to see how, through ceremonial activities, women knit the threads of the village social tapestry. Women do this on a regular basis, not just in staging their own ceremonies but through helping one another.

Finally, there is the personal tie to the mother expressed in the last lines of the proverb. The emotional meaning of this tie is evident not just in this proverb but in the many lamentations for the mother sung on the village stage by female bards during the entertainment part of village ceremonies. One that is particularly moving in the mournful cadence of the music and voice of the female singer is about coming home from far away and finding one's mother gone and the ancestral house of one's birth boarded up. It ends with these verses:

> *If my dear mother is at home*
> *My worries are over.*
> *When I am sad, she soothes my heart.*
> *When I need her, she gives advice.*
> *Without her I am nothing.*
> *With whom will I talk?*
> *I feel so lost, I can only cry.*
> *It is late, I must hurry home.... Oh, Mother.*

The Role of the Mother's Brother

In 1896, E.B. Tylor wrote an article entitled "The Matriarchal Family System" in which he concludes that because the mother's brother holds household authority in matrilineal societies like the Minangkabau, we cannot speak of matriarchy. In my book, *Women at the Center*, I argue that Tylor's conclusion was based on the misleading definition of matriarchy as female rule—misleading, because the definition was devised with patriarchy in mind rather than being based on observing behaviour and worldviewin societies like the Minangkabau in which the dominant social symbols and ceremonies are women-centred.

Matriarchal values in societies like the Minangkabau constitute a system of social interaction in which no one social group holds final power over another. The Minangkabau fit what Riane Eisler (1987) calls a "partnership" society. Final power rests in *adat*, not in people. Matrilineal *adat* is considered sacred and cannot be changed. Uncles have authority, but so does Bundo Kanduang. The authority shared between the Mamak (mother's brother) and Bundo Kanduang is interdependent. One cannot operate without the other; both show mutual respect. This is the Minangkabau way based on their system of *tali budi* (good relations).

The Minangkabau way holds *adat* up as the final arbiter, the law to which all are subservient. When the Mamak meet in the village council house to settle disputes, the titled male leaders refer to the body of law codified by the original *adat* lawgivers, sons of the first Bundo Kanduang. This body of law establishes a procedure for the resolution of disputes according to *mupakat*, or consensus decision-making in search of the truth. Mutual agreement is the ultimate sovereign in Minangkabau life. Anyone who stands in the way of truth by acting discourteously or resorting to the use of force is exiled from the community or shunned.

The primary function of the Mamak is to resolve disputes, negotiate marriage with their sisters, confer titles on new candidates, and engage males from other lineages in an official exchange of speeches at *adat* ceremonies. In addition to his role along with senior women in negotiating marriage, theoretically it is the responsibility of the Mamak to look after the young people of his clan by helping them find spouses. In practice, this job falls to the mothers involved in a potential union.

In a dispute settlement, the Mamak of a village resolves competing claims over land that can lead to harsh words and outright conflict in the village. The process is careful and deliberate for the proceedings must follow consensus decision-making in the search for the truth, in accordance with the saying:

Loosen that which is tight,
So that the sound is like a tinkle rather than a crash.

With respect to the members of his own immediate extended family, the man who inherits the Mamak title oversees the management and use of ancestral land in conjunction with his sisters. Because this puts him in a position where he could abuse clan interests for his own profit, the man chosen to receive a title must display more than the correct genealogical link. He must be deemed honest, truthful, straightforward, and strong enough to uphold the rules of *adat*.

A man who breaks these rules by selling land without the appropriate agreement from his female relatives suffers the consequences of the curse of the ancestors. The symbolism of the curse seems to have been devised with the Mamak in mind. On the one hand, the Mamak is likened to a tree; on the other hand, the curse of the ancestor refers to the illness that afflicts those who break the oath of the ancestors to respect matrilineal rights to property. The fate of the man who breaks this oath is likened to the decay and slow death of a tree bored in the middle by bees.

Conclusion

Based on observing *adat matriarchaat* in Minangkabau village life, I object to the western definition of matriarchy as female rule (see Sanday 2008). Defining matriarchy as the mirror image of patriarchy is based on two faulty assumptions.

The first assumption is that women must be like men to occupy a central position in society. The second is that social prominence for either sex is founded only in social power as we know it, which always means power over people. Neither assumption is compatible with the role that democratic values and maternal meanings play in Minangkabau daily life.

Defining matriarchy either in terms of female rule or by reference solely to mother goddesses blinds us to the social complexities of women's actual and symbolic role in partnership societies. Not finding cases in which women are rulers in society or in heaven, mainstream scholars looked no further and proclaimed universal male dominance. This is a mistake, because it underrates the vital role that maternal meanings play in upholding the social fabric and human well-being in many societies.

If we think of Minangkabau social meanings as forming an intricately woven tapestry of values, the mutually supportive role played by *adat matriarchaat* and Islam stands out as a major theme. One provides a defense against the destructive consequences of western capitalism and the other guards against falling lockstep into a simplistic anti-western Islamism. The synergy of the connection acts as a hedge against the decline of either. Backed by religion, *adat* is better able to withstand the global capitalist formations sweeping Indonesia. With solid roots in *adat* practice, cultural Islam is better able to withstand militant Islamist trends. The *adat* ceremonies organized by women play an essential role in this struggle by reminding young men, who might otherwise be guided by the seductive pull of political Islam, of their cultural roots and responsibilities. In a world where young men in many countries seem to have lost their cultural bearings by turning to indiscriminate violence, it is a relief to know there are societies like the Minangkabau.

Although I went to West Sumatra looking for female power, I came home many years later with a more nuanced understanding of what matriarchal values can do in the world. It is not female power *per se* that counts. Values are the key. If competitive, combative values rule—such as the cowboy mentality which suffuses North America's presentation of its national self in today's world—it doesn't matter which sex rules because the end result will be the same: assertiveness, violence, and preemptive warfare. On the other hand, if working on behalf of equality, human rights, children, the world's poor, and against environmental depletion, are values that drive social thought, it also doesn't matter who is at the helm for we all know, male and female alike, that this is the only way to protect a gradually disintegrating world for future generations. Our concern should not be with who rules, but with protecting the vulnerable in the interest of peace and social well-being for all. If this goal were one of the world's priorities, we would enjoy an unparalleled era of peace.

Peggy Reeves Sanday is a pioneering feminist anthropologist and a Professor of Anthropology at the University of Pennsylvania. Her landmark book, Female Power and Male Dominance: On the Origins of Sexual Inequality *(1981) is a classic in its field. She has received numerous awards and is a member of the Board of Scholars of* Ms *Magazine. In her view, anthropology has to do with Enlightenment and she is a critic of the concept of universal male dominance. Her most recent book,* Women at the Center: Life in a Modern Matriarchy *(2002), is based on more than two decades of primary research among the Minangkabau people of West Sumatra who describe their society as matriarchal.*

[1] This is my interpretation of the proverb based on discussions with many *adat* experts.

[2] J. J. Bachofen and Lewis Henry Morgan presented strong arguments for sovereign female authority in the mid-nineteenth century. Bachofen introduced the notion of maternal law, which he defined as government of the family and of the state in his 1861 book *Das Mutterrecht* (see Bachofen 1967). Morgan described mother-right among the matrilineal Iroquois and, like Bachofen, spoke of *gynecocracy* in early human society. Although, this might seem to credit Bachofen and Morgan as the discoverers of matriarchy defined as female rule, neither actually used this term. According to the classicist Stella Georgoudi (1992: 450-451), although matriarchy is considered to have been Bachofen's great discovery, compared by French feminists in the early twentieth century with Columbus' discovery of America, the term does not appear in his work. Rather, as Georgoudi points out, matriarchy was forged later in the nineteenth century by analogy with patriarchy. As far as I can surmise, E. B. Tylor (1896) is the first to use this term in the context of anthropological analysis.

Although Bachofen and Morgan didn't actually use the term matriarchy, they can be credited with the association of matriarchy with female rule because of the degree to which both conflated gynecocracy and mother-right. As Georgoudi notes, Bachofen used these terms side by side as if to say these were inextricable characteristics. Thus, where he found matrilineal kinship, Bachofen assumed gynecocracy.

Lewis Henry Morgan, the father of American anthropology, can be credited with the most extensive and earliest examination of the social meaning of matrilineal descent. His famous *League of the Iroquois* was first published in 1851, ten years before Bachofen published *Das Mutterrecht*. In his later work, however, Morgan seems to have been influenced by Bachofen when he spoke of Iroquoian mother-power and claimed that mother-right and gynecocracy among the Iroquois is not overdrawn (1965 [1881]: 66).

The notion that mother-power represents an ancient phase of human life, illustrates the second most important attribute that came to be associated with matriarchy: its evolution prior to patriarchy. For example, Bachofen associated mother-right with the pre-Hellenic peoples and patriarchal forms with the more advanced Greek culture (1967: 71). His preference for one over the other is seen in his conclusion regarding the triumph of paternity, which he said liberates the spirit from nature and sublimates human existence over the laws of material life (109).

References

Abdullah, Taufik. 1972. "Modernization in the Minangkabau world: West Sumatra in the Early Decades of the Twentieth Century." *Culture and Politics in Indonesia*. Eds. Claire Holt, Benedict Anderson, and James Siegel. New York: Cornell University Press. 179-249.

Bachofen, J. J. 1967. *Myth, Religion, and Mother Right: Selected Writings of J. J.Bachofen.* Princeton: Princeton University Press.

Eisler, Riane. 1987. *The Chalice and the Blade: Our History, Our Future.* San Francisco: HarperCollins.

Georgoudi, Stella. 1992. "Creating a Myth of Matriarchy." Ed. Pauline Schmitt Pantel. *A History of Women: 1. From Ancient Goddesses to Christian Saints.* Cambridge: Harvard University Press. 449-463.

Hakimy, Pak Idrus. 1985. Personal Interview.

Jakarta Post, The. 2002. Opinion Page. Summer issue.

Morgan, Lewis Henry. 1851. *League of the Ho-dé-no-sau-nee, or Iroquois.* 1965. Rochester: Sage and Brother.

Morgan, Lewis Henry. 1881. *Houses and House Life [House-Life] of the American Aborigines.* 1965. Chicago: University of Chicago Press.

Sanday, Peggy Reeves. 1981. *Female Power and Male Dominance: On the Origins of Sexual Inequality.* Cambridge: Cambridge University Press.

Sanday, Peggy Reeves. 2002. *Women at the Center. Life in a Modern Matriarchy.* New York: Cornell University Press.

Sanday, Peggy Reeves. 2008. "Matriarchy." *The Oxford Encyclopedia of Women in World History.* Ed. Bonnie G. Smith. New York: f0 `Oxford University Press.

Tylor, Edward Burnett. 1896. "The Matriarchal Family System." *Nineteenth Century* 40: 81-96.

USRIA DHAVIDA

The Role of Minangkabau Women

I would like to introduce to the history of the Minangkabau term, *Bundo Kanduang*. The oldest men in a Minangkabau clan are given the title, *Datuak;* the oldest women in the clan or family are given the title, *Bundo Kanduang.* Bundo Kanduang is a symbolic title that confers honour to Minangkabau women who have children and are the oldest women in the tribe or clan. These are mothers who possess revered qualities of motherliness and of leadership.

Bundo Kanduang is an icon for the Minangkabau people, as is the temple, for example, for our nation, Indonesia. According to Minangkabau tradition, Bundo Kanduang was the first queen who lived with her sons in the first village and established the first kingdom under the rule of *Adat* (Minangkabau matriarchal principles). It was the famous kingdom of Pagarruyung, whose influence spread throughout central Sumatra. The Minangkabau are the descendants of the first Bundo Kanduang, and they have the same clan name following the matrilineal system. Each clan mother is also called Bundo Kanduang in honour of her position within the clan. She is respected by everbody. In general, nobody treats women badly.

The Bundo Kanduang or clan mother must meet certain criteria: she is the wise woman in her family, in her clan. She is able to differentiate the good and the bad, and nurture and guard her family. There is a saying in Minangkabau that shows the influence of woman as a mother: *If in the beginning of the river the water is clean, then at the ending the water is also clean.* It means "like mother, like children." When the mother is doing good, her children will also do good.

Another saying shows the central position of women in the Minangkabau world. Woman is the main pillar of the big, communal house. This "main pillar," this woman, holds the house together. After getting married, she has to be intelligent and wise, for she has to keep her husband in her soul and she has to educate and guide the children and the family. This points to the function of Bundo Kanduang as role model: she has to manage her own household as well as the communal one, putting things in their places. If there is no Bundo Kanduang, then love is not good, it will become dry. A Minangkabau woman is a symbol of pride in her family. In Minangkabau society, women's roles are very noble. A Minangkabau woman is always respected at every stage of her life.

We call the matrilineal system *Tambo*. We have good reason to practice the matrilineal system in Minangkabau. The main reason is that it is much easier to trace someone's family tree through the mother's line than through the father's. Another reason is that matrilineal family relations limit individualistic ethics, that is, you must not do everything individually, but in agreement with your siblings. Minangkabau women stand for the safeguarding of the existence of this matrilineal system and, by this heritage, women care for the continuity of *Adat*. Giving women a high position, treating women with respect, prevents begging from others for sustenance, prevents homelessness and prostitution among children, and undermines male misbehaviour, crime, and domination.

Today, Minangkabau are followers of Islam. According to Islam, as stated in the Koran 49.1-13, women are appraised by God as being similar to men. Allah says: "We have created all humankind out of a male and a female, and made you tribes and nations that you may know each other!" So, women as members of the society have to have a good relationship with Allah according to our belief. That means, how can we do the best thing for everybody around us? By having good relations with our husbands and good relations with our children, and taking care of our religious community. That is the role of women in general.

Traditionally, our communities, our villages, and towns—*Nagari* in our language—have been independent and self-determined units. But in recent times, the Indonesian government undermined this independence by centralist laws, thus weakening our *Nagari* system and the autonomy of Minangkabau women. Then, after 30 years of centralism, the government returned to the *Nagari* de-centralized system with its "Back-to-*Nagari*-program." We now call this time the "after-centralist period." Since 1991, with the implementation of Law 22, Minangkabau women are regaining some of their original autonomy. The new de-centralization system is giving Minangkabau women back their official role as Bundo Kanduang. This is an improvement in the way the government pays attention to women. The reason behind this new program is to shelter the state from the dangers of globalization, which changes everything.

But the special role of Minangkabau women can only be realized by by improving the quality of their education and by the empowerment of women in all fields: social, economical, and political. Doing so will also lead to the improvement of the quality of life within their families and clans.

Usria Dhavida is a Minangkabau and mother of a girl and boy who are now students. She studied linguistics and museology, and worked for 29 years at the Museum of West Sumatra in Padang, Indonesia, which collects and protects the Minangkabau cultural heritage. Today, she is the head of the museum. She is also an activist, and is particularly involved in organizations that are concerned with women, children,and social affairs.

RUXIAN YAN

The Kinship System of the Mosuo in China

The Mosuo inhabit the Lugu Lake area on the borders of Yunnan and Sichuan Provinces in Southwestern China. It is a hot tourist site nowadays, but in the 1960s when we first visited, it was an isolated area with poor transportation conditions. It took us ten days to walk from the seat of Lijiang County to Lugu Lake.

The Mosuo call the lake *xie na mi* meaning "Mother Lake." They call the mountain situated at the north shore of the lake *gan mu* meaning "Female Mountain," and consider it the guardian of the Mosuo. The Female Mountain is surrounded by a number of male mountains that are its companions. In this area, women are considered superior and mothers are highly respected. Big trees are female, and smalls ones male; big mountains are "mother-mountain," while small mountains are identified as male. The matrilineal blood ties are paramount. A Mosuo proverb says: *(We) do not worry about the lack of sons while water does not flow without daughters; having daughters is more significant than having sons for daughters are the roots.* The Mosuo consider the matrilineal system as the most natural, most perpetual, and most sacred tie among all human relations. In their mind, mother is the loftiest among all female relatives and the maternal uncle is the loftiest among all male relatives. Part of their wonderful tradition is to respect elders and care for the young. They hold the unity of the matrilineal relatives as the source of a happy life for all.

The first Mosuo household we visited in the Aguwa village was the Yijie's with sixteen members. I habitually asked Gaocuomi, the female head of the household, the family's surname. She answered that, "we don't have any surname. Just call us the Yijie's." The head of the township who acted as our guide explained to us that, "Yijie is the name of a female ancestor ten generations ago, used as the name of this household." They belong to a *siri* (sub-clan) called Sadabu. Sadabu is the name of a more ancient ancestor." I then asked Gaocumi, "How many children do you have?" "Ten," she answered. I was surprised and confused because I was told that the birth rate of Mosuo women was low. The first person I had ever talked to seemed to be an extreme exception. The head of the township explained again that, "She actually gave birth to only one son. The rest of the children are her sisters'. Mosuo women take all their sisters' children as their own. The children in turn treat all of them as their mothers."

The answers to these two simple questions suggested that the Mosuo concept of kinship was different from those of the partriarchal groups that we were familiar with. We immediately decided to move from the guesthouse of the local government to the Mosuo household so we could closely observe and experience their household structure and day-to-day life.

The Matrilineal Kinship System

The kinship system, also called the kinship terminology system, is a kind of social norm that uses a set of particular vocabulary to indicate the blood or affinal relationships among the people of a certain social group. The matrilineal kinship system of the Mosuo is used within their matrilineal blood groups of *er* (clan), *siri* (sub-clan), and *yidu* (matrilineal household). It includes the following terminology[1]:

Relation to the ego	Appellation	Meaning
Great-grandmother	^{2}sz^2	Great-grandparent
Mother's mother	e^{2}zi^1	Grandmother
Mother's maternal uncle	e^{2}phu^2	Granduncle
Mother	e^{2}mi^2	Mother
Maternal uncle	e^{2}v^2	Maternal uncle
Daughter (female call)	mv^1	Children
Son (female call)	zo^2	Son
Granddaughter (female call)	zu^{1}mi^2	Granddaughter
Grandson (female call)	zu^{1}v^2	Grandson
Great-granddaughter (female call)	zu^{1}mi^2	Granddaughter
Great-grandson (female call)	zu^{1}v^2	Grandson
Elder sister	e^{2}mv^3	Elder sister
Elder brother	e^{2}mv^3	Elder brother
Younger sister	go^{2}mi^2	Younger sister
Younger brother	gi^{2}zz^2	Younger brother
Sisters	e^{2}mv^3, go^{2}mi^2	Sisters
Brothers	e^{2}mv^3, gi^{2}zz^2	Brothers
Sister's daughter (female call)	mv^1	Daughter
Sister's son (female call)	zo^2	Son
Sister's granddaughter (female call)	zu^{1}mi^2	Granddaughter
Sister's grandson (female call)	zu^{1}v^2	Grandson

Sister's daughter (male call)	zi^3mi^2	Niece
Sister's son (male call)	zi^3v^2	Nephew
Sister's granddaughter (male call)	zu^1mi^2	Granddaughter
Sister's grandson (male call)	zu^1v^2	Grandson
Mother's elder sister	$e^2mi^2gz^3$	Big mother
Mother's younger sister	$e^2mi^2tci^1$	Little mother
Mother's sisters	e^2mi^2	Mother
Mother's sister's daughter (older than ego)	e^2mv^3	Elder sister
Mother's sister's daughter (younger than ego)	go^2mi^2	Younger sister
Mother's sister's son (older than ego)	e^2mv^3	Elder brother
Mother's sister's son (younger than ego)	gi^2zz^2	Younger brother
Mother's sister's granddaughter (female call)	mv^1	Daughter
Mother's sister's grandson (female call)	zo^2	Son
Mother's sister's great-granddaughter (female call)	$zu^1 mi^2$	Granddaughter
Mother's sister's great-grandson (female call)	zu^1v^2	Grandson
Mother's sister's granddaughter (male call)	$zi^3 mi^2$	Niece
Mother's sister's grandson (male call)	zi^3v^2	Nephew
Mother's sister's great-granddaughter (male call)	$zu^1 mi^2$	Granddaughter
Mother's sister's great-grandson (male call)	zu^1v^2	Grandson
Grandmother's sister	e^2zi^1	Grandmother
Grandmother's brother	e^2phu^2	Granduncle
Grandmother's sister's daughter	e^2mi^2	Mother
Grandmother's sister's son	e^2v^2	Maternal uncle
Grandmother's sister's granddaughter (older than ego)	e^2mv^3	Elder sister
Grandmother's sister's granddaughter (younger than ego)	go^2mi^2	Younger sister
Grandmother's sister's grandson (older than ego)	e^2mv^3	Elder brother
Grandmother's sister's grandson (younger than ego)	gi^2zz^2	Younger brother
Grandmother's sister's great-granddaughter (female call)	mv^1	Daughter
Grandmother's sister's great-grandson (female call)	zo^2	Son
Grandmother's sister's great-granddaughter (male call)	zi^3mi^2	Niece
Grandmother's sister's great-grandson (male call)	zi^3v^2	Nephew
Great-grandmother's sister	$^2sz^2$	Great-grandparent
Great-grandmother's brother	$^2sz^2$	Great-grandparent

Great-grandmother's sister's daughter	e^2zi^1	Grandmother
Great-grandmother's sister's son	e^2phu^2	Granduncle
Great-grandmother's sister's granddaughter	e^2mi^2	Mother
Great-grandmother's sister's grandson	e^2v^2	Maternal uncle
Great-grandmother's sister's great-granddaughter (older than ego)	e^2mv^3	Elder sister
Great-grandmother's sister's great-granddaughter (younger than ego)	go^2mi^2	Younger sister
Great-grandmother's sister's great-grandson (older than ego)	e^2mv^3	Elder brother
Great-grandmother's sister's great-grandson (younger than ego)	gi^2zz^2	Younger brother
Great-grandmother's sister's great-great-granddaughter (female call)	mv^1	Daughter
Great-grandmother's sister's great-great-grandson (female call)	zo^2	Son
Great-grandmother's sister's great-great-granddaughter (male call)	zi^3mi^2	Niece
Great-grandmother's sister's great-great-grandson (male call)	zi^3v^2	Nephew
Mother's partner	e^2v^2	
Maternal uncle's partner	e^2mi^2	
Ego's partner	a^2cia^2 a^2du^2	
Partner's daughter (male call)	zi^3mi^2	
Partner's son (male call)	zi^3v	
Partner's mother	e^2mi^2	
Partner's maternal uncle	e^2v^2	

The above terminology includes one lineal line and four collateral lines.[2] It encompasses all ranks of matrilineal social structures. The principle of classifying relatives according to these categories can be further extended. However, regardless of whether the relation is close or remote, the appellations used are always the same as those of the lineal line blood relatives. As a result, all the collateral blood relatives are included into the range of the lineal line blood relatives. This kind of kinship terminology has the following features:

The great-grandmothers and the great-grandchildren have the most distant relationship up and down the terminology chart. All the ancestors before, and all the descendants after these two categories, are incorporated into the categories respectively. This means, all generations before the great-grandmothers are called "great-grandmothers" while all generations after the great-grandchildren are also called "great grandchildren."

The female ego is the centre in both the direct line and the collateral line kinship relations. That is, the basic reference for the genealogy can only be a female because only women have children. We can trace up from oneself to the mother and the mother of the mother while we can trace down to the daughter and the daughter of the daughter. The brothers of each generation are included in the lineal line. However, the sexual partners of the mothers, oneself, and the daughters are not included. Neither are the sexual partners of male members of the household. Within a *yidu*, both sexes of the same generation are siblings. All the relatives of the collateral lines are classified the same way.

The first and by far the most important characteristic of this kinship system is that there is no difference between the lineal line and the collateral line. The first collateral line indicates the relations between the sisters' descendants and oneself: if I am a woman, my sisters' children are theirs as well as mine. They call their biological mother and me "e²mi²." In the same way, the children of my sisters' daughters are their grandchildren as well as mine. Namely, I take my sisters' children as my own and treat them as such.

Second, in this Mosuo system, children belong to their mother and her *yidu*. So a man's next generation is his sisters' children instead of his own. He calls them nieces and nephews while they call him maternal uncle.

Third, the sisters of one's mother are the mothers to one. That is, sisters of both the lineal line and the collateral line all take the position of mother to each other's children.

Fourth, the children of one's mother's sisters are one's siblings. The second collateral line indicates the relations between the descendants of my mother's sisters and me. Regardless if I am a woman or a man, the sisters of my mother are all my mothers, and their children my sisters and brothers. Furthermore, the children of these sisters are my children if I am a woman, while they are my nieces and nephews if I am a man.

Fifth, the sisters of one's grandmother are all taken into the category of grandmothers so as to avoid leaving out any collateral matrilineal relatives of this generation. The third collateral line indicates the relations between one and one's grandmother's sisters as well as their descendants. In the same way, the children of these grandmothers are one's mothers and maternal uncles, while these mothers' children are one's siblings.

Finally, although the blood ties are more distant by going further upward or downward on the collateral lines, the use of kinship appellations are exactly the same as those of the same generation with one's lineal line relatives. Take the fourth collateral line as an example. It indicates the relations between the sisters and their descendants of my great-grandmother and me. Namely, the sisters of my great-grandmother are my great-grandmothers; their daughters are my grandmothers; their granddaughters are my mothers; and, their great-granddaughters my sisters. Their sons are different generations of maternal uncles. So are other collateral relatives.

Consequently, although the matrilineal blood relatives could have many collateral lines, there are only thirteen basic terms in the Mosuo system. They are great-grandmothers and great-grand maternal uncles ("$^2sz^2$"); grandmothers ("e^2zi^1"); grand maternal uncles ("e^2phu^2"); mothers ("e^2mi^2"); maternal uncles ("e^2v^2"); sisters ("e^2mv^3, go$^2mi^2$"); brothers ("e^2mv^3, gi$^2zz^2$"); daughters ("mv^1"); sons ("zo^2"); nieces ("zi$^3mi^2$"); nephews ("zi$^3v^2$"); granddaughters ("zu$^1mi^2$"); and, grandsons ("zu$^1v^2$").

The Social Foundation and the Evolution of the Mosuo Kinship System

The matrilineal system of the Mosuo has a solid practical basis and a deep historical basis. According to historical record, the ancestors of the Mosuo arrived at the Lugu Lake area in the fourth century. Six ancient *er* or matrilineal clans settled in a place called Sibuanawa to the north of Lugu Lake, and then and then migrated south in three pairs. These three groups practiced intermarriage. At the beginning, the members of an *er* lived together in the same community. When the population grew, *er* formed a subgroup called *siri*, and the members of a *siri* lived together in the village. The fission continued and an even smaller group, *yidu*, derived from *siri*. The social function of a *yidu* is like a family. It is the epitome of a matrilineal clan, the unilateral consanguinity of a maternal blood relative group. When we conducted our investigation in 1963, most *yidu* consisted of brothers and sisters who were born from the same female ancestor, and the children of the sisters. The average size of the *yidu* was seven to eight people; however, as many as twenty to thirty people can live in a *yidu*. *Yidu* is still the basic production and living unit among the Mosuo today.

In a *yidu*, the head is most commonly a female. If she is not the oldest generation in the household, her mother and mother's sisters and brothers are also included. In a typical Mosuo house, old women and children sleep in the main room where all group activities are held. There are small rooms for each adult woman, but no place for male adults unless they are *lamas* (Tibetan Buddhist monks) or are too old to have sexual life. Male adults are expected to spend nights with their sexual partners while work for and live their daily life with their maternal *yidu*. All children belong to their mother's *yidu* and they call their mother's sisters mother and their mother's brothers maternal uncle, who are responsible for raising and educating them, and providing financial and emotional supports. There is neither an affinal kin in the *yidu* nor affinal terminology in the Mosuo kinship system.

Although the matrilineal clan, *er*, collapsed a long time ago, most people know to which *er* they belong. *Siri* existed for a long period after the collapse of *er*, functioning as the kin group of mutual production and consumption. The *yidu* derived from *siri*; it had a smaller number of people and tighter blood connections. Thus, *siri* was no longer the form of group in which people lived their daily life, yet it sill played a role of ceremonial importance. People of the same *siri* hold ceremonies to worship their ancestors together. And they are not allowed to have sexual relations.

As a practical entity of production and living, the *yidu* keeps the characteristics and the customs of the matrilineal clan alive and more specific:

1. Women are at the centre. The statuses of women and men are equal. The genealogy is passed down through the maternal line. The head of the household is called *dabu* and is usually the mother or a capable daughter. The head of the household is responsible for planning production activities, such as what to plant, how many seeds and fertilizers to use, and arranging the daily life of the household.

2. The properties belong to all the members of the *yidu*. Everyone does the work according to her/his ability, and the whole *yidu* consume together.

3. Dividing of the *yidu*. When there are so many people in a household that it causes some inconveniences, a daughter *yidu*, *a po*, will separate from the mother *yidu*, *a wo*. The *a wo* will help the *a po* build up a new house. She will be given a certain amount of land, domestic animals, and tools, while the major properties remain in the *a wo*. Little conflict is caused when dividing the properties.

4. Naming of the *yidu*. Most *yidu* are named after an ancestor, especially a female. Some of them take the names from animals or the places they live.

5. Dwelling of the *yidu*. Members of a *yidu* live together in the same compound centred by women. Namely, old women and children live in the main room; elderly maternal uncles live in the upper room; and each adult woman has her private room. However, although each adult man has a seat in the main room in daytime, there is no bedroom for him, as he should spend nights at his partner's room in her *yidu*.

6. The common cemetery. Each *yidu* has a burial ground in the cemetery of the *siri* in which they belong. The Mosuo cremate those who died naturally, put their ashes into hemp pouches, and bury them into the common ground according to the order of their seats by the hearth of the household when they were alive. Namely, the older generation is seated in the upper place and the younger generation the lower, while females are seated on the right side and males on the left. This shows that the people of the same matrilineal blood kin are never separated from each other, even in death.

Apparently, all these characteristics are inherited from the matrilineal clan. The *yidu* members see themselves as inseparable; they go through thick and thin together. There is a deep sense of intimacy and security in the their consanguinity. This extends to the entire Mosuo community. All old and young, sick and handicapped, are taken care of. There are few conflicts between household members or neighbours. All the people offer their care and help to those affected in times of difficulty or disaster. Mother's love is the core of humanity. It nurtures the material and spiritual bases of the Mosuo matrilineal system, which has existed for centuries and will exist for a long time to come.

Rethinking the Origin of the Kinship System

The origin of the kinship system is a topic that has been debated for a long time. It is the premise of this paper that the debate has concluded with the victory of Lewis Henry Morgan's theory of bilateral origin. John Ferguson McLennan's unilateral origin theory lost because he failed to provide examples. However, the very existence of the Mosuo *yidu* and their practices of the pure unilateral matrilineal kinship system call for the re-examination of this issue.

The American Lewis Henry Morgan (1818-1881) was the founder of kinship study. He collected kinship terminologies for over two hundred societies, created general terminology lists, and established a research methodology. He observed that the origin of the kinship system is bilateral and clearly pointed out that it originated in the Malayan system, which he called "the simpler, and, therefore, the older form" (1997: 484) among classificatory kinship system.

The British anthropologist John Ferguson McLennan (1827-1881) held a different viewpoint. He argued that there had been a period of promiscuity in the process of human evolution, and then matriarchy arose. Therefore, tracing the genealogy from the maternal line was earlier than from the paternal line. However, the one who initiated the point of matriarchy was the Swiss anthropologist and sociologist Johann Jakob Bachofen (1815-1887). In his book *Myth, Religion and Mother Right,* Bachofen held that marriage had not existed in primitive societies so it was hard to identify who the father was, and the blood relation could only be determined through mother. Consequently, the kinship relation could only be traced through the maternal line.

Interestingly, each scholar agreed that there was a group marriage period in early human history. The discrepancies lay in that Morgan thought there were relevant marriage rules even at that time. The maternal line, paternal line, and affinal line were all clear and could be expressed by kinship terminology. McLennan, on the other hand, did not believe there were marriage rules during that period. He maintained that there were only matrilineal relatives at the time. However, there was no adequate evidence to prove this point.

In fact, Morgan brought up a hypothesis regarding the relations between a woman and her children, between her and her mother and her mother's mother, between her and her siblings, and between the children of her daughter and her granddaughters—all these relations could be expressed by appropriate terminology. This hypothesis started a whole new kinship system, which was based on blood ties and had nothing to do with marriage rules. This was a wonderful hypothesis. Unfortunately, he could not obtain any physical evidence. Although he firmly believed that the partially consanguineal and partially affinal Malayan system was the most ancient kinship system based on the data he had at the time, Morgan left a profound question: if the consanguineal system was indeed a kinship system, where had this lost system existed.

The exciting answer was, China: it was there and is still there among the Mosuo people who live by Lugu Lake in Southwest China. In fact, it was never lost, but we did not realize this until we conducted field work research in that region. I and my colleagues found the missing link that caused the error in Morgan's theory on kinship system and provided solid evidence for the matrilineal kinship system. The Mosuo kinship system is exactly like Morgan's hypothesis, that is, the "unilateral" kinship system. In this system, all maternal blood relatives, no matter how close or remote, are classified into a category of five-rank kinship relation. To the female ego, those who are one generation older are all mothers and maternal uncles; those who are two generations older are all grandmothers and maternal granduncles; those who are the same generation with the female ego are all brothers and sisters; the next generation are daughters and sons while those who are two generations younger are granddaughters and grandsons. The whole series of relatives are connected by maternal blood ties and have nothing to do with marriage principles. Therefore, there are no patrilineal terms or affinal terms in the system. This system is apparently simpler than the Malayan system, and it is just as Morgan suggested, "a kinship system that is clearly based on blood relations."

The Mosuo kinship system had not changed after the establishment of clan exogamy because the basis of the kinship system was the maternal blood tie. Two terms were added to the original terminology: niece and nephew. This clearly marked that men had no direct descendant and the clan commune was passed down through the maternal line. More importantly, a large number of *yidu* exist today. They are not families but the products of the constant fission of matrilineal clans, therefore forming small matrilineal blood groups.

Although coexisting families (families consisting of two matrilineal lines due to brothers taking wives into the household) and patrilineal families appeared in Mosuo region due to the influence of the central dynasties, the matrilineal *yidu* still held the dominant position. Patrilineal terminology emerged and some terms were borrowed from neighbouring ethnic groups. Nevertheless, even in the patrilineal families, most children called their father, e^2v^2 (maternal uncle), and their paternal aunt, e^2mi^2 (mother), while affinal terminology virtually did not exist.

In conclusion, the development of the Mosuo kinship system reveals that the early form of the matrilineal system is unilateral, namely a maternal, kinship system. Patrilineal kinship terminology was gradually developed along with the establishment of the father/son relation. However, the bilateral system has not yet completely formed among the Mosuo up to now. We believe that the "early period," when the kinship system was counted only according to the maternal line, was the early and middle stages of matrilineal clans. In that time, the matrilineal clan functioned as both the unit of production and living, and the basic cell of Mosuo society. That is, people within the clan participated in daily economic activities together and lived under the same roof. The matrilineal blood tie provided the natural connection to the system. The sexual relation between women and men was the sexual partnership established between clans. The relation between the two parties was loose and unstable, and did not lead to a common life. The clan, based on the matrilineal blood tie, was all that mattered at the time. The members lived together closely as a unit, and were buried together when they died. That was the foundation of unilateral kinship relation.

The Mosuo kinship system and the matrilineal blood kinship structures, the clan and the *yidu*, which the kinship system was developed from, is the kinship structure that is more ancient than Tulannian kinship system and Iroquian bilateral kinship system. It filled the missing linkage of the kinship system based on maternal line only. It is not only significant in exploring the history of matrilineal clan system but also crucial in examining the rich maternal culture.

Translation by Liu Xiaoxing

Ruxian Yan is a Professor of Ethnology at the Institute of Nationality Studies of the Chinese Academy of Social Sciences, Beijing. Her decades-long research has focused on the social structures of ethnic groups in China, especially the matrilineal system among Mosuo people in Southwest China. She is actively involved in national and international academic activities and has served as an executive committee member of the Chinese Women's Federation, vice-chairperson of the Women's Committee in the Chinese Academy of Social Sciences, council member of the Chinese Ethnological Society, the Chinese Folklore Society, and the Chinese Association of Marriage and Family.

[1]The pronunciation of the kinship terminology uses International Phonetic Symbols. The number on the upper right corner of the letter is the tune of the syllable.
[2]There is no affinal appellation within a *yidu* as this kind of relationship is not recognized. For example, a man visiting his girlfriend addresses her relatives in the same way as she does, but he is counted neither as a family member nor as a relative.

References

Bachofen, Johann Jakob. 1967. *Myth, Religion and Mother Right. Selected Writings of J. J. Bachofen.* Trans. Ralph Manheim. London: Routledge and Kegan Paul.

McLennan, John Ferguson. 1886. *Studies in Ancient History: Comprising a Reprint of Primitive Marriage.* London: Macmillan and Co.

Morgan, Lewis Henry. 1997. *Systems of Consanguinity and Affinity of the Human Family.* Lincoln: University of Nebraska Press. 484.

LAMU GATUSA

Matriarchal Marriage Patterns of the Mosuo People of China

The Mosuo have live at the shores of Lake Lugu, in Southwest China, for more than 1600 years according to documents of the Han Dynasty. The population is about 30,000. They have their own distinct language, but no script. Most practice their native Daba religion while some adhere to Tibetan Lamaism. Due to the mountainous terrain they inhabit, the Mosuo have not had much contact with the "outside world" except through the ancient "Tea Horse Road." Many of their daily needs are met through trading with a caravan. This caravan takes an ancient route that heads to the north and meets the following places: Yongning-Lijiang-Zhongdian-Deqin-Mangkang-Zuogong-Leiwuqi-Naqu-Lhasa. There is also a southern route, which is further; it takes the caravan one whole year to make the journey to Tibet and back. The Mosuo community has been isolated for a long time and has lived a self-reliant and self-managed lifestyle, clear evidence of the validity of its culture and traditions.

When the army of the Yuan Dynasty advanced from three different routes from the north to the south to fight the Dali regime, one of Kublai Khan's routes reached the Mosuo area. The perception of the Mosuo among the leaders of the army was that of a peaceful community, because of their policy of non-resistance. (In fact, the Mosuo had no ability to resist.) The area where the Mosuo lived was named Yongning, "a place of eternal peace and stability." The army of the Yuan Dynasty took camp for a time in the valley in Yongning, called Riyuehe, which means "the place where sun and moon are in harmony." Here the army was able to recover and the Mosuo were not bothered.

Lamaism gained influence at the end of the Yuan Dynasty, which had some impact on the cultural development of the Mosuo. The Mosuo accepted into their culture whatever brought improvements to their daily life. For example, the religious leadership of Lamaism was kept separate from the political leadership of the local area. Lamaism was seen as a religion that gained strength through families who adopted its values. Each family set up a special room for the recitation of the Lama scriptures and they would visit the temples only on festival days.As such, the influence of Lamaism and the Tibetan culture on matrilineal Mosuo culture was limited. As a result, sixty percent of the Mosuo still live in matriarchal families today.

Matriarchal Family Patterns

The Mosuo have preserved a harmonious family structure. The matriarchal family is composed exclusively of matrilineal members, including grandmother, mother, maternal aunts and uncles (mother's brothers and sisters), and the children of the mothers and of the sisters. No members from the paternal side are part of the family. The members of a matrilineal family belong to a mother or her sister's children. Children remain in the maternal home throughout their lifetime and work there together with their brothers and sisters. The mother is in charge of the economics of the family and its just distribution. If there are several sisters in a family, one of them will be elected as the *Dabu*, the matriarch, the woman who is the smartest, most capable, and impartial of them all. The brothers of the mother are responsible for the religious activities and rites around the year.

There is a clear division of labour between men and women. Women are responsible for household duties and men for heavy labour. Any income gained by work is handed to the clan-mother, the *Dabu*, who uses it to meet the family's needs, such as clothing, food, housing, and services which they can not provide for themselves. Divorces, quarrels, and strife are not known in Mosuo communities. The benefits of this kind of family culture are listed below:

1. There is great support among all members of the family. Each member is a descendant of the mother. The relationships between members is free and easy. They get on well with each other and without strife among brothers, wives, uncles, or nephews.

2. Marriage is based on love. It is not affected by political, economic, or religious factors. Elders never interfere with the choices of the young. The only exception is the case of being too closely related, or members of the same clan. In such a case, an intervention will be made by the mother's brother. This intervention is accepted and, as a result, struggles over marriage issues never occur.

3. Mosuo families care for their own. The young and the old are looked after very well and disabled people have a special place in the community as they are seen as messengers sent by God.

4. The population increase is steady but slow. Men and woman are equal. Boys are not regarded as more important than girls; girls, actually, are preferred. The fertility rate is not high. The children are common to the sisters who live together. In this way, a gender balance is kept perfectly.

5. The birth process is easy. Many of the young Mosuo live the custom of "visiting marriage," and bear their children when they are in the best physical condition. As soon as a young woman is pregnant she shares her mother's bedroom in order to avoid being "visited" again; this is to protect the embryo.

6. The property of the family always stays intact. Matriarchal families gather great financial strength in spite of the size and many needs of its members. The setting up of separate families would incur great expenses and divide the acquired wealth.

7. A clear division of labour encourages all the members who are engaged in different jobs according to their own special abilities. Some members set up businesses, but all work is completed with ease and attention.

8. There is a reasonable arrangement between work and the rest of life. Mosuo people are simple, honest, and unspoiled. People often sleep without shutting their doors, and no one pockets anything found on the road. Mosuo greatly enjoy the plentiful provisions of nature, and a happy peaceful family life.

As a result, some scholars hold that Mosuo communities are free of six problems which face modern society: 1) the problematic social status of the two genders; 2) the situation of the elderly, often left alone or ill-treated; 3) family conflicts and domestic violence; 4) crime, such as sexual harassment, theft, murder, and arson; 5) estrangement of family members and humans in general from one another, leading to possible civil war; and 6) environmental problems.

There are, however, even in Mosuo communities, shortcomings and contradictions which I will discuss below.

Love and Marriage Among the Mosuo

"Visiting marriage" can be defined in a simple way: Women and men marry freely. The lovers meet at night at the woman's house and at dawn the man leaves to go home to his maternal family. The couple do set up a new family and do not share property. Any children resulting from the union of the couple are the woman's children; the man helps to raise the children of his sisters. On the basis of not having any economic ties, or political or family pressures influencing their decision, erotic love and affection are the only basis of their relationship. As a result, any development in the relationship which results in them separating in no way impacts on the life of the children.

Mosuo separate the issue of emotions and the material world with its economic requests. As a result, the only factor which influences the choice for a partner is love and affection. A woman or man's wealth is not a factor in the choice of a partner as goods or property belong to the clan house.

The philosophy of Mosuo life is expressed in the following sentences from the Daba scriptures: *Love is without fault, love is nectar in the blossom, salt in the soup, and brings joy to the world.* The Mosuo follow the laws of nature: water can not be held back from flowing, a tree can not be rescued if it is dying. People enjoy the life that has been given to them. Women have the right to choose their partners among the Mosuo. If a woman is loved by two men at the same time, the one who is not chosen does not hold ill feelings, because he loves her sincerely and holds no grudges as he makes no demands of his love. He may get a chance later on if he is patient enough. He gains something just by loving, even if his desire is not fulfilled. The heart can only be conquered by another heart; everything else will hurt the heart. Mosuo people understand that love is a fragile feeling. Friendship is nurtured with tenderness and affection. People who experience jealousy might make fun of their opponent, but without hostility.

As a result of such attitudes and ideas, love and marriage are truly free for Mosuo women, and Mosuo men and women are regarded as a happy people who know how to love. In fact, Mosuo women are gentle, kind, uncomplicated, capable, and hardworking. A Mosuo woman obtains status and authority through her diligence and intelligence instead of having it bestowed on her by others. It is said in a poetic way that her deepest emotion is:

> *Like good tea made with fresh water*
> *which slowly sends forth a delicate fragrance,*
> *like a spring which brings forth streams of water,*
> *like the taste of the most mysterious fruit of all,*
> *like a flying bird in the field,*
> *not a peacock in a cage.*

Matriarchal Attitudes and Thought

In patriarchy, man is fundamental and woman nonessential; man is the seed and woman is the carrier; man is the superior sky and woman is the inferior earth; man is the shining sun and woman is the pale moon. The focus is on the man; the woman is only an appendage. The worst expression of this attitude is man is perceived as holy and woman is unclean and able to defile the holiness of man. Women are insulted and abused by the many vicious labels patriarchal society puts on them.

These ideas do not exist in the Mosuo matrilineal culture. I would like to provide a few insights into matriarchal attitudes and thoughts. On the first page of the ancient Daba scriptures are the following sentences:

> *Water is the source and trees have the roots.*
> *Life can't be separated from the mother.*
> *It won't hurt if flesh clashes with flesh,*
> *but it will hurt if flesh knocks against bone.*

These words illustrate the differences between a matriarchal family and a patriarchal family. In matriarchal families, difficulties among the members can be easily negotiated, because they all come from the same mother and are more considerate of each other. It is different in patriarchal families; here, persons may be hostile to each other, such as the wife and her husband's mother or the different wives of brothers. A differing family composition is the explanation for this.

An elderly Mosuo woman once said:

> *The woman is source and man is course; female is bone and male is blood.*
> *Why? Because new life emerges from the woman! A person's shape is completed inside the woman's body. People will grow up after birth but the*
> *structure of the body, the arms, feet, nose, ears, mouth, and all the other*

organs are completed before birth. The whole course of the creation process is completed within the mother. The father provides a little seminal fluid which can be compared to blood, sweat, and water and will disappear quickly. New life from the mother is more permanent.

The most important rites of passage in Mosuo culture—birth, adult initiation, and death—reflect the words of this elder. For example, in the Mosuo clan-house, there is a special room for the birth of children. The same room is also used as the deathbed for the mother. The entire family is happy about the new birth, especially the mother and her sisters. Male family members are not allowed to participate in the birth process; they are not even allowed to enter this birth room, the origin of the new life. All the female relatives from nearby villages will visit the mother and baby in the first month, bringing chicken, eggs, brown sugar, and butter. After the baby has completed its first month of life, an important rite of passage will be held where women play a leading role. Male members keep silent and do not take part in the performance of this rite. Otherwise they would be laughed at. The thought of "female being source and male being course" is advocated from the beginning to the end of the birth rite, as if the arrival of a new life has nothing to do with men.

Another great festival for the Mosuo is the adult initiation rite, which is held when a girl turns thirteen. This process enables the girl to become an adult family member. Now she can express her opinion, and is no longer given special care. At this special celebration, the mother's brothers invite Lama and Daba to bless the child with a ritual. However, the mother dresses the daughter in the special festive clothes of a young woman and gives her a special treasure to hold in her hand. After the rite the mother will take the child to relatives and receive many gifts. Male members do not have this kind of honour bestowed on them.

Funerals are different, however. Men arrange the funeral procession no matter who the deceased is. Women avoid taking part in funerals. Here, strong matriarchal thought is revealed. The place for new life is sacred; men can not take part in it. And woman do not witness the end of life, or disease and decay leading to death. Only men in Mosuo culture confront death.

Survival: Flexibility in Different Approaches

The matriarchal family and marriage patterns of the Mosuo people are not immutable. They are not a living museum, and life is full of changes. A philosopher once said: "The only permanency in life is change." The Mosuo are a small ethnic group of 30,000 people surrounded by much larger groups. In the past they faced the onslaught of the Han culture, Tibetan culture, and Yi culture. It can be problematic for the Mosuo to conserve their matrilineal culture and continue to survive and grow.

If, for example, a family has only male descendants and all of them practice "visiting marriage," the clan-house will not have any children. Mosuo people, however, have developed measures to deal with this situation. A brother's lover/wife—one who is virtuous, fair, and capable—may be selected as *Dabu*. After a trial period, all family members will accept her and the life of the family can be continued. If family members are not satisfied with this approach, they will train a female successor from a maternal relative's family to enable the family to have descendants. This family will thus become a coexistent family with a matrilineal part and a patrilineal part, if a male family member marries a woman from a different clan. However, the family will go back to the matrilineal pattern if there are several female members born into the next generation. A matrilineal family with only one son who marries a woman from the Mosuo community will change into a patrilineal family that may go back to being matrilineal when the third generation produces enough girls. A family with only daughters will let one of them marry a man who lives in her clan-house, and the others will practice "visiting marriage" as usual. This flexibility serves to maintain matriarchal culture and reflect the wisdom of this small ethnic group.

Sometimes it is difficult for the Mosuo people to keep out the influence of foreign cultures. During the period of the Great Culture Revolution in communist China (1966-1976), the central government carried out what was called the "Marriage Movement," according to which only patrilineal marriage of one man and one woman was permitted (the patriarchal marriage pattern). The government dispatched working teams to publicize policies and supervise the execution of the same in Mosuo villages. Mosuo matriarchal families with their matrilineal marriage patterns were regarded as a primitive. Those who didn't follow the new policy would not be provided with their daily needs, such as tea, salt, sugar, cloth, and so on. Sometimes three generations in one family went to obtain their marriage certificates at the same time. Afterwards, many Mosuo people went back to their own homes and ignored the marriage certificates and new policy as soon as the working teams left, because traditional convictions and culture could not be eradicated in such a brief time. However, due to government pressures, some Mosuo did observe the new regulations and suffered much emotional stress as a consequence. After the Great Culture Revolution ended, the government allowed the local traditions to be practiced again. The Mosuo recovered from this upheaval and went back to the tradition of "visiting marriage."

Any culture will continue to exist as long as it has vitality. A culture develops through mutual exchange with its social environment. It will not lose itself, if cultural exchange is based on equality for both sides. The Mosuo culture is now confronted with new challenges and has to find a new road into the future.

Following Tradition and Facing the Future

Mosuo people still follow matriarchal patterns and the concept of "visiting marriage." But tourism has brought the latest onslaught to Mosuo culture. People from many different cultures are now visiting the Mosuo. The influence of television, newspapers, telephone, and Internet are also taking their toll on Mosuo values and traditions. This is happening on a daily basis and we need to observe it and learn from it. Fortunately, only one village has been badly affected by these changes: the fishing village Luo Shui. Most other Mosuo villages are outside of the main tourist areas. This is the reason why research into these changes is so vital for understanding not only the process by which they occur, but how they influence and affect Mosuo culture.

In 1983, the Chinese Government set up the Lugu Lake Provincial Tourism Area in Luo Shui County in order to boost the region's economy. However, the Mosuo people did not know how to generate money from toursim in spite of government programs to educate them. They regarded the tourists as friends and as such entertained them and were ashamed to receive money for this. One village elder said to me: "The government encourages us to develop tourism, but we do not know how to do it." During this time one woman, Ceng Lacuo, had her own ideas about how to go about it. She started a small hotel in her house with twenty beds and began to receive tourists, usually men. This caused upheaval in the village. Although it is natural for Mosuo women to receive men in their houses, the Mosuo did not want Ceng Lacuo to charge for this as they felt it would give them a bad reputation. Furthermore, the elders of the villages felt that older people and children would suffer the most as the demands of this economic venture might lead to their neglect. Finally, Ceng Lacuo agreed to take responsibility for any problems, and the village committee agreed to let her go ahead with her plans. She earned 30,000 Yuan without any of the anticipated problems materializing. This is a huge sum of money for the Mosuo.

As a consequence, many other Mosuo villages also set up private hotels. This, however, caused problems because now these villages were competing for cus-tomers, and formerly harmonious communities became competitive communi-ties. To deal with this problem, the women who owned hotels and the elders got together to work out a solution. They came up with the idea that the owners of hotels should distribute their boats and horses among the families who did not have hotels, thereby enabling them to earn some money from the tourists by offering boat trips and horseback riding. This helped them to be on good terms again with each other. Tourism thus took off in Luo Shui County.

One of the results of this boom is that many non-local people married Mosuo women because of the considerable wealth generated by tourism. Family quarrels and even separations became more common, and the Mosuo now face more dif-ficult challenges. Some companies set up in the area and began to employ Mosuo people during the tourist season. The clan mothers saw this as an opportunity for their children to gain knowledge and encouraged their children to pick up jobs with these companies. Many Mosuo girls worked in Kunming, Shengzhen, Shanghai, and Beijing for years before returning to their villages. They clearly saw the difference in how they were treated at home and how unhappy they felt when they were away from home. This experience of discovering that the sparkling modern world does not keep its promises turned them into advocates for their own culture.

Preservation of one's culture and seeking cultural, social, and economic development are the two sides of one coin. Preservation without development leads to powerlessness. On the other hand, the loss outweighs gains if development is carried out without preservation of the traditional culture. How can we find a balance between development and preservation? This is the problem Mosuo people face today. To reject modern education is not the answer. Further, tourism alone can not be the only answer to the need for development or to gain access to mainstream society.

It is possible that the traditional Mosuo culture will disappear in a few decades. There are several shortcomings in Mosuo culture that threaten its survival. First, the life of the family is the centre of attention to the detriment of the larger community. For example, Luo Shui County has no cultural facilities that promote and help preserve our cultural heritage, even though financial resources are available. Second, the main focus is on traditional family education and modern education in schools is rejected though it would give youth access to science and technology. Third, because of the strong position of the mother in Mosuo families, children do not develop a strong sense of independence and have little pioneering spirit. Their potential for individual achievement is limited, especially after leaving their community, for the most part because the competitive consciousness that exists in the outside world is not at all part of the harmonious Mosuo culture. Fourth, Mosuo population is on the decline. If there are one or two children in a family already, the women will not have more children. Mosuo people who intermarry with people from other ethnic groups will lose their children to these other groups because of two reasons: Mosuo men leave the children to the mothers as usual. But intermarried Mosuo women have to leave their children with their partner's families, too, because these families are patrilineal. If these current trends continue, this ethnic group will die out.

I do not believe that the Mosuo can avoid colliding with modern civilization; we must, then, adjust and reconstruct our culture. We should learn to choose and develop in a sustainable way, and find a path between tradition and modernization. It is of paramount importance that the situation at Lugu Lake is studied and researched as the impact of outsiders increasingly changes the face of Mosuo culture. Mosuo people are aware that they should hold the paddles of their own boats.

Translation by Wang Jun and Jutta Ried

Lamu Gatusa is Mosuo and is an associate professor at the Social Sciences Research Institute of Yunnan Province in Kunming, China. He devoted his studies to his own Mosuo people in order to preserve their unique social and spiritual heritage. In 1993, he took part in research travel with the International Academy HAGIA to the Mosuo as an Indigenous anthropologist. He is also a writer and has received awards for his work on Mosuo culture. He is a member of the Chinese Writers' Union and the Chinese Minority Nationalities Writer's Union.

Mosuo Family Structure

I f you "google" "Mosuo" on the Internet, there is a tremendous amount of information about my people. However, all the information I find on-line or in books about the Mosuo is usually wrong. What is more, in some way, I feel that my people are being insulted. Sometimes I laugh, sometimes I am curious, and sometimes I find it painful.

First of all, when people talk about the Mosuo, they are usually referring to the Mosuo who live in the Lugu Lake area. Actually, Mosuo people live in both Yunnan and Sichuan provinces. In Yunnan about 30,000 Mosuo people reside in places like Lugu Lake, Yongning, Labo, Yankouba, and Xinyingpan; another 10,000 Mosuo people inhabit Zuosuo in Sichuan province.

Second, people are curious about my people. They think we Mosuo women have sex with a lot of men, and that our children do not know who their fathers are, especially after the publication of Ms. Yangerchenamu's book, *The Walk From Girls' Kingdom*. Most readers of this book misinterpret Ms. Yangerchenamu and conclude that all Mosuo women are like her and have many sexual partners. This book troubled me when I was in college. People came to me and asked me how many lovers I had and whether I knew my father. I had a difficult time explaining to them what our culture is really like. In this paper about Mosuo family structure, I hope to provide readers with a better understanding of my culture.

I also am aware that there are researchers who have an interest in the matriarchal family, and they are doing very good research. They provide much accurate information and contribute to an understanding of my culture. I do appreciate what they have done. But deep in my heart, I always feel there is something still lacking. I appreciate that this opportunity to explain what I know about my own people. I do not claim to be an expert on the matriarchal family, but as a Mosuo, I can talk about my people from my own perspective.

An Overview of Mosuo Marriage Systems

To talk about family structure, we have to talk about marriage. Marriage systems are influenced by the development of a society, its economy, and politics. Many people think all Mosuo people practice what we call "visiting marriage." This is not always the case. Actually, in different Mosuo areas, there are different kinds of marriage systems. These different marriage systems lead to different family structures. The main system, visiting marriage, is practiced by 60 percent of Mosuo people, which conforms to a matriarchal family structure. In the second marriage system, visiting (matriarchal) and monogamous (patriarchal) patterns coexist in a complex family structure. Lastly, there is a patriarchal (monogamous) family structure, which is most common in China.

Visiting Marriage System and Its Family Structure

Visiting marriage represents the main marriage system of Lugu Lake, including Sichuan Zuosuo and Yongning area. Men and women spend their whole life with their respective matriarchal families. In the evening, after having dinner in his own home, the man will go and stay with his sexual partner during the night. The next morning he will go back home. The man and woman involved in visiting marriage address each other as lovers. Their relationship is not like that of a husband and a wife. They are simply sexual partners. This kind of marriage does not include a legal or economic relationship. The mother's side of the family is responsible for the upbringing of any children that result from this relationship.

A matriarchal family is normally made up of three or four generations, all of whom are descendants of a common great-grandmother. They share the same surname, which comes from their mother. Property is shared between them. A woman of high moral standard and learning is selected to be in charge of family affairs. Mosuo people call this woman *Dabu*. *Dabu* is responsible for putting food on the table and dealing with important family issues. The male members of the family will give all their earnings to *Dabu*, and *Dabu* will decide what gifts partners may give their *axias* (lovers) when they meet at night**.**

In Chart One, the *Dabu* is the oldest woman in this family named *Bimalamu*. *Heidewudu* visits her during the night, and they produce five children who are brought up in *Bimalamu's* family. Among the children, there are two daughters and three sons. The sons visit other women, and their *axias'* families will bring up their children. *Akaguqu* and *Bemami* visit the two girls, Jiacuma and Cidanshi. These visits will lead to five more children in this family. Later on in life, other men will visit their daughters. For example, Danshi is visiting Ajia, who is the daughter of Jiacuma. In this way, the matriarchal family is continued.

Coexisting Marriage System and Its Family Structure

Mosuo people live in remote areas. The average altitude is above 2,500 metres. Our living environments are quite harsh. Most Mosuo people, except those who live around Lugu Lake, earn a living through various means; all of us, however, live off the land. As a result, the marriage system is adjusted to adapt to the living environment. This can lead to a mixed marriage system in which patriarchal and matriarchal family structures coexist. This kind of marriage system mostly

Chart One

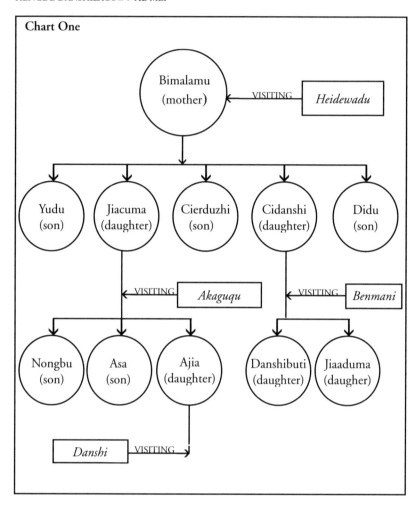

happens in the Labo area where proves more challenging. For instance, there is often no electricity and the water supply is inadequate. Couples might first practice visiting marriage, then after negotiation, plan to marry. There are two possible family structures: one generation of the family is all sons, or alternately, one generation of the family is all daughters.

One generation has only sons: In this situation, they have to find a girl to continue this family so that in the future she can take charge of family affairs. So they find a girl to marry one of the sons. In Chart Two, in the oldest generation, Jiacuma is practicing visiting marriage. She bore two sons, Danshinongbu and Asa. In order to continue the family they found a young woman, Yiji, to marry one of the sons. Then Asa and Yiji have two daughters and a son. Those two daughters may practice visiting (matriarchal) marriage again, and the other son Danshinongbu is likely to practice visiting marriage, too.

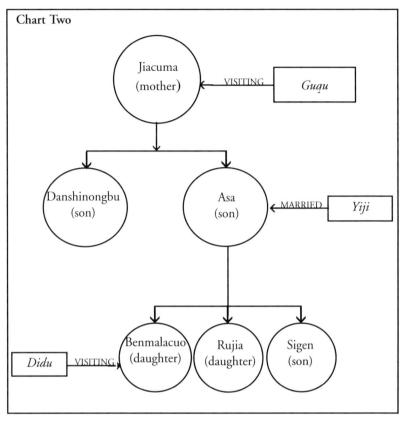

Chart Two

One generation only has daughters: They need men to fetch firewood from the mountains and plough the fields. Men are needed for their labour. In this case, a family generation that has only girls has to find a man to marry one of the girls, so that the family can have a better life. In Chart Three, the mother Garuma practices visiting marriage. She has three daughters. One of them, Erqima, is married to Gumadanshi, a man the family has found to be her husband. Jiaaduma, the other daughter, is practicing visiting (matriarchal) marriage with Cirdanshi.

Patriarchal Marriage System and Its Family Structure

The patriarchal (monogamous) marriage system is similar to the marriage system in the rest of China. Mosuo people who live around Ninglang County in Yankouba and Xinyingpan, and people like me who work out of Mosuo villages, follow this marriage system in which the daughters have to leave their families when they marry. Mosuo who do not live in Mosuo communities must have a marriage certificate in order to live together. In Chart Four, the mother Cierduma comes from outside the family, and Dumami and Ajiami, the wives, who

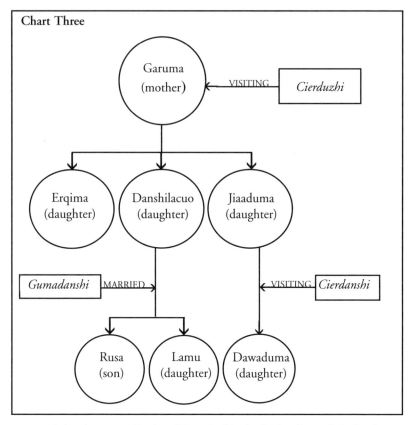

Chart Three

are married to her sons, Guci and Luzoduzhi, also had to leave their families to marry into this clan. Garuma, her daughter, joins another family by marrying Cierduzhi.

Facing Challenges

Just ten years ago, the local government decided to open the Mosuo culture to the outside world to enable local Mosuo people to have a better life. All of a sudden, the Mosuo area became a tourist destination. At present, the Mosuo culture faces great challenges because of this "development" strategy.

In formerly remote areas like Lugu Lake, cultural resources are in jeopardy. Local governments want to increase the economy quickly, but don't want to protect cultural artifacts, because they are not regarded as contributing to the overall economy. It is estimated that 280,000-300,000 tourists visit the Lugu Lake area annually, where less than 1,000 Mosuo people live. Local people cannot handle the impact caused by this opening of their culture to outsiders.

Local residents welcome the people from outside who are willing to pay to glimpse at a culture which is thousands of years old. They feel that it's an easy

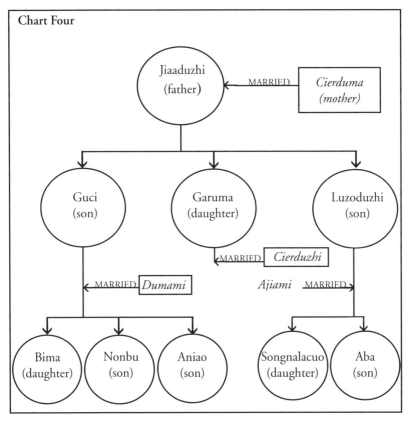

Chart Four

Jiaaduzhi (father) — MARRIED — *Cierduma (mother)*

Guci (son) — Garuma (daughter) — Luzoduzhi (son)

MARRIED — *Cierduzhi*

MARRIED — *Dumami*

Ajiami — MARRIED

Bima (daughter) — Nonbu (son) — Aniao (son) — Songnalacuo (daughter) — Aba (son)

way to earn money. If their everyday Mosuo lifestyle has become an attraction for other people who like to spend time and money to come and look, they will are pleased. The combination of all the above factors, however, results in the diminution and abuse of cultural resources. There is no driving force to improve or change the situation, let alone to optimize the use of cultural resources.

Even though the economic base in these areas has improved, Mosuo culture is vanishing rapidly. Because of tourism, Mosuo people are influenced by outsiders. The clan and family structure is changing drastically. Further, the Mosuo matriarchal family is dying out. It will probably disappear in a few years.

With the development of technological and economic globalization, Musuo consciousness is experiencing great changes. Some Mosuo people no longer value their own culture. Mosuo youth are inevitably impacted by outside culture. For me, this is not a positive development.

There are also problems with the education system. Students have to pay for their high school education. However, most Mosuo people live in the mountains and can not afford tuition, so students drop out school and find a job instead. Young women find jobs such as cleaners, babysitters ,and other low-skilled, low-paying jobs in the cities. With Mosuo women working, only the old, the very young, and some of the men stay at home. What happens to the matriarchal family structures?

Protection of Cultural Heritage Urged

Mosuo people lack funds and the technical expertise to protect our cultural heritage. Most importantly, we need to invest in the protection of our cultural resources. But the government budget is squeezed. Statistics show that the central government now boasts about 400,000 culture sites, including 750 sites under the state's top protection and 99 renowned historic cities in the western part of China. The central government is so far unwilling to make the large investment necessary to protect Mosuo culture. Local governments are not doing anything, and non-governmental investments have not been available on a large scale.

I am not a governor. It is impossible for me to find a great way to change the situation immediately. However, I love my people and my culture from the bottom of my heart. That is why I am so worried about the disappearance of our culture. I don't think we can rely on the government. We are just a small group of people compared with the 56 other ethnic groups in China. Our voice is too weak to be heard. As far as I know, Mosuo culture is unique in the world, and the world has a stake in preserving it. For us, it is a matter of just trying to survive against the odds.

At present, there are some organizations around Lugu Lake trying to preserve Mosuo culture. I wish them well. But they are not very effective. I believe that educating my people about the importance of our culture is critical and it is how I hope to contribute to the preservation of Mosuo culture. I am thinking about some of the following projects that could be initiated with partners:

1. Starting an art program in which older people can teach the younger generation ancient songs and dance heritage.
2. An educational program to teach four- to seven-year-old children o Mosuo language, and another program to reduce the current students drop-out rate.
3. A Mosuo religion project. For me this is urgent. We have no written language; we educate Mosuo people through oral speech in the Daba religion. I do not want our oral tradition to disappear for the coming generations. I will try to protect it.
4. Found a performance group to dance and sing for tourists, so they have a chance to understand Mosuo culture.
5. Open a data centre to collect and store information on Mosuo culture and the environment.

However, to protect cultural resources requires not only money but also technical expertise. Modern technology must be used to protect our precious cultural heritage. We smust record and preserve as much as we can in print, photographs, recordings, and videos; set up folklore villages and museums; and establish institutions to preserve and study ethnic cultures.

I know I have presented an ambitious agenda. I cannot do it alone. I welcome your suggestions. I welcome your help.

Hengde Danshilacuo / He Mei was born in Labo Ninglang in 1978. She attended her village elementary school, then was chosen to go to a top class in Tuodian. In 1990, she started at Ninglang No. 1 Middle School. In 1996, she went to the Yunnan Institute for Nationalities in Kunming. After graduating in 2000, she went back to her county city to become a teacher at Ninglang Hengde No. 1 Middle School. In December 2003, she received a Ford Foundation Fellowship from the International ellowship Program. Since January 2004, she has been pursuing her Master's degree in Educational Administration Program, at the College of Saint Rose.

SHANSHAN DU

Frameworks for Societies in Balance

A Cross-Cultural Perspective on Gender Equality

Questions concerning the equality/inequality of men and women comprise an enduring humanistic inquiry—from Plato's philosophical exploration of gender roles in his ideal society, to Marx and Engels' social and historical accounts of the origin of sexual inequality, to the increasingly heated debate among feminists over competing visions of gender equality. Despite all these inquiries, in the vast majority of human societies, gender equality has been relatively underdeveloped in ideologies, social institutions, and gender roles. At the beginning of the twenty-first century, mainstream academic voices and popular opinion alike still tend either to deny, or are ambiguous about, the existence of gender-egalitarian societies.

Is there any gender-egalitarian society on earth? Proposing answers to this question constitutes an integral part of the debates over major academic inquiries and feminist endeavours. Despite their scarcity, societies do exist that are documented to have achieved remarkable levels of gender equality. Early anthropological literature documented the Andaman Islanders of the Indian Ocean (Radcliffe-Brown 1922), and the Iroquois (Mann 2000). As I will show below, more recently, following the declining influence of the notion of universal female subordination since the late 1980s (Mukhopadhyay and Higgins 1988), ethnographic studies of gender-egalitarian societies have greatly increased.

What can we learn from these societies? What are the possible socio-cultural frameworks that facilitate gender equality not only in dominant symbolism and social structures but also in people's daily practices? In this article, I intend to explore these questions by offering four types of frameworks that empirically foster gender equality.[1] I term these: "maternal centrality," "gender complementarity," "gender triviality," and "gender unity." I have tentatively constructed this classification in order to expand our current analytic capacity regarding the diversity of gender equality. My research indicates that while rooted in different gender ideologies and expressing sexual equality in diverse ways, these frameworks all promote harmony and interdependence between men and women and they discourage the development of gender-based competition and hierarchy. In other words, gender-egalitarian societies are also societies in balance.

Frameworks of Gender Equality

Maternal Centrality

I term the first type of egalitarian framework "maternal centrality," which greatly overlaps with "matriarchy" as defined respectively by Dan McCall (1980: 252), Heide Goettner-Abendroth (1999), and Peggy Reeves Sanday (2002: 237). Typically associated with societies that are characterized by matrilineal descendant rule and matrilocal residence pattern, the socio-cultural framework of maternal centrality tends to highlight gender difference. Rather than stressing the symmetrical complementarity between the two sexes, the symbolism of this model tends to elevate the female principle over its male counterpart, a phenomenon that is particularly salient in matrilineal kinship structures. The principle value of this framework is placed on the characteristics that are commonly associate with maternity, such as life-giving, nurturance, connection, and harmony.

Despite the asymmetrical gender symbolism that favours the female, the framework of maternal centrality does not lead to male subordination. Instead, this model promotes gender equality by glorifying the maternal power that links the members of a society to the source of life, rather than ranking them according to sex difference (Sanday 2002: 230). Maternal centrality fosters the interdependence of male and female in layers of cross-sex bonding, especially in that of mother-child and siblings relations. The expansion of the mother-centred connections and values result in matrilineal kinship groups at different levels. Within such mother-centred networks of relationships, men and women are identified primarily as partners with shared interests, benefiting from harmony and interdependence rather than from competition for domination. Societies that have been documented for their coherent socio-cultural expressions of maternal centrality include the Minangkabau of Indonesia (Sanday 2002), the pre-colonial Iroquois (McCall 1980; Mann 2000), and the Mosuo of Southwest China (Cai 2001; Yan and Song 1983). I highlight the Minangkabau case here as it is particularly well-documented and analyzed for the contemporary era.

The cultural framework of the Minangkabau revolves around the mother-child bond; the nurturing of the newborn is believed to be the source of fertility, growth, and social well-being (Sanday 2002: 214). Specifically, maternal features that are associated with nurturing and growth constitute the core of what is defined as "power" in Minangkabau culture. Asymmetrical gender symbolism that favours the female is well-exemplified by the association between the origin of Minangkabau and an apical ancestress who is taken to represent "the repository of the vital life-force, the centripetal force around which social connections and access to land are formed for each generation" (Sanday 2002: 237). Additionally, both men and women are similarly expected to possess certain characteristics that are commonly associated with femininity, especially nurturing and politeness. The centrality of Minangkabau women in social life is manifested not only in the fact that land ownership and lineage membership are passed down to the next generation exclusively through the female line, but also in the social and symbolic significance of women's roles in various social and ritual contexts. Nevertheless, Minangkabau men are not devalued within the maternal centred society. In contrast to the western association of "power" with domination and masculinity, Minangkabau men are valued as equal members of the society, and are especially appreciated for their contribution as brothers and mothers' brothers in the public and educational domains. In fact, the common association between men and public domains, and the significant role of the mother's brother in matrilineal societies, were often misinterpreted in earlier anthropological literature as signs of gender inequality, expressed by husband and brother competing for authority over women (Richards 1950). By contrast, valuing above all nurturing, growth, and harmony, the maternal-centred socio-cultural framework of the Minangkabau fosters interdependent and egalitarian partnerships between the two sexes, rather than producing male subordination. Remarkably, the Minangkabau have maintained this orientation while being adherents to Islam, a religion that historically has tended to produce a notably patriarchal orientation (Sanday 2002). The commitment of the Minangkabau to gender equality while remaining faithful Muslims makes a careful examination of their case especially compelling.

Gender Complementarity

The perceptions of the two sexes as "different-but-equal" are evident in another model, which I term "gender complementarity." I suggest that the framework of gender complementarity generates equality between men and women by promoting symmetrical reciprocity of the two sexes. Similar to that of maternal centrality, the framework of gender complementarity also highlights gender difference symbolically and socially. By stressing the reciprocal interdependence of the two sexes, the complementarity principle not only symbolically highlights the differences between men and women, it also institutionalizes gender separation in social and economic domains. This principle also resembles that of maternal centrality in perceiving each sex as fully reliant on reciprocity with the other and attaching equal value to both men and women as well as to the different roles they play. Specifically, by placing core values on the interdependence between the sexes, the complementarity principle identifies men and women as reciprocal partners with shared interests—both benefiting from their harmonious cooperation—rather than as competitors with conflicting interests. Different from that of maternal centrality, however, the gender symbolism of the framework of complementarity tends to be symmetrical.

The "dual-sex" system of some pre-colonial Igbo groups, especially those who live in Midwestern Nigeria, seems to represent the most coherent application of the principle of gender complementarity (Okonjo 1976). Traditional Igbo gender ideals made sharp symbolic distinctions between men and women, serving to maintain and perpetuate the reciprocal system between the two sexes in all major domains of the society (Nzegwu 1994; Okonjo 1976).

In the economic arena, men and women grew their own crops, contributing complementarily to the family and community and engaging in intense economic reciprocity. The principle of gender complementarity was also widely realized in the realm of social organization. Men and women had their own kinship institutions, age grades, and secret and titled societies to manage their own affairs and to interact with each other as equal partners in a variety of social institutions (Okonjo 1976). Most dramatically, a male monarch (*obi*) and a female monarch (*omu*) functioned as complementary political entities that jointly governed various local political units that were also divided by sex. Being unrelated to each other and living in their own palaces, these two monarchs represented the highest authorities in the region to deal with the affairs of the members of their own sex. In other words, the king and the queen, together with the two monarchies that they ruled, symbolized and operated as the complements of Igbo society as a whole, rather than as two competitive kingdoms (Nzegwu 1994; Okonjo 1976). Remarkably, the well-known Igbo ritual called "sitting on a man" (the "women's war" in the context of anti-colonial protests), by which women gather to sing songs of ridicule to a man for transgressions such as wife-beating, was traditionally used to maintain harmony within the dual-sex systems, rather than expressing institutional confrontations between men and women.

In sharp contrast to "maternal centrality" and "gender complementarity," which promote harmony and balance between the sexes while highlighting their differences, the next two frameworks that I will discuss below foster gender equality by minimizing the socio-cultural significance of sexual difference, especially in gender roles (Du 2004).

Gender Triviality

I term the third type of egalitarian framework "gender triviality," by which I mean the scarcity and social insignificance of the symbolic elaboration of "men," "women," and their relationships in a given culture (Du 2002). Every known society distinguishes "male" from "female," at least biologically and linguistically. However, this fact by no means suggests that gender is universally and uniformly judged significant, as is commonly assumed in the dominant Western discourse. From a cross-cultural perspective, the degrees of conspicuousness and significance of gender constitute a spectrum on which gender triviality occupies an extreme end.

Within the framework of gender triviality, sex difference is socially and culturally insignificant because men and women are primarily considered as individuals and members of a community regardless of their sex difference. By minimizing gender differentiation in both ideological and practical arenas, gender triviality leaves little space for discrimination against the members of either sex. In other words, gender equality is achieved effortlessly within such a socio-cultural framework, that is, simply by ignoring gender itself. Based on the principle of gender triviality, gender equality manifests itself in the form of "same-thus-equal"—that

is, men and women are equal because of the gender-blind attitudes of the dominant ideologies and institutions.

I observe that the egalitarian societies that trivialize gender tend to highly
value individual autonomy and collective cooperation. The Vanatinai Islanders
of New Guinea provide a well-documented example of such a society (Lepowsky
1993). In accordance with the scarcity of gender symbolism in the society, gender-blindness is closely associated with the Vanatinai ideal personalities, including characteristics that promote both individual autonomy (such as strength,
wisdom, and magical power) and communal solidarity (such as sharing, generosity, and nurturing) (Lepowsky 1993: 116, 119, 283). The ideological triviality
of gender is also reflected in the overlapping of sex roles. Most significantly,
individuals who possess desirable characteristics often attain the prestigious titles
"big men" or "big women" through their extraordinary hard work and generosity. At the same time, there is a high degree of tolerance of idiosyncrasy and
variation among all members of the society. The tendency to trivialize gender is
also institutionalized sociologically to a great extent. Specifically, the Vanatinai
matrilineal system is counterbalanced by other gender-blind institutions such as
the relatively unusual bilocal pattern of postmarital residence, which obligates
a married couple to live alternately with their two natal families for many years
(Lepowsky 1993: 47).

To date, I have identified two additional societies as "gender-trivial": the Aka
of the Western Congo, and the Okinawans at Henza. The Aka people are characterized by a similar unelaborated gender ideology (Hewlett 2000) and an ethical orientation toward collectively grounded individualism (Hewlett 1991). The
core values of the Aka include individual equality, independence, autonomy,
sharing, and cooperation (Hewlett 1991: 27-28). Both men and women regularly participate in net hunting and in intensive and intimate care of infants. The
depth of this society's patrilineage is remarkably shallow, corresponding to weak
lineage identity (Hewlett 1991: 22) and close relations between a married couple
and their relatives from both sides. The autochthonous Okinawans at Henza
exhibit related strategies of trivializing gender (Sered 1999).

Gender Unity

The final type of gender equality I have identified to date is one I term "gender
unity." I suggest that while distinguishing men from women and recognizing
certain superficial differences between them, gender-unified societies minimize
the symbolic and social significance of sex differences. In particular, the unitary
principle maximizes gender similarities and mutuality by highlighting the entities that are made complete by incorporating both male and female. Accordingly, the two sexes are defined as essentially similar and are bound to each other
in value, interest, obligation, authority, and social status. In other words, gender
equality is fostered in the unity of the two sexes, rather than being achieved by a
careful distribution of equal power and prestige between males and females.

As I will elaborate in the second passage of the article, my major fieldwork to date has been with the Lahu, a society that is organized around the principle of gender unity. Elsewhere, I have catalogued consistent socio-cultural elaboration of gender unity as recorded among the Andaman Islanders (Radcliffe-Brown 1922) and some indigenous Andean groups living in Ecuador (Hamilton 1998) and Bolivia (Harris 1978). Reminiscent of the Lahu expression, "Chopsticks only work in pairs," some Andean cultures express the principle of gender unity by phrases such as "It takes two wings to fly" (Litherland 1999).

Gender Unity Among the Lahu People

My fieldwork research focuses on the Lahu, a Tibeto-Burman-speaking people in Yunnan, Southwest China. The subsistence pattern of the Lahu is usually a mixture of farming, raising of domestic animals, gathering, hunting, and fishing. Lahu villages generally lack stratification, and the major markers for hierarchical status are generation and age. Monogamous marriage is practiced, and households constitute the centre of village life, serving as basic units for production and consumption.

The Lahu egalitarian value of male and female is deeply rooted in their dyadic worldview centring on the concept "pairs," which suggests a single entity that is made of two similar yet distinguishable components. This worldview is organized around the principle of gender unity, or, male-female dyads. Such a dyadic perspective highlights the similarities and harmony between the two components, which identify with each other through their shared membership and joint function in the whole. When applied to Lahu cultural perceptions of men and women as well as their relationships and roles in society, such an ideology produces gender equality as a byproduct (Du 2002).

The dyadic principle provides the fundamental order for Lahu cosmology. According to Lahu mythology, just as the supreme god of creation (Xeul Sha) is a male-female dyad, so are all the other entities and beings in the universe, including the Sun (female) and the Moon (male), the earth (female) and the sky (male), as well as the original ancestors of human beings. Conforming to the dyadic cosmological order, joint gender roles in managing the supernatural realms is believed a matter of course. While the paired supreme god forms the top of the spiritual power framework ruling the universe, deities or spirits that are subservient to the paired supreme gods also operate in male-female units, including the paired spirits or deities of a household, a village, and a region. The cosmological order of male-female unity is coherently elaborated in the Lahu indigenous religion, which combine beliefs in a supreme god, parental spirits, and animism. Overall, Lahu cosmology perceives the world in terms of male-female dyads, as expressed by their motto that "everything comes in pairs, aloneness does not exist." Interestingly, even the Buddha worshipped in some Lahu village temples has been transformed from Gautama to Xeul Sha, that is, the paired indigenous gods (Du 2003; Wang and He 1999: 179).

Applying the dyadic cosmological order to the life cycle, Lahu perceptions of personhood revolve around monogamous marriage in both the social and spiritual realms. Specifically, the Lahu threshold for adulthood is the wedding, which unites two socially immature individuals into a single social entity and transforms them into full members of society. After the wedding ceremony, the couple simultaneously achieves the social rank of "adult" and is expected to share responsibility, prestige, and authority when they go through the life journey together. After fulfilling their joint responsibilities in life, a couple is believed to be able to reunite in the afterlife. Holding the honourable and authoritative position of "parental spirits," the deceased couple jointly enjoy offerings and ritual respect from their children and children-in-law. Since the eternal bond between husband and wife constitutes the essence of ideal human life, those who die before marriage or before fulfilling marital responsibilities are considered the worst failures at life and are said to be marginalized as lone souls in the afterlife.

The cosmological emphasis on the entity of husband and wife correlates with the ideal of joint roles and authority of the two sexes, as is encapsulated in an oft-cited metaphor: "Chopsticks only work in pairs" (Du 2000). The equal contribution of each stick in a pair of chopsticks in their joint performance of tasks echoes the Lahu naturalization of joint gender roles in all possible arenas, including pregnancy, childbirth (the husband serves as midwife), childcare, domestic chores, subsistence work, and leadership. Additionally, the uselessness, and thus powerlessness, of a single chopstick serves as a metaphor for the joint power and authority that are accorded men and women. Such a value is expressed by the traditional belief that households, villages, as well as the whole universe are manageable only when "a pair of male-female masters rules together." While a co-headship of husband and wife in the household is still widely practiced, the tradition that requires married couples to hold political and spiritual posts in the village and the village cluster has been threatened by interventions of the Chinese state and is now retained in only a few areas (Du 2002; Wang and He 1999).

Implications of Gender-Egalitarian Studies

The preceding sections have discussed several types of gender-egalitarian frameworks derived from a selection of ethnographic data from different continents and my own fieldwork on the Lahu people. Rather than intending to provide a few pigeonholing models, I hope that my preliminary classifications may encourage more comparative studies on the equality between men and women, a critical component in both humanistic inquiries and major theories of social sciences. I argue that more systematic comparison and theoretical analysis of known gender-egalitarian societies can serve both scholars and activists who work to propose feasible parameters of gender equality that may be possible elsewhere. The contributions of such studies can be broken down into three interrelated aspects.

Most importantly, they help to break through the enduring and deeply rooted western emphasis on hypothetical *utopian* societies that has prevented us from recognizing the existence of extant gender-egalitarian societies. I argue that the difficulty in recognizing the existence of gender-egalitarian societies is rooted in western utopian ideals towards gender equality, which, ironically, often turn the notion of the universality of female subordination into a self-fulfilling prophecy. Such a tendency has been exacerbated by the double standard used to measure gender equality and hierarchy—that is, while gender equality must be perfect to exist, gender hierarchy can exist in any degree. Under the shadow of this utopianist bias, very few scholars who have encountered gender-egalitarian societies directly acknowledge those societies as such, thus further weakening the impact of their studies. Comparative studies of gender-egalitarian societies can contribute greatly to the removal of the utopian blinders that hinder our recognition of gender-egalitarian societies.

Furthermore, gender-egalitarian studies can enhance our understanding of the diverse meanings of "gender equality" across cultures. Such studies can demonstrate that not only do gender-egalitarian societies exist, they also differ in the respective socio-cultural frameworks that foster equality between men and women. These explorations can also reveal that these different underlying principles of gender equality are rooted in the diversity of cultural perceptions of men and women and their relationships. Accordingly, comparative studies of gender-egalitarian societies can provide insight into the recent academic effort to develop both general and specific indicators of gender equality in cross-cultural settings.

Finally, by recognizing the existence of more distinct frameworks for gender equality, gender-egalitarian studies encourage individuals from different socio-cultural backgrounds to reflect on the goals, challenges, and strategies for promoting gender equality in their own societies. Such reflections may contribute to more constructive dialogues between non-western women and feminists in the dominant societies of North America and Europe. An increased recognition of the diverse meanings and manifestations of gender equality can expand the horizons of cross-cultural communications regarding how to define, assess, and achieve gender equality in particular socio-cultural contexts.

I would like to thank the American Council of Learned Societies for offering me a Charles A. Ryskamp Research Fellowship to support this study. I also thank Heide Goettner-Abendroth and Alma Gottlieb for their comments. The major ethnographic examples I have found to date in my research derive from societies located in East Asia and the Pacific, Southeast Asia, Africa, and Central and South America. While the socio-cultural conditions of the vast majority of these societies are contemporary, some exist only in historical records.

Shanshan Du is associate professor of Anthropology at Tulane University (U.S.A) and winner of the Elsie Clews Parsons Prize (American Ethnological Society) and the Syl-

via Forman Prize (Association for Feminist Anthropology). Her book, "Chopsticks Only Work in Pairs": Gender Unity and Gender Equality Among the Lahu of Southwest China *was published by Columbia University Press in 2002.*

References

Cai, Hua. 2001. *A Society Without Fathers or Husbands: The Na of China.* 1997. Trans. by Asti Hustvedt. New York: Zone Books.

Du, Shanshan. 2000. "'Husband and Wife Do It Together': Sex/Gender Allocation of Labor Among the Qhawqhat Lahu of Lancang, Southwest China." *American Anthropologist* 102 (3): 520-537.

Du, Shanshan. 2002. *"Chopsticks Only Work in Pairs": Gender Unity and Gender Equality Among the Lahu of Southwest China.* New York: Columbia University Press.

Du, Shanshan. 2003. "Is Buddha A Couple? The Lahu Gender-Unitary Perspectives of Buddhism." *Ethnology: An International Journal of Cultural and Social Anthropology* 42 (3): 253-271.

Du, Shanshan. 2004. "Traditional Village-Level Political Organization and Its Transformations among the Lancang Lahu." *Contributions to Southeast Asian Sociology* 12: 65-93.

Goettner-Abendroth, Heide. 1999. "The Structure of Matriarchal Society. Exemplified by the Society of the Mosuo in China." *ReVision* 21 (3): 31-35.

Hamilton, Sarah. 1998. *The Two-Headed Household: Gender and Rural Development in the Ecuadorean Andes.* Pittsburgh: University of Pittsburgh Press.

Harris, Olivia. 1978. "Complementarity and Conflict: An Andean View of Women and Men." *Sex and Age as Principles of Social Differentiation.* Ed. J. S. La Fontaine. London: Academic Press. 21-40.

Hewlett, Barry S. 1991. *Intimate Fathers: The Nature and Context of Aka Pygmy Paternal Infant Care.* Ann Arbor: University of Michigan Press.

Hewlett, Barry S. 2000. Personal communication.

Lepowsky, Maria. 1993. *Fruit of the Motherland: Gender in an Egalitarian Society.* New York: Columbia University Press.

Litherland, Katherine. 1999. Personal communication.

Mann, Barbara A. 2000. *Iroquoian Women: The Gantowisas.* New York: P. Lang.

Matisoff, James A. 1988. *The Dictionary of Lahu.* Berkeley: University of California Press.

McCall, Dan. 1980. "The Dominant Dyad: Mother Right and the Iroquois Case." Ed. Stanley Diamond. *Theory and Practice: Essays Presented to Gene Weltfish.* New York: Mouton Publishers. 221-262.

Mukhopadhyay, Carol C., and Patricia Higgins. 1988. "Anthropological Studies of Women's Status Revisited: 1977-87." *Annual Review of Anthropology* 17: 461–495.

Nzegwu, Nkiru. 1994. "Gender Equality in a Dual-Sex System: The Case of Onitsha." *Canadian Journal of Law and Jurisprudence* 7 (1): 73-95.

Okonjo, Kamene. 1976. "The Dual-Sex Political System in Operation: Igbo Women and Community Politics in Midwestern Nigeria." Eds. N. J. Hafkin and E. G. Bay. *Women in Africa*. Stanford: Stanford University Press. 45-58.

Radcliffe-Brown, A. R. 1922. *The Andaman Islander*. Cambridge: Cambridge University Press.

Richards, Audrey. 1950. "Some Types of Family Structure Amongst the Central Bantu." Eds. A.R. Radcliffe-Brown and D. Forde. *African Systems of Kinship and Marriage*. Oxford: Oxford University Press. 207-51.

Ruxian, Yan, and Song Zhaolin. 1983. *Yongning Naxizu de Muxizhi* (*The Matrilineal System of the Naxi in Yongning*). Kunming: Yunnan People's Publishing House.

Sanday, Peggy R. 2002. *Women at the Center: Life in a Modern Matriarchy*. Ithaca: Cornell University Press.

Sered, Susan. 1999. *Women of the Sacred Groves: Divine Priestesses of Okinawa*. New York: Oxford University Press.

Wang, Zhenghua, and Shaoying He. 1999. *Lahuzu Wenhua Shi* (*The History of Lahu Culture*). Kunming: Yunnan Nationalities Publishing House.

**Part V
Past—Theory of History**

RIANE EISLER

The Battle Over Human Possibilities

Women, Men and Cultural Transformation

M any of us agree that the issue of what is possible or impossible for us as humans is critical for our future, and whether we have one. In an age of escalating terrorism, warfare, nuclear and biological weapons, soaring global overpopulation, and unprecedented environmental, economic, and social challenges, many of us are also aware that our present course is not sustainable. Therefore, many of us worldwide are working for cultural transformation, for a shift to a more peaceful, equitable, and sustainable way of relating to one another and our Mother Earth. But the question—and it is a fundamental question—is whether such a shift is possible. This question has been a central focus of my research (Eisler, 1987, 1995, 2000, 2002).

According to some popular sociobiological theories, a shift to cultures that are less violent, more gender-balanced, and more equitable goes against human nature. As much as we might like it to be different, the argument goes, to believe anything else is naive and unrealistic because of ancient evolutionary imperatives we carry in our genes. This negative position is also buttressed by some archaeologists and cultural historians who claim that human society always was, and by implication always will be, violent and inequitable.

I will briefly examine these arguments from the perspective of the cross-cultural and historical study carried out by me and some colleagues over three decades. Drawing from transdisciplinary research, I will look at cultural evolution from the perspective of two underlying possibilities for structuring social systems: the contrasting configurations of the *domination model* and the *partnership model*. I will propose that narratives about our cultural origins are not just of academic interest; they reflect and guide how we think, feel, and act. Theories that deny the possibility of more equitable, peaceful, and gender-balanced societies work to constrict human possibilities; such theories serve to maintain cultural patterns orienting towards the domination model of top-down rankings ultimately backed up by fear and force. I will also show that so-called "women's issues" are not, as we have been led to believe, secondary to "the important issues," but of central importance in shaping policies, quality of life, and our future.

My method of inquiry, the study of *relational dynamics*, differs in key ways from most studies of human society. Rather than looking for simple causes and effects, it looks for interactive patterns that are self-organizing, self-maintaining, and, during periods of severe disequilibrium, capable of transformative change. It draws from a larger database than most studies. Instead of examining one period or place at a time, it takes into account the whole span of our history—including prehistory. It also takes into account not only the public, political, and economic sphere but also the private sphere of our day-to-day family life, and other intimate relations. And, unlike most studies that have aptly been called "the study of man," it takes into account the whole of humanity—both its female and male halves.

Two Basic Cultural Patterns: The Domination Model and the Partnership Model

Drawing from this larger database, I found that cross-culturally and historically cultures fall on a continuum of two basic possibilities for structuring relationships, beliefs, and institutions: the *partnership model* and *the domination* or *dominator model*. Because I drew from a database that gives equal importance to both the female and male halves of humanity, I also saw that one of the core differences between these two models is the cultural construction of the roles and relations of women and men. This is why I sometimes use the gender-specific terms *androcratic*, or ruled by men, and the neologism *gylanic*, which derives from the Greek *gyne* (woman) and *andros* (man) linked by the letter *l* for *lyen* (to resolve) or *lyo* (to set free), signalling that the female and male halves of humanity are linked rather than ranked.

No culture orients completely to either model. But the degree to which it does profoundly affects beliefs, institutions, and relationships—from intimate to international. This is so regardless of differences in geographical locations, time periods, religion, economics, politics, or levels of technological development.

The four core elements of the domination configurations include an authoritarian social and family structure; rigid male-dominance; a high level of fear and built-in violence and abuse (from child and wife beating to chronic warfare); and, a system of beliefs, including beliefs about human nature, that make this kind of structure seem normal and right. Difference, beginning with the fundamental difference between the female and male halves of humanity, is equated with superiority or inferiority.

The European Middle Ages and fundamentalist regimes such as the Taliban are both examples of religious cultures that orient closely to the domination model. But the same configuration can be found in secular societies. And here too the subordination of women is a central theme. When the Nazis came to power, they too called for a return of women to their "traditional" place (a code word for subservient) in a "traditional" family.

As we move toward the partnership side of the partnership-domination continuum, we begin to see a very different cultural configuration. The four core elements of this configuration include a more democratic and egalitarian family and social structure; gender equity; a low level of institutionalized violence and abuse (as there is no need for fear and force to maintain rigid rankings of domination); and, a system of beliefs, stories, and values that supports and validates this kind of structure as normal and right.

Again, we find cultures orienting more to this model in many different settings. They can be tribal societies such as the Teduray of the Philippines, agrarian cultures such as the Mosuo of China and the Minangkabau of West Sumatra, or industrial societies such as Sweden, Norway, and Finland (Min 1995; Eisler, Loye, and Norgaard 1995; Schlegel 1998; Goettner-Abendroth 1999; Pietila 2001; Sanday 2002; Esiler 2007).[2]

None of these are ideal societies. But Nordic nations, in contrast to the United States and other wealthier nations, do not have huge gaps between the haves and have-nots. They not only have more political and economic democracy, but these nations also have a much more equal partnership between men and women. For example, women in Sweden, Norway, Finland, and Iceland make up 35 to 45 percent of their respective legislature—more than anywhere else in the world.

Among the Teduray, anthropologist Stuart Schlegel found elaborate social mechanisms for the prevention of cycles of violence. The Teduray recognized that violence could occasionally erupt. But violence is not integral to male socialization and men are not ranked over women. Nor do they have tribal hierarchies of domination. Instead, there are elders—both female and male—who are highly respected because of their wisdom and who play an important role in mediating disputes.

Similarly, among the Minangkabau of West Sumatra, mediation for violence non-escalation helps maintain a more peaceful way of life. Again, the Minangkabau do not rank men over women. On the contrary, as anthropologist Peggy Reeves Sanday (2002) extensively documents, women play a major social role. As among the Teduray, violence is not part of Minangkabau child-raising practices. For the Minangkabau, nurturance rather than violence is viewed as inherent in humans and nature.

This takes me to an important point about the interactive dynamics of social systems. This is that, as the status of women rises, so also does the status of values and activities such as empathy, nonviolence, and caregiving that are, in domination-oriented cultures, unacceptable in men because they are stereotypically associated with "inferior" femininity.

But all the different qualities and behaviours are part of our genetic repertoire. The real issue is what human possibilities are culturally supported or inhibited by the prevailing system of beliefs and social institutions—within the family, education, religion, politics and economics.

Genes, Experience, and Findings from Biological and Social Science

This does not mean that genes do not matter, individually and collectively. But we humans are not, as some sociobiologists and evolutionary psychologists claim, robots of selfish genes ruthlessly trying to replicate themselves (Dawkins, 1976; Barkow, Cosmides, and Tooby 1992; Wright 1994).

War, these theorists say, is adaptive. It came about because it has "evolutionary payoffs" in the competition of genes to reproduce themselves. Male dominance, too, they claim, is built into our genes. They claim the same for rape, arguing that primate males "naturally" seek to control females to ensure *their* genes, and not those of other males, are passed on (Thornhill and Palmer, 2000; Pinker 2002). All this, they argue, is the inevitable result of our genetic heritage from what they call our ancestral environment millions of years ago.

These claims fail to note that all human behaviours—including caring and nonviolence—have evolutionary roots, or we would not be capable of them. Instead, they highlight those behaviours appropriate for dominator relations. They also ignore the fact that one of our closest primate relatives, the bonobo chimpanzee, has a social organization that is *not* male dominated and chronically violent.

Like common chimpanzees, bonobos share approximately 98.4 percent of their genes with humans. But they are a much less tense, less-violence-prone, primate than the common chimpanzee. For example, in contrast to chimpanzees, where males have been observed killing infants, there are no instances of infanticide among the bonobos (de Waal and Lanting 1997: 118-121). Females, particularly mothers, play key social roles.

But there is much more that is wrong with theories that claim we are driven to male dominance, inequity, and chronic violence by genetic imperatives rooted in our primate heritage. Perhaps most critically, these theories discount the importance of environmental influences—sometimes even claiming that parenting does not matter in how our brain, and with it our behaviours, develop.

Astonishingly, this position ignores evidence from neuroscience showing that the human brain develops out of the interaction of genes and experience, which in turn is heavily influenced by the human creation we call culture as mediated by the family, education, religion, politics, and economics. It even ignores evidence that the behavioural expression of individual genetic predispositions is largely dependent on experience. Findings from anthropology, sociology, and psychology further contradict claims that our genetic heritage inevitably leads to behaviours and cultures that are violent and inequitable. For example, cross-cultural surveys such as those of anthropologist Peggy Reeves Sanday (1981) and sociologist Scott Coltrane (1981) show great cultural variability in the relations between women and men, rates of violence, and general social structure.

Sanday and Coltrane found statistically significant correlations that verify the foundational importance of gender roles and relations to a culture's character.[1] For instance, they found a statistically significant correlation between greater sexual equality and a greater male involvement in childcare, which in turn often correlated with a cultural construction of masculinity that is not disassociated from all that is "soft" or stereotypically feminine.

Nonetheless, in different permutations, narratives that make it seem as if the domination model is the only possible cultural form periodically resurge. Indeed, these resurgences are a notable feature of times of regression to the domination model—times like the period we are experiencing worldwide today.

The Battle Over Cultural Origins

If we look at modern history through the analytical lens of the partnership-domination continuum, we see that, while this is not brought out in conventional historical analyses, all the progressive social movements have been challenges to an entrenched tradition of domination.

This takes me to the current resurgence of the argument that archaeological evidence supports the conclusion that violence, male dominance, and unjust social arrangements are universals that have been with us since prehistoric times.

Again, this position is not new. And neither is the position that it is not true. The mid- and late-nineteenth century was a time of strong partnership movement in Europe and the United States. At the same time that writings on humanism, feminism, and socialism challenged entrenched traditions of domination, a number of scholars proposed that mythical and archaeological evidence points to a time when human society was not one of domination and exploitation. These scholars wrote of matriarchies that preceded patriarchies; equitable and peaceful societies in which women were not dominated by men (Bachofen1861; Morgan 1877; Engels 1884; Gage 1893). But toward the end of the nineteenth century, there was a strong movement to discredit these matriarchal theorists. This came along with an anti-feminist crusade, a religious movement that had as its goal the creation of a Christian state, a massive re-concentration of wealth in the hands of industrial "robber barons," and a cultural push to re-establish the old "macho" masculinity that, as Theodore Roszak (1969) wrote, combined the vilification of women with the glorification of male violence that eventually culminated in the bloodbath of World War I (Roszak 1969; Dijkstra 1986; Eisler 1995).

But the movement toward partnership resurged with renewed vigour in the second half of the twentieth century. Along with the civil rights, peace, economic equity, women's liberation, and women's rights movements, came a new wave of assertions that patriarchy is not the only cultural possibility. And, again, part of these movements was the assertion that there were prehistoric societies in which men did not dominate women—societies that were also generally more egalitarian and peaceful.

During the 1960s, British archeologist James Mellaart (1967) reported his discovery of the Anatolian town of Çatal Hüyük, an advanced Neolithic site where he reported finding many female images and no signs of destruction through warfare for almost 1000 years. This was followed by the publication of the work of Lithuanian-American archaeologist Marija Gimbutas (1991, 1999) on what she called the pre-Indo-European Civilization of Old Europe, where she reported that between circa 7000 and 3500 BCE there developed a complex social organization, in which female figures and symbols were foremost, and peace seems to have been the general norm. Others, such as Alexander Marshack (1991), who revised earlier interpretations of Paleolithic art, and Nikolas Platon (1966), who excavated the generally peaceful Minoan civilization that flourished on Crete until circa 1400 BCE, also reported the presence of what they called Goddess figurines in prehistoric cultures. But in the closing decades of the twentieth century, came yet another campaign to demolish interpretations of prehistory and ancient history that did not present a top-down, male-dominated, chronically violent system as the only human possibility. Many scholars returned to the view that cultural evolution is driven by genetic imperatives that make a top-down, male-dominated, chronically violent social organization the only possibility. Or, they argued that although the early hunting-gathering stage of culture was more egalitarian and peaceful, technological and social complexity inevitably led to war and domination.[2]

As in the late nineteenth century, this twentieth-century backlash against narratives that support the possibility of partnership or *gylanic* relations was not an isolated event. It was part of a larger cultural backlash. It occurred at the same time as fundamentalist religious leaders launched a virulent anti-feminist crusade and agitated to get women back into their "traditional" place. As in the late nineteenth century, there was also an enormous re-concentration of wealth—this time in multinational corporations with more assets than most nations, and in a new class of billionaires with a combined wealth equal to the combined wealth of the majority of people on the planet (UNDP 1998: 29-30).

In short, the efforts to counter challenges to dominator narratives about human possibilities did not take place in a cultural vacuum. This does not mean there was a conspiracy between archaeologists and regressive religious, political, and economic forces seeking to return us to a time when most men and all women "knew their place." But because of pressures for dominator systems, the cultural climate, including the academic cultural climate, was no longer supportive of those who looked at prehistory through a different lens.

Ideology and Interpretation

Of course, no one can be certain of what happened thousands of years ago. Indeed, even when there are written records, we cannot fully rely on them as accurate, much less complete, accounts. They, too, reflect the writers' views, and his or her personal history and professional training. Further, certain viewpoints fall academic rewards system for certain views rather than others. Above all, interpretations are often influenced by the prevailing cultural assumptions, which are often projected onto earlier societies.

For example, when the Paleolithic "Montgaudier baton" (a fourteen-and-one-half inch engraved reindeer antler) was found in the 1880s by the famous French prehistorian Abbé Breuil, he reported that he saw on it a series of "barbed harpoons." But when Alexander Marshack (1991) looked at these carvings again through a magnifying lens that made it possible to more clearly make out worn areas, the "weapons" turned out to be line drawings of plants. As Marshack wrote: "Under the microscope, it was evident that these were impossible harpoons; the barbs were turned the wrong way and the points of the long shafts were at the wrong end. However, they were *perfect* plants or branches, growing at the proper angle and in the proper way at the top of a long stem." So, according to Marshack, the images on this ancient object had little to do with killing. They reflected our ancestors' interest in, and celebration of, the coming of Spring—or, as Marshack put it, "the birth of the New Year" (1991: 173).

This concern with the renewal of life also seems to be reflected in many of the beautiful animal cave paintings of the Paleolithic, which show male and female animals in pairs, with females sometimes depicted as pregnant. This is also evident in the carvings generally known as Venus figurines: stylized female figures highlighting woman's life-giving powers. Yet some scholars today argue that these carvings were just representations of women, with no mythical significance—or even that they were just dolls.

But to say that a work such as the Venus of Laussel, carved at the entrance of a cave sanctuary or ritual site, is merely a representation of a woman with no mythical significance, or something meant for children's play, does not make sense. Like other Venus figures, the Venus of Laussel is a wide-hipped, large-bellied, possibly pregnant, nude. She is not a portable figure, and hence cannot have been meant as a doll. Her left hand points to her clearly delineated vulva, and in her right hand she holds a crescent moon notched with thirteen markings: the number of the lunar cycles of a year as well as of a woman's menstrual cycle. As Elinor Gadon and other scholars noted, this prehistoric figure, and the ceremonies performed in the Laussel cave, must have had something to do with women's menstrual cycles and the cycles of the moon (Gadon 1989). They were most probably associated with the recognition that woman's life-giving power plays an important role in the great cyclic drama of birth, sex, death, and rebirth.[3]

There are also conflicting interpretations of the next phase of cultural development: the Neolithic. It is difficult to establish the social and economic structure of prehistoric societies from archaeological remains. But we can draw some conclusions from the relative size and arrangement of dwellings as well as from the relative size of burials and the "grave gifts" in them. Based on these sources, Mellaart (1967) wrote that although some social inequality is suggested by the size of buildings, equipment, and burial gifts, this was "never a glaring one." Similarly, Gimbutas wrote of "tightly knit egalitarian communities" in Old Europe, noting that "the distribution of wealth in graves speaks for an economic egalitarianism" (Gimbutas 1991: 94, 324). Platon (1966) wrote that excavations of later Minoan sites not only showed a generally high standard of living and a high status for women, but also a general absence of signs of destruction through warfare.

Gimbutas and Mellaart also concluded that while the earlier Neolithic cultures they excavated were not violence-free, they were not warlike. These interpretations contrast sharply with those of archaeologists such as Brian Hayden, who wrote that the Old European sites described by Gimbutas must have been top-down chiefdoms in light of their size, craft specialization, and other advanced features. Indeed, one of Hayden's major assumptions has been that Neolithic societies were chronically warlike and can best be understood in terms of a "Big Man complex," which he believed is "founded upon self-interest, desire for power and materialism" (Hayden 1998: 251-253).[4]

These kinds of interpretation not only ignore the evidence for a more egalitarian social structure, but the general absence of fortifications as well as of scenes depicting and idealizing violence in the art of the early and middle Neolithic. In contrast to later art, there is a general absence of scenes of men killing each other in "heroic battles" or idealizing strong-man rule. Instead, we find a great variety of images of nature, as well as a profusion of female figures often emphasizing vulvas and breasts, pointing to a cultural focus on the power to give and nurture life rather than the power to dominate and take life.

Nonetheless, proposals that the prevalence of these female images reflect cultures in which women were not dominated by men are today fiercely disputed. Even beyond this, Paleolithic cave carvings that scholars such as Marshack and Gimbutas classified as vulvas are being reclassified as merely cleft ovals or ovals with slits, although phalluses are still described as phalluses. In the same way, Neolithic female carvings that Mellaart and Gimbutas classified as Goddess figurines are being described as female dolls, even though male figurines are recognized as having ritual significance. And, the old assumption that the appearance of the archaic state, and with it "high civilization," brought with it male dominance, chronic warfare, and slave-based economies is being revived, despite the fact that there are no indications that this was the case in the highly advanced civilization of Minoan Crete.

The High Civilization of Minoan Crete

Although Minoan society was socially complex and technologically advanced, with clear signs of centralized government, it was, in key respects, different from other high civilizations of that time. As Greek archaeologist Nanno Marinatos noted, the lack of fortifications indicates not only peaceful coexistence among the Minoan city-states but also that religion rather than violence was the primary means of enforcing the authority of the rulers. Also interesting is that there are no martial female deities in Minoan iconography (1993: 104, 149). This, too, is in contrast to later high civilizations, where female deities such as Ishtar and Athene are already warrior goddesses.

We have to make a distinction between two different kinds of hierarchies. Hierarchies based on force or the threat of force, I have called *domination hierarchies*. More flexible and less authoritarian hierarchies I have called *actualization hierarchies*, which have a greater complexity of functions and higher levels of performance. In hierarchies of actualization, respect and accountability flow not only from the bottom up but also from the top down. It is this second kind, the actualization hierarchy, that better describes the administrative and religious structure at ancient Minoan sites (for example, the Palace of Knossos), which apparently also served as a centre for crafts, trade, and resources distribution.

A Minoan art work of particular interest in this connection is the so-called procession fresco. Here the central figure (with arms raised in benediction) is *not* on an elevated pedestal (as later "divine kings" characteristically are shown) or of a larger size than the approaching figures bringing it offerings of fruit and wine. Equally interesting is that the central figure in this fresco is female rather than male.

Accordingly, some scholars have written about a queen or queen/priestess as the representative of the Goddess officiating in the famous "throne room" of the Palace of Knossos. As Helga Reusch (1985: 334) points out, the griffins on each side of the "throne" are almost universally associated with goddess figures. The lilies and spirals on the walls are also typical Goddess symbols and the smallness of the "throne" (actually a gracefully carved stone chair that is not elevated) also suggests that a woman may have been its occupant. However, as Archeologist R. F. Willetts (1977) further points out, it is also highly probable that male hierarchies had co-existed with the palace priestesses, some in charge perhaps of trade and maritime affairs, others serving as priests. What all this points to is a partnership-oriented or *gylanic* society where both women and men played leading roles, with men probably playing a larger role in trade and administration, and women in religion.

From Past to Present and Future

Using the analytical framework of the partnership-domination continuum, the cultural transformation theory introduced in my books traces the evolution of western societies from prehistory to the present in terms of the underlying tension between the two models as two basic alternatives for organizing society. Like chaos theory, cultural transformation theory highlights that social systems are self-organizing and self-maintaining, but that during periods of disequilibrium they are capable of transformative change. It proposes that cultural evolution is not a straight-line upward movement from barbarism to civilization, as we are often taught, but that it has from the beginning consisted of the tension between the partnership or *gylanic* and the dominator or *androcratic* models as two underlying possibilities for all societies—from the tribal to the technologically advanced (Eisler 1987, 1995, 2000). Cultural transformation theory further proposes that there is evidence of cultural transformation during a time of disequilibrium in prehistory when the original course of civilization, not only in the West but also in other early centres of civilization, shifted from a partnership to dominator direction.

Here I want to conclude by looking at the application of cultural transformation theory to our present and future. Because in our time of massive technological and social dislocation another fundamental shift is possible—to a world orienting more to partnership rather than domination.

Largely because of the dislocation and disequilibrium brought on by the shift to industrial technologies that accelerated in the West during the eighteenth century, modern history has seen many challenges to entrenched traditions of domination: the "divinely ordained" rule of kings over their "subjects"; the rule of men over women in the "castles" of their homes; the enslavement of one race by another; and, the use of warfare as a means for one nation to control another. These challenges brought many gains we today take for granted.

However, the movement toward partnership has not been linear. It has been more like a spiral upward movement, with periodic dips or regressions to the domination model. In the West, the most visible regressions have been those of Hitler's Germany and Stalin's Soviet Union. Today, we are in a time of global regression to the domination model.

It is precisely during periods of regression that we need to be proactive rather than just reactive. This requires a systemic approach—one that takes into full account what we have been examining: the foundational importance of how a culture structures the roles and relations of the female and male halves of humanity.

In the *first stage* of the modern partnership movement, the emphasis was primarily on dismantling the top of the dominator pyramid—on economic and political relations in the so-called public sphere. Far less emphasis was placed on the so-called private sphere of relations—the relations between women and men, and between them and their sons and daughters—relations that were seen as secondary "women's issues" and "children's issues." As a result, we still lack the solid foundations on which to build a truly democratic, equitable, more peaceful world.

It is not coincidental that for the most violent and repressive regimes and would-be regimes of modern times a top priority has been "getting women back into their traditional place" in a "traditional family," a code word for a family where top-down control and severe punishments are taught children as normal, moral, and inevitable. The reason, simply put, is that it is in family that people first learn and continually practice either dominator or partnership relations.

But a way of structuring relations into rigid rankings of domination—be it man over woman, man over man, race over race, nation over nation, or man over nature—is not tenable at our level of technological development. This is why we urgently need to move to a crucial *second stage* in the challenge to traditions of domination: a politics of partnership that encompasses *both* the public and private spheres of human relations and focuses intense attention on shifting gender relations from domination to partnership.[5]

There has already been much progress in moving toward partnership, as evidenced by the changes in the West from the Middle Ages to today. There is, today, an unprecedented strong grassroots movement in all world regions toward family and social structures that are closer to the partnership than domination model. But, as I have briefly outlined, much more attention must be given to the cultural construction of the roles and relations of the two basic halves of humanity as foundational to a more sustainable, equitable, and peaceful future.

Congresses such as this are important contributions to this urgently needed focus on gender roles and relations as integral to the kind of cultures and world we create. Cultural transformation does not happen by itself. It comes about through human agency, and every one of us can play a part. Awareness that a cultural organization based on partnership—on mutual respect, accountability, and benefit, rather than on fear, domination, and violence—is possible, and that so-called women's issues are central rather than peripheral, is basic to the construction of the kind of world we so want and need for ourselves, our children, and generations to come.

Riane Eisler is best known for her bestseller The Chalice and the Blade: Our History, Our Future *(1987), which has been translated into eighteen languages, Riane Eisler is president of the Center for Partnership Studies. She has taught at the University of California, is a fellow of the World Academy of Art and Science, and is a founding member of the General Evolution Research Group. She has done pioneering work in human rights, especially in regards to women and children. She has received many honours, including the Humanist Pioneer award and honorary membership of the World Commission on Global Consciousness and Spirituality. Furthermore, she co-founded the Spiritual Alliance to Stop Intimate Violence. Her most recent book,* The Real Wealth of Nations: Creating A Caring Economics, *was published in 2007.*

[1]I want to emphasize that when we speak of statistically significant correlations, this does not mean invariable correlations, but rather central tendencies. Because cultures involve a very large number of variables, we can expect some variations from central tendencies. For example, some societies with an ideology of male dominance where women had some economic power still tended to have a relatively high degree of male aggression, including aggression against women.
[2]Engels had proposed a variation of this theory in Origins of the Family. More recent articulations are Meillassoux (1972); Boulding (1976) ; Lerner (1986).
[3]André Leroi-Gourhan (1971), director of the Sorbonne's Center for Prehistoric and Protohistoric Studies, also concluded that Paleolithic art expressed an early religion in which feminine representations and symbols played a central part. He wrote that "characteristically the female figures and symbols were located in a central position in the excavated chambers. In contrast, the masculine symbols typically either occupied peripheral positions or were arranged around the female figures and symbols." For a more detailed discussion, see Eisler (1987).
[4]For a detailed critique of Hayden, see Marler (1999).
[5]This integrated partnership political agenda focuses on four cornerstones: partnership gender relations; partnership childhood relations; partnership economics; and cultural beliefs, myths, and stories that support partnership. In my most recent book, *The Power of Partnership* (2002), I present some key strategic build-

ing blocks to put each of these cornerstones in place and show how every one of
us can help with their construction.

References

Bachofen, J. J. 1861. *Myth, Religion, and Mother-Right.* Trans. Ralph Mannheim.
Princeton: Princeton University Press.

Barkow, Jerome, Leda Cosmides, and John Tooby, editors. 1992. The Adapted
Mind: Evolutionary Psychology and the Generation of Culture. New York:
Oxford University Press

Boulding, Elise. 1976. *The Underside of History: A View of Women Through Time.*
Boulder, CO: Westview Press.

Coltrane, Scott. 1996. *Family Man: Fatherhood, Work, and Gender Equity.* New
York: Oxford University Press

de Waal, Frans B. M. and Frans Lanting. 1997. *Bonobo: The Forgotten Ape.*
Berkeley: University of California Press.

Dawkins, Richard. 1976. *The Selfish Gene.* New York: Oxford University Press.

Dijkstra, Bram. 1986. *Idols of Perversity: Fantasies of Feminine Evils in Fin-de-
siecle Culture.* Oxford: Oxford University Press.

Eisler, Riane. 1987. *The Chalice and The Blade: Our History, Our Future.* San
Francisco: Harper & Row.

Eisler, Riane. 1995. *Sacred Pleasure: Sex, Myth, and the Politics of the Body.* San
Francisco: Harper Collins.

Eisler, Riane. *Human Possibilities: Who We Are, Were, and Can Be.* Work in progress.

Eisler, Riane. 2000. *Tomorrow's Children: A Blueprint for Partnership Education
in the 21st Century.* Boulder, CO: Westview Press.

Eisler, Riane. 2002. *The Power of Partnership: Seven Relationships that Will Change
Your Life.* Novato, CA: New World Library.

Eisler, Riane. 2007. *The Real Wealth of Nations: Creating A Caring Economics.*
San Francisco: Berrett-Koehler Publishers.

Eisler, Riane, and Daniel S. Levine. 2002. "Nurture, Nature, and Caring: We
Are Not Prisoners of Our Genes." *Brain and Mind* 3 (1): 9-52.

Eisler, Riane, David Loye, and Kari Norgaard. 1995. *Women, Men, and the Global Quality of Life.* Pacific Grove, CA: Center for Partnership Studies.

Engels, Friedrich. 1972. *Origin of the Family, Private Property and the State.*
1884. New York: International Publishers.

Gadon, Elinor. 1989. *The Once and Future Goddess,* San Francisco, Harper &
Row

Gage, Matilda Joslyn. 1972. *Woman, Church and State: A Historical Account of
the Status of Woman Through the Christian Ages with Reminiscences of the Matriarchate.* 1893. New York: Arno Press Inc.

Gimbutas, Marija.1991. *The Civilization of the Goddess.* San Francisco: Harper
Collins.

Gimbutas, Marija. 1999. *The Living Goddesses*. Ed. Miriam Robbins Dexter. Berkeley: University of California Press.

Goettner-Abendroth, Heide. 1999. *Das Matriarchat II.1. Stammesgesellschaften in Ostasien, Indonesien, Ozeanien (Matriarchy II.1. Matriarchal Societies in East Asia, Indonesia, and Pacific Area)*. Stuttgart: Verlag Kohlhammer.

Hayden, Brian. 1998. "An Archaeological Evaluation of the Gimbutas Paradigm." *The Pomegranate* 6: 35-46.

Lerner, Gerda. 1986. *The Creation of Patriarchy*. New York: Oxford University Press.

Leroi-Gourhan, André. 1971. *Prehistoire de l'Art Occidental*. Paris: Éditions D'Art Lucien Mazenod.

Marinatos, Nanno. 1993. *Minoan Religion: Ritual, Image, and Symbol*, Columbia: University of South Carolina Press.

Marler, Joan. 1999. "A Response by Joan Marler to Brian Hayden's article, 'An Archaeological Evaluation of the Gimbutas Paradigm.'" *The Pomegranate* 10: 37-46.

Marshack, Alexander. 1991. *The Roots of Civilization*. Mount Kisco: Moyer Bell.

Meillassoux, Claude. 1972. "From Reproduction to Production: A Marxist Approach to Economic Anthropology." *Economy and Society* 1: 93-105.

Mellaart, James. 1967. *Catal Huyuk: A Neolithich Town in Anatolia*. New York: McGraw Hill.

Min, Jiayin, ed. 1995. *The Chalice and the Blade in Chinese Culture: Gender Relations and Social Models.* Beijing: China Social Sciences Publishing House.

Morgan, Lewis Henry. 1977. *Ancient Society.* 1877. New York: H. Holt and Company.

Platon, Nicholas. 1966. *Crete*. Geneva: Nagel Publishers.

Pietila, Hilkka. 2001. "Nordic Welfare Society – A Strategy to Eradicate Poverty and Build Up Equality: Finland as a Case Study." *Journal Cooperation South* 2 (2): 79-96.

Pinker, Steven. 2002. *Blank Slate: The Modern Denial of Human Nature (Selection)*. New York: Viking.

Reusch, Helga. 1985. "Zum Wandschmuck des Thronsaals in Knossos." *Minoica: Festschrift zum 80 / geburtstag von Johannes Sundwall.* Berlin: Akademie-Verlag. 334-358.

Roszak, Theodore. 1969. "The Hard and the Soft: The Force of Feminism in Modern Times." *Masculine/Feminine: Readings in Sexual Mythology and the Liberation of Women.* Eds. Betty Roszak and Theodore Roszak. New York: Harper and Row. 92-93.

Sanday, Peggy Reeves. 1981. *Female Power and Male Dominance: On the Origins of Sexual Inequality.* Cambridge: Cambridge University Press.

Sanday, Peggy Reeves. 2002. *Woman at the Center: Life in a Modern Matriarchy.* Ithaca, NY: Cornell University Press.

Schlegel, Stuart. 1998. *Wisdom from a Rain Forest.* Athens: University of Georgia

Press.

Thornhill, Randy and Craig Palmer. 2000. *A Natural History of Rape: Biological Bases of Sexual Coercion.* Cambridge, MA: MIT Press.

Ucko, Peter J. 1968. *Anthropomorphic Figurines of Pre-dynastic Egypt and Neolithic Crete with Comparative Material from the Prehistoric Near East and Mainland Greece.* London: Andrew Szmidla.

United Nations Development Program (UNDP). 1998. *Human Development Report 1998.* New York: Oxford University Press.

Willetts, R. F. 1977. *The Civilization of Ancient Crete.* Berkeley: University of California Press.

Wright, Robert. 1994. *The Moral Animal: Why We Are the Way We Are.* New York: Vintage.

JOAN MARLER

The Iconography and
Social Structure of Old Europe

The Archaeomythological Research of
Marija Gimbutas

L ithuanian-American archaeologist Marija Gimbutas (1921-1994)[1] was
a pioneer in the study of the symbolic imagery of the earliest farming
peoples of Europe. In her view, the settlement patterns, burial evidence,
and iconographic imagery of the Neolithic[2] farmers of "Old Europe"[3] reflect
peaceful, matrilineal, egalitarian social structures in which women were honoured at the centre of ceremonial life. Her primary research and interpretations
of European prehistory have been at the centre of the most crucial debates on
European genesis for half a century.

As an Indo-European specialist, Gimbutas was well acquainted with the patriarchal social structure, warfare, population movements, and material remains
of later Bronze Age peoples whose appearance signalled the end of Old Europe.
Her Kurgan Hypothesis, first presented in 1956 and refined over several decades,
combined archaeology and linguistics to determine the homeland of Indo-European speakers and to explain the Indo-Europeanization of Europe.[4]

Gimbutas's comparative study of the contrasts between Old European and
Indo-European material artifacts, habitation and burial patterns, symbolism, and
social structures convinced her that the androcratic system that spread throughout Europe during the Bronze Age did not arise as a consequence of internal development of the earlier Old European societies. The profound transformation
of ideology, symbolism, and social structure that marked the end of Old Europe
resulted from a progressive collision of diametrically different social systems.

Gimbutas refused to use the term "matriarchy" to describe the social structure
of Old European societies because of its common association with the nineteenth-century concept of domination by women. Nevertheless, her descriptions of Old European cultures closely resemble the definition of matriarchal
societies as given by Heide Goettner-Abendroth (1995, 1998: 45) and Peggy
Reeves Sanday (1998, 2002).

Old Europe

Between the seventh and fifth millennia BC, communities throughout southeast Europe developed mixed horticultural economies,[5] villages with well-built

283

houses, an abundance of sculptural and ceramic art, craft specialization including weaving and metallurgy, and elaborate ritual traditions. There is abundant evidence for long-distance trade and for the use of a linear script within a ritual context. Examples of long-lived Old European societies include the Sesklo culture in the Balkan peninsula, c.6500-5500 BC, followed by the Dimini culture, c. 5500-4000 BC; the Starčevo culture of the central Balkans, c. 6300-5300 BC, followed by the Vinča culture c.5400-c.4100 BC; the Cucuteni-Tripolye culture, c.5050-3500/3200 BC in Moldavia and the Ukraine; the Butmir culture in Bosnia, c.5300-4300 BC; the rich Karanovo sites in central Bulgaria from the early sixth to the mid-fifth millennium BC (see Gimbutas 1991); and, the Linearbandkeramik, stretching across central Europe, c.5500-4500 BC, among others.[6] Although distinctive Neolithic cultures developed over a large geological region, Gimbutas and other scholars have documented similar patterns of economy, social structure, and ritual activity (Gimbutas 1991; Whittle 1985: 64; Milisauskas 2002). Considered together, the non-Indo-European societies, which Gimbutas referred to as the "civilization of Old Europe," reached a florescence of cultural development during the fifth millennium BC made possible by long-term dynamic stability.

Between 1967 and 1980, Marija Gimbutas directed five major excavations of early Neolithic sites in Bosnia, Macedonia, Greece, and Italy.[7] The development of calibrated radiocarbon dating revealed the true antiquity of these developed societies. Gimbutas's Greek excavations at Sitagroi and Achilleion yielded hundreds of anthropomorphic figurines and abundant ritual equipment reflecting "the small, ragged remnants of a rich fabric constituting the mythical world of their time" (see Gimbutas 1986: 225-301, 1989: 171-250). At that time, the Neolithic sculptures found throughout southeast Europe were typically considered to be "curiosities of art history with no standard method of description and interpretation" (Bánffy 2001: 53). Their contexts were sometimes not even recorded. As Gimbutas remarked, "I saw thousands of figurines lying in boxes in museum storerooms, completely ignored and not understood" (personal communication).

In the mid-1950s, Christopher Hawkes articulated a hierarchy of difficulty in archaeological interpretation. According to his "ladder of reliability," Hawkes declared religious practices and spiritual beliefs the most difficult to reconstruct (Hawkes 1954: 161-162). This prescription became embedded in archaeological thinking and as the "New Archaeology" gained favour, archaeologists developed a "timidity regarding cult and religon" (Bertemes and Biehl 2001: 12-13). By the 1960s, it was deemed unscientific for archaeologists to investigate the beliefs of prehistoric people. At the same time, excavations of Neolithic sites throughout southeast Europe were unearthing thousands of exquisitely painted ceramics, temple models, altars and offering vessels, stylized anthropomorphic sculptures, often with animal masks and costumes engraved with symbolic designs. Gimbutas considered it impossible to adequately understand the early societies that produced these extraordinary remains without studying their abundantly preserved symbolism. She, therefore, devoted the remaining thirty years of her life to an in-depth investigation of the iconography and social structure of the earliest farmers of Europe whose distinctive cultures virtually disappeared during the transition to Bronze Age societies.

Methodology

In the absence of written texts, an understanding of the nonmaterial aspects of culture is not possible through the description of artifacts alone. Gimbutas, therefore, developed *archaeomythology,* an interdisciplinary approach to scholarship that combines archaeology, mythology, ethnology, folklore, linguistic paleontology, and the study of historical documents. This methodology is informed by the following assumptions: Sacred cosmologies are central to the cultural fabric of all early societies; deeply rooted beliefs and rituals expressing sacred worldviews are often slow to change; and archaic patterns can survive as substratum elements into later cultural periods. Moreover, an interdisciplinary approach provides a corrective: If an interpretation based upon one or more disciplines does not hold up according to the findings of another, the initial interpretation must be reexamined.

In Gimbutas's view, prehistoric images are not mute, but speak a language of visual metaphor. Since Neolithic symbols are remnants of once-living contexts, they should not be studied in isolation, but are best understood "on their own planes of reference, grouped according to their inner coherence" (Gimbutas 1989: xv). In *The Gods and Goddesses of Old Europe* (1974) and *The Language of the Goddess* (1989), Gimbutas discusses Old European symbolic elements as part of a "cohesive and persistent ideological system" that crosses the boundaries of time and space. Extremely ancient rituals and myths that have endured into the historic period offer invaluable opportunities for studying the function of prehistoric imagery.

In the folk culture of Lithuania that Gimbutas experienced as a child, the ancient songs, stories, dances, seasonal celebrations, communal rituals, sculptures, textile patterns, even architectural features are elements of a complex fabric of ancient beliefs arising from an abiding respect for the earth. She observed people kissing the earth in the morning and in the evening as though the earth was their actual mother. The life-giving, death-wielding, and regenerative powers of nature are expressed in both anthropomorphic and zoomorphic forms. In the Baltic pantheon, for instance, Laima, the cosmic goddess of Fate, who controls the powers of creation, is a shape-shifter who can appear in human form, or as a bear, sacred tree, or waterfowl. She can be touched as stone, or heard in the voice of the cuckoo. The Earth Mother Žemyna, related to seasonal awakening, creates life out of herself and represents justice and social conscience. The death goddess Giltine can appear as a slithering snake or in human form standing at the head of a dying person. Ragana, the death goddess who oversees regeneration, is a seer who sometimes appears as a snake or bird of prey. Vaizgantas, the male god of fertility, rises, dies, and resurrects as the flax (Gimbutas 1999: 213). Gimbutas's early experience of these ancient beliefs within a still-living context informed her study of Old European symbolism.

The Context of Old European/Neolithic Symbolism

A profusion of dynamic designs painted and incised on well-fired Neolithic ceramics and sculptures of the sixth-fifth millennia BC feature rhythmically interconnecting spirals, zigzags, circles within circles, egg shapes, and serpent forms coiling and uncoiling. Similar patterns are found in regional variations throughout central and southeast Europe in Butmir, Karanovo, Bükk, Cucuteni-Tripolye, Linearbandkeramic, and other Neolithic traditions.

In *The Language of the Goddess* (1989) Gimbutas states, "Symbols are seldom abstract in any genuine sense; their ties with nature persist, to be discovered through the study of context and association. In this way we can hope to decipher the mythical thought which is the *raison d'être* of this art and basis of its form" (xv). What was the underlying context and mythical thought of early horticultural societies that gave rise to Neolithic imagery?

The creation of reliable food production and sustainable communities required a] fine-tuned responsiveness to ecological conditions and the progressive development and transmission of traditional knowledge. Early human communities were continually concerned with the fragility of life and the need to renew the generative processes of nature (Gimbutas 1989: xvii). Human survival depended upon an intimate and respectful relationship with the seasonal transformations of the natural world—the fertility of the soil, the abundance of water, the climate, the teeming presence of birds, animals, plants, forests, glades, and myriad life forms. From this perspective, it is no surprise that many Neolithic artifacts feature interconnected, cyclic patterns.

Some are elegantly abstract, while others combine plant, animal, and human forms. Similar motifs have been created by indigenous peoples on every continent of the world who share a sacred relationship with the living world. These designs often express an uncanny resemblance to writings by quantum physicists who describe the universe as a web of relationships between the various parts of a unified whole. Physicist Fritjof Capra, for instance, identifies dynamic patterns on the micro and macro levels that continually change into one another in a "continuous dance of energy" (1983: 81, 91). David Bohm speaks of the "implicate order" within the universe as analogous to a hologram in which the entire cosmic web is enfolded within each of its parts (Capra 1983: 95).[8] Anthropologist/ecologist Gregory Bateson (1972) refers to the self-organizing dynamics of the universe as "the pattern that connects."

Gimbutas writes that Old European symbolism is lunar and chthonic, built around the understanding that life on earth is in eternal transformation, in constant and rhythmic change between creation and destruction, birth and death. "The concept of regeneration and renewal is perhaps the most outstanding and

Butmir culture vase, c. 5000 BC, Bosnia.
Courtesy: Gimbutas collection, with permission.

dramatic theme we perceive in this symbolism" (Gimbutas 1989: 316). The "mythical thought" at the basis of Neolithic art can be identified as expressing concepts of the sacred, and a consciousness of respectful participation with the cyclic processes of the natural world.

Spirals, elegant curvilinear designs, and myriad symbolic forms are found on ceramics, sculptures, even household implements throughout Old Europe. According to evidence on figurines, great attention was given to body decoration and to ritual costume (see Gimbutas 1991: 269-281). The spirals incised on buttocks and labyrinthine patterns on the legs, backs, and torsos of terracotta figurines may reflect traditional practices of scarring or the use of pigments on living bodies. Such practices would reinforce a *felt participation* (Ricoeur 1978) in the replication of the Neolithic worldview.

Well-composed, dynamic designs are also found on temple models and on actual houses and communal shrines, such as those of the Vinča, Tisza, and Karanovo cultures, where structures were painted inside and out with great swirling designs and formal geometric patterns, even three-dimensional spirals (Hodder 1990: 54-55).

At the fifth millennium BC site of Casciorarele, on an island in the Danube in southern Romania, a two-roomed ceremonial building (16 x 10 meters) had

Cucuteni pot, Romania c. 4400 BC. Photo: J. Marler.

one room richly painted with designs. One wall had a raised clay area painted with red and cream spirals, and two wooden columns plastered with clay rose from the floor elaborately covered with interlocking curvilinear patterns. The walls were decorated with red eggs, concentric circles, and spirals that Gimbutas associates with regeneration (Gimbutas 1991: 258-262; Whittle 1985: 154).

P. Bourdieu's (1973; Williams 2003) study of Berber houses is instructive as a way of appreciating the Old European cultural environment. He discovered that children brought up surrounded by traditional imagery within Berber houses absorbed Berber concepts through "an education of attention" that focused their perceptions. In a similar way, the myriad figurines, zoomorphic sculptures, miniatures, ritual items, and household implements painted with symbolic designs created a human environment rich with mythic significance.

Female Iconography

According to Balkan archaeologist Henrieta Todorova (1978: 83), more than 90 percent of the identifiable Neolithic figurines found in Bulgaria are female. Of the 250 anthropomorphic sculptures from Gimbutas's excavation at Sitagroi, Greek Macedonia, none can be identified as male (Gimbutas 1986b: 226; Hodder 1990: 61). Of the 200 figurines found at the Sesklo site of Achilleion in Greece, only two are assumed to be male due to the absence of female attributes (Gimbutas et al. 1989: 198). Throughout southeast Europe, Anatolia, and much of the circum-Mediterranean world, a similar pattern obtains.

The significance of the female presence is emphasized throughout Old Europe by elaborately incised Cucuteni figurines; enthroned female Tisza sculptures culture engraved with complex textile designs; hundreds of Vinča sculptures stylized as bird-women, masked as mother bears, anthromorphic vessels, and thousands of other images indicating a gendered relationship between the human, animal, and mythic realms.

Gimbutas is not the only archaeologist who recognizes a connection between the vast number of female images and women's centrality within the domestic and horticultural realms. While some colleagues, such as Ian Hodder (1990: 61-63) are willing to acknowledge economic and social implications, Gimbutas goes further to insist that female images are metaphoric of sacred concepts. The refined stylization of form and posture of many of these sculptures, their ritual and ubiquitous contexts, the frequent use of masks and exaggerated female attributes suggest the expression of a complex sacred concept that Gimbutas calls "goddess."

These images may also have expressed polyvalent meanings concerning ancestral lineage, female sovereignty, the sacred source of life, or other attributes essential for ethical and cultural continuity. See Peggy Reeves Sanday (this volume) for a related discussion about the social power of maternal symbols.

Although goddesses are well-known from the Greek and Roman periods, the idea that the sacred source of life may have been venerated as female at the dawn of European prehistory, with a relative absence of male imagery, challenges the charter myth of Western civilization in which male dominance in both human and mythic realms is assumed. The term "goddess" for many researchers is opaque and problematic, conjuring a utopian fantasy about a matriarchal fertility cult (i.e., Meskell 1995). In actuality, Gimbutas repeatedly insisted that the concept of goddess is not limited to fertility and motherhood, nor did she refer to Old Europe as matriarchal. Gimbutas defines "the Goddess," in all her manifestations, as a symbol of the *unity* of all life in Nature. "Her power

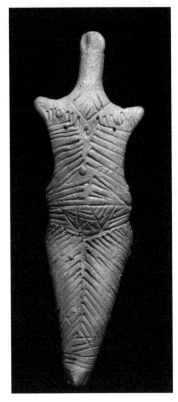

Engraved female figure from the Late Neolithic site of Scânteia, Moldavia, NE Romania, 4350-4200 BC.
Photo: J. Appelbaum,
Institute of Archaeomythology.

was in water and stone, in tomb and cave, in animals and birds, snakes and fish, hills, trees, and flowers. Hence the holistic and mythopoetic perception of the sacredness and mystery of all there is on Earth" (Gimbutas 1989: 321).

Gimbutas's excavation at the seventh-sixth millennium BC site of Achilleion in Thessaly provided *in situ* contexts for specific types of anthromorphic sculptures. She was, therefore, able to formulate a classification system based on morphology and style and to identify twenty categories of figurines associated with seven distinct deities. Sculptures indicating pregnancy, for instance, were found near circular hearths, outdoor ovens, and in places where grain was stored, ground, and baked into bread. The fecundity of the womb and the grain that nourished the community were clearly associated. Hybrid zoomorphic figures combining a woman's body with a bird or animal mask were found in house shrines, possibly as protectors. Male images from other Old European sites, often in ithyphallic posture, are interpreted by Gimbutas as "gods" that are consorts of the youthful goddess in her springtime aspect. However, evidence for males as fathers during this period is absent. "My archaeological research does not confirm the hypothetical existence of the primordial parents and their division into the Great Father and Great Mother" (Gimbutas 1982: 316).

Many anthropomorphic sculptures have no sexual characteristics. Others appear to combine both male and female attributes—such as several from the Starčevo culture, c. 5000 BC, as well as sculptures from the Gumelnitsa culture in Romania. The combination of male and female elements may suggest a unity, wholeness, a fluidity of gender, or one who is "self-generating." There are also doubles, most generally two females fused into one body, suggesting a bonding between women or between mother and daughter.

Social Structure

Settlement and cemetery evidence as well as linguistic, mythological, and historical research indicate that non-Indo-European Neolithic societies were matrilineal, matrifocal, and egalitarian. Gimbutas called this social system *matristic* (Gimbutas 1991: 294-296, 324-349; 1999: 112-125). She writes,

> We do not find in Old Europe, nor in all of the Old World, a system of autocratic rule by women with an equivalent suppression of men. Rather, we find a structure in which the sexes are more or less on equal footing, a society that could be termed a *gylany* [in which] the sexes are 'linked' rather than hierarchically 'ranked.' I use the term *matristic* simply to avoid the term *matriarchy*, with the understanding that it incorporates matriliny. (1991: 324)

In Gimbutas's view, sacred beliefs are mirrored by social structure (1991: 342). The absence of evidence of male dominance and the predominance of ritual activity associated with female imagery is evidence of a mother-kinship system and ancestor worship. Caches of female figurines, such as those from the Cucuteni culture, may reflect a council of women who functioned as guides of community life (see Gimbutas 1991: 344).

Settlement evidence

The transmission of cultural memory throughout the duration of Old Europe nurtured finely developed cultural traditions, a symbiosis with specific landscapes, and cooperative balance between community members. "These were old histories of tradition, renewal and reaffirmation ... [with] little evidence for overt lineage or other internal differentiation" (Whittle 1996: 121). Colin Renfrew describes the farmers of this period as "egalitarian peasants," whose societies "probably embodied no hierarchical ordering whatsoever: certainly their material culture does not reflect it..... [T]here is no reason to suggest the existence in them of hereditary chieftains, and certainly none to warrant a specialized functional division of population into warriors, priests and common people" (1987: 253).

At the local level, internal differentiation is not readily apparent within individual settlements in terms of either layout or structure. Larger buildings did exist although they contain no evidence of chieftains, and were most likely used as communal buildings or shrines (Gimbutas 1989, 1991: 331; Whittle 1985: 63). Often, ceremonial buildings are virtually indistinguishable from residences except for more elaborate decorations and a greater abundance of ritual artifacts (Marangou 2001: 155; Whittle 1985: 151, 153). The pattern of communal chapels attended by several households of women has endured to the present-day in the Aegean I Islands (Gimbutas 1991).

Burial evidence

During the Early Neolithic, particularly in the Balkans, women, children, and youths were buried under house floors and between buildings. Habitation areas were, therefore, realms of the ancestors as well as of the living. When cemeteries of kin-related burials came into use, there is no evidence of spatial hierarchy in which rich and poor graves are placed in separate areas (Gimbutas 1991: 331; Whittle 1985: 89). Until cemeteries began to appear around 5000 BC, the burials of adult males are conspicuously absent. As Alistar Whittle [is?] has noted, "Notions of human community may have been sanctioned by links to a divine community of sacred beings, from whom descent was derived" (1996: 8). Whittle's emphasis on the significance of ancestors is somewhat consonant with Gimbutas's interpretation of the veneration of ancestors within a mother kinship system.[9]

Old European graves in central Europe demonstrate that male burials are associated with trade items and tools, whereas women's graves include pottery tools, quern stones, and symbolic items. Nevertheless, the division of labour between males and females reveals a certain fluidity: quern stones for grinding grain are sometimes found in male graves while stone celts for woodworking also appear in female graves (Gimbutas 1991: 133). In the later Neolithic, the egalitarian pattern of kin-related burials continued in the megalithic graves of western Europe where communities of ancestors were honoured in large-stone monuments.

Historical evidence

A major tenant of Gimbutas's theory is that the deeply rooted Old European cultural traditions did not produce the patriarchal system that later took hold. The dramatic transformation in Neolithic social structure, economy, language, and religious beliefs that took place during the fourth and third millennia BC was not simply the result of internal development of elite dominance out of simpler, egalitarian societies. Gimbutas's Kurgan Hypothesis describes a progressive collision between two entirely different ideologies and social systems. After the introduction of androcratic structures and the demise of Old Europe, matristic patterns endured in some regions as substratum features into the historical era.

Ancient sources from Herodotus in the fifth century BC to Strabo in the first century AD, describe cultures practicing inheritance and royal succession through the female line; matrilocal and group marriage combined with common ownership; metronymy (naming through the mother in which the father is not recognized); endogamy (marrying within the same kinship group); the importance of a queen's brother (no husband, only a consort), and the high status of women, particularly in Minoan and Etruscan societies (Gimbutas 1991: 349).

Matrilineal succession continued in such non-Indo-European societies as the Minoan, Etruscan, Pelasgian, Lydian, Lykian, Carian in western Turkey, Basque in northern Spain and southwest France, and the Picts in Britain before the Celts. Matrilineage and prominent female deities are also found in Indo-European-speaking societies such as the Celts, Teutons, Slavs, and Balts who absorbed matricentric and matrilineal traditions from the rich substratum of Old European populations (Gimbutas 1991: 344).

Beneath the intertwined layers of Indo-European and Christian influences, many Old European elements are preserved in myths and folklore that speak of a veneration of the earth, female deities, and women as cultural and religious leaders guiding their communities. These lingering themes occur not only in ancient Greek and Roman mythologies but also in Basque, Old Irish, Welsh, Gaulish, Norse, German, Baltic, and Slavic traditions (Gimbutas 1991: 324).

As late as the early twentieth century, "the Basque priestess, *serora*, and her female helpers inhabited caves and grottos where they were consulted as oracles and prophetesses. Their status was higher than that of the Catholic priest" (Gimbutas 1991: 343).

Conclusion

According to the archaeomythological research of Marija Gimbutas, the matristic social patterns that endured into the historic period in Europe did not develop out of the patriarchal social system that spread throughout Europe during the Indo-Europeanization of the continent. The settlement patterns, burial evidence, and iconographic imagery of the Neolithic farmers of "Old Europe" reflect peaceful, matrilineal, egalitarian social structures in which women were honoured at the centre of ceremonial life. "There is no question that Old European sacred images and symbols remain a vital part of the cultural heritage of Europe ... the matrix of much later beliefs and practices" (Gimbutas 1991: 320).

Although Gimbutas refused to use the term "matriarchy" in order to avoid the nineteenth-century definition of "rule by women," her descriptions of Old European cultures are harmonious with the concept of matriarchal societies as re-defined by Goettner-Abendroth, Sanday, and other authors in this volume.

Joan Marler was born in northern California in 1947. She teaches Archaeomythology at California Institute of Integral Studies in San Francisco where she is on the faculty of the Women's Spirituality, Philosophy, and Religion M.A. and Ph.D. program. She is the Executive Director of the Institute of Archaeomythology and is the editor of From the Realm of the Ancestors: An Anthology in Honor of Marija Gimbutas *(1997).*

[1]Marija Gimbutas (née Alseikaitė) was born in Vilnius, Lithuania, in 1921, and received a classical education in linguistics, folklore, ethnography, and archaeology. She left Lithuania as a refugee in 1944 with her husband and infant daughter. After the war, she enrolled at Tübingen University where she earned a doctorate in archaeology, combined with ethnography and comparative religion. In 1949, the young family immigrated to the United States. From 1950 until 1963 Gimbutas worked as a researcher in East European Archaeology at Harvard University, where she devoted herself to the question of post-Paleolithic European origins. She became a formal Research Fellow in 1954. During her years at Harvard, Gimbutas's knowledge of Eastern European archaeology and languages placed her in a unique position to produce *The Prehistory of Eastern*

Europe (1956), *The Balts* (1963), *Bronze Age Cultures in Central and Eastern Europe* (1965), *The Slavs* (1971), and other texts. Before she produced these works, the prehistory of Eastern Europe had been available to Western scholars only in fragmentary form due to political and linguistic barriers (Marler 2001: 89). After the publication of *Bronze Age Cultures,* Gimbutas turned her attention to an in-depth investigation of the Neolithic societies of southeast Europe (see Gimbutas 1974/1982, 1989, 1991). For the complete bibliography of Marija Gimbutas see Marler 1997.

[2]Although "Neolithic" literally refers to the "new lithic" technology of ground stone tools, the definition of a Neolithic society in most regions of Europe refers to the transition to a sedentary lifestyle, food production via village gardens and domesticated animals, and the use of ceramics.

[3]Gimbutas coined the term "Old Europe" to indicate the earliest farming cultures of Europe before the influence of Indo-European speakers. She considered the earlier non-Indo-European societies to be diametrically different in terms of language, ideology, economic patterns, material culture, and social structure from the Bronze Age cultural patterns that replaced them.

[4]For a concise discussion of Gimbutas's Kurgan Hypothesis, see Marler 2001, 2006.

[5]"Mixed horticultural economies" refers to gardening combined with animal husbandry and a measure of hunting and gathering in the surrounding environment.

[6]For the chronologies of Central, Southeastern, and Eastern Europe, see Ehrich (1992: 356-406).

[7]Between 1963 and 1989, Marija Gimbutas was Professor of European Archaeology at University of California, Los Angeles. Her excavations took place through the auspices of UCLA.

[8]In concert with this concept, Dragos Gheorghiu has recently suggested that encoded artifacts can function as holograms to be used for cultural interpretation (2001: 73).

[9]Alasdair Whittle takes a literal interpretation of figurines as representing specific ancestors in contrast to Gimbutas's view of figurines as visual metaphors.

References

Bánffy, Eszter. 2001. "Notes on the Connection between Human and Zoomorphic Representations in the Neolithic." *The Archaeology of Cult and Religion.* Eds. P. F. Biehl and F. Bertemes. Budapest: Archaeolingua. 53-72.

Bateson, Gregory. 1972. *Steps to an Ecology of Mind: Collected Essays in Anthropology, Psychiatry, Evolution and Epistemology.* San Francisco: Chandler Publishing Co.

Bertemes, Françoise, and Peter F. Biehl. 2001. "The Archaeology of Cult and Religion: An Introduction." *The Archaeology of Cult and Religion.* Eds. P. F. Biehl and F. Bertemes. Budapest: Archaeolingua. 11-24.

Bourdieu, P. 1973. "The Berber House or the World Reversed." *Rules and Meanings*. Ed. M. Douglas. Harmondsworth: Penguin. 98-110.

Capra, Fritjof. 1983. *The Turning Point: Science, Society, and the Rising Culture.* Toronto and New York: Bantam Books.

Ehrich, Robert W. 1992. *Chronologies in Old World Archaeology, Vol. 1.* Chicago: University of Chicago Press.

Gheorghiu, Dragos. 2001. "The Cult of Ancestors in the East European Chalcolithic. A Holographic Approach." Eds. P. F. Biehl and F. Bertemes. *The Archaeology of Cult and Religion.* Budapest: Archaeolingua. 73-88.

Gimbutas, Marija. 1956. *The Prehistory of Eastern Europe. Part I: Mesolithic, Neolithic and Copper Age Cultures in Russia and the Baltic Area.* American School of Prehistoric Research, Harvard University Bulletin No. 20. Cambridge: Peabody Museum.

Gimbutas, Marija. 1963. *The Balts. Ancient Peoples and Places, Vol. 33.* London: Thames and Hudson.

Gimbutas, Marija. 1965. *Bronze Age Cultures in Central and Eastern Europe.* The Hague: Mouton.

Gimbutas, Marija. 1971. *The Slavs. Ancient Peoples and Places, Vol. 74.* London: Thames and Hudson.

Gimbutas, Marija. 1974 and 1982. *The Goddesses and Gods of Old Europe.* London: Thames and Hudson; Berkeley: University of California Press.

Gimbutas, Marija. 1986. "Mythical Imagery of Sitagroi Society." Eds. C. Renfrew, M. Gimbutas, and E. Elster. *Excavations at Sitagroi.* Berkeley: Institute of Archaeology, University of California. 225-289.

Gimbutas, Marija. 1989. *The Language of the Goddess: Unearthing the Hidden Symbols of Western Civilization.* San Francisco: Harper and Row.

Gimbutas, Marija. 1991. *The Civilization of the Goddess: The World of Old Europe.* Ed. Joan Marler. San Francisco: HarperSanFrancisco.

Gimbutas, Marija. 1997. *The Kurgan Culture and the Indo-Europeanization of Europe. Selected articles from 1952-1993.* Eds. M. R. Dexter and K. Jones-Bley. *Journal of Indo-European Studies* Monograph No. 18. Washington, DC: Institute for the Study of Man.

Gimbutas, Marija. 1999. *The Living Goddesses.* Ed. M. R. Dexter. Berkeley: University of California Press.

Gimbutas, Marija, Shan Winn, and Daniel Shimabuku, eds. 1989. "Achilleion. A Neolithic Settlement in Thessaly, Greece, 6400-5600 BC." *Monumenta Archaeologica 14* Berkeley: Institute of Archaeology, University of California.

Goettner-Abendroth, Heide. 1995. *Das Matriarchat I.* Stuttgart: Kohlhammer.

Goettner-Abendroth, Heide. 1998. "Cultures of the Goddess: A Discussion." *ReVision* 20: 45.

Hawkes, Christopher. 1954. "Archeological Theory and Method: Some Suggestions from the Old World." *American Anthropologist* 56: 155-168.

Hodder, Ian. 1990. *The Domestication of Europe.* Oxford: Blackwell.

Marangou, Christina. 2001. "Sacred or Secular Places and the Ambiguous Evidence of Prehistoric Rituals." Eds. P. F. Biehl and F. Bertemes. *The Archaeology of Cult and Religion.* Budapest: Archaeolingua. 139-160.

Marler, Joan, ed. 1997. *From the Realm of the Ancestors: An Anthology in Honor of Marija Gimbutas.* Manchester: Knowledge, Ideas and Trends (KIT).

Marler, Joan. 2001. "L'Eredità di Marija Gimbutas: una Ricerca Archeomitologica sulle radici della Civilità Europea." *Le Radici Prime dell'Europa: Gli Intrecci Genetici, Linguistici, Storici.* Eds. G. Bocchi and M. Ceruti. Milan: Bruno Mondadori. 89-115.

Marler, Joan. 2006. "The Beginnings of Patriarchy in Europe: Reflections on the Kurgan Theory of Marija Gimbutas." *The Rule of Mars: Readings on the Origins, History and Impact of Patriarchy.* Ed. C. Biaggi. Manchester: Knowledge, Ideas and Trends (KIT). 53-75.

Meskell, Lynn. 1995. "Goddesses, Gimbutas and 'New Age' Archaeology." *Antiquity* 69: 74-86.

Milisauskas, Sarunas. 2002. *European Prehistory: A Survey.* New York: Kluwer Academic/ Plenum Publishers.

Renfrew, Colin, Marija Gimbutas, and Ernestine Elster, eds. 1986. *Excavations at Sitagroi. A Prehistoric Village in Northeast Greece, Vol. 1. Monumenta Archaeologica 13* Berkeley: Institute of Archaeology, University of California.

Ricoeur, P. 1978. "The Metaphorical Process as Cognition, Imagination and Feeling." Ed. S. Sacks. *On Metaphor.* Chicago: Chicago University Press. 141-157.

Sanday, Peggy Reeves. 1998. "Matriarchy as a Sociocultural Form." Paper presented at the 16th Congress of the Indo-Pacific Prehistory Association, Melaka, Malayasia, 1-7 July.

Sanday, Peggy Reeves. 2002. *Women at the Center: Life in a Modern Matriarchy.* New York: Cornell University Press.

Todorova, Henrieta. 1978. *The Eneolithic Period in Bulgaria in the Fifth Millennium BC.* Trans. V. Zhelyaskova. Oxford: BAR International Series, No. 49.

Whittle, Alasdair. 1985. *Neolithic Europe: A Survey.* Cambridge/London: Cambridge University Press.

Whittle, Alasdair. 1996. *Europe in the Neolithic: The Creation of New Worlds.* Cambridge: Cambridge University Press.

Williams, Mike. 2003. "Growing Metaphors: The Agricultural Cycle as Metaphor in the Later Prehistoric Period of Britain and North-Western Europe." *Journal of Social Archaeology* 3 (2): 223-255.

ANNETTE KUHN

Nefertiti – "A Beautiful Woman Has Come"

Matriarchal Power in the Spiral of History

This paper is about a tiny segment of a larger project, "Making Women's History Visible," aimed at the foundation of a Museum of Women's History. I hope to show the basic elements of a matriarchal pattern in history and to grasp decisive moments of the continuity and change of matriarchal power within history. The early historical origins of human consciousness and of a matriarchal pattern can be detected in the short reign of the Egyptian Queen Nefertiti. Let's keep in mind that the basic elements of a matriarchal pattern originate in one's first awareness of one's self as a woman, and in history as it exists up to the present-day. Three introductory thoughts may help illustrate this presumption: Woman's body as the symbolic representation of matriarchal power; the notion of giving birth as the origin of history and historical thought; and, matriarchal universality linked to Nefertiti's praise of Isis.

Woman's Body: The Symbolic Representation of Matriarchal Power

The tiny, little statue called "Venus of Willendorf," created about 22,000 years BCE, is rather well known. It is only one of many thousands of similar figures found nearly worldwide that date back to an early time in human history. These figures symbolize woman as the image of life and the world in a universal way. The heavy breasts of the "Venus of Willendorf" emphasize her nourishing power. Her braids, which resemble embroidered stars wrapped around her head, symbolize the universe. Her triangular womb functions as a sign of birth, signifying the conception of life as an indivisible entity composed of living, dying, and regaining life.

This statue is a good example of the invention of symbols in human history, of the human capacity of creating a symbolic world. It reveals the early self-consciousness of women, and their awareness of their body. This awareness is the starting point for the invention of a symbolic world; one that reflects a feminine vision.

This thought is fundamental to my discussion of matriarchal power and of the continuity of a matriarchal pattern within history. Women in early history experienced their own body as the source of life and as a vital part of their own history, and of the history of the universe. They transformed this basic experience into artifacts we admire today.

This idea of the female experience and representation of the female body as the foundation of our human culture and its symbolic representation is the key to my thoughts on a matriarchal pattern in history and to my interpretation of matriarchal power throughout history. Sticking to these themes, I will discuss traces of these body-bound signs of matriarchal power within later cultures, concentrating on ancient Egyptian society and the female heritage of Queen Nefertiti. We have many images of her, and possibly of her grandmother, a woman called Thuyu. The figure of Thuyu is depicted in a similar manner as the Venus of Willendorf, holding her breasts as a sign of nourishment and everlasting life —a clear example of the continuation of matriarchal symbolic system.

Giving Birth: The Origin of History and Historical Thought

I am arguing that later attempts to develop symbol systems derive out of the basic matriarchal symbols, and are, thereby, fundamental to later religious and theoretical thought. I am aware of the obvious patriarchal, monotheistic, and logocentric appearance of our dominant religious and political ideologies. Patriarchal worldviews do not, in my way of thinking, contradict this basic assumption. The Egyptian concept of creation, recorded in written form around 1000 BCE, is based on matriarchal symbology and can still today be interpreted as a universal vision of an inhabited earth.

The creation scene in Figure 1 shows the three stages of the sun: the rising of the sun, the midday sun, and the setting sun, moving within the circle of the universe. The universe itself is depicted as a pregnant woman's body, encircled by streams of water, constantly being renewed by the two goddesses of the northern and the southern part of Egypt. Eight men or gods are shown toiling the fertile earth.

This matriarchal creation myth is rooted in the earliest experiences of women giving birth. It is the key to my understanding of the matriarchal power upheld during the reign of Queen Nefertiti. The universal matriarchal framework and the matriarchal symbolic world, showing the male sun receiving strength and power by passing through the female body, are essential to the understanding of these images. During her reign, Nefertiti presents herself to her people as a goddess-like queen. She appears as a universal body and the incarnation of the creative female power. For a short time within history, Nefertiti was the most influential woman of the ancient world (Tyldesley 1999). She publicly demonstrated the basic attributes of her matriarchal power by showing her womb, navel, and breasts as symbols of her natural body and her royal heritage. Birthgiving, represented by the symbols of womb, navel, and breasts, was the centre of her matriarchal view of life, history, and government.

It is not surprising to find many images of women giving birth and nourishing their male and female children in the history of Egypt. Such images show unknown, ordinary Egyptian women in similar poses or positions as that of statues

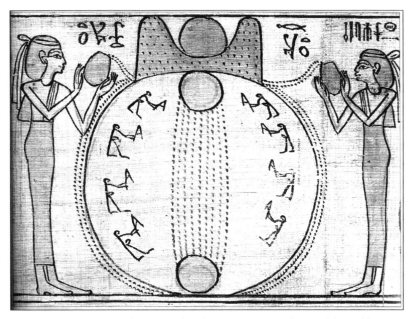

Fig. 1: The course of the sun within the Egyptian universal view of the world.

depicting Isis with her son Horus. Both reflect the centrality of birth within the Egyptian concept of life and history. The idea of power is bound to the image of Isis giving birth to her child Horus, nourishing him, and protecting his life. It reminds us of images of the Virgin Mary and Jesus, images revealing the hidden matriarchal centre of Christian belief.

Figure 2 depicts the Egyptian creation myth, the story of the birth of the sun. Nut gave birth to her son, Re. At his birth the morning sun was red as the blood of his birth. By noonday, Re became a man of full strength and gave light to the world. Here we see him, born out of the mouth of Nut, who in turn is shown bending over the earth. According to this matriarchal myth, Nut opened her mouth and devoured him, making once again the evening heaven, also red as blood. The next morning the sun rose again (Goettner-Abendroth 1995: 44f). Here we also see Hathor, the goddess of love, as the creative force of life. Giving birth, "for the love of the world," as Hannah Arendt puts it (Young-Bruehl 1982), is depicted as the main force in history.

Matriarchal Universality: Nefertiti and the Praise of Isis

The last of my introductory thoughts reflect the unique quality of matriarchal universality. We must keep the images of Isis breastfeeding her son Horus, or the story of the Egyptian god Re (also called Atum or Aton) in mind. In one beautiful image is the Goddess Isis, the heavenly Queen and Mother, the sun is visible in her crown. The moon, in turn, is shaped like the horns of the cow. Just as in

Fig. 2: The birth of the sun.

the creation myth, the sun must be held in place by a feminine symbol of life. Isis symbolizes the wholeness of life, including life after death. She is shown raising her hand, protecting and blessing the universe, bearing the *uraeus* or cobra snake, a symbol of power, on her forehead. The *uraeus* is said to spit fire into the eyes of the enemy. Isis represents a conception of universality, which is far more open and inclusive than the later patriarchal religious and intellectual concepts that claim universality.

This matriarchal idea of universality is basic for all later conceptions of matriarchal power and its symbolic expression. Isis praises herself as the sole goddess, reigning from one end of the earth to the other; she is the inventor of the universe, the one who sees everything. In the hymns of her self-praise she stresses her power: "Nothing happens without my consent" (Regler-Bellinger 1995: 269). The hieroglyph for Isis is the throne, also a symbol of the seat of birth-giving.

This concept of matriarchal universality is the key to understanding power during the reign of Nefertiti. Queen Nefertiti was welcomed as the "beautiful woman, who has come, beloved by the great sun disc who is in jubilee" (Tyldesley 1999: 37). Nefertiti was perceived to be the incarnation of Isis. Daily she gave birth to the king and the sun, which helped make all things flourish on earth (Jacq 2000: 99).

Attributes of Matriarchal Power During the Reign of Nefertiti: Handling Patriarchal Ambitions

The Greek historian Herodot in the fifth century BC was shocked by the freedom Egyptian female citizens enjoyed: "The women go to market and take part in trading, whereas men sit at home and do the weaving." Herodot concluded: "The Egyptians seem to have reversed the normal practices of mankind" (Fletcher 1999: 34).

This male-dominated view of the "normal practices of mankind" has prevailed for centuries. Instead of generalizing this judgment I shall reverse it, speaking of birth as the source of matriarchal power, of the "Holy Marriage" as the bond of power between women and men in everyday life, and of the Egyptian belief in the renewal of matriarchal power .

This method reflects two different ways of viewing history, distinguishing clearly between a patriarchal and a matriarchal approach. My endeavour is to put these two ways of seeing our historical past together again. Ancient Egyptian society was a combined patriarchal-matriarchal society—much like societies in the Middle East of this time, and of later societies up to the present—that used elements from both traditions. Sometimes the two systems worked together, and other times, the two worked against one another. In order to put these two views together I must focus on the less well-known matriarchal traditions.

During the reign of Nefertiti and Akhenaten (1353-1335 BCE) the development of Egyptian society was, to a certain extent, based on men striving for male-conceived power. These basic facts cannot be overlooked. The Amarna Period named after the new capital city at el-Amarna, was, religiously and culturally, a period of peace and general welfare. It came to an end when General Horemheb took over around 1319 BCE. Horemheb tried to eradicate all signs of Queen Nefertiti and the power she exerted. His efforts were in vain. For us today, Nefertiti exemplifies a feminist way of invoking matriarchal power within a society bent on ambitious patriarchal aims.

Queen Nefertiti was aware of the inclusive view of matriarchal power. She saw the world as a whole and considered patriarchal ambitions a secondary system of power she had had to deal with in an intelligent way. She invented new and differentiated terms of trade between men and women, visible when observing her life as a woman, wife, mother, queen, and priestess more closely.

Queen Nefertiti's Double Heritage

Queen Nefertiti was accepted by the people of Egypt as their legitimate queen by birth. She was "the Hereditary Princess, Great in Favour, Lady of Grace,

Endowed with Gladness. The Sun God Aten rises to shed favour on her and sets to multiply her love. The great and beloved wife of the King, Mistress of South and North, Lady of the Two Lands. Nefertiti, may she live forever" (Tyldesley 1999:1).

This is the description of Nefertiti as the legitimate hereditary princess found in the tomb of Apy. Her legitimacy as queen is based, first of all, on the Egyptian concept of heritage bound solely to the mother. Yet we know nearly nothing about Nefertiti's real mother. Maybe Tuju is the mother of Queen Tjeje, an influential woman at the court of Queen Tjeje and King Amenophis III and a priestess of the Goddess Hathor. Most likely Nefertiti's real mother was known to the women at court. The smile on the mask of Tuju suggests that we should be satisfied with the little knowledge we have. We are acquainted with the knowing motherly smile in history: the smile of Sarah, who bore Isaac in her old age; the smile of Elisabeth, the barren mother of John the Baptist; and, the knowing smile on the faces of Egyptian women. An ancient Egyptian myth speaks of the goddess Neith, whom, upon seeing her creation, smiled. In later creation myths we miss these telling stories of smiling women, mothers, and goddesses. Did God, for many of us the image of a male creator, smile? Today we speak in a rather ambivalent manner of the smile of Medusa (Garber 2003).

Fig. 3: Queen Nefertiti at the summit of her power, shown in Amarna style.

Nefertiti had two mothers: an earthly and divine mother. The goddess Isis was her divine mother. As Queen of Egypt, Nefertiti was the incarnation of the Goddess Isis, following as closely as possible the example of Isis just as the Egyptian queens before her did. Nefertiti gave life to daughters, and was responsible for their nourishment and well-being. Just as the Goddess Isis, the source of matriarchal power, Nefertiti ruled according to her double heritage. She reigned in her own right and in cooperation with her husband Akhenaten, copying the legendary life of Isis.

The Holy Marriage

Strangely enough, Egyptologists complain about the lack of testimonies on marriage ceremonies in ancient Egypt. This observation is quite contrary to the abundance of contemporary sources reassuring us that the royal marriage was the foundation of regal power. The marriage ceremony expressed the terms of trade between the wife and the husband, and reflected the old tradition of the Holy Marriage with the woman functioning as the source of power, a role she shared with her husband.

Many contemporary statues depict the royal couple as a loving, attractive, and happy couple, marrying according to the matriarchal ceremonial tradition of the Holy Marriage, centred around the cult of Isis (Goettner-Abendroth 1995:53f.). The young prince, Akhenaten, was about 16 or 17 years of age when he married Nefertiti and, as such, in images of the couple he appears younger than Nefertiti. She, instead, is depicted as the Goddess Isis, the loving wife, mother, and goddess, who chose her lover and gave him new life in the sign of the *ankh*, the symbol for eternal life. Thanks to Gerda Weiler and later feminist scholars, we can trace the further development of the matriarchal core of the Holy Marriage within many other societies, especially among the Jewish and Christian people (Weiler 1989: 115 f.).

Nefertiti demonstrated publicly the central meaning of her love marriage for all of Egyptian society. Her marriage reflected the matriarchal concept of power. Queen Nefertiti created a new iconographic style, one that depicted the loving royal couple occupied in different occasions of daily life: enjoying dinner with family members, playing with their children, or riding out in their royal carriage. She expected these images to be venerated in public. One popular relief shows the young queen driving with her husband in an open chariot; the couple kissing one anther beneath the rays of the sun god.

This public demonstration of royal love is essential to the refined culture of her time. It is further reflected in the new individualized style of Egyptian love poems from this period (Kischkewitz 1976). For the Egyptian people, Nefertiti was the royal bride who gave new life to her lover, the king, who in turn, as the Isis myth tells us, awoke every morning anew as the rising sun.

The idea of a Holy (love) Marriage in its down-to-earth appearance symbolizes the presence of matriarchal power. Arguing here that love between the queen and the king is vital to the maintenance and the transformation of matriarchal power within history, we must take a further glimpse into the public presentation of the everyday life of the royal couple.

Family Life in Days of Joy and in Days of Sorrow

Certainly one of the most conspicuous traits of the co-regency of Nefertiti and Akhenaten is the public demonstration of intimate family scenes. Queen Nefertiti is shown in another relief, the "Window of Appearance," surrounded by three of her daughters. One of her daughters is lovingly tickling her chin, while the whole royal family is conveying the blessings of the sun god to the people. The rays of the sun god are extended arms holding the *ankh*, the sign of bounty and everlasting life. This scene depicting a happy family functioned as a model for the Egyptian people, and as a mirror of regal matriarchal power that renewed itself in daily life.

The six daughters of Nefertiti are shown again and again. But there is no mention of a son. This might have been viewed as a "catastrophe" (Tyldesley 1999: 54). Nefertiti's status as the "King's Wife" was dependant on her role as the mother of royal children. But daughters, not sons, were vital to the carrying over of regal power. The eldest daughter Meritaten, the "King's bodily Daughter whom he loves," is depicted as the image of her mother Nefertiti. Born of the "great King's Wife, whom he loves, Mistress of the two Lands, Nefertiti." Meritaten is shown dressed in a flimsy robe, similar to the extravagant dress of her mother, and holding a small-scale sistrum. She is the the perfect miniature of Queen Nefertiti. Both mother and daughter are seen as priestesses, offering to Aten, the sun god.

The experience of death is also as a part of family life, documented in public images of the royal family's periods of deep sorrow and mourning. Mourning is a joint duty of the queen and king, also depicted on reliefs, in moving scenes such as the death of a princess who died at childbirth. For example, on the upper level of one relief we see Akhenaten and Nefertiti with their right arms raised to their heads in grief. Outside the room a woman is shown, cradling a tiny baby in her arms. In the background male and female mourners are assembled. In the scene below, the stiff body of a dead young princess is lying on a bier. Akhenaten grasps the arm of Nefertiti, in a supportive gesture of grief and solidarity. Again we see a group of mourning women and presumably two men, supporting a woman overcome by grief.

The experience of death is depicted as a shared experience of the royal couple. In the poem, "Hymn to the Sun," ascribed to Akhenaten, death is described as the sun going down, going through the body of the Mother called Neith: "You go down as Aten. You embrace your Mother, Your Mother embraces you." This does not mean that the dead give up their individuality and return to a state of pre-existence (Assmann 2000: 38). This image of the sun and the mother goddess is an expression of the matriarchal concept of power, a reflection of the symbolic world of ancient Egypt.

Queen Nefertiti: A Priestess and the Incorporation of Matriarchal Power

During her reign, Queen Nefertiti presented herself to the people of Amarna as a symbol of power, culminating in the worship of the god Aten. A limestone statue of Nefertiti and Akhenaten show the royal couple as they enter their new residence. Nefertiti is wearing her blue crown with the *ureaus* snake and is depicted as smaller than her king.

Fig. 4: Queen Nefertiti legitimizes her power together with King Akhenaten through offerings to the Sun God Aten.

This marked difference in size, typical of the Egyptian statues of the royal couple, cannot be interpreted as a sign of inequality. The power between the queen and the king is shared between the two. These images of the co-regents make us aware of the specific quality of matriarchal power. These images depict the female act of support in the handing over of matriarchal power to the king, out of hope that he is capable of using/harnessing/taking over his share of the regal power. The most significant gesture of giving over matriarchal power is Nefertiti holding the hand of Akhenaten her "son," her lover, and her husband, symbolizing that she is endowing the king with her innate, matriarchal might.

We can trace this act of endowing the king with matriarchal power in many images showing Queen Nefertiti and King Akhenaten in their daily life as they perform rituals and offer sacrifices to their goddesses and gods. We see the queen anointing the king with oil, a ritual act as well as a scene from everyday life, a well-known gesture that symbolizes the transfering over of the gift of matriarchal power. The worship of the Sun God, Aten, is the most important ritual, legitimizing the rule of Nefertiti and Akhenaten. An image depicting both Nefertiti and Akhenaten giving offerings to the Sun God Aten gives an impression of the division of power between the queen and the king and, at the same time, of the indivisibility of matriarchal power. It thereby reveals the essential difference between matriarchal power and the power represented by her royal husband.

305

Both Akhenaten and Nefertiti give offerings to the Sun God (see Figure 4). Akhenaten holds a tray with the two protective goddesses of Egypt, Nekhbet and Wadjet. These two goddesses could also represent the goddesses Isis and her sister Nephthys. Both goddesses wear the double feather of the Goddess Ma'at, the Goddess of Truth and Justice, the symbol of just rule and cosmic order in the world. With the help of these Goddesses, the king bids Aten, the Sun God, to accept his offerings and renew and strengthen his regal power.

Nefertiti's offering differs fundamentally from the image of legitimizing male power thanks to the help of the goddesses as an intermediating power. The Queen and priestess Nefertiti is not dependant on male interference. She offers herself as a Queen and as a Goddess. On her tray Nefertiti presents herself as the Queen and as the incorporation of the Goddess Isis. As the incarnation of the Goddess Isis, Nefertiti represents power in the matriarchal tradition of giving life, and extending one's own power to one's children and beloved, without losing anything within the cycle of giving and receiving.

Nefertiti symbolizes in a bodily and symbolic sense, matriarchal power. She is the "beautiful woman, who has come," and she is "pure of hands, the Great king's wife whom he loves, the Lady of the Two Lands." She is the beloved of the "living Sun Disc." Her power is comparable to the circular and spiral motions within the universe. The Queen receives the sun's power and is, at the same time, contrary to the King, the source of power, and not dependant on him as a ruler. During the reign of Queen Nefertiti, matriarchal power lay in her hands. She entrusted her power to a man, whom she called her brother, her husband, and her son. Following the example of Isis is this praise: "My hands laid on this child are the hands of Isis, just as she laid her hands on Horus, her Son," a popular way to say thanks for the presence of Isis and the Isis cult in Egyptian life (Papyrus Berlin, 3027).

Matriarchal Power Today:
The Continuity of Matriarchal Power Within the Spiral of History

I have been discussing a view of matriarchal power via a feminist framework of history. In concluding, I will suggest a means of generalizing this "doubled vision" of history (Gadol 1984) and of rediscovering matriarchal power as a force in history today.

During Nefertiti's and Akhenaten's reign, Egypt enjoyed years of peace. Yet it was neither a time without conflict nor a timeless model for a peacekeeping society. Therefore, I shall point out one controversial issue regarding the sharing of power between Queen Nefertiti and her King before making a few general remarks on the continuity of matriarchal power up to the present-day.

Historians are at a loss when analyzing a statue showing Nefertiti at the summit of her regal power. Is she depicted as male or female? Is she bisexual? Androgynous? Did she, after approximately thirteen years of regency, usurp the power she had freely given over? The co-regency after the move to Amarna is described as "revolutionary." But at about the thirteenth year of reign, Nefertiti seems suddenly to vanish from sight.

Nicholas Reeves (2001: 165) has discussed this sculpture of Queen Nefertiti (see Figure 5), in which she is shown holding the rod and the whip, the traditional signs of power endowed to the king by the ruling queen. It is the traditional way of demonstrating the transition of female power, originating in the story of Isis, who sent Osiris away to cultivate the land of Egypt. Egyptian kings are traditionally depicted with these attributes but also with female traits—accentuating the female breasts and showing no male genitals. In this manner, it was possible to represent regal power invested to men without making use of patriarchal ideas of force and subordination.

In this monumental statue, Nefertiti once again holds the rod and the whip, which she had handed over to her husband, the king. Here we are confronted with the main

Fig. 5: Nefertiti symbolizing matriarchal power.

question concerning matriarchal and patriarchal power. Are they interchangeable? The question of the interchangable quality of matriarchal and patriarchal power seems to lead us, on a symbolic level, to a dead end.

During the Amarna period, female and male images became more and more individualized. Both women and men were conscious of their own need for self-expression. The process of female and male "emancipation" seems to have reached a turning point. I shall argue that Nefertiti carried on the old tradition of matriarchal power, accommodating the matriarchal pattern to the needs of the day. Nefertiti certainly did not suddenly vanish. Maybe she took over sole regency after the early death of Akhenaten. We can leave this controversial question open. Surely in this monumental statue she represents legal and feminine power within a matriarchal concept of sharing, of giving up and of taking over power according to the necessities of life.

As far as I know, this statue has never been seriously considered a symbolic expression of the female power within a matriarchal symbolic tradition. It has been put aside as "an asexual colossus" (Tyldesley 1999), interpreting both Akhenaten and Nefertiti as one indistinguishable entity or body, leaving the basic question unanswered. In this way, both Nefertiti and Akhenaten lose their identity as a real person in history. Looking for a way out of this dilemma, I will not argue within the well-known, dualistic male construction of the "two bodies" of the king, the natural and divine body. Within a feminist view of history and my concept of the continuity of, and the transformations within, a matriarchal symbolic world, I will argue that the female body symbolizes a far wider, more universal and more humane concept of power.

Three last points support my idea of the matriarchal concept of power as the essential foundation of democratic societies up to the present-day.

Political Potential° of a Matriarchal View of Women's Power in History

The cosmic view of the world in ancient Egypt can easily be traced back to early images of the female, and stories regarding matriarchal power. Images showing the Goddess Isis spreading her wings over the universe, protecting life on earth and holding the midday sun, often accompanied by the two protective goddesses of Egypt, sum up some of the leading ideas on matriarchal power. Within this cosmic view, power is divided between women and men according to a universal plan that women invented and which men must, for their own good, abide by. This cosmic view, particular to Egyptian cultre four or five thousand years ago, can help us generalize this perception of matriarchal power within the spiral of time, in realizing that monotheism as a power has proven a misleading patriarchal illusion. An illusion that has led us to dualistic ways of thinking, of the world divided into heaven and hell, good and bad. It is an illusion that accepts damnation, violence, war, and destruction as a necessary force in history, and monotheism as a sign of cultural progress. This view is only half the story, and certainly the worse half.

The matriarchal view of power is based on a more open, more inclusive framework, claiming the rights of women and men to live according to their own visions of humankind—a vision of enjoying and loving life, of trusting, respecting, and loving one another, of cherishing equality as the fruit of cultivating human diversity. Seeing this matriarchal pattern within history, I become aware of the continuity of women's power in history and above all I detect women's capacity to stick to a policy of human survival.

This paper on the reign of Nefertiti together with Akhenaten is part of a women's history project, which focuses on the survival of women. I am arguing that women today are surviving thanks to to a tradition of matriarchal power that has existed throughout the ages and continues still alive today.

Matriarchal power is inscribed in our history and is part of our vision for an inhabited world of peace today. Maybe the ancient Egyptian cosmic view and its matriarchal concept of power can be of help. The little scarab beetle holds the sun as a symbol of matriarchal power in the spiral of time and of history (Weiler 1990: 135). According to an old Egyptian story, the scarab daily pushes its eggs into the heaps of manure expecting new life to develop day-by-day in the warmth of the manure. The little beetle—she never gives up. The ancient Egyptians knew that they needed the guiding hands of a woman. Otherwise, the sun doesn't shine.

Following the enforced flight of her family from Nazi-Germany in 1937, Annette Kuhn's childhood was deeply influenced by the experience of emigration to the UK and then to the United States. She returned in 1948 to Germany and became, at the age of thirty, the youngest professor in Germany in the Department of History at the University of Bonn. In 1986, she gained the first professorship in the Studies of Women's History and has since developed a critical feminist theory with numerous publications to her credit. She was visiting professor at the University of Bern in Switzerland and the University of Minnesota in the USA. Since her retirement in 1999, she is working on the foundation of a Museum for Women's History.

References

Assmann, Jan. 2000. *Der Tod als Thema der Kulturtheorie.* Frankfurt: Edition Suhrkamp.

Fletcher, Joann. 1999. *Ancient Egypt, Life, Myth, and Art.* London: Duncan Baird Publishers.

Fromm, Erich. 1994. *Liebe, Sexualität und Matriarchat.* München: Deutscher Taschenbuch Verlag.

Gadol, Joan M. Kelly. 1984. "The Doubled Vision of Feminst Theory." *Women, History and Theory: The Essays of Joan Kelly.* Chicago: University of Chicago Press.

Garber, Marjorie, and Nancy J. Vickers. 2003. *The Medusa Reader.* New York, London: Routledge.

Goettner-Abendroth, Heide. 1995. *The Goddess and her Heros. Matriarchal Mythology.* Stow: Anthony Publishing Company.

Goettner-Abendroth, Heide. 2004. *Inanna, Gilgamesch, Isis, Rhea. Die großen Göttinnenmythen Sumers, Ägyptens und Griechenlands.* Königstein: Ulrike Helmer Verlag.

Jacq, Christian. 2000a. *Nofretes Schwestern. Eine Kulturgeschichte der Ägypterinnen.* Reinbek bei Hamburg: Rowohlt.

Jacq, Christian. 2000b. *Nofretete und Echnaton. Ein Herrscherpaar im Glanz der Sonne.* Reinbek bei Hamburg: Rowohlt.

Kischkewitz, Hannelore. 1976. *Liebe sagen. Lyrik aus dem ägyptischen Altertum.* Leipzig: Reclam.

Regler-Bellinger, Brigitte. 1995. *Die Himmelsherrin bin ich. Gebete und Hymnen an Göttinnen.* Bonn: Verlag Gisela Meussling.

Reeves, Nicolas. 2001. *Akhenaten: Egypt's False Prophet.* London: Thames and Hudson.

Tyldesley, Joyce. 1999. *Nefertiti: Unlocking the Mystery Surrounding Egypt's Most Famous and Beautiful Queen.* London: Penguin Books.

Wacker, Marie-Theres. 1991. "Feministisch-theologische Blicke auf die neuere Monotheismus. Diskussion, Anstöße und Fragen." Eds. Marie-Theres Wacker und Erich Zenger. *Der eine Gott und die Göttin: Gottesvorstellungen des biblischen Israel im Horizont feministischer Theologie.* Freiburg: Herder. 17-48.

Weiler, Gerda. 1997. *Ich brauche die Göttin.* Königstein: Ulrike Helmers Verlag.

Weiler, Gerda. 1989. *Das Matriarchat im Alten Israel.* Stuttgart: Verlag Kohlhammer.

Weiler, Gerda. 1996. *Der enteignete Mythos. Eine feministische Revision der Archetypenlehre C. G. Jungs und Erich Neumanns.* Königstein: Ulrike Helmers Verlag.

Young-Bruehl, Elisabeth. 1982. *Hannah Arendt: For the Love of the World.* New Haven: Yale University Press.

Part VI
Matriarchal Societies of the Past

MICHAEL DAMES

Footsteps of the
Goddess in Britain and Ireland

"Ysbaddaden, Chief Giant of Wales, has a daughter called Olwen."
So says the fable, "Culhwch and Olwen," written in the fourteenth
century from older oral sources. Wherever Olwen walks, four white
trefoils or clover flowers spring up behind her; therefore, her name is *olwen*,
"white track," says the storyteller. Her return from the underworld is marked
and matched by emerging clover plants. Their four-fold array connotes the
cardinal directions visited by Olwen in her wanderings. In a sense she *is* the
nation's fertile meadow. Britain, as the sixth-century monk Gildas explained, is a
beautiful bride, decked out for her forthcoming wedding.

Olwen's admirer Culhwch is set more than thirty difficult tasks before her
father will consent to the marriage, yet these are accomplished in time for the
ceremony to take place at Welsh *Calan Mai*, May Day, the traditional start of
the Celtic "Summer Half" of the year. Her father Ysbaddaden, whose name
means May Bush, or Hawthorn, is then decapitated. Representing the previous
year, his lopped boughs, still dripping with blood-red berries, accept the need
for a fresh start.

In the British Isles, as elsewhere, the goddess sows and reaps a field of
metaphors. Metaphor involves exchange, the give-and-take of shared identity. So
Goddess=flower means this=that. A general principle of interpenetrating values
is thereby advanced. Olwen silently advocates a poetry of being. Her footsteps
are the stitches that sew a world exhausted by aggressive rivalry into a renewed
garment of hope.

Her journey embodies a narrative, suggesting that the interchangeability and
interdependence of all material phenomena is rooted in, and arises from, a spirit
of divine coherence, expressed through mythic dramas of the deities, wherein
everything is conceived, born, flowers, comes to fruition, and sinks into decay.
These events serve as sacred prototypes and exemplars for comparable changes
in the ordinary world.

Supervising this endless cycle of death and renewal in Irish myth, sits the
mother of the pantheon called An, Anu, or Danu. In Wales she is called Don.
Olwen is, indirectly, one of her daughters. From Annwn, the Welsh underworld of
underlying truths, Olwen appears to permeate the world of surface phenomena,

where her cloak may be spun from golden sunlight, corpse worms, horse hair, wheat straw, mountain streams, blades of new grass, tongues of fire, moonbeams, coils of clay, and the songs of her devotees. She is both immanent within every petal *and* hidden below the level of human consciousness, or placed deep in the Otherworld.

How can these archaic forms of understanding have any relevance to the modern world, given its different approach to knowledge and its addiction to secular materialism? What purpose does the retelling of long abandoned tales have in the context of a book on matriarchy? Myth, by definition, comes from a pre-Socratic era and speaks directly of sacred revelation from the godhead, via poet or seer, to human community. In this transmission the objective detachment central to scientific method is unknown. Instead, myth seeks the fusion of subject with object. The listener is *engrossed,* intellectually and emotionally, body and soul, in the story, thereby achieving union with the divine.

Instead of analysis and the maximum reduction of variables sought in scientific experiment, the goddesses of Britain and Ireland stood for synthesis. Their narratives incorporate paradox, ambiguity, polar opposites, and contradictions, thereby offering a comprehensive fabric in which joy and grief, night and day, and winter and summer, match the complexity of human experience. Consequently, both the verbal and the visual symbols employed are polyvalent and multifaceted. Thus, when Olwen's walk is reactivated and represented by human May-time ritual celebration and performances, the event takes on all-embracing significance, far exceeding the narrow "functionalism" of most contemporary British archaeologists' outlook. By misapplying their instrumentalist training to the exclusion of older perspectives they tend to miss the point of prehistoric society's outlook, in which issues of farming technique, farm animals, practical tool-making, and architecture are all regarded as sacred gifts and derivatives of the original knowledge pool, presumed to be divine. To the mythic mind there is nothing so useful as deity. A single clover flower can be an encyclopaedia. A few footsteps in the dewy grass may lead, if followed, to *everything* necessary.

The goddess who walks across the land is also the land in its entirety. Even the merely allegorical figure Britannia, who appears on coinage in the second century AD, and still presides over Britain's 50 pence piece, is a superhuman metaphor, a version of the English landscape from John O'Groats to Land's End, viewed as a living anthropomorphic being, a comprehensive organic entity. This female who represents the island *is* the island, just as the goddess Ériu *is* Éire, alias Ireland.

In mythic usage, symbols enjoy a flexibility of scale, as they span the full range between macro and microcosm. For example, the little crucifix hanging on a Christian breast can stretch to the edges of the Christian cosmos. On an intermediate scale, the goddess in Wales frequently appears as a giantess carrying a load of boulders in her apron. When she accidentally drops these, they become the stones and covering cairn of a Neolithic burial chamber. In this way, the superhuman female of nineteenth-century folklore and place names reunites the deity of the New Stone Age, five thousand years older. Plainly the goddess in Britain can stride across time, as well as space. To the question: "Who built the chambered tombs?" both give the answer: "I did."

The monarch, whose head always appears on the obverse side of Britain's Britannia coins was traditionally regarded as "married" to the land deity. This arrangement was converted into the Christian "divine right" of kings, the issue over which Charles I lost his head. Similarly, in Tara, Ireland, a megalithic stone called *Lia Fáil* was said to roar when the rightful claimant to the throne sat on it (her) as a prelude to the *banais rigi*, or king-goddess wedding, symbolizing the fusion of secular and sacred power, without which chaos would ensue.

After the abandonment of such rites, now considered absurd, the contract between the British counterpart of Greek Ge, the earth goddess, and a respectful concern for our *ge*ography, has also markedly declined. Exploitation has replaced loving care, while the former morally responsible *husband*man (or farmer) has turned to factory farming, cynically indifferent to the abusive quality of the new relationship. Many British folktales warn against aiming heedless blows at the "land lady" (earth). At Llyn Fan y Fach, Breconshire, a harvest goddess is seen floating on the lake by a young man, who woos and weds her. Her dowry is a herd of Otherworld cattle. His farm prospers, until, although forewarned, he strikes her three times for no good reason, whereupon she vanishes and his prosperity turns to ruin. This "old wives tale" now serves as a message addressed to a society, heading towards ecological disaster. Whether on a local or international level, the goddess's forgotten transits have never been more relevant.

The earliest goddess figurines found in Britain date from c.23,000 BP. They are three images carved out of deer and wild horse bone. Arranged in a group around a male skeleton, which was covered in red ochre and accompanied by the skull of a mammoth, all lay in Paviland Cave, on Gower Peninsula, South Wales. Like a trio of Romano-British Matres, the carvings have hips, waists, and breasts. One wears the suggestion of a smile, another carries traces of a decorative binding, implying that the symbol was engaged in ritual action. The limestone headland rising over the cave has been interpreted as a topographical image, a holy mountain, and a display of the earth mother's pregnant anatomy.

At Nab Head, Pembrokeshire, Mesolithic figurines carved c.10,000 BP bring the same impulse nearer the advent of agriculture, when focus of worship upon the mysteries of germination becomes of central concern in Britain, as elsewhere in Eurasia, and often expressed through images of the earth mother, squatting or sitting, about to give birth to the harvest child. This double image, combining agriculture and human parturition was appropriately often made of clay. Mother Earth was more than a figure of speech. Envisaged in human shape, her image could range in scale from miniature to gigantic.

Her pregnant womb is portrayed on a monumental scale at the tallest human construction in prehistoric Europe, Silbury Hill, near Avebury, Wiltshire.

Silbury Hill, Wiltshire, UK, August 2002.
Photo: Greg O'Beirne (source: Wikimedia Commons).

The material used to create this forty-two-metre high edifice was dug, c.4600 BP, from a surrounding quarry, deliberately shaped to resemble the rest of her head, neck, and body. The quarry floor consists of a thin layer of naturally occurring clay, impervious to water. Therefore, seeping from the surrounding chalk strata, subterranean water turns the dry pit into a lake. Behold! The Lady of the Lake! Her womb-mountain is reflected in her water body, from which it was raised. Rippled by every breeze, her moat image accepts the gold and silver jewels bestowed on it by sun and moon.

This great cultural achievement has a natural counterpart in a nearby sacred spring, the Swallowhead source of the river Kennet. This outpouring from the Underworld, or Annwn, probably inspired Silbury's location. The spring's emergence depends on the same layer of clay which the hill builders located in order to create their "Mother Moat."

Four hundred metres south of Silbury, the Swallowhead water flows from an underground channel only 45 centimetres high, at the base of a wall of exposed chalk rock, 1.5 metres tall, topped by a one-metre mass of coombe rock and soil. At the foot of this natural amphitheatre the Kennet is born. From here the shallow water threads its way around grasses and lumps of sandstone and trickles twenty-two paces between an old hawthorn and a willow tree, to meet a river much bigger than itself. This river has travelled four miles from the north, but it is called Winterbourne, not Kennet. Winterbourne is *turned into* Kennet by the modest contribution from Swallowhead. Recent geological studies and the eighteenth-century folk tradition agree about this.

From the earliest times, human beings have worshipped at, in, and before water-issuing caves, because the cave epitomizes those states of transition which are compelling and of universal interest: light-dark, enclosed-open, in-out, life-death. These pairings and paradoxes have sexual references in the broadest sense, and the symbolic amalgam is also contained in the name "Swallowhead."

Swallowhead is perhaps the most physically memorable inland cave-spring to be found anywhere on the chalk, and because, in Ernst Cassirer's (1965) words, "all the sanctity of Mythical Being goes back ultimately to the sanctity of the origin" (105) we can see why the Silbury birth woman was built beside it.

The sixteenth-century topographer John Leland (1957 [1540]: 85) emphasized the connection: "Kennet riseth at Selbiri hille bottom," while the early eighteenth-century antiquarian William Stukeley (1743) again and again links Swallowhead to Silbury, although to do so contributes nothing to his theory that Silbury was a hero's tomb: "The person that projected the forming of this vast body of earth … pitched upon the foot of the Chalk hill, by the fountain of the Kennet.… At Silbury Hill [the river] joins the Swallowhead or true fountain of the Kennet, which country people call by the old name of Cunnit and it is not a little famous among them" (19). Further on he writes: "Silbury Hill, where the real Head of the Kennet is" (34-35).

This pairing is further supported by the frequency with which Irish Harvest Hills were associated with holy springs, and also by the siting of the Great Goddess temple at Eleusis: "But now let all people build me a great temple …upon a rising hillock above the Kallichoron" (Stukelely 1743: 316). Scholars agree that the Kallichoron was a well.

With the help of the Avebury peasants of Stukeley's day we may yet discover the Kennet as Cunnit, and the Swallowhead as Cunt. The name of that orifice is carried downstream in the name of the river. Cunnit is Cunnt with an extra i. As late as 1740, the peasants of the district had not abandoned the nomenclature, and the old name was in use all down the river to Hungerford, in 1723. The antiquity of the form is clearly shown by the Roman riverside settlement called Cunetio—their principal town in the entire Kennet valley.

The rediscovery of the Silbury Hill treasure depends on unearthing what Eric Partridge (1951), in his *Concise Dictionary of Slang,* describes as "the most notable of all vulgarisms…. Since 1700 it has, except in the reprinting of old classics, been held to be obscene, i.e., a legal offence to print it in full" (198). Unable to take the risk Partridge settles for C*NT, but perhaps he should not have included the word at all, because J. S. Farmer (1966: xxxi) affirms that it is not slang, dialect or any marginal form, but a true language word, and of the older stock. Other language stocks show:

Latin	*CUNNUS* (E.A. Andrews, *Latin English Lexicon,* 1854)
Middle English	*CUNTE* (F. H. Stratman, *Middle English Dictionary,* 1891)

Old Norse	*KUNTA* (Ibid.)
Old Frisian	*KUNTE* (Ibid.)
Basque	*KUNA* (A. Griera, *Vocabulario Vasco*)

Although the dreaded C*NT (the medieval cleric's mouth of Hell) was not, and is not, admitted into the *Oxford Dictionary* fragments of the world which she generated are included:

CUNABULA: cradle, earliest abode, the place where everything is nurtured in ts beginnings, associated with:
CUNINA: the goddess who protects children in the cradle (Roman)
CUNCTIPOTENT: all-powerful, omnipotent
CUNICLE: a hole or passage underground (obsolete)
CUNICULATE: traversed by a long passage, open at one end
CUNDY: (N. English dialect) a covered culvert; inquire into, explore, investigate, to have experience of, to prove, test, make trial of, to taste (obsolete)
CUNNING: (in its earliest sense) to know, possessing a practical knowledge or skill; able, skilful, expert, dextrous, clever; possessing a magical knowledge or skill.

The Silbury designers had to satisfy an awe-inspiring list of demands. They had to build in the immediate vicinity of the sacred spring. They had to tap the underground water supply, and find the only strata of chalk that could be cut into large blocks. They were asked to construct on an unprecedented scale, so that the Hill could be seen clearly from the other monuments in the ritual cycle, such as the West Kennet long barrow, whose chambers are arranged to describe a hollow image of the squatting mother, here seen giving birth to death. Equally important, the promise of maternal fulfilment had to be offered to those gathering on May Day at the Avebury Henge, which served as a "wedding ring." Therefore, the Silbury summit *is* visible from the centre of the Henge's south circle. Furthermore, Silbury as a mighty sculpture had to be modelled in an unmistakably figurative idiom to *look* like the Mother of the Universe, combining supreme intelligence (eye) with her role as giver of physical life, with her womb doubling as "world mountain."

The primary reason for building Silbury has yet to be described, for if Silbury failed to give birth, the builders would have regarded the whole achievement as inadequate. At the traditional start-of-harvest eve, which preceded the Quarter Day, August 7, midway between summer solstice and autumn equinox, and now called Lammas, the completed structure is put to the test.

So let us go to the Hill on Lammas Eve, at the start of August, when a full moon, regarded in British folklore as its "pregnant" state, coincides with Lammas, and see if the "harvest child" will appear. The sequence of events outlined below takes account of the Silbury latitude 51° 24' and may be witnessed by moving round the periphery of the terrace, incorporated into the original design of the Hill, just below its flat summit. It presupposes that the ditch should be clear of silt though, in some years, such as 1971, the August water level may rise above the sediment accumulated since Neolithic times.

On the night of August 7-8, the goddess gave birth and gave birth *for all to see.* Nothing less than total theatre was required and provided. The theme was to be the same every year—namely the birth and nourishment of the harvest or "first fruits" child. Heavy cloud could ruin the performance, but every effort was made to ensure the action could be seen and understood by the audience participators. In this respect the scale of the "Mother stage" was crucial. It had to be broad enough to absorb all known variations of Lammas full moon behaviour, while avoiding the consequent danger that the actress with the most dynamic part (the goddess as moon) would muddle up her moves. The Lammas Eve sun, going down in the north west shortly after 7:30 p.m., aligns with a pronounced curve in the otherwise straight moat edge, corresponding to her neck, to which the setting sun contributes a length of golden-orange "hair," as a moat reflection, snaking towards the mound.

After this show has disappeared, there is a pause, lasting about 30 minutes, during which the observers move to the south east edge of the terrace to await moonrise. At 8:00 p.m. the moon's upper edge shows itself at 109°. At 110°, the full disc occupies the Silbury moat, its light falling across the thigh and indicating the vulva. (And the vulva lies precisely on a due north-south axis, joining the Avebury Henge to Swallowhead.) By 10:00 p.m. the reflection has fallen on the Mother's big left knee, and when the last stain of twilight has given way to true darkness, at 10:45 p.m., the moon is hanging over the narrow gap between her "knee" and "child," both defined by the causeways which are features of the Neolithic plan. The "child," who doubles as a monumental "first grain" of wheat, waits to be defined and so born by moonlight on the inter-causeway moat of the squatting goddess. By midnight, the infant's head appears as a full round lunar reflection on the inter-causeway moat. At the same moment, it is seen suspended over the Swallowhead. Silbury Mother and river Mother are in harmony, and share the child-making, while affirming, in the inter-causeway moat as "ditch-phallus," the bisexuality of the great creator. For, in addition to being part of the goddess, the phallus also stands as "son" to feminine matter. He discloses the mystery of masculinity that has hitherto been hidden within. The god springs from the darkness of the maternal womb. In Wiltshire folklore he is called King Sel. A world in balance accepts and cherishes the male.

Seen from the south rim of the terrace shortly after midnight, the moon is at its highest altitude, lying at 180° where the mother's and baby's navel might be found. This was the moment to cut the umbilical cord, to declare the birth achieved, and also to cut the first heads of new corn, severing them from the earth in which they had been rooted. Perhaps wheat grew on the summit itself, to be ceremoniously decapitated at this time, when the reflected disc defined the baby's navel.

Here was the great moment, the classical demonstration of the goddess's power of generosity, where riverhead, lunar pulse, and temple image combined. We may hear the echo from Demeter's temple at Eleusis: "At Eleusis, in the course of the night the hierophant shouts: 'Holy Brimo has born a sacred child, Brimos!' that is, the mighty gave birth to the mighty one" (Hippolytus, second century AD). This moment was accompanied, according to Pindar, by "the showing of the great and marvellous mystery of perfect revelation, in solemn silence: cut wheat."

No wonder the Wiltshire moon-rakers, characters from local folklore, looked into their ponds and streams and saw silver treasure, long after their behaviour had come to be regarded as the depths of rustic folly, for they had inherited a mighty tradition, and were in love with moonshine, with good reason. The corn child can still be seen by Lammas full moon, swaying over Swallowhead-Cunnit. The very name Cunnit helps to bring to mind the *cununas,* the young girls who, in Transylvania, personified the harvest babies. They wore a spherical crown of wheat, and sang:

Two girls have cut down
Ripe wheat, high as a wall
From where the cununa comes.

The little cununa, glittering like gold
Must slake its thirst
With water from the mill
With wine from the inn
And with water from the stream.

The little cununa must drink, and so must the Silbury child. To do so it had only to descend the original Neolithic steps into the moat. But babies prefer milk and, by 1:00 a.m. on the Silbury birth night, the child's moon head has moved to the west end of the inter-causeway moat, and is demanding to be fed. If the Neolithic child is not to starve, where is the milk? None is to be had on the broad, dry, west causeway but, accompanied by the first sign of dawn, the moon indicates the nipple at 3:17 a.m. The anxious wait for milk is over once the moon has touched the tip of the breast with white light. For the next hour, the breast fills with white light.

A flight of Neolithic steps, each 30 cm high, was found by A. C. Pass (1887: 251), and led to the bottom of the six-metre deep breast. At this place he discovered stags' horns, the Neolithic symbols for maternity. The steps and the implied immersion suggest a ritual, involving representative human mothers, mimetically engaged with the Great Mother. This annual event may be reflected by local seventeenth-century folklore which states that "Silbury was built while a posset (or bowl) of milk was seething" (Aubrey 1862: 333).

As the Silbury start-of-harvest night drew to a close, the reflected moonlight was removed from the moat breast by the growing shadow, cast by the high rock wall forming the outer edge of the breast lobe. When the moon had dropped to within 8° of the horizon, the water was left in darkness, while the outermost crest of the ditch, defining that part of her anatomy, continued to glisten with silver light and, therefore, became the centre of attention. This was now focused on the natural soil line, and the cornfields beyond, and so away to the southwestern horizon, where eventually the moon would set.

The genius of the Silbury designers is nowhere better demonstrated in this use of moonlight and shadow to create an apparent flow of fecundity, where birth moved from the specific monumental Mother, to the Mother in her extended form—the entire landscape, awaiting harvest. The goddess casts her eye and her example over the island as a whole, as a visceral and intellectual endowment. Such an attitude receives divine confirmation at Bath, the Roman Aquae Sulis, where the native eye goddess Suil (Celtic *suil*, "eye," a word from which Silbury probably got her current name) merges with Minerva's wisdom at the famous hot spring.

By contrast, the dualistic split advocated by Descartes between abstract thought and physical process—a schism introduced by Socrates and Plato, is now orthodox in western culture. Nevertheless, the steaming waters still flow freely from the eye and vulva of Sulis—Minerva at Bath. There, head and body are conjoined, even today. This reunion of idea and thing and of insight and embodiment, is much needed in every realm of contemporary life, not least in the field of British and Irish Archaeological studies. But how can it and the modern world expect to rediscover the art of synthesis if it relies too heavily on an analytical methodology, while ignoring the poetic, pre-scientific spirit of Antiquity, perpetuated by the folk tradition?

While enjoying and benefiting from scientific procedures, perhaps it is time to adopt a pluralistic methodology, composed of different strands, in which science becomes one among several. This pluralism would offer an open welcome to subjective and intuitive responses, as valid means towards achieving empathy with lost societies and with neglected or despised routes towards understanding. In doing so, it would affirm that the human family is essentially one. What draws it together is more significant than what splits it apart. A shared sense of wonder is an inheritance that we should be encouraged to reclaim. Then we might step into the footprint left by Olwen.

The Irish scholar, Thomas O'Rahilly (1949) has made a convincing case for enlarging Olwen's range beyond underworld and earth surface, to include the sky. He derives her name from Eurolwyn, its alternative form, which means "Golden Wheel" (304). It turns out that she was also a sun goddess. The wheel of her chariot was her all-seeing, travelling eye.

This is confirmed in "Culhwch and Olwen," when the shepherd Custennin says: "She comes here every Saturday to wash her head, and in the bowl where she washes, she leaves all her rings. Neither she nor her messenger ever comes for them" (Jones and Jones 1949: 93). What are these rings? They are the daily circuits, the spun gold of her sunbeams, as she passes. Then "She was sent for. And she came, with a robe of flame-red silk about her, and around the maiden's neck a torque of red gold … yellower was her head than the flower of the broom … who so beheld her would be filled with love for her."

Whether on foot, or in her sky car, she envisages and marks out a dynamic track, joining elements and hemispheres together, in one image of adorable unity. There is no limit in space or time, to the goddess as a working metaphor, combining grace, elemental power, comprehensive affection, and the skill to return.

Michael Dames is an artist, writer, and pre-historian who has earned degrees in Geography and British Archaeology. From 1971 to 1976 he was Senior Lecturer in History of Art at the Birmingham Polytechnic. From 1977 to 1987 he was active in several art projects to illustrate the synthesis between landscape and the human figure. He is best known for his books The Silbury Treasure *(1976),* The Avebury Cycle *(1977), and* Mythic Ireland *(1992). His recent publications include:* Merlin and Wales (A Magicians' Landscape) *(2002);* Taliesin's Travels *(2006);* Roman Silbury and the Harvest Goddess *(2007); and forthcoming in June 2010,* Silbury: Resolving the Enigma *(The History Press).*

References

Aubrey, J. 1862. *Topographical Collections, 1659-70.* London.
Cassirer, Ernst. 1965. *The Philosophy of Symbolic Forms.* Trans. Ralph Manheim. New York: Yale University Press.
Dames, Michael. 1976. *The Silbury Treasure: The Great Goddess Rediscovered.* London: Thames and Hudson.
Farmer, J. S. 1966. *A Dictionary of Slang.* London.
Jones, G. and T. Jones. 1949. "Culhwch and Olwen." *The Mabinogion.* London: Dent.
Leland, John. 1957. *Journey Through Wiltshire.* 1540. London.
O'Rahilly, Thomas Francis. 1949. *Early Irish History and Mythology.* Dublin: The Dublin Institute for Advanced Studies.
Pass, A .C. 1887. *Wiltshire Archaeological Magazine* 23: 246-247.
Partridge, Eric. 1989. *A Concise Dictionary of Slang and Unconventional English.* 1951. 4th edition. Berlin: Langenscheldt.
Stukeley, William. 1743. *Abury, A Temple of the British Druids, With Some Others, Described.* London: W. Innys, R. Manby, B. Dod, J. Brindley.

KURT DERUNGS

Landscapes of the Ancestress

Principles of Matriarchal Natural Philosophy and Landscape Mythology

The method of landscape mythology is a result of storytelling research and all fields of knowledge dealing with "layers of time" and therefore with the oldest cultures, which the author has explored and taught for the past twelve years. In the field of history of language there is a whole branch of research: "archaeology of language," i.e., the etymological research which reconstructs the cultural origin and original meaning of a word. In the same way, research into myth and fairytales has a long tradition of bringing out the oldest layers of a story. Enhancing the structure of the storytelling and its archaic motives reveals consistent interpretations and brings them, once again, to consciousness. Thus, next to language etymology we can also speak about a storytelling etymology.

Geographical names as well as mythological tales have a strong reference to local landscapes and regions.Until now, geographical names have not received much attention as part of the social and cultural backgrounds of myth. But these landscapes have an even older substratum—with totally different patterns of thought—that is not accessible to conventional methods. By researching the human environment relationship of the myth, the author makes a pioneering step, by combining language and storytelling etymology with the etymology of landscape. Through Landscape Mythology we reach the roots of a culture in a given geographical area. This has been shown in different regions and brought about the discovery of the mythical landscape of the Old Testament.

The author has systematically enlarged the field of Landscape Mythology (or Landscape Ethnology) and created an integral system of knowledge. It contains principally three traditional specialist fields: ethnology; archaeology; and mythology.

As in the way of interdisciplinary research, each field is creating new multi-layered challenges, and thus avoiding an isolated approach. Integrating modern Matriarchal Studies into the field of Landscape Mythology is a new approach, leaving behind old patriarchal modes of knowledge and patterns of thought.

In this way Landscape Mythology is a branch of modern Matriarchal Studies, or depending on one's viewpoint and emphasis, Matriarchal Studies is an important building block of Landscape Mythology. In addition to the specialist fields listed above, the following fields of knowledge are also of importance: totemistic traditions; shamanistic traditions; and matriarchal mythology and customs.

These explain many phenomena within the Landscape Mythological approach in an integral circle of understanding. Especially in matriarchal myths and customs, we can find sociological traces and social coherence of the culture under discussion. All three fields are influenced by principles of matriarchal societies and mythology, meaning these principles explain and give reason to the remnants of archaic layers or customs in kinship totemism, in shamanism and the mythology of matriarchal peoples.

Matriarchal societies are sacred societies as they do not make a distinction between the sacred and the profane. In this vein, there is no artificial distinction made between humans and nature, or culture and nature. Furthermore, matriarchal societies are, socially and politically, kinship societies. This principle is also expressed in the kinship-like approach to the environment and phenomena of nature. The principles of the matriarchal kinship group are not only assigned to the clan or tribe, but also to nature and the landscape. The landscape, or more precisely the worldview derived from the landscape, reflects in many ways mythological knowledge and viewpoints, which have been informed or are still informed by matriarchy. Therefore, it is possible using this method of Landscape Mythology, to re-discover this old knowledge and natural philosophy.

This has revolutionary consequences for traditional customs and archaeological finds: the primacy of the landscape. For example, archaeological digs will concentrate not so much on the individual habitat, but will look for the connections and speciality in the landscape that serves as a pattern of interpretation.

From the principles of the matriarchal mother clan and its traditions (mythology and customs) further characteristics and attributes can be deduced. These are visible again and again in landscape mythology: direct veneration of nature; ancestral veneration and in particular the adoration of a godlike ancestress; and body analogies.

Especially in reference to the last two characteristics, one can see the relationship between kinship relations and appearances in the landscape. This will be shown with three examples: 1) the Black Woman in Vietnam; 2) The Island of the Pregnant Woman in Malaysia; 3) the Landscape Ancestress of Lenzburg, Switzerland. The first two examples are both in Southeastern Asia, and, therefore, ethnologically and sociologically within the classical area of matriarchal societies.

Landscape Mythological Examples

The Black Woman of Vietnam

When looking at the history of landscape and language in Southeastern Asia, we can find traces of matriarchal mythology and a natural philosophy. The name of the river "Mekong" literally means "Mother of all water-bodies" and signifies the appearance and attributes of the great ancestress in Southeast Asia. In the Mosuo mythology in Southwestern China, the Mekong is in consort with the rivers Salwen and the Jang-Tse-Kiang. All three are mythologized and referred to as three sisters; they emanate from the geographical area of their springs in the "Nest of the Mother," which means the lap of the landscape goddess of the region.

In the north of Vietnam we discovered a large delta close to Hanoi that is fed by three rivers: the White, the Red, and the Black River. These names refer to the appearance of the rivers, but are also the cult colours of matriarchal societies per se (clothing, textiles, ceramics, and symbolism). The rivers symbolize the three-fold landscape ancestress, a goddess-triad. The three unite as one, the Red River, and flow into the ocean. This is a concrete example of how the content of matriarchal mythology has been transferred into the landscape.

In the southern part of Vietnam, in the Mekong delta, we find a holy mountain called Ba Den. This name means literally "Black Woman Ancestress"—the mountain is locally revered as a holy landscape ancestress. The cultural roots of this region are extended even to the indigenous Cham people, a people partly organized according to matriarchal patterns who originally worshipped this holy goddess mountain. In the process of domination by patriarchy, the ancestress mountain was occupied by Buddhist monks. They transformed the Black Ancestress of the suppressed Cham people into a Buddhist Mother-Goddess, depicted with a black face.

In the centre of Vietnam we can find the Black Ancestress once again. Close to the seaport of Nha Trang—situated in a temple district—we find a consecrated mount used for cult purposes. The ancestress is sometimes addressed as Ba Den or Po Ino Nagar. The word *nagar* is indicative of an animal symbol of the black landscape ancestress. It means "snake" or "dragon"—the classical animal of the underworld of the Earth and Sea Goddess.

Po Nagar, or Ba Den, is venerated inside the temple district, but she can actually be seen from there in the landscape: To the question where the "reclining woman of the heavens" could be seen, we were told that she did not exist at all in this area and we would be better off going inside the temple and praying. By sheer tenacity we finally ended up talking to an invalid beggar who makes his living around the temple. He gladly pointed out a hill, which clearly showed the body of a reclining woman—the Sea Goddess Po Nagar or Ba Den. This Po Nagar in central Vietnam also originates from the matriarchal Cham people.

The Cham, like the Fu-Nan people inhabiting the Mekong Delta are austro-asiatic in descent. The Fu-Nan are described as dark, curly-haired and naked by Chinese travellers in the first century. They worshipped standing stones (*menhirs*) as ancestress and ancestor and were skilful farmers. There is proof of a snake cult (*Naga*) and totemism, as well as a Naga Queen called Liu Yeh. She was conquered and married by an Indian Brahman who later founded his own dynasty. This report describes how the Fu-Nan and their Queen were taken over by patriarchal Indian cultures. The Indian Brahmans changed the aristocratic

From the hill of the temple district in Nha Trang (Vietnam):
View of the form of the lying ancestress and Sea Goddess Po Nagar

Fu-Nan and the Cham into a God-Kingdom including a ruling dynasty, the caste system, Indian gods, and widow burning (*suttee*). In spite of that the people stayed true to their matriarchal traditions and, for a long time, Brahmanism did not play a very important role. In the southern part of Vietnam, Cham villages can still be found. They are surrounded by mounds, as though fences; the dwellings of the daughters are grouped around the dwelling of the mother. The men move into the house of the women. One compound includes kitchen and store rooms, the house with the rice barn, the wedding room, and the living quarters for the kin-group of the youngest daughter.

The veneration of nature of the Cham in pre-Buddhist and pre-Hindu times includes ancestral stones, the Naga-snake cult, as well as totem and shamanistic practices. Furthermore, holy mounts and mountains, the Black Woman and Po Nagar were worshipped. The latter is an Earth-Mother-goddess, the great ancestress of the country, who also makes her appearance as Uroja. The name *Uroja* literally means "Mother's Breast," a motif which appears repeatedly on jewellery and décor. Po Nagar is the creatress of the world and appears even in the form of the Naga-snake. She is also a rice goddess, a protective goddess of the city Nha Trang, and, she reigns over all mountain-tops and tablelands of the region.

The Brahmans attempted to transform her into a Hindu goddess by subordinating and changing her into a Uma, the Shakti of Shiva, or into a

Durga, meaning a Muk Juk or Black Mistress. In spite of this, the mythology of the Uroja and Po Nagar remained:

> Po Ino Nagar is the highest revered goddess. She arose out of a heavenly cloud and the sea. Among the 97 men she married, Po Yan Amo is her lover. From the union with her spouses she bore 38 daughters—all became goddesses like their mother. Po Ino Nagar is the goddess who created the earth, the costly incense, the plants, and the grain. Owing to the heaven's affection for incense, grain, and sandalwood, the goddess throws a grain of rice during a ritual offering to honour the heaven and the grain, equipped with cloud-white wings, rises up to. She disperses her gifts and favours everywhere. (Cham)

The Black Woman—Uroja, Ba Den, or Po Nagar—is not only worshipped in Vietnam as a mountain or as a female body mound, but also as a black stone in caves. We find one of these cult stones approximately fifty kilometres south of Hanoi, in the perfume pagoda, which is situated, significantly, in the landscape of the White, the Red, and the Black River. Here, the Buddhist monks are unaware of the local veneration and mythology or play down its importance with unconnected fairy stories. Locals, and again, "simple folk," tell us that a black stone can be found in the cave. Furthermore, there are two stalactites with the names: "Milk-breast of the Mother" (also Lap of the Mother) and "Mother-Brother." In this way, the stalactites and the black stone embody the former matriarchal ancestress of the region and her male partner, the uncle on the mother's side. Societal order and worldview as well as nature and culture are merging, and the principles of matriarchal mythology can be sensed in stone.

The Island of the Prenant Woman in Malaysia

In the north of Malaysia, a country of matriarchal people, we find a group of islands called Langkawi, in the border region with Thailand. In the south of this group we find an island called "The Island of the Pregnant Woman" on which there is a sacred lake. From above, the lake appears as an almond-shaped mandorla—meaning a large vulva, and represents the lap of the ancestress. What Po Nagar represents in the landscape of Vietnam, the same phenomena can be found here. According to the legends, the ancestress of Langkawi appears as a fairy-like princess who married a mortal prince. Her first child died shortly after birth. Out of sorrow she put the dead child in the crystal clear water of the lake and blessed it. Then she vanished to the heavenly fields. However, she left behind a gift—that all childless women who bathe in the holy lake may conceive.

Many women of the area make pilgrimages to the lake and drink its water to become pregnant. On this island, highly visible from the sea, there is a range of hills suggesting the form of a reclining woman. Interestingly, this can also be said of the whole island; if one looks at the island from a macro perspective, we

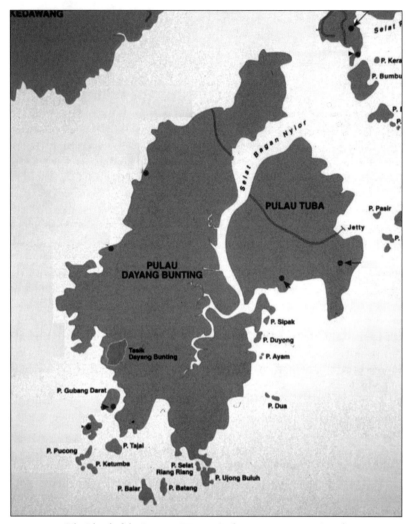

The Island of the Pregnant Woman (Pulau Dayang Bunting) in the Langkawi archipelago (Malaysia) has the body shape of the great goddess.

recognize the outline of a female body, which is doubtless the goddess ancestress of the region. Clearly one can see the head, two legs, and distinct buttocks. The lap-lake is situated in the generative area of the body of the landscape ancestress, and, also very significantly, a small meandering river represents the vulva and uterus of the goddess.

We have thus re-discovered one of the largest body analogies of the ancestress, for in the mythology of the people this island has always been the island of a god-like fairy. Only after patriarchy took hold of the island through Brahmanism, Buddhism, Islam, and modern industrialization, did the island become disenchanted and desecrated. The direct nature worship of the goddess is prohibited in order to force the people into an abstract belief in the afterlife.

The Landscape Ancestress of Lenzburg

Near Lenzburg, a half an hour's drive west of Zurich, in the heartland of Switzerland, we can find a most unusual range of hills. A great number of stone chest graves were found close to the hills and were judged by archaeologists to be about 6000 years old. More than a hundred skeletons of women, men, and children of different ages were excavated. Most of them were buried in groups: several persons were entombed lying side by side and on top of one another in one stone chest. However, a specific sepulture draws our attention: the people buried in the stone chests were all found in the foetal position, the so-called squatting position. It is interesting to note that all were laid on their left side as if they were just sleeping. Their bodies were oriented towards the nine-year lunar cycle.

The neolithic site of Lenzburg is of great significance in Europe. The excavation forty years ago was of careful diligence and is well-documented. In spite of the archaeologically exact exploration many questions remain unanswered: the riddle of Lenzburg cannot be explained by a single scientific discipline. Since 1996 I have been giving particular attention to this region and—by applying landscape mythology—I can demonstrate the multi-layered nature of this cult site. Furthermore, the principles of matriarchal mythology are evident and so allow primal decoding of the landscape. The different perspectives leading to a deeper understanding will be outlined here; the results will emerge in a synthesis.

Inherently the name "Lenzburg" draws more attention as we discover that the vocable root *lind* "water" originated from the (pre)Celtic period. Indeed the region proves to be extremely aquatic. Furthermore, the word *lind* has extended meaning: we know the expression "lindworm" refers to "dragon snake." In the landscape, water bodies, hills, and mounds are symbolized and refer to that mythological animal also characteristic of Lenzburg. There is a myth of a huge dragon snake living in the conic castle-hill (Schlossberg). It is the mythic animal of the earth goddess. Though her name is not transmitted, we may name her "Lentia"—from the place-name, "Lenzburg." She reminds us of Po Nagar in Vietnam who is represented as a snake woman. Just as the island goddess of Langkawi shows up as a snaking vulva-river, the myth of Lenzburg tells that the hill with the castle (Schlossberg) is perceived as a huge vault where the snake is guarding the hereafter paradise. The hill Schlossberg is, however, not the only "cave-hill" of this region. Facing it is the Goffersberg hill, a long drawn-out plateau resembling a bulge or a vault. According to the myth, every December— or rather winter solstice—the hill opens its vault from which St. Nicholas steps out and enriches the people with gifts and presents. The Goffersberg hill is an opening and closing mount: a typical female mount with chthonic hoards of the earth goddess. As St. Nicholas, she appears now masculinized and Christianized. In another myth, however, it is said that he is associated with a mystical "Frau

Hilde" who was visited by many lovers. Close to the Goffersberg hill there is a legendary deep fountain where women drink and conceive from the water—an analogy we know from the holy lake on The Island of the Pregnant Woman of Langkawi.

Near Goffersberg hill we find a path leading to a third hill, called Bölli. Unfortunately, this one is, sadly, overbuilt. All three hills—Schlossberg, Goffersberg, and Bölli—form together a closed system in the landscape. Walking in this system, one is overwhelmed by the natural setting of space and ambience. Facing this triple system to the west is a separate mount called Staufberg. According to the myth it is connected to the realm of death and afterlife and is additionally associated with a male elected by the "white woman" in the spring time (Eastern) to become her partner.

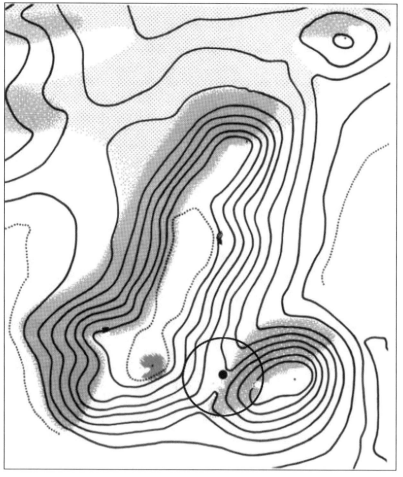

The three hills of Lenzburg (Switzerland) appear together as the body of a lying landscape ancestress. In her lap the deceased are buried in foetal position.

The decryption of the neolithic site of Lenzburg can be now understood with the principle and concept of body analogies applied in the landscapes of Po Nagar in the harbour of Nha Trang and of The Island of the Pregnant Woman of Langkawi. Looking at the three hills Schlossberg, Goffersberg, and Bölli from a macro-view, we discover the shape of the lying body of the landscape ancestress. Her head is the Bölli hill, her body outstretched like the long drawn-out Goffersberg hill, and finally her huge, pregnant belly is the Schlossberg hill with the snake of life. The stone tombs are exactly placed in the landscape body, where, in analogy to the female body, her uterus—the generative part of the ancestress—would be. Here in her lap the deceased were arranged in the foetal position in the stone chests—in the motherly earth in order to achieve rebirth by the landscape goddess's vitality.

Like the landscape ancestress, the buried lie on their left side. In the Lenzburg system, she lies in the eastern part, i.e., towards the recurring life, while the male Staufberg is to the west in accordance with the setting sun, and thus representing the other world, the hereafter. The landscape goddess would ensure rebirth. This is the reason why the deceased were buried as embryos in the pregnant bulging hill. Earlier people believed in the rebirth of their ancestors who would return to the clan as little children born by the young women of the maternal clans. In analogy to this, their local mythology depicts the landscape goddess with the spiral snake of life, symbolizing the eternal cycle of death and rebirth. The deceased went back to where they came from—in the stone chests embedded in the lap of the earth goddess—and waited, "sleeping" in the meantime for their juvenescence. Here they would be reborn as little children conceived in the soulful water or at the cult stone. In this way the old matriarchal mythology of rebirth is portrayed.

Relevance of Landscape Mythology

Like modern matriarchal studies, landscape mythology is a very innovative science. Within cultural history it leads us to the matriarchal roots of culture, which have not been researched by any previous study of patriarchal specification. These one-dimensional sciences claim that we have no way of finding out about such old knowledge. But with the holistic approach of landscape mythology we continue to find traces of old traditions, clearly indicating a matriarchal mythology, a goddess culture, and the worship of the great ancestress. Landscape mythology reveals and gives evidence of the fact that the earliest societies were matriarchal, and whose remnants and traces can still be found today. The historical-cultural depth structure of the landscape was and is the landscape of the ancestress. At the same time landscape mythology points out—even here in Europe—that matriarchal traces and traditions are not only found in the Far East, but are also on our own doorstep. This delineates the huge area of European ethnology. It is worth continuing the pioneering work in this field as we are dealing with an almost lost cultural inheritance. It describes our ancestry and a different way of relating to the landscape—beyond the present destructive relationship between humans and the natural world.

Translated by Isabelle and Kurt Derungs and Barry S. Simon

Kurt Derungs lives and works in Switzerland. He has studied anthropology, linguistics, philosophy, and history and holds a doctorate in ethnology. For more than twelve years, he has been developing a new field of knowledge that he calls Landscape Mythology, taking Modern Matriarchal Studies into account. He founded, together with Isabelle My Hanh, the publishing house Edition Amalia in 1995. In 2002, he designed the exhibit "Lenzburg—Landscape of the Goddess." Since 2003, he has been lecturing at the University of Applied Science in Bern. <www.derungs.org>

References

Cohen, Claudine. 2003. *La femme des origines: Images de la femme dans la préhistoire occidentale.* Paris: Editions Herscher.

Crawford, O. G. S. 1991. *The Eye Goddess.* Oak Park: Delphi Press.

Dames, Michael. 1976. *The Silbury Treasure: The Great Goddess Rediscovered.* London: Thames and Hudson.

Dames, Michael. 1977. *The Avebury Cycle.* London: Thames and Hudson.

Derungs, Kurt. 2000. *Landschaften der Göttin: Avebury, Silbury, Lenzburg, Sion. Kultplätze der Grossen Göttin in Europa.* Bern: Edition Amalia.

Derungs, Kurt. 2002. *Mythen und Kultplätze im Drei-Seen-Land.* Bern: Edition Amalia.

Derungs, Kurt. 2003. *Mythes et Lieux de Culte au Pays des Trois-Lacs.* Yens sur Morges: Editions Cabédita.

Derungs, Kurt. 2003. "Die Natur der Göttin." Ed. Edwin O. James. *Der Kult der Grossen Göttin.* Bern: Edition Amalia.

Derungs, Kurt, und Isabelle My Hanh Derungs. 2006. *Magische Stätten der Heilkraft:Marienorte mythologisch neu entdeckt. Quellen, Steine, Bäume und Pflanzen.* Grenchen: Edition Amalia.

Devereux, Paul. 2000. *The Sacred Place.* London: Cassell and Co.

Früh, Sigrid, und Kurt Derungs. 2003. *Die Schwarze Frau: Kraft und Mythos der schwarzen Madonna.* Zürich: Unionsverlag.

Gimbutas, Marija. 1989. *The Language of the Goddess: Unearthing the Hidden Symbols of Western Civilization.* San Francisco: Harper and Row.

Gimbutas, Marija. 1999. *The Living Goddesses.* Ed. M. R. Dexter. Berkeley: University of California Press.

Goettner-Abendroth, Heide. 1995. *The Goddess and her Heros. Matriarchal Mythology, Fairy-Tales and Poetry.* Stow: Anthony Publishing Company.

Goettner-Abendroth, Heide. 1998. *Matriarchat in Südchina: Eine Forschungsreise zu den Mosuo (Matriarchy in South China: Monograph of Mosuo Matriarchal*

Society). Stuttgart: Verlag Kohlhammer.

Goettner-Abendroth, Heide, und Kurt Derungs, eds. 1999. *Mythologische Landschaft Deutschland.* Bern: Edition Amalia.

Goettner-Abendroth, Heide, und Kurt Derungs, eds. 1997. *Matriarchate als herrschaftsfreie Gesellschaften.* Bern: Edition Amalia.

James, Edwin O. 1959. *The Cult of the Mother-Goddess.* London: Thames and Hudson.

Khôi, Lê Thành. 1981. *Histoire du Viêt Nam.* Paris: Sudestasie.

Michell, John. 1975. *The Earth Spirit.* London: Thames and Hudson.

My Hanh, Isabelle. 1995. *Kinder Küche Karma. Die Frau im Buddhismus und Konfuzianismus. Zwischen Matriarchat und patriarchaler Ideologie.* Bern: Edition Amalia.

Molyneaux, Brian L. and Piers Vitebsky. 2000. *Sacred Earth, Sacred Stones.* London: Duncan Baird Publishers.

Pollack, Rachel. 1997. *The Body of the Goddess.* Shaftesbury: Element Books. *The Encyclopedia of Malaysia* – Volume 4: *Early History.* Singapore: Archipelago Press.

KAARINA KAILO

The "Helka Festival"

Traces of a Finno-Ugric Matriarchy and Worldview?

His story / history
My story / mystery
    —Adele Aldridge

May 20, Ascension Day, also called Holy Thursday, is an official religious day in Finland, the significance of which has changed for the average person in the course of history—and even more so as herstory has given way to master narratives. Like many holy days, it has become more or less a holiday, a day off. However, in the distant and hazy past this period and the notion of "ascension" appears to have had a spiritual, concrete, and down-to-earth meaning. The roots of Ascension as the upward spiral of nature's cycles of growth have persisted against the odds in the Ritvala village in Sääksmäki, Finland.

The purpose of this article is to revisit this special festival in light of the most distant gynocentric, possibly matriarchal elements that one can detect in the ritual's historical layers. Matriarchies and gynocentric imaginaries are not identical, but they provide heuristic tools through which we might imagine or become sensitized to a psychic and gendered geography and paradigm of "elsewhere," contrasting with the taken-for-granted patriarchal social contract, sex/gender systems, and imaginaries. As all research into the distant past is, at best, educated guesswork, including non-gynocentric research, the value of research into matriarchies is part of an important process of academic archaeology. Every informed, if speculative new step in that direction helps future scholars reconstruct past societies, slowly allowing a more full and scientifically well-rounded, gender-sensitive picture to emerge out of history. While matriarchies have been defined with specific historical criteria, gynocentrism is a general description for feminist approaches that focus on women's culture and contributions. It represents a politics of difference where women's qualities and worth are not measured by how similar they are to men or how much they share with male-defined notions of power, politics, and social life. Gynocentrism refers to values, practices, and ways of organizing life that reflect women's culture, conditioning, and specific outlook, although not in a biologically deterministic way, and recognizing the heterogeneity of the category "woman." The work of Marija Gimbutas (1974, 1985), as well as that of Heide Goettner-Abendroth (2004, 2007), provide theoretical and empirical lenses that lend much support to such comparative cross-cultural research. Because one of the ways to strengthen and legitimize Christian patriarchy in Finland has been to rename and/or devalue female *haltias* (guardians of game and nature) and to replace them with male gods or Christianized female characters, my method consists also in re-visiting/ re-evaluating the various embodiments of "pollution" or impurity in research on prehistory. It seems, wherever one finds strong Church condemnation, forbidden practices, trivialization, denigration, or denial, we are approaching the matriarchal notion of the divine, the taboo, the veiled or suppressed Sacred Feminine. The site of alleged devil worship is likely to often be the site of the Sacred Feminine.

Defining "Matriarchy":[1] Traces of a Life-Centred Philosophy and Worldview:

Goettner-Abendroth has studied matriarchies for over 30 years and, based on this work, has listed a number of defining features of such a worldview (2004, 2007). She looks upon matriarchies as non-hierarchical, horizontal societies based on matrilineal kinship. She points out that the Greek word *arché* has a double meaning: "beginning" as well as "domination." She concludes that one can translate "matriarchy" accurately as "mothers from the beginning." I begin by outlining the broader context of a Finnish or Finnic worldview and a set of key concepts that may refer back to gift and give-back economies. This refers to a worldview that promoted social bonds and interdependency of all sentient beings as its core "social contract." I focus on the relationship between Helka as a Finnish creator goddess, goddess of Iron, mother of the maidens, and her mythic, patriarchal foil, Louhi. The latter has come to personify the negative, shadow aspects of the Goddess. The festival, like the goddess whose positive, life-enhancing, and healing dimensions have been suppressed and replaced for the most part with death-wielding destructive ones, bears strong evidence of the overwriting and appropriation of an originally matriarchal or life-centred worldview and way of life.

Description of the Ritvala Helka Festival

Young girls have been organizing *helkajuhlat*, the Helka feast, complete with a maidens' procession since the Middle Ages—or as it is claimed, "since time immemorial." The tradition was still going strong as recently as the 1950s. "The world will end when Helka of Ritvala is no longer," says an old Finnish proverb about the Whitsuntide feast in the parish of Sääksmäki. To describe the festival in its typical form, on Whitsunday the maidens of the village, in national costume, gather at the village crossroads from which, singing ancient Helka songs, they first wander a short way down each road and return to the starting point. Finally they move off in procession towards Helkavuori ("Helka Hill"). This makes a cruciform figure of the route they walk. On Helkavuori the girls make a circle and finish the song they were singing on arrival (Hiekkanen). After the procession, there is an open-air feast that conforms faithfully to old Finnish tradition with folk dances, folk songs, and instrumental folk music. It is worth noting that Ritvala is the only village in Finland to have kept alive the ancient fertility festival rituals with its procession of young maidens and songs in the *Kalevala* style. The ways, beliefs, and customs of the Helka Feast may have evolved during a particular period of pagan history, subject to Christian influence flowing from the West. On Ascension Day, all streets, yards, and shelters were cleaned and the village ways were covered with spruce. Elders remember times when the entire village was covered with leaves, birch branches, and flowers. One of the major scholars of the Helka fest, Viljo Tarkiainen (1922), has pointed out that it was essentially a women's festival. Elias Lönnrot (cited in Tarkiainen 1922: 11) reported that only honourable and chaste young girls were allowed to participate. Men did not command the ordinary Whitsunday psalms, rather, the song tradition was passed on by word of mouth from the older to the younger women. Foremost were the singer maidens who held hands or held each other by the elbow, in rows of three or four, or five, sometimes six to eight girls. Those not singing would follow at the back. As soon as the procession started, the foresingers would start with the initial hymn and as it was repeated, they would direct themselves towards the Helka mountain, at the side of the fields. In the meantime, the menfolk had, according to ancient custom, prepared a bonfire out of twigs. Once at the mountain, the singer girls would form a tight circle so no man could intervene and sang their songs to the end. There is speculation that the fire kindler had as his task to make each girl jump across the fire (Reinholm cited in Enäjärvi-Haavio 1953). Then the girls would dance, frolic, and sing around the fire, until it was time to return to the village. With three Helka hymns, the program was extensive enough to last three nights. There could be two processions with similar songs and rituals carrying on this tradition simultaneously, sometimes even together.

Although many scholars recognize today that the festival contains pagan elements as its most distant layer, it has also been pointed out that in its modern form, it has affinities with the mediaeval field-blessing processions of the Catholic Church. The Helka Feast thus condenses superimposed rites which have been added and modified during the course of time. However, the features that lend themselves most clearly to an analysis of matriarchal traces, analyzed together, are the following:

•spring renewal and rebirth rites;
•*hela valkeat* or the Whitsunday bonfires;
•*hela* or clamouring;
•the central role of young girls;
•the affinities of the girls' procession with Greek initiation rituals for

the *arctoi* at Brauron;
•the focus on eros as the connective, life-enhancing, fertility-oriented principle of the festival;
•the giving of gifts to the Earth, and the Spring fertility dances in honour of nature's creative forces;
•and, the exclusion of boys (girls forming a tight circle) from the core activities.

There is much to support the view that the Ritvala Helka festival was, in its origins, a Spring rite. Timo Heikkilä (2004), for one, infers that it is part of a broader life-centred worldview focused on the symbolism of nature's "furry" powers representing growth. The central role of young girls points to a worldview where the feminine elements of the cosmos were the most valued by virtue of their links with the death/life cycles of nature. The cyclical worldview was based on a system of time measuring where the periodically recurring phenomena, for example the menstrual cycle, the bear's hibernation and rebirth, were central. Women were highly valorized in archaic times in Northern Europe, because they represented the principle of life and the fertility on which any group's survival depended (Kailo 2006, 2007). As Goettner-Abendroth has emphasized, one must not refer only to a simple fertility cult in this regard, however, but to a complex spiritual and material worldview that must not be reduced to its most widely-circulated, stereotypical features (1995, 2007). Many feminist scholars agree that women's religions cannot be judged and classified using the criteria of patriarchal religions. In fact, Goettner-Abendroth doubts that matriarchies were "religions" in any organized, institutionalized sense. She believes it is more accurate to refer to a balance-oriented worldview beyond the patriarchal hierarchies. In the cosmos and on Earth, matriarchal people observe the cycle of life, death, and rebirth. According to the matriarchal principle of connection between macrocosm and microcosm, they see the same cycle in human life. Their concept of nature and of the human world most often lacks the dualistic way of thinking that separates "spirit" and "nature" or "society" and "nature." Goettner-Abendroth notes that the matriarchal principle lacks among other things the dualistic concept of morality that defines what is "good" and splits off what is "evil." From the matriarchal perspective, life brings forth death, and death brings forth life again—everything in its own time. Female and male are also seen as a cosmic polarity. It would never occur to a matriarchal people to regard one sex as inferior or weaker to the other (Goettner-Abendroth 1987). The following comments lend support to the Helka feast having affinities with matriarchal life-celebrating performances as described by Goettner-Abendroth:

> The concept of time is cyclic rather than linear, and the cycle of the seasons, with its phases of waxing and waning, of life and death and revival, is the basic pattern of all thought. On the level of rituals, matriarchal mythology is enacted in mystery plays performed by the

priestesses, who are led by the sacred priestess-queen, the image of the goddess herself. The priestess-queen is accompanied by the sacred king, the "heros" (Greek) of the goddess and giver of joy and fertility. Both are joined together in ritual festivals which follow the seasonal cycle: Initiation in springtime (spring equinox), Sacred Marriage in summer (summer solstice), Death of the "heros" in autumn (fall equinox), and Rebirth/Return/Resurrection of the "heros" in winter (winter solstice). (1987: 3)

Lönnrot (1832) believes that the Ritvala Helka Fest is an ancient sacrifical festival that was, in order to avoid famine, a sacred duty to perform. The repetitions and turn-takings or chain-singing modalities within the song tradition, as well as the back-and-forth movement of the circular procession suggest that the tradition goes back to a worldview, where time was not conceived in an obsessively linear and progress-oriented way. Tarkiainen (1922) notes that it is as if the very mountains, back woods (*korvet*) echoed back, mirroring these children's songs. Furthermore, the cyclical rituals served to help crops ripen into the final harvest through various means of raising nature's "eros," the mysterious power at the root of creation.[2] In his *Mythologia Fennica* (1785), one of the earliest collected and published mythologies of the Finns, Cristfried Ganander describes archaic healing dramas, in which the word *synty* (genesis) was central and which, in addition to origins and narratives being related to genesis, also refer to deceased beings (cited in Pentikäinen 1987: 178). The notion of beginnings is so central to ancient Finns that any ailment, for it to be exorcised and healed, must be traced back to its origins. One has to know the deep words of origin (*synnyt*). It is possible then that at an early stage, the Goddess at the root of it all was equally central. After all, the notion of rebirth or knowing the origins harks back to the matriarchal ethos of periodic renewal and the celebration of "beginnings."

A central feature of matriarchies was likewise to promote or ensure growth by honouring the powers of nature, and honouring guardians of game, animals, and nature. That is why gifts were given to the spirits and guardians presiding over nature and its produce. As Goettner-Abendroth (2004, 2007) also suggests, matriarchies have been and still are gift-circulating societies, where social bonds serve to create group cohesion and the recognition of the interdependency of all sentient beings. Out of the features of the traditional Finnish-Karelian and Ingrian worldview, one should foreground the central shamanistic and dynamistic concepts that are intimately connected with a cyclical worldview. The universe was seen to be governed by supernatural powers and spirit beings, with whom one had to live in harmony. In the most distant layers of the Finnic universe, we find numerous *haltias* and goddesses of creation, birthing, healing, and sustenance. The notion of raising the powers of nature to enhance growth is a central aspect of Finnish shamanism, and to such an extent it might be argued that matriarchy is not alone in having such traits. However, shamanism as other archaic worldviews are not generally analyzed in terms of gendered approaches, and it could be that more recent shamanistic rituals and ways of living contain in them the "evolved" features of gynocentric societies. The feminine concept to do with the growth-inducing creative/procreative powers is present in the so-called *hela* (clamour) accompanying the rite and the songs (or maybe incantations?) of the Helka festival.

Helavalkea, Hela Clamouring

In archaic times ancient Finns used to burn *helavalkiat*, Whitsuntide bonfires, thereby trying to help the sun stay on its course as a source of power and energy, and to celebrate first the Spring equinox, and later, the summer solstice. The burning of bonfires and the clamouring carried out by the young girls at the Helka festival served, according to Tarkiainen (1922), for example, to catch the attention of gods or *haltias*, to raise the energies of nature, to ward off evil spirits, or all of this together. Some believe that the role of clamouring also had to do with purifying nature of any negative spirits or influences that might hamper the harvest. The fields have in the most distant layers been presided over by earth goddesses, although male gods have taken over in this sphere as well.

Much of the symbolism of the Helka festival reflects the world renewal rituals of other Northern, particularly Indigenous peoples, and the eros-related dimension has to do with a kind of *hieros gamos*—sacred marriage between earth and sky, male and female. One need not interpret this as an image of heteronormativity but as a kind of yin/yang play of cosmic forces. Maybe the clamouring (*helanhuuto)* served also to agitate nature, humans, and animals in order to inspire them to copulate and procreate. The *helavalkea* was a magic bonfire which was also connected with love-raising magic, and the festival is in fact associated with sexual games, which consists of boys and girls trying to catch and take hold each other (Tarkiainen 1922: 19). There is a great deal of evidence of the love-raising magic in the Finnish Folk poetry collections. As in many other countries with similar processions for young girls, the young would tie wreaths, throw them into water, and wait to see what they prophesied. *Helanhuuto* or the *hela* clamour has given way to refrains in songs that are Christianized in other respects. In other words, maybe they were powerful expressions of the women's voices as the muscles of their souls, calling forth equally strong erotic energies. Turning them into hymns has been a similar process of taming nature's powers, as is the taming of women themselves. The Finnish *Kalevala* describes in the view of Paavo Liski (Liski and Marjatta 1986), for example, the transformation of Louhi, "evil matriarch," into a tame and more peaceful dove.

Many elements of the Festival embody ways and values that are more compatible with matriarchal values than others. Since such details as the *helavalkea* or Whitsuntide bonfires and the *hela* yells (*helahuuto*) are likely pagan phenomena, one can posit that we are dealing with a gender-neutral shamanistic, animistic past in these layers. Is it possible that the bear feast, of which there is a wealth of material, represented a historic stage of the give-back, life-oriented societies of the past, which were mostly male-only activities and rituals, while the Helka Fest was the female exclusive gender ritual? As Goettner-Abendroth notes, Goddess worship is a free-form artistic expression that celebrates, individually or collectively, the creative life force itself. The bear hunt, for its part, has to do already with a strong trait of patriarchy—killing rituals and violent bloodshedding. Women's menstrual rituals have not in many cultures involved the taking of life; women menstruated straight into the ground as an offering to the Earth. Perhaps the female-oriented initiation rituals of the young girls dancing in honour of a Goddess—like the Greek Brauronia—was the prototype of a mother-daughter-bear spouse ceremony that men imitated and finally supplanted. Perhaps the celebration of the life force came to be replaced by a culture focused on such ego-related concepts as competition between neighbouring nations, giving as a means of preventing war, and other "deficit"-type interpretations of ritual activity. Is that how women were excluded from the father-son oriented rituals of primal beginnings that changed the focus of the entire gender system? As Goettner-Abendroth (1987) notes:

> Matriarchal mythological systems were repeatedly brought to life on a seasonal-cyclical basis in the great cultic dramas and public celebrations of their cultures, and are thus alien to the constructing of institutions with a privileged class of priests, high above the degraded class of 'believers', which leads to spiritual-intellectual imperialism.(11)

The assumption persists that matriarchies are the mirror image of domination-oriented and hierarchical patriarchies, but Goettner-Abendroth reminds us that this is clearly not the case. The female-exclusive nature of the Helka festival is also likely not evidence of a worldview and social system based on excluding the males, at least not in the way that the bear ceremonial has evolved into an exclusionary and hierarchical event. Perhaps gradually, after the focus on mothers and daughters, there were male and female specific rituals, and the celebration of life and growth did not contain the kind of notions of mastery over nature and "the other" that characterizes patriarchies. There is support for such speculation within comparative ethnographic studies.[3] However, mainstream research, because of its general gender-blindness, does not facilitate such speculation. Michael Branch notes that instead of pure types of religion, we find combined forms which, however, well-adapted and functional, still retain elements from an earlier developmental phase. Vertical heritage exists and indeed survives, changing its form and function according to the conditions of horizontal adaptation and acquiring a niche in the new tradition-ecological environment (cited in Honko, Timonen, Branch and Bosley 1993: 66). Although no mention is made of matriarchy, Branch notes, echoing many other scholars, that characteristic of the earliest form of religion is a close but flexible relation to nature (cited in Honko et al. 1993: 67).

What indeed is the earliest religion? Branch notes that the religious authority is the multifunctional shaman in whose person, for example, priest, leader, healer, and technician are united. Can we not see the Finnish goddesses or *haltias*, Helka/Louhi/Kave as the combined figure holding all these positions? For Branch, the hunter's right to kill game is in the hands of the "lord of animals" or his female counterpart, who has the power to allocate the inexhaustible wealth of nature. To retain his valour, the hunter and fisherman must appease him [sic] by a proper approach to nature, a correct handling of game, and a sacrifice before and immediately after each catch. In a more developed system, each species of economic importance may have a divine guardian who must be approached in the proper way when hunting or fishing that species (cited in Honko et al. 1993). Branch notes that there are for the hunter-gatherers no fixed shrines. Offerings take place at temporary sites along the route. Images of spirits and ancestors, made of wood and cloth, are kept at home (cited in Honko et al. 1993: 67).

It is not easy to tease out explicit references to a matriarchy or worldview centred on the Sacred Feminine from the above. However, it is typical of the mainstream research on archaic times to leave out the very possibility that something radically "other" may have preceded the weather god, sky god/ mother earth system, i.e., a worldview beyond strict or hierarchical dualisms. The reasons can be unconscious resistance to such a possibility in addition to the lack of convincing evidence. However, informed speculation that does not refer to either patriarchy or matriarchy is not thereby neutral or objective. Whatever is gender-"neutral" ends up lending support to the often-made argument or assumption that matriarchies have never existed. Patriarchy remains an implicit norm. Gender-"neutral" speculation on the past reproduces willy-nilly the androcentric norm, i.e., the ideological assumption that patriarchy and violent societies are the general norm. Men have had more power to develop disciplinary methods and approaches, and it is unquestionable that the ethos deriving from male upbringing, or what Genevieve Vaughan (1997) calls "the masculation process" , is reflected in the assumptions projected into past societies. Feminist projections are no less speculative, but at least tend to recognize the speculative nature of all research on past societies as informed guesswork.

According to Timo Heikkilä (2004), however, one of the few scholars in Finland who have considered matriarchy as a possibility and who has elaborated on it, the Helka Festival has been a cult of agrarian people, a cult he calls the cult of the Holy Barley (*ohra*). The spring rite would thus echo back to such fertility rituals and also to a series of Goddess figures converging on the two sides of the cyclic world, decay/death and growth/rebirth. For Heikkilä, the raising of barley is one of the central themes of the cult: the ascendance of the Earth towards the Sky through the spirit of crops. He believes that this theme is contained in a Helka song from Southwest Finland (Varsinais-Suomi): *"hei hei helatorstai,/ nouse ohra/ylene hyvä ruis"* (Hey Hey Whitsun barley, come on and rise/grow high, good rye).[4] Barley was the first plant sewn, and maybe the reason why the celebration of Ritvala Earth cult was built around the entire idea of the growth of the Earth. Heikkilä argues that one needed rituals in order to maintain a thought system and relationship with the Earth, through which one might most appropriately sum up the most essential principles of natural activities. Through rites one prepared and attuned oneself psychically with the natural processes and became intimately aligned with the annual cycle. Rites served to create a quality of attention, where the relationship between humans and nature remained a vigorous sounding board for daily activities. The Earth was looked upon as a feminine organism that was highly respected. An old custom of donning a Sunday outfit when going out for the harvest, still practiced a hundred years ago, reflects this ceremonial attitude. The Ritvala Festival as a dramatic visualization of the Earth's growth cycle has been only one aspect of the cult's broader significance; the other dimension concerned being human as part of creation and as the product of the same forces that bring life forth.

Helka—The Goddess of Origins, Iron, and Mother of Luonnotar

The word *Helka* also gives clues as to the semantic links uniting different pagan aspects of the festival. While many dimensions of the ritual have been analyzed, the linguistic associations between *hela, Helka*, and related terms in Finnish mythology have remained relatively unfocused. On the level of religion and worldview, matriarchal societies are, according to Goettner-Abendroth, characterized by mythologies of the mother-goddess. At the rural stage of development, one always finds the mythology of a chthonic goddess, an earthly mother like Gaia or Rhea, while at the urban stage of development, we find an astral mythology, with the triple moon-goddess as its dominant figure (Goettner-Abendroth 1987: 3; 1995).

As Heikkilä argues, Ritvala's Helka has likely been part of a feminine cult of the earth with the life-producing and light aspect of the Goddess *Maaemo* (Mother earth), and her specialized aspects linked with birth-giving, above all Helka-wife and the Golden woman (*Helka-vaimo, Kultainen nainen*). The dark counter images of the life-giving feminine are present in the image of the Finnic *Pohjolan emäntä*, Mistress of the North Farm, also called *Louhi*. *Annikki* is another female being of Finnish mythology who has been the representation and embodiment of growth, love, and inspiration. The very name of the festival, Helka, refers to a goddess which the compiler of Finnish mythology, Cristfried Ganander (1789), in *Mythologia Fennica*, has defined as the mother of *Luonnotars*, daughters of nature. Their role was precisely that of maintaining the wholeness of nature. According to Ganander:

> Helka, no doubt refers to Helga or Olga, alias sacred Helen: "The Finns describe her as the good, priski, chosen wife, i.e. she is considered to be a most exemplary chosen woman and wise old woman, who can together with Mary stop bleeding from wounds or iron-related damage."

Helka is clearly related to the other cross-cultural aspects of the primary Goddess, midwifery, and healing: "In Savo a Helka figure mixed up with Virgin

Mary has been called upon to come and help during delivery, echoing the role of the Golden Woman" (Heikkilä 2004: 402, cf. SKVR 45: 117-130).

Heikkilä (2004) points out that among Finno-Ugric peoples the term for mother-goddess has varied, and he mentions such variations as *Kältas, Kaltas, Sorni-Kaltes, Kyldys, Kaltsj,* and *Pugos Anki.* A few scholars have noted that the mother of Lemminkäinen, reduced in Lönnrot's *Kalevala* to a nameless, sacrificing mother, is in the old poems nothing less than a sage and a hierophant, initiating a candidate through death and rebirth towards shamanistic knowledge. The fact that she does not, for example, have the name, as in folk poetry, of Suonetar (Goddess or Haltia of Veins), reflects the patriarchy's overwriting of a more gynopositive history and tradition, and of limiting women's role to idealized motherhood, instead of maintaining her combined status as mother and spiritual authority. The proper name "Helka" also echoes back to the Scandinavian complex where *Hel, helka,* and healing form an ideational chain of associations. The Swedish activist, artist, and writer Monica Sjöö (1999) elaborates on the meaning of the word *Hel,* and the German *Holle* in *Return of the Dark/Light Mother or New Age Armageddon?* She allows us to infer that "Helga" and "Helka" are part of this word complex. She presents the hypothesis that to the Scandinavian and Germanic peoples, Frau Holle, or Hel, was the fairy queen or Goddess of the Otherworld, and one entered her realm through the Neolithic mounds and long barrows underneath various sacred mountains. Sjöö (1999) argues that Hel's uterine fiery shrine or cauldron/well (associated also with the uterus) was turned into the image of hell by Christians (33). The Helka Festival echoes Frau Holle to the extent that mounds and mountains, to which processions were directed, have been the classic passage-ways to the realm of the dead, nature in its state of winter sleep, and dead relatives.[5]

Paul Shephard and Barry Sanders (1985) have unearthed intruiging links between Old English *burlic* and *beran* and a series of other related terms converging on bear, beginnings of life, the source of procreation and creation, iron, biers of death and, as I claim, the underworld space of mothers and matriarchies (xv). In shamanism, women as healers and shamans mastered the realms of the upper, middle, and lower worlds and ensured the renewal of the cycles of growth. If Helka has represented the healing, positive side of Mother Earth and nature, the patriarchal co-optation of the mythology has focused only on the old and gap-toothed dame of *Pohja,* called also "Old Woman." The meaning of the Helka Hill to which the young girls march can be unravelled by considering in a broader way the abode of the decaying side of the goddess, and the meaning of hills related to shamanistic worldviews. To quote Ásgeir Magnússon (1989):

> Valhöll could very well have had an earlier existence, before the [The Æsir-Vanir] war. Let's look at the word höll (palace, hall). Höll is of the same root and meaning as holl (hill), hól (hall, hollow) hellir (hollow, cave), hulin (hidden), Hulda (hidden one), Holla, hell and Hel. (Bjarnadottir 2002: 127)

An Icelandic scholar, Ásgeir Blöndal Magnússon, further notes:

The image reflected from all these words and names is in fact an empty, enveloping space, a tomb or womb. So from this we can see that "Valhöll" can mean "the round cave," or "the hall of the vulture of falcon," or "the hollow vulva," or "the hidden round place," or "the evolving space," or "the chosen hall," etc. (Magnússon qtd. in Bjarnadottir 2002: 127)

Whichever of these translations we choose, *Valhöll is a tomb-womb space, it is the Goddess' womb of regeneration*. Hel has the same meaning. It is a hollow place, or the goddess of that hollow place. Hel is half-blue (or black) and half-white, which shows well her regeneratrix nature. We can assume that there was a time when Hel and Valhöll were the same, or "Hel was the goddess of Valhöll, the womb lying Freyja's fertile Fólkvangur (Valley of the Dead)" (Bjarnadóttir 2003: 127). The central role of women in the spiritual culture may well have its epitome in the Ritvala Helka feast, where both the guardians of the event and the participants are exclusively female.

In the course of history, the role of Helka has been taken over by Virgin Mary, while the Mother Goddess/Earth Goddess in her various forms has been reduced to the principle of death, death of nature, and castrating threats (to male monopolies of creation and innovation), frozen nature, and a personification of the icy Northern winter. Helka then is also the guardian of iron, and it is significant that in many contexts iron is a metaphor for that which is earth-like (cf. Sanders and Shephard [1985: x] who relate "bear" also to iron, *fer*). It is worth noting also, when looking for the affinities between Helka and iron that the Ritvala Helka Hill consists of coarse gravel that is particularly strong in iron. People have known that iron has links with substances found in blood, and thus Helka is found in incantations to do with stopping bleeding. Helka, then, condenses a wealth of etymological, linguistic, gynocentric, matriarchal word complexes and meanings ranging from "holy" to healing, wholeness, blood, iron, creation, bear, hill, and Hell. Quite a different meaning from the simplistic notion of evil and death, to which patriarchal lore has reduced the Goddess in her triple faces.

Conclusion

Re-ligio means "re-binding" the ties to God. But such a re-binding of important ties is only necessary if the primary ties have gotten lost. And these primary ties could only get lost, if at some pint the deity changed—into somebody very remote, very majestic, very superior, very alien, and very transcendent, somebody who must be sought—in short, if the deity is somebody fundamentally other than our Selves. (Goettner-Abendroth 1987: 13)

The relevance of the name "Helka" in the Helka Festival, the Great Goddess complex of Scandinavian and the broader European societies, condenses a many-sided positive, woman-empowering imaginary that represents psychic healing and renewal for the modern women who feel orphaned by patriarchal religions and imaginaries. Matriarchal religions have often been labelled as "fertility cults," a designation Goettner-Abendroth has exposed as misleading and insulting. For matriarchal religion, far from being an inferior culture of inferior people, as is often suggested, is in fact a fully developed independent system of religious mythology. Furthermore, today, the concept of fertility is understood very narrowly, as having to do solely with the production of crops, vegetables, domestic animals, and children. Yet the matriarchal concept of fertility incorporates life, death, and the revival of the whole universe: it implies a truly integrating cosmology. Matriarchal mythologies are better characterized as "religions of rebirth," with all the far-reaching mystical and metaphysical implications of this concept (Goettner-Abendroth 1987: 3).

If matriarchy refers, indeed, to "mothers in the beginning," the various manifestations of the primal sources of life converge in the creatrix figure *Kave, Luonnotar* who also heals. As the word's etymology suggests, *Helka*, as the root of healing, also refers to the politics of balance and gift circulation, keeping the cosmos together, whole, thanks to a holistic outlook. As Bruce Lincoln (1986), notes in his survey of Indo-European traditions and the notion of healing:

> It is not just a damaged body that one restores to wholeness and health, but the very universe itself.... The full extent of such knowledge is now revealed in all its grandeur: the healer must understand and be prepared to manipulate nothing less than the full structure of the cosmos. (118)

This view is typical of many Indigenous nations, including Finno-Ugric peoples, whose worldview does not originally contain the splits of spirit and matter, religion and medicine, and so on, characteristic of the master imaginary and the Western schismogenesis (Kremer 2008). As many scholars, among them, Jürgen Kremer, have shown:

> [Healing] is in obvious ways related to the etymology of "to heal," which is connected with the German "heilen," and the Indoeuropean root *kailo-, referring to a state and process of wholeness (the word "whole" also being related to this root). But "to heal" is also connected to "holy" (as is German "*heilen*" to "*heilig*," or Icelandic "*heill–heil–heil'g*"), which points to the older layers of understanding healing through remembering the history of language. (188, fn 11)

Kremer adds that "healing—in the indigenous sense of the Indo-European root word: *kailo, whole and holy—is just one particular aspect of this indigenous conversation with all beings (spirits)" (Kremer 2008: 150).

Helka can be seen to represent the healing of women's cultural memory. Helka is the Goddess of iron weaving the bearshirt for protection—one might read her also as the iron will we need to reintroduce (paradoxically) a more responsible ethos around the global village. To conclude, personal healing comes when we consciously unite the hidden and repressed parts of ourselves and of our culture. Likewise, our culture can be healed through an honestly and multi-dimensionally explored archeohistory—and herstory. This is the gynocentric meaning of doing research on prehistoric societies beyond the patriarchal demand for absolute proof.

Kaarina Kailo teaches at the Oulu University, Faculty of the Humanities, and has held several positions in Modern Languages and Cultures and in Women's Studies both in Canada and Finland (Simone de Beauvoir Institute, University of Montreal, and Oulu University, Finland). She acted as professor of Women's Studies and multiculturalism at Oulu University from 1999-2004. She has published over 70 articles and co-edited or edited numerous books on topics ranging from minority-majority relations, Indigenous literature, culture and postcolonialism, eco-feminism, women, globalization and technology, feminist perspectives on bear cults and bearlore, gift economy, mythology (Kalevala) and feminist literary criticism. Most recently, she is the editor of Wo(men) and Bears: The Gifts of Nature, Culture and Gender Revisited *(Inanna Publications, 2008).*

[1]For a discussion of the possibility of a women's land, Terra Feminarum in the North (or closely related issues on matriarchy), see Kailo (2006); Von Bremen (1917 [1975]); and Tacitus (1955 [98 AD]: 45).
[2]This life force has different names in different cultures. In Finnish, everything is believed to have its *väki* (lakes, mountains, people, animals etc.), but it is the strongest among women and bears. This may be because they are representatives of rebirth and of strong powers. On *väki,* see Kailo (2006) and Apo (1993), among others.
[3]See the writings of the "First World Congress on Matriarchal Studies," 2003 in Luxembourg, at <www.hagia.de>.
[4]In 2006, the book documentation of this congress came out, in German. See Goettner-Abendroth (2006).
[5]My free translation from the Finnish.
[6]The Finnish word *noita* (witch) referred originally to a wise man or woman who resorted to the technique of falling into a *lovi* (trance), or an ecstasy ending in fainting. The term *lovi,* which literally means a crevice, a hole, or a cut, referred to the gap between Heaven and the Underworld. According to Finnish mythology, this gap was a kind of gateway to Hades (Tuonela, Manala). Falling into a trance meant that the soul of the person travels to the Underworld to meet the souls of the dead who, in turn, could offer wisdom otherwise unattainable. The Underworld was governed by the female goddess, known as *Pohjolan emäntä*

(Mistress of the North) or *Louhi*. (The North was often regarded as a synonym for the Underworld.) People believed that at the very beginning of the world the Mistress of the North created all of humanity's adversities: illnesses, crop failures, etc. Shamans and witchdoctors, among them many female witches, were supposed to fight the evil spirits of Louhi. By conjuring or "singing" incantations the seer sends the misfortunes back to the gloomy north, or the Underworld, where they belonged.

References

Abercromby, John. 1898. *Pre- and Proto-Historic Finns, Both Eastern and Western, With the Magic Songs of the West Finns.* n.p. London.

Apo, Satu. 1993. "Ex Cunno Come the Folk and Force: Concepts of Women's Dynamistic Power in Finnish/Karelian Tradition." *Gender and Folklore: Perspectives on Finnish and Karelian Culture. Studia Fennica Folkloristica 4.* Eds. Satu Apo, Aili Nenola and Laura Stark-Arola. Helsinki: Finnish Literature Society, 1998. 9-27.

Bjarnadóttir, Valgerður. 2003. "The Saga of Vanadís, Völva and Valkyrja: Images of the Divine from the Memory of an Icelandic Woman." Unpublished Masters thesis, California Institute of Integral Studies.

Daly, Mary. 1987. *Webster's First New Intergalactic Wickedary of the English Language.* Boston: Beacon Press.

Enäjärvi-Haavio, Elsa. 1953. *Ritvalan helkajuhla. Jälkeenjääneen käsikirjoituksen täydentänyt ja painoon toimittanut Martti Haavio.* Helsinki: WSOY.

Ganander, Cristfried. 1792. *Mythologia Fennica.* Suom. Pentikäinen J. Tampere, Recallmed Oy.

Gimbutas, Marija. 1985. "Pre-Indo-European Goddesses in Baltic Mythology." *Mankind Quarterly* 26 (1/2): 19-25.

Gimbutas, Marija. 1974. "The Gods and Goddesses of Old Europe 7000 - 3500 BC." *Myth, Legends and Cult Images.* London: Thames and Hudson.

Goettner-Abendroth, Heide. 1987. *Matriarchal Mythology in Former Times and Today.* Freedom: Crossing Press.

Goettner-Abendroth, Heide. 1995. *The Goddess and Her Heros. Matriarchal Mythology.* Stow: Anthony Publishing Company.

Goettner-Abendroth, Heide. 2004. "Matriarchal Society: Definition and Theory." Ed. Genevieve Vaughan. *The Gift. Athanor* 15 (8). Rome: Meltemi.

Goettner-Abendroth, Heide, ed. 2006. *Gesellschaft jn Balance. Dokumentation des 1. Weltkongresses für Matriarchatsforachung.* Stuttgart: Kohlhammer and Edition Hagia.

Goettner-Abendroth, Heide. 2007. "The Relationship Between Modern Matriarchal Studies and the Gift Paradigm." *Women and the Gift Economy: A Radically Different Worldview is Possible.* Ed. Genevieve Vaughan. Toronto: Inanna Publications. 99-107.

Hiekkanen, Markus. 2002. "Sääksmäki ja keskiajan uskonnollinen kulkue." 17

July 2006 Online: <http://www.saaksmaki-seura.fi/hiekkanen2002.htm>.

Heikkilä, Timo. 2004. *Aurinkolaiva. Lemminkäisen myytti ja Ritvalan kultti.* Helsinki: Basam Books.

Heikkilä, Timo. 1999. *Kalevalan metafysiikka ja fysiikka.* Helsinki: Like.

Honko, Lauri, Senni Timonen, Michael Branch and Keith Bosley. 1993. *The Great Bear: A Thematic Anthology of Oral Poetry in the Finno-Ugric Languages.* Pieksämäki: SKS.

Kailo, Kaarina. 2008. "The Unbearable Gaze: Archaic Bear Ceremonials Revisited." *Wo(men) and Bears: The Gifts of Nature, Culture and Gender Revisited.* Ed. Kaarina Kailo. Toronto: Inanna Publications. 243-315.

Kailo, Kaarina. 2006. "Kave, Louhi ja Pandoran lipas—miesnäkökulmaisen mytologian uudelleenarviointia." Myyttien Hyrinässä. *TAIDA, Oulun yliopistopaino.* 79-111.

Kremer, Jürgen. 2008. "Bearing Obligations." *Wo(men) and Bears: The Gifts of Nature, Culture and Gender Revisited.* Ed. Kaarina Kailo. Toronto: Inanna Publications. 145-199.

Lincoln, Bruce. 1986. *Myth, Cosmos, and Society.* Boston: Harvard.

Liski, Paavo and Herva Marjatta. 1986. "Kalevala on maailman humaanisin ja hyväntahtoisin paikka (Kalevala is the World's Most Humane and Well-Intentioned Place)." *Kirjokannesta kipinä. Kalevalan juhlavuoden satoa (A Spark off the Bright-Coloured Lid: The Harvest of the Kalevala Anniversary Year).* Helsinki: SKS. 157-161.

Magnússon, Ásgeir Blöndal. 1989. *Íslensk orðsifjabók.* Reykjavík: Orðabók háskólans.

Shephard, Paul and Barry Sanders. 1985. *The Sacred Paw: The Bear in Nature, Myth, and Literature.* New York: Viking Penguin.

Schibli, S. 1990. *Pherekydes of Syros.* Oxford: Oxford University Press.

Sjöö, Monica. 1985. "The Goddess/es of the Northern Peoples, Part I and II." *Arachne* 13-19.

Sjöö, Monica. 1999. *Return of the Dark/Light Mother or New Age Armageddon? Towards a Feminist Vision of the Future.* Austin: Plainview Press.

Suomen Kansan Vanhat Runot (SKVR) I-XIII. Suomalaisen Kirjallisuuden Seuran kansanrunousarkiston kokoelmat. Suomalaisen karhuperinteen primaarilähteet. Suomen Kirjallisuuden Seura. [Finnish Peoples' Folk Tales].

Suomen Kansan Vanhat Runot (SKVR) VII. Raja-ja Pohjois—Karjalan Runot 4. Tautiloitsut toisinnot 1550-3207.

Tacitus 1955 [98 AD]. Trans. Edwin Linkomie. Helsinki.

Tarkiainen, Viljo. 1922. *Ritvalan Helka. Juhla ja Virret.* Porvoo: WSOY.

Vaughan, Genevieve. 1997. *For-Giving: A Feminist Criticism of Exchange.* Austin, TX: Plainview Press.

Von Bremen, Adam. 1917 [1075 AD]. *Jkr. Gesta Hammaburgensis Ecclesiae Pontificium* ("Hamburgische Kirchengeschichte"). 1917. Hannover und Leipzig.

Wall, Kathleen. 1988. *The Callisto Myth from Ovid to Atwood Initiation and Rape in Literature.* Kingston and Montréal: McGill-Queen's University Press.

LUCIA CHIAVOLA BIRNBAUM

Dark Mother, Dark Others, and a New World

The Case of Sardinia

A fter the publication of my book *Dark Mother: African Origins and Godmothers* in 2001, I started taking students to on-site explorations of some of the book's themes, and I have come to realize the importance of cultural and political phenomena on African migration paths in Europe. I have also been struck by the significance of return migrations of Semites for understanding world history. My research has encompassed Sicily, Sardinia, and elsewhere in Italy, Spain, and France, places where I have found a similar pattern:

•African migration paths marked by menhirs and dolmens;
•signs of the African dark mother (the colour ochre red and pubic V) ;
•stone images of the dark mother after 25,000 BCE;
•images of black Madonnas and other dark woman divinities in the common epoch;
•African healing water rituals;
•great prehistoric art remembered in modern art;
•and, early heresies which are remembered in contemporary transformative cultural and political movements.

This essay, focusing on Sardinia, is part of a book in progress, *The Future Has an Ancient Mother: Legacy of Caring on African Migration Paths Around the Mediterranean.* The book is intended to stimulate others to consider my hypothesis of the significance of African migration paths in other places in the world.

My work on the legacy of African migrations to the islands and countries of Europe is based on the consensus of world scientists that modern humans, homo sapiens sapiens, emerged in south and central Africa in 100,000 BCE. L. Luca Cavalli Sforza (1994) and other geneticists have proven through DNA that Africans, after 50-60,000 BCE migrated to all continents, taking their beliefs with them. This research converges with the work of archaeologist Emmanuel Anati (1995) on the rock art of the world, as well as my research in feminist cultural history that major signs of the African dark mother in art and artifacts

La dea madre, late paleolithic-early neolithic photo of the ancient mother of Sardinia. Museo Archeologico Nazionale di Cagliari. Photo: Wallace Birnbaum.

are the colour ochre red and the pubic V, which point to women's ability to generate life.

My work also converges with the scholarship of Marija Gimbutas's (1999) confirmation of many images of women divinities in Europe, and of the world studies of Heide Goettner-Abendroth (1991, 2000) on matriarchy, a word whose original meaning she identifies as "mothers in the beginning." This essay is particularly indebted to Emmanuel Anati's discovery of the archaeological site at Har Karkom, where Africans in 40,000 BCE created the oldest sanctuary we know at Mt. Sinai—place of origin of the world's dominant religions—a sanctuary characterized by dolmens and menhirs incised to look like humans.[1]

Sardinia

Geologically, Sardinia is the oldest part of Italy. Africans in migration probably arrived in Sardinia before 50,000 BCE, moving inland from the seacoast about

4300-3000 BCE. They engaged in the obsidian trade (the black gold of antiquity), and sculpted figurines of their divinity, who may be seen today in the national museums of Cagliari and Sassari. Early on they developed art depicting a woman deity and animals such as bulls and rams as sacred. In Sardinia we visited some of the 140 collective burial places that are associated with dolmens. When our study tour visited Pranu Mutteddu, we were hushed into silence as we viewed the rows of sixty menhirs converging on underground burial tombs at Goni.

After African migrations to Sardinia, the other significant migrations were of Semites, originally African, in return migrations. After 2300 BCE, Semites (a language group, also called "peoples of the sea" or the Shardana) from Ur in West Asia, swept through Europe carrying images of a nurturing dark mother (offering her breasts), and settled in Sardinia. After 1500 BCE Canaanites (called Phoenicians by the Greeks) from Syria, Palestine, and Lebanon, took icons of the dark mother all over the "known world," in a peaceful trading empire whose base was Carthage in Africa, and whose hub was Sardinia.

Although the dark mother was subsequently subordinated and whitened by Greeks, Romans, and the Christian church, her memory continued to be transmitted in the common epoch by subaltern classes. This was achieved not only in sustaining images of black Madonnas and other dark women divinities of the world, but in folk art, through crafts, stories, rituals, dance, and song, which conveyed her values: justice through nurturance, compassion, healing, equality, and transformation.

In Sardinia in the Barbagia—the oldest and unvanquished interior of the island—the memory of the dark African mother has been kept in figurines, and in rituals, notably dance (the *lestru, dillu, passu torrau, ballu thoppu, boche seria*, and *boche notte*), and in songs transmitting the lyrics of poets as well as improvised lyrics with non-words that end in "ma," the oldest sound in the world. Music of the Barbagia is very similar to the rap music of contemporary African-Americans. The typical canto, sung by a tenor of the Barbagia, imitates sounds of animals and nature: for example, the sound of a bellowing ox, bleating sheep, whistling and hissing wind; sounds that hark back to the primordial singing of Africa, as well as those places Africans and their descendants migrated, such as Oceania.[7]

Semitic Shardana: "Peoples of the Sea"

The people who created the thousands of *nuraghi*, cone-shaped structures that have become the symbol of Sardinia, have been the subject of a good deal of speculation. A book recommended to me by Sardinian scholars, Leonardo Melis's *Shardana: I Popoli del Mare* (2002), has been helpful because of its extensive documentation. The people known as "peoples of the sea," according to Melis, are the Shardana, who gave Sardinia its name. The Shardana were Semites, whom Melis identifies as the lost tribe of Dan, a Semitic tribe who venerated a dark mother.

Little idols of the Great Mother in Sicily. Museo Archeologico Nazionale di Cagliari. Photo: Wallace Birnbaum.

Fleeing a three-hundred-year famine in Ur (Mesopotamia) the Shardana expanded after 2300-2000 BCE into the Anatolian peninsula, then into central and northern Europe, leaving clues to their presence in names; e.g., from the Danube (Dan) and the Dniepr (Dn) rivers, to the Baltic and Scandinavia into Ireland ("Danny Boy"). Another group of these Semitic Shardana went south to Syria and the Dead Sea, then into Greece, Crete, Sicily, Corsica, and Sardinia (where they settled), and thence, in a reprise of early African migrations, to the northern coast of Africa.

According to Melis, the Shardana arrived in Sardinia 2300–2000 BCE, about the same time as they arrived in Tuscany and Latium on the mainland of Italy, as well as on the Balearic Islands off Spain, and on Crete and Cyprus. For this paper, it is sufficient to note that these Semites, like everyone else, were African in origin, and revered a woman divinity. The woman divinity of the Shardana is glimpsed in Bronze Age cruciform figurines offering Her breasts; figurines very similar to those of other African migration paths in Europe.

The "peoples of the sea" or Shardana have been described as violent. This claim is unclear because the 7000 beehive-shaped megalithic structures (*nuraghi*) associated with Shardana settlements bear no evidence of weapons. The Shardana are enigmatic; their warrior shields resemble women's breasts, complete with nipples. Icons of Shardana warriors feature four eyes. Prof. Diane Jenett, of the Institute of Transpersonal Psychology, in Palo Alto, California, pointed out to me that four eyes are characteristic of the earlier eye goddess of Tell Brak in Iraq (c.3000 BCE).[3]

The point at hand for Mediterranean, Sardinian, Sicilian, Italian, and world history, is that the Shardana, in Sardinia, an island that archaeologists regard as a museum of the prehistory of Europe, venerated a dark mother, whom Melis calls Mater Mediterranea. The connection with African beliefs is suggested in that menhirs and dolmens were central icons of *nuraghic* communities. Figurines of women in *nuraghic* communities hold the solar disk, the symbol of African veneration of the sun. The figurines also hold their breasts in an African nurturing gesture, and, there is evidence that they engaged in African water rituals. Further, *Nuraghi* of Sardinia resemble sanctuaries in Zimbabwe in Africa.

In Sardinia, the belief in the dark mother and her values appears to be continuous from prehistory to the present. Ancient caves where early African migrants lived were later called *Domus de Janas* by the Romans; today these caves are popularly considered the dwellings of women with supernatural powers. In Sardinia, the early Christian church at Saccargia was originally megalith in form. Inside the church at Saccargia (rebuilt in the Middle Ages), we saw two black Madonnas.

Semitic Canaanites

Canaanites in Sardinia (whom the Greeks called Phoenicians) arrived after the Shardana, mixed with them, and shared the belief in the dark mother that characterizes Sardinian history. Sardinia during the presence of the Canaanites was the hub of a peaceful trading empire based at Carthage in Africa. Reaching the Spanish Levant in the west, Cyprus in the east, and Tuscany and Sicily in Italy, the Mediterranean network was characterized by a shared belief in the dark mother (see Moscati 1995).

Casting aside a millennia of slurs,[4] the Canaanites were Semites, who came (after the expansion of the Shardana) to Sardinia from Syria, Palestine, and Lebanon, founding coastal settlements where they enjoyed good relations with the ancient African peoples of the interior as well with the Semitic Shardana (see Moscati 1993). Semitic Canaanites offer a dramatic case of how defeated peoples are treated by chroniclers who write history for the winners. Defeated earlier by the Israelites, vanquished later by the Romans, maligned in Judeo-Christian scriptures, Canaanites have been disparaged ever since by historians

Black Madonna of Saccargia, Church of Saccargia.
Photo: Wallace Birnbaum.

who mindlessly repeat spurious libels.[5] What happened to the Canaanite belief in the dark mother after Canaanites were vanquished by the Israelites? My research in submerged beliefs suggests that the memory of the dark mother remained in the suppressed beliefs of Palestine and Israel, as well as in the beliefs of subaltern classes of Europe—peoples whose genetic and/or cultural inheritance held a memory of early African migrations and later Semitic migrations. Beliefs, that, are suggested in the values associated with the early icons of the dark mother and with the folklore of the black Madonnas: justice with nurturance, healing, equality, and transformation.

Italians, in a 1988 exhibit under the direction of Sabatino Moscati, *I Fenici*, took the lead in revisiting the Canaanites, displaying a stunning collection of sarcophagi, jewelry, scarabs, amulets, ivory and bone articles, bronzes, metallic cups, glassware, ceramics, and figurines of a nurturing woman divinity offering her breasts.[6] The historic exhibit and catalogue edited by Moscati support my hypothesis that belief in the dark African mother is accompanied by great art. The exhibit did not address the issue of African origins, the shared Canaanite ancestry of both Palestinians and Israelis, or their shared suppressed belief in the dark mother.

Recent research has uncovered the pervasive presence of icons of a woman divinity in early Syria and Palestine (Weiss 1985).The University of Pennsylvania Museum has produced a postcard book, *Facing Antiquity: Canaan and Ancient Israel,* which illustrates Canaanite artifacts found in Israel—notably figurines of women offering their breasts, the pubic V, and mother and child figurines. These artifacts are very like African and Canaanite art found in Sardinia, Sicily, Spain, and elsewhere in the ancient Canaanite network. Western historians, perhaps blinkered by the unscientific notion of a white race,[7] try to differentiate characteristics and cultures of West Asian Canaanites from those of African Carthaginians. For Moscati (and for me) this is an impossible task—the artifacts are alike.[8]

Canaanite Astarte, whose West Asian antecedents were Cybele, Inanna, and Anat, easily melded with the African Isis and Tanit. Semites worshipped these icons of the dark mother along with her male consort. Worshipping Isis meant worshipping the "trinity" that was comprised of Isis, Osiris, her husband, and Horus, their son, a trinity that differs from the father, son, holy ghost of Christian doctrine. It is the African version of the trinity—mother, father, son—that has persisted in the vernacular Christian beliefs of Italians, the French, the Irish, and others, of the popular trinity of Mary, Joseph, and Jesus.

Semitic influence in Sardinia dates from the *nuraghic* (Shardana) culture after 2300 BCE followed by Canaanites in the millennium before Mary and Jesus. In the common epoch, Semitic moors from West Asia and Africa returned to the islands and countries embraced by the Mediterranean. In *Dark Mother*, I discuss the Basque enclave in Spain that resisted Aryan incursions; earlier, the Basque area of Spain extended east in Spain and into France. The Basque influence came with the Catalans to Sardinia (in Spain there is a major sanctuary of a black Madonna at Montserrat outside Barcelona), re-enforcing earlier beliefs in the African dark mother (Barcelona was founded by African Carthaginians). In the twentieth century the dark mother's legacy of justice and equality was re-enforced by the Sardinians Antonio Gramsci and Enrico Berlinguer who brought her values to Italian, and world, politics.

Intuitions of D. H. Lawrence on his trip to Sardinia in 1921 have helped me trust my own; for example, the attraction (from prehistory to the present) of men to women that led not to violent conquest in some cases, but to imitation, and the political legacy of the dark mother. At a carnival Lawrence noted a man dressed in a woman's peasant costume with a "ribboned whip" and "frilled drawers." He came across "male Sardinians wearing Phrygian stocking caps," reminding me that French revolutionaries wore this same cap that remembers devotees of the Anatolian mother divinity.[9]

In Sardinian women Lawrence found "something shy and defiant and un-

Phoenician necklace. Photo: Wallace Birnbaum.

get-table," reminding me of my sense of the ancient wisdom and the *forza* (strength) of Sardinian and Sicilian women, when I was researching Italian feminists in the 1970s and '80s (Birnbaum 1986). Italy, and Sicily and Sardinia in particular, reminded Lawrence of something old, "so primitive, so pagan, so strangely heathen and half-savage.... Man has lived there and brought forth his consciousness there and in some way brought that place to consciousness.... Strange and wonderful chords awake in us and vibrate again after many hundreds of years of complete forgetfulness" (Lawrence 1997: 116-117).

The chords, ultimately African, can still be heard in Sardinia, resonating in the mamuthone masks (whose smiles, after centuries of foreign domination are contorted into twisted mouths) and in the carnival ritual that Sardinians share with the Basques of Spain: men wearing black masks and sheep fleeces, climbing hill and dale, and clanging huge bells on their backs. In Sardinia, as elsewhere, the veil covering the pagan substratum of Christian festivals is very thin. The first of May—the day of the mother—was transformed by the church into a celebration of Sant'Efiso. Yet in Cagliari on the first of May, the ancient music of shepherd flutes, the *launeddas*, remembers the dark mother.

Sardinians are at once ancient and, yet, look to the future. They put signs of the ancient civilization of the African dark mother into their handicrafts, producing beautiful rugs, tapestries, costumes, jewelry, and arresting bread and pasta shapes. They paint murals to convey outrage at social injustice while images, rituals, handicrafts, and politics remember the dark mother and her values: justice with nurturance, compassion, healing, equality, and transformation.

Lawrence helps us see these values of the dark mother before patriarchy tried to allocate different characteristics to men and women and separated humans from animals. Nurturance, for example. Lawrence noted a "black-gowned St. Anthony nursing a boy child … he looked a sort of male Madonna." He realized that Sardinians held "non-patriarchal views of sexuality … men in close breeches dancing together … men dressed like women during carnival, when scarlet [colour of the dark mother] cloth is everywhere." He observed that in Sardinia, as late as 1921, pigs had to have tickets to travel on a bus, "as if Christian." At the same time, Lawrence helps us understand male anxiety in patriarchal cultures about women. He admired Sardinian women in scarlet and rose-pink striding along, yet, the Britisher added, "I would not like to tackle one of them" (Lawrence 1997: 130, 144-145).

Sardinia helps us understand the influence that Africa held in Mediterranean regions, an African influence that lived on in African descendants—in the Shardana who created the high civilization of the Bronze Age in Sardinia, then in the Canaanites, who created a high civilization and trading empire "without any of the characteristics of conquest." Until very recently, historians have repeated, and repeated, lurid and untrue tales about Canaanites sacrificing infants to the nurturing goddess, Tanit. Peaceful traders, Canaanites sailed with their West Asian divinity Astarte, and African divinities Isis and Tanit, and established entrepôts and settlements, yet left other people to their own beliefs, to govern themselves in democratic assemblies.

Network rather than empire, Canaanites coming out of Syria, Palestine, and Lebanon reached Cadiz in Spain in 1110 BCE, Utica in Africa in 1101 BCE, and about the same time, Lixus on the Atlantic coast of Morocco. They established their base at Cartage in Africa in 811 BCE, the same year they founded Palermo, my ancestral maternal place in Sicily. Later, in 654 BCE, Canaanites founded Ibiza off eastern Spain, an island with a treasure of icons and artifacts of the African dark mother that has become the festive gay capital of the world. Looking for silver in Spain, tin in Cornwall in Britain, and amber in the Baltic, Canaanites are said to have circumnavigated Africa in their journeys taking images, as well as the just and egalitarian values of the dark mother everywhere in the ancient world.

Although Greeks never came to Sardinia, their mother/daughter divinities Demeter and Core reached the island via North Africa. The Romans brought the Aryan legacy of hierarchy, violence, and subordination of the dark mother to Sardinia as well as everywhere else. Christianity brought a mixed legacy where the new religion was interpreted differently by dominant and subordinated classes. The subaltern culture put its own gloss on Christianity by remembering the pagan dark mother via black Madonnas and in stories and rituals transmitting pagan values of justice through nurturance, compassion, healing, equality, and transformation. At Monastir today, Sardinians live as primitive Christians following these pagan values.

A random sampling of Canaanite artifacts in the museums of Sardinia includes the sign of Tanit at Nora, as well as many figurines of women offering their breasts at Sulcis, Monte Sirai, Tharros, Castagnino, and Nora. Canaanite

357

jewelry celebrated the African Isis, as well as her husband Osiris, and their child Horus. Other African themes are evident in a figurine of a woman encircled with serpents; earrings with a falcon as Horus, pendant with the eye of Horus, and amulet with Horus; lions; ankh at Sulcis; figurine of a woman holding a solar disk to her breast at Monte Sirai; enthroned divinity at Cagliari; winged sphinx; scarab of Isis enthroned; scarab with seated lions, scarab with ankh, many scarabs with Isis and Osiris; amulets of cats, falcons, a cow nursing a calf, of Sekhmet; razor of Isis and Osiris; and, a pitcher whose spouts are hands offering breasts.[10]

The legacy for Europe of African migrations in Sardinia is vividly seen in feminist precursors Eleonora d'Arborea and Grazia De Ledda. The political heresy that continues to unsettle the sleep of the dominant classes of the world to the present is the communism grounded on Sardinian beliefs in the values of the dark mother of Antonio Gramsci, major Marxist theorist, and of Enrico Berlinguer, communist premier of Italy in the 1970s.

Eleonora d'Arborea in the fourteenth century refused to acknowledge the rule of the Aragonese and united Sardinians in resistance to the Spanish invaders. Eleonora's name, Sa Judikessa, points to the value of justice. Considered the mother of Sardinia, she promulgated the *Carta du Logu* in 1392. Written in the Sardinian language, the charter affirmed equal rights and equal legal status of all women and men. Grazia De Ledda at the age of fifteen began to write down the ancient customs of the Barbagia and won the Nobel Prize in 1926, the second woman writer to have done so.

Antonio Gramsci, perhaps the major Marxist theorist of our time, was born at Ales in Sardinia near an obsidian mountain (ancients associated the prehistoric obsidian trade with the dark mother). Founder of the Italian communist party, Gramsci's prison writings stress the significance of subaltern folk beliefs in justice and equality for the cultural revolution that necessarily precedes, or accompanies, authentic political revolution. Enrico Berlinguer, Italian communist prime minister of the 1970s and 1980s, also born in Sardinia at Sassari, offered a model of uncorrupted communism. He proposed an "historic compromise" between communism and religion, and "Eurocommunism."

When our study tour viewed Santa Cristina's well in Sardinia, a student on the tour exclaimed, "Totally Tanit!" The early Christian well, remembering African water rituals, is formed precisely in the shape of the African/Semitic woman divinity Tanit of Cartage. In the 1970s, in one of those curious upwelling of ancient beliefs, the ankh, or figure of Tanit, became the symbol of international feminism.

Lucia Chiavola Birnbaum is a Sicilian-American feminist cultural historian and professor in the Women's Spirituality program in Philosophy and Religion at the California Institute of Integral Studies in San Francisco. She has devoted recent historical research to the rescue of submerged beliefs that point to transformation and wrote several books on this topic. She is the author of Liberazione Della Donna: Feminism in Italy *(1986), which won an American Book Award from the Before*

Columbus Foundation; of Black Madonnas in Italy *(1994), which won the Premio Internazionle di Saggistica Salvatore Valitutti; and of Dark Mother: African Origins and Godmothers (2001), which was translated into Italian as* La Madre O-Scura *(2005), and into French as* La Mere Noire *(2008),*

[1]For an extensive bibliography of this scholarship see the first chapter of my *Dark Mother: African Origins and Godmothers* (Birnbaum 2001).

[2]A singing group has brought this ancient form to Europe and the United States. We heard Tenores de Oniferi at Freight and Salvage Coffee House in Berkeley, California, on October 26, 2003.

[3]In her Christian version, the eye goddess became Santa Lucia (aee chapter 5, Birnbaum 2001).

[4]The slurs, or libels, of the Canaanites, are similar to those cast historically on the Jews until these were dispersed in the twentieth century, after the Holocaust and World War II.

[5]The major libel that Canaanites sacrificed infants to their woman divinity, Tanit, has been refuted by contemporary archaeologists. When I visited a *tophet* in Mozia, it was an infant cemetery alongside an adult burial ground. See Moscati (1995: 19) for a revised view of *tophets.*

[6]See the *I Fenici* catalogue of the 1988 exhibit at Venice. Direzione scientifica di Sabatino Moscati.

[7]See works of L. Luca Cavalli-Sforza (1994), who, with other world geneticists, documented in the DNA that we are one human race, and that skin colour differences are due to climate. See Birnbaum (2001) for a discussion of this scholarship.

[8]See *I Fenici*, 1200 photographs of Canaanite artifacts from Spain, Sardinia, Sicily, Cyprus, and Carthage.

[9]See *I Fenici*. See especially, pg. 63.

[10]See *I Fenici*.

References

Anati, Emmanuel. 1995. *Il Museo Immaginario della Preistoria. L'arte Rupestre nel Mundo.* Milano: Jaca Book SPA.

Birnbaum, Lucia Chiavola. 1986. *Liberazione Della Donna: Feminism in Italy.* Middletown, CT: Wesleyan University Press.

Birnbaum, Lucia Chiavola. 1993. *Black Madonnas: Feminism, Religion and Politics in Italy.* Boston: Northeastern University Press.

Birnbaum, Lucia Chiavola. 2001. *Dark Mother: African Origins and Godmothers.* Lincoln: iUniverse.

Birnbaum, Lucia Chiavola, ed. 2005. *She is Everywhere!: An Anthology of Writing in Womanist/Feminist Spirituality.* Lincoln: iUniverse.

Cavalli-Sforza, L. Luca. 1994. *History and Geography of Human Genes.* Princeton, NJ: Princeton University Press.

Gimbutas, Marija. 1999. *The Living Goddess.* Edited and Supplemented by Miriam Robbins Dexter. Berkeley: University of California Press.

Goettner-Abendroth, Heide. 1991. *Das Matriarchat II, 1. Stammesgesellschaften in Ostasien, Indonesien, Ozeanien.* Stuttgart: Kohlhammer-Verlag.

Goettner-Abendroth, Heide. 2000. *Das Matriarchat II, 2. Stammesgesellschaften in Amerika, Indien, Afrika.* Stuttgart: Kohlhammer-Verlag.

Lawrence, D. H. 1997. *Sea and Sardinia.* New York:Penguin Books.

Melis, Leonardo. 2002. *Shardana: I Popoli del Mare (Shardana: The People of the Sea).* Prima Tipografia Mogorese.

Moscati, Salvatore. 1993. *Il Tramonto di Cartagine: Scoperte archeologiche in Sardegna e nell'area mediterranea.* Turin: Società Internazionale.

Moscati, Salvatore. 1995. *Italia Punica.* With Sandro Filippo Bondi. Milan: Rusconi Libri.

Weiss, Harvey, ed. 1985. *Ebla to Damascus: Art and Archaeology of Ancient Syria.* Seattle: Smithsonian Institution in association with University of Washington Press.

VICKI NOBLE

How the Amazons Got Their Name

Birth, death, and regeneration were themes of central importance to the late Lithuanian archaeologist, Marija Gimbutas, whose documentation of Neolithic sites in Old Europe posed such a powerful challenge to patriarchy's origin story (see Gimbutas 1999). Earlier scholars had also recognized the Goddess or female ancestress at the centre of the early peaceful civilizations of the ancient world, but Gimbutas had the good fortune to be able to use Carbon 14 and tree-ring dating methods, which are much more accurate than anything prior to their discovery in the mid-twentieth century. With these modern dating methods, and from her position as an internationally renowned authority on the European Bronze Age, Gimbutas was able to observe that there was an earlier layer of material quite distinct from the "weapons, weapons, weapons" (as she put it) that she had been digging up from Bronze Age sites. Curious to investigate this discovery for herself, she set about excavating at a site called Achilleion in northern Greece. I remember her excitement as she described to me in an interview how she bent down and picked up from the ground her first female figurine that had been exposed in a rainstorm at the site.

The backlash in archaeology toward the work of Gimbutas, still very strong today, is a testimony to the breathtaking power of the paradigm change she was suggesting. Whereas traditionally scholars had seen only war, male domination, class stratification, competition, aggression, greed, and centralized top-down government as innate to the development of human civilization, Gimbutas saw peaceful, cooperative, female-centred societies without noticeable differences of wealth or prestige in burials or habitation sites. Finds from the peaceful Neolithic period are highly refined and show an evolved artistic development and religious sensibility. Artifacts include thousands of female figurines, plus many temple models, exquisitely decorated vessels in all shapes and sizes, and seal stones. Many of the ceramics are inscribed with an indecipherable Old European script, predating Sumerian Cuneiform by at least two thousand years. These early cultures appear to have been forcibly disrupted in waves and either destroyed or displaced by people who entered the region from east of the Black Sea. In this light, it is interesting that rock art found in eastern China's Tarim Basin has recently been identified as hypothetically identical to the cultural complexes near the Black Sea, suggesting migrations from what is today Bulgaria (Davis-Kimball 2002: 164). Blue-eyed, blonde, light-skinned European-type mummies dating to the second millennium BCE have been found in the Tarim Basin oasis sites near the rock art (Mallory and Mair 2000). Some of them are wearing tartan plaid wool twill clothing, preserved by the salt in the sand, like kilts in Scotland today.

Gimbutas never used the word "matriarchy" to describe her findings, choosing instead the lesser-charged word "matristic" to describe societies where women were positioned at the centre and were responsible for many significant contributions to culture. She wrote, however, that "the worship of a female deity as the creatress of life mirrors the matrilineal, or mother-kinship, system that most likely existed" (1999: 112) in Paleolithic and Neolithic times. "The mother and the mother-daughter images are present throughout Old Europe," she says, "while the father image, so prevalent in later times, is missing" (Gimbutas 1999: 112). Always ahead of her time, she presumed that "in many societies females did not mate for life with their male sexual partners..." and that "the mother and her kin automatically are the focus of the family, and the family structure is matrilineal" (Gimbutas 1999: 112).

At an important early site from the seventh millennium BCE in northern Greece called Nea Nikomedeia (which translates literally as "New Victory of the Wise Woman"), the largest building, filled with ritual artifacts and surrounded by six smaller buildings, had been labelled by other archaeologists as the house of a "chieftain" or a "big man." Gimbutas challenged this view by describing the building as a "shrine" that would have been kept by "the female members of the families living in the surrounding houses," just as Christian Orthodox women still tend the family shrines on the Aegean Islands today (Gimbutas 1999: 117). Gimbutas posited that a council of priestesses was sometimes overseen by a central priestess, often enthroned, whose role was to embody or enact the part of the goddess in rites and ceremonies for the community. "Communities of priestesses and women's councils, which must have existed for millennia in Old Europe and in Crete, persisted into the patriarchal era, but only in religious festivals" (Gimbuta, 1999: 120).

Fast forward to the first millennium BCE, the Iron Age, when most of the peaceful female-centred civilizations are now long-gone, scattered to the four directions, leaving only hints and traces in the eighth century BCE tales of Homer, Hesiod, and the later classical mythologies of Greek and Roman times. But it is also this same period that is rich with legends and images of the Amazons—those fierce fighting women on horseback whom the Greeks depicted more frequently than any other subject on their painted pottery and the edifices of their magnificent temples. The Greek historian Herodotus wrote during the fifth century BCE about all kinds of strange customs he saw or heard about the women living in lands beyond Greece. These so-called "barbarian" women had more freedom than the Athenian women, who by this time were not much more than slaves in their own homes. Remnants of matriarchal culture are also found in historians' reports of Etruscan women (living in central Italy at the same time) who "raised their own children, whether they knew the father or not," and Etruscan inscriptions referred to individuals by the mother's name only (Gimbuta, 1999: 122).

My research has shown a strong and continuous cultural connection linking Africa, Europe, and Asia across the Silk Road for several thousand years. This link involved particularly the function of female shamanism, documentation for which is richly evident in the archaeological excavations, art, written records, and human burials from Italy, Crete, Egypt, and Mycenaean Greece to Turkey, Central Asia, India, and Tibet (see Noble 2003). When nomadism became prevalent in the first millennium BCE, mounted warriors of the Central Asian steppes travelled in huge decentralized confederations of tribal people like the Scythians and the Saka, to name some of the most well-known. These nomads, apparently organized in patriarchal clan structures, often overtook the Indigenous people they found living in agricultural areas near rivers and around lakes. One profound colonizing strategy they used was marriage. At least two Scythian chieftains have been found buried with Indigenous priestesses, in an example of the widespread practice of "bride stealing" which has come all the way down to the present day as part of the wedding traditions in Central Asia.

Who Were the Amazons?

It used to be widely believed that the Amazons were all-female tribes who burned off one breast in order to shoot their bows better, but there has never been any archaeological evidence to support this idea. Scholars had mistranslated the word Amazon as "without a breast," leading to the sensationalized stories. Linguists today have translated the word as "without a husband" (Davis-Kimball 2002: 118), and it is my theory that incoming patriarchal tribes, such as the Scythians, would have naturally perceived the matriarchal customs of any Indigenous remnant populations as "those without husbands," thereby naming them Amazons. The central feature distinguishing the Scythians from the Sauromatians or Sarmatians, for example, female-centred peoples living in southern Russia and northern Kazakhstan from the sixth to the fourth centuries BCE, would have been the Scythian patriarchal clan structure and its institution of marriage and the consequent subjugation of women. Archaeologists have unearthed rich burials of high-ranking autonomous priestesses along the Dniepr River north of the Black Sea from the fifth century BCE, exactly at the time of the nearby "royal Scythian burials," which included the so-called "intermarriages" (probably abductions) I have described at more length elsewhere (Noble 2005). Similarly, Gimbutas states, "the Old European matristic and the Indo-European patristic deities existed side by side for millennia with very little intermingling" (Gimbutas 1999: 199). Even today in Russia and most of Europe, the old Goddess traditions co-exist with Christianity and are obvious in the rituals (especially weddings), and the songs, dances, and folk arts.

The Biological Base of Matriarchy

A fascinating book, *The Tending Instinct*, authored by a woman scientist, Shelley E. Taylor (2002), presents the idea that "women's bonds with one another are maintained, in part, by the affiliative neuro-circuitry" in the brain and nervous system (111). The concept that women need each other to survive, and the evolutionary development that this assumption implies, is investigated thoroughly in this book, providing a scientific basis for matriarchy as an organic social structure that is biologically based. The conclusions of the first study, "Tend and Befriend," carried out by Taylor and her research group show that the "inclination of women to bond together may be far older than we imagine" (91), and that there is "an evolutionary heritage that has selected for female friendship. Women and children have literally stayed alive over the centuries because women form friendships" (90). Subsequent studies reported in the book show in stark undebatable terms that women "get much of their social support from their ties with other women, and are only somewhat benefited, both emotionally and in terms of health, from their ties with men" (86).

While this is heartwarming in a feel-good kind of way for all of us who value "girlfriends" in whatever way we define that term, the findings are actually much more radical and imply, among other things, that women should not simply "tend and befriend," but should be governing society. A call for the return to matriarchal organizing structures is the sub-text of this research, nothing less. It is troubling and somewhat ironic to juxtapose the results of this research against women's current isolation in individual nuclear families. Taylor (2002) states unequivocally what we all know on some level, "Women who are isolated from other women can be in danger" (104). Mara Keller, in an anthology on the roots of patriarchy edited by Cristina Biaggi (2005), reports that "In the United States, domestic violence is the leading cause of injury to women, *causing more injuries than muggings, stranger rapes, and car accidents combined* (my emphasis). Each day, on average, three women are murdered by a husband or boyfriend. More than four million women are battered by their partners each year, one woman every nine seconds" (Keller 2005: 226). (And 25 percent of these are pregnant!) In case you have your doubts, "The overwhelming majority of domestic violence (92 percent) is by men against women" (Keller 2005: 226).

There something seriously wrong with this picture. This scenario is happening inside of consensual relationships, inside of America. Women in the U.S. don't have "arranged" marriages—we choose our mates! Yet it would seem that an American woman's home is the most unsafe place in the world for her, and the scariest person in her life is the one who professes to love her the most. How else are we to read this, except as an end result of a colonization process that, over time, has robbed us of our discernment? The statistics cited by Keller include further implications of this untenable situation—that in households where a man is battering a woman, he is also hurting her children; that women who are abused tend to abuse their children; that the children of abused women attempt suicide more of the time and are 50 percent more likely to abuse drugs and alcohol. Clearly domestic abuse is not "merely a women's issue."

It seems time to lay to rest the tired mythology of the Amazons as male-hating females living in all-women tribes, burning off one breast in order to shoot better, and maiming or giving away their boy children. While colourful and sensational, these stories do an injustice to the many real-life matriarchal tribes trying to sustain their original way of life in the face of great danger during the patriarchal transition—a transition that is even now not fully realized as we can see from the numerous contributions offered at the two recent World Congresses on Matriarchal Studies. Just as Genevieve Vaughan (1997, 2008) has stressed under the rubric of the "gift economy" paradigm, Taylor reports that

> nearly invisible women's networks ... provide the lifeblood of communities under stress. At their core are older women who cook, nurse sick children and adults, take people in who are temporarily homeless, and care for others' children when they are out seeking employment or working. (2002: 109)

What better time than now to reinstate the archetype of the Amazons, to inspire and invigorate our imaginations in terms of what response we might make to our current conditions. The Amazons were a resistance movement—a refusal to abandon the ancient ways, and a profound commitment to the deep truth of women's wisdom and the cyclic rhythms of natural law that lie at the base of biological life. If we love this planet, and if we value life itself, let us resurrect the Amazon in each of us today. Like a deep underground spring, may the spirit of the warrior woman erupt in each of us to challenge the hegemony of patriarchy in every aspect of our lives.

Vicki Noble is a feminist healer, teacher, artist, writer, and co-creator (with Karen Vogel) of the bestselling Motherpeace Tarot Deck. *She is author of several well-known books including* Shakti Woman: Feeling Our Fire, Healing Our World *and* Motherpeace: A Way to the Goddess. *Her latest research encompasses the subjects of Amazons, matriarchy, and female shamanism. She is a professional astrologer, and she teaches female shamanism and archaeomythology in the Women's Spirituality Masters program at the Institute for Transpersonal Psychology in Palo Alto, California.*

References

Davis-Kimball, Jeannine (with Mona Benan). 2002. *Warrior Woman: An Archaeologist's Search for History's Hidden Heroines.* New York: Time Warner.

Keller, Mara. 2005. "Violence Against Women and Children in Religious Scriptures and in the House." *The Rule of Mars: Readings on the Origins,*

History and Impact of Patriarchy. Ed. Cristina Biaggi. Manchester: Knowledge, Ideas and Trends (KIT). 27-42.

Gimbutas, Marija. 1999. *The Living Goddesses.* Edited and supplemented by M. R. Dexter. Berkeley: University of California Press.

Mallory, J. P., and Victor H. Mair . 2000. *The Tarim Mummies: Ancient China and the Mystery of the Earliest Peoples from the West.* London: Thames and Hudson.

Noble, Vicki. 2003. *The Double Goddess: Women Sharing Power.* Rochester: Bear and Co., Inner Traditions.

Noble, Vicki. 2005. "From Priestess to Bride: Marriage as a Colonizing Process in Patriarchal Conquest." *The Rule of Mars: Readings on the Origins, History and Impact of Patriarchy.* Ed. Cristina Biaggi. Manchester: Knowledge, Ideas and Trends (KIT). 187-206.

Taylor, Shelley E. 2002. *The Tending Instinct: Women, Men, and the Biology of Our Relationships.* New York: Times Book/Henry Holt and Co.

Vaughan, Genevieve. 1997. *For-Giving: A Feminist Critique of Exchange.* Austin: Plainview/Anomaly Press.

Vaughan, Genevieve, ed. 2007. *Women and the Gift Economy: A Radically Different Worldview is Possible.* Toronto: Inanna Publications.

MARGUERITE RIGOGLIOSO

In Search of the Libyan Amazons

Preliminary Research in Tunisia

W hen most people think of "Amazons," they envision mythological warrior women who marched on Athens and were immortalized in Greek literature and art. Few people are aware, however, that ancient texts also speak of much earlier Amazons in "Libya"—the term Greek writers used variously to refer to all of North Africa (sometimes with the exception of Egypt) or to the entire continent of Africa itself. Most literature on the Amazons describes the later, better-known warriors, who are said to have dwelt in Asia Minor around the Black Sea near the ancient "Thermadon" River.[1] This paper focuses instead on the "Libyan" Amazons of North Africa. In this preliminary study, I draw on ancient texts, archaeology, ethnography, linguistics, and my own explorations in Tunisia in March 2005 to make the case that the Libyan Amazons were most probably real warrior women who existed in history.

Libyan Amazons in Diodorus Siculus and Tassili Rock Art

Female warriorhood in Africa is hardly the stuff of fantasy but has a long-documented history in that continent, from Hatshepsut's rule as pharaoh in Egypt in the late fifteenth century BCE to the military leadership of Yaa Asantewa, who fought the British in Ghana in the early twentieth century of the Common Era.[2] The earliest and most comprehensive account of the Libyan Amazons is found in the work of the Greek historian Diodorus Siculus (b. 80 BCE). Diodorus acknowledges that most people of his day were likely to be skeptical about the existence of such Amazons (3.52.2), but affirms that many poets and historians of both early and later periods wrote of them. He specifically says he takes his own account from that of Dionysius of Mitylene.[3]

Diodorus's chronicle (*Library* 3.52-55) describes a nation of North African Amazons in which women held political and military leadership and served exclusively as the society's warriors, evincing great prowess with the bow, arrow, and horse. These Amazons were nomadic pastoralists and lived on an island named Hespera, located in the marsh Tritonis. Diodorus details the conquests in North Africa and West Asia made by the queen of one group of these Amazons,

Myrina, and he mentions another Amazon tribe, the Gorgons, whose queen was Medusa.

According to Diodorus, the Amazons of Libya ultimately were vanquished in a series of defeats in Thrace and North Africa such that they disappeared entirely "many generations before the Trojan War" (3.52.2), when the later Thermadon Amazons were at their peak. Dating the Trojan War to approximately 1250 BCE, that would put the disappearance of the Libyan Amazons in the Bronze Age, perhaps the fourteenth century BCE. We can assume from this that the Libyan Amazons were in their full vigour earlier in the Bronze Age, and that they hailed perhaps from even remoter times.

Ancient rock art located in Algeria attests to the presence of warrior women during precisely the period Diodorus describes. A massive Bronze Age painting from Sefar in the Tassili n'Ajjer, for example, reveals, upon close inspection, a striking combat scene in which the figures shooting at one another with bows and arrows have breasts, indicating that they are women (Lhote 1959: 148; Lajoux 1963: 164-168). Female archers also appear elsewhere in the Tassili paintings from this period. I identify the Africanoid[4] archer from Tin Abotéka (Lajoux 1963: 171), for example, as female, given that she has a hint of a breast. Furthermore, I identify figure 57 of Lhote (1959), which carries a bow, as female, as she, too, has a faint suggestion of a breast and is characterized by steatopygia (fleshy thighs and buttocks), a typically female body characteristic.[5]

Amazonian Auses in Herodotus

Writing several centuries earlier than Diodorus in the fifth century BCE, the Greek historian Herodotus provides ethnographic descriptions in his *Histories* attesting to cultures of his day bearing Amazon-like characteristics.[6] Particularly noteworthy in this regard are the Auses, whom Herodotus places, like the Amazons of Diodorus, around the shores of a lake named Tritonis, which was fed by the River Triton. According to the historian, the Auses held an annual festival in honour of Athena (4.181) (whom he confirms more than once [2.62; 4.181] was the very same as the Egyptian goddess Neith, as did Plato [*Timaeus* 21e] and others). In this ritual, young maids (*parthenoi,* or virgins) divided into two groups and fought each other with "sticks and stones." The death of any maiden resulting from this combat signalled that she was not a "virgin." Before the fight, the Auses picked out the most beautiful girl, dressed her publicly in a full suit of Greek armour and a Corinthian helmet, put her in a chariot, and drove her around Lake Tritonis. The Auses held that this combat ritual had come down to them from time immemorial, indicating that both it and the tribe's worship of Neith were quite archaic.

Herodotus mentions that all of the tribes of Libya lived "on meat and milk" (4.188), which recalls Diodorus's descriptions of the Amazons' pastoral lifestyle, and lends credence to the possibility that the Auses were part of the very same group. He then comments further on religious practices, noting that the nomads living around Lake Tritonis (again, including the Auses) made ritual sacrifice: first, to the sun and the moon, second, to Athena/Neith, and, third, to Triton and Poseidon.

Herodotus further states his belief that the robe and aegis of the Greek Athena were in fact copied directly by the Greeks from the dress of the Libyan women of this area. The "aegis" refers to a protective garment worn over the dress. Herodotus says that while Athena's aegis was rendered as cloth with snakes for tassels, the Libyan women's aegis was made of red-dyed goatskin fringed with thongs of hide. What he is describing has been identified as one of the earliest forms of human armour (Herodotus 1920: 4.189.1, fn 1). That the Libyan women of Lake Tritonis regularly wore a combat-ready clothing would correspond with the possibility that they were Amazons.

Herodotus goes on to mention that "Libyan women" (read: the Amazons he has just been describing) were particularly skilled at uttering ceremonial cries during religious ceremonies, a practice the Greeks learned from them. The term for this practice is the onomatopoeic Greek *ololugé*, meaning a cry of triumph or exultation. It has its analogue in the Semitic *Hallelu*, which has survived in the Christian *Hallelujah* (Herodotus 1920: 4.189.1, fn 2). It is what is also known in North Africa today as the *zagharit* (Bates 1970: 154), commonly referred to in English as "ululating," and is essentially accomplished by rapidly trilling the tongue against the roof of the mouth or top lip while uttering a high-pitched, single-toned sound. Herodotus implies that such ritual vocalizing was done in honour of Neith/Athena, and one may not unreasonably assume it was used during the combat ritual among the Ause maidens. Thus, I suggest it may have been a form of ritualized war cry to invoke Neith/Athena during battle.[7]

Given all of these sacred associations among the Auses, Robert Graves (1960: 44, sec. 8.1) posits that the annual combat of the maidens of the tribe represented much more than what Herodotus's rather superficial account relays. He suggests, and I agree, that these girls were in fact virgin "priestesses" who annually vied for the position of "high priestess." This indicates that both warriorhood and priesthood were strongly associated among the Libyan Amazons.

What is particularly striking in this section of Herodotus is the convergence in Ause culture of matriarchal characteristics[8] and armed combat involving women, as evidenced in the fight between the maidens, the dressing up of one of the maidens in armour, and the veneration of what we will shortly confirm was in part a war goddess. He locates the tribe near Lake Tritonis, which Diodorus identifies as the Libyan Amazons' homeland. This is as close to an ethnographic description of Amazons in the work of any ancient writer that we find.

The Amazon Goddess Neith/Athena

An analysis of the attributes and genealogy of the Auses' goddess Neith offers further information about the possible nature of Libyan Amazon society. In the Egyptian pantheon, Neith was possibly the oldest divinity, and there is evidence that she existed before recorded history (Lesko 1999: 57). She was regarded by the Egyptians as an eternal and infinite being who was the ruling power of heaven, earth, and the underworld, and every creature and thing in them (Budge 1969: 459). To her is ascribed the famous inscription at Sais: "I am everything that has been, and that is, and that shall be, and no one has ever lifted my veil" (Plutarch, *De Iside et Osiride* 4).

But Neith was probably not an Egyptian divinity originally: During the Old Kingdom the Egyptians describe her as being from "Libya"—that is, the area stretching from the oases of western Egypt to the Atlantic coast of Morocco. They depict her, in the words of Herman Kees, "as if she was [sic] the chieftainess of the neighboring people with whom the inhabitants of the Nile Valley were at all times at war" (1961: 28).[9] This latter characterization brings to mind the possibility that Neith herself may have been a Libyan queen who subsequently became divinized in African fashion. Deceased female heads of clans have long been revered among the Tuareg, one of the Berber/Amazigh groups thought to be descendants of the indigenous peoples of North Africa. To this day, various Tuareg sub-groups consider themselves descendants of a single female eponymous ancestress, one of whom is Tin Hinan, venerated by the Tuareg at what is thought to be her grave in Algeria.[10]

Significant to this discussion is the fact that in Egyptian times, Neith was known as Mistress of the Bow and Ruler of Arrows, which probably also reflects her original iconography in Libya. The earliest symbol associated with her was two click beetles, head-to-head, over two crossed arrows, and the crossed arrow motif endured as a part of her symbolism (Lesko 1999: 46; Budge 1969: 30-31, 451). Certainly this would make her a goddess not only of the hunt, but also of warfare, and it may be in this capacity, in particular, that she served as patroness of the Amazons.

Neith's martial aspect and many of her other North African associations were retained in her Greek manifestation as Athena. According to Greek genealogy, Athena gestated in the womb of her mother Metis, a Titan Goddess who presided over wisdom and knowledge. Zeus swallowed Metis while she was pregnant with Athena (Hesiod, *Theogony* 886-890), but he was subsequently plagued by a severe headache as he walked by the river Triton. It was here that Hephaestus took an axe and split open Zeus's skull (Pindar, *Olympian* 7.65), from which Athena sprang with a mighty shout, fully armed, and leapt toward the river Triton (Apollodorus 1.3.6).

Apollonius Rhodius, the third-century BCE epic poet, offers another account of Athena that confirms her Libyan origins and provides further important Amazon-related details. He reports that the pre-Hellenic peoples in Greece, the Pelasgians, indeed believed that Athena was born beside Lake Tritonis/River Triton in Libya (*Argonautica* 4.1310). He adds that they believed she was found and nurtured by three nymphs dressed in goatskins. The Pelasgians maintained that, as a girl, Athena killed her playmate, Pallas, while engaged in combat (Apollodorus 3.12.3). Apollodorus adds the detail that Pallas was the daughter of the river god Triton, thus affirming that the episode took place at the Lake Tritonis/River Triton. As a token of her grief, Athena placed Pallas's name before her own and became Pallas Athena. According to this story, her worship came to Greece from North Africa by way of Crete.

That Athena was consistently said to be "born" by Lake Tritonis/River Triton affirms her African provenance. The motif of the "goatskins" worn by the women who raised her confirms her association with the Auses, and her armour connects her with battle and the Amazons, in particular. Her emerging with a "mighty shout" also links her to the Amazons, in that this sound may have been a ululation, that is, the Libyan cry of battle and triumph mentioned earlier.

I propose that the combat between Athena/Neith and Pallas was the very ritual that Herodotus describes of Ause girls fighting in honour of Athena/ Neith to determine who among them were true virgins—or perhaps, as Graves suggests, priestesses. Could such a "legend" thus be referencing an actual historical biography in which Athena/Neith and Pallas were real women of the very distant past? Did Athena/Neith win the title of "high priestess" by killing Pallas in the maidenhood ritual? And upon her death, was she immortalized as the sacred ancestor/goddess of the Amazons who was invoked for all sacred ritual and warfare?

Vestiges of the Libyan Amazons in Tunisia

Ethnographic, linguistic, archaeological, topographical, and semiotic investigations of North Africa reveal what may well be numerous allusions to and vestiges of ancient Amazonian society. One of the most striking survivals may reside in the names traditionally used by indigenous North African Berber peoples to identify themselves as a cultural group: *Tamazigh* (also *Tamazirt*), which refers to the language, and *Imazighen* (sing. *Amazigh*) which refers to the people themselves. Peoples of one of the Berber groups, the Tuareg, call themselves *Imuzagh, Imuzag, Amashaq,* or *Amazagh* (Hagan 2000: 75). There is some evidence that all of these and related terms were used to designate the native Libyans in the Egyptian and Graeco-Roman periods. Egyptians referred to the Libyans as *Mashwesh*, of which Imazighen is most likely a cognate (Hagan 2000: 32). In the classical period, Herodotus (4.175-95) mentions tribal names *Macae, Maxyes,* and *Machlyes,* also likely cognates.[11] Later, under the Romans, the widespread tribal name *Mazices* and its variants, such as *Maces*, may have been cognates as well, and may have been terms used to refer to indigenous Africans in general (Brett and Fentriss 1997: 5). I would argue, then, that the term used by the Greeks to describe the warrior woman, *Amazon*, does not mean "one without a breast," contrary to Diodorus's (3.53.3) claim,[12] but rather was a garbled attempt to transliterate *Amazigh/Imazighen* into the Greek language.[13] This would be in keeping with Greeks' general habit of making transliteration errors when encountering foreign names, a phenomenon other scholars have noted (e.g., Smith 2003). That the term *Amazon* may well come from the ancient

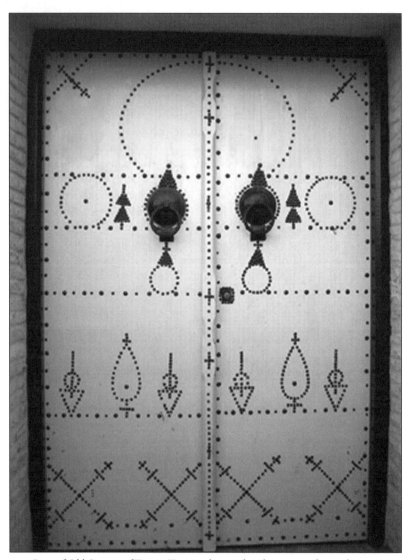

Door of Old Quarter of Tozeur, Tunisia, decorated with arrows and crossed arrows.
Downward facing arrows resemble the fibulae worn by Berber/Imazighen women
to secure their mantles. Photo: Marguerite Rigoglioso.

name denoting the entire scope of indigenous North African peoples suggests
that, far from being a minority group, the Amazons may have dominated ancient
North Africa, or that North African culture at one time had a strong female
warrior element.

Some identify the legendary Lake Tritonis with the *chotts* or salt lakes (now
much desiccated) of Tunisia, particularly the Chott el Jerid (e.g., Camps 1982:

548); others identify it with the Bou Ghrara Gulf, an inland sea off the eastern coast of Tunisia (e.g., Agence Nationale du Patrimoine 1996: 16). In either case, contemporary Tunisia seems to be the general location associated with this ancient lake, and thus with the Libyan Amazons and their ancient goddess, Neith/Athena.

In my explorations of Tunisia in March 2005, I indeed found numerous signs that may be suggestive of an Amazon legacy there. Symbols on the old wooden doors of the Ouled el Hadef, or Old Quarter, in the town of Tozeur, located near the Chott el Jerid, for example, are particularly suggestive in this regard. The doors, which date to the fourteenth century, reveal a panoply of prophylactic designs in nails, including horseshoes (for good luck), fish (to ward off the evil eye), female figures resembling goddesses found on ancient European art, and, most interesting to this discussion, arrows, crossed arrows, and tridents.

Although the architecture of the old quarter in general is Islamic, these symbols seem to bespeak of a pre-Islamic antiquity. I propose that the arrows and crossed arrows may be a remnant of the ancient veneration of Neith, and that the tridents are a vestige of the veneration of Poseidon and Triton. The crossed arrow motif can be found, as well, on a detail of one of the traditional women's dresses found in the Museum of Arts and Popular Traditions in Houmt Souk on the island of Jerba, located off the coast due east of Tozeur.

Also in Eastern Tunisia, silver brooches known as fibulae, commonly designed with a long spike sometimes ending in a triangle, have a striking arrow-like appearance. These items, which indicate a woman's status, are worn by Berber/Imazighen women on each side of the upper chest to hold the mantle in place (Courtney-Clark 1996: 130-31). Symbols of the matriarchal Tuareg people, which appear profusely on jewelry as well as decorative and utilitarian objects, include in many cases what may also be interpreted to be arrow tips, as well. Neolithic/Early Bronze Age arrowheads have indeed been collected in abundance particularly around the *chotts* of Tunisia (Smith 1982: 389, 394), confirming the longstanding presence of the bow and arrow in this region.

Another interesting symbol with Amazonian resonances found throughout Tunisia is what I term, after the Greeks, the *pelta*. The Greek *pelta* was a small shield, shaped like a half moon, which was used in combat and which appears in the hands of Amazons in works of ancient art. Occasionally it was peaked at the inner part of the crescent to resemble an ivy leaf (Xenophon *Anabasis* 5.4.11).

That the *pelta* symbol may have originated in ancient Libya, possibly among the Amazons, is suggested by *pelta*-shaped designs on traditional textiles and jewelry of the Berbers/Imazighen. Such a motif appears as an amuletic Tuareg symbol, for example.[14]

In this latter case, the *pelta* is incised with further motifs, such as the triangle, which, according to Malika Grasshoff (a.k.a. Makilam 1999: 48-53), represents to the Berbers/Imazighen the female vulva and the magical life powers. The Berber/Amazigh *pelta* also greatly resembles the image of the bird goddess found throughout matriarchal Neolithic Old Europe and Minoan Crete (see,

Tuareg amulet resembling the Amazonian pelta or shield, decorated with sacred symbols similar to those found on Old European art. Photo: Marguerite Rigoglioso.

for example, Gimbutas 1989: 8, 39, 95, 191, 295), again attesting to its possible connection with women, the sacred female, and matriarchal culture.

The peaked *pelta* also appears as a repeating motif on a necklace housed at the Museum of Arts and Popular Traditions on the Tunisian island of Jerba. It is among a collection said to be made by the island's Jewish artisans, whose presence on the island may date back to 566 BCE.[15] Could the immigrant Jews have picked up the *pelta* motif from the local Berbers/Imazighen? The *pelta* shape additionally appears embroidered on a traditional bridal shawl housed in the small Berber Museum in Tamezret in southeastern Tunisia.

This particular shawl also features lunar crescents, another common Berber/Amazigh symbol, which recall the symbol of Ta-Nit, the goddess associated with the ancient Phoenician city of Carthage in northern Tunisia (c. fifth century BCE). Like Neith, Ta-Nit was worshiped as an armed deity (Meyerowitz 1958: 132), and her name in fact may be a cognate of the Libyan Neith/Nit, suggesting

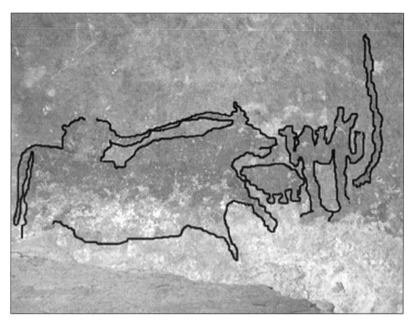

Prehistoric rock painting from the rock shelter of Chaabet el Marek, Ghomrassen, Tunisia. Note double orant figures, adjacent snake, and human figure either riding a horse or leading a bovine animal. Photo: Marguerite Rigoglioso.

that the two goddesses were one and the same (Bertholon and Chantre 1913: 612, 618) and that they both reflected the warrior aspect of women. A further connection between Ta-Nit and indigenous North African culture can be seen in the fact that the orant, or upraised arm posture, in which the Carthaginian goddess is usually depicted, continues today as a ritual dance gesture among the Berbers/Imazighen where it is called the "Aza" (Hagan 2000: 23). Moreover, contemporary Berbers/Imazighen have adopted the orant sign as a symbol of resistance against political oppression (Hagan 2000: 54).

I found this gesture in closer proximity to Tunisia, not far from Chott el Jerid/ Lake Tritonis. In the rock shelter of Chaabet el Marek, north of the town of Tataouine in the village of Ghomrassen, is an ancient rock painting of two orant figures in red ochre, one of whom has protrusions sprouting from the head.[16]

The two figures are depicted with a person of unidentifiable sex who is either riding horseback or leading a bovine animal with a harness. Immediately next to the two orant figures is a snake. Given that the snake and the cow were of the epiphanies of the Amazon goddess Neith,[17] and that the orant gesture was a sign of Ta-Nit (a form of Neith), the entire constellation suggests the presence of the sacred female, perhaps Neith herself. Could the scene represent a blessing of the person (woman?) riding the horse/leading the bovine? What is the meaning of the double orant figures? Could this relate to the fact that all over the world the female deity is frequently depicted as a complementary or opposing pair (e.g.,

Isis/Nephthys, Demeter/Persephone, Inanna/Erishkegal)?

Neith/Athena was also regarded as the divine matron of weavers (Lesko 1999: 56). Wallis Budge (1969: 451) speculates that her very name may be connected with the root *netet*, "to knit, to weave," and that two symbols that often appear above her head may in fact be weaving shuttles. For the Berber/ Imazighen women of Kabylia, weaving is still very much a magical art. We may see a vestige of the Auses' ancient worship of Neith, sun, and moon in the Kabyle women's contemporary view of weaving as an act that unites "sun" and "moon" (representing the masculine and the feminine) in the drawing together of threads (Makilam 1999: 42). An observation on the Tunisian flag is interesting in this regard, as well: it contains the symbol of the lunar crescent encircling a star/sun; both motifs regularly appeared in the iconography of Ta-Nit, as well.

A fragment of a legend associated with a megalithic site on the Tunisian island of Jerba calls to mind the Greek version of Medusa, who was named by Diodorus Siculus as the queen of the Amazonian Gorgon tribe of ancient Libya. This site, just east of the town of Sedouikech, consists of a long avenue of two parallel rows of megalithic stones of unknown antiquity, most likely dating at least to the Bronze Age, if not earlier. A well whose outline bears a resemblance to a uterus and fallopian tubes, or to two vulva-shaped basins, lies nearby.[18] That this avenue of megaliths was most likely considered a sacred site is attested to by its continued ritualized use by the local Berbers/Imazighen, who leave burnt offerings, candles, and other signs of religious activity directly on the stones.

The local legend relates that the sixteenth-century hermit Sidi Satouri, whose mausoleum lies some 500 yards to the southwest of the site, once turned to stone members of a wedding party who interrupted him at prayer (Jacobs and Morris 2001: 384). A local informant I spoke with added the detail that nearby residents consider the megalithic stones of the site to be the remains of the wedding party's petrified guests. Women typically visit the hermit's mausoleum to have wishes granted by the ancestral saint, particularly the wish to conceive children.

In this we see an entire constellation of motifs associated with women and female fertility: the uterine well, the pregnancy-granting tomb, and the "wedding" story. Moreover, stones were always associated with Amazon religion. Meteorites and other baetyls were venerated by Amazons in antiquity, including the Black Stone venerated as Cybele/Artemis in Pessinus in Phrygia, and a similar black stone venerated by Amazons on an island off ancient Colchis (Apollonius Rhodius *Argonautica* 2.1172-77). Both of these latter stones were central pillars in Amazon ritual, and recall an event recounted by Diodorus (3.59.8) of the Libyan Amazon queen Myrina setting up altars to Cybele on Samothrace.

Another detail suggesting a possible Amazonian connection with the site is that of the hermit turning the guests to stone. For, in Greek legend, it was Medusa who had the power to turn men to stone through her gaze (Ovid *Metamorphoses* 4.792-802). After beheading Medusa, the Greek military hero Perseus turned an entire dinner party of King Polydectes of Seriphos to stone by displaying her head (Apollodorus 2.4.3). Even the late patriarchal Greek legend confirms

Medusa's Libyan provenance by naming her as one of the three Gorgon "sisters" who dwelt there (Hesiod *Theogony* 270-280). Could the motif of Sidi Satouri freezing his guests for all time, then, somehow be related to the history of the Libyan Queen Medusa?

As an interesting coda to the theme of the megaliths of Jerba, in March 2005, when I visited the tomb of Sidi Satouri, I heard two Berber/Imazighen women ululate as punctuation to a ritual they conducted in the inner sanctum of the mausoleum. The high-pitched, aggressive sound immediately sent chills down my spine, as it struck me as a highly incongruous element in a ritual of petition to a dead hermit. I immediately had the impression that it was a battle cry, and thus it was particularly striking to me to later learn about the ululating of the Amazonian Ause women. That the custom of ritually ululating has been retained by Berber/Imazighen women in North Africa may serve as one small piece of evidence to demonstrate that they descended in part or whole from the Amazons.[19]

Stories of the seventh century CE military leader Kahina[20] are a well-documented part of North African history and suggest that female warriorhood may never quite have died in this part of the world. According to historical accounts, Kahina ruled the whole of Ifriqiya (contemporary Tunisia) and, with her army, temporarily repulsed the Arab invasion of the continent. She was also a spiritual leader who exhibited prophetic abilities (Hannoum 2001: 1-28). The warrior-priestess combination echoes the figure of the Libyan Amazon Queen Myrina, who set up rites in Samothrace and elsewhere.

Certainly North Africa has a long history of female rulers, holy women, and queens, quite a number of whom were warriors who participated directly in battle. Berber/Amazigh culture, in particular, contains many matriarchal elements, and historically the Tuareg included female tribal heads and heads of camps. In my ongoing work, I continue to investigate the cultures of the Berbers/Imazighen and others of North and Central Africa in my search for possible remnants of the Libyan Amazons.

The Challenge of the Amazon Image for Matriarchal Studies

Africa has had a long tradition of matriarchy, probably going back to prehistoric times,[21] and, as I have argued here, seemingly a long tradition of amazony. Not all African matriarchies have included female warriorhood, and not all African amazony has had its development under conditions of matriarchy. Thus, it would be an error to lump matriarchy and amazony together.

The issue is an important one, especially given the tendency in the collective imagination to equate matriarchy with female violence and female-on-male abuse and repression. We do see the Libyan Amazons portrayed in this latter way by Diodorus Siculus, but this depiction does not represent how matriarchy functions in general. Heide Goettner-Abendroth (2004) in fact has discovered that matriarchies are usually societies of peace, and speculates that they may always have been so since the earliest human times.[22]

Diodorus's account of bloodthirsty and imperialistic Libyan Amazon tribes as cultures that amount to "reverse patriarchies" indeed presents a problematic picture for the feminist scholar of conscience who abhors warfare of any kind and is not interested in promoting female warriorhood or lauding women's participation in it. The first point to be made in this regard is that one must remember that the history of the Libyan Amazons was written by males who were fully indoctrinated into the patriarchal mindset of ancient Greece. Richard Smith (2003: 497), who has written eloquently on the ancient Libyans, confirms that from the Greek historian Herodotus to the Arab historian Ibn Battuta, male commentators on North Africa consistently observed the high position of women there and uniformly discredited the feminine power that they witnessed. Thus, it may be that Diodorus's negative descriptions of Libyan Amazons are somewhat overdone and distorted. The second point is that it is unknown whether amazony developed spontaneously or was rather a response on the part of peaceful matriarchal societies in Africa to Bronze Age patriarchal incursions.

The ultimate purpose of this work is surely not to glorify warfare or women's role in it, but simply to demonstrate that women once had a type of agency so inconceivable today that it has been consigned to the realm of "fiction." My hope is that such agency may be reclaimed and transmuted into more effective social forms.

Marguerite Rigoglioso is the author of the The Cult of Divine Birth in Ancient Greece *(Palgrave Macmillan, 2009). An instructor at the California Institute of Integral Studies, the Institute of Transpersonal Psychology, and Dominican University of California, she teaches pioneering courses on female deities and priestess traditions of antiquity. She has travelled to Europe and North Africa on numerous occasions to conduct research on these topics, and has published related articles in journals and anthologies, including the* Journal of Feminist Studies in Religion, *which granted her 2005 article on Persephone in Sicily an honourable mention for the New Scholar Award.*

[1]Their homeland was variously posited as western Asia Minor (present-day Turkey) or northeast Asia Minor along the Black Sea (Bennett 1967: 12)—the latter being the legendary location of the ancient Thermadon River.
[2]See, e.g., Alpern (1998), Clarke (1988), Hannoum (2001), Radford (1967), Redd (1988), Williams and Finch (1988), and Wimby (1988) for studies on African female warriors and political leaders.
[3]It is conjectured that Dionysius of Mitylene (a locale that, interestingly, bears the name of a Libyan Amazon), surnamed Scytobrachion, lived either shortly before the time of Cicero (c. 106-43 BCE) (and was instructed at Alexandria), or as far back as the fifth century BCE. Attributed to him were works recounting the military expedition of Dionysus and Athena, and a prose work on the Argonauts

in six books. He may also have been the author of the historic cycle poems, lost epics recounting ancient history up to the twelfth century BCE. (Smith 1873, "Dionysius" entry, sec. 34). One translator of Diodorus's history, C. H. Oldfather, dismisses Dionysius's account as a mere "mythical romance" (Diodorus Siculus 1935: 246, fn 2), but I choose to view Dionysius as, if not a historian proper, someone who faithfully recorded ancestral genealogy. It is to be acknowledged that Diodorus has also had his ancient and contemporary detractors, among them Pliny, who accuses him of interlacing lies with truth. His histories have been dismissed by some as "mythology" (Kelly 1991: 48, 259). However, I take his accounts for the most part seriously (acknowledging that they may include distortions here and there). Diodorus himself at times refers to Dionysius's storytellings alternatively as "legend" and "mythology," but one detects in his work an implication he believes they were historical. I embrace his euhemeristic approach to religious legend.

[4]I use the term "Africanoid" to denote a physiognomy that includes dark brown skin, kinky hair, full lips, and a flat nose. I avoid the more common term, "negroid," because of the attachment of "inferiority" to the phenotype that often goes with it. See Drake (1990: xi).

[5]One that is also particularly common among Africanoid women.

[6]Herodotus, like Diodorus Siculus, also has had his ancient and contemporary detractors, who depict him as a sensationalist, if not an out-and-out fabricator of so-called ethnographic and historical information. My approach is generally to accept his observations as containing a good measure of truth, and to attempt to cross-reference his claims with other literary and archaeological sources. In some cases, he's all we've got, and I see no need to dispute him on every single point even though some of his descriptions sound exotic. Indeed, it is the very fact that his ethnographic descriptions, frequently based on oral sources, in many instances reveal cultures and cultural characteristics in direct opposition to those of ancient Greece, which was highly patriarchal, that to my mind make them particularly valuable, especially when they pertain to women's social roles. I question whether the discrediting of his work may in some cases reflect more about the cultural biases of androcentric historians than it does about the reality of ancient North African life. Henri Lhote (1959: 187), who was an expert on the ins and outs of the Saharan terrain, believes that from a geographical and geological point of view, in any event, Herodotus "had at his disposal very accurate information," information most likely obtained from the caravan men who travelled the region. Ironically, however, even Diodorus, whom I have similarly defended, accuses Herodotus of interlacing lies with truth, which admittedly complicates things. For a discussion of the validity of Herodotus's work, see, for example, Verdin (1975) and Momigliano (1966).

[7]Smith (1907: 431) conjectures that the Libyan *ololugé* was generally a cry of ritual lamentation for sacrificial victims.

[8]For example, Herodotus says the Ause women were "common property" (4.181) and that tribe members engaged casually in sexual relations and did not live

together as married couples. Paternity was determined only when a child was fully grown, and was assigned by group decision among the men according to the man whom the child most closely resembled. If we penetrate through the androcentric veil in his passage, we read in it the description of a matriarchal society. Such societies are typically characterized by the sexual freedom of their female members, communal childrearing practices, and greater importance attributed to the maternity than the paternity of the child.

[9]I acknowledge that numerous Egyptologists contend that her first appearance is purely Egyptian, but I believe this represents an unwillingness to consider the possibility more generally that the indigenous peoples of North Africa, that is, the ancestors of today's Berbers/Imazighen, may have helped found Egypt. See Hagan (2000) for an intriguing exploration of the possible Amazigh/Berber roots of Egyptian civilization.

[10]For information on Tin Hinan, see, e.g., Brett and Fentriss (1996: 206-07), Gautier and Reygasse (1934). For controversy regarding the geographical location of her tomb and her historical dating, see Gast (1973).

[11]Hagan (2000: 69) also refers to spellings such as *Maziques, Masax, Mazaces, Mazikes,* and *Mastites.*

[12]Diodorus said the term comes from *a-mazos* (without a breast), and that it derives from the fact that Amazons seared the breasts of young girls so that they would not develop and be a hindrance in warfare. However, Bennett (1967: 13), a philologist, states that this etymology is false.

[13]Austrian archaeologist and Amazon scholar Gerhard Pöllauer notes this linguistic correspondence on his website, "The Amazons" (1997-2006), particularly at <http://www.myrine.at/Berber/berber.html>, as does Walker (1983: 24).

[14]I am indebted to Gerhard Pöllauer (personal communication, March 2005) for initially making the connection between the peaked *pelta* and this Berber/Amazigh motif.

[15]The date of the arrival of the first Jews to Jerba is disputed; some believe it was 566 BCE, following the fall of Jerusalem to Nebuchadnezzar, others say 71 CE, when the city was taken by Titus. Today about 1500 Jews inhabit the island of Jerba. Historically, Jewish artisans worked there as jewelers (Morris and Jacobs 2001: 382).

[16]These may be ostrich feathers, typically depicted as head adornment on ancient North African art. See, e.g., Lhote (1959: figs. 44, 47)

[17]In Egypt, serpent imagery is associated with Neith, as can be seen in a spell from the Egyptian *Book of the Dead,* imagery from Tutankhamen's tomb, and the Hymn to the Diadems (Lesko 1999: 56). Neith is depicted in bovine form, for example, in Coffin Text spell 15, in Herodotus's descriptions of her festival at Sais, and on the wall of the temple to the god Khnum at Esna (Lesko 1999: 55, 59, 60).

[18]Pöllauer (2005: 8) first noted this correspondence in the shape of the well.

[19]Today, however, the cry is used to mark events such as births and deaths, the reception of startling or happy news, the entry of a notable person into a camp

or village, etc. (Bates 1970: 154 fn 2).

[20]Her name has been transliterated in various ways: Kahena, El Cahena, El-Kahena, El Kahéna, al-Kahina. In its North African pronunciation, there is sometimes no article: al-kahina or kahina (Hannoum 2001: xix). Her tribe may also have descended from Jews.

[21]Bates (1970: 112-113) confirms the strong probability that among North Africans, matriarchy "was at some early period widely established."

[22]See Goettner-Abendroth (2004, *passim*) for a development of this idea.

References

Agence Nationale du Patrimoine. 1996. *Tunisia Saharan: Gafsa and the Gafsa Region*. Tunis: Edition Regie 3.

Alpern, Stanley B. 1998. *Amazons of Black Sparta: The Women Warriors of Dahomey*. London: Hurst & Company.

"The Amazons." 1997-2006. *The Amazon Research Network.* Online: <http://www.myrine.at/Amazons> Accessed: 22 March 2006.

Bates, Oric. 1914. *The Eastern Libyan: An Essay*. 1970. London: Frank Cass and Co. Ltd.

Bennett, Florence Mary. 1967. *Religious Cults Associated with the Amazons*. New York: AMS Press, Inc.

Bertholon, L., and Ernest Chantre. 1913. *Recherches Anthropologiques dans la Berbérie Orientale*. Lyon: A. Ray.

Brett, Michael, and Elizabeth Fentriss. 1997. *The Berbers*. Malden: Blackwell Publishing.

Budge, E.A. Wallis. 1904. *The Gods of the Egyptians*. Vol. 1. 1969. New York: Dover Publications, Inc.

Camps, G. 1982. "Beginnings of Pastoralism and Cultivation in North-West Africa and the Sahara: Origins of the Berbers." *The Cambridge History of Africa*. Ed. J. Desmond Clark. Vol. 1. Cambridge: Cambridge University Press. 548-624.

Clarke, John Henrik. 1988. "African Warrior Queens." *Black Woman in Antiquity*. Ed. Ivan van Sertima. New Brunswick: Transaction Publishers. 123-134.

Courtney-Clark, Margaret. 1996. *Imazighen: The Vanishing Traditions of Berber Women*. London: Thames and Hudson.

Cooper, A. M. 1987. "Canaanite Religion, an Overview." *The Encyclopedia of Religion*, Vol. 3. Ed. Mircéa Eliade. New York: Macmillan. 35-45.

Diodorus Siculus. 1935. *Library of History*, Books II.35-IV.58. Trans. C. H. Oldfather. Cambridge: Harvard University Press.

Drake, St. Claire. 1990. *Black Folk Here and There*. Vol. 2. Los Angeles: Center for Afro-American Studies, University of California.

Gast, Marceau. 1973. "Témoignages Nouveax sur Tin Hinane, Ancêtre Légendaire des Touareg Ahaggar." *Revue de l'Occident Musulman et de la Méditeraneé* 13-14: 395-400.

Gautier, E. F. and Maurice Reygasse. 1934. "Le Monument de Tin-Hinan." *Annales de l'Académie des Sciences Coloniales* Vol. VII. Paris, Société d'Éditions.

Gimbutas, Marija. 1989. *The Language of the Goddess.* San Francisco: HarperSanFrancisco.

Goettner-Abendroth, Heide. 2004. "Matriarchal Society: Definition and Theory." *Il Dono/The Gift: A Feminist Analysis.* Ed. Genevieve Vaughan. *Athanor: Semiotica, Filosophia, Arte, Letteratura* 15 (8). Rome: Meltemi Editore.

Graves, Robert. 1960. *The Greek Myths.* New York: Penguin Books.

Hagan, Helene. 2000. *The Shining Ones: An Etymological Essay on the Amazigh Roots of Egyptian Civilization.* Philadelphia: Xlibris.

Hannoum, Abdelmajid. 2001. *Colonial Histories, Post-Colonial Memories: The Legend of the Kahina, a North African Heroine.* Portsmouth: Heinemann.

Kees, Herman. 1961. *Ancient Egypt: A Cultural Typography.* Ed. T. G. H. James. Chicago: University of Chicago Press.

Kelly, Donald R. 1991. *Versions of History from Antiquity to the Enlightenment.* New Haven: Yale University Press.

Lajoux, Jean-Dominique. 1963. *The Rock Paintings of Tassili.* Cleveland and New York: The World Publishing Company.

Lesko, Barbara. 1999. *The Great Goddesses of Egypt.* Norman: University of Oklahoma Press.

Lhote, Henri. 1959. *The Search for the Tassili Frescoes.* London: Hutchinson and Co.

Momigliano, Arnaldo. 1966. "The Place of Herodotus in the History of Historiography." *Studies in Historiography.* London: Weidenfeld and Nicholson. 127-142.

Makilam. 1999. *Symbols and Magic in the Arts of Kabyle Women.* Trans. Elizabeth Corp. Aix-en-Provence: Edisud. Online: <http://www.makilam.com>.

Mercante, Anthony S. 1978. *Who's Who in Egyptian Mythology.* New York: Clarkson N. Potter, Inc.

Meyerowitz, Eva L.R. 1958. *The Akan of Ghana: Their Ancient Beliefs.* London: Faber and Faber Limited.

Morris, Peter, and Daniel Jacobs. 2001. *The Rough Guide to Tunisia.* London: Penguin Books.

Pöllauer, Gerhard. 2005. "Research Report: Southern Tunisia 2005." *The Amazon Research Network.* Online: <http://www.myrine.at/Amazons>. Accessed: 22 March 2006.

Redford, Donald B. 1967. *History and Chronology of the Eighteenth Dynasty of Egypt.* Toronto: University of Toronto Press.

Redd, Danita R. 1988. "Hatshepsut." *Black Woman in Antiquity.* Ed. Ivan van Sertima. New Brunswick: Transaction Publishers. 188-226.

Smith, Philip E. L. 1982. "The Late Paleolithic and Epi-Paleolithic of Northern Africa." Ed. J. Desmond Clark. *The Cambridge History of Africa,* Vol. 1. Cambridge: Cambridge University Press. 342-409.

Smith, Richard. 2003. "What Happened to the Ancient Libyans? Chasing Sources across the Sahara from Herodotus to Ibn Khaldun." *Journal of World History* 14 (4): 459-500.

Smith, William. 1873. *A Dictionary of Greek and Roman Biography and Mythology.* London: John Murray. Perseus Digital Library. Online: <http://www.perseus. tufts.edu/cgi-bin/ptext?doc=Perseus%3Atext%3A1999.04.0104> Accessed: 21 March 2006.

Smith, W. Robertson. 1907. *Religion of the Semites.* Third Ed. London: Adam and Charles Black.

Verdin, H. 1975. "Hérodote historien? Quelques interprétation récentes." *L'Antiquité Classique* 44: 668-85.

Walker, Barbara. 1983. *The Woman's Encyclopedia of Myths and Secrets.* San Francisco: HarperSanFrancisco.

Williams, Larry and Charles S. Finch. 1988. "The Great Queens of Ethiopia." *Black Woman in Antiquity.* Ed. Ivan van Sertima. New Brunswick: Transaction Publishers. 12-35.

Wimby, Diedre. 1988. "The Female Horuses and Great Wives of Kemet." *Black Woman in Antiquity.* Ed. Ivan van Sertima. New Brunswick: Transaction Publishers. 36-48.

CHRISTA MULACK

Matriarchal Structures in the Hebrew Bible

Having attended the first World Congress on Matriarchal Studies in Luxembourg, I am glad to be able to follow up on a subject that has become more and more important to me these last two decades. In this paper, I often refer to a German friend of mine who died some ten years ago. Her name is Gerda Weiler, and I shall refer to her studies as well as to mine. In the late seventies we both worked on very similar subjects without, however, knowing each other. My thesis was subtitled "Matriarchal Presuppositions of the Image of God." It dealt with the matriarchal grounds of the Kabbalah. When Gerda and I met for the first time, each of us had just published her first book. Gerda was twenty years older than I but our mutual interest in matriarchal studies was the basis from which grew a very interesting friendship where age did not matter.

Let me now turn to the first part of this paper that deals with some of the problems we have to deal with on approaching any close reading of the Bible.

Main Problems with Bible Study

Studying ancient literature, like the Bible, can be compared to an archaeological excavation. We have to be prepared to peel away many layers of patriarchal writing. This reminds me of an ancient myths that tells the story of how inherent female power was swallowed, conquered, and/or distorted by a male figure. It is the Greek myth about the Olympian god, Zeus, who raped and then swallowed the pregnant Metis. Metis was known as the original goddess of wisdom—infinitely wiser than all the gods. "She knew, moreover, the art of changing shape, which she put to use whenever Zeus approached" (Campbell 1982: 151). After she changed into a white mare and then into a white swan, Zeus feigned admiration for her capability and asked if she could also change into a small fly. Of course, she could. And when she did, he swallowed her for fear that if her child was born this would be the end of his power. Nevertheless, after another god split Zeus's head open with a double axe, Metis' daughter, the Goddess Athene, sprang from his brain, fully armed, and shouting a battle cry. "Zeus thereafter, continued to claim that Metis, still sitting in his stomach, was giving him the benefit of her wisdom" (Campbell 1982: 151).

This is a striking picture that reflects not only what happened to matriarchal cultures worldwide, but what we also continue to deal with today. We can interpret Metis as a symbol of matriarchy, a social and spiritual pattern that was swallowed by patriarchal priests as well as artists, writers, philosophers, and so on. Whenever we search for matriarchal wisdom we come across written sources that offer only substitutes for this original wisdom, substitutes that come from male brains, who claim Athene as their own, one who had the "ability to inspire excellent males to excellent patriarchal deeds" (Campbell 1982: 159). Knowing of no mother, Athene refers to a male origin, to a god who claimed to be the first and final source of original wisdom that came from his stomach, where Metis was imprisoned.

Though "two-in-one," the union of Zeus or Metis is not a real union, for a union is not possible if it comes about as a result of rape and imprisonment. In this enforced union, female wisdom is no longer in a position to speak for herself. In later centuries, Gnostic myths took up this problem and spoke of the imprisoned Sophia, a later Greek goddess of female wisdom.

Another example is the Apollonian conquest of the holiest place in Greece, Delphi; "delphi" meaning "uterus." By sword, Apollo, the god of light, took over this cryptic place of female prophecy, where priestesses sat above a crevasse that released vapours from its deepest depths sending mysterious messages that were perceived as coming from the holiest of places: the womb of mother earth. After the patriarchal conquest, these messages from the Great Mother were delivered only after they had been interpreted by Apollo's male priests.

The prison that I am dealing with in this paper is the Bible. The myths I have just described give us an impression of what historically happened to matriarchal societies, and we need to keep this in mind when studying the Bible. Here we are confronted with some of the first literature of the conquerors: layers of patriarchal regulations and laws that claim to come from the Lord, the one and only God (the Father), with myths of conquest and defeat as well as family sagas. Yet, once we have learned about the differences between patriarchal and matriarchal myths and structures, we are able to discern a residue of mystery that remains lurking through these patriarchal layers, emanating from the archaic symbols of former times—"as though speaking silently, to say: 'But do you not hear the deeper song?'" (Campbell 1982: 25).

We will only hear it if we know that it is there. And herein lies the main problem: The idea of a matriarchal period before patriarchy took over has been denied for centuries.

This holds true also in mainstream feminist theology. Even the term "goddess" a taboo, a taboo that incorporates the notion of all-encompassing female power. Most academic feminist theologians refuse to break this taboo. But this is exactly what we must do if we want to find buried matriarchal layers of biblical texts.

There is another point I would like to make: Most texts are not as old as they appear at first glance. They are mainly a creation of Jewish authors after the exile in the sixth century BCE, even if they point to events of a much earlier period.

The texts that were written before the sixth century were edited according to pastoral needs of post-exilic times. Exegetic studies that fail to look behind the pastoral intentions of authors and editors may serve as a Sunday sermon, but they will not do justice to deeper dimensions of biblical literature.

Gerda Weiler (1989) and I (Mulack 1983-1988, 1985) have dug much deeper than most feminist and other theologians. And, in doing so, we developed what I have called a matriarchal thealogy. It can be compared to psychoanalysis that aims at uncovering suppressed parts of the psyche, particularly disturbing complexes that go back to early childhood. They have to be brought up into consciousness to inaugurate a healing process. With matriarchal thealogy it is almost the same. It is concerned with the deepest layers of biblical texts rendering them accessible to our collective consciousness by means of a profound exegesis. And, in fact, this work can be healing, too.

The Text Behind the Text

Most stories from the Bible have many layers on top of original texts. They were edited with various tactics of concealment. The matriarchal message, as well as the original intentions of the text, have thus been distorted and hidden by editorial work.

This holds true for many of the Sara and Abraham stories. They are not based on historical memory or fact, as most readers are made to believe, but are mainly a construct of saga collectors who combined various texts that had one mutual core: matriarchal cultic liturgy (Weiler 1989: 123). Texts that originally served cultic purposes were transformed into family sagas. Indeed, most of the family sagas in the Bible are adaptations of cult legends. "Priestesses and priests have made use of those texts as direct instructions for cultic performance. They have passed on the tradition from one generation to the next" (Weiler 1989: 32).

We all know these priestesses. They are the women in the Bible who have only borne one son: Sara, Rebekka, Rachel and Hannah, the mother of Samuel. They all are reflections of priestesses, "who gave birth to a son, representing nature. One son only, because there is only one world or one creation.... Quite often the double-face of life we experience in death and life, darkness and light, in disappearing and reappearing is reflected in the birth of twins" (Weiler 1989: 115). In our case, they twins are Rebekka's sons, Jakob and Esau.

Many of the texts that were found in Ras-Shamra, Ugarit, offer a variety of parallels to biblical accounts and cultic texts from matriarchal times, early myths that point to a matriarchal mythology that may be called universal. It is

> the myth of the queen of heaven and her terrestial son-lover, her brother or her consort, telling the cultic drama with parallels all over the world. This is not at all surprising, for everywhere in the world the seasons follow a certain rhythm. To archaic people the dying of nature was quite frightening. So they tried to enact this drama, burying the

deceased cultic son of the goddess and guiding him into the underworld. They offered him sacrifices that would allow him to survive. For his rebirth they trusted in the goddess. The highlight of seasonal festivities was then the awakening of nature with the celebration of the divine marriage of the goddess and her consort. (Weiler 1989: 32)

Many biblical texts conceal this cultic consummation from matriarchal times. The biblical story of earth's first couple, Eve and Adam, is an example. In Genesis 2, we are told that "a man shall leave his mother and father and cling to his wife; and they shall be one flesh" (v. 24). These words can only be understood in a matriarchal context (where men leave their homes to "visit" their wives in the maternal clan house); in patriarchal societies, it is the women, and not the men, who have to leave the family in order to marry.

In the third chapter of Genesis we read about Eve in paradise, a synonym for matriarchal times. We find her in a garden, near a tree with the fruits of life and knowledge. The garden, the tree and the fruit are three matriarchal symbols for a woman's body; symbols that also suggest the divine marriage of which even the name "Eve," the Hebrew *Chawwa*, is a reminder. *Chawwa* means *mother of life, tutor,* and *the source of meaning.* These are female attributes.

The serpent is a symbol of divine counsel in the religion of the goddess. Even in the biblical story, the serpent can be seen as the guardian of the tree. After learning from the serpent about the fruit of knowledge of good and evil, Eve agrees to eat from it. By passing the fruit on to Adam she was far from committing "original sin." In matriarchal spirituality, this act is ymbolic of choosing a consort for the ritual of the divine marriage. In later Gnostic interpretations, Eve is presented as a daughter of the Goddess Sophia, since she had saved Adam from leading an unconscious life, like an animal.

The divine marriage was celebrated under the blessing of the Great Mother—heaven and earth. In the Genesis text this blessing, however, becomes a curse, which in Hebrew is the same word. The the longest part of the paradise myth is composed of Yahweh's reprimand, punishing Eve with pain at childbirth and with the desire for her husband, followed by his rule over her—three aspects in a woman's life that would have been unknown to her before. Yahweh then curses the serpent for having seduced Eve to eat the fruit of knowledge, condemning the serpent to creep on her belly and eat dust all the days of her life. These words describe the downfall of the serpent from a divine to a perfidious animal—a downfall that in Christian belief is considered to be the downfall of the entire human species.

Yahweh then curses Adam because he listened to Eve instead of Yahweh. This rivalry runs through the whole Bible as well as through Judaism and patriarchy as a whole. The sorrow and pain Eve is condemned to experience in childbirth is now paralleled by the sorrow Adam is condemned to by having to till the soil and eat bread produced by his own sweat until he dies (Genesis 3, 14-19).

In her book *Reinstating the Divine Woman in Judaism,* Jenny Kien (2000) shows that earlier blessings from the Goddess can be recognized behind Yahweh's curses. The serpent goddess once invited Eve to eat from her fruits and thus become wise by knowing the difference between good and evil. She blessed Eve with sexual desire that would make her the creatress of life. This is actually what her Hebrew name *Chawwa* means, along with tutor and source of meaning. Adam, too, as her consort, was blessed by the goddess. She charged him to become a distributor of life by tilling the soil. He would then be able to bring home the fruits of the earth and thus help to renew human life. This is what still shines through the Yahwistic layers: a completely different—even opposite—origin story.

In the case of the paradise myth, the idea of a different origin story gets support from another biblical text called "apocryphic" because it was not canonized. It is part of the so-called wisdom literature edited by a writer called Jesus Sirach (24,16-24). Here, as well as in other parts of wisdom literature, we learn quite a lot about Sophia or, in Hebrew, *Chochmah*, the Great Goddess of wisdom, who plays a very important part in later Gnostic literature. Sophia is an opponent to Yahweh, contradicting the Yahwist's concept of prohibitions, threats, and curses. Introducing herself as the tree of knowledge, Sophia invites man to eat from her fruits in order to become wise. According to her, the consequences would not be original sin and death, but well-being and eternal life. She says:

> *Come to me, you who long for me get satisfied on my fruits.*
> *My memory goes back to the farthest generations.*
> (i.e., Eve and Adam—matriarchal times)
> *Those who listen to me will not fall into sin.*
> *Those who bring me into light will have eternal life.* (Jes. Sir. 24)

Wisdom speaks in a tongue very different from Yahweh. Sophia encourages eating the fruit, whereas Yahweh forbids it. She wants people's satisfaction, including eternal life—he their obedience by threat of death. She goes back to the farthest times when she was known and appreciated—matriarchal times—when Yahweh was not known. Although this text was written much later than the paradise myth, traces of an an older matriarchal origin story can be detected. This existence of this version suggests that matriarchal patterns and traditions continued to exist partly in the open and partly underground. Opposition to the "new" religions must have been quite strong, otherwise this text would not have been passed on as it was never part of the official canon.

There is another text in the Bible that openly refers to the matriarchal tradition of divine marriage. I am speaking of the Song of Solomon.

The Sacred Song Behind Folklore

It is surprising that this text was preserved and taken up into the biblical canon, since it is the only text in the Bible that unfolds and celebrates eroticism and sexuality as a world creating power as well as a dynamic element in the lives of women and men (see Winter 1983). There are three facts that helped to preserve this wonderful love song: The contents (1) of the original text as well as its use (2) were being distorted, and furthermore it was ascribed to (3) the wise king Solomon—three changes that allowed it to be canonized. But there is a fourth point—a change in interpretation.

During the last 2000 years, Jewish Bible scholars have invested much energy to interpret the Song of Solomon's clearly sexual message as a metaphor of God's love for his people. Yet, neither as a cultic song between the goddess and her consort, nor as a profane love song that was very popular in the taverns of Israel, could the song have passed the hurdle of canonization. It has mainly survived because of these allegorizations that changed its meaning into a purely spiritual relationship between God and his people. Christian theologians followed Jewish scholars in this by replacing the Jewish people with the Christian community.

For non-scholars it is hardly possible to realize from the biblical version that the Song of Solomon originally described the ritual of divine marriage. So it has been rearranged by some scholars, like Gerda Weiler, during the last few decades. Weiler was certain she discovered the original order of the lines in the song, so that its cultic background was revealed. To give you an idea of the intense feelings expressed in this famous love-song, let me just quote from two parts:

At the end of the first scene of the cultic mystery play, the priestly Queen sings a yearning song:

> *O that thou wert as my brother,*
> *that sucked the breasts of my mother!*
> *When I should find thee without,*
> *I would kiss thee;*
> *yea, I should not be despised.*
> *I would lead thee,*
> *and bring thee into my mother's house,*
> *into her chamber*
> *where she once gave birth to me:*
> *Here I would cause thee to drink*
> *of spiced wine of the juice of my pomegranate.* (8.1-2)

The juice of pomegranate refers to the love potion the priestess is going to prepare for her consort. In this song, the mother's chamber becomes a centre point of the divine marriage. The Queen-Mother is represented by her daughter. The place of origin of their relationship is the mother's chamber, a cultic space that plays an important part even in cultic love. Further on, her consort replies:

> *Set me as a seal upon thine heart,*
> *as a seal upon thine arm:*
> *for love is strong as death;*

jealousy is cruel as the grave..
The coals thereof are coals of fire,
which hath a most vehement flame.
Many waters cannot quench love,
neither can the floods drown it;
if a man would give all the substance of his house for love,
would it be right to condemn him?
(8.5-7)

These words are evidence of a time in which women and men expressed their love in a passionate and tender way without being intimidated by any form of rigid morality.

Worldwide we find corresponding parallels. We come across sacred couples, whose love is praised in equally abounding metaphors. We know for example Inanna and Dumuzi in Sumer, Ishtar and Tammuz in Babylon, Aphrodite and Adonis in Greece, Isis ond Osiris in Egypt, Baal and Baalat in Canaan, Jahwe and Ashera in Israel—mythical names that stand for the cult of divine marriage.

Without doubt this song comes from a matriarchal era, even if the version in the Bible conceals this fact. Let me finish this section of the paper with one my favourite verses expressing a wisdom that is needed today:

I charge you, O daughters of Jerusalem,
that ye stir not up, nor awake my love,
until it pleases herself. (8.4)

The Matriarchal Heros Behind the Patriarchal Lord

As mentioned previously, many biblical writers have rewritten cultic texts and turned them into family sagas that were then assumed to be factual, historical reports. This method of historizing was also applied to archaic reports on the symbolic death of God-Kings. Patriarchal consciousness being exclusively historically-orientated deprived cultic texts of their cultural context.

This is clearly evident in the story of David, a biblical king of paramount importance. An awareness of matriarchal cults and values helps us to discern a very different picture of the king. At Sunday school, children learn about this modest and pious young man who played gentle songs on the harp for his monarch, King Saul, in order to lighten the King's distress and depression.

Even though King Saul made various attempts on his life, David remained a loyal to him, responding to his threats of murder with steadfast kindness. Being an obedient servant of the Lord, David finally succeeds, with the assistance of God's grace, to become king and transform Israel into an ancient empire. His characteristics are described as follows: unconditional obedience, absolute loyalty to God, adaptability, humbleness, and love. He is of a rather small, yet, handsome appearance. On the basis of a patriarchal consciousness, all these characteristics are usually related to the female. But then this very agreeable person is paralleled to a completely different figure: a brutal conqueror, ruthless warrior, and cold-blooded murderer, who is ready to kill two hundred Philistines, because his future father-in-law, Saul, demands a like number of foreskins in return for his daughter's hand.

David, a professional warrior, leads a troop of hired soldiers—runaways and criminals—for whom war has become their only purpose for living. Before his name became a proper name, the word *david* meant "the commander." He was a commander who spent all his life with this dangerous gang, guiding them to robbery and manslaughter after having destroyed their dignity and extinguished their personality while demanding absolute obedience in return (see II Sam. 23). Having changed this "army" into a gang of bondsmen lacking in will-power, David used of them without qualms for raids, thus satisfying his immense lust for power.

How can we explain this contradictory characterization of one person? Behind the gentle, humble, and peace-loving David flashes the ancient myth of the matriarchal cultic king. And since the historical David was bound to the old cults celebrating various divine marriages his personage melted with the cultic *heros* (Greek).

As we learn from the Song of Solomon, the consort of the high-priestess was a shepherd who tended the cattle that belonged to her temple. He was then made a shepherd of his people. David, too, was said to have been outside tending the sheep when the prophet Samuel came to anoint him as king. When he played the harp for King Saul, we recognize the old cultic instrument on which the former sacred king used to play. In the psalms that the Bible mainly ascribes to David, we may also discover "lectures about the lapse of the matriarchal cult" (Weiler 1989: 197).

Psalm 18, for example, reflects very clearly its origin in a matriarchal cultic song, where we find once more almost exactly the story of David. When we read: "When the waves of death encompassed me, the floods of evil made me afraid; the snares of hell prevented me and the ropes of death overpowered me" (II Sam. 22.5), we can hear "the cultic lamentation of the dying king, who suffers in the underworld" (Weiler 1989: 197).

The cultic tradition this psalm refers to is very old and reflects the original, matriarchal myth. As Weiler has stated, "The cultic song originating from matriarchal tradition was suggested to have been sung by David. It was still the same old song, in autumn when the rain fell and the new year began" (2000: 198).

These songs were subsequently silenced, for the Lord of the prophets was a lonely autocrat, who withdrew from the goddess's embrace and then denied being dependent upon her. However, though the prophets went to a lot of trouble to suppress the goddess, the people did not forget her—not yet. Her memory stayed alive in the Bible, although only from (male) prophets' point of view.

The Queen of Heaven Behind the Lord of History, or, Women Refuse to Follow the Lord

The prophets proclaiming that Yahweh alone and none else should be worshipped were a very small group. We can trace them back into the eighth century BCE, where Hosea apparently was the first prophet who threatened his people because they preferred to worship the goddess and her consort. One hundred and fifty years later the prophet Jeremiah did the same, only his threats were far worse. The book of Jeremiah gives us some important hints not only with regard to goddess worship, but also to women's reminiscences of matriarchal times.

During the early sixth century, the Babylonian King Nebuchadnezzar and his troops were on their way to Jerusalem. While approaching the eastern gates, people in town were in despair discussing what they should do: Leave the city through the western gates and escape to Egypt, or remain in town risking death or imprisonment?

For Jeremiah the issue was clear. He favoured the second solution as he regarded the Babylonian king and his troops as the arm of the Lord, who intended to punish his people for their unfaithfulness. (This is a problem "Yahweh-alone-prophets," as we call them, have lamented over for the last two centuries.) According to Jeremiah, trying to escape from the wrath of the Lord was another crime and, furthermore, not possible: no one can escape the Lord's judgment. If the people went to Egypt they would be killed there. Jeremiah made it quite clear that no one would survive. In the end, he succeeded in intimidating many of the people and, as a result, they decided to stay in Jerusalem and submit to the Lord's will. There were some, however, who refused to submit—neither to the prophet, nor to the Lord, or to the Babylonian troops. They escaped and took the prophet with them to Egypt. There Jeremiah predicted their complete annihilation. He proved wrong, as we know. Realizing that his people participated in the rites of the Queen of Heaven as celebrated in Egypt, he warned them that they would "be consumed by the sword … by famine … and pestilence and thus fall in the land of Egypt … from the least even unto the greatest…" (Jeremiah 44,12-13).

But then the people of Jerusalem stood up against the prophet and the women spoke for themselves saying:

> As for the word that you have spoken to us in the name of the Lord we will not listen to you. But we will certainly do whatsoever comes from our own mouth, that is to burn incense to the queen of heaven, and to pour out drink offerings to her, as we have done, we, and our fathers, our kings, and our princes, in the cities of Judah, and in the streets of Jerusalem: for then we had plenty of victuals, and were well, and saw no evil. But since we left off to burn incense to the queen of heaven and to pour out drink offerings to her, we have wanted all things and have been consumed by the sword and by famine. And when we burned incense to the queen of heaven, and poured out drink offerings unto

her, did we make her cakes to worship her and pour out drink offerings unto her without our men? (Jeremiah 44.15-19)

The women had had enough of being patronized by the prophets and their strange idea of a single male god. On this occasion they give us what may be the oldest analysis of patriarchy as a warlike society causing starvation and evil. They realized the context between a patriarchal image of a male god and the subsequent patriarchal imperative that covers the earth with wars, starvation, and distress. Here, the women remembered that when they worshipped the Queen of Heaven they had never experienced the misery that befell them with the imposition of patriarchal religious beliefs. While the prophet blamed goddess worship for all the destruction they had experienced, the Judaeo women were certain the destruction was the result of a male monotheistic religion, an issue that comes up in matriarchal studies even today.

I think the women of Jerusalem who spoke up against the "Yahweh-alone-prophet" are behind all of us who do matriarchal research, especially as this research confirms that in matriarchal societies, justice and peace had once found a home. Whenever we are being reproached for projecting our desires for peace into a distant past, we need to remember these women from Jerusalem some 2600 years ago who confirmed that there once were peaceful societies with a much higher quality of life that were lost once patriarchy took over.

Christa Mulack is a writer and lecturer living in Hagen, Germany. Her doctoral thesis was entitled: "The Femininity of God: Matriarchal Presuppositions of the Image of God." She has held teaching assignments at several universities and has been working on the issue of matriarchy for the past twenty years.

References

Campbell, Joseph. 1982. *The Masks of God. Vol. 3: Occidental Mythology.* New York: Penguin Books.

Kien, Jenny. 2000. *Reinstating the Divine Woman in Judaism.* Florida: Universal Publishers.

Mulack, Christa. 1983-1988. *Die Weiblichkeit Gott. Matriarchale Voraussetzungen des Gottesbildes.* Stuttgart: Verlag-Pomaska-Brand, Schalksmühle.

Mulack, Christa. 1985. *Maria - Die geheime Göttin im Christentum.* Stuttgart: Verlag-Pomaska-Brand, Schalksmühle.

Weiler, Gerda. 1989. *Das Matriarchat im Alten Israel.* Stuttgart: Verlag Kohlhammer.

Winter, Urs. 1983. *Frau und Göttin. Exegetische und ikonographische Studien zum weiblichen Gottesbild im alten Israel und dessen Umwelt.* Göttingen: Vandenhoeck & Ruprecht.

SUSAN GAIL CARTER

Amaterasu-o-mi-kami, Japanese Sun Goddess

The Matristic Roots of Japan

Of all the world's main religions, only in Shinto is a goddess preeminent without a male consort. Amaterasu-o-mi-kami, the Japanese Sun Goddess, has been worshipped throughout Japan for thousands of years. Even today, rituals in homage to her are observed publicly and privately by both the Japanese Emperor and the general public. In our time, and from a western, feminist perspective, this fact is remarkable.

Amaterasu-o-mi-kami's main shrine at Ise had been established sometime in the fifth century CE, a century or two before her myths were first written down, in the late 600s and early 700s CE. Some scholars suggest that her oral myths were perhaps already 2,000 years old when they were first recorded in written chronicles. This leads to the question of whether there were certain characteristics present in Japan's prehistoric past that shaped her myths, and allowed a female *kami* (or deity) to emerge and then survive in what became a strongly patriarchal society.

There is ample evidence that matriarchy or a matristic culture[12] preceded patriarchy in Japan. A number of scholars have referred to early Japan as a matriarchal, matrilocal, matrilineal, and/or a "feminine" culture at least through the Heian period (up to 1185 CE), but rarely with adequate elaboration.[2] It is also known that Japan has had eight reigning empresses, the most recent in the eighteenth century. Further, there is ample evidence of female *kami* (deity) worship in Japan for well over 1,300 years.

Matristic Cultural Characteristics

For this investigation into Japan's prehistory and early history I developed and used a set of seven cultural characteristics as a template in which to explore Japanese culture.[3] These cultural characteristics are:[4]

- matrifocality, matrilocality, and/or matrilineality
- egalitarianism
- nature-embeddedness
- peacefulness

•female veneration
•worship of female *kami*
•little or no separation between secular and sacred.

All of these cultural characteristics likely existed in Japan's prehistory.[5]

By a matristic culture I mean a culture that is matrifocal, matrilocal, and matrilineal, that is, the responsibility for social values and/or familial identity is ascribed to its female members. Women are recognized as both bearers of children and bearers of culture, serving their communities significantly and importantly, in farming, arts and crafts, and religious and social functions. For these contributions they are respected and honoured.

A matristic culture is also egalitarian. In such a culture the sexes may work side by side and consider each other in terms of complementarity, with neither subordinate to the other. The relationship might also be based on serial reciprocity or alternating dominance for balance. At the very least, in an egalitarian culture there are no elaborate political hierarchies.

Matristic cultures tend toward peacefulness. Instances of disagreement, conflict, or violence among members are dealt with through formal intervention and mediation rather than through armed conflict.

Matristic cultures value life itself and recognize the interconnectedness of all life forms. Through this interconnection, humans are one part of a greater life energy that is also connected to its source, and the cosmic power of deities are perceived as embodied within each individual and all of creation in the natural world. Overall, the culture is deeply embedded in nature's manifestations.

Embodiment of life is honoured and is associated with females through the gestation and birth process; the female becomes a symbol for all life. As such, the female form is considered venerable, and artistic re-creations of the female form may be used as a way in which to put forward the culture's understanding of and intentions for survival and continuity. In this way the female form may be deified and becomes "goddess," looked to for the fulfillment of daily human needs. The worship of male deities is by no means precluded, but it is the female deity or deities who become primary communal spirits for matristic cultures and the major focus of their religious celebration and ritual.

Finally, a matristic culture embraces a way of life in which there is little or no apparent separation between the secular and the sacred. Life is celebrated daily because it is sacred and daily life is part of a larger, continuous cycle.

Japan's Early Culture: The Jomon Period

Japan had an extremely long prehistoric period, with a flourishing culture spanning perhaps some 16,000 years.[6] (Indeed, the prehistoric period far exceeds in duration all of the other proto-historical periods and the historical period combined.) Writing was not introduced in Japan until around 400 CE—and was not extensively used until the 600s by the developing government. Likewise, other technology such as metallurgy was also introduced quite late in comparison to most other parts of the world.[7]

The Jomon period (16,500 BCE-300 BCE) is now considered the beginnings of Japanese culture, and can be highly informative when looking for Japan's matristic roots. There is some evidence for all of the matristic cultural characteristics in the Jomon period, with these characteristics diminishing or falling away as we proceed into the historical era.

The Jomon culture is thought to have been egalitarian. Uniform dwellings and unpretentious graves from this period point to a classless society. There is no indication from this time of any unequal status between genders: neither women nor men were considered superior to the other as a class.

There is evidence of limited forms of agriculture, hunting/fishing/gathering practices, and continuously used settlements (some for more than a thousand years in one place), which demonstrate that the Jomon people's survival depended on their knowledge of nature and living in harmony with it. From the archaeological specimens of animal and plant food remains, it is clear that the Jomon knew how to utilize, tend, and even augment the natural resources around them. Further, some artifacts suggest nature worship.

The Jomon culture appears to have been peaceful. Settlement locations have no apparent superiority or advantage from a military strategic point of view. Rather, there is a relationship to the procurement of food, water, and shelter. Even though Jomon architectural remains show that the Jomon had the technical knowledge and capacity to build strong and large structures, there are no indications of defensive fortifications. Nor have any archaeological excavations to date yielded any signs of overt warfare.

Archaeological finds support the possibility of both household and community ritual or ceremonialism in Jomon settlements, suggesting little or no separation between the secular and the sacred. Altars, communal structures, stone circles, and caches of broken figurines and polished stone axes offer loose analogies to ceremonial practices that survive to this day in folk observances of rural Japan. The abundance of ritual objects such as fantastic pottery vessels and female figurines support the possibility of regular ritual practices.

Importance of the Female

The other three cultural characteristics—matrifocality, matrilocality, and matrilineality; female veneration; and female *kami* worship—all point to the importance of females in the culture, and are evidence of early goddess and sun worship. These cultural characteristics can be interpreted as the beginnings of Amaterasu-o-mi-kami.

Perhaps the earliest rendering of the female form in Japan can be found on river cobbles from the late Paleolithic/Incipient Jomon period.[8] Incised stones, with delineated breasts, were found in a cave along with a bowl, and are thought to have been used ritually. Stones like these may have been the forerunners of the later clay *dogu*[9] figures found in the Jomon period.

It is these *dogu* figures that I believe point to both female veneration and goddess or female *kami* worship at this time. By the 1990s, over 10,000 *dogu* figures had been found throughout Japan.[10] When one considers that the size of Japan is smaller than the state of California, this number is impressive, and demands our attention.

Dogu figures date from the early to the late Jomon periods (the middle of the Initial Jomon phase, ca. 7,500-5,000 BCE, to the end of the Late Jomon, ca. 2,000-1,000 BCE). The earliest are rather plaque-like with rough features. They then became more carefully made, followed by a period in which they were fashioned quite elaborately. The latest figures found date from around 700 BCE. The figures range from a few inches to about a foot in size, and are usually in a standing position with only a few in a crouching position. They are overwhelmingly considered female; of the over 10,000 figures found, only a handful might be considered male. Many have ample bellies, hips, and breasts, perhaps indicating pregnancy, and they are decorated with symbols and colours that may represent fertility and abundance, such as the colour red, triangles, and pubic triangles, and symbols such as spirals, running spirals, and dentil (or saw-tooth) patterns. Changing from flat, solid, and simple, to ample, hollow, and ornate, *dogu* appeared over thousands of years, throughout much of the Jomon period.

While scholars agree that the purpose of these *dogu* was most probably ceremonial, there has long been speculation about their use, with ideas including medicine dolls to attempts at birth control. More recently the idea of them as earth goddesses is being embraced, and this understanding has been reflected in the labelling of the Jomon period artifacts exhibit at the Tokyo National Museum.[11] All agree that their purpose was most probably ceremonial.

Also found from the Jomon period are interesting stone circles, some of which are called sundials. The fixed position of the stones in each of these circles, nearly identical in position to each other, suggests deliberate placement for a specific purpose. They may have been sundials used to measure the seasons of hunting, gathering, and planting. Some *dogu* have been found in the circles, as well as a few pits believed to have been burials, which suggests ceremonial use. From above, these stone configurations look like sunbursts, and may be the first signs of sun worship in the culture. It is possible to speculate that circles such as these may have informed the Jomon people about the seasons for planting, gathering, fishing, and hunting which were so important to their survival. It should not be forgotten that the ancient word for "saint" or "sage" in Japanese is *hijiri*, which literally means, "to know the sun."

It is significant that fertility and the sun are two aspects that are combined in the form of Amaterasu-o-mi-kami. The archaeological evidence of the *dogu* figures and the sundial stone circles inform my conclusion that the Jomon culture may have provided fertile ground for the myth and worship of Amaterasu-o-mi-kami to emerge. The evidence supports the idea that early forms of her myths and a form of sun worship may have already been in place in the Jomon period.[12]

Dogu, H. 36 cm. Final Jomon. Ebisuda Tajiricho, Miyagi Prefecture, Tokyo National Museum, Tokyo Kokuritsu Hakubutsu-kan. (Illustration by Marilyn Higginson).

Dogu figures from the prehistoric Jomon Period (16,500 – 300 BCE) are evidence for very early female kami (deity) worship and possibly sun worship. This extensively decorated female figure is a drawing of an accurate reproduction from the Final Jomon period (purchased from the Tokyo National Museum, author's collection). The spirals and other designs were most likely associated with birth, regeneration, and new growth.

The Sun Goddess Emerges and Survives

Many of the matristic cultural characteristics declined over the centuries as Japan developed into a nation state. This development was accompanied by ever increasing social stratification and political hierarchy, as the gradual shift from a matriarchal to a patriarchal society took place. However, through the subsequent periods of proto-history and history, the Shinto religion remained nature-embedded, and Amaterasu-o-mi-kami continued to survive as the preeminent deity of the Shinto pantheon worshipped by the common people, the Japanese court, and Imperial family.

However, the remaining cultural characteristics from prehistory alone cannot fully explain why Amaterasu-o-mi-kami emerged as female: politics in its early history may have also played an important role.

We know that there were various forms of sun worship throughout early Japan. The Yamato clan (which came to be the Japanese Imperial family) claimed Amaterasu-o-mi-kami as their clan *kami (uji-gami)*, and unified the developing nation state under the auspices of sun worship and Amaterasu-o-mi-kami. She may have survived because the Yamato clan maintained its power, and she served as a bridge between the past and the present when Japan was first developing as a nation.

Further, the historical chronicles of Japan, the *Nihongi* and the *Kojiki,* were started and completed during the reigns of two empresses in the early 700s CE.[13] It is possible that those who held influence in the court wanted to further legitimize female Imperial power and position by having a female *kami* preeminent in the Shinto pantheon, and used Amaterasu-o-mi-kami to their political advantage accordingly.

It is also important to note that one of the primary reasons these chronicles were written was to legitimize the Yamato clan and growing Imperial rule. The chronicles detail the account of Amaterasu-o-mi-kami sending her grandson down to earth to tend the earthly plain as she does the heavenly one. It was important to the Imperial family that the lineage of the Emperor be traced back to Amaterasu, proving the rulers' divinity, and, thus, the right to rule. This would again point to the importance and continuance of matrilineality in Japan into the historic era. In these chronicles, Amaterasu-o-mi-kami myths are detailed and the Sun Goddess is portrayed as the ancestress of the Imperial family. Amaterasu stood as the symbol of the new ruling power, and, at the same time, represented the older traditional powers of the life-giving sun, fertility, and motherhood. Drawing on this rich and ancient tradition, the Sun Goddess continued to be worshipped for the gift of agricultural fertility and abundance as in times past, and also came to be worshipped as the mother of the new nation.

As already mentioned, the later historical periods in Japan became much more rigidly hierarchal and patriarchal. A militaristic and feudal society emerged. The growing influences and adoption of many Chinese practices and beliefs from Taoism and Confucianism diminished the importance of women's roles in Japanese society. The matristic society of ancient Japan gradually gave way to one in which women were subordinate to men. It was not until the Meiji Reformation of 1868, when political power was restored to the Emperor that some of women's agency was partially restored.

When this history is considered, it is even more remarkable that Amaterasu-o-mi-kami has survived and is part of what might be called the dominant culture, sanctifying the sovereignty of the Emperor, and remaining the preeminent *kami* of the Shinto pantheon. Amaterasu-o-mi-kami seems to be exceptional in this regard. In many other spiritual traditions once important goddesses (and their powers) were greatly diminished, they often became mere consorts, sisters, wives, or mothers of a more powerful male deity, and no longer served as primary or preeminent dieties. Amaterasu-o-mi-kami's spiritual reign and survival today can, in part, be attributed to the remaining characteristics of an earlier matristic culture, that is, female *kami* worship and nature-embeddedness still prevalent in the Shinto religion.

Amaterasu-o-mi-kami Today

Today *norito* prayers[14] are still recited to Amaterasu-o-mi-kami as they have been for over a thousand years. In various ceremonies the Japanese Emperor continues sun worship rituals and the worship of Amaterasu-o-mi kami. An example of this can be seen on the occasion of the annual First Fruits Festival held in the autumn season at the Ise Shrine and during which continuing rituals demonstrate that the Shinto religion remains nature-embedded. In a later part of the First Fruits Festival, rice grain from a paddy on the Imperial Palace grounds in Tokyo, some of which is planted and harvested by the emperor himself, is taken and offered to the Sun Goddess with an oral petition for continued abundance and blessing.

Female *kami* worship and the worship of Amaterasu-o-mi-kami continues to be practiced by the general public. Today, over six million people visit Amaterasu-o-mi-kami's Grand Shrine at Ise annually, one of the oldest places of continued worship in existence. She is worshipped at thousands of shrines in the Japanese archipelago, often symbolized by her *shintai* or *kami* body, the round shining mirror. The sun, another of her symbols, remains on the national flag as a large red circle on a white ground.

Female Ascendance to the Chrysanthemum Throne?

In regard to Matriarchal Studies, many pertinent questions are often raised: Even if we can prove that matriarchy preceded patriarchy—or that there are still matriarchal cultures alive today—why might this matter? How does this have relevance in our modern lives? How might this inform contemporary society today? In the case of Japan, Amaterasu-o-mi-kami's continuing spiritual presence can still inform political, religious, and social discourse in interesting ways.

In December 2001, after eight years of marriage to Japan's Crown Prince, Prince Naruhito, the Crown Princess Masako gave birth to a baby girl, Princess Aiko. At that time the Crown Prince and Princess had yet to produce any male offspring, and the Crown Prince's younger brother, Prince Akishino, had two daughters. There had been no males born to the Imperial family since the birth of Prince Akishino in 1965, thus there was no male heir to the throne to follow the current Crown Prince in the world's oldest hereditary monarchy, and current Japanese law forbids a female Emperor.

The female gender of this new royal child in 2001 caused public debate among

Japanese commoners and national leaders alike. Questions arose as to why a female could not accede to the throne, or why the high priest of the national cult must be male when the Sun Goddess herself is female (see Sayle 2000: 84-91). Political polls at that time indicated that the general population overwhelmingly found such a solution acceptable.[15] Many politicians, including Prime Minister Koizumi (serving in 2001), repeatedly declared that they were in support of reversing the law that had been in place since the late nineteenth century as well as an additional edict put forth in 1947 that forbids a female to accede to the throne. Even older female members of the royal family spoke out in favour of a reversal. One elder princess went so far as to publish an article in a popular women's magazine voicing her approval. A government panel, which included university professors in addition to politicians and bureaucrats, considered how the Imperial Household laws and governmental laws might be changed to allow for this.

All of these considerations were quite quickly placed on hold when the Crown Prince's brother, Prince Akishino, and his wife, Princess Kiko, made the announcement in the spring of 2006 that they were expecting another child in the autumn of that year. Regardless of heated speculation on whether or not the expected child would be a boy or a girl during her pregnancy, there was little surprise when Princess Kiko gave birth to a son (Prince Hisahito) in September, 2006—the first male born to the Imperial family in forty-one years. Further debate about possible changes to allow for female ascendancy to the Chrysanthemum Throne has since been tabled indefinitely.

Regardless of the unfolding events of recent history, or the result of this most recent debate, it remains evident that the Japanese Sun Goddess, who has reigned for millennia, is alive in the minds of the Japanese people and still looked to as a model. Amaterasu-o-mi-kami and her myths, taught in public schools as fact until the end of World War II, continue to shape the social, political, and spiritual lives of the Imperial family as well as the common people of Japan. Looking to Japan's ancient past and its matristic roots from which Amaterasu-o-mi-kami emerged it may still be possible for a female to ascend to the Chrysanthemum throne. Time will tell.

Susan Gail Carter is an associate professor at the California Institute of Integral Studies in San Francisco, where she teaches interdisciplinary courses in the humanities, women's spirituality, and community activism. In addition to presentations on her thesis/dissertation research, she has presented nationally and internationally on topics such as community-based learning, engaged spirituality in higher education, and the critical intersections of women's spirituality, women's studies, and the processes of social change.

[1]"Matristic culture" is a term I have applied to seven cultural indicators based largely on Marija Gimbutas' description of a goddess civilization. See fn 3.

[2]These historians who have referred to early Japan as "matriarchal," "matrilineal," and/or "feminine," have rarely adequately elaborated or substantiated their claims. Nor have they placed such periods in a larger historical context. For examples, see Sansom (1958: 17); O. Reischauer (1988: 41-42, 1981: 205). These examples suggest that historians have not applied the "matriarchal theory" to Japan in a thorough or critical manner. This point is further discussed in my dissertation: *Amaterasu-o-mi-kami: Past and Present. An Exploration of the Japanese Sun Goddess from a Western Feminist Perspective.*

[3]To assist in my investigation, I relied on the work of scholars such as the late archaeomythologist Marija Gimbutas (1991), whose groundbreaking work covered the prehistory of Old Europe; philosopher Heide Goettner-Abendroth (1995, 1998: 44-48, 1999: 31-35), who has done so much to further Matriarchal Studies and bring it to world attention through her publications and two "World Congresses on Matriarchal Studies," 2003 and 2005; and anthropologist Peggy Reeves Sanday (1981, 1998), whose large-scale cross-cultural work on over 150 cultures, as well as her more recent work on the modern-day matriarchal society in West Sumatra are so important to the discussion of matriarchal societies.

[4]All of these characteristics or indicators are discussed by Marija Gimbutas in *The Civilization of the Goddess.* For her comments and/or discussion of "matriliny" see pp. x, 324; for "egalitarianism" see p. x; for "nature-embeddedness" see p. 228; for "peacefulness" see p. 48; for "female veneration" see pp. 222-23; for "goddess worship" see pp. 222-223; (and for "god worship" p. 249); for "no separation between secular and sacred" see p. x. In my definition of "matristic," the characteristic or cultural indicator of goddess worship is not a necessary element, as it is in Gimbutas' definition, but it is a probable one. I use the term "female *kami*" when discussing female deities in Japan. (See also Appendix B of my dissertation under, "Definitions of Selected Terms" for more discussion of "goddess civilization.")

[5]The scope of this article does not allow for a lengthy discussion of each of the Japanese periods in regard to the cultural indicators. More detailed information can be found in my dissertation work.

[6]The invention of fire-proofed clay vessels is the indicator for the Jomon period's inception, but the starting date continues to shift backward in time (see Kenrick 1995: 21.) Further, recent Carbon-14 testing now supports a date of 16,500 BCE for the beginning of the Jomon period (see "A Potted History" 1999: 79).

[7]It should be noted that the late introduction of iron and bronze took place simultaneously in Japan.

[8]The start of the Incipient Jomon period is commonly recognized as 10,000-7,500 BCE. However, some scholars suggest it began ca. 16,500 BCE. (See fn 5 above.)

[9]*Dogu* literally means puppet or doll.

[10]Due to the backlog in cataloguing artifacts and publishing data from the efforts of archaeologists working in Japan, it is difficult to ascertain how many of a certain type of artifact have been discovered.

[11]The Tokyo National Museum has labeled their large collection of *dogu* figures (in Japanese) as "goddess figurines, venerated as objects of earth mother worship (*jibonshin shinko*)." There is also an English explanation stating: "*Dogu* (figurines) and other clay objects of the Jomon period have long been studied as religious relics of the Jomon people's spiritual world. There are different opinions about the identity of the *dogu,* including that they were worshipped as an earth goddess since many of them represent well-fleshed women ... that they represented a god in the Jomon period."

[12]I assert that Amaterasu-o-mi-kami's myths are brought from prehistory into the historical era here, as they were considered already ancient when first written down. For further discussion see Philippi (1969: 4-5).

[13]The Kojiki and the Nihongi were completed in 712 and 720 CE respectively, during the reigns of Empress Gemmei, who reigned 708-715 CE, and Empress Gensho, who reigned 715-724 CE.

[14]Although the Shinto religion does not have scripture or dogma, the norito are a collection of prayers which were first written down ca. 800 CE, and were already considered ancient at that time.

[15]On December 12, 2001, the *Mainichi Shimbun* (a popular newspaper) reported that, "A whopping 86 percent of those polled believed that the Imperial House Law should be amended to allow a female member of the world's longest ruling monarchy to ascend the throne" (<http://www12.mainichi.co.jp/mdn/search-news/842245/Princess-0-5.html> Retrieved December 15, 2001). Public opinion remained overwhelming in favour of changes to allow for a female Emperor.

References

"A Potted History." 1999. *Economist* 24 April: 79.

Aston, W. G. 1972. *Nihongi*. Rutland/Tokyo: Charles E. Tuttle Company, Inc.

Carter, Susan Gail. 2001. *Amaterasu-o-mi-kami: Past and Present. An Exploration of the Japanese Sun Goddess from a Western Feminist Perspective*. Ph.D. dissertation, California Institute of Integral Studies. United States–California. Dissertations & Theses @ California Institute of Integral Studies–NCCPL. (Publication No. AAT 3004465).

Gimbutas, Marija. 1991. *The Civilization of the Goddess: The World of Old Europe*. San Francisco: HarperSanFrancisco.

Goettner-Abendroth, Heide. 1995. *The Goddess and Her Heros*. Stow, MA: Anthony Publishing Company.

Goettner-Abendroth, Heide and Joan Marler. 1998. "Cultures of the Goddess: A Discussion." *ReVision* 20 (3) (Winter): 44-48.

Goettner-Abendroth, Heide. 1999. "The Structure of Matriarchal Societies, Exemplified by the Society of the Mosuo in China." *ReVision* 21 (3) (Winter): 31-35.

"Imperial Harvest." 1996. *San Francisco Chronicle* 3 October: A9.

Kenrick, Douglas Moore. 1995. *Jomon of Japan: The World's Oldest Pottery.* London and New York: Kegan Paul International.

Philippi, Donald L. 1969. *Kojiki.* Tokyo: University of Tokyo Press.

"Princess Kiko is expecting fall birth." 2006. *The Japan Times* 8 February. Online: <http://search.japantimes.co.jp/cgi-bin/nn20060208a1.html>.

Reischauer, Edwin O. 1981. *The Japanese.* 1977. Cambridge: The Belknap Press.

Reischauer, Edwin O. 1988. *The Japanese Today: Change and Continuity.* 1977. Cambridge: The Belknap Press.

Sanday, Peggy Reeves. 1981. *Female Power and Male Dominance: On the Origins of Sexual Inequality.* Cambridge: Cambridge University Press.

Sanday, Peggy Reeves. 1998. "Matriarchy as a Sociocultural Form: An Old Debate in a New Light." Paper presented at the Sixteenth Congress of the Indo-Pacific prehistory Association, Melaka, Malaysia, 1-7 July. Online: <http://www.sas.upenn.edu/~psanday/matri.html>.

Sansom, George. 1958. *A History of Japan To 1334.* Stanford: Stanford University Press.

Sayle, Murray. 2000. "Letter from Japan: A Dynasty Falters." *The New Yorker* 12 June: 84-91.

Part VII
The Origins of Patriarchy

JAMES DEMEO

Saharasia

The Origins of Patriarchal Authoritarian Culture in Ancient Desertification

G eographical study of human behaviour has revealed a global pattern of
social violence strongly correlated to regions of major climate change
during early prehistory (DeMeo 1986, 1998). This conclusion developed from one of the first comprehensive studies to produce global maps of human behaviours and social institutions related to family life, sexuality, childrearing methods, and the status of women. I specifically focused upon traumatic and
repressive attitudes, behaviours, social customs and institutions that were also, as
part of my work, cross-culturally correlated with violence and warfare. My focus
was upon the biological needs of infants, children, and adolescents, the repressive and damaging effects that certain social institutions and classes of harsh
natural environments have upon those needs, and the behavioural consequences
of such repression and damage.

The geographical approach to the origins of violence, as presented in my publications and briefly summarized here (DeMeo 1986, 1998, 2002), has confirmed the existence of an ancient, worldwide period of relatively peaceful social
conditions, where warfare, male domination, and destructive aggression were
either absent, or at extremely minimal levels for most of the world, most of the
time. Moreover, this approach has made it possible to pinpoint those times and
places on Earth where human culture transformed from peaceful, democratic,
egalitarian conditions, to violent, warlike, despotic conditions, as well as the
environmental, ecological conditions prevailing during those transformations.

Unarmoured Matrism Versus Armoured Patrist Culture:
The Roots of Violence in Childhood Trauma and Sex-Repression

A major starting point for my research was the sex-economic theory of Wil-
helm Reich (1935, 1942, 1945, 1947, 1949, 1953, 1967, 1983). Reich's theory,
which developed within but later diverged from psychoanalysis, identified the
destructive aggression and sadistic violence of *Homo sapiens* as a completely ab-
normal condition, resultant from the traumatically-induced chronic inhibition
of respiration, emotional expression, and pleasure-directed impulses.

According to Reich's sex-economic viewpoint, a chronic characterological and muscular *armour* is set up in the growing human according to the type and severity of painful trauma he or she experiences. The biophysical processes which normally lead to full and complete respiration, emotional expression, and sexual discharge during orgasm are chronically blocked by the armour, to a greater or lesser extent, leading to the accumulation of pent-up, undischarged emotional and sexual (bioenergetic) tension. The dammed-up reservoir of internal tension drives the organism to behave in a generally unconscious, distorted, self-destructive, and/or sadistic manner (Reich 1942, 1949). The above processes occur whenever, and only whenever, attempts are made to irrationally deflect or mould human primary biological needs or urges away from their original pleasure-directed goals, according to the demands of "culture." The denial of the breast to an infant, the beating of a child for defecation or sexual expression, or the forced marriage of young girls to old men ("child betrothal," "bride price") are examples.

Pain-inflicting and pleasure-censoring rituals and social institutions have been present in most, but by no means all, historical and contemporary cultures. There are, for instance, a significant minority of cultures studied by anthropologists which neither inflict pain upon infants and children, consciously or otherwise, nor repress the sexual interests of adolescents or adults. Of great interest is the fact that these are also nonviolent societies, with stable but non-compulsive, generally monogamous family bonds, and congenial, friendly social relations, but without sadomasochists, pedophiles, and other distortions of behaviour.

Malinowski (1927, 1932) first pointed to such cultures as a rebuttal to Freud's assertion of a biological, pan-cultural nature for childhood sexual latency and the Oedipal conflict. Reich (1935) argued that conditions within Trobriand society proved the correctness of his clinical and social findings relating sexual repression to pathological behaviour. Other ethnographic descriptions of similar cultures have been made (Elwin 1947, 1968; Hallet and Relle 1973; Turnbull 1961; Goettner-Abendroth 1998). James Prescott's (1975) and my own (De-Meo 1986, 1998: 51) global cross-cultural studies have confirmed these findings: Societies which heap trauma and pain upon their infants and children, and which subsequently repress the emotional expressiveness and sexual interests of their adolescents, invariably exhibit a spectrum of neurotic, self-destructive, and violent behaviours. By contrast, societies that treat infants and children with great physical affection and gentle tenderness, and which view emotional expressiveness and adolescent sexuality in a positive light, are psychically healthy and nonviolent. Indeed, cross-cultural research has demonstrated the difficulty, perhaps the impossibility, of locating any disturbed, violent society that does not also traumatize its young and/or sexually repress their adolescents and the unmarried.

In addition to my review of the ethnographic-anthropological literature, a separate systematic survey was made of published global historical and archaeological compendiums, independently confirming the above correlations, between childhood traumas, sex-repression, male-dominance, and family violence, in the descriptions of various warlike, authoritarian and despotic central states (DeMeo 1986, 1998). From similar historical data, Gordon Taylor (1953: 83) developed a dichotomous schema of human behaviour in various societies. Using Taylor's terminology and expanding upon his schema according to sex-economic findings, such violent, repressive societies are identified here as *patrist*, and they differ in almost every respect from *matrist* cultures, whose social institutions are designed to protect and enhance the pleasurable maternal-infant and male-female bonds. Table 1 gives a contrast between extreme forms of patrist (armoured) and matrist (unarmoured) culture.

Most aspects of patrism interfere with the biology of the infant and child in a manner generally unseen elsewhere in the animal world, and some clearly increase infant and maternal mortality and morbidity. Besides the painful or pleasure-reducing rites given in Table 1, it is important to note that most patrist societies possessed, at some time in their recent or distant past, severe psycho-pathological social disorders designed for the socially-approved, organized discharge of murderous rage towards children and women (i.e., ritual murder of children, widows, "witches," "prostitutes," etc.), with a complement deification of the most aggressive and sadistically cruel males (totalitarianism, divine kingship). And there are many contemporary cultures that continue to express such conditions in a fully blown form, or exhibit residues of such conditions.

Given that clinical, cross-cultural, and historical evidence indicates that adult violence is rooted in early childhood trauma and sex-repression (see DeMeo 1998 for a comprehensive review), and does not exist where maternal-infant and male-female bonds are protected and nurtured by matrist social institutions, a question naturally arises as to how the cultural complex of trauma, repression, and violence (patrism) could have gotten started in the first instance. Patrism, with its great outpouring of violence toward infants, children, and women, which is passed from one generation to the next through painful and life-threatening social institutions, must have had *specific times and places of origins* among some, but not all of the earliest human societies. The assumed absence of an innate character to patrism, which derives from the chronic blocking, inhibition, and damming-up of biological urges, demands that this be so. Matrism, however, which springs from freely-expressed, unimpeded and pleasure-directed biological impulses, and which therefore is innate, would have been global in nature, ubiquitous among all of humankind at the earliest times. Indeed, natural selection would have favoured matrism, given the fact that it does not generate the sadistic urges that lead to deadly violence toward women and children, nor does it disturb the emotional bonds between mothers and infants, which impart distinct psycho-physiological survival advantages (Klaus and Kennell 1976; LeBoyer 1975; Montagu 1971; Stewart and Stewart 1978a, 1978b; Reich 1942, 1949).

Confirmation and support for the above starting assumptions and inferences exists in the geographical aspects of the global anthropological and archaeological data. For example, certain aspects of matrism and peaceful social conditions

Table 1: Dichotomous Behaviours, Attitudes, and Social Institutions

Trait	Patrist (armoured)	Matrist (unarmoured)

Infants, Children, & Adolescents:	Less indulgence
	Less physical affection
	Infants traumatized
	Painful initiations
	Dominated by family
	Sex-segregated houses
	  or military
		More indulgence
		More physical affection
		Infants not traumatized
		No painful initiations
		Children's democracies
		Mixed-sex children's
		  houses or age villages

Sexuality:	Restrictive attitude
	Genital mutilations
	Female virginity taboo
	Adolescent lovemaking
	  severely censured
	Homosexual tendency plus
	  severe taboo
	Incest/pedophile tendency
	  plus severe taboo
	Coercive concubinage
	  and prostitution
		Permissive attitude
		No genital mutilations
		No female virginity taboo
		Adolescent lovemaking
		  freely permitted
		No homosexual tendency
		  or strong taboo
		No incest/pedophile tendency
		  or strong taboo
		No concubinage or
		  coercive prostitution

Women:	Limits on freedom
	Inferior status
	Vaginal blood taboo (hymenal,
	  menstrual & childbirth)
	Cannot choose own mate
	Cannot divorce at will
	Males control fertility
	Reproductive functions
	  denigrated
		More freedom
		Equal status
		No vaginal blood taboo
		
		Can choose own mate
		Can divorce at will
		Females control fertility
		Reproductive functions
		  celebrated

Cultural & Family Structure:	Authoritarian
	Hierarchical
	Patrilineal
	Patrilocal
	Compulsive lifelong
	  monogamy or polygyny
	
	Military structure
	Violent, sadistic
		Democratic
		Egalitarian
		Matrilineal
		Matrilocal
		Noncompulsive monogamy or
		  occasional polygamy
		  (polygyny or polyandry)
		No full time military
		Nonviolent, no sadism

Religion & Beliefs	Male/father oriented
	Asceticism, pleasure-avoidance
	  pain sought & emphasized
	Inhibition
	Fear/hatred of nature
	Full time religious specialists
	Male shamans/healers
	Strict behaviour codes
		Female/mother oriented
		Pleasure welcomed and
		  institutionalized
		Spontaneity
		Nature cherished and embraced
		No full time religious specialists
		Male or female shamans/healers
		Absence of strict codes

had previously been identified in the deepest archaeological layers of some regions, with demonstrated transitions toward more violent, male-dominated conditions in later years. While some researchers have either been unaware of these newer findings, have tended to ignore them, or have merely objected-without-substance to their implications, a growing number of studies have demonstrated major social transitions in ancient times, from peaceful, democratic, and egalitarian conditions, to violent, male-dominated, warlike conditions (Bell 1971; Eisler 1987a, 1987b; Huntington 1907, 1911; Gimbutas 1965, 1977, 1982; Goettner-Abendroth 1995; Stone 1976; Velikovsky 1984).

My work revealed distinct global geographical and time-ordered patterns in these archaeological transitions, wherein entire regions were transformed from matrism to patrism within the same general time periods, or where the transition to patrism swept across major portions of a continent, from one end to the other, over a period of centuries (DeMeo 1986, 1998). Of significance was the finding that the largest and most dramatic of these cultural transformations occurred in specific Old World regions (notably in North Africa, the Near East, and Central Asia, around 4000-3500 BCE), *in concert with major environmental transformations, from relatively wet to arid conditions.* The existence of these timed environmental and cultural transitions was most important, given other evidence which suggested that severe drought and desertification had the potential to traumatically disrupt maternal-infant and male-female bonds, just as certainly as any harsh and painful patrist social institution.

Social Devastation in Regions of Drought, Desertification, and Famine

Other lines of evidence lead to the conclusion that severe and repeated drought and desertification, which promotes famine, starvation, and mass migrations among subsistence-level cultures, must have been a crucial factor which would have gradually, or even rapidly, pushed early matrist cultures towards patrism (DeMeo 1998: chapter 3). For example:

1) Eyewitness reports of culture-change occurring during famine and starvation conditions indicate a resultant breakdown of social and family bonds. Colin Turnbull's (1972) heartbreaking account of the Ik peoples of East Africa is most clear on this point, but other, similar observations have been made (Cahill 1982; Garcia 1981; Garcia and Escudero 1982; Sorokin 1975).

2) Clinical research on the effects of severe protein-calorie malnutrition of infants and children indicates that starvation is a trauma of the most severe proportions. A child suffering from marasmus or kwashiorkor will exhibit symptoms of contactlessness and immobility, with, in the most extreme cases, a cessation of body and brain growth. If the starvation has lasted long enough, recuperation to full potential may not occur after food supply is restored, and mild to severe physical and emotional retardation may result. Other effects of famine and starvation upon children and adults have been noted to include reductions in general emotional vitality and sexual energy, some effects of which may per-

411

sist even after food supply is restored. Importantly, *the infant biophysically and emotionally withdraws and contracts under conditions of famine and starvation in a manner nearly identical to the equally traumatic effects of maternal deprivation and isolation.* Both sets of experiences have clear, lifelong effects that disturb the ability of adults to emotionally bond with both mate and offspring (Aykroyd 1974; Garcia and Escudero 1982; Prescott, Read, and Coursin 1975).

3) A number of other traumatic factors specifically related to the hard life in deserts and droughty regions were identified. One major example was the use of the restraining, head-moulding, back-pack cradle by migratory peoples of Central Asia, which appears to have inadvertently led to the dual traumas of infant cranial deformation and swaddling. Infant cranial deformation as a social institution mostly died out around c.1900 CE, but swaddling today appears to persist in the same general regions. The archaeological record suggests that cranial deformations and swaddling subsequently became institutionalized parts of childrearing tradition in those same areas (DeMeo 1998; Dingwall 1931; Gorer and Rickman 1962). Indeed, painful cranial deformations and swaddling became an identifying mark and cherished social institution of such peoples, to persist even after they gave up the nomadic existence for a settled lifestyle. Other major social institutions, such as male and female genital mutilations (circumcision, infibulation), were also found to be geographically centred on, and have their earliest origins within the great Old World desert belt (DeMeo 1986, 1998).

In the process of making the above determinations, it became increasingly apparent to me that early matrist social bonds might have first been shattered among subsistence-level cultures which had survived the devastating effects of severe, sequential droughts, desertification, and prolonged famine. With the progressive, generation-after-generation disruption of maternal-infant and male-female social bonds by hyperaridity, famine, starvation, and forced migrations, there would be a consequent development and intensification of patrist attitudes, behaviours, and social institutions. And these would gradually replace the older matristic ones. Patrism would have become fixed into the character structure just as hyperarid, desert conditions became fixed into the landscape. And once so fixed, patrism would remain with the afflicted people, irrespective of subsequent climate or food supply, given the behaviour-affecting, self-duplicating character of social institutions. Patrism would thereafter appear in the moister regions of plenty by virtue of irruptions of migrating, warlike peoples from adjacent desert regions.

The Geographical Aspects of Anthropology and Climatology

My preliminary cross-cultural review of behaviour and social institutions in a sample of 400 different subsistence-level, aboriginal cultures from around the world (taken from Textor 1967) and a more systematic and definitive global analysis derived from 1170 different cultures, using cultural data from Murdock's *Ethnographic Atlas* (1967), fully validated the matrist-patrist social organizational structure given in Table 1, with a high level of significance (see the large *Correlation Table of Sex-Economic Factors* in DeMeo 1986 and 1998). These standard cross-cultural analyses also confirmed the severe desert-patrist correlation, but also showed it was *not* valid for all semiarid lands or even hyperarid deserts of limited geographical size (i.e., the Atacama and Namib), where food and water supplies could be obtained by making a short journey. Moreover, wetland regions adjacent to the largest, most hyperarid deserts were found to be partly or entirely patrist in character, a fact that was later explained in the demonstrated migrations of peoples *out of the deserts* (DeMeo 1986, 1998). Murdock's *Ethnographic Atlas* did not contain any maps, and was composed almost exclusively of descriptive tabular data on aboriginal peoples living in their native regions. Data for North and South America, and Oceania, in large measure, reflected native, pre-European conditions. Murdock's data was gathered from hundreds of reliable ethnographic sources published roughly between 1750 to 1960; his data has been critically reviewed and subject to cross-checking and correction by other scholars, and is today widely used for cross-cultural social theory testing.

In my final analysis, which led to the development of a specific *World Behaviour Map*, each of the 1170 individual cultures was separately evaluated (by computer) according to 15 different variables, which approximated the matrist-patrist schema previously given in Table 1. Cultures exhibiting a high percentage of patrist characteristics for the 15 variables received an appropriately high score, while cultures with a low percentage of patrist characteristics (with a high degree of matrism) received an appropriately low score. Latitudes and longitudes were obtained for each culture, and a regional percent-patrist average was extracted for each 5° by 5° block of latitude and longitude. Figure 1, the World Behaviour Map, emerged from this procedure (DeMeo 1986, 1998).

The patterns on the World Behaviour Map were independently supported by separate maps of each of the 15 variables used in its construction, and by maps of other related variables (Male Genital Mutilations, Female Genital Mutilations, Infant Cranial Deformation and Swaddling, Areas Influenced or Occupied by Arab Armies, and by Turkish Armies) previously presented with more detailed discussion (DeMeo 1986, 1998). The World Behaviour Map clearly demonstrates that patrism was neither ubiquitous nor random in its worldwide distribution. Old World cultures were clearly more patrist than those in either Oceania or the New World. Furthermore, the area of most extreme patrism in the Old World is found in one large, contiguous swath, stretching across North Africa, the Near (Middle) East, and into Central Asia. Of major significance is the fact that *this same geographical territory encompasses what is today the most intense, widespread, and hyperarid of desert environments found on Earth.*

Maps of environmental factors related to extreme desert conditions demonstrate distributions very similar to that of extreme patrism on the World Behaviour Map. Figure 2 is, for instance, a map identifying the most hyperarid of desert environments as determined from the Budyko-Lettau dryness ratio (Budyko 1958; Hare 1977).

Fig. 1:
The World Behaviour Map

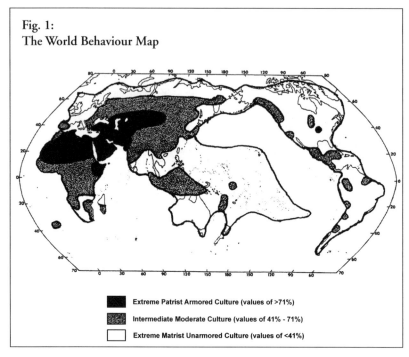

■ Extreme Patrist Armored Culture (values of >71%)

▨ Intermediate Moderate Culture (values of 41% - 71%)

□ Extreme Matrist Unarmored Culture (values of <41%)

This ratio contrasts the amount of evaporative energy available in a given environment relative to the amount of precipitation. It is a more sensitive indicator of stress within arid environments than those used in more standard climate classification systems, which may mislead one into thinking that all "desert" environments are similar in nature. Maps identifying other stressful environmental extremes, such as greatest precipitation variability, highest mean monthly maximum temperatures, vegetation-barren regions, regions of lowest carrying capacity, regions of desert soils, and uninhabited regions show very similar distributions of their most intense, widespread aspects within this same extreme desert-patrist territory (DeMeo 1986, 1998). I have given the name *Saharasia* to this broad expanse of correlated extreme climate and culture.

The Geographical Aspects of Archaeology and History

The highly structured distributions on the World Behaviour Map suggested that global patrism developed earliest within Saharasia, after which it was carried outward by migrating peoples to affect surrounding moister regions. The testing of this hypothesis regarding climate, behaviour, and mass-migrations in ancient times necessitated the creation of a new database composed of information on ancient climatic conditions, the migrations of peoples, past social factors relevant to the treatment of infants, children, and women, and tendencies towards male dominance, despotism, sadistic violence, and warfare. A new da-

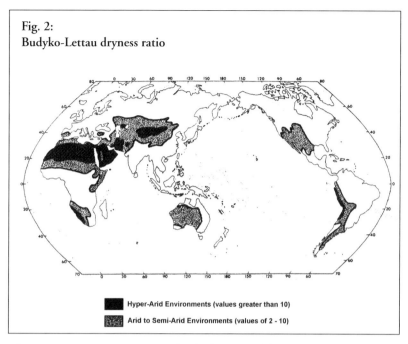

Fig. 2:
Budyko-Lettau dryness ratio

■ Hyper-Arid Environments (values greater than 10)
▨ Arid to Semi-Arid Environments (values of 2 - 10)

tabase containing over 10,000 individual time- and location-specific notecards
was developed and assembled chronologically; each card contained information
from the archaeological or historical literature identifying artifacts and/or ecological conditions for specific field sites or regions at specific times. Over 100
separate authoritative sources were consulted and outlined to compose this new
database, which allowed identification and comparison of ancient conditions
across broad geographical regions for similar time periods. Times and places
of widespread ecological and cultural transition, as well as the migrations and
settlement patterns of peoples, were thereby identified. My predominant focus
was on Saharasia and its moister Afro-Euro-Asian borderlands, but a significant
amount of data was also collected for Oceania and the New World (DeMeo
1986, 1998).

From the patterns observed in this database, it was clear that patrism developed its most widespread early expressions within Saharasia, at the same time
that the landscape underwent a major ecological transition, from relatively wet
to arid, desert conditions. Evidence from dozens of archaeological and paleocli-
matic studies indicates that the great desert belt of modern day Saharasia was,
prior to c.4000-3000 BCE, a semiforested grassland savanna. Large and small
fauna, such as elephant, giraffe, rhino, and gazelle, lived on the highland grasses,
while hippopotamus, crocodile, fish, snails, and mollusks thrived in streams,
rivers, and lakes. Today, most of this same North African, Middle-Eastern and
Central Asian terrain is hyperarid and often vegetation-barren. Some of the now
dry basins of Saharasia were then filled with giant lakes at levels tens to hundreds

of metres deep, while the canyons and wadis flowed with permanent streams and rivers (DeMeo 1986, 1998).

But what of the peoples who inhabited Saharasia during the wetter times of plenty? The evidence is also clear on this point: *These early peoples were almost entirely peaceful, unarmoured, and matrist in character.* Indeed, I have concluded that there does not exist any clear, compelling or unambiguous evidence for the existence of significant widespread or persisting patrism within any major region of Earth prior to c.4000 BCE. Only the most isolated and temporary of examples can be documented (DeMeo 2002). However, strong evidence exists for early and widespread peaceful matrist social conditions. These inferences are made partly from the *presence* of certain artifacts from those earliest times, which include: the sensitive and careful burial of the dead, irrespective of sex, with a relatively uniform grave wealth; sexually realistic female statues; and naturalistic, sensitive artwork on rock walls and pottery which emphasized women, children, music, the dance, animals, and the hunt. In later centuries, some of these same peaceful matrist peoples would progress technologically, and develop large, un-fortified agrarian and/or trading states, notably in Crete, the Indus Valley, and Soviet Central Asia. The inference of matrism in these early times is also made from the *absence* of archaeological evidence for chaos, warfare, sadism, and bru-tality, which becomes quite evident in more recent strata, after Saharasia dried up. This latter archaeological evidence includes: weapons of war; destruction layers in settlements; massive fortifications, temples, and tombs devoted to big-man rulers; infant cranial deformation; ritual murder of females in the tombs or graves of generally older men; ritual foundation sacrifices of children; mass or unkempt graves with mutilated bodies thrown in helter-skelter; and caste strati-fication, slavery, extreme social hierarchy, compulsory polygyny and concubi-nage, as determined from architecture, grave goods and other mortuary arrange-ments. Artwork style and subject matter of the later, dry periods also changes, to emphasize mounted warriors, horses, chariots, battles, and camels. Scenes of women, children, and daily life vanish. Naturalistic female statues and artwork simultaneously become abstract, unrealistic, or even fierce, losing their former gentle, nurturing, or erotic qualities; or they disappear entirely, to be replaced by statues of male gods or god-kings. Artwork quality as well as architectural styles decline for Old World sites at such times, to be followed in later years by monumental, warrior, and phallic motifs (DeMeo 1986, 1998).

With a few special exceptions, the overwhelming bulk of early evidence for chaotic social conditions and patrism on Earth can be found in those parts of Saharasia which began to dry up first, namely within, or very close to Arabia and Central Asia. These are discussed below, and in detail elsewhere (DeMeo 2002), but they are *exceptions which prove the rule:* Severe desertification and famine trauma greatly disturbed the original matrist social fabric, and promoted the development of patrist behaviours and social institutions; patrism was, in turn, compounded and intensified by widespread land-abandonment, migratory adjustments, and competition over scarce water resources.

The Genesis of Patrism in Saharasia

After c.4000-3500 BCE, radical social transformations are apparent in the ruins of previously peaceful, matrist settlements along river valleys in Central Asia, Mesopotamia, and North Africa. In each case, evidence for increasing aridity and land abandonment coincides with migratory pressures upon settlements with secure water supplies, such as those at oases, or on exotic rivers. Central Asia also experienced a shifting in lake levels and river beds coincidental to climatic instability and aridity, stimulating abandonment of large lakeshore or irrigation agricultural communities.

Settlements on the Nile and Tigris-Euphrates, as well as in the moister highland portions of the Levant, Anatolia, and Iran, were invaded and conquered by peoples abandoning Arabia and/or Central Asia, which continued to dry out. New despotic central states emerged thereafter. Tomb, temple, and fortification architecture, with evidence for ritual widow murder (eg., mother murder, when performed by the eldest son), cranial deformations, emphasis on the horse and camel, and growth of the military occurs following such invasions in almost every case I have studied. As these new despotic central states grew in power, they expanded their territories, sometimes to conquer the nomadic pastoral tribes still present on the desiccating steppe. Some of these despotic states periodically invaded into the wetlands adjacent to Saharasia to expand their territories. They either conquered local peoples in the wetlands or, failing to do so, stimulated defensive reactions among them, which can be seen in the subsequent appearance of fortifications, weapons technology, and an intermediate level of patrism in those wetlands. Other despotic Saharasian states eventually vanished from the history books as aridity intensified and dried up their subsistence (DeMeo 1986, 1998, 2002).

The Diffusion of Patrism into the Saharasian Borderlands

Patrism appeared in the wetter Saharasian borderlands after it first developed within the desiccating Saharasian core. As aridity gripped Saharasia, and as the armoured, patrist response increasingly gripped Saharasian peoples, migrations out of the dry regions increasingly put such peoples into contact with the more peaceful peoples of the moister Saharasian borderlands. Increasingly, the migrations out of Saharasia took place in the form of massive invasions of the more fertile border territories. In these borderlands, patrism took root not by virtue of desertification or famine trauma, but by the killing off and replacement of the original matrist populations by the invader patrist groups, or by the forced adoption of new patrist social institutions introduced by the invading, conquering peoples. For example, Europe was sequentially invaded after c.4000 BCE by Battle-Axe peoples, Kurgans, Scythians, Sarmatians, Huns, Arabs, Mongols, and Turks. Each took a turn at warring, conquering, pillaging, and generally transforming Europe towards an increasingly patrist character. European social institutions progressively turned away from matrism towards patrism, with the far western parts of Europe, notably Britain and Scandinavia, developing patrist conditions much later and in a more dilute form, than either Mediterranean or Eastern Europe, which were more profoundly influenced by Saharasian peoples.

Across the Old World, in the moister parts of China, peaceful matrist conditions likewise prevailed until the coming of the first extreme patrist Central Asian invaders, the Shang and Chou, after c.2000 BCE. Subsequent invasions by the Huns, Mongols, and others would reinforce patrism in wetland China. Japanese culture remained matrist a bit longer, given the isolating influence of the China Sea and Korean Strait, until the coming of the first invading patrist groups from the Asian mainland, such as the Yayoi, around c.1000 BCE. In South Asia, the peaceful, largely matrist settlements and trading states of the Indus River valley collapsed after c.1800 BCE, under the combined pressures of aridity and patrist warrior-nomad invaders from arid Central Asian lands. Patrism spread thereafter into India, and was intensified in later centuries by Hunnish, Arab, and Mongol invasions, which also came from Central Asia. Matrism similarly predominated in Southeast Asia until the onset of progressive patrist migrations and invasions, by both land and sea, from the patrist kingly states of China, India, Africa, and Islamic regions. In sub-Saharan Africa, available evidence suggests that patrism first appeared with the arrival of various southward-migrating peoples, around the time that North Africa dried up and was abandoned. Pharaonic Egyptian, Carthaginian, Greek, Roman, Byzantine, Bantu, Arab, Turkish, and Colonial European influences also increased African patrism in later years (DeMeo 1986, 1998).

The geographical patterns in these migrations, invasions, and settlement patterns are most striking. Two major patrist core zones appear in the data after c.4000 BCE, one in Arabia and the other in Central Asia, the respective homelands from which Semitic and Indoaryan peoples would migrate. These were also the first parts of Saharasia to start desiccating, though other portions of Saharasia would begin to dry up and convert to patrism within a few centuries. Elsewhere I have shown another historical aspect of these irruptions of desert warrior nomads, in maps of the territories occupied at one time or another by Arab and Turkish empires. The territories of these two groups, who were the last of a series of invaders coming from Arabia and Central Asia, encompass fully 100 percent of desert Saharasia, spilling outward into its moister borderlands (DeMeo 1998: 104).

These facts of geography explain why matrism was preserved to a greater extent in those regions most far removed from Saharasia. Regions at the periphery of Saharasia (particularly islands), such as England, Crete, Scandinavia, the Asian Arctic, Southern Africa, Southern India, Southeast Asia, and Island Asia, demonstrate a later historical acquaintance with or adoption of patrism, and a consequent dilution of patrism with pre-existing native matrist social institutions. From the various sources used to construct my database, Figure 3 was developed, suggesting patterns of diffusion of patrism within the Old World. The vectors are only a first approximation, but are in agreement with prior studies on the migrations and diffusion of peoples. These geographical patterns, taken from the literature of archaeology and history, are independently supported by a very similar spatial pattern in the more recent anthropological data, as previously given in Figure 1, the World Behaviour Map.

Fig. 3:
Patterns of diffusion of patrism within the Old World

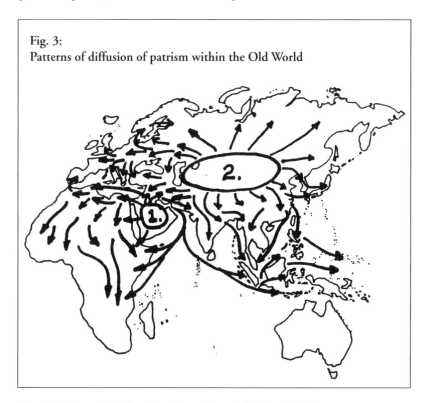

The Diffusion of Patrism into Oceania and the New World

These observations regarding the migrations of patrist peoples may be extended to include the trans-oceanic diffusion of patrism from the Old World, through Oceania, and possibly even into the New World. A map of the suggested migratory pathways is given in Figure 4, which assumes no source region for patrism other than Saharasia. This last map was derived from the various maps presented above, including the World Behaviour Map, and from other sources (DeMeo 1986, 1998). Additional research will clearly be needed to confirm or clarify these suggested pathways.

It is significant that patrism in the Americas was identified in the ethnographical data, and on the World Behaviour Map primarily among peoples who lived along the coasts or among peoples whose ancestors developed their earliest patrist

419

communities on coastal regions, or on major river systems—all of which implies navigation by boat. Furthermore, it is significant that the early patrist peoples of the Americas were the very same cultures for whom others have argued, on the basis of material culture, artwork, or linguistics, a pre-Columbian connection with the ocean-navigating patrist states of the Old World. This suggests, the earliest peoples to migrate into the Americas were peaceful and matristic in character, with patristic groups arriving only later, after c.4000 BCE, and settling predominantly along coastal or river-valley regions (DeMeo 1986, 1998).

Fig. 4:
The Global Diffusion of Patrism from Saharasia

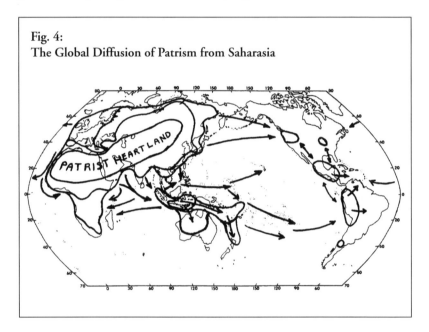

More Recent Archaeological Findings

Space does not permit any detailed discussion of several key but isolated examples of social violence that have been identified by archaeologists for time periods well before my c.4000 BCE marker date for the first genesis of widespread patrism and social violence. However, they are not exemplary of any widespread or persisting social condition, and as I have shown elsewhere (DeMeo 2002), they all appear to have developed within earlier epochs of climatic instability and drought-desert-famine conditions (i.e., Jebel Sahaba, SE Australia), or they are found among peoples who directly migrated away from a desert or drought-affected region (i.e., the Ofnet-Schletz-Talheim massacre sites are linked with early migrations out of the Middle East). Once again, they are "exceptions which prove the rule" of a drought-desert-famine mechanism for temporary and isolated examples of patrism and social violence during those earlier periods. Such findings do not overturn my Saharasian discovery, but instead, strengthen it (DeMeo 2002).

Conclusions

The findings summarized here strongly suggest the earliest human societies were peaceful and egalitarian in nature, where violence was the rare exception, rather than the rule. This implies the innate portions of behaviour are limited to the pleasure-directed aspects of life and social living, which impart distinct survival and health advantages to the growing child, which nurture bonds of love between men and women, and thereby function to preserve genuinely civil society. These are the matrist behaviours and social institutions, which support and protect the bonding functions between newborn babies and their mothers, which nurture the child through its various developmental stages, and which encourage and protect the bonds of love and pleasurable excitation which spontaneously develop between the young male and female. From these pleasure-directed biological impulses come other socially cooperative tendencies, and life-protecting, life-enhancing social institutions. Such impulses and behaviours, which are pro-child, pro-female, sex-positive and pleasure-oriented, have been demonstrated to exist in more recent times predominantly outside the bounds of the Saharasian desert belt. However, my work strongly suggests they once were the dominant forms of behaviour and social organization everywhere on the planet, before the great Old World desert belt of Saharasia developed. Given the new evidence presented here, patrism, to include its child-abusive, female-subordinating, sex-repressive, and destructively aggressive components, is best and most simply explained as a contractive and pathological emotional and cultural response to the traumatic famine conditions that first developed when Saharasia dried up after c.4000 BCE, a response which subsequently spread out of the desert through the diffusion of traumatized and affected peoples, and their damaged social institutions.

James DeMeo is director of the Orgone Biophysical Research Lab in Ashland, Oregon, which he founded in 1978. He studied Environmental Science at Florida International University, and received his doctorate in Geography from the University of Kansas in 1986 where he specialized in the social and environmental aspects of desertification. He was formerly on the faculty of the Geography departments at Illinois State University and the University of Miami, and has undertaken extensive field work in the deserts of the South Western U.S.A., and in Israel, Egypt, Namibia, and the Horn of Africa. He has published articles on the issues of energy resources, health, cultural history, environmental problems, and experimental life-energy research.

[1]Some time after my major findings had been accepted and published as a dissertation through the University of Kansas (DeMeo 1986), I learned of Riane Eisler's (1987a) study *Chalice and the Blade*, which identified *dominator* and *partnership* types of social organization. These are nearly identical in concept to the respective patrist and matrist forms of social organization as defined here. Subsequently, Brian Griffith's work *The Gardens of Their Dreams: Desertification*

and Culture in World History (Griffith 2001) was published, independently corroborating the findings presented in my *Saharasia*.

[2]The fifteen variables were: Female Premarital Sex Taboos, Segregation of Adolescent Boys, Male Genital Mutilations, Bride Price, Family Organization, Marital Residence, Post-Partum Sex Taboo, Cognatic Kin Groups, Descent, Land Inheritance, Movable Property Inheritance, High God, Class Stratification, Caste Stratification, and Slavery.

References

Aykroyd, W. 1974. *The Conquest of Famine*. London, Chatto & Windus.

Bell, B. 1971. "The Dark Ages in Ancient History, 1: The First Dark Age in Egypt." *American Journal of Archaeology* 75 (1): 1-26.

Budyko, M.I. 1958. *The Heat Balance of the Earth's Surface*. Trans. N. A. Stepanova. Washington DC: U.S. Dept. of Commerce.

Cahill, K. 1982. *Famine*. Maryknoll: Orbis Books.

DeMeo, J. 1986. *On the Origins and Diffusion of Patrism: The Saharasian Connection*. Dissertation. University of Kansas, Geography Department. Xerox available from Natural Energy Works, PO Box 864, El Cerrito, CA 94530.

DeMeo, J. 1998. *Saharasia: The 4000 BCE Origins of Child Abuse, Sex-Repression, WarfareandSocial Violence, in the Deserts of the Old World*. Ashland:Natural Energy.

DeMeo, J. 2002. "Update on Saharasia: Ambiguities and Uncertainties in 'War Before Civilization.'" *Pulse of the Planet* 5:15-40.

Dingwall, E. J. 1931. *Artificial Cranial Deformation*. London: J. Bale, Sons & Danielson, Ltd.

Eisler, R. 1987a. *The Chalice and the Blade*. San Francisco: Harper & Row.

Eisler, R. 1987b. "Woman, Man, and the Evolution of Social Structure." *World Futures* 23 (1): 79f.

Elwin, V. 1947. *The Muria and their Ghotul*. Calcutta: Oxford University Press.

Elwin, V. 1968. *The Kingdom of the Young*. Bombay: Oxford University Press.

Garcia, R. 1981. *Nature Pleads Not Guilty*. Vol. 1 of the *Drought and Man* Series, IFIAS Project. New York: Pergamon Press.

Garcia, R., and J. Escudero. 1982. *The Constant Catastrophe: Malnutrition, Famines, and Drought*. Vol. 2 of the *Drought and Man* Series, IFIAS Project. New York: Pergamon Press.

Gimbutas, M. 1965. *Bronze Age Cultures in Central and Eastern Europe*. The Hague: Mouton.

Gimbutas, M. 1982. *The Goddesses and Gods of Old Europe*. Berkeley: University of California Press.

Gorer, G., and J. Rickman. 1962. *The People of Great Russia: A Psychological Study*. New York: W. W. Norton.

Goettner-Abendroth, H. 1995. *The Goddess and her Heros: Matriarchal Religion in Mythology, Fairy-Tales and Poetry*. Stow: Anthony Publishing Co.

Goettner-Abendroth, H. 1998. *Matriarchat in Südchina. Eine Forschungsreise zu den Mosuo* (*Matriarchy in South China: Monograph of Mosuo Matriarchal Society*). Stuttgart: Verlag Kohlhammer.

Griffith, B. 2001. *The Gardens of Their Dreams: Desertification and Culture in World History*. London: Fernwood/Zed Books.

Hallet, J. P., and A. Relle. 1973. *Pygmy Kitabu*. New York: Random House.

Hare, K. 1977. "Connections Between Climate and Desertification." *Environmental Conservation* 4 (2):81-90.

Huntington, E. 1907. *The Pulse of Asia*. New York: Houghton-Mifflin.

Huntington, E. 1911. *Palestine and its Transformation*. New York: Houghton-Mifflin.

Klaus, M. H., and J. H. Kennell. 1976. *Maternal-Infant Bonding: The Impact of Early Separation or Loss on Family Development*. St. Louis: C. V. Mosby.

LeBoyer, F. 1975. *Birth Without Violence*. New York: Alfred Knopf.

Malinowski, B. 1927. *Sex and Repression in Savage Society*. London: Humanities Press.

Malinowski, B. 1932. *The Sexual Life of Savages*. London: Routledge & Keegan Paul.

Montagu, A. 1971. *Touching: The Human Significance of the Skin*. New York: Columbia University Press.

Murdock, G. P. 1967. *Ethnographic Atlas*. Pittsburgh: University Pittsburgh Press.

Prescott, J. 1975. "Body Pleasure and the Origins of Violence." *Bulletin of Atomic Scientists* (November):10-20.

Prescott, J., M. Read, and D. Coursin. 1975. *Brain Function and Malnutrition*. New York: J. Wiley & Sons.

Reich, W. 1971. *The Invasion of Compulsory Sex-Morality*. 1935. New York: Farrar, Straus & Giroux.

Reich, W. 1973. *Function of the Orgasm*. 1942. New York: Farrar, Straus & Giroux.

Reich, W. 1973. *The Sexual Revolution*. 1945. New York: Octagon Books.

Reich, W. 1970. *The Mass Psychology of Fascism*. 1947. New York: Farrar, Straus & Giroux.

Stewart, D., and L. Stewart. 1978a. *Safe Alternatives in Childbirth*. Chapel Hill: NAPSAC.

Stone, M. 1976. *When God Was a Woman*. New York: Dial.

Sorokin, P. 1975. *Hunger as a Factor in Human Affairs*. Gainesville: University of Florida Press.

Taylor, G. R. 1953. *Sex in History*. London: Thames & Hudson.

Textor, R. B. 1967. *A Cross-Cultural Summary*. New Haven: HRAF Press.

Turnbull, C. 1961. *The Forest People*. New York: Simon & Schuster.

Turnbull, C. 1972. *The Mountain People*. New York: Simon & Schuster.

Velikovsky, I. 1984. *Mankind in Amnesia*. New York: Doubleday.

HEIDE GOETTNER-ABENDROTH

Notes on the Rise and Expansion of Patriarchy

To understand the rise and development of patriarchy it is first of all necessary to have knowledge of the non-patriarchal, or matriarchal, societies
they originated from. The second crucial point is to avoid explaining the
rise of patriarchy in a mono-causal way—that is, not to look for one single reason
for this worldwide and long-lasting transformation. The question of patriarchy's
rise can only be answered if the many constituent causes that contributed to it
at each step of its complicated development are taken into account. At different
times, on different continents, during the period of transition to patriarchy, new
and different constituent causes effected multiple changes.

Patriarchies are societies of domination, and it is a myth that they are universal. This is merely a pillar of patriarchal ideology. To explain the rise of patriarchy
means to explain the rise of domination, and this is not at all an easy task. On
the contrary, because the patterns of domination are dependent on so many
interrelated conditions, long periods of time had to pass before these forms of
social organization were invented and perfected.

This article will look at theses about the rise of patriarchy and evaluate their
merits: the main ones are (1) recognition of biological paternity; (2) technical
innovation; (3) cattle herding; (4) social differentiation based on division of labour; and, last but not least, (5) men's character defects.

Criticism of Theses on the Rise of Patriarchy

Biological Paternity

There is much to say against the thesis that the recognition of biological paternity led to the change from matriarchy to patriarchy. In order to recognize paternity and patrilineal genealogy, women have to be isolated, locked away, and live
monogamously. This happened historically quite recently, and only under the
pressure of domination. In order to establish this paternity recognition system,
an enforcement staff must be organized to suppress and subject the majority of
the people. This process includes the usurpation of culture and re-interpretation
of religious ideas so as to enable the rulers to produce their own ideology. These
are complicated social strategies directed against women. Thus, for recognition

of paternity to happen, domination must have been accomplished first.

Furthermore, biological fatherhood was sometimes understood in matriarchies, but it was of no importance because it was eclipsed by "social fatherhood." In matriarchal societies, the mother's brother, the maternal uncle, is the "social father" of his nephews and nieces, who share his clan name. The biological "father" in our sense does not have the same clan name as "his" children do, so he is not seen as being akin to them. Additionally, patriarchy could not have developed based on a few individuals becoming aware of their biological fatherhood. This is because the social pre-conditions for patriarchal paternity, such as taking away the women from their mother clans, confining them with one sole husband, and prohibiting them from having lovers, must all be in place in order for biological paternity to become significant. Clearly, biological paternity and patrilinearity presuppose patriarchal domination for their enforcement but could not, by themselves, produce it.

Technical Innovation

An equally weak argument is that the introduction of a single technical innovation such as the plow, which depended on men's physical strength to operate, led to the rise of patriarchy. But anthropological evidence proves that women in matriarchal societies were by no means the artificially acculturated "weaker sex" (Briffault 1969; Goettner-Abendroth 1998). Furthermore, in many matriarchal societies the men do the plowing and other heavy work without the rise of any patriarchal tendencies. It is by no means plausible that a complex social structure like matriarchy could have changed into another complex social structure like patriarchy simply because of a new working technique.

The same objection is true for the argument that horse-riding and cattle-breeding, which came along with pastoral cultures, led to the rise of patriarchy. Though this thesis has been favoured by many scholars (e.g., Engels 1972; Bornemann 1975), much historical and anthropological evidence contradicts it.

Pastoral nomadic society did not create an original and independent culture by itself, as is widely believed. Rather, this type of society was derived from the matriarchal agricultural societies, which bred domestic animals much earlier. It was developed in regions which are too barren to establish agriculture, but it remained heavily dependent on it, because humans need vegetable food. In fact, nomadic society itself once had a matriarchal structure, and in some cases, this has lasted until today. For example, the Tuareg people of the Central Sahara lived until recently as a pastoral nomadic society. With their neighbours they were warlike, riding on camels and horses and robbing people. However, they preserved their age-old matriarchal social patterns up to the present day. They live matrilineally and matrilocally in tents, and the herds of camels, goats, and sheep belong to the women (Claudot-Hawad 1984, 2001; Goettner-Abendroth 2000). Similar patterns are valid for some pastoral peoples of Siberia and Mongolia. In the case of Old Tibet, pastoral nomadic society remained a marginal part of a matriarchal agricultural society in the river valleys, and was dependent on it (Goettner-Abendroth 1991, 1999). So cattle-breeding and horse-riding by themselves cannot be the reason for the rise of patriarchy, because they do not explain the rise of male domination.

Cattle Herding

There is also the thesis that ownership of large cattle herds provided the power base for the first patriarchs (Engels 1972). But in egalitarian societies—from which the patriarchies have developed—the initial accumulation of large amounts of property in the hands of a few is not possible, because the other members would actively resist it. Many examples from different kinds of still existing egalitarian societies provide evidence of such resistance (Sigrist 1979; Howe 1978). The patterns of domination have to be established first, and egalitarian economic principles abolished; then, and only then, is it possible for someone, against the will of the majority, to accumulate private property on a large scale.

Division of Labour

Just as implausible is the thesis that, in the course of history, a complex division of labour and a corresponding social differentiation led to patriarchy. This implicitly presumes that matriarchal societies must have been more "primitive," because they came into existence before patriarchal ones did. This linear progression theory of the historical development of human cultures is pure fiction. If it were true, we would now have the most perfect society of all.

From this point of view, the development of history is distorted. Many different forms of society are omitted, including those that have fostered different special skills and have now vanished without successors. Furthermore, Neolithic matriarchal societies (from 10,000 BCE) included the first urban centres in Anatolia, Palestine, and Southeastern Europe to exhibit a high degree of division of labour and of social differentiation. This high degree of culture would not have been found among the patriarchal troops of warriors that conquered them.

Men's Character Defects

A few last questionable theses should be presented at this point. One of these is that the nature of men is "aggressive and wicked" as demonstrated by the fact that they have invented the patriarchal society of warfare and domination. A similar argument is that matriarchy made men uncomfortable because in matriarchal societies men were marginalized. So they allegedly revolted, and the matriarchy was overthrown and patriarchy established. This argument assumes that the feelings of matriarchal men are the same as the feelings of patriarchal men of contemporary civilizations. In our society, men tend to think they are marginal unless they are the focus of their mothers' care, the focus of women's lives, and the focus of society in general. But it is different with the feelings of matriarchal men, because the patterns of matriarchal societies are different. There is no historical or ethnological evidence in favour of these biological or psychological arguments.

Notes on Serious Arguments

There are some other, more relevant arguments that show us how to solve the problem. The archaeologist Marija Gimbutas (1991, 1997) has provided much evidence from the cultural area of Western Asia and Europe from 4500 till 2500 BCE. This period of two millennia is characterized by three waves of migrations by Indo-European herding peoples with a patriarchal social organization, who advanced from the steppes of Southern Russia to the matriarchal urban cultures in Eastern Europe and then into the Central and Western parts of Europe. She has described the consequences for the matriarchal cultures of Old Europe—these urban centres were completely destroyed.

But how did this begin? What was the reason that made the Indigenous peoples of Central and Western Asia give up their native, matriarchally organized agricultural societies (demonstrated by archaeological evidence going back to 7,000 BCE) and to survive as herders and horsemen? And what induced them to leave the steppes of Southern Russia for a long-term catastrophic migration towards the west?

According to Gimbutas (1991), the Indo-European peoples hunted the wild horse and domesticated it, and in this way they achieved a new source for food and a new mobility that gave them the opportunity for increased migration. But in spite of her well-documented description, based on archaeological findings and linguistic research, Gimbutas could not convincingly explain how this nomadic culture actually developed, and how it became patriarchally organized. Her central thesis in this regard is: "Horse riding changed the course of European prehistory" (354). But this falls short of being an explanation for the rise of patriarchy. This is a much more complex social development than could have been invented by some horse-riding thieves with a propensity toward violence. Unfortunately, Gimbutas uncritically incorporates Engels' theory that some technical innovation and wealth that derived from cattle would automatically bring patriarchy along with it.

So we still have the question of what induced certain Indigenous peoples in Central and Western Asia to give up their native matriarchal agricultural societies and become a nomadic hunting and herding culture supported by the use of horses. We have to look deeper to find an answer.

At this point, let me make a distinction between "regulated migration" and "catastrophic migration." "Regulated migrations" are, for example, those undertaken by Paleolithic peoples who followed the migration routes of wild game. Another example of "regulated migrations" are those of the agricultural Neolithic peoples who moved to a new place to found a new settlement whenever a village or a city had become too big for the tilled land that surrounded it. These movements of migration opened up land, mostly along the courses of rivers and the coasts, to be cultivated by humans.

In contrast to this, "catastrophic migrations" are caused by wide-ranging natural catastrophes that do not necessarily happen suddenly, but rather creep forward slowly with devastating effects. Such natural catastrophes are the drying up, flooding, or freezing of huge areas of land—possibly caused by the shift of the earth's magnetic poles.

In his work, the geographer James DeMeo (1998, 2002) has demonstrated this. According to De Meo, the profound climatic changes in Central and Western Asia, and the consequent hunger-driven migrations, were the catalyst for social violence, wars, and the development of patriarchy. This is a very interesting theory, because it is founded not on speculations, but on solid geographical evidence.

However, I am critical of the way DeMeo uses his theory too generally. The kind of patriarchalization that occurred in Central Asia and Europe was unknown in South and North America, and in the Pacific area. There were different catalysts for the development of patriarchy in those regions, and these processes still need to be researched.

We also have to explain why, if they depended on catastrophic change, the invention of violence, war, and patriarchy did not develop earlier? In the long history of humanity (about six million years) such wide-ranging catastrophes have occurred repeatedly (for example, the Ice Ages). Because of such catastrophes, whole cultures and peoples have had to move on, again and again, or else remain and perish. But these upheavals did not cause patriarchy to develop at that time.

Generally, I think, in his theory, DeMeo clearly explains the constituent causes of the rise of violence, but his theory falls short of explaining the rise of patriarchy. It is not possible to explain the latter by giving a setting of *physical and psychological* causes only (according to W. Reich's theory), because patriarchy is a new structure of society. Therefore serious socio-historical argumentation is needed to explain it, following its different developments in different continents.

Developing the Outline of an Explanation

Based on the theoretical steps set out by Gimbutas and DeMeo, which are of great value to further research on this topic, and relying on my own interdisciplinary research, I want to suggest a step-by-step scenario that describes how patriarchy could have arisen:

First Step
Geographic research like DeMeo's demonstrates that at around the time of 5000-4000 BCE or even earlier, Central and Western Asia experienced a change of climate, which turned vast areas into dry steppe and desert. The mountain ranges of Central Asia once had much more water and fertile land than they do today. The plains once had rich agricultural regions, and flourishing agricultural cities once existed even in the now desolate Gobi desert. But during this period, about six to seven thousand years ago, the source of nourishment, the ground itself, literally dried up under the feet of the large populations who lived there.

They were forced to emigrate in order to survive.

Such migrations, even if they are "catastrophic," come to pass very slowly. It is quite likely that with every step these people took in the movement towards arable land, they tried at each new place to till the soil in the attempt to build a new settlement. But the expanding steppe caught up with them again and again. This fight for survival, in a land that was becoming more and more inhospitable, must have lasted for generations. But it was hopeless, and slowly it must have led to the complete breakdown of matriarchal agriculture.

Second Step

In times of trouble, human societies tend to turn from more developed forms to older and simpler ones, and this could have been the case here. When there was no more land to be cultivated, these peoples, in their distress, returned to Paleolithic practices, and became hunters and gatherers of the steppe. In any given group, if the men, as "secondary hunters"—because hunting was not their original culture—succeeded in nourishing the whole population through their hunting prowess, then the role of those men would have become important. But their new importance did not yet add up to patterns of domination and patriarchy.

In terms of their historical development, it is much more likely that men did *not* succeed in nourishing all members of their clans. Then they may have separated themselves from the women, children and old people, leaving all food and resources to them. It is a matriarchal principle that in times of distress matriarchal men leave their clans not to be a burden for women and children—regarded as more important for the future of the community—and try to survive on their own (for example, the Tuareg practice this in times of severe draught; see Goettner-Abendroth, 2000). The female clan members stayed behind and tried to survive with their hereditary techniques of agriculture—and presumably perished. Large clan structures typical of matriarchies could not be maintained under such conditions, and the social structures broke down.

As disorderly troops of hunters, the men migrated further to the west or to the south. Further, whole peoples migrated in ox-carts with their herds, to find new homeland, fertile and empty, where they—if they had been successful—could have re-organized their traditional culture. In this way the position of women, who had lost their old culture of agriculture and the matrilineal clans and clan houses, completely declined. Some Indo-European peoples arrived in Northern India in this state of affairs.

Of course, the taming and riding of horses played an important part in this process, but it was not its main cause. And, as with hunting, even if the role of men did become more and more important in this migratory process, that does not by itself explain the development of patriarchal structures.

Third Step

Even after the development of a pastoral culture in the steppes of Southern

Russia, the Indo-European people continued to move toward the west. The only explanation is that even the steppes of Southern Russia did not turn out, in the end, to be the new homeland, because they were drying up, too. So the peoples were forced to continue their catastrophic migration with or without their cattle. This is how they arrived in the highly developed urban cultures around the Black Sea, in Eastern Europe, and in Northern India.

They may have looked in wonder upon the abundance and wealth manifested in these places. This was indeed the land they had always longed for. But, of course, it was not empty!

Now another constituent cause came into play. As long as enough empty land had existed to absorb catastrophic migrations in human history, the situation did not lead to extreme changes. For example, during the Ice Ages, peoples migrated into southern regions, and returned when the ice-fields withdrew, where they continued to practice their traditional cultures. But now it was a different story for the migrating peoples, who could not find enough empty fertile land to absorb their migration. For, right at this crucial time, about 5000 BCE, the increased human population density on earth had reached a critical level. There no longer was empty fertile land on which the emigrants from spreading deserts could settle.

Fourth Step

In this situation, what should the migrating peoples do? Should they now turn back to the steppe and desert, prey to hunger and death, or should they instead take up arms—this time against other humans rather than animals—and take possession of these already occupied green lands? At this crucial time in their struggle for existence, the second possibility was chosen: for the first time in history, for their own survival, men waged war on other humans. So it is not a special form of culture—such as a horse-riding, pastoral culture—that necessarily tends toward brutality and brings forth war all by itself, but it is rather the necessity to survive that generates such actions.

The peaceful urban cultures were not prepared for such attacks, and so they found themselves helpless victims. Of course, some degree of peaceful immigration and a sort of co-existence also could have taken place. But with wave after wave of uprooted peoples arriving and pushing their way into the fertile regions, there was little hope for a solution in which there could be enough for everybody and the possibility of peace.

This was the invention of war.

Fifth Step

In many cases the invaded villages and cities were simply robbed and burnt down. But this is not the best solution, because it leaves behind wasted land. A much more strategic solution was to conquer the region, and now a new structure developed: the invention of classes. The small group of rulers who belonged to a foreign people became the upper class by pure violence, and a large group of the vanquished Indigenous people, who were forced now to work for the rulers, constituted the lower class. At this point, and only then, patriarchy begins, since the first structure of domination has been invented. Simultaneously, patriarchal consciousness begins, which celebrates violence and domination. It is based on two axioms: "All power comes from weapons" and "War is the father of everything."

Sixth Step

But the Indigenous peoples, greater in number and interrelated, would not have tolerated such foreign rule for long if the dominating group of warrior-kings had not developed further techniques of domination. Moreover, the usurpers now claimed credit for the development of the subjugated people's culture, arguing that before they arrived, no culture had existed at all, and insisting that they were the ones who had led the people out their state of brutish dullness into the right culture. This is the basis of patriarchal ideology.

It is clear that only warrior-kings with the ability to develop such domination techniques could have maintained their rule. The others would have been assimilated or expelled—as the history of all these mounted, warlike peoples show who invaded Eastern Europe. After a short, victorious period of robbing and burning they collapsed and had to withdraw into the steppe; they could not establish themselves by building societal structures of duration. Those who invented the new domination techniques could do it, and a central point of the development of their domination was the discrimination directed against women. In the matriarchies, women had always been the bearers of all culture. Now that their matriarchal clans were destroyed, they were raped and dragged as helpless individuals into patriarchal clans, isolated from social life and robbed of their grown-up children, until they existed only as locked-up beasts of birth. Such was the process of inventing paternity and patriarchal genealogy, which consolidated the victory over women and matriarchal society.

Notes on the Expansion of Patriarchy

I would like to discuss a last question here: The worldwide expansion of patriarchy over the past 6000 years or so of human history has constantly created chaos such as wars, conquests, oppression, and civil conflicts laboriously choreographed by the rulers of the day. In its relatively short history, patriarchy has proved to be extremely turbulent and unstable, as shown by the quickly changing "world empires" with their high consumption of human lives. Why has such a violent, destructive form of society been so successful in propagating itself all over the world?

The answer is: Where patriarchal structures of domination were established, these peoples with their strict military organization put pressure on their neighbours, threatening to dominate them. The initial, occasional pressure from the natural environment that once pushed peoples to migrate now turned into a constant pressure exerted by the human environment upon non-patriarchal peoples. The course of history worldwide shows it clearly: patriarchal societies based on strategic thinking and military organization have unremittingly threatened their neighbours with conquest, have in fact conquered them, and have thus destroyed their social order.

Other peoples, under similar pressure from patriarchal neighbours, have fought against it. However, this self-defense has forced them to adopt the strategic and military techniques of their patriarchal neighbours. Such structures of resistance, which sometimes arise in wars of liberation, have changed matriarchal societies from the inside. First of all, the importance of women, who normally do not belong to the warrior caste, declines. From being protectresses of all life, they turn into creatures who have to be protected.

The stronger the pressure on such a society, the more important chiefs and warriors become in the process of time, since it is they who have to do all the fighting for autonomy. Thus, the old structure of society, which was based on equality and peace, ceases to exist, while patriarchal patterns creep in and slowly develop into a full patriarchy. These are the reasons why patriarchal structures of domination—once they have been established—have become a worldwide epidemic.

Looking at it like this, it seems we are facing an extremely difficult future. Today the overpopulation of the earth has reached a much higher critical level, with the industrial nations as overpopulated as the countries of the so-called "Third World." At the same time, climatic catastrophes on a large scale are already underway. Neither nature nor the international structures of human society are in balance. What can be done about these problems? How can we deal with the patriarchal superstructure, today called "globalization," in a highly armed world?

Answers to these questions are rare. And yet the only sensible thing that can still be done is to break up the dangerous superstructure of industrial patriarchy that rules the world today, and to create small, economically independent units. These could dissolve the superstructures from below. In a materially simpler way of life lies the possibility of self-education and the education of others towards a new culture: "culture" in the sense of a humane life in small communities, like affinity groups, clans of siblings by choice, and regional networks based on matriarchal values, which foster mutual attention and assistance and a high ethical level of interaction and relationship with nature.

Matriarchal cultures give us the best examples and the widest array of suggestions for this future. They show the kind of social and cultural intelligence that is the only thing worth developing, and that maybe can open the way to new possibilities. In this sense, I think education for a new matriarchal culture is urgently needed, in order to detach us as thoroughly, and as quickly as possible from the context of the patriarchal barbarism that surrounds us.

Translation by Heide Solveig Goettner and Karen P. Smith

References

Bornemann, Ernest. 1975. *Das Patriarchat*. Frankfurt: Verlag Fischer.

Briffault, Robert. 1969. *The Mothers*. 1927. New York: The Macmillan Co.

Claudot-Hawad, Hélène. 1984. "Femme idéale et femmes sociales chez les Touaregs de l'Ahaggar." *Production pastorale et société* 14: 93-105.

Claudot-Hawad, Hélène. 2001. *"Eperonner le monde». Nomadisme, cosmos et politique chez les Touaregs."* Aix-en-Provence: Edisud.

DeMeo, James. 1998. *Saharasia: The 4000 BCE Origins of Child Abuse, Sex-Repression, Warfare and Social Violence, In the Deserts of the Old World*. Ashland: Natural Energy.

DeMeo, James. 2002. "Update on Saharasia: Ambiguities and Uncertainties." "*'War Before Civilization'.*" *Pulse of the Planet* 5: 15-40.

Engels, Friedrich. 1972. *Origin of the Family, Private Property, and the State*. 1884, 1890. New York: International Publishers.

Gimbutas, Marija. 1991. *The Civilization of the Goddess: The World of Old Europe*. Ed. Joan Marler. San Francisco: HarperSanFrancisco.

Gimbutas, Marija. 1997. *The Kurgan Culture and the Indo-Europeanization of Europe. Selected articles from 1952-1993*. Eds. M. R. Dexter and K. Jones-Bley. *Journal of Indo-European Studies* Monograph No. 18, Washington D.C.: Institute for The Study of Man.

Goettner-Abendroth, Heide. 1991 and 1999. *Das Matriarchat II.1. Stammesgesellschaften in Ostasien, Indonesien, Ozeanien (Matriarchy II.1. Matriarchal Societies in Eastern Asia, Indonesia, and Pacifique Area)*. Stuttgart: Verlag Kohlhammer.

Goettner-Abendroth, Heide. 2000. *Das Matriarchat II.2. Stammesgesellschaften in Amerika, Indien, Afrika (Matriarchy II.2. Matriarchal Societies in America, India, Africa)*. Stuttgart: Verlag Kohlhammer.

Goettner-Abendroth, Heide. 1998. *Matriarchat in Südchina. Eine Forschungsreise zu den Mosuo (Matriarchy in South China, Monograph of the Mosuo Matriarchal Society)*. Stuttgart: Verlag Kohlhammer.

Goettner-Abendroth, Heide. 2005. "Patriarchy as Society of Domination. Notes on its Rise and Development." Ed. Cristina Biaggi. *The Rule of Mars: Readings on the Origins, History and Impact of Patriarchy*. Manchester: Knowledge, Ideas and Trends. 27-42.

Howe, J. 1978. "How the Cuna keep their Chiefs in Line." *MAN* 13. Royal Anthropological Institute of Great Britain and Ireland.

Sigrist, Christian. 1979. *Regulierte Anarchie*. Frankfurt: Verlag Suhrkamp.

Part VIII
Matriarchal Politics

Declaration on Matriarchal Politics

O n the last day of the Second World Congress on Matriarchal Studies, "Societies of Peace," held in San Marcos, at the Texas State University in 2005, a political declaration was developed. The speakers and many participants expressed their ideas on how to generate concrete alternatives and practical solutions to the patriarchal system of exploitation, and what steps could be taken to promote the re-establishment of peaceful societies. This declaration emphasizes the political significance of both of these congresses and of modern Matriarchal Studies.

What Matriarchal Politics Mean

Heide Goettner-Abendroth (Germany)

What is matriarchal politics? It is based on modern Matriarchal Studies and its aim is to create an egalitarian economy and a peaceful society. How this can be achieved is clearly demonstrated by matriarchal societies whose patterns have lived over millennia. Their economics, politics, social organization, and spirituality are inseparably connected, and the purpose of all of it is to provide a good life for everybody.

Economically, the lesson of matriarchies is to develop a new subsistence economy, based on local and regional units. It is self-sufficient and creates circles of gift-giving. Women are the mainstays of these economic structures. Regionalization under the guidance of women is a way to a matriarchal economy.

On the social level, we learn from matriarchies to create and support communities that are based on affinity. They are formed on the basis of a spiritual-philosophical rapport between the members, who feel like siblings by choice. They form a symbolic matri-clan, because these clans are initiated, created and lead by women. The decisive factors are the needs of women and children who are the future of humanity. Men are intergrated as equal members.

On the political level, the matriarchal consensus principle is of utmost importantce for a truly egalitarian society. It is the foundation for building new matriarchal communities. The symbolic matri-clans are the true decision-makers, even if the consensus principle is broadened onto local and regional levels.

On the cultural level, the lesson of matriarchies is to leave behind all hierarchical religions with a claim to the total truth. Instead, it is necessary to regard the world as holy, to love and to protect it, because everything in the world is divine. Matriarchal spirituality includes matriarchal tolerance: nobody has to "believe" anything. There is no dogma, but the participation in the continuous, manifold celebration of life and the visible world.

In that way, we can create working "matriarchal models" which are the component parts of a new humane society. <www.hagia.de>

Collective Political Declaration (read by Genevieve Vaughan)

International Matriarchal Politics stands against white supremacist patriarchal capitalist homogenization and the globalization of misery. It stands for egalitarianism, diversity, and the economics of the heart. Many matriarchal societies still exist around the world and they propose an alternative, life affirming model to patriarchal raptor capitalism.

The movement to preserve ethnic cultures should recognize the specificity and importance of matriarchies and the contributions these societies make to the sanity and health of the world. Instead they are being attacked by wave after wave of colonization. For example, WalMart is locating into Juchitàn, where markets controlled by women and integrated into life-affirming relationships and practices will be taken over and erased. Under the disguise of progress, this economic colonialism tricks the people into giving up their precious cultural achievements in favour of false promises of jobs and a better life.

In mutual respect and honouring our diversity, we call on all women to make an activist commitment to preserve existing matriarchies and to recognize themselves as matriarchal peoples caught in the trap of patriarchal capitalism.

We oppose policies of governments and businesses that dispossess people of their spiritual and economic heritage including the treasure of Indigenous languages. Capitalist patriarchy is breaking the laws of Mother Nature, invading sacred places, and plundering the biodiversity that has been the sustenance of, and under the stewardship of, indigenous peoples for millennia. We assert that it is a moral act to pull up and eliminate transgenic corn, and we stand in solidarity with our sisters everywhere in the assertion of a matriarchal morality that recognizes and rejects the lies of patriarchy, lies that mask exploitation as benevolence, and the bringing of death as the bringing of life. We know the difference.

Three Different Viewpoints on Matriarchal Politics

The Viewpoint of the International Researchers on Matriarchy

The statements are about:
•developing modern Matriarchal Studies as a new socio-cultural science, that includes a vision and an outline of a new society based on

justice and peace;
•the research strategies to create and expand this new paradigm, and at the same time, to form an alternative scientific community by collaboration and networking;
•the plans for future education; for example, the introduction of this new field of knowledge into schools, colleges, and universities.

Veronika Bennholdt-Thomsen (Germany)
Economic globalization is a project of the big international capital and its followers to create one single worldview worldwide, which says, profit sustains life. Matriarchal Studies are crucial in the opposition against this overthrow of human values. Its research reveals the social principles that create and support a moral economy and a peaceful society in past and present. It shows how a motherly economy and society, a motherly world looked like and how it can be developed. It is still women who bear children, they have daughters and the sons have mothers. This guarantees that compassion and caregiving will not die out completely. However we have to be aware of the far reaching social, cultural, and economic dimensions of mothering, as well as of its contradictions. Matriarchal Studies contribute to this knowledge.

Genevieve Vaughan (USA / Italy)
It is important to include the idea of the gift economy in Matriarchal Studies because it gives the possibility of a point of view from which to criticize the market and Patriarchal Capitalism. It also gives an explanation of the values of women as the superstructure of an alternative economic structure. Women in Patriarchal Capitalism can consider ourselves matriarchs who have been deprived of our cultures and social structures yet continue to practice the gift economy and embrace its values, at least to some extent. In this capacity we can join with our Indigenous sisters to stand against the economy of hate and domination whenever and wherever possible.

Claudia von Werlhof (Austria)
Patriarchy began with war. With capitalist patriarchy it became a global war system that is destroying life on earth. If we want to have a chance to build up a post-patriarchal civilization we have to stop patriarchy by starting to throw it out of ourselves. Otherwise we would not have the strength we need to throw patriarchy out of the world as well.

Ruxian Yan (China)
In the ancient time, maternal instincts forged humanity. In the future, maternal instincts will still lead humanity to sublimation.

Xioaxing Liu (China)
The existence of current matrilineal communities demonstrates that people

can actually live a productive and humane life in the same time in the modern world. The matrilineal and matriarchal studies will help us to recognize and to choose a better way of life.

Carolyn Heath (Great Britain)

Rationality (logos) and intuition (mythos) are two complementary dimensions of mind. In the western world, intuition has been sacrified to rationality. Balance must be restored by seeing how rationality and intuition may complement each other in every human being.

Indigenous people with non-hierarchical gender patterns may well provide a working model of a harmonious society for the western world, one in which the power-balance between men and women is equal: "Not equal and alike, but equal and opposite" (Labouvie-Vief 1994).

Karen Smith (USA / Switzerland)

Much of modern Matriarchal Studies owes a debt to existing matriarchal cultures. These cultures have been created and maintained over millennia, by indigenous peoples—in the midst of surrounding cultures that have threatened and oppressed them. They have undergone great hardship, suffering, and attempted genocide—in order to protect and defend these very traditions that we as researchers are finding to be so important to our work.

To fulfil our responsibility to these cultures, modern matriarchal researchers must attend to, and support these peoples, in whatever way the peoples themselves suggest.

Cécile Keller (Switzerland)

Modern Matriarchal Studies offers a new perspective on specific areas such as matriarchal medicine. Matriarchal medicine treats people holistically, and includes the social context, the natural world, and the cosmos itself. In this way, matriarchal medicine contributes not only to individual well-being, but to the entire society.

Peggy Reeves Sanday (USA)

The voices of Indigenous peoples must be heard in Matriarchal Studies so that we can understand both the unity and the diversity in matriarchal practices, social structures, and worldview.

Antje Olowaili (Germany)

Mother Earth does not belong to us. We belong to her because she has brought us forth, therefore we have to share her fruits with all humans and animals. Sharing is important because we are all brothers and sisters.

All nature is female. That's why she has to be protected just as women have to be protected. Nature and women are the same. Therefore, a person who venerates Mother Earth also respects and protects women as her reflection.

Vicki Noble (USA)

Knowing of the existence of matriarchal societies in the ancient past grounds us in a biological basis for peaceful human evolution organized around the female. Recognizing the presence of living matriarchal cultures in our own time supports our faith in human nature and provides a much-needed alternative model to stimulate our collective imagination. Let us go forward with conviction and courage to break with tradition and create new forms that honour natural processes and the sacred knowledge of woman and nature.

Susan Carter (USA)

This second World Congress has confirmed my conviction that it is more important than ever that we take what we have shared here out into the world. Through the combination of our academic research in Matriarchal Studies, our personal stories about our lives living within existing matriarchal societies, and our deep soulful, heartfelt desire to manifest practical application of this information for social change on a planetary level, we can each individually and collectively create a world in which all beings thrive.

Annette Kuhn (Germany)

My main aim is to show the continuity of women's power within history. This aim implies a re-definition of power on matriarchal terms and a double view of history, evaluating the creative, mental, and moral powers of women within our symbolic and social world and based on the background of patriarchal attempts to take over.

James DeMeo (USA)

The study of both matriarchal and patriarchal societies must proceed on an objective, scientific foundation, so as to best separate out myth from fact. Cross-cultural evaluations, to review specific practices, are one such objective indicator. The claim that a matriarchal society is more desirable or better than another social model must proceed from a clear detailing about just what it is we value in a society: higher women's status, greater overall freedom for everyone, low violence, absence of cruel sexual mutilations, and so forth.

Only with such scientifically critical and objective approaches can the study of matriarchal societies hope to defeat academic obstructionism, and benefit the world.

Marguerite Rigoglioso (USA)

This Second World Congress on Matriarchal Studies confirms that matriarchy exists in the present day as a real and valid social structure. Our collective research into history, mythology, iconography, and linguistics provides increasingly persuasive evidence that matriarchy was the original social structure of humanity. Given the more positive and wholesome nature of matriarchy as a social system in contrast to the present patriarchal social system that dominates most of the world, it is imperative that education about matriarchy be disseminated globally.

Kaarina Kailo (Finland)

To create fertile conditions for post-capitalistic peaceful societies, we need to expose the horrendous honour/shame system, which is the psychological anchor of asymmetrical and violent gender relations. By attributing honour to the violent control of women's life and sexuality, these systems support war and oppression. We need to adopt matristic notions of honour based on ecological, social, cultural, and biological sustainability, gift circulation, and the life-enhancing, egalitarian principles of matriarchal cultures, adapted to diverse cultural contexts. We need to respond to the needs of Mother Earth.

Paola Melchiori (Italy)

It is important to actualize the matriarchal cultures, meaning to identify the aspects of matriarchal cultures that could be helpful to us *now*, today and in this world. This means to confront its basic concepts and practices with those of modern feminism, identifying where the ideas are compatible or in conflict, and in which aspects. The combination and critical confrontation of the knowledges and practices of feminism, matriarchal studies and Indigenous women can be of enormous help in imagining a new society. These knowledges and practices are particularly invisible as much as they are instead important in the new social movements such as the social forums and the Indigenous movements.

Heide Goettner-Abendroth (Germany)

Despite all the hostility directed against modern Matriarchal Studies, it is not possible to disregard its findings. It presents us with a well-balanced, egalitarian and basically peaceful society which can exist without life-destroying inventions like wars of conquest and the rule of dominance. This is why I am convinced that matriarchy will be successful in the struggle for a humane world.

Michael Dames (Great Britain)

All that I can offer is a handful of soil. Soil can be regarded as the fifth element, in which air, fire, earth and water meet and mix, to form the seed-bed of new life and hope. Similarly, when Male and Female collide and coalesce on this ground, bitter distinctions may turn to love.

The Viewpoint of Indigenous Researchers from Matri-centred Societies on Different Continents

The statements are about:
- the significance of modern Matriarchal Studies for indigenous peoples; i.e., that these studies discover the deep structure of the traditional matri-societies all over the world;

•to visualize matriarchal patterns as models for a peaceful society of the future;
•to intensify the criticism of patriarchal patterns, from which Indigenous peoples have suffered and are still suffering;
•the strengthening of Indigenous net-working and political aims.

Barbara Alice Mann, Bear Clan of the Ohio Seneca, Iroquois (USA)

It is profoundly demoralizing to Indigenous peoples from matrilineal cultures to find their thousands of years of history ignored, dismissed, or downplayed by academic statements that present patriarchal oppression as a "given" since "time began," when, in fact, their own cultures serve as known and knowable templates for societies based on co-operation and mutual respect. Tacitly regarding patriarchy and domination as "the norm" sabotages efforts to present alternative models as legitimate. Therefore, Matriarchal Studies must first explore and best document known models of open, egalitarian, participatory, and shared cultures, with any references to domination, oppression, and patriarchy as purely secondary and non-formative.

Wilhelmina J. Donkoh, Akan (Ghana, West Africa)

Matriarchal Studies provides a positive and exciting medium for the study of matrifocal societies. As a scientific and analytical tool it projects the positive values inherent in such systems without alienating other elements that they entail. Through the medium of Matriarchal Studies, matri-centred societies are elevated into mainstream discourse rather than as a sub-culture.

Makilam, Berber (Algeria / France / Germany)

The disciplines of social sciences should come to a consensus on a definition of matriarchy and its structures. It is important to have more interdisciplinary sharing on matriarchal research with Indigenous peoples. It needs to be accepted that the basis of life is female, and women's ability to bear children has to be protected, and reproductive technology should not be allowed to replace mothers.

Savithri Shanker de Tourreil, Nayar (Kerala, Southwest India)

Let us all be deeply aware of the tending instinct and live every moment honouring this instinct, acting according to the intuition that is born from this instinct. Moreover, let us do our best always to invite, incite, and instigate all human beings, male and female, who are in our own personal universe, to consider the tending instinct our life principle and our constant motto for every kind of action.

Patricia Mukhim, Khasi (Meghalaya, North East India)

We have just discovered our common heritage and a common ancestress. We need to unite and support one another. Help us to stop the World Bank and other financial institutions from exploiting us. This is an appeal to all.

Usria Dhavida, Minangkabau (Sumatra, Indonesia)
It really was a great coming to this conference because we were ablet o meet many different peoples of this world talking about woman/mother, and Matriarchal Studies. To me, the differences are the good thing to know so that we can get information that we did not have before.

Endri, Minangkabau (Sumatra, Indonesia)
The role of globalization is huge in my society, the Minangkabau of West Sumatra. Today, *Adat*, our matriarchal law and customs, is still strong, and so is religion. The two support one another in a way that lessens the bad influence of globalization. It is important for the peoples of the world who care for matriarchal traditions to erect barriers against the effects of globalization.

Rosa Martha Toledo, Juchiteca (Oaxaca, Mexico)
We need to remember that we are all Goddesses. The power resides in the interior of each one of us. We are sacred and powerful, that is our strength. We do not need to defend ourselves aggressively, because nothing can hurt or offend us if we are strong at the core. We love life, we accept joy and pain as two sides of the same coin. We do not want war, because we do not believe in violence as a path to peace. We want a world in which our daughters and sons can grow healthy and happy.

Mariela de la Ossa, Kuna (Kuna Yala, Panama)
After having heard the experiences of other cultures, I have come to the conclusion of how our Vaquito Foundation can help preserve the Kuna culture on the islands of Kuna Yala. I have learned that we must keep western culture and education from dominating our traditions and customs and how to take a strong role in diffusing our culture for the benefit of future generations.

Bernedette Muthien, Khoesan (South Africa)
Matriarchies encompass completeness, harmony, and interdependence of all creations. And hence scholarship should balance with, and be relevant to actual communities of (grassroots) people, rather than predatory cannibalization of ancient infinite wisdom and sacredness. In this compassionate, respectful way, Matriarchal Studies can be the most powerful revolutionary movement we have ever had. Matriarchy is less "hail the goddess," and more "love the self (and others) as an embodiment of the divine."

Gad A. Osafo, Akan (Ghana, West Africa)
I am a woman and I am a man. You are a man and you are a woman. Both parts make it human. The present patriarchal dominated models of global developments are evidently noxious. Immediate, official actions to arrest and reverse this trend is therefore of paramount importance, if we want our grandchildren to acknowledge and honor us as ancestors and elders. It is critical that matriarchies

are conscientiously given more room in global development. Congresses like this, which address this issue, should therefore be encouraged and supported to sow the seeds for a better future.

Doña Enriqueta Contreras, Zapoteca (Oaxaca /Mexico)
Respect should not be lost. We must strive to maintain equality of gender in order not to lose respect. Respect all living beings, animate and non-animate, so that respect will duplicate in other contexts, and in order to help from escalating aggression. We must respect sacred sites because they have been alive for thousands of years supporting and reinforcing women's spirituality. Unity, communion and communication go hand in hand with the search for peace and tranquillity in re-establishing the environment for which we are looking.

Yvette Abrahams, Khoekhoe (Namibia, South Africa)
With regard to the overall direction of Matriarchal Studies, the topic is too big to do justice to in a few sentences. I can only say what I am doing in may own research, which is that I am worried about the greenhouse effect. Apparently South Africa is due to become one of the two driest areas in the world by 2015, it will become desertified. So I will hopefully complete the research I am doing on the plants of the Eastern und Southern Cape in the next two years and increasingly study our desert and semi-desert plants after that. So we can know what to grow for food. In that way I am preparing for the troubles that are coming and trying to preserve as much of our matriarchal culture as possible.

Hengde Danshilcuo (He Mei), Mosuo (Yunnan, China)
Start where we are, with what we have, do what we can.

The Viewpoint of Women in Patriarchal Societies Worldwide

The statements are about:
• the significance of modern Matriarchal Studies for women in patriarchal societies; i.e., that these studies present a completely different kind of society than they are used to living in;
• their identities as women, their concepts of history and worldviews;
• their awareness of still existing matriarchal patterns in their own lives, and in the lives of other women;
• the creation of new matriarchal patterns and their significance for the political empowerment of women in general.

Uschi Madeisky and Gudrun Frank-Wissmann (Germany)
Our careers as filmmakers took us to several matrilineal/matriarchal societies. There we experienced matriarchal consciousness for the first time. We received our second socialization from the Khasi, the Garo, the Kunama and the Palauan women. This rescued us from the handicap we inherited from patriarchies. For

this we are grateful to our many mothers and sisters. But we also experienced that all these societies are forced to give up their roots and values by Christian missions with a powerful support. Therefore we call on all sisters to join the Association for the protection and promotion of matrilineal/matriarchal societies and their values because these societies provide us with the insides we need to live in a peaceful world. <www.ur-kult-ur.de>

Mary Margaret Navar (Texas / USA)

From the passing ancestor clouds above, to the foam floating on a cup of chocolate, life is filled with sacred opportunities. Let us seize them with respect and passionately pull them to the center of our hearts, bodies and spirits so that we might be fed and have enough to feed others by giving with gentility and compassion—one world, one heart.

Lydia Ruyle (USA)

The ancient mothers are calling each of us to remember and return the soul to the images and stories of the divine feminine, the goddess. If you want to change reality: just do it! That is what crones do. They don't whine, they just do it.

Maria Teresa (Mexico)

Stop the killings of the women in Juarez! It is our birthright to have safety, and the birthright of our young daughters who have to work in these factories. And that they can get home safely after work. Step out of your heads into your hearts and support us, we are women like you. Our daughters are dying. I ask for help, letters to the governor of Chihuaha, articles in your press! Mexico is not helping. Include birthright and safety in the declaration. Women there want support from the international community. I learned patriarchy is not universal. But the market economy is making it become universal.

Ana Isla (Peru / Canada)

We have ignored the situation that it is patriarchy in which we are living. Development has amounted to an attack on the last Indigenous lands. Latin America is destroying the biodiversity. Ecotourism is destroying every last religious site. Genetic material being destroyed and IP's are a target for extermination. We need to link oppression by the patriarchy to capitalistic oppression.

Amejo Amyot (USA)

We declare: to acknowledge, to value, to see the importance of traditional crafts as the deepest connection to intuitive knowing, to Mother Earth. Write a declaration that we can take to the women and children in the schools.

Beebe Frazer (USA)

I declare that every baby has the right to be greeted to the planet in a circle of love and gentleness—rather than in an environment of machines and monitors and an overriding fear of pain and disease. I declare that each woman has the right to feel the divine power of her blood mysteries of menarche, childbirth, and menopause. I declare that the holy ceremonies of birth and death are given back into the hands of women, as it has been and still is in matriarchal cultures.

Frieda Werden (Canada)

Communication and stories are mothering tools and also a human right of all peoples. We declare against the use of global telecommunications to plant a monoculture of patriarchal stories modeling accumulation and violence. We declare in support of community media with equal access for all—especially women.

Author unknown

As we, each in our own way, work to move the concepts of matriarchy into the popular consciousness, let us confront patriarchy everywhere with expressions of love, creativity, and joy. A vigorous celebration of life is a most effective weapon in the hands of modern day non-violent amazon warriors.

Caresse Bennett (USA)

We declare that it is no longer acceptable to define any human being as superior to another. It is no longer acceptable to define any person as acceptable to exploit—whether that person be disabled, of a different race, an elderly person, a woman, or of any other differentiated group. We will form networks and alliances between women and men of all nations who love and respect the Divine Feminine and live up to her principles. And who are willing to create life-based, successful, economic models that help to see that there are alternatives. We declare that we will look to the wisdom of the Indigenous peoples worldwide to help us to create the new models.

Jean Hamilton (USA)

I agree that global capitalism and market economy is an outcome of patriarchy. We have to underscore our sense of urgency in opposing the spread of harmful effects of global capitalism on both the earth (e.g. global warming) and on the cultures and well-being of Indigenous peoples. Matriarchal cultures hold the key to helping us all. We need to learn how to preserve that knowledge, how to simplify, down-size, and to live in a more sustainable way, how to create women's spaces and real communities—as existing patriarchal societies (USA) start to crumble. Thus, I believe, we must both theorize and take action. What we do now is urgent! My path is to create women's land and a women's community in New Mexico.

Maria Suarez (Costa Rica)

The purpose of this conference is to unite us. The academic research which was presented here should be shared with people outside.

Another point: In matriarchy the body was central, but in patriarchy this is denigrated. The beauty culture and business also is a new form of colonization. It has profound effects on the way it divides women. In many ways patriarchy makes women sick, so a part of our struggle has to be to heal ourselves. Militancy can burn us out quickly, so we have to heal ourselves. For this reason, there exist women's health collectives in Costa Rica. <www.fire.or.cr>

Peggy Reeves Sanday (USA)
Speaking truth to power. I wrote a book about sex and privilege on campus. You can't always change things by being sweet. Speaking out derives from the strength I gained and what I learned from the Minangkabau. So I want to do a popular film on this subject.

Jeanne Johnson (USA)
Walking away from patriarchy one step at a time! Each one is powerful where you are. Each one teach one.

Author unknown
We can create a women's walking circle. This means to act as host for meetings neighborhoodwise. Share numbers so when you want to go for a walk with someone, call a number. On the walks, we can tell them about the matriarchy.

Author unknown
Teach girls about their divinity, present other positive models of femininity.

Annette Kuhn (Germany)
Don't believe what is written in the history books. Teach what you know by your own experience. Matriarchy is the force that keeps all of this going. If patriarchy were victorious, we would vanish. Gift economy is the basis of what we are doing. I am building a Museum of Women's History. <www.hdfg.de>.

Linda Christiansen-Ruffman (Canada)
Start rebuilding the women's movement. Figure out most egregious evidence of patriarchy in your communities and start resisting it, and include everybody's wisdom. Information, knowledge and wisdom are different, pay regard to the distinction. In Canada we have started to use CEDAW.

Chiquie Estrada (USA)
We have an early education school for children to learn responsibility and ecology. They are using the Montessori model which is based on maternal love, just like gift giving and just like matriarchy.

Sally Jacque (USA)
Stay local in your community. Be known in the community so you can bypass

all the institutions that are employed to stop you from helping people in crisis situations. Meet together, so you can strategize about how to be able to take action, because it will be more and more necessary now that Mother Nature is speaking.

Dona Enriquetas Contreras, Zapoteca (Mexico)

Giving birth. I have been attending births for 50 years. My grandmother was also a midwife and she had 22 children. She lived for 115 years, and no one showed her how to birth. She spoke her own language. I have six children, and no one is going to show me how to give birth. We decide for ourselves and we are no one's instrument. Science is one thing, but conscience is another.

People pay the doctor so they can give you the illness. We exhibit ourselves and the doctor decides how we give birth. This violates a spiritual rule. I invite young women and all mothers here to engage in the task from this day forward to begin education from the very nucleus of our families. We have to be right, physically and spiritually so we can offer something to others. We have a heart that beats and a divine light and we are connected with the entire universe. That is why we are called "women." These values are so important, and we can't buy them at any marketplace in the U.S. So if we seek cure for all these epidemics then we have to fights against the pestilence that is hurting us.

The importance of this gathering is that each and every one of us transmit the words of everyone here and, in this way, transmit a good future. So we can begin to make our change. No neighbour is going to fix what is broken in my house. That is something I must fix in my own house. Every interaction is sacred. Women are a garden of flowers. We need the value of respect.

***

Thanks to all those who supported both of the World Congresses on Matriarchal Studies in the most generous way, and to those on whose lifelong research they were based. The congresses were great successes. The short and longterm consequences of these extraordinary events cannot be anticipated at this point.

May the example of matriarchal societies show us how to leave patriarchy behind, and may women lead the way again to societies of peace!

HAGIA: International Academy for Modern Matriarchal Studies and Matriarchal Spirituality (Germany)

The International Academy HAGIA was founded in 1986 by Dr. Heide Goettner-Abendroth. It is dedicated to exploring the long history of matriarchal societies and cultures past and present. Historically, matriarchal cultures have existed worldwide, and some of them continue to exist even today. In her life's work, Heide Goettner-Abendroth has developed a coherent theoretical basis that combines the different aspects of modern Matriarchal Studies, convincingly presenting it as a new socio-cultural science. It is only recently that modern Matriarchal Studies has become an international field of exploration based within a scientific framework. Her own matriarchy research, and that of many international guest lecturers, is presented dynamically and attractively in seminars, as well as in the international study trips offered by Academy HAGIA. In terms of social and cultural structures, modern Matriarchal Studies opens up a fundamentally different perspective on life, culture, and society, creating a new paradigm. It makes us aware of the patterns in our own patriarchal societies and personal lifestyles; these can then be understood, confronted and changed, and in the long term, can change patriarchal societies as a whole. Therefore, the activities of Academy HAGIA are at once intellectual, political, artistic, and spiritual at once. Every Academy event includes aspects of both history and society, and creates a living connection to the natural world around us. Dr. Goettner-Abendroth and the Academy HAGIA organized the First World Conference on Matriarchal Studies, "Societies in Balance," held in Luxemburg in 2003. The Second World Conference on Matriarchal Studies, "Societies of Peace," held in San Marcos and Austin, Texas in 2005, was organized by Genevieve Vaughan and the Foundation for a Compassionate Society. See: www.hagia.de.

The Foundation for a Compassionate Society (Austin, Texas, USA)

The Foundation for a Compassionate Society was founded by Genevieve Vaughan in 1987 as an attempt to practice the gift economy in the here and now. She hired many local, national and international feminist activists to carry out projects in a co-ordinated way with the goal of giving the gift of social change and addressing problems created by patriarchy. These projects, which included media, meeting and office spaces, activist organizing, and conferences, involved many cultural and political areas. The Foundation closed its doors in 2005 although the Goddess Temple of Sekhmet in Nevada still continues with Genevieve's support as an example of the gift economy and Alma de Mujer Retreat Center, FIRE (Feminist International Radio Endeavor), and WINGS (Women's International News Gathering Service) continue independently. See: www. gifteconomy.com.